ON THE

CULTURE AND COMMERCE

OF

COTTON IN INDIA,

AND ELSEWHERE

ON THE

CULTURE AND COMMERCE

OF

COTTON IN INDIA,

AND ELSEWHERE;

WITH AN ACCOUNT OF THE

EXPERIMENTS MADE BY THE HON. EAST INDIA COMPANY
UP TO THE PRESENT TIME.

BY

J. FORBES ROYLE, M.D. F.R.S.

GYAN

Published by

Gyan Publishing House
5, Ansari Road
Daryaganj, New Delhi-110002
Phone: 011-47034999, 9811692060
E-mail: books@gyanbooks.com

Distribution Network
gyanbooks.com
India, USA, Canada, UK, Australia, France

ISBN: 978-81-212-7771-6 (PB)
First Published, 1851

2nd Impression 2023

Printed at: Gyan Press, Delhi.

ON THE CULTURE AND COMMERCE OF COTTON IN INDIA AND ELSEWHERE

Author: J. FORBES ROYLE

ON THE

CULTURE AND COMMERCE

OF

COTTON IN INDIA,

AND ELSEWHERE;

WITH AN ACCOUNT OF THE

EXPERIMENTS MADE BY THE HON. EAST INDIA COMPANY UP TO THE PRESENT TIME.

APPENDIX:

PAPERS RELATING TO THE GREAT INDUSTRIAL EXHIBITION.

BY

J. FORBES ROYLE, M.D. F.R.S.,

Late Superintendent of the Hon. E. I. C.'s Botanic Gardens at Saharunpore;
One of the General Secretaries of the British Association for the Advancement of Science;
Professor of Materia Medica and Therapeutics in King's College, London.

LONDON:
SMITH, ELDER, & CO., 65, CORNHILL.
1851.

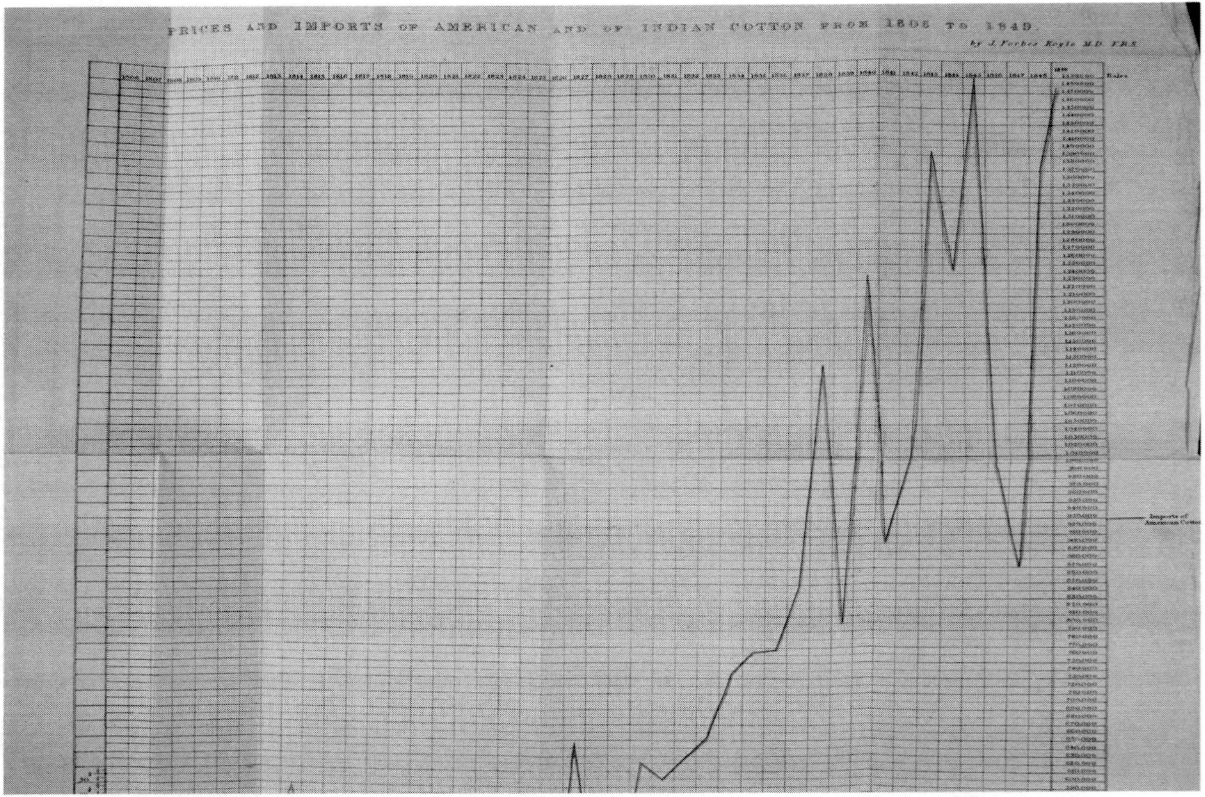

PRICES AND IMPORTS OF AMERICAN AND OF INDIAN COTTON FROM 1806 TO 1849.
by J. Forbes Royle M.D. F.R.S.
Bales
Imports of American Cotton

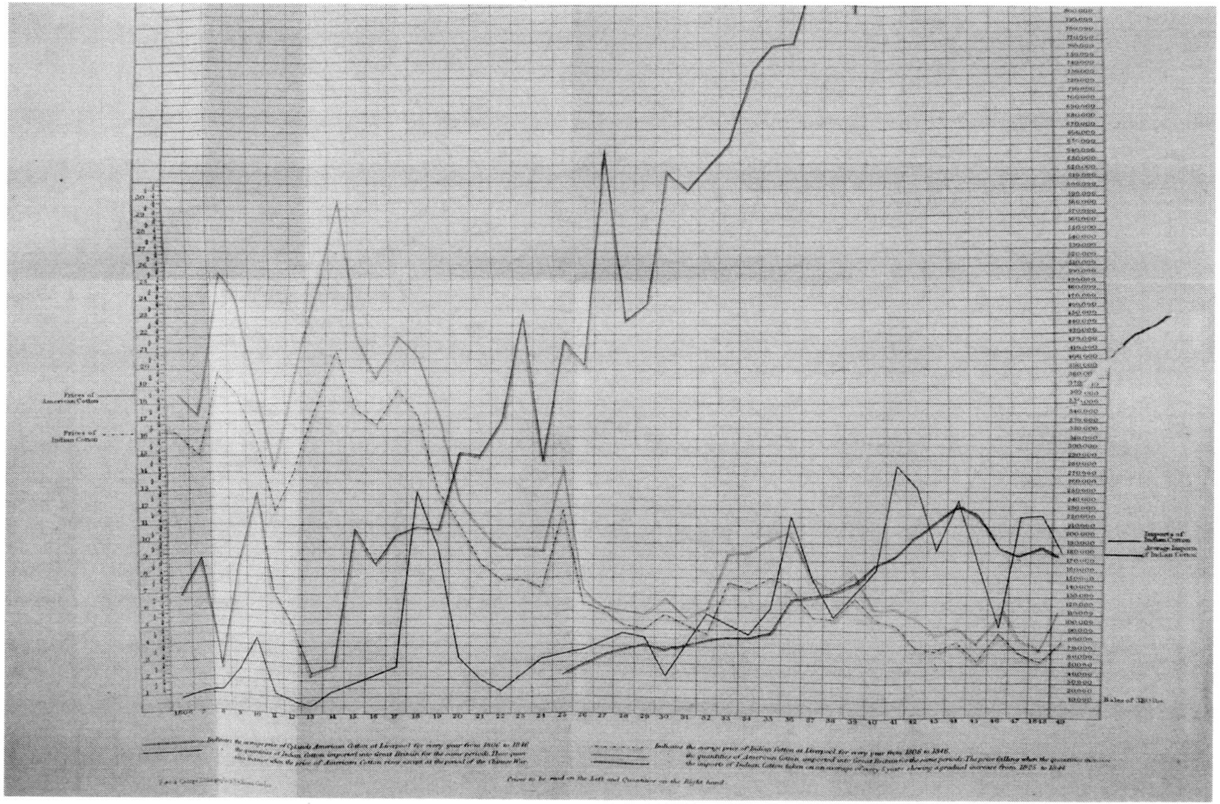
Prices of American Cotton
Prices of Indian Cotton
Imports of Indian Cotton
Average Imports of Indian Cotton
Indicates the average price of Uplands American Cotton at Liverpool for every year from 1806 to 1846
the quantities of Indian Cotton imported into Great Britain for the same periods. These quantities increase when the price of American Cotton rises except at the period of the Chinese War.
Indicates the average price of Indian Cotton at Liverpool for every year from 1806 to 1846.
the quantities of American Cotton imported into Great Britain for the same periods. The price falling when the quantities increase
the imports of Indian Cotton taken on an average of every 5 years showing a gradual increase from 1825 to 1844
Prices to be read on the Left and Quantities on the Right hand

DEDICATED

TO

THE CHAIRMAN, DEPUTY-CHAIRMAN,

AND

COURT OF DIRECTORS

OF THE

East India Company;

WHOSE

PERSEVERING EFFORTS FOR A LONG SERIES OF YEARS,

TO

IMPROVE THE CULTURE OF COTTON IN INDIA

HAVE AT LAST RESULTED IN BRINGING THE EXPERIMENT TO SO SUCCESSFUL AN ISSUE IN SOME OF THE DISTRICTS, AS TO REQUIRE ONLY TO BE FOLLOWED UP BY THE LEGITIMATE EFFORTS OF THOSE SPECIALLY INTERESTED IN THE IMPROVEMENT OF THIS GREAT STAPLE,

BY THEIR MOST OBEDIENT SERVANT,

THE AUTHOR.

PREFACE.

Though the subject of this work requires no apology, discussing, as it does, the means of increasing the supply of the raw material of one of our most important manufactures, yet it may seem to have been treated of at greater length than was necessary. This was far from the author's intention; but the subject has grown under his hands, partly from the introduction of some collateral subjects, but chiefly from his having obtained, by the liberal permission of the Court of Directors of the East India Company, much new and important information from the several cotton districts of India.

The various statements which have been made respecting the causes which interfere with the extended exports of cotton from India, and the repeated experiments made by the East India Company to improve its culture in India, followed by apparent or alleged failure, have rendered it necessary to investigate the subject under three different heads. These were intended at one time to have formed three separate parts, and to have been published separately.

I. The commercial causes which influence the irregular imports of Indian cotton, as dependent on the crops of

American cotton, and on the nature and condition in which Indian cotton is brought into market.

As failures are stated to have followed nearly all the attempts made by the Indian government to grow American cotton in India, some of the results obtained have been given in an early part (p. 96 to p. 116) of the work, before the account of the experiments themselves. But it was necessary to investigate the physical causes which prevented success; this has been done under the second and third heads:—

II. Cultivation of Cotton; including the different species of cotton plants, and the peculiarities of soil and climate, as well as of culture, which they require; and adding a brief exposition of the principles of culture in general, in order that planters may be able to investigate for themselves the causes of success or failure in particular localities.

III. Experimental Culture of Cotton in India. Under this head, the author has taken notice of the several experiments which have been made in different parts of India for the improved culture of the Native or for the introduction of American cotton. As the author believes he has noticed every district in India which produces cotton to any considerable or even to very little extent, this part of the work has become more extended from his having introduced information respecting the statistics of Indian cotton from almost every district of India. This he has been able to do in consequence of his having been favoured, through the liberality of the Court of Directors of the East India Company, by having access to the replies of Collectors of Revenue to the six queries (*v.* p. 90) circulated by them throughout India in the year 1847.

In conclusion, the author calls attention to the able 'Note on the Land Revenue of India,' for which he is indebted to Francis W. Prideaux, Esq., of the East India House, and which gives so clear a general view of a subject so little understood, and so often misrepresented.

He has also to express his obligation to the late J. Thomson, Esq., of Clitheroe, for the beautiful engraving of the fibre of cotton, as drawn by Mr. C. Varley.

He takes this opportunity of stating, that the publication of this work has been delayed for some months past, at first in consequence of severe and long-continued indisposition; and lastly by duties connected with the Great Industrial Exhibition.

As tending to display the varied natural products of India, many of which may, like cotton, become extensive articles of commerce, the author has published the Papers and Lists which he prepared on the first proposal of the Exhibition in the summer and autumn of 1849.

CONTENTS.

PART I.

PART II.

CULTIVATION OF COTTON.

PART III.

EXPERIMENTAL CULTURE IN INDIA.

LIST OF PLATES.

ON THE

CULTURE AND COMMERCE OF COTTON IN INDIA.

MATERIALS for food and for clothing, both equally necessary for man in a civilized state of society, are yielded in probably equal proportions by the animal and vegetable kingdoms. The flesh of various animals, wool and silk of different kinds being contributed by the former, as the cereal grains, pulses, and roots, with flax, hemp, and cotton are yielded by the latter, and form the food and clothing of millions of the human race. Though the first coverings of men may have been formed of skins, the wool of sheep and the hair of goats were early employed for such purposes in Northern Asia and Southern Europe, as silk no doubt was in China. Hemp was cultivated in the north of Europe and flax in Egypt, while COTTON has, from the earliest periods, been considered to be characteristic of India. Though the uncertain nature of Hindoo chronology prevents us from even guessing at the period when it was first employed, there is little doubt that it must have been so from the earliest ages of Hindoo civilization: for being indigenous in their country, it could not fail to be noticed by its inhabitants; first from the brilliancy of its golden inflorescence; and secondly, from the dazzling whiteness of its bursting fruit. This being filled with seeds, enveloped in a material so soft, so white, and so fibre-like as cotton, could hardly fail to be gathered even by the most incurious. On gathering, one would almost involuntarily twist it into a thread, and thus appear to rediscover the patriarchal art of spinning. Other plants have their useful flax-like fibres concealed under bark, or in other vegetable matter: but cotton, on the bursting of the pod, like wool at the birth of the lamb, is at once revealed to view. As this must be separated from its skin, so the other requires only to be pulled off its seed, to be ready for being spun into thread. The father of History, in his account of

India, says, "the wild trees in that country bear fleeces as their fruit, surpassing those of sheep in beauty and excellence: and the Indians use cloth made from these trees."

Having a thread, the art of weaving would be readily discovered, as that of platting rushes, slender stems and strips of leaves, seems to have been universally practised. But much ingenuity must have been expended before even the most common loom was invented. Weaving was well known to all the civilized nations of antiquity; as to the Egyptians, the Assyrians, the Chinese, and Hindoos. The culture of flax, and the processes of weaving, are represented in the ancient monuments of Egypt; and Joseph was by Pharoah arrayed in fine linen. The Israelites, on their departure from that country, were acquainted not only with weaving, but with dyeing. The curtains of the Tabernacle were blue, purple, and scarlet. The former art is sometimes stated to have been discovered in Assyria, and its results we see represented in the monuments disinterred by the energy of a Layard, and interpreted by the genius of a Rawlinson. They are noticed in the not less creditable relics of the ancient Hindoos, that is their Vedas and the Institutes of Menu.

But the art of weaving was not confined to the old world, for Columbus found cotton abundant on his first arrival in the West Indies; and the early Spanish historians describe it as forming the chief clothing of the Mexicans; and cotton fabrics of different kinds formed a part of the presents sent by Cortez to Charles V. Magellan saw it among the Brazilians; and it has of late years been discovered in the ancient Peruvian tombs, along with cloth of a black and white check, not unlike some modern patterns. We may, therefore, readily concede, what botanists maintain, that the Indian and American cotton plants are perfectly distinct as species. Though a common kind was grown at an earlier period, the United States are described as receiving their fine cotton seeds from one of the West India islands about the year 1786. The culture was soon carried from the *sea islands* of the coast of Carolina into the interior and *uplands* of Georgia, and shortly afterwards from the Atlantic states to those which lie along the Gulf of Mexico, and latterly into Texas.

Celebrated as India has been, from all antiquity, for the

production of cotton, and for the excellence of her calico, as well as for the marvellous beauty of her muslin manufacture, it seems unaccountable to see Indian cotton occupying the lowest place in price currents, and described as inferior in quality, dirty in condition, and deficient in supply. We hear, moreover, of her hitherto matchless fabrics, and the much desired objects of commerce for probably 3000 years, beaten out of even her home market by the comparatively recent but now gigantic cotton manufactures of England. The latter effect has no doubt been produced by the joint influence of the persevering ingenuity of her mechanics, and the untiring power of steam, aided by an abundant supply of the raw material from a variety of sources. The alleged failure of India to produce increasing quantities of superior cotton has been ascribed to a variety of causes:—to the depressing effects of fiscal regulations, and to the want of easy means of transit; sometimes to the baneful influence of middlemen, and the extortionate demands of money-lenders; seldom to poverty of soil or to unsuitableness of climate, or to the unfitness of Indian cotton for English machinery. Some who complain seem to forget the possibility of change, even in an age of innovations, for they adduce grievances which have years before been abolished, and state as general facts, what on examination, prove to be only local incidents. Few inquire whether the native cultivator participates in the anxiety which is displayed for his improvement, or is likely to be rewarded for any extra labour he may bestow on a new culture, or the merchant for the risk he incurs in exporting to an ever-varying market. In such a case, the difficulty of ascertaining the truth is as great as it is important that it should be ascertained, in order that impediments should be removed, and exertion applied to improve the culture of a plant and to the careful picking of its produce, as this could hardly fail to be of benefit to the natives of the country, and to the extension of their commerce.

Next to the grain of the cereal grasses, Cotton is probably the natural product upon which the comfort and prosperity of several nations depend more than upon any other. It may be sufficient to observe, that if it is beneficial for America to produce, and for England to purchase, the raw material for her gigantic manufacture, it is equally so for India to consume what she produces within her natural limits, with the aid and for the use of her hundred millions of cotton-clad inhabitants. To those who have not paid attention to the subject, it may appear that we exaggerate its importance, when we connect the welfare of nations with what may to them appear so very trivial a matter as the hair, or rather wool-like covering, of a seed; but let us for an instant, without on the present occasion mentioning all the countries where cotton is produced, take a glance at the great producers and consumers of this not less elegant than useful product of the vegetable kingdom.

§ 1. Rise of the Cotton Manufacture in Great Britain.

To England, a regular supply of cotton, and its price, is a subject of paramount importance, even though the manufacture here is of comparatively recent origin; for any interruption in the supply of the raw material is not a question of mere inconvenience, or of the profitable employment of capital, but one of vital statistics; for it deprives hundreds of thousands of her industrious population not only of regular employment, but of their daily bread. In order fully to appreciate the importance of this manufacture, we may briefly notice its origin and rapid extension, as well as connect this with its effects on India.

The cotton manufacture was no doubt established in India long before we find it noticed in any reliable history. The natives of that country early attained excellence in the arts of spinning and weaving, employing only their fingers and the spinning-wheel for the former; but they seem to have exhausted their ingenuity when they invented the hand-loom for weaving, as they have for ages remained in a stationary condition. From India the culture of the plant and the manufacture of cotton spread into the south of Persia and into Egypt. By the Mahomedans both were carried wherever their arms extended their conquests. Mr. Baines, whom we have chiefly consulted for the historical facts, observes it as "extraordinary, that a branch of industry so apt to propagate itself, should have lingered 1300 years on the coast of the Mediterranean, before it crossed that sea into Greece or Italy."* Cotton seems

* History of the Cotton Manufacture in Great Britain. By E. Baines, jun., Esq.

to have been first cultivated in Spain by the Mahomedans as early as the 10th century, and the manufacture to have been established in Italy in the beginning of the 14th century.

It has been stated that the cotton manufacture has existed in England for three centuries, for the making of cottons at Manchester and Bolton is spoken of in the years 1520 and 1552; but there is undoubted evidence that the "cottons" of Manchester, like the Kendal and Welsh "cottons" of the present day, were a coarse kind of "woollens." The exact period of the introduction of the cotton manufacture into England is unknown, but cotton-wool, for the purpose of making candlewicks, was imported as early as 1298, and from the Levant frequently at the beginning of the 16th century. Though no mention earlier than 1641 has been found of the true cotton manufacture, Mr. Baines is of opinion that the art was imported from Flanders by the crowd of Protestant artisans who fled from Antwerp in 1585, some of whom settled in Manchester, and were patronised by the clergy of its church. In 1641 the manufacture seems to have been well established at Manchester, for several kinds of cotton goods were supplied for the home as well as for the foreign market. About 1739 and 1740, East Indian yarns, we learn, were commonly used for the finer kinds of goods, and "up to the year 1760, the machines employed were nearly as simple as those of India." In 1766, the annual value of the cottons made was estimated at £600,000.

But at this period a rapid increase was about to take place, from the numerous happy inventions which were to abridge labour and multiply produce. In 1738 Wyatt and Paul took out a patent for spinning by rollers; thirty years later, Arkwright perfected a similar machine; carding by cylinders was invented by Paul in 1748, and from 1764 to 1767, Hargreaves completed the spinning-jenny. When these several machines were invented, yarns could be supplied in any quantity and of improved quality, so that weavers could obtain as much as they required and at a reasonable price, and manufacturers could use warps of cotton; for up to about the year 1773 linen yarn was used as the warp for nearly all cotton goods in this country. About this time, the imitation of Indian calicoes was successfully attempted, and "Blackburn became the principal mart for that description of goods" which "now constitutes by far the largest branch of the manufacture." (*Baines*, l. c., p. 332.) The machines hitherto invented not being adapted for the finer kinds of yarn, the *mule*-jenny was invented and completed by Crompton in 1779.

Attempts were made, as early as 1780, both in Lancashire and Glasgow, to manufacture the more delicate and beautiful muslins of India, with weft spun by the jenny; but the "attempt failed, owing to the coarseness of the yarn. Even with Indian weft, muslins could not be made to compete with those of the East. But when the mule was brought into general use in 1785, both weft and warp were produced in this country sufficiently fine for muslins," and they soon "so completely succeeded as to banish all fear of the competition of Indian goods." In this year Arkwright's machines were thrown open to the public. Though invented by others, they owed their perfection to his finishing hand. The astonishing extension of the manufacture which immediately followed, shewed that the nullification of the patent was a great national advantage.

Water was early substituted for hand-power in turning the machines. This was, in its turn, supplanted by the all-pervading agency of steam, and the factory system became, by degrees, established in England.

Hitherto the cotton manufacture had been carried on almost entirely in the houses of the workmen, as it still is in India, and has been from the remotest period. The series of ingenious inventions seem to have reached their culminating point in the self-acting mule, which seems a thing instinct with life,—drawing out, twisting, and winding-up many thousand threads with infallible precision and unfailing strength. But the cotton manufacture would necessarily have been brought to a check, from the difficulty of training hands fast enough to weave all the cotton that was spun into thread. But the invention of the power-loom by Dr. E. Cartwright, not himself a mechanic or a manufacturer, overcame even this difficulty, and the only impediment then experienced was, from the necessity of frequently stopping the machinery, in order to dress the warp with starch.* This was at first effected by a

* "The consumption of flour in the cotton manufacture is estimated at not less than 42,301,584 lbs. a year, or 215,824 barrels (of 196 lbs.), or 177,256 loads (of 240 lbs. each)."—*Burn's Commercial Glance for* 1832. "Bengal flour (then) lately introduced into this country, is found to answer well for dressing."—*E. Baines*. "If 2½ oz. of flour

dressing-machine, and now by an improved sizing apparatus. Every difficulty, as it occurred, was overcome, and each then assisted in still further extending, and, at the same time, cheapening the cotton manufacture, and thus magnifying the power and prosperity of Great Britain; at the same time inflicting disastrous consequences on even so anciently established and apparently perfect a manufacture as that of the calicoes and muslins of India. So early as 1793 we find a Select Committee of the Court of Directors of the East India Company upon the subject of the cotton manufacture, stating that "every shop offers British muslins for sale, equal in appearance, and of more elegant patterns, than those of India, for one fourth, or perhaps more than one third, less in price."

Having thus taken a cursory view of the history of the manufacture in this country, we may briefly notice the different operations to which the cotton is subjected, and, for this purpose, we shall use Mr. Baines's words: "Let us briefly review the different processes through which the cotton goes, in its conversion into cloth, all of which are performed in many of the large spinning and weaving mills. The cotton is brought to the mill in bags, just as it is received from America, Egypt, or India, and is then stowed in warehouses, being arranged according to the countries from which it may have come. It is passed through the *willow*, the *scutching-machine*, and the *spreading-machine*, in order to be opened, cleaned, and evenly spread. By the *carding-engine* the fibres are combed out, and laid parallel to each other; and the fleece is compressed into a sliver. The sliver is repeatedly drawn and doubled in the *drawing-frame*, more perfectly to straighten the fibres, and to equalize the grist. The *roving-frame*, by rollers and spindles, produces a coarse and loose thread, which the *mule* or *throstle* spins into yarn. To make the warp, the twist is transferred from cops to bobbins, by the *winding-machine*, and from the bobbins at the *warping-mill* to a cylindrical beam. This beam being taken to the *dressing-machine*, the warp is sized, dressed, and wound upon the weaving-beam. The latter is then placed in the *power-loom*, by which machine the *shuttle*, being provided

be allowed for sizing each pound of twist yarn, it will take 28,437,500 lbs. of flour, or 118,500 packs, or 79,000 quarters of wheat per annum; being nearly ½ per cent., or 1-200th part of the whole wheat consumed in the United Kingdom."—*J. Baynes.*

with cops of weft, the cloth is woven."—(*Baines*, l. c., p. 243.) It is obvious that if the fibre, or staple as it is called, of different cottons vary in length or in strength, some may be able to undergo this rough treatment, while others may escape from it, and yet be well suited to the delicate fingering of the human machine.

§ 2. Imports of Cotton into Great Britain.

Every difficulty that has occurred has been successively overcome; but one great difficulty still remains, that is, a regular supply of the raw material, not only at moderate prices, but in annually increasing quantities. Mr. J. Baynes, in 1846, calculated that, "The consumption of cotton, for the last thirty years, has increased at the compound ratio of 6 per cent. each year, thereby doubling itself every twelve years." The supply of cotton ought, therefore, to continue to increase regularly, in order to keep the manufacturing population in full and healthy employment. This great object, it appears to us, can only be effected by multiplying the sources, and having so extensive a basis of supply as to counter-balance any local peculiarities of seasons, and to make the annual increase of several places keep pace with the annually increasing demand. Before proceeding to consider the capabilities of different countries to meet, not only the ordinary but this constantly increasing consumption, it will be instructive to take a cursory view of the way in which the present enormous and comparatively sudden demand has hitherto been met.

Though we have notices of the import of cotton in small quantities at earlier periods, in the year 1697 it amounted only to about two millions of pounds. In 1775, the average import was only four times what it had been in the beginning of the century, and chiefly from the Mediterranean and Levant. In the year 1786, the quantity imported amounted to 19,475,025 pounds, in the following proportions, from—

British West Indies	5,800,000
French and Spanish Colonies	5,500,000
Dutch "	1,600,000
Portuguese "	2,000,000
Smyrna and Turkey	5,000,000
Total	19,900,000

"The purposes for which the cotton was used, in the year 1787, are thus stated." (*Baines's Hist.*, p. 216.)

Calico and Muslins	11,600,000
Fustians	6,000,000
Mixtures with Silk and Linen	2,000,000
Hosiery	1,500,000
Candle-wicks	1,500,000
Total	22,600,000

The first notice we have of cotton being imported from India is in 1783, when 114,133 pounds were obtained from thence; but in the year 1790, as much as 422,207 pounds, in consequence of an order from the Court of Directors of the East India Company. The export of cotton from the United States was little thought of at this period; for in 1792, Mr. Jay, the American negotiator of a commercial treaty between the United States of North America and Great Britain, stipulated that no cotton should be imported into the latter from the former: the object being to prohibit, in American vessels from the United States, such articles as they had previously imported from the West Indies. But small quantities of the short staple cotton had, previous to this, been grown in North America.

In 1784, an American ship, which imported 8 bags of cotton into Liverpool, was seized, on the ground that so much cotton could not be the produce of the United States." (*Macgregor's Commercial Statistics*, vol. iii, p. 453.) In 1790, 81 bags were exported to Europe from the United States. The total of the imports into this country in that year amounted to 31,447,605 pounds, and increased in 1800 to 56,010,732 pounds. Though the import increased so much at the end of the century, it did not materially increase for the next fourteen years—being on an average, 66 millions of pounds annually, until the conclusion of the war in 1814. In 1815, the import amounted to 100 millions of pounds. Subsequent to this period, the increase has not only been rapid, but most extraordinary, as may be seen in the average for periods of five years.

		Average increase.
From 1815 to 1819 . .	118,267,611 lbs.	
„ 1820 „ 1824 . .	152,201,829 „	33,934,218 lbs.
„ 1825 „ 1829 . .	205,665,011 „	53,463,182 „
„ 1830 „ 1834 . .	280,918,826 „	75,253,815 „
„ 1835 „ 1839 . .	415,039,185 „	134,120,359 „
„ 1840 „ 1844 . .	586,507,757 „	171,468,572 „
„ 1845 „ 1849 . .	629,144,967 „	43,637,210 „

The author is indebted to the kindness of G. R. Porter, Esq., of the Board of Trade, for informing him that the imports from all countries have been, for the years 1847, 474,707,615, for 1848, 713,020,161, and for 1849, 775,469,000 lbs.

In the year 1846, when Mr. J. Baynes made his calculations, and when there was a deficiency of cotton, in comparison with the consumption, he said: "If the consumption of cotton continues to increase in the same ratio which it has done during the last twelve years—all other things being the same—the cotton required twelve years hence, say for the year 1858, will be—

		To be supplied—	
Great Britain . .	3,200,000 bales.	From United States	5,055,000 bales.
Continent . . .	1,656,000 „	„ other sources	755,000 „
United States . .	954,000 „		
	5,810,000 „		5,810,000 „

or upwards of 5,000,000 of bales of cotton from the United States twelve years hence."

The latest progress of consumption and supply has not kept pace with these anticipations.

During the year 1849 there were imported—

From the United States	1,477,512	bales of 330lbs.
„ Brazil	163,445	„
„ East Indies	182,079	„
„ Egypt	72,727	„
„ West Indies and other parts . .	9,485	„
Total	1,905,248	„

A manufacture employing so vast an amount of raw material must necessarily be of immense importance. In the year 1824, Mr. Huskisson considered the total value of the cotton manufacture to amount to £33,500,000. This has since been considered too high an estimate for that period. Mr. M'Culloch, in the year 1833, estimated its value to be £34,000,000, and the amount of capital employed in the manufacture to amount to about the same sum; and Mr. E. Baines, who arrived at his result by a totally different process, valued it at £31,338,693 in the same year, and considered Mr. M'Culloch's estimate of £34,000,000 as the amount of capital invested in the manufacture to be very moderate. The population of the counties where the chief cotton manufactures are carried on was only 781,850 in the year 1780, but in fifty years it had increased about two millions, for it amounted to 2,753,685 in the year 1831. "The number of individuals directly employed in the manufacture, with those dependent on them for subsistence, must amount to 1,500,000," and now it is supposed to be as much as one tenth of the population. The exports of cotton goods are valued at twenty-five millions a year, or one half of the exports of the produce and manufactures of Great Britain, and employ 300,000 tons of shipping for freight. It is stated that, up to the year 1834, cottons to the enormous value of £570,000,000 had been sent from this country to foreign markets, thus furnishing materials for clothing to the people of almost every region of the globe, at the same time benefiting the nation itself by the production of clothing at so much less cost, and of so much better quality, than that to which the mass of the people had been accustomed.

Considering the variety of interests at stake, and the numbers of people employed, directly and indirectly, it is not surprising that any deficiency of the raw material should be contemplated with so much apprehension, not only in Lancashire, but throughout the country; and as the largest supplies come from America, so are the crops of that country looked to as signs of progressive prosperity or of approaching difficulties. The failure of the American crop in the year 1846, as in the very last season, caused a considerable rise in the price of cotton; and it was calculated that in that year an advance in price of 2*d.* a pound required an increased payment by this country of £4,000,000 sterling. In this year the increase in price has caused many spinners and manufacturers of coarse yarns and heavy goods, either to stop their mills or to work short time, and of course to throw many of their workmen out of full and regular employment. It has been well ascertained that, "with high prices of the raw material, the present enormous production of cotton manufactures will not, and cannot, be taken off by the markets of the world."—(*Manchester Guardian*, Jan. 23, 1850.) Such being the paramount importance of a regular supply and moderate price of the raw material, we cannot but expect that the enlightened Government of this country must have been assured that such methods as were appropriate to its various colonies had been adopted for extending this supply; and that the Directors of the East India Company cannot but have promoted the culture of cotton in the magnificent empire intrusted to their sway. Merchants and manufacturers, also, so keenly alive to what is not only for their own interest, but for the benefit of all, must individually and collectively have concerted such measures as were suitable to the different natures and habits, as well as to the different states of civilization of the several nations of the globe. They, better than any other class, know that even commerce, though it never flourishes more than when left free and unshackled, yet in many situations would never have existed if it had not in a measure been forced, by the more civilized taking to those who are less so, the produce of their skill, to exchange for the rude product of some distant land. Of nations possessing a soil and climate fitted for such a production, some require only to be informed of, others to be induced to do, what is obviously for their own benefit.

§ 3. Origin and Progress of the Culture of Cotton in America.

Though the cotton manufacture of England was at its origin supplied with the raw material from the Levant, and subsequently from the West Indies and South America, the United States soon became the principal exporters of what appears to have been an exotic to their soil, though an ordinary short-staple cotton is stated by Mr. Seabrook "to have been grown in Virginia in a limited way, at least 130 years before the Revolution." In Wilson's account of the 'Province of Carolina in America,' published in 1682, it is stated, "that cotton of the Cyprus and Malta sort grows well, and a good plenty of the seed is sent thither." Mr. Spalding of Sapelo Island, near Darien in Georgia, has stated that his father was one of the first to cultivate the long-stapled, or sea-island cotton, in 1787, from seed received from the Bahamas. The seeds of probably the same cotton carried into the interior and upland parts of Georgia, from the poor soil and drier climate, and the necessary modifications of culture, produced what is known as *uplands* cotton. The culture spread thence into the states which abut on the Gulf of Mexico. There the rich soil and moist climate required the cultivation to be suited to it; but everything being congenial, and fresh seed introduced from Mexico, the largest known returns per acre have been obtained.

In England, the invention of machinery by Wyatt, Hargreaves, and Arkwright, from 1739 to 1769, and the consequent establishment of the factory system about 1785, greatly increased the demand for cotton wool. This demand could hardly have been supplied if the culture had not been so vigorously taken up by the Americans; but even they, with their deficiency of labour, would never have been able to free from its seed the quantities of cotton which they grew, if it had not been for the invention of Whitney's saw-gin in 1793. This is justly stated to have done as much for the cultivators of America as the above inventions did for the cotton manufacturers of England; but he was not better treated in the new, than his brother inventors usually are in the old world.

But this fortunate conjunction of an extensive demand with the means of supplying it, the latter occurring among a people ready and able to take advantage of the opportunity, soon established the cotton trade of the United States on an extensive and also secure basis, because it was founded on the excellent quality of the raw material.

Mr. Macgregor, in his valuable Commercial Statistics, vol. iii, p. 452, mentions, that "among the provincial trade returns we find that among the exports of 'Charles Town,' from November 1747 to November 1748, were 7 bags of cotton wool, valued at £3 11*s.* 5*d.* per bag. In 1754, some cotton was exported from South Carolina. In 1770, there were shipped for Liverpool 3 bales from New York, 4 bales from Virginia and Maryland, and 3 barrels full of cotton from North Carolina." From the official returns it appears that the first arrival of cotton wool in Liverpool, the produce of the United States, took place in 1770, and consisted of 2000 lbs. Fourteen bags arrived during the year 1785. And the total import during the six years from 1785 to 1790 inclusive, was 1441 bags, weighing about 150 pounds each; but the supply was neither uniform nor extensive, the import in 1789 having exceeded that of the following year 731 bags."—(*Macgregor*, l. c., p. 465.)

In the year 1791, 189,316 pounds of cotton were exported from the United States, but in 1794 the quantity had increased to 1,601,700 pounds; and by the end of the century to nearly 18,000,000 of pounds. The production of cotton has continued annually to increase, and probably now amounts to about a thousand millions of pounds, or to about 2,500,000 bales; of this a quantity, which has been steadily increasing from year to year, and now amounts to about 500,000 bales, is retained for home consumption. The remainder is exported, chiefly to Europe, but by far the largest proportion to this country.

As it is desirable to have the means of comparing the progress of the different cotton-growing States one with another, as well as of observing the general increase, and how the crops of particular seasons affect the commerce and manufactures of other countries, we insert the following tables. In these, the States are arranged geographically, in order afterwards to weigh the influence of physical causes in limiting or extending the powers of production. In the first table, we may see that the Southern Atlantic States, though they increased their culture very rapidly, yet were very soon equalled by the Gulf States, though these began the culture at so much later a period. The author has compiled this table from *Commercial Statistics*, iii, p. 462.

I. *Estimated Crops of Cotton in America, in lbs., from* 1790 *to* 1834, *given in Millions and Tenths.*

Years.	Virginia.	N. Carolina.	S. Carolina.	Georgia.	Florida.	Alabama.	Mississipi.	Louisiana.	Tennesse.	Arkansas.	Total estimated American Crop.
1791	—	—	1·5	·5	—	—	—	—	—	—	2· lbs.
1801	5·	4·	20·	10·	—	—	—	—	1·	—	40· „
1811	8·	7·	40·	20·	—	—	—	2·	3·	—	80· „
1821	12·	10·	50·	50·	—	20·	10·	10·	20·	—	170· „
1826	25·	10·	70·	75·	2·	45·	70·	55·	45·	·5	348·5 „
1834	10·	9·5	65·	75·	20·	85·	85·	62·	45·	·5	467·5 „

In the following table, the imports of American cotton into Great Britain, from 1834 to the present time, are given in bales. These are estimated to have weighed, on an average, 330 lbs. from 1833 to 1842 inclusive; but the average weight, at present, is 385 lbs.* Here we see that the Atlantic States have either diminished their exports of late years, or have remained stationary; while the Gulf States have increased theirs to an enormous extent. The same fact is thus exhibited :

Actual Average of the Eighteen Crops, from 1824 *to* 1841.

	First 6 Years.	Second 6 Years.	Third 6 Years.
South Atlantic States	433,000 bales	522,000 bales	529,000 bales
Gulf States	253,000 „	504,000 „	1,030,000 „

* Thus, 358 lbs. per bale for Uplands or Georgia, &c.; 437 lbs. for New Orleans and Alabama; 360 lbs. for Sea Island. (*Messrs. Holt's Circular.*) The planters commonly calculate 400 lbs. to a bale.

Under the head of New Orleans, the produce of Louisiana and of Mississipi are included, as well as of some of the interior States, as of Tennessee, which is brought down the river Mississipi.

II. *Growth of Cotton in the different States of America, from* 1834 *to* 1849, *in Bales.*

Years.	Virginia.	N. Carolina.	S. Carolina.	Georgia.	Florida.	Alabama.	Mississipi.	New Orleans.	Texas.
1834-35	33,170	34,399	203,166	222,670	52,085	197,692	—	511,146	—
1835-36	29,197	32,557	231,237	270,121	79,762	236,715	6,889	474,747	—
1836-37	28,618	18,004	196,377	262,971	83,703	232,243	7,755	593,259	—
1837-38	32,000	23,719	294,334	304,210	106,171	309,807	19,675	711,581	—
1838-39	22,200	11,136	210,171	205,112	75,177	251,742	16,432	568,562	—
1839-40	26,900	9,394	313,194	292,693	136,257	445,725	6,767	946,905	—
1840-41	21,800	7,865	227,400	148,947	93,552	320,701	1,085	813,595	—
1841-42	21,012	9,737	260,164	232,271	114,416	318,315	727,658		—
1842-43	15,639	9,039	351,658	299,491	161,088	481,714	1,060,246		—
1843-44	15,600	8,618	304,870	255,597	145,562	467,990	832,172		—
1844-45	25,200	12,487	426,361	295,540	188,693	517,196	929,126		—
1845-46	16,282	10,637	251,405	191,911	141,184	421,966	1,037,144		27,008
1846-47	15,819	6,061	350,200	242,789	127,832	323,462	705,979		8,317
1847-48	8,952	1,518	261,752	254,825	153,776	436,836	1,190,733		39,742
1848-49	17,550	10,041	458,117	391,372	200,186	518,706	1,093,797		38,827

In the third table, the aggregate crop and exports for the last twelve years are given, in order that we may afterwards see how these affect the exports from India in the same or following years. These are taken from the Circular, for the year 1849, of Messrs. Tetley, the eminent brokers of Mincing-lane:

III. *The Crop of Cotton Wool in the United States of America, with the Export, for the last Twelve Years.*

YEARS.	CROP.	EXPORT.		
		Great Britain.	France.	Continent.
1837-38	1,801,497	1,165,155	321,480	88,994
1838-39	1,360,532	798,418	242,243	34,028
1839-40	2,177,835	1,246,791	447,465	181,747
1840-41	1,634,945	858,742	348,776	105,759
1841-42	1,684,211	935,631	398,129	131,489
1842-43	2,378,875	1,469,711	346,139	194,287
1843-44	2,030,409	1,202.498	282,685	144,307
1844-45	2,394,503	1,439,306	359,357	285,093
1845-46	2,100,537	1,102,369	359,703	204,720
1846-47	1,778,651	830,909	241,486	168,827
1847-48	2,347,634	1,324,265	279,172	254,824
1848-49	2,728,596	1,537,901	368,259	321,684

The energetic planters of the southern states of the American Union cannot but be deeply interested in a culture which gives such extensive occupation to their slave population, the more especially as it is subject to a multitude of accidents from the vicissitudes of seasons and the depredations of insects. Thus, though the crop has so greatly increased when viewed in a series of years, yet considerable fluctuations occasionally take place in the quantity produced. It has been said that a good crop, with the advantage of a mild winter, as compared with a bad season and early frosts, makes a difference of from 6 to 700,000 bales. In 1838 a severe frost, occurring on the 7th of October, severely injured the crop. In 1845 the crop was nearly 2,400,000 bales, but in 1846 only about 1,800,000 bales, making a difference of 600,000 bales, all destroyed, it is said, by caterpillars. The present crop is expected to be not above 2,100,000 bales, against 2,700,000 of the previous year. These fluctuations in quantity necessarily produce great variations in price. Thus, the lowest price at Liverpool of New Orleans cotton was—

In June, 1845	$3\frac{1}{2}$*d.* per lb.	In June, 1848	$3\frac{1}{4}$*d.* per lb.
„ 1846	$4\frac{3}{8}$ „	„ 1849	$3\frac{7}{8}$ „
„ 1847	$5\frac{3}{4}$ „	In Dec. 1849	5 „

The American planter necessarily suffers from any depreciation in the value of his produce, though he is in some measure remunerated for the smallness of a crop by the increase in price which almost necessarily ensues, when any deficiency in quantity is experienced. But still he complains, and apparently with justice, of the continued decline which has taken place in prices. Mr. Woodbury, Secretary of the United States' Treasury, has shown that the average prices at the places of exportation for each period of five years has been—

1791-1795	$15\frac{5}{8}$*d.* per lb.	1816-1820	13*d.* per lb.
1796-1800	$18\frac{1}{8}$ „	1821-1825	8 „
1801-1805	$12\frac{1}{2}$ „	1826-1830	5 „
1806-1810	$9\frac{1}{2}$ „	1831-1835	6 „
1811-1815	$7\frac{1}{2}$ „		

Since then still lower prices have been obtained. Mr. Turner stated to the Committee of the House of Commons, that he had bought ordinary Orleans cotton on one occasion as low as $3\frac{1}{2}$*d.*, and that its average price for the years from 1843 to 1846 might be considered to have been about 4*d.* The planter anxiously inquires whether such depression is likely to be permanent, and also whether other cultures, such as that of the sugar-cane, are not more profitable. And though at first he endeavours to meet low prices by the production of iucreased quantities, yet as prices continue to decline, he concludes that cultivation must diminish unless a rise takes place, for at the above low rates he asserts that it does not pay. Probably if it had not been for the extension of territory and the richness of soil of the southern states, some diminution would have taken place generally, as its culture has not of late increased much in the Atlantic states, indeed it has in many parts diminished, as the soil became less fertile, and the farmer's slaves or stock required renewing.

But as the planter occasionally enjoys the benefit of an increased price for his produce, endeavours are constantly made to advance prices by sending unfavorable reports of the prospects of the crop. Such reports are eagerly re-echoed by the active body of speculators, and they are said to be sometimes assisted by the bankers of the Southern States making advances on the cotton in the interior, in order to enable the planters to keep it for a time out of the market. "Similar statements continue to be made from year to year, and are usually unfounded. Prices, moreover, which have been forced up by speculators, alternately break down through the combined influence of the increased supplies (from India and elsewhere), and of the diminished consumption which inevitably results from a heavy advance in the price of the raw material."—(*Manchester Guardian.*)

Unsuitable as low prices may be to the American planter, and disastrous as a deficient supply always is to the manufacturer, the irregularity of prices is most discouraging, not only to the merchants but to the cultivators of a distant country like India. For before any large quantity can arrive from thence, the fall in price will in many cases have taken place, and the Indian exporters will suffer, as they often have done. So, also, if the cultivator should, by the demand of one year, have been induced to extend his breadth of culture, he will find that even before his crop can be gathered, the price has fallen and the great demand for his cotton apparently ceased, from the preference given for the cleaner cotton of America.

CULTURE OF COTTON IN INDIA.

Vastly important as cotton is to England and to America, it is not less so to India, though Indian cotton is but little esteemed by our manufacturers. It forms but a small part of the imports into this country, but a more conspicuous feature of those into China; the two quantities together, however, make but an insignificant portion of what is produced in the country. For it may be seen cultivated in patches in almost every part of its wide extent, in some provinces forming nearly one fourth part of the *khureef*, or wet season crop, and necessarily an important item in the agriculturalist's returns. But it is also of great importance to the manufacturing population, and to the people themselves. Its hundred millions of inhabitants are clothed in home-grown cotton, in the hot weather, and in the rains in calicoes and muslins, and in winter in an additional quantity, for their calico coats are padded with cotton. At night they lie on beds and pillows stuffed with cotton, and instead of blankets they cover themselves with quilts of calico padded with the same material. In place of doors and windows they hang up curtains padded with cotton. Awnings and carpets, tents and tent ropes, the coverings of carriages, the housings of elephants, and the halters of horses, are all made of cotton.

Mr. Woodbury, Secretary to the United States' Treasury, calculated the cotton crop of India as amounting, in the year 1834, to 185,000,000 pounds; but this is far short of the truth, unless the crop for export only is intended. For in the year 1818, 90,000,000; in 1836, 80,000,000; and in 1841, upwards of 100,000,000 pounds were exported to this country, besides considerable quantities, as 50,000,000 also in 1818 to China, and a little into Nepal and the Sikh territories. These were only the surplus of what was required for the use of the inhabitants and for the manufacture of cotton goods which were in the same years exported to different parts of Asia, and some even to Europe. Major General Briggs,* who has paid considerable attention to the subject, and is well acquainted with the habits of the natives of India, estimates that they require

* Gen. Briggs, in a paper read before the Royal Asiatic Society, stated that the ordinary dress of a male Hindoo consists of—

not less than 375,000,000 pounds, for only a single dress weighing two pounds and a half, and that as much more cotton will be required for all the other purposes for which it is employed; making the annual crop amount to 750,000,000 pounds. But he adds that Dr. Wight, considers that each individual in India consumes twenty pounds of cotton for those different purposes per annum, and that this "would be equivalent to about 3,000,000,000 annually used in the country." This, however, appears too high an estimate, as the number of those who use less than twenty pounds greatly preponderates over those who use so much. In N. W. India it is calculated that if a district produce only 5 lbs. for each individual, it is barely sufficient for the wants of the people, and that 2 lbs. is not enough for the poorest

A dhoty	4	square yards		
Doputta	8	„		
A Turban	12½	„		
Not less than	24½	„	weighing above	3½ lbs.
Add to this, the sary, or female dress	8	„	„	1½ „
We have	32½	„	„	5 „

Those who do not wear the dhoty invariably wear a cotton waistband, besides a loose gown and trousers; and he assumed 2½ lbs. to be worn by each well-clad person, which must be below the truth. To the Cotton Committee, he replied:

"1343. From your knowledge of the people of India, can you say whether the consumption of cotton amongst them is very extensive; in fact, that cotton is used by them to a much larger extent than it is amongst the population of this country for a great variety of articles?—It is used for all the purposes that hemp and flax, and hair and wool, are used in this country. The home consumption is something enormous. I exhibited at the Asiatic Society the cloth of a man's dress and a female's dress, and the weight of those two was five pounds; the average dress of each inhabitant, therefore, was two and a half pounds; and if we multiply that by the population, assuming it to be 150,000,000 over the whole of India, it will amount to 375,000,000 of pounds. But it is used for beds, pillows, cushions, awnings, canopies, and ceilings, draperies and hangings, carpets, screens, curtains, quilting and padding of every description, both for padding clothes and for saddles, for tents, ropes for tents, halters for horses, and, in fact, applied to all the purposes that hemp and wool are used for in this country. I assumed at that time, without any correct data, that it would require at least as much more annually for such purposes, which would make an amount of 750,000,000 pounds. But I find that Dr. Wight states, who has had a much better opportunity of judging than I had, that each individual in India consumes 20 pounds of cotton for those different purposes per annum, which I have estimated at 5 pounds. Now, for the limited quantity that I have stated, it would require 312,000 tons of shipping to move it; but, if Dr. Wight is right in estimating it at four times the amount, that would be equivalent to about 3,000,000,000 annually used in the country."

peasant. The quantity produced must evidently be immensely large, and that which is exported bears but a small proportion to what is consumed in the country. But if so large a quantity of cotton wool is used up by the people themselves for clothing and coverings, it is evident that, in a country where spinning and weaving are all done by hand, multitudes of the natives must be employed in the cotton manufacture of India. A writer in the 'Examiner,' well acquainted with India, and who considers the population to amount to 120,000,000, estimates that allowing ten shillings for the annual worth of every person's wardrobe, it would amount to £60,000,000 of manufacture, which is equal to the highest value that has been set upon that of this country. We need not at present consider whether this is too high an estimate, nor attempt to calculate the number of acres which must annually be under cultivation to produce the immense crop of Indian cotton. But it may be admitted that the culture appears to be of sufficient importance to command the attention of the agriculturalist, the more so as the different qualities of his produce can all be used up, the best for weaving and the worst for padding. Such considerations may, however, make him indifferent to the demands of foreign commerce.

We have hitherto spoken of India as a great country, growing immense quantities of raw material, and making it up into useful clothing for her teeming population; also long famous for exporting her elegant fabrics to the most civilized nations of ancient as of modern times. In the present day, however, we often hear the country talked of only in the light of a cotton farm, whose business it should be to supply the raw material to England whenever it is required, and to take back her manufactured goods in any quantities that the makers choose to send. If we consider the disastrous consequences which ensue in England upon the occurrence of a short supply, and of an increased price, of cotton, it is not surprising that not only those who are engaged in the manufacture, but that the public, should feel interested in the field of culture being enlarged. So that the irregularities of supply, dependent as these chiefly are on vicissitudes of climate, might be neutralised; and also that the manufacturer should be more independent of the intervention of untoward political events. India, notwithstanding its enormous distance, is generally looked to as the country which, from its great extent, and apparently illimitable powers of production, is capable of counter-balancing the existing irregularities of supply and price. As the occasional deficiencies of America, and the consequent demands of England, have frequently occurred, and for a series of years, it is eagerly asked why India does not, like America, send, not only a regular but a regularly increasing supply of cotton. It is not doubted that it must be the wish, and would be for the benefit of the Indian farmer to share more largely in a commerce which the American planter makes a principal object of desire, indeed nearly monopolises. That he does not do so is ascribed by some, as we have stated, to mismanagement, and by others to the absence of a regular demand and of remunerative prices. Of the demand for cotton in general, there can be no doubt. If India, therefore, has anything to complain of in this respect, it must be owing to the nature of Indian cotton, or to the state in which it is sent to market. As the whole question may be found to hinge upon such points, we shall inquire into their truth before discussing questions of price, or of improvements in culture or cleaning, or the alleged impediments to the increased imports of Indian cotton.

Nature and Present Condition of Indian Cotton.

It is evident that, before proceeding with the question whether India is capable of supplying more cotton for the manufactures of Europe, it is necessary to determine whether the manufacturers themselves do actually require, in large quantities, such cotton as the natives themselves use, and which India could most easily send: or whether it is some other kind or condition of cotton which is to be grown, or prepared, in India. The questions, it is clear, are very different; one dependent upon causes which have been, or may still be, in existence; the other, probably, on the proper application of knowledge and principles derived from other sources. We shall first discuss the nature and present condition of Indian cotton, and then proceed to improvements in cleaning and in culture of the different kinds of cotton, and ascertain of what quality and at what prices these can be produced in India.

With regard to the quality of Indian cotton, it will readily be admitted that some of it at least must be fitted for the purposes of cotton manufacture, if we consider only the substantial appearance and well-known durability of the far-famed Indian calicoes, or the delicacy of texture of the still more celebrated muslins of Dacca, as it was and still is, or of the Chunderee of the present day. These are described by Tavernier as "so fine, that you can hardly feel them in your hand;" while they have been described more poetically as "webs of woven air," and were attempted to be depreciated by an English writer of the 17th century calling them "only the shadow of a commodity." It may happen, however, that cotton, well fitted for such purposes when spun by the delicate fingers of the Hindoo, may yet be unfit for the iron handling of machinery. As it is, the weaver of the southern provinces depends for a part of the success of his manufacture upon the softness of his climate, while the stern Mahomedan of north-west India immures himself in underground workshops, of which the air is artificially moistened, in order to produce the beautiful fabrics which are prized by, and still adorn, the wealthy of his land.

It is probable, however, that the cotton of different provinces of an extensive country like India may differ so much, that what is produced in one part may be fit for the purposes of the English spinner, while he may be unwilling to employ another, even though esteemed for many native manufactures. The extent and regularity of the foreign demand for Indian cotton will often depend, in a great measure, upon the proportion brought to market of that which is of the best quality to that which is indifferent; and it is very certain that the best commodity may be sent in so dirty or adulterated a state to market, as greatly to depreciate its value, and interfere with its regular employment.

Indian cotton is well known to have certain good qualities of its own. By the natives of India it is esteemed for wearing well; in this country it is valued for its colour. Mr. Bazley, in reply to a question by a member of the Cotton Committee, stated that "the Indian cotton is always of a rich creamy colour, and for its colour it is frequently used as a mixture to improve the colour of the worst or low American cotton." It is also thought well of for taking some dyes better than American cotton, and for its thread swelling in the process of bleaching; so that cloth made with it becomes more substantial in appearance. This property has long been known to the weavers of India. Thus Mr. Bebb, who was Resident at Dacca and afterwards a Director of the East India Company, stated, in 1789, that "the general distinction in quality the natives make, is, whether the thread made therefrom swells or not in the bleaching. That which is in the neighbourhood of the city (Dacca) to the eastward is reckoned not to swell, if it be not used the same season that it is gathered. The thread made of cotton produced in the south-east swells in bleaching, but less than the Hindostan cotton. The thread in the country west and north-west swells much in bleaching, more especially if it be hard twisted." These facts are interesting, as showing the minute attention paid by the natives of India to the cotton employed in their calicoes and muslins. But they do not prove the fitness of Indian cotton for English machinery, because most of it has one great defect, that is shortness of fibre, or of staple as it is called, which, though capable of being twisted between the fingers, may yet be blown away during the various processes of machine spinning.

In wishing to ascertain the fitness of Indian cotton for English manufactures, it is useless to adduce the opinions of any but of those who have seen its practical working. For brokers even, who have spent their lives in the employment, are fallible, and spinners do not pronounce a final opinion on a sample of cotton, until they have seen by experiment the quantity of yarn it produces in proportion to the waste. But on this point we have excellent evidence from the Presidents of the two Commercial bodies of Manchester, though we have to regret that it is not in favour of Indian cotton; but the truth is at all times preferable to mystification. Mr. Bazley, President of the Chamber of Commerce of Manchester, examined by the Committee of the House of Commons on the growth of cotton in India, and who uses only the finest kinds, as he stated, "perhaps no spinner has bought as largely as I have (cotton) at 1*s*. 6*d*. per lb.:" and the author has been told that "Gardner and Bazley's is of the very highest class of yarns." With respect to the quantity of cotton imported from India,

Mr. Bazley stated that it was, upon an average, about 10 to 13 per cent. of the whole quantity imported into the country, but that the Indian cotton is so inferior, that the consumers have a table arranged to enable them to see, at a glance, what price they ought to give for it relatively to the American Orleans, or to the "Boweds." Thus, the spinner of No. 20 yarn says, when the Surat cotton is at 3*d.* a pound, it is his interest to give $3\frac{1}{2}$*d.* a pound for American, for that he obtains from Surat only 12 ounces of yarn, whilst from American he obtains $13\frac{1}{2}$ ounces.

Surat and American Cotton, at equivalent prices.

1 lb. Surat, yielding 12 oz. yarn.	1 lb. American, $13\frac{1}{2}$ oz.
3*d.*	$3\frac{1}{2}$*d.*
$3\frac{1}{8}$	$3\frac{3}{8}$
$3\frac{1}{4}$	$3\frac{3}{4}$
$3\frac{3}{8}$	4
$3\frac{1}{2}$	$4\frac{1}{8}$
$3\frac{5}{8}$	$4\frac{1}{4}$
$3\frac{7}{8}$	$4\frac{1}{2}$
4	$4\frac{3}{8}$
$4\frac{1}{8}$	$4\frac{5}{8}$
$4\frac{1}{4}$	$4\frac{3}{4}$
$4\frac{1}{2}$	$4\frac{7}{8}$
$4\frac{3}{4}$	$5\frac{3}{8}$
5	6

It does not, however, appear, from this table, whether this difference of price is owing to the intrinsic inferiority of the Indian cotton, or to the dirty state in which it is usually sent to market. Both causes have, no doubt, their influence. For Mr. Bazley, in reply to questions, stated that it was found by experience, that the waste in using Surat cotton is 25 per cent., whilst from the American the loss is $12\frac{1}{2}$ per cent.; that is, that from every 100 lbs. of Surat cotton which the spinner takes into his mill, he produces 75 lbs. of yarn; and that from every 100 lbs. of American cotton, he produces $87\frac{1}{2}$ lbs.; also that the same machinery produces a larger quantity of yarn from the American cotton than from the Surat cotton, and when asked whether that does not arise from the smaller number of breakages, he replied—

"635. Yes; and from the American cotton requiring fewer turns from the spindle, and for the quantity of yarn coming through the rollers, less twist per inch.

"636. Are you aware whether the consumption of the Surat cotton is confined almost exclusively to the manufacture of the weft, that which runs across the piece, and not the warp, which is lengthways, in consequence of the Surat being so short in the staple?—In very coarse numbers the Surat is applied to warp purposes, but as the numbers increase, generally there is a mixture of the American with the Surat for weft."

A portion of the loss seems, however, to be made up, for Mr. Bazley further says:

"639. Is it always easy to distinguish one from the other by the colour?—Yes, it is. From Surat cotton, which cost $3\frac{1}{4}$*d.*, the yarn No. 20 is worth $5\frac{7}{8}$*d.*; and from American cotton, which cost $4\frac{1}{4}$*d.*, the yarn is worth $6\frac{1}{2}$*d.* You see that in using the American cotton, the spinner has actually a less amount for working the cotton than he has in the case of the Indian cotton; those are numbers 30; one is Surat, and the other American—[*handing in two other specimens*]—the Surat cotton for 30 cost $3\frac{1}{2}$*d.*, and the yarn is worth 7*d.*; the American cotton for 30 cost $4\frac{1}{2}$*d.*, and the yarn is worth $7\frac{3}{4}$*d.*; in that case the spinners have $3\frac{1}{2}$*d.* for making the Surat cotton into yarn, but for making the American cotton into yarn only $3\frac{1}{4}$*d.*"

"640. *Chairman.*] Do you suppose that the difference of a farthing is compensated or more than compensated by a smaller amount of loss in working up the American cotton?—Clearly by the greater turn off."

Provided that greater care was taken in cleaning the Indian cotton, it was stated that a speedy rise in price would take place in Liverpool. But mere cleaning is not sufficient, for some cotton from the neighbourhood of Agra, which had been "cleaned admirably," was yet stated to be unsuited to the English market, and, like the general produce of India, inferior.

"734. What increase would be necessary of such cotton as you could buy and profitably work up, to affect the price of the American cotton?—Probably from 10 to 25 per cent. of increase.

"735. How great an improvement in the cotton would be necessary to give you an article from India that you could buy and work up: you say that you do not buy much now?—An improvement of from 10 to 25 per cent. would, I should say, vastly increase the consumption of Indian cotton; I now speak of the quality."

"745. Mr. *Bolling.*] From your knowledge of the state of

trade, do you think that the import of Indian cotton into this country is likely to increase at all, as long as the native-grown cotton is adhered to?—I have seen some of the native cotton that is very little inferior to the American—the Surats; but I am satisfied that the quality of the cotton must be greatly improved before we can use it to advantage."

Mr. Aspinall Turner, President of the Commercial Association of Manchester, was next examined. He, on the contrary, has "been a large consumer of Indian cotton for many years, and indeed was not aware of any one in Manchester consuming more Indian cotton than himself." He, however, does not give a more favorable character of the Indian cotton, as fitted for general purposes. In the first place, Mr. Turner stated that there is very little refuse, technically called waste, in using American cotton, for most of it could be disposed of, for "the purposes of inferior spinning;" while, of the Surat, a large portion comes which cannot be worked into inferior or coarse articles. But some of this, the author believes, can be used for wadding, and for paper-making. It is unfortunate that the word "Surat" is frequently used to signify Indian cotton generally, because the best kind of Indian cotton, which is nearly equal in quality to middling Uplands, is produced in the neighbourhood of Surat, and brings a higher price than any other Indian cotton from indigenous seed.

We shall immediately adduce Mr. Turner's opinion respecting the dirty state of Indian cotton. With regard to its quality, he said, "I do not think that there will be a very great increase in the importations of Indian cotton, if the quality remains of an inferior description, as hitherto;" but "if you can improve the quality of the Indian cotton, so as to meet the American cotton in the market, it will never fall off." So Messrs. Hollinshed and Tetly, the well-known brokers of Liverpool, in their circular for 1847 inform their constituents that, "of Surat cotton it is worthy of remark, that the consumption has been greater than in any former year, a sure indication of a bad trade." Major-General Briggs, well acquainted with the subject, and warmly disposed towards India, at a General Court of the East India Company, held on the 20th February of the present year, remarked: "As to the complaint of the Manchester gentlemen that they could not get cotton from India, that was owing entirely to the fact, that the cotton which they required was not such as the natives of India used."

Mr. R. W. Crawford, a Bombay merchant, took a contrary view to the great spinners of Manchester, for he stated, that "it is a question more of reduction in price at present than of improvement in quality;" and on being asked whether the spinners in Lancashire would purchase cotton for spinning in this country, such as is grown in India at present, and to the exclusion of American cotton, provided it was cheap enough, replied, "Yes, if they could buy it cheap enough for those purposes," and also, "if the cotton were cheap enough, its quality is sufficiently good to afford material for the spinning of three fourths of all the cotton spun in this country at the present time." "Q. 2759. For the great bulk of the trade they use the lower numbers?—Yes, the great bulk of the trade spinning under 20's." So Mr. Chapman, Manager of the Great India Peninsular Railway Company, in his 'Statement of Cotton Facts,' addressed to T. Bazley, Esq., as Chairman of the Chamber of Commerce, Manchester, states, "that cotton of good quality, for English use, is always to be had in Berar (Central India, 300 to 400 miles from Bombay) at about $1\frac{1}{2}$*d.* per lb., ranging of late years from $1\frac{1}{4}$*d.* to $1\frac{7}{8}$*d.* The quality of this cotton is such, that at a certain relative difference of price (averaging about 15 per cent. less for Indian than American), it can be used instead of American for more than 50 per cent. of our manufactures," that is, it will afford material for all yarns under No. 20. This is a question that can be decided only by spinners and manufacturers; the author regrets that he has been unable, notwithstanding numerous inquiries, to obtain confirmation of the correctness of this opinion, though he would rejoice to do so, as the question would then be comparatively easy, especially as the cottons of Broach and Surat, districts situate close to the sea-coast, produce cottons which are considered superior in quality to those of the far distant territories of the Nizam. The author, however, has no doubt, from facts which will be afterwards adduced, that some of the indigenous cotton of India is fitted for the purposes described, and a portion of it for even higher numbers; but he believes that the great mass of the cotton produced in India is not so fitted from the shortness of staple. But an important practical inference may be deduced from the fact of the indigenous cotton of one part of India being longer in the staple than that of another, as they are both produced by the same species of plant. For if so, it becomes an important point to determine the physical states in which such cotton is produced, and to ascertain whether the same peculiarities of soil and of climate, with suitable culture, cannot be found in other parts of India.

With regard to the dirty state in which Indian cotton is sent to market, we shall see, that in the unchangeable East, things still are as they long have been. Thus, in 1803, we find it stated, "The native sort was not well cleared from seeds and extraneous matter." (*E.I.C.'s Cotton Papers*, p. 28.) In 1810, when a large quantity of cotton had been imported by the East India Company, we find the Court of Directors writing to Bombay, "that no excuse will hereafter be admitted by us for the foulness, dirt, and seeds, which are suffered to remain mixed with the cotton; and it is our positive order, that the commissions be not paid to any commercial resident whose provision of cotton shall be faulty in this particular," (l. c. p. 35 and 36.) That no improvement has taken place, even up to the present time, with the great mass of Indian cotton, is clear from the evidence of Mr. Turner, who stated, "that in the spinning establishment of which I am at the head, we are in the habit of throwing upon the waste land an amount of dirt, for which we have paid 7,000*l.* per annum, chiefly consisting of soil, sand, dirt, and various extraneous matters which have been introduced, I suppose, or have never been cleaned out of the cotton." (Q. 789.)

The author, in a paper read before the Statistical Section of the British Association at Oxford, June 28, 1847, said: "Thus, at other times, we are told, that the chief impediments to an increased consumption of Indian cotton, is the dirty state in which it reaches the manufacturer; this dirtiness being dependant, in the first instance, on the careless manner in which it is first collected, and then housed; or it is owing to the fraudulent additions made to it by the bunyas or wakarias, who purchase it from the ryots. Thus, it is sometimes adulterated with seed, cotton in seed, fine sand, or finely-powdered salt, scattered over it at intervals; as the dews of night are allowed to fall upon it when spread out in an open court or yard, and before the sun is up it is packed into bales. Sometimes an inferior is mixed with a superior kind of cotton, by a process technically called 'flogging.' Further injury is sustained by the daily unloading when conveyed on bullocks. These, moreover, are described as eating up the cotton 'by mouthfuls out of the bales;' also that 'the brinjaries and cartmen themselves steal largely;' and finally that even the boatmen, in conveying the cotton from the tender to the ships, steal a good deal of cotton, as 'canoes and small boats come alongside, under one pretence or another, and receive the bundles previously prepared and secreted.' The same thing takes place in the conveyance of cotton from Broach to Bombay, as liquor boats come alongside those conveying the cotton, and exchange some of their arrack for cotton, which is abstracted from the bales, and its weight supplied with sand, mud, or salt water."

We may now produce proofs of the above statements, and see how all this dirt gets admission into the cotton. We shall take the evidence of those chiefly who are practically engaged in the subject, and shall see how much the cultivator is in fault, and how little he is encouraged to take any pains in improving the state of this great staple. We refer not to one, but to the principal cotton districts of India, some situated near the coast, others far in the interior, but all labouring under the same reproach of sending dirty cotton to market.

The province of GUZERAT may first command our notice, as being one of the principal cotton districts of India, and having within it both Surat and Broach, the two places most celebrated for the goodness of the indigenous cotton. All parts of the district are, moreover, within a short distance of the sea-coast of the Gulf of Cambay. The produce is, moreover, conveyed only in carts and in the dry weather, it cannot, therefore, suffer from the state of the roads; while the freight from Broach to Bombay, as stated by the Bombay Cotton Committee, is as low as from London to Hull. Mr. Vaupell, who describes himself as having had several years' occupation and experience in the cotton trade (from 1818 to 1826), has published the result of his observations in the 'Transactions of the Agricultural Society of Bombay.' Mr. Vaupell says: "The cleanliness of the article depends mainly upon the attention bestowed in the gathering; but the cotton, as it comes from the gin, is beautifully clean, and if forthwith taken to the screws and packed in bales, would be all that could be desired; but it is generally either put into burkees or dokras (large gunny or cloth bags), in carts; and while so doing, is adulterated with seed, cotton in seed, fine sand, or finely-powdered salt, scattered over it at intervals. Another mode of adulteration is, by having the entire area of the yard, or court, daily fresh cow-dunged about sunset in the evening; and the cotton, as it comes from the churkas, spread thereon before the ground is half dry. The dews of the night are then allowed to fall upon it; and early next morning, before the sun is up, it is packed into bales. This process, besides tinging and soiling the cotton with the wet cow-dung and earth, adds considerably to the weight of the article, while it materially injures it both in fibre and cleanliness.

"The cultivator has, generally speaking, no immediate inducement to render the produce of his fields unfit for the market, for in most cases he disposes of the cotton in seed, in the state in which it is gathered; from that moment his concern about it ceases, and it rests with the purchaser, or middleman, to prepare it for the exporter." These "agents employed between the grower and the exporter are generally Bannians, who, to the eastward of the Gulf of Cambay, are termed Wakarias. It is these people who find their interest in adulterating the cotton previous to disposing of it to the exporter." "Of late years the quality of the produce has deteriorated considerably, more particularly in respect of cleanliness."

This view is fully confirmed in the 'Letter of the Bombay Chamber of Commerce to the Government of that Presidency,' dated Jan. 21, 1841, from which the author also quoted in the above paper.

"The baneful influence of these Wakarias or Middlemen, is considered by the Bombay Chamber of Commerce as the principal cause which impedes the extension and improvement of the culture and trade of cotton in Western India, and which they characterize, 'as the state of hopeless pecuniary bondage in which the ryots are kept from one generation to another to the Wakarias and village Bunyans.' These men make advances to the ryots to enable them to sow their cotton, and to pay their assessment, purchasing the produce always before it is gathered, more frequently before it is ripened, often before it is even sown. It is the same class of persons, the Wakarias, to whom most of the frauds enumerated above are to be attributed, and till the baneful influence of these men is supplanted, either by the gradual settlement of a superior class of agents in the districts, or by bringing those districts, by the aid of steam, within the immediate and certain reach of the European merchants, all other measures, it is feared, will fail." Again, par. 55, "With the employment of all other modes of encouragement, this the committee consider to be after all the great, almost the only eventually effectual, remedy for the numerous causes, whether arising from poverty, from ignorance, from negligence, or from fraud, which at present obstruct the improvement in cotton."

Merwanjee Hormusjee, who "served for several years, and with distinguished credit, as native agent for the provision of the Company's China and British Cotton investments," under Mr. Pelly, and who has since done much for the improvement of cotton, ascribes, "the principal cause of the cotton of India not fetching prices equal to that of America, &c., "to the very careless manner in which it (the cotton) is gathered from the plant, and immediately after thrown into deep pits (kullees) dug for the purpose, and in which it becomes mixed up with clods of earth, imbibes the night-dues (dews) whereby its colour and quality become injured." Dr. Gibson, who is so well acquainted with the habits and modes of thinking of the Natives, says, (*House of Commons' Return*, p. 60,) "They prefer the tolerably certain return received for the inferior article, to the trouble and expense required to produce cotton of superior cleanness." Dr. Johnston, Civil-Surgeon at Ahmedabad, attributes, (l. c.) among other causes, the little improvement in the gathering of cotton in Guzerat, "to the better return which the merchant in Bombay finds for the uncleaned and cheaper cotton, than he does for the cleanly-gathered and dearer article." Mr. Vibart, the Revenue-Commissioner of Bombay, (*Return*, p. 66,) writes, that "the cultivators find that as ready a sale is obtained for cotton in a dirty and adulterated state as when brought to the market in a clean and first-rate condition, while the difference of price between the two articles does not repay them for the additional time and labour."

The Southern Mahratta country, lying to the south, as

Guzerat does to the north of Bombay, is the next district which we shall notice: it contains within it the district and town of Dharwar. From thence much of the cotton, known in the market as Coompta cotton, is obtained. The distance is about 100 miles to the port of shipment, and the expenses of conveyance were stated, by Mr. Mercer, to be 10 rupees for 784 lbs. of cotton, which cost from 40 to 50 rupees, but that they would not be more than 5 rupees if a cart-road was made all the way, that is, down the mountain-side. This road has been made, and the expenses must therefore be reduced.

Mr. Shaw, collector, of Dharwar, in 1843, wrote, "That a cultivator that will clean and tend his jawarree (millet) and wheat-field, will leave his cotton plantation to take care of itself, gathering the wool at the close of the season, some of which has fallen, and been lying for days on the ground, some scarcely in a fit state to be picked; neither can he understand that it is of any kind of importance it should be otherwise, although he knows full well, were he to pursue this course with his jawarree, or wheat, that he would be a sufferer, as the persons who purchase the one consume it on the spot, whilst the cotton is bought by an indifferent agent, shipped to a distant market, and there fetches just perhaps a remunerating price."

Messrs. Mercer and Blount, two of the American planters who have contributed so much to the improvement of the cotton of India, on their return had an interview with the Commercial Association of Manchester. Mr. Blount stated that the ryots "leave all the cotton in the field until the whole is ripe, and then they make one gathering of it; they get together the fresh and the old, making no distinction between the cotton and the dirt." Mr. Mercer stated that the person who usually advanced money to the ryot was himself a poor man. "He obtained this money from the banker, and buys the cotton from the ryot in connexion with a large merchant, whose business it is to screw down the middleman to the lowest figure he can. The latter has no margin to go on; and on the slightest fluctuation of price, he has recourse to the expedient of scattering in seed and putting water on the cotton, to increase the weight. The native merchant afterwards does not hesitate, if his profits do not promise to be large, to add a little sand and water also, and thinks there is nothing like having good weight when he delivers it (the cotton), and he knew many instances where the cotton had been repacked and the same system carried on."

Mr. Shaw says (l. c., p. 483), "It is, moreover, to me a mystery that a mercantile community like that existing in Bombay, should contentedly continue purchasing ill-cleaned and badly-cultivated cotton-wool at the Presidency, when an individual or company may here, on the spot, purchase cotton grown, if they please, under their own instructions, clean it, screw it, and ship it, at nearly half the price."

Before proceeding further, it is desirable to notice the quantities of cotton which are imported into, and afterwards exported from Bombay. The Cotton Committee appointed there in 1846, give in their Report, dated March 1847, a detailed account of the sources whence cotton is obtained, and packed and screwed into bales in the Island of Bombay previous to being re-exported. Thus—*Abstract of Statement* A:

Average Annual Imports into Bombay for thirteen years, ending with 1846.

From Guzerat	59,873,024
„ Conkun (Concan) .	30,763,610
„ Malabar and Canara	11,684,583
„ Cutch and Scinde .	5,397,438
„ All other quarters .	110,366
Total	107,829,021

The average exports for the same years are stated by the Committee in their Report, to have amounted to 117,303,364 pounds, and that the largest export was in 1843-44, and amounted to 171,453,725 pounds; and that the smallest export was in 1834-35, and "That the first eight months of the current year 1846-47, is proportionately much lower than any year immediately preceding it." With respect to the discrepancy between the imports and exports the Committee observe, p. 11: "In completion of these statistical records of the Cotton trade of Bombay, we beg leave to submit to government the following further information, which has been placed at the disposal of the Committee in the course of its inquiries:

Statement (H) showing the quantity of Cotton imported into Bombay by sea from 1834 to 1846 inclusive, to have been .	12,515,868 cwts.
Statement (I) showing the quantity sent in over the Sion Causeway from 1st May 1839 to 31st Dec. 1846, to have been: India maunds 220,199 22a., or	161,805 cwts.
Total .	12,677,673 cwts.

Or 937,896 cwts. less than the quantity which appears according to Statement (A)."

The Committee also observe: "That the decline in quantity has been accompanied for seven years by a gradually increasing decline in value also." With regard to this observation, it is probable that the former is only a consequence of the latter. For the Committee afterwards refer to "the healthy action produced upon the market by the comparatively small advance in the prices paid at Liverpool in August and September last, an advance which was quite sufficient to leave considerable profit to the exporter, with some benefit to the cotton trade also."

The quantity of cotton produced in Guzerat was estimated, in the year 1789, to have been about 43,000 candies (of 784 lbs.), of which from 25,000 to 30,000 bales were exported. The price at that time of Ahmood and Broach cotton is stated to have been, at Surat, in March, Rs. 95 per candy, and in April, Rs. 98, but which fell before the season closed, in May, to Rs. 88 or Rs. 90. The price at Broach was from Rs. 12 to 15 less, according as the cotton had been brought by sea or by land to Surat. (E. I. C.'s papers, p. 10.) The zillah of 'Baroche' was acquired by conquest and cession in 1802-3 and in 1817; Lieut.-Colonel Williams, who surveyed it from 1816 to 1820, writes that "kuppas (seed-cotton) has of late years become a primary object of cultivation in this collectorate, as well as in the adjoining purgunnah, in consequence of the advance in its price from Rs. 45 to about Rs. 70 per bar (960 lbs.)" "The quality of all the cotton of the collectorate is the same, but its value is affected by its being gathered and kept free from all kinds of dirt, leaves, &c.; it is divided by the Commercial Department into three classes, according to the degrees of its cleanness; and the first class, or toomel (picked), fetches 4 rupees per bar more than the third class, which is called "rasee."—'*Survey*,' p. 42.

The average exports of cotton from the different ports of Guzerat to Bombay, from the year 1834 to 1846, were about 60,000,000 of pounds, but in 1840-41, amounted to upwards of 96,000,000. A candy of cotton (784 lbs.), which had been as high as Rs. 165 in 1817-18, was sold in Bombay, in 1846, as low as 67 rupees; but the average at that time was 75, and is now about 80 rupees.

The Guzerat cotton, as it is sometimes all called, is produced within the Collectorates of Surat, Broach, Ahmedabad, and the contiguous native states; for instance, that which comes from Gogo is the produce of Kattywar, while some Candeish cotton is occasionally sent down by the Comdabarree Pass into the Surat Collectorate, and is from thence forwarded by sea to Bombay.

Under the head of Cutch and Scinde are included the produce of the former province, and the extensive native districts contiguous thereto, including all cotton exported from Kattywar, excepting that from Gogo.

The cotton which comes from the Conkun, or is exported from the ports under the Tanna and Rutnagerry Collectorates, such as Oomergaum, Tanapoor, Mahim, Bassein, Callian, Salsette, Caranja, Panwell, Rygur, Rajapoor, Anjunwell, Rutnagerry, Viziadroog, Malwan, and Vingorla, is the produce of the Collectorates of Candeish and of Sholapore, but to a much greater extent of the western parts of Berar, as far south as Shorapore (not Sholapore): some of this is known at Bombay as Bursee cotton.

The cotton from Canara and Malabar, exported from the various ports of the extended coast, and known as Coompta cotton at Bombay from the principal port, is the produce of the Collectorates of Belgaum and of Dharwar, commonly called the Southern Mahratta country, as well as of the most southern part of Berar; and likewise of Bellary and the neighbouring districts of the Madras Presidency, to which these two Collectorates indeed belong.

The average exports from Canara to Bombay amounted for the thirteen years ending with 1846 to about ten millions of pounds annually, and from Malabar to somewhat less than a million annually for the same period, having been only 728 pounds in 1837-38, though much higher in other years.

" Another item of great importance in the calculation of the cost of the cotton of Western India remains now to be considered; namely, the expense of conveying it from the various districts of its production to Bombay, as the port of shipment. We find, with respect to the cost of bringing cotton to Bombay by sea, whether from the ports of Guzerat to the northward, or those of the Conkun and Canara to the southward, that the ordinary rates of freight on native craft are sufficiently low, excepting occasionally towards the close of the fair season, to preclude the possibility of any reduction of practical utility being effected under this head. Three rupees per candy of seven cwt. appears to be about the average rate throughout the season from Broach, Tunkaria Bunder and Coompta, a rate which, if we suppose every candy of cotton to be carried 250 miles by sea, will be found not to exceed three fourths to seven eighths of a penny per ton per mile, and not more, we understand, than would be incurred in sending the same cotton a similar distance in the United Kingdom, or say between London and Hull, when the navigation is not closed for one third of the year, as it is in this country."

If we proceed further southward into the territories of the MADRAS PRESIDENCY, we find the same methods pursued. Mr. Sullivan, then (in 1840) a Member of Council at Madras, observes in a Minute, that "Dr. Wight gives 70 and 90 rupees the candy of 500lbs. as the price paid for the Bourbon and indigenous cotton of the South of India; these are the prices paid to the brokers; the prices paid to the growers do not exceed 40 or 50 rupees, about 2¼*d.* per lb., while the price realized by the exporter is from 6*d.* to 11*d.*" It is quite clear from this that what is wanted, as Dr. Wight observes, is "more competition among buyers, and somewhat higher prices to growers." The distance from Coimbatore to Cochin, the port of shipment, is 150 miles, 90 of cart-road and 60 of backwater. The expenses, according to Mr. Petrie, are 6¾ rupees for cart and boat for a bale of cotton from Coimbatore to Cochin.

Mr. Fischer, who has long been settled in the interior, and is described by the Madras Government as having extensive annual contracts with the cotton growers of the Salem and Coimbatore districts, gives it as his opinion, in a letter, dated 14th May 1841, to the Chief Secretary of the Government of Fort St. George, "that the general inferiority of our cotton is to be attributed mainly to the manner in which the trade in this article is at present carried on, namely, by the medium of a succession of brokers, from the dubash of the Madras agent to the village chetty, who advances to the ryot in his hour of need, whereby but the smallest per-centage of profit remains to the ryot after each of these middlemen has made his own profit; and, consequently, the ryot has no sufficient inducement to bestow any other care than to reap the greatest possible quantity from his cotton-field." (*Return*, p. 315.)

Mr. Petrie, in his evidence before the Cotton Committee in 1848, having referred first to the carelessness of the natives in gathering their cotton, and to his having succeeded in inducing them to take more pains, stated that "the up-country market is badly regulated; good articles do not always sell at their real value, and the price, even for the best cotton in the market, is but little more than it is for the worst; cotton that would be sold in England at 4½*d.* per lb., and cotton that would only bring 3*d.*, will sell there within 3 or 4 per cent. of the same value; the cultivators know this, and therefore they have no object in bestowing more care and labour." (*Report*, p. 198.)

Mr. Finnie, one of the American planters, who had transferred his services from the Bengal Presidency to that of Madras, describes, in a letter to the latter Government, the state of the trade at Tinnivelly, the most southern cotton district, and from whence the cotton is shipped by the southern port of Tuticorin: "Here (Tinnivelly) the field is occupied by European agents, who instead of encouraging the people to bring clean cotton, give a premium indirectly on the dirtiest trash. A contract is made, usually by the house itself, with the chetties for such a quantity of cotton of such a quality, and the very lowest sum is fixed. The chetty, finding he cannot get a price that would justify the delivery of such cotton as he has contracted for, agrees to it, well knowing that they must take such as he chooses to deliver to them at the time. He knows they have their engagements to meet; they have made their arrangements; a ship is perhaps waiting; the presses are idle, and he brings in his cotton to the agent who has merely to receive it.

"The cotton is produced by the ryot. He is always in his banker's books, as deep in proportion to his means, as his European master, and can do nothing without aid. The brokers, or cotton cleaners, or gin-house men are the middlemen between the chetty and the ryot. The chetties, being monied men, make an advance to the broker. The broker is particular in classifying the seed-cotton, and pays for it according to cleanliness, and then he has much of the trash and rotten locks picked out, not to make the cotton better, but because the rubbish chokes the churka and prevents it from working. The good cotton is then separated from the seed; and the bad stuff, which had been taken away from the good, is beaten with a stone to loosen up the rotten fibre from the seed, and then it is passed through the churka. The good cotton and this bad stuff are both taken into a little room 6×6, which is entered by a low door about 18 inches by 2 feet, and a little hole, as a ventilator, is made through the outer wall. Two men then go in with a bundle of long smooth rods in each hand, and a cloth is tied over the mouth and nose; one man places his back so as to stop the little door completely, to prevent waste, and they both set to work to whip the cotton with their rods, to mix the *good and bad together* so thoroughly, that a very tolerable article is turned out. Even after all this bedevilling, if the people get a living price for it, they let it go as it is. But, as is usually the case, they are shaved so close, that they are driven to resort to another means of realizing a profit. They add a handful or two of seed to every bundle, and this is delivered to the chetties, and the chetties deliver it to the European agents, and the European agents save their exchange, and their object is gained. The cotton is taken by the manufacturer at a low price, because he knows not what he is buying."

Mr. Mercer has also stated, and Mr. Finnie confirms the statement, "that an inferior and dirty cotton is the more profitable article to the native trade, and even to the European merchants." The Marquis of Tweeddale, at that time Governor of Madras, observes upon this statement, "It is manifest from this, and from the inferior condition in which the cotton wool of India continues to be sent to the British market, that the interests of the dealer or broker, and the merchant, are not identical with those of the manufacturer or the Government.

"The object of the latter is to raise and bring into the market an article of such quality and at such a cost, as may stand in permanent competition with American cotton. The merchant and agent has no object in the transaction, but his immediate profits in any one year; and if the inferior article yield him as handsome or even a better profit than a selected and better article would do at a higher price, he will doubtless take it off the growers' and native dealers' hands to any extent, and it is hopeless to look for any permanent improvement under this system."

The exports of cotton from the Madras Presidency have never amounted to very large quantities; but still some was exported, even when much was imported from Berar and Nagpore for the use of the manufacturers of Masulipatam, and of other parts of the northern Circars. In the year 1812, the Madras Board of Trade applied for reports from Commercial Residents and Revenue Collectors, for information respecting cotton culture and commerce in the various collectorates of the Madras Presidency. (*E. I. C. Papers*, p. 398.) From their replies, General Briggs has calculated that about 25,000,000 of pounds were grown in the several districts, and that it was sold for $2\frac{1}{4}d.$, $3d.$, and $4d.$ a pound. During the thirteen years, ending with 1846, about 13,000,000 of pounds were annually exported from Madras, with about 3,000,000 of pounds from the Port of Tuticorin. Of late years Cochin has also become a port of export for cotton. In the present day much cotton is grown, and much more might be grown, in the southern districts of Salem, Coimbatore, and Tinnivelly, and is of a better quality than that grown in the western and northern districts of the Presidency, and has been sent to Liverpool and Manchester at an expense of about $3\frac{1}{2}d.$ a pound.

Though the provinces of Bengal, Behar, and Benares have long been famous for their manufactures of cotton goods, and have grown considerable quantities of cotton for their own use, they yet imported much from the tracts of country lying along both sides of the Jumna river, and from the distant regions of Central India, which used to be and still is brought to and conveyed down the Ganges. Though the cotton of the Bengal Presidency is not well fitted for the purposes of the English manufacturer, much of it may become so, as we hope afterwards to be able to show. Our present object is to adduce evidence only respecting the state in which the natives themselves produce their cotton, as being that in which it enters the market in competition with that of other parts of the world.

If the soil and climate were found suitable for the production, Bengal, from its vicinity to the sea and ample water-carriage, is admirably situated for the culture of even the superior kinds of cotton. But there seems never to have been enough grown even for home consumption, or Bengal would not have been an importer of cotton; but much of this must, no doubt, have been required for the extensive manufactures of cotton goods which used to be exported to all parts of Asia, and even to Europe. In the present day Bengal imports yarns from Europe, instead of cotton from Central India, and is perhaps by this means enabled to keep up a manufacture which might otherwise have been entirely destroyed. It is curious to observe that, in the late depressed state of the cotton market in this country, the finer yarns were those for the Indian market, and were the only ones in demand.* In 1789 the price of cotton at Dacca was from $5\frac{1}{2}$ to $6\frac{1}{2}$ rupees a maund. In 1831 we learn from Mr. Lamb, long resident there, that its price had fallen from 5 to $3\frac{1}{2}$ rupees, and that the culture was not at all in favour with the farmers.

Though some cotton must undoubtedly have always been grown in Bengal itself, a quantity seems also to have been imported by sea from Surat, for in 1789 we learn, by a letter from the Governor in Council at Bombay, that "of late years cotton has not been in great demand in Bengal, consequently little or none has been sent thither." So from Dacca at the same period, we learn from Mr. Bebb, that Surat cotton was formerly brought to this port, but that none has arrived for several years, and probably will not in future. By Mr. Taylor, we are told that "the first imports by the Ganges seem to have taken place in 1783."† From the reports which were at that time called for of the extent of the culture of cotton, it would

* "In 30s, 40s, and 50s mule twist, suitable for India, the market is steady, prices being well sustained by the adequacy of the demand, to take up the production as it becomes disengaged." (*Manchester paper*, March, 1850.)

† These statements are taken from a work, entitled 'On the Culture and Manufacture of Cotton Wool, Raw Silk, and Tobacco in India,' ordered to be printed, in 1836, by the Court of Directors of the East India Company. It consists of extracts from reports and letters from the authorities in India, from 1788 to 1836. It will be quoted as the East India Company's Papers, to distinguish it from 'The Return,' called for by the House of Commons, which carries on the history from 1836 to 1847, and from the 'Report of the Cotton Committee of the House of Commons of 1848.' The later references are from official documents which have been received subsequent to the above dates, and for the use of which the author is indebted to the liberality of the Court of Directors of the East India Company.

appear that only about 7,000,000 of pounds were produced in the provinces of Bengal, Behar, and Orissa, which at that time formed the whole of the Bengal Presidency. But it is evident that this estimate must be incorrect, as the supply could not have been sufficient for even the most moderate consumption for each individual. Much was grown then as now in small patches near houses for home consumption, spun into thread by the women, and wove into cloth by members of the family. In 1799 it is stated, that "the weavers at present depend upon the country cotton imported into Bengal for seven eighths of the quantity used in their various manufactures." This cotton was brought either from the Deccan, that is, Central India, or from Calpee, the produce chiefly of the districts of Etawah and of Bundlecund, also of Jaloun and Jhansee, and of other Mahratta states immediately to the westward of the Jumna. These imported cottons were required not only for the manufactures of Bengal, but also for those of Behar and Benares. In 1802 we learn that Allahabad was formerly the mart for these cottons, but that of late, in consequence of the exactions experienced by the merchants, Mirzapore had become so. In that year the three districts of Currah, Carah, and Etawah, were ceded by the Nawab Vizier to the East India Company. At that time 180,000 maunds, each of 96lbs., were received from Nagpore, and 270,000 from Calpee. It was stated that this quantity was sufficient for the use of the manufacturers, but that if the import amounted to 600,000 maunds, as in the year 1802, then the price remained sufficiently low to allow of export to China. In 1803 we find the first notice of the export of cotton from Calcutta to China, though only to the extent of about 2,000,000 of pounds. It increased to 18,000,000 in 1806, and continued between 22,000,000 and 26,000,000 from 1814 to 1818, and rose to 44,000,000 in 1836, but has since then sunk to about 14,000,000 from the year 1838 to 1845, or on an average for the thirteen years ending with 1846, to 20,000,000 of pounds annually.

In the accounts of the cotton trade of Dacca in 1798 by Mr. Bebb, then collector of Dacca, afterwards a Director of the East India Company, and in that of Benares by Mr. Duncan, who was subsequently Governor of Bombay, we learn that much of the cotton which was used both in Bengal and Benares, was obtained from Mirzapore, a town situated on the right bank of the Ganges, and a few miles above Benares, to which it had been brought both from the south-west, or Central India, and from the north-west. The same trade follows in the present day the same course, into which indeed it is directed by the physical features of the country. Mr. Money, collector of Mirzapore, in an official letter dated the 6th of June 1848, writes:—

"Mirzapore is well known to be the largest cotton mart on this side of India; large quantities are received annually from Amroutee, Nagpore, Bundlecund, Agra, Furrackabad, and other places, and are usually dispatched from hence to Ghazeepore, Patna, Moorshedabad, and Calcutta. The Dakhan trade, however, has been on the decline, as will be seen from the imports, as obtained from the custom-house:—

Year.	Cottons.
1845-46	351,810 maunds of 96 lbs.
1846-47	256,754 "
1847-48	180,906 "

"There is at present a stock of nearly four lacs of maunds in the bazaar, a larger quantity than there has been for many years, and more is daily arriving. The demand is languid, and the prices very low and falling. The best Bundlecund could be landed in Calcutta, cleaned, and picked for shipment, in half-screwed bales, at Co.'s Rs. $7\frac{1}{12}$ to Rs. 10. Ten years ago such cotton would have sold for Co.'s Rs. 16. The abolition of the export duties led people to expect a fair demand; but the state of things in China has stopped shipment, and the cotton trade of this side of India is but a wreck of what it was, and unless some change take place, cotton will cease to be an export. The internal consumption is small in the district, as there are no manufactures. The expenses of conveyance from Mirzapore to Calcutta (distant 700 miles) are, one rupee four annas per maund. The wholesale price of cotton, after deducting commission, exchange, and brokerage, is:—

Western Cotton.			*Southern Cotton.*		
Agra . . .	7	12	Nagpore . . .	8	14
Bundlecund . .	8	0	Amroutee . .	8	10
Furrackabad . .	7	14	Saugor . . .	7	0"

With this we may contrast the prices of these same cottons, as given by Mr. Duncan in 1798:—

Western Cotton.				*Southern Cotton.*			
Julwan	14	5	8	Nagpore	16	6	7
Gohrah	14	2	5	Amrootie	15	2	10
Misserpore	13	11	10	Hurdeynuggur	14	5	8
				Bhenomghur	14	5	8

"The market at Mirzapore," Mr. Duncan writes, "is chiefly influenced by the selling rate at Bogwangollah near Moorshedabad, to which large quantities are always exported from this country, and where Beoparies, or traders, from Dacca, Calcutta, &c., usually repair to purchase this article." (l. c., p. 369.

In consequence of the diminished exports from Calcutta, it has been inferred that there must have been diminished production in the countries whence cotton was in former times obtained. But the cotton of Central India finds its way more easily to Bombay than it could do in former times. With regard to the alleged diminution of production in the Doab and Bundlecund, there seems to be considerable doubt in the minds of those best qualified to judge. Mr. Hamilton Bell, a gentleman who has been long engaged in mercantile pursuits in the Doab, in a letter dated 7th November 1846, addressed to C. Allen, Esq., Officiating-Secretary to the Agra Government, writes as follows:

"I support my opinion of undiminished cotton cultivation in our own districts on several grounds. It may be assumed as undeniable, that in the North-West Provinces much more land is now under cultivation than was the case thirty years ago, and, from all I can learn, the usual proportion of one fourth of the khureef crop is still general. I imagine we may consider the population considerably increased in the last thirty years, and, although the superior and middle classes are certainly much impoverished, I believe the condition of the mass of the population improved."

"My personal, not inattentive, observation, extending locally over the last twenty-three years, supports this impression. The wages of labour have certainly increased, and many old Kisans (cultivators), with whom I constantly converse when out in the districts, have lamented to me the degeneracy and profusion of the present times, remarking, that in their younger days the lower classes were exclusively fed with the inferior description of grain, whereas now, barley and even wheat have become the common food of the hired labourer. The improvidence of the native character is opposed to accumulation in the agricultural class, for any other purpose than marriage or religious ceremonies. They spend what they earn, and I conceive it as not an unfair assumption, that those who feed better will seek better clothing. If they can afford to spend more on their food, we might conjecture they would appropriate more for their clothing; but if we were to consider the same amount as previously disbursed for their apparel, this would establish a vastly enlarged demand, and a proportionate increase of consumption of the raw material for their manufactures."

"We are also still very large importers of cotton, as the Custom-house books can establish. The cottons to the south-west are superior to our produce, and sell for better prices; but this must be more than counterbalanced by charges of transport; and these importations, if they are undiminished, would establish an increased consumption, as our export trade has nearly ceased. I am inclined, therefore, to think that my impression of undiminished internal production is not a mistaken one."

These observations apply chiefly to the Jumno-Gangetic Doab, a portion of which has always been a cotton exporting country, and is ready to become so again, should a demand arise, and be backed by remunerating prices, or by such as would pay as well as other cultivation. But in other parts of the upper provinces, cotton does not seem in favour as an object of culture, and is as carelessly collected as in any other part of India. Mr. Reade, commissioner of the Benares division, writes, 16th August, 1848, "In this division the cultivation of cotton is little more than nominal; it is most commonly mixed up with other crops; it is nowhere carefully tended; in many places it is an object of superstitious aversion; and often, when the plant contrives to struggle to maturity, it is left, after being stripped of a portion of the bolls enough to supply present domestic purposes, to be devoured by cattle." Mr. Pidcock, commissioner of the Bareilly division, says, "The cotton now grown in Rohilcund is inferior in quality and staple, and it is so full of impurities as greatly to deteriorate its value, and to render it unfit for the English manufacturer." "These impurities are almost all attributable to carelessness in gathering." So even in Bundlecund, Mr. P. Edgeworth, an excellent observer, and lately collector of Banda, writes, 20th Jan., 1848, "The collection of cotton is most slovenly; it is often allowed to fall on the ground, and is always more or less mixed with the dried leaves and other dirt."

When the author was in the north-west provinces, the culture of cotton seemed nowhere to be a principal object with the ryot. A little was grown everywhere, but sown broadcast, and mixed with two or three other crops. The cotton was generally allowed to hang until it got mixed with dried and brittle leaf, and much of it to fall on the ground, so that it would be hardly possible to clean it without much hand picking.

Mr. Mercer, one of the American planters, bears testimony to its being there considered an unimportant crop, for he says, "Cotton is, in Bundlecund, regarded with indifference, and as one of the riff-raff crops, whose failure or not is of no consequence." (*Return*, p. 217.) Mr. Finnie, who was first engaged in endeavouring to cultivate the American cotton in the Doab, and afterwards in superintending a model farm at Agra, says of the natives, "In order to insure a better price for the article, which has cost them, at least, additional trouble in gathering, we must create a market for the superior article which they produce, for it is well known that the present cotton merchants make no difference in the value of foul and clean cotton." (L. c., p. 221.)

The capabilities of these districts are, however, considerable. In a report from the Board of Revenue to the Government of the North-West provinces, in reply to queries sent out by the Court of Directors, it is stated, "The area cultivated for cotton is reported at 1,002,040 acres, which may, it is estimated, be extended to 1,689,662 acres; but this includes territory which affords no supplies for Europe, the exports being derived from a tract which extends no higher, within the Doab, than Allyghur; but on the south-western side, or right bank of the Jumna, includes districts of the Allahabad, Agra, and Delhi divisions, as far as Rohtuck, which contain important marts. Exportation is also spoken of as taking place from Rohilcund, but it seems to be limited to the western portion of Budaon, and to the mart of Chundowsee, in Moradabad; and, as the whole produce is of inferior quality, Rohilcund may be left altogether out of the account. The more northern and western districts, in the places in which cotton is grown, generally require it for their own consumption, or for places in their vicinity; and when there is a surplus it is exported to the states westward. The hill districts on the north produce little or none; and with respect to the remaining division of Benares, however well situated it is as respects exportation, and whatever may in future be effected in realization of the commissioners' expectation, various prejudices have hitherto operated against its natural advantages, so that the quantity it at present yields is quite insignificant." The Doab, therefore, and countries on the right bank of the Jumna, remain, as heretofore, the sources whence a supply may be obtained, though the exports have declined, in consequence of diminished prices. The expenses of conveyance by the river (300 miles) from Calpee to Mirzapore are about one rupee a maund.

Various causes have been assigned for the diminished supply from Bundlecund, but it is extremely difficult to arrive at the truth without an examination of details. In the first place, much of the cotton which formerly came down the Ganges was the produce of central India. This is now carried more easily westward to Bombay, as we shall afterwards see. Bundlecund itself no doubt suffered for years from the ill consequences of the heavy assessment levied by the official zeal of the collector of 1815. This assessment was much diminished by Mr. Pidcock and by Mr. C. Allen, and the district is stated, by Mr. Lowther, the present commissioner of the Allahabad division, to be "rapidly recovering." But even the assessment does not account for all the difficulties under which the province has laboured. Mr. Lowther, in a letter, dated 12th Sept., 1846, to the Government of Agra, in reply to inquiries instituted by the orders of the Court of Directors, states, that he is informed by Mr. Bruce, who was attached, from 1808 to 1834, to the commercial residency at Calpee, and afterwards exclusively engaged in the purchase of cotton on his own account, as well as on commission for several agency-houses in Calcutta, that Bundlecund first became less productive in 1834, on the discontinuance of the Company's trade, as is stated by Mr. Sullivan, in his evidence (Q. 4,520) to have been the case also in Coimbatore. Mr. Bruce is of opinion, however, that the first check was received in 1819, from the heavy losses (estimated by him at 3 millions) sustained by speculators in Great Britain. Again, by the failure, in 1833-34, of all the principal agency-houses in Calcutta, as they were the chief exporters of cotton to China. In addition, the district has suffered under a series of physical afflictions, which would be sufficient to account for much diminution of culture, if any has been experienced. There was first a drought in 1829, a famine in 1833, and another in 1837; numbers of the population were subsequently carried off by cholera. "A disastrous succession of calamities," as remarked by Mr. H. Bell, "against which no agricultural population in India could possibly make head." In addition to these, we find that the demand in Bengal for the cotton of India has ceased, in consequence of the large imports not only of the calicoes of Europe but also of yarn and twist, upon which the native weavers are now chiefly employed on, in districts where much cotton is not grown. The export of raw cotton to Europe from Calcutta has nearly ceased, and that to China has greatly diminished; and, more than all, prices have declined, as in all other parts of India. But notwithstanding all these discouraging circumstances, Mr. Lowther states that cotton still remains the staple product of the district. Mr. H. Bell, also, is of opinion that it is not a declining cultivation, more being required for home consumption. The natives say that as extensive an area is cultivated as formerly, but that the plants are less productive. This is probably owing to defective cultivation, and partly to unpropitious seasons, which there is reason to believe have become more dry than heretofore, as we shall afterwards endeavour to explain.

With regard to the quantity exported, Mr. Lowther annexes to his letter two tables—one exhibiting the amount of duties collected at the old Cawnpore Custom-house from 1818-19 to 1830-31, including the produce both of the Doab and of Bundlecund. In this there is considerable variation from year to year, but no great change during the whole period, having amounted in 1818-19 to Rs. 116,685, and in 1829-30 to Rs. 116,164; but the highest amount, Rs. 217,395, occurred in

1820-21, and the lowest, Rs. 57,889, in 1827-28. In the other table the duties collected on cotton at the Calpee Custom-house are given from 1835-36 to 1845-46. In this we observe, that though the rate has not been uniform, yet that a considerable increase has taken place within the above period, having amounted to Rs.108,624 in 1835-36, and to Rs.174,443 in 1845-46. Upon which Mr. Lowther remarks upon the two tables, that, "by comparison, it would appear that of late years the trade in Bundlecund has greatly increased," and concludes by stating, "that before the company's trade was discontinued it is estimated that British Bundlecund produced annually something more than a lac of (100,000) bales of cotton, and about the same quantity was grown in the Jaloun and Jhansi states;" also, that "the article is so cheaply produced in Bundlecund, that if a demand were created for it there would be no difficulty in increasing the cultivation much beyond its former extent."

The Lieut.-Governor of the North-West provinces, in reference to Mr. H. Bell's opinion, records his own in the following words:—"It will be seen that his Honour is disposed to concur in the latter opinion, that the cultivation had not decreased, but that the increased consumption of cotton manufactures had taken off all that was before exported, and had kept pace with the increasing import. Every inquiry went to prove that the people were more numerous than they had been and were much better clothed."

In the Cotton papers (p. 16) published by the East India Company, we learn that, in 1796, the average cost of cotton cleared from the seeds at Jolloan and Calpy, in the Mahratta country, may be estimated at eight sicca rupees per maund of 102 sicca weight to the seer." Mr. H. Bell writes, that at the beginning of the century the price was from 7 to 9 rupees, and that these are the present rates, and that 8 rupees per maund to the ryot gives him a fair profit, and one with which he is satisfied. Though there is this uniformity, if we compare the first-mentioned periods with the present time, considerable fluctuations have in the interim taken place. "During the short period of the American war large quantities of cotton were shipped to England, prices ran high, and were maintained in the bazar long after the exciting cause had ceased, as the natives did not comprehend the grounds of the speculation." Mr. Bell probably refers to the speculations of 1817-19; for the price varied from 13 to 17 rupees from 1816 to 1839, and in one year, 1820, rose as high as 27 rupees. But none of this increased price ever reached the ryots, "being absorbed by the village Bunnier, the dealer with the Ryutt, the more considerable trader to whom he sells, and the buyers in the great mart, in which the latter realises his return." A regular fall in price has, however, taken place since 1843, and has remained at from 8 to 10 rupees per maund.

The Board of Revenue of the North-West provinces calculate the expenses on cotton from Calpee to Calcutta, to be—

Price, in mart, per maund	8	0	0
Charges to Mirzapore	0	15	7
Ditto from Mirzapore to Calcutta	1	4	0
	10	3	7

"This gives a cost in Calcutta, taking the maund at 80 tolas and the rupee at 1*s.* 10*d.*, of 2.733 pence per pound."

Mr. Bruce, in a letter to Mr. Lowther, dated the 15th March, 1848, says, "If the associations and manufacturers who have been memorialising and soliciting the authorities in England, regarding the increase of cultivation of cotton in India, actually wish for it, and will guarantee that all that may be produced through my exertions in this country will be taken by them, and paid for here, and will send out responsible agents to receive charge of the cotton, either here or at Calcutta, I will engage and undertake to produce for them as much real good marketable cotton as they may require, and not cost them, when landed in England, more than about 3½*d.* per lb., which I think very moderate, considering the Indian cotton generally realises from 4½*d.* to 5½*d.* per lb. in England."

The Doab, as well as Bundlecund, has always grown considerable quantities of cotton, and will be able, as we hope to show, to grow it of a better quality as soon as the Ganges Canal, that most magnificent of works for irrigation, is completed. At present the Doab cotton is so short in staple as not to be well fitted for the purposes of the English manufacturer, and is not so esteemed as that of the countries west of the Jumna by the natives themselves. Mr. H. Bell, in recently recommending to the Agra Government the improvement of the culture of cotton in the Doab, gave it as his opinion, that "no Desee cotton (meaning the cotton of the district) should be permitted to be cultivated." The cotton of Jaloun and Jhansi was formerly much celebrated. Koonch is now the great mart in that direction, and it is surrounded by the Jaloun territory. Mr. Bell, after making careful enquiries, ascertained that the cotton of Baugchenee was that which is at present most in repute with the natives of those parts, who give about $7\frac{1}{2}$ per cent. more for it than for the other best kinds. The district is on the south of the Chumbul, near Dholpore, and therefore probably very similar in soil and climate to that of Jaloun and Jhansi, which are not very distant. Mr. Bell further thought that it might be landed at Liverpool, in a clean and desirable condition, for about $3\frac{1}{2}d.$ per pound. As these districts, as well as Bundlecund, lie to the westward of the Jumna, and have always been famous among the natives for their cotton, it is probably owing to some physical peculiarities of soil, or of climate, that the cotton is produced of a better quality, for we cannot discover that it has the advantage of any more careful culture or cleaning.

From these districts we may proceed into the interior, and trace to its source the cotton which used formerly to be brought to Allabahad, and of late years to Calpee and Mirzapore. The SAUGUR and NERBUDDA territories, which are under British rule, and lie southward and westward of Bundlecund, extending over 3 degrees of longitude and as many of latitude, may next command our attention. In the table of the present prices at Mirzapore of Saugur cotton, we see that it occupies the lowest place; but from this fact we cannot be sure whether this is owing to its being of inferior quality, or to its being in a dirtier state than the other cottons brought to that mart. The tract of country is irregular in shape, but much of it must be favorable for the growth of cotton, stretching as it does between Scindia's territories and Malwah on the north, and Nagpore and Berar on the south. Colonel Sleeman, the distinguished commissioner in charge of the district, writes, on the 19th July 1848, in reply to the queries sent by the Court of Directors in 1847: "There is little difference in the quality of the cotton in the different districts under my charge; and the difference of price at the different places arises almost altogether from their different distances from the markets on the Ganges and Jumna (Calpee and Mirzapore), and the difference of duties to which their cotton is liable in passing to them." The Jaloun district surrounds Koonch, of which the merchants buy up the cotton, as well as that from the Gwalior districts. Nursingpore is 300 miles from Mirzapore. In all the districts the quantity might probably be doubled, if there was a demand for the cotton. The prices in the several districts, the expenses of conveyance to the marts on the river, and the quantity of land under cultivation, are given in the following table, from the reports sent to Colonel Sleeman:—

	Price per maund.	Expenses of conveyance.	Under cultivation.
Jaloun	5 4	0 12	1,13,201 beegahs
Gwalior ceded districts	5 8 to 6 0	. . . .	25,099 or
Jubbulpore	5 4	1 12	33,652
Saugur	6 8	2 8	50,000 acres.
Nursingpore	5 0	2 14	37,338 „

Respecting the nature and condition of the cotton of these districts, we have the testimony of Mr. Mercer, the American planter, who, in marching along the great road from Mirzapore to Jubbulpore, daily met with carts and bullocks carrying cotton from Central India, as well as from Jubbulpore, Nursingpore, and Saugur, to the great mart on the Ganges. On the 30th Dec. he "met several hackeries (carts) of Jubbulpore cotton, very inferior, short, and fuzzy; not well cleaned." Three days afterwards he again "saw several hackeries of Jubbulpore: knew it, before enquiring, by the open bags and loose package." On the 10th Jan. he "met several hackery loads of cotton from Nagpur, very well cleaned and soft-feeling cotton, but short and uneven." When in the Maheer valley, he mentions "the cotton-fields as the best he had then seen," and "generally planted without any mixture of other plants." The cotton of Nursingpore is, however, "considered the best in Jubbulpore, on account of its strength, body, and colour." At Nursingpore he says the country has been decidedly more of the character of a cotton country, as cotton appears to be the staple crop of many villages, though invariably planted with urrhar" (Cytisus Cajan, or pigeon pea). He found cotton cultivated all along his route to Hoshunabad, and from that to Baitool: at Paltrata, without any admixture, and looking a great deal better than ordinary. But with regard to the care bestowed in storing it, he says, "The cotton in every village is piled on scaffolds, raised 8 or 10 feet from the ground: the natives say, to protect it from rats and white ants. It is accordingly exposed to rain, dews, and sun, which cannot benefit the staple."

In the foregoing notices of the cotton trade of the Ganges, we have seen that Bengal and Benares were supplied with cotton from Central India as well as from the Doab and Bundlecund, and that these displaced the cotton which came by sea from Surat, as early as the year 1783, that is, about the very time that the demand was springing up in England. For many years afterwards, or indeed until the conclusion of the Mahratta and Pindarrie wars in 1818, most parts of the above tracts were in too disturbed a state to encourage the peaceful progress of commerce, and therefore cotton did not then travel westwards to Bombay, and also on account of the transit duties to be paid in passing through the several native states and Jaghire villages. But in addition to the trade to Mirzapore, much cotton was taken to the southward and eastward for the extensive manufactures of the Northern Circars. Indeed, we find a Committee at Fort St. George, in 1790, remarking "with concern that the raw material for *the coast investment* is procured, in a great measure, from *foreign countries*," that is, chiefly from Nagpore, "as being best adapted to the coast manufacture, but being of a higher price, is mixed by the weavers with cotton the produce of the Circars."

This trade has in a great measure ceased, and that to the Ganges has greatly diminished; but that to the westward, from the security of property, the shorter distance, and the removal of some of the transit duties, has greatly increased. Little of this cotton is produced within the British territories, but abundantly in those of the Rajah of Nagpore and of the Nizam of Hyderabad.

The only account which we have seen of the province of NAGPORE, is in the notes communicated by Major Wilkinson, Resident at that capital, to the then private Secretary of Lord Ellenborough, dated 2d June 1842. Major Wilkinson states, that there are two extensive cotton marts in the territory of his Highness the Rajah of Nagpore, viz. Hingunghat and Arvee, the former fifty and the latter seventy miles from the capital. The cotton brought to the Hingunghat market is grown in districts which lie to the south-west of Nagpore, and separated from the territories of the Nizam by the Wurda river. That which is taken to the Arvee market is grown in districts to the westward of Nagpore, and on the upper part of the same river. Some cotton is also brought there from the contiguous districts of Berar. The cotton collected at Arvee is taken to Mirzapore and to Bombay, as is that which is collected at Oomrowtee. The cotton from Hingunghat is taken to Mirzapore, where it is called Nagpore cotton. The Arvee cotton is called Oomrowtee, both at Bombay and Mirzapore, in consequence of following nearly the same route. "A small quantity of Hingunghat cotton was one year taken to Bombay, where it fetched a higher price than any of the Berar cottons. The Hingunghat or Nagpore cotton sells at a higher price at Mirzapore than cotton brought from any other part of India, except Hindeenugger, which is near Saugur." The quantity taken to Hingunghat varied in the season of 1837-38 to that of 1841-42, from about 12,867½ bhojas to 19,146½ bhojas, of which from 600 to about 7,000 bhojas were taken to Mirzapore, 2,000 to Cuttack, and the remainder retained for home consumption. At Arvee, from 6,000 to 9,000 bhojas were collected in 1840-41, the whole of which was taken to Mirzapore. In 1841-42, up to the month of June, 6,000 bhojas had arrived, of which there were taken to Mirzapore 3,300 bhojas, and to Bombay 2,700 bhojas.*

Mr. Mercer, in the journey from Mirzapore, to which we have already referred, met the cotton of Nagpore and that of the Nizam's dominions along with that of the Saugur and Nerbudda territories, and though on the same road, conveyed on bullocks instead of in carts. Of the cotton of Nagpore, mentioned as from Hingunghat, he says of a drove of 900 bullocks, "All the cotton I have seen from that place is of very good quality indeed, and better cleaned than is usual in Indian cottons;" and again, of another drove of 500 bullocks, he observes, "Cotton very good, just the same as all the Nagpore cotton I have seen. It is of fair length and fineness, colour excellent,

* Three Oomrowtee bhojas are equal to one Bombay candy of 784 lbs.

and if a little better cleaned, would certainly equal good Mobile or upland Georgia. It has none of the harshness so common in the cottons of the north-western provinces." He mentions afterwards that he had just heard from Mr. Hamilton, a merchant at Mirzapore, that, at that place, the Hingunghat cotton fetches $1\frac{1}{4}$ rupees more than that of Oomrowtee. When at the latter place, Mr. Mercer learnt that the cotton merchants there "account for the superiority of Hingunghat cotton, from the care in gathering and growing, and the very superior land in that district." The appearance of the plant wherever he had seen it, was precisely that of the Oomrowtee plant.

Oomrowtee and Khamgaum are the two great northern marts for cotton, the one being on the east and the other on the western frontier of BERAR, in the Nizam's territories. But Oomrowtee, being the largest mart, has its name generally applied to distinguish the cotton of the whole country. The countries of Central India being situated at a distance from the sea-coast, with the worst kind of carriage for so bulky an article as cotton, and yet able to supply large quantities of it, and at a cheap rate, would indicate the presence of improved culture and careful cleaning or a favorable state of fiscal regulations. None of these seem to be the case, and therefore we must infer a very favorable soil and climate, with the absence of other more profitable objects of culture. As we propose examining these questions in a subsequent part of this essay, we shall at present enquire only into the state in which the cotton of the Nizam's territory enters the market, in order to see how it influences, or is influenced by, the trade of other countries.

Mr. Mercer, in 1843, when he examined the Oomrowtee cotton, at Mirzapore, found that "the samples, though leafy, were pretty free from other impurity, and of very good colour, fine, soft, and, though uneven, of pretty good length and strength." On his journey he mentions droves of bullocks carrying Oomrowtee cotton to Mirzapore. Between Ellichpore and Oomrowtee he found cotton to be the chief object of culture, and the mode of cultivation approaching that of America; for instance, the cotton planted without admixture, and sown in rows of a cubit, or a little less, in width, thinned to a single stalk in a place, and, according to the statement of the ryots, occasionally ploughed between." But, " in regard to gathering, they seem generally very careless and slovenly, allowing a great deal to waste, and taking little pains to keep it clean. They store it in large wattle baskets without covering, in their stack-yards amidst all their other crops, collecting a due share of all the chaff, trash, and broken leaves that necessarily abound there." " In many of the larger Bazaar villages I saw immense heaps of it lying without shelter, merely enclosed around, exposed to innumerable clouds of dust, and sometimes to a shower of rain ; near these heaps sat dozens of people running the churka, making the vile masses still more filthy."

Captain Dorin, Supt. of Roads in Berar, in a report dated July 1848, says—" The reason that the cotton is exported to Mirzapore in preference to Bombay, though the land journey is much longer, is to avoid the extremely heavy and arbitrary duties levied upon it and every other species of merchandise passing through the Nizam's territories, and which are avoided in going to Mirzapore, as the road crosses the frontier about 30 miles from Oomrowtee and enters the Nagpore country."

With respect to any care bestowed in picking and cleaning, he says, " An advance is always made, and from this advance arises one of the great evils of the cotton trade. The money having been advanced by the purchasers, who buy the cotton in large quantities for exportation, they are obliged to take whatever produce is brought to them, or lose their money ; and the Muhajuns, who are the principal cleaners of the cotton, and the ryots, who cultivate it, knowing this, mix with the clean and good cotton all sorts of rubbish and the bad and inferior cotton of the last year, which admixture can never be again entirely separated ; and this it is that makes the Berar cotton so much inferior in the market price to the Surat cotton ; to which it is, when properly cultivated and gathered, hardly inferior. The cultivators again, when they have received advances, are frequently not allowed to gather the cotton in small quantities, as the pods ripen, but are obliged to wait until the crops have been assessed, and by this time much of the cotton is frequently spoiled by the pods falling off, and dry leaves, &c., getting mixed with them."

Captain Meadows Taylor, in a valuable report from Shorapore, a principality subordinate to the Nizam, and situated in the south-west of Berar, where he is stationed on special duty, writes, in July 1848: "The only way to avoid this, and to pick the cotton clear of these incumbrances and dirt, would be to gather it early, and when the leaves and seed-vessels are not quite withered; this, however, is not attended to, nor, indeed, unless the people could be assured of a constant demand and possibly superior price, under the local purchasers and directions of capitalists from Bombay, would they alter their present careless mode of proceeding. The cultivators seem, however, to have little inducement to take greater care of or to grow more cotton." Captain Dorin further says: "The cotton cultivation has of late years fallen off very considerably, and whenever I have asked the ryots why land which I had seen under cotton cultivation was planted with Jowaree, or other grain, they have invariably replied, that the cotton cultivation did not now pay them, if they cultivated it properly, allowing the land to lie fallow every second or third year; and the restrictions as to gathering it, and the necessity they were under of selling it to the people who had made them advances, together with the high arbitrary duties, and the difficulty of transporting it, when gathered, were so oppressive, that they preferred cultivating any other crop. Should, however, these restrictions be removed, it would be difficult to say to what extent cotton might not be cultivated in Berar."

Captain Reynolds, who acted as revenue officer in Berar for 10 years, and was chiefly stationed at Hingolee, represents, in his evidence before the cotton committee of the House of Commons, the transit duties as the greatest impediment to improvement:—"The contractors of the transit duties made whatever demands they pleased;" besides these there were "many single villages held by jageerdars, who had an *imperium in imperio*, and again collected a different rate of duty from that claimed by the revenue contractors. You would suppose that the cotton would naturally take the route indicated by the main road—the route is not dependant upon your having made a carriage road, but upon the route defined by the Hoondakars, who have contracted for the duties—numerous complaints used to be made to him of the vexatious delay on the part of the collectors of the transit duties, and on the part of the jageerdars, who would very summarily overthrow a dozen loads of produce, and keep them in pawn till the duty that they demand had been paid by the carrier." In fact, if it was not for the system of Hoondakuree, fully explained by Capt. Reynolds (v. H. of C. Report, pp. 37 and 416), by which arrangements are made for the conveyance of goods to their destination, including one with the contractors of transit duties, even the present degree of trade could not take place. But everything tends to keep the cultivator in subjection to the purchaser of his cotton.

Captain M. Taylor writes, that in the country south of the Kistnah there are probably 70,000 beegahs cultivated with cotton. The cotton of the more southern and south-western parts of this tract goes principally to Coompta on the coast, via Bellary, Dharwar, &c., along with the produce of the Bellary, Dharwar, and other districts of the southern Mahratta country. It is known as Coompta cotton in the Bombay market. But a portion of the cotton of the south of the Kistnah, as of Raichore, &c., is sent north and north-east to those districts of Telingana (that is, the Northern Circars on the coast of the Bay of Bengal), where cotton is not cultivated, but where it is required for local manufacturing consumption. A considerable quantity is required for the Gudwall district, where there are manufactures to a large extent, and for those districts further to the eastward which border upon Kurnool. Though some of the cotton of these districts is conveyed in carts, the greater part of it is so on bullocks, which he considers one of the greatest impediments to the extension of the commerce. As a cart-road has been made down the Ghauts to Coompta, it is probable that some portion of the cotton of the interior may get an easier exit to the coast; but Captain Taylor advocates the making of a direct cart-road to Viziadroog, where, he says, there is a port large enough to admit large ships, which might come in and take the cotton direct to Europe, instead of its going first to Bombay.

In reference to the extension of culture, Captain Taylor says, "I am satisfied by frequent discussions with the people of all classes, that provided there was a ready market for cotton, and the price was regularly maintained, by a steady demand, to a remunerative rate, the cultivation of it would be preferred to almost any other. The lands at present neglected would be improved, those which are waste broken up, and Jowaree (*Sorghum vulgare*, the Durra of the Arabs) 'which is the other great staple of the district,' to some extent superseded by cotton, to secure a return which would be regular and permanent, and which, in reference to its intrinsic value, would not be liable to any great fluctuation of price. These causes would, I am strongly of opinion, give a gradual increase of from 30 to 50 per cent. on the present cultivation, if not more."

Captain Taylor further states that the country north of the Bheema supplies the marts of Sholapore, of Bursee, and of Wyrag. The greater portion of what is known as Bursee cotton in the Bombay market, is the produce of these districts north of the Bheema.

Oomrowtee is described by Captain Reynolds (Report, p. 37) as a place of trade "the most flourishing in that part of India. It swarms with Marwaree firms, and most of the influential Sahookars (bankers) of Upper India, as well as of Bombay, have correspondents or branch houses there. The celebrated Dhunraz made Oomrowtee his head-quarters, and was extensively engaged in cotton speculations. His subordinates were established in every pergunnah in the Berar valley, and they made advances to the cultivators, or assisted them in paying their kists (portions of rent), on agreement that the produce of their cotton-fields should be placed at the disposal of their employer. Oomrowtee was the depot for the raw cotton; there were large warehouses for storing it as it arrived from the country, and it was cleared from the seed, packed, and dispatched to the coast, either by way of Mirzapore to Calcutta, or direct to Bombay. The price of cotton at this mart is about 54 rupees for 750lbs. Mr. Mercer states that he learned from the Brinjarras, that they get about 7 rupees per bullock for carriage from Hingunghat and Oomrowtee to Mirzapore, but that the rate varies, according to the season, from 5 to 9 rupees. A bullock-load is about 240lbs., Mr. Mercer says 4 maunds.

The price of cotton at Khamgaum, which is the most westerly of the two great marts of Berar, is said to vary from 15 to 20, rising sometimes even to 30, Hyderabad rupees, for a pullah of 240 pounds. The whole of the cotton of Western Berar and of Berar Balaghaut, and a portion of that of Eastern

Berar is exported by this mart, viâ Ahmednugger, to Bombay, which is 300 miles distant, at an expense of from 5 to 8 rupees the pullah, though higher rates are occasionally demanded. The carriage is chiefly in the hands of the Brinjarras, the great carriers of Central India. Mr. Fenwick, of Khamgaum, late of the Nizam's military service, states that carts have of late come much into vogue, and are preferred, on account of their travelling three and four times the distance a day that Brinjarra bullocks can. Perhaps a third or more of the cotton from Khamgaum is now carried on carts. But a greater difficulty is experienced from the uncertainty of the seasons; too dry a season not allowing the bullocks to travel for want of fodder, while unseasonable wet inundates the country, and renders the roads impassable. But even with these difficulties, Mr. Fenwick states that about 28,000,000 of pounds of cotton were exported from the westward of Berar, besides what was sent to Mirzapore from Oomrowtee.

In Shorapore, which is the most southern of the districts usually included within the territories of the Nizam, the price is about 53 rupees for a candy of 784lbs. This, Captain Taylor states, is carried either in carts to Sholapore, and from thence to Panwell, incurring a further expense of Rs. 14 10 an., and then costing Rs. 67½., at a time when Coompta and Bursee cottons, which are of the same quality, were selling at Bombay for 80 rupees the candy; or it is sent on bullocks to Sunkeshwur, near Kolapore, and thence to Rajapore, in the Concan, where it is shipped to Bombay; but the expense is considerably greater, and the adventure is repaid by the return load of kirana, or groceries, in which are included spices, &c.

We have thus made a circuit along the far-extended coasts of India from Guzerat on the west, to the mouths of the Ganges on the east, and then up that high road of the commerce of Hindostan to Rohilcund on one side, and Bundelcund on the other. From thence we crossed southwards and westwards, along the Saugur and Nerbudda territories, into Nagpore and Berar, whence the cotton finds its way, on one side, to Mirzapore, and, on the other, to Bombay and Coompta. In this extended survey, we have purposely abstained from questions of soil and of climate, as well as of culture, as better suited to the second part of this Essay, where we shall enter on such details, and examine into the suitableness of the several districts for improved culture, and into any results of this nature which have already been obtained. But nowhere have we seen the business arrangements of this extensive commerce at all of a satisfactory nature. The culture, we shall find, is better in some parts than in others; but the gathering of the crop is everywhere careless, and the cleaning and packing systematically worse, where the commerce is most extensive. The cultivator, who, in many of his ways, seems to combine the independence of the freeman with the indifference of the slave, is, however, little interested in the quality, and seldom in the extension of his crop. The middleman, with perverse ingenuity, seeks to change the nature of his purchase, and thinks to add to its value by making additions to its weight; but he succeeds in deceiving only himself. The European manufacturer, taught by long experience, has ceased to expect a pure article, and therefore never gives the price which he otherwise would for cotton of the same quality; and all the expenses of carriage, freight, and insurance have to be deducted from this lower price. Such seems to be the case, not in one, but in all the cotton districts of India, some near the coast, others far in the interior; a few being of comparatively recent acquisition, the rest long incorporated within the regular British territories, and some still subject to the irregularities of native rule. It is often asserted that it is the want of roads and the expensive carriage on bullocks which has prevented the extension of cotton cultivation in India: but every part of Guzerat is near the coast; Coimbatore is not far from, and Tinnivelly is on, the coast; Bundelcund and the Doab have always been open to the Ganges. All these, except the last, produce good cotton, and carts are everywhere the ordinary carriage of the country. Dharwar, though not very distant from the coast, was unable, till of late, to send its produce the whole of the way by carts. The cotton of Central India, therefore, alone of the good cotton districts, depends entirely upon bullock carriage. But nowhere do we find the trade on a satisfactory footing, for everywhere we hear complaints of a want of demand as well as of remunerative prices, for the cotton produced. Seldom do we find the purchaser for the European market coming in contact with the producer of the raw material, so that the latter might have the assurance of being rewarded, for any extra labour he felt inclined to bestow, by one who was a judge of and valued an improved article for the English manufacturer.

Some, indeed, ascribe the whole of the difficulties, and the unimproved state of Indian cotton, to the continued purchases, by the European merchants, of the very dirty and adulterated article. Those, however, who are resident at Bombay, rebut this charge, and explain the peculiarities of their position, in a letter from the Bombay Chamber of Commerce to the Government of that Presidency, dated 21st January, 1841. In this document, extending to seventy-three paragraphs, they describe how difficult it is for the merchants resident in the capital to come in contact with the cultivator in the country, for they are "a small body, not exceeding forty in number, belonging to about twenty firms, so that each firm has only, on an average, two resident members, a number barely sufficient for the transaction of their local business;" and they are, moreover, "in most cases the agents of others, whose orders they must comply with."

"The merchants here, therefore, are guided in their purchases by the orders received from their constituents at home, and the execution of these orders is always limited to time;" they are, therefore, "wholly dependent on the cotton to be found at Bombay, whatever be its quality."

Other circumstances, besides, exercise an imperative influence on the purchases, such as "the general state of exchanges, the individual urgency for a remittance of produce in return for cargoes received here, the rate of freights, the necessity for loading ships, &c." The price of cotton is not within his control. He may offer for good cotton a price which is high in relation to the average price of the day, and this is invariably done; but this average price is wholly out of his control, depending, in some degree, on the state of the China, or on that of the Liverpool, market. This latter is regulated by causes wholly independent of the quality of the Bombay cotton sent them," being "generally regulated by the price of the American cotton; and this last depends not only on the greater or less amount of the supply, but on the state of the money market in Great Britain and America, and the banking operations of the two countries." "Instead, therefore, of tracing the production of bad cotton to the door of the Bombay merchant, and stopping there, those who advocate these views should carry it further, namely, to the Liverpool market, exchanges, freights, the Bank of England, the cotton growers of America, the banks of the United States, &c."

Exports and Imports of Indian Cotton.

Such being the nature of Indian cotton in the opinion of Manchester spinners, and such the carelessness of the growers —and such the culpability of the first purchasers, and such the state of its commerce in the opinion of merchants of Bombay, —it is not surprising that the trade should be occasionally in a declining state, though it does seem unaccountable that its true nature should usually be so little understood and so superficially investigated. Neither do we get much information when we refer to the representations of public bodies, who are themselves interested in the commerce; though it may seem presumptuous in one not personally interested in the matter, thus to think, and so to express his opinions.

The Chamber of Commerce of Manchester addressed the Court of Directors of the East India Company on the 7th Dec. 1838, on the subject of the imports of cotton from India, and stated that "The quantity of cotton imported into Great Britain in the first eleven months of the present year amounts in value to £14,000,000 sterling in its unmanufactured state;" but that "the cotton from India amounts to about £600,000, or only 5 per cent. of the whole value of cotton imported, about 90 per cent. of our supply being drawn from foreign sources."

So in the year 1846, some of the merchants resident in Bombay addressed the Government of that Presidency, and, after referring to a former communication in which they had called their attention "to the state of decline into which this most important branch of our export trade appeared at that time to be falling," adduced the small number of bales shipped in 1846 in comparison with 1844. This, they add, "will abundantly show that our apprehensions were not unfounded, and that the causes which then appeared to exercise so very prejudicial an influence on the cotton trade, have not lost their force, but, on the contrary, are still in full and active operation."

A Committee was appointed by the Bombay Government, and consisted chiefly of mercantile men, with two members of the Bombay Civil Service. They were appointed to inquire into and report on the extent and causes of the decline represented to have taken place in this trade, and to suggest any remedial measures which, in their opinion, may with advantage be applied to it. The Committee was authorized to communicate with the Revenue Commissioners, and with the collectors of districts. Their Report, dated the 23d March 1837, was ordered to be printed by the House of Commons on the 21st July of the same year. The members of this Committee appear to the author to have unnecessarily restricted their attention to "the export trade in cotton from the port of Bombay" as "distinct from the local consumption;" because, so far as the growers, that is, the suppliers, of cotton are concerned, the regularity, nature, and extent of the two demands must considerably influence both the quantity, the kind, and the condition of the cotton sent to market. The Committee take their statistics from "the year 1834, in the early part of which the trading privileges of the Honorable Company ceased, and from which time the course of the trade in cotton, as in every other commodity, has been left free to the operations of the ordinary considerations by which commerce in general is commonly governed." Some of the statements of the Committee we have already referred to, and shall do so to others in the course of our inquiries.

The Committee take the exports of the year 1846 as indicating the loss sustained by the port of Bombay in the less amount spent in the shape of cooly and boat hire, in the purchase of hemp and gunnies, in screwing charges, freight, and insurance. Whence about 5,400,000 rupees, or £540,000 less, is annually employed in the trade of the port, diminishing the ability of the buyers who frequent this market to take off its imports, and affecting the exchanges in England and China in a corresponding degree. Such calculations place, in a very clear point of view, the vast amount of the interests which are bound up in the cotton trade of India, and how important it is that everything should be done to remove impediments, and to make such improvements as will place the culture and trade on something more stable than its present basis. But the year 1846 does not appear to afford any true indication of the real state of the trade, as there does not seem to have been any *regular* decrease of the export of cotton from the port of

Bombay, nor are any reasons assigned by which we might be led to discover the cause of the decline of the Cotton Trade of India. In scientific investigations it is not found that an isolated fact will explain the causes of natural phenomena, unless we can prove that it is a natural concomitant, and not an accidental coincidence. In the present case, if either of the bodies which have been referred to had taken the year 1836 in the one case, or the years from 1841 to 1844 in the other, their calculations would have been inapplicable. Indeed, in the very year that the Bombay Committee made their report, the export of cotton had more than doubled, indeed, almost trebled, itself in 1848, and we have no doubt that, in the present year, they will be as high as they have ever been.

At the same time that the Bombay Committee were investigating this subject in India, the author, without any knowledge of their being so engaged, was endeavouring in this country to account for the anomalies of the trade, as well as for the various discrepant statements made on the subject even by well-informed men.

The author was led to this investigation, by conceiving that it was of little use to make expensive and repeated experiments for the cultivation of cotton in India, unless the trade was on such a footing as to give a regular and reasonable encouragement to the growing of better kinds, or to the improved picking of what is at present cultivated. Having considered the long list of untoward circumstances which attend the growing, picking, cleaning, packing, and selling of cotton, it appeared to the author that they were sufficient to have "long since annihilated the cotton trade of India, especially as it had to contend against that of America, where cotton is produced abundantly, and of excellent quality, at moderate prices; which is, moreover, carefully picked, well cleaned, and substantially packed, with both the culture and the trade often in the same hands, and these characterised by energy enlisted in the cause of self-interest." Without referring at present to other points, it may be sufficient to mention that India, in addition to its much greater distance from this country, suffers in the contest from the far greater productiveness of the American cotton soils, the returns in America being from 250 to 400 lbs., whilst in India they are not more than from 50 to 100 lbs., of clean cotton per acre.

But that the Indian cotton trade has not been annihilated even by such formidable competition, must be dependent either on the inherent goodness of the cotton or the cheapness with which it can be produced, or the causes assigned for the diminished imports must be incorrect or exaggerated. Of the causes assigned some are permanent in nature, as the assessment on land, and the difficulties of conveyance, while others are fluctuating, as seasons and *prices*. The latter, though usually not alluded to, have probably more influence than any others; because it may be justly inferred in most cases, that if bad seasons produce insufficient crops, the farmer is usually remunerated by improved prices. The Indian cultivator of cotton, however, does not necessarily derive any benefit from high prices in bad seasons, as far as the export to Europe is concerned; for he may be told that the season has been favorable in America, the crop abundant, and the price of good New Orleans cotton low, and therefore he must be satisfied with a still lower one for his dirty and inferior Indian cotton.

Before endeavouring to explain the anomalies of the Indian cotton trade, it is first necessary to ascertain the facts of the case, and this not for one or two, but for a series of years. Thus, when we hear of continually decreasing imports of Indian cotton, it is desirable to determine the period from which this diminution commenced. In examining the exports of cotton from India to this country for a series of years, the author observed that, instead of showing a regular decrease, they presented a series of rapid alternations, at one time high and at another, often immediately afterwards, low; proving that these exports were influenced by some fluctuating cause, as, for instance, favorable or unfavorable seasons, or high or low prices. But if these had reference only, as in most other cases, to the country where the produce was cultivated, then an unfavorable season and a short crop ought to have been accompanied by high prices, and the Indian cultivator might have been sufficiently remunerated, and encouraged to proceed with his culture on an improved and extended scale. This, however, is not the case. Though the Indian cultivator does occasionally suffer from unseasonable weather, being unable to sow his crop from want of, and sometimes having it destroyed by excess of rain, he is often met, as far as this country is concerned, with low prices, even when he is himself suffering from a deficient crop. Though few probably are now induced to extend their cultivation, from the irregularity of the demand, yet it must be very discouraging to have a short crop valued less than a large one might be in some other years. Indeed, if it were not for the compensating effects of the large consumption in India, and the regular assignment of raw cotton for export to China, no increased supply would at any time be obtainable for the fluctuating demands of the English manufacturer. When, therefore, any considerable quantity is suddenly obtained, it must be by taking a part of that which is intended for China, or retained for home (that is Indian consumption), and in most instances by increasing the price to the natives of India.

By further investigation, the author found that the demand for Indian cotton for the English market seemed to be influenced chiefly by the prices of American cotton; that is, whenever there was a tendency in American cotton to rise in price, then the exports from India were observed to increase: the rise in price of American cotton depending, as we have seen, upon the more or less favorable season in America, with which the Indian cultivator is in no way concerned, except in its being frequently the reverse of what he wishes for.

In the first place, it is desirable to ascertain whether the alledged decreasing imports of Indian cotton are connected with the great diminution which has taken place in the price of American cotton (as we noticed at p. 16) ever since the great increase in cultivation which followed the conclusion of the war, when the demand for cotton became so greatly augmented in this country. The general rate of decrease in the price of all kinds of American cotton we have already seen, l. c.; but it is desirable to observe the price of American short staple cotton in comparison with what are commonly called Surats; as in the following table:

	Upland. Ordinary to Good.	Surat. Ordinary to Good.
Average price for 14 years, from 1808 to 1821	15¾*d.* to 24*d.*	13*d.* to 18½*d.*
„ 4 years, ending 1825 .	6¼ „ 13	5½ „ 10¼
„ „ 1829 .	5 „ 7¾	3¾ „ 6¼
„ „ 1833 .	5½ „ 8⅞	3½ „ 6½
„ „ 1837 .	6⅜ „ 11¾	4¼ „ 8½
„ „ 1841 .	6⅞ „ 8¾	3½ „ 6¾

From these data it has been observed, by Mr. W. Laird, that the average variation for the first 14 years, from 1808 to 1821, is $2\frac{3}{4}$*d.* per lb. less on Surat than on Upland cotton; and for the twenty years from 1825 to 1841, the average price of Surat cotton has varied $\frac{7}{8}$ of a penny less than Upland cotton. We further observe, that though there is a gradual decrease in price from the earliest to the latest period, yet there are occasional risings after a fall has taken place, even when the more marked discrepancies are made to disappear by the method of taking averages. The differences in price are therefore much more conspicuous when observed in a long series of years.

Messrs. Collmann and Stolterfoht observe, in their excellent Cotton Circular, that " we ventured the opinion in our last septennial, that the prices of cotton seemed to move in cycles of seven years, and the following comparison of the highest and lowest prices of fair Upland cotton in each year will apparently bear us out in that supposition, viz. :—

Period of Low Range.						
1826.	1827.	1828.	1829.	1830.	1831.	1832.
d. *d.*	*d.* *d.*	*d.* *d.*	*d.* *d.*	*d.* *d.*	*d.* *d.*	*d.* *d.*
$6\frac{1}{4}$ to $8\frac{1}{4}$	$5\frac{1}{2}$ to $7\frac{1}{4}$	$5\frac{1}{2}$ to $6\frac{5}{8}$	$5\frac{3}{8}$ to $6\frac{3}{8}$	$6\frac{1}{4}$ to $7\frac{1}{8}$	$5\frac{1}{4}$ to $6\frac{3}{8}$	$5\frac{1}{4}$ to $7\frac{1}{4}$
Period of High Range.						
1833.	1834.	1835.	1836.	1837.	1838.	1839.
d. *d.*	*d.* *d.*	*d.* *d.*	*d.* *d.*	*d.* *d.*	*d.* *d.*	*d.* *d.*
$7\frac{1}{4}$ to $11\frac{1}{4}$	$8\frac{3}{8}$ to $10\frac{1}{4}$	9 to $11\frac{1}{4}$	$9\frac{1}{2}$ to $11\frac{3}{8}$	6 to $10\frac{1}{4}$	$6\frac{1}{2}$ to $8\frac{1}{4}$	$6\frac{5}{8}$ to $9\frac{3}{4}$
Period of Low Range.						
1840.	1841.	1842.	1843.	1844.	1845.	1846.
d. *d.*	*d.* *d.*	*d.* *d.*	*d.* *d.*	*d.* *d.*	*d.* *d.*	*d.* *d.*
$5\frac{3}{4}$ to $6\frac{3}{4}$	$5\frac{5}{8}$ to 7	$5\frac{1}{4}$ to $5\frac{3}{4}$	$4\frac{3}{8}$ to $5\frac{1}{4}$	$4\frac{1}{8}$ to 6	$4\frac{1}{8}$ to $4\frac{5}{8}$	$4\frac{1}{4}$ to $7\frac{1}{8}$.

" The reason why we began our table in 1826, the year of the excessive speculation, is because it offered a starting point after the completion of an important epoch in the cotton trade."

In connection with this, it is extremely interesting to recall the observation made by the Bombay Cotton Committee of 1846, " That the decline in quantity has been accompanied for seven years by a gradually increasing decline in value also."

Indian cotton, however dirty its state or inferior its quality, has yet a value in its own country for consumption in the various ways we have enumerated (p. 18), or for export to China. Thus, prices at Bombay in 1843-45, though they were affected by low rates at Liverpool, yet maintained a higher standard than would have been the case if the cotton depended on the export trade only. The prices, we may observe, vary, being low at the beginning of the year, and high towards autumn.

					The lowest.			The highest.	
					rs.	*an.*		*rs.*	*an.*
1843-44,	the price of	Guzerat Cotton was,	in	Feb.	12	8;	in March	16	8
"	"	Cutch	"	Sept.	10	8	April	15	8
1844-45	"	Guzerat	"	Jan.	10	12	Aug.	14	4
"	"	Cutch	"	Jan.	10	12	Sept.	13	8
1845-46	"	Guzerat	"	May	10	4	July	12	0
"	"	Cutch	"	May	9	0	Nov.	11	8

By these prices at Bombay in 1843-46, the lowest being $2\frac{1}{4}d.$ to $2\frac{3}{4}d.$ a pound, and the highest being from $3\frac{1}{4}d.$ to a little above, we perceive that there can have been no inducement, except as an object of exchange, to export to Liverpool during these three years, when the price has been so low, frequently not more than $2\frac{1}{2}d.$ per pound.

But besides high prices at Liverpool, local causes enhance the price of cotton in India in particular seasons, as they do of all other products in other parts of the world. Thus Dr. Burns in his Report of the Operations at Broach from 1844 to 1845, published in the 'Journal of the Agricultural Society of India,' vol. v, p. 45, traces the diminished shipments from Broach chiefly to unfavourable weather in the interior:—

"I have obtained the monthly shipments from Broach for the two last seasons, and which show a deficiency of 25,336 bales in the season of 1843-44 compared with that of 1842-43, which although, I believe, not entirely depending on the bad season, is mainly to be ascribed to it." So Mr. Fenwick, in a letter published in 1847, at p. 59 of the Report of the Bombay Railway Company, states, "It is the actual fact, that from the want of water and forage on the road, owing to the scanty preceding monsoon, a large quantity of the cotton from Berar could not be carried to Bombay."

The prices in different parts of India are well shown in a table prepared by Mr. Chapman, and given at p. 357 of his evidence, a part of which we here insert. Those of Bengal cotton (which we have omitted for the convenience of space), are usually a little lower than the other Indian cottons, as are also those at Khamgaum. These we have seen vary a good deal, and are stated by Mr. Chapman to have been 1·25 to 1·45 pence per pound in 1846-47, and 2·30 to 2·88 in 1836-37. The prices in the southern Mahratta country were stated to be as low (1·25) by Mr. Mercer, in reply to the question put to him by the author in 1844, vide *House of Commons' Report*, p. 6.

Prices of Cotton in India and Liverpool, for the Years specified, in Pence, per lb. avoir.

N.B. The Rupee is taken at 23 Pence.

Year.	Broach.	Bombay.		Calcutta.	Madras.	Liverpool.	
	Ryot's Price.	Average Import Price.	Average Export Price.	Average Export Price.	Average Export Price.	Prices of Surat and Madras Cotton.	Prices of American Uplands.
1834-35	4·12	2·86	4·58	2·61	3·36	5¼ to 7¾	7½ to 9½
1835-36	3·46	3·27	5·09	3·00	3·21	6⅝ " 8¾	9 " 11¼
1836-37	3·83	2·98	3·52	2·46	3·74	5½ " 8½	9 " 12
1837-38	2·65	3·20	3·30	2·55	3·40	4¼ " 6	7 " 8¾
1838-39	3·53	3·43	3·24	2·53	3·61	5½ " 6½	6¾ " 9
1839-40	2·46	3·11	3·58	2·83	3·54	4¾ " 6¼	5¾ " 7¾
1840-41	3·16	3·25	3·50	2·91	3·07	4 " 5	5¼ " 7
1841-42	2·06	2·90	3·10	3·05	2·77	3 " 5	4⅝ " 6¾
1842-43	2·21	2·70	2·95	2·79	2·68	3¾ " 4½	4 " 6
1843-44	2·43	2·97	2·82	2·80	2·51	3⅛ " 4⅛	4⅜ " 6
1844-45	2·21	2·71	2·62	2·79	2·72	4 " 4¼	3⅜ " 4⅝
1845-46	2·21	2·35	2·44	2·78	2·44	2½ " 3⅜	3⅜ " 4½
1846-47	2·21	2·35	2·33	—	—	4½ " 6	6 " 7½

It is evident that when so small or no margin is left to the merchant in India, he cannot calculate safely, and therefore does not make regular engagements for the English market with the growers of cotton. As this uncertainty of price tends to discourage purchasers at the capitals, so it will those who buy up cotton in the districts where it is grown, and necessarily tend to prevent any great and continued increase of cultivation, and render the merchant dependent, in a great measure, upon the surplus of what is grown for home consumption or for export to China.

Mr. John Peel, of the house of Peel, Cassels, and Co., of Bombay, but himself resident near Manchester, stated at a meeting there on the 10th of May 1848, that "he could say from his own experience for several years, that it had not been possible to import native East Indian cotton into this market, except with a heavy loss, in more than one year out of five. If a large quantity of this cotton was imported into this country, the price was at once lowered, and the object of the importer, which was of course profit, was at once defeated;—the spinners would not take the native cotton when they could help it."—*Manchester Guardian, May* 13, 1848. This is just what occurred in the year 1809, and will probably continue to occur, unless the best Indian cotton only is sent, and that in a clean state, or the quality of the whole is much improved.

If we place the exports from India, or the imports into England, in parallel columns with the prices of American uplands cotton, or, indeed, with the prices of Indian cotton, because these in the Liverpool market depend on the former, we shall observe that though a large crop of American cotton produces moderate if not low prices, and a short crop diminished exports and high prices, yet with Indian cotton the reverse is the case. When prices are high, the imports of Indian cotton are large; but when prices fall, the imports into this country become greatly diminished, though extraordinary circumstances of a political or commercial nature may interfere with what now appears to be the natural course of the trade. The close connexion between prices and imports is more conspicuous since the establishment of steam communication. It is to be observed, that it is the high or low prices of one year that affect the imports of the next, and also that what were considered low prices at one period, would be thought very satisfactory at the present time.

	Surats.			Surats.	
1816 —	34,000	. . 15*d.* to 17*d.*	1830 —	35,189	. . 4⅛*d.* to 5⅛*d.*
1817 —	117,995	. . 15 „ 19	1832 —	109,285	. . 4⅜ „ 6
1818 —	227,300	. . 8 „ 14½	1834 —	88,136	. . 6½ „ 8
1819 —	178,300	. . 7½ „ 10½	1835 —	118,187	. . 5½ „ 7½
1820 —	57,300	. . 7¼ „ 9	1836 —	219,043	. . 4 „ 7½
1821 —	29,700	. . 6½ „ 8½	1837 —	141,761	. . 4½ „ 6½
1822 —	19,300	. . 5¾ „ 6¾	1838 —	108,435	. . 5½ „ 6½
1823 —	80,387	. . 3¾ „ 5¼	1845 —	155,039	. . 2½ „ 3⅜
			1846 —	94,643	

Though prices have, upon the whole, declined so much, the quantities of cotton imported into this country have, upon an average of years, not fallen off. This is probably owing to the diminution of profit and expenses; as, in freight, in inland carriage, in transit duties, and in the expenses of packing and screwing, for the price to the cultivator has not varied greatly, if distant periods are compared; but one which was found discouraging to the exporter a few years since, is found to act as an excitement to the trader at the present time. The dirty condition in which Indian cotton is sent to market always operates as a discouragement; for lower prices are paid for it by the manufacturer than he would be willing to give, if he knew that he was purchasing a pure article, and all the expenses have to be charged upon the low as they would be upon a higher-priced article.

Thus we see, that though from 1834 to 1836 fair prices were obtainable, but with a tendency to fall, and that 220,000 bales were imported in the last-mentioned year, yet in 1840, very fine cotton brought only $4\frac{1}{2}d.$ to $5d.$, while in 1845, only $3\frac{1}{4}d.$ was obtainable for Indian cottons, and the imports went down to 94,000 bales in 1846. But when prices began to rise in the autumn of 1846, and the December mail arrived at Bombay, the price there of cotton and the rates of freight both rose, the latter on 16th February, 1847, to £7 a ton to Liverpool; and as the cotton crop of that season was large, the freight was expected to be high the whole of that season. During it, indeed, large quantities were exported, and 210,000 bales received in this country. But, as we have before said, the cultivator feels nothing of these paroxysmal starts; before he can take measures for increased cultivation, the prices will have again fallen, and he will remain hopeless as before, until some fresh difficulty in America directs attention to his neglected produce.

But notwithstanding the accumulated difficulties under which the cotton trade labours and has laboured for a series of years, we cannot find that, on an average of years, the imports of Indian cotton into this country have at all diminished. In fact, at no time (if we except the ruinously speculative transactions of 1817 to 1819), have the imports been so large, notwithstanding the continued decrease in price, as in 1835 to 1837, in 1841 to 1844, again in 1847, and as we may safely say they will be in 1850. To place this in a clear point of view, we shall reprint a table prepared by Messrs. T. and H. Littledale in 1841. Here the imports and consumption of the year and of the latter per week are given. The excess of imports above consumption, as is well known, is re-exported to the continent.

EAST INDIAN COTTON.

Year.	Import.	Consumption.	Per Week.	Surat's Prices.	Year.	Import.	Consumption.	Per Week.	Surat's Prices.
1816	34,000	11,440	220	15 to 17	1829	80,387	35,204	677	3¾ to 5¼
1817	117,995	71,552	1376	15 „ 19	1830	35,189	50,700	975	4⅞ „ 5⅞
1818	227,300	83,720	1610	8 „ 14½	1831	76,654	35,932	691	3½ „ 5
1819	178,300	57,200	1100	7½ „ 10½	1832	109,285	56,680	1090	4⅜ „ 6
1820	57,300	71,552	1376	7¼ „ 9	1833	94,743	69,680	1340	5 „ 7¼
1821	29,700	49,192	946	6½ „ 8½	1834	88,136	53,508	1029	6½ „ 8
1822	19,300	48,880	940	5¾ „ 6¾	1835	118,187	55,952	1076	5½ „ 7½
1823	38,650	41,236	793	6¼ „ 7½	1836	219,043	72,384	1392	4 „ 7½
1824	50,900	34,632	666	6 „ 7¾	1837	141,761	77,948	1499	4½ „ 6½
1825	59,374	51,636	993	5½ „ 7¼	1838	108,435	91,988	1769	5½ „ 6½
1826	64,662	30,160	580	5½ „ 6¼	1839	132,832	107,276	2063	4½ „ 6
1827	73,544	30,992	596	4 „ 5¼	1840	216,495	113,776	2188	3⅞ „ 5½
1828	84,642	35,776	688	3¾ „ 5	1841	274,984	150,176	2888	3⅛ „ 5

For the last 5 *weeks the average consumption has been* 3,562 *per week.*

The same fact will appear still more clearly, if we adopt the system of taking averages as has been done by Mr. W. Laird, taking the figures from the year 1825 to 1841 inclusive, from Messrs. Marriott and Co.'s Circular. The author has added those from 1841 to 1849 from Messrs. Tetley's Circular.

Years.	Quinquennial Average Imports of Cotton.		Annual Imports.
	American.	East Indian.	
1825	356,618 bales.	39,597 bales.	....
1826	375,420 „	46,515 „	....
1827	438,882 „	57,363 „	........:..
1828	437,886 „	66,613 „	84,641 bales.
1829	473,580 „	72,522 „	80,422 „
1830	512,664 „	67,685 „	35,212 „
1831	555,364 „	70,083 „	76,654 „
1832	551,554 „	77,231 „	109,285 „
1833	594,190 „	79,251 „	94,683 „
1834	648,568 „	80,801 „	88,122 „
1835	677,568 „	97,401 „	118,433 „
1836	708,965 „	125,879 „	219,157 „
1837	752,277 „	132,374 „	145,063 „
1838	845,549 „	135,122 „	108,879 „
1839	861,856 „	144,061 „	131,731 „
1840	956,025 „	163,723 „	216,495 „
1841	983,536 „	174,911 „	274,984 „
1842	1,020,648 „	197,455 „	255,129 „
1843	1,065,280 „	212,066 „	181,993 „
1844	1,162,225 „	233,438 „	238,693 „
1845	1,213,580 „	221,167 „	155,039 „
1846	1,231,432 „	185,119 „	94,643 „
1847	1,202,479 „	178,465 „	221,959 „
1848	1,197,866 „	187,181 „	227,572 „
1849	1,243,798 „	176,253 „	182,079 „
1850	1,200,000 ? „	200,000 ? „	250,000 ? „

It is necessary to mention, that the figures differ slightly in the different circulars, being made up independently and issued before the official accounts are published: but they all confirm each other in every material point.

The foregoing table is formed by adding the imports of five years together, dividing by 5, and taking the result as the average for the last year. Thus, to obtain the average for 1825, the imports of the years 1821, 1822, 1823, 1824, and 1825 are added together, and then divided by the number of years, and so on for other years.

"The result shows an increase in the American crop imported into this country in 1841 of 626,918 bales, or 175 per cent. in round numbers, over the crop of 1825, and an increase in the East Indian crop in 1841 of 135,314 bales, or 350 per cent. in round numbers, over the crop of 1825, or the East Indian crop in seventeen years has increased double in proportion to the American." These observations, made in the year 1841, when the imports from India were increased in consequence of the Chinese war, are still applicable, though not to the same extent; but still the average of the five years previous to 1849 is nearly the same as for 1841.

If it be true, as it is stated, that the imports of Indian cotton have diminished in consequence of the operation of the land-tax and the want of sufficient roads, these being permanently acting causes, we ought to observe a continued diminishing import of Indian cotton, in proportion to the great fall which has taken place in price. But this is not the case; for if we look at these quinquennial averages, we find that there is a gradual increase up to the year 1844, when the annual and the average imports are nearly the same. Since then the average has fallen, in consequence of the low import of the year 1846, and has remained about what it was in that year.

The author ventured, from the prices of cotton in the latter part of 1846, to state that "the increased price of cotton in this country will cause large importations, and the average import will again rise." He may say the same of the present season, and that it will be to a greater extent, as the unfavorable prospects of the American crop were early known to some, and orders sent to India for cotton. The connexion between prices and imports is better shown by a diagram than by description.

Diagram of the Prices and Imports of Cotton.

The author finding himself puzzled with the multitude of facts which required to be considered with respect to each year's imports of cotton, was induced, in order to understand, if possible, what appeared the anomalies of the Indian cotton trade, to mark the quantities imported in the several years on ruled paper, of which the horizontal divisions should mark quantities, and the vertical ones the years in which these quantities were imported: the result was the line coloured yellow in the accompanying diagram. Having previously observed, when placing the prices in parallel columns with the imports, that these seemed to depend on the prices, he introduced the latter into the same diagram, making the horizontal divisions which marked quantities on the right, to indicate prices on the left hand, and the result was the line coloured green. Subsequently, the lower uncoloured line was added to indicate the prices of Indian cotton. This line, it may be observed, conforms very closely to the former, but approaches nearer to it as the prices become lower. By these lines it will be at once seen how closely the imports of Indian cotton depend upon the prices of American cotton, and that the imports of Indian cotton have not decreased upon the whole, as the blue line indicating the quinquennial averages clearly shows. To complete the statistics of the prices and imports of American and of Indian cotton, the annual imports of the American were introduced, and are coloured pink. By this it will be seen, that though the quantities have greatly increased, the price has greatly diminished, and, therefore, the American farmer has been remunerated by the quantity of produce, instead of the high rate at which he used to sell it. It was at this time supposed that the limits of production, at such prices, had been reached, as it was confidently stated that at such the culture did not pay. The imports fell in 1846, since then they have again increased; but those of 1845 still remain the highest. Another line might have been introduced, though hardly necessary, to indicate the quinquennial average imports of American cotton, of which the figures are given above. These show a regular rise up to 1,231,432 in 1846, when it falls to 1,197,866 in 1848, but rises again in 1849 to 1,243,798, though it will probably fall as low as in 1844 for the present year.

From this diagram it appears, that when the price of American cotton is low, the imports of Indian cotton have been small, but when the price of American cotton has increased, then the quantities of Indian cotton have likewise become generally augmented. The only exception in recent times is in 1841, at the period of the Chinese war, which caused a diminution of the exports from Bombay to China to the amount of 30,000,000 lbs., all of which was sent to this country, and ought to have sold comparatively well, as there was rather a short crop in America; but the year 1841 was one of distress and failure in the cotton trade, and hence the continued low price both of American and of Indian cotton. The prices being low, a diminution of imports took place in 1843, but a slight increase followed in 1844, probably in consequence of the threatening state of affairs with America.

Having thus the statistics of the Indian and American cotton trade in a manner pictorially represented, we may endeavour to understand the anomalies of the former by the help of this diagram. Though Indian cotton yarns had, to a considerable extent, been imported into this country from the begining of the century—as 114,000 lbs. in 1703, 219,879 lbs. in 1707, but afterwards in diminishing quantities, probably on an average of 20,000 lbs. annually, to the year 1744, and only to the extent of 2814 lbs. in 1760 (v. p. 5), raw cotton does not seem to have been imported until the year 1783. From the table of imports of cotton into Great Britain (p. 80), it appears that in the 5 years ending with 1775 the average import (under 5 millions of pounds) was only four times more than what it had been in the beginning of the century; but in the ten years from 1780 to 1790 it had increased five-fold—that is, to 30,000,000. From this time until the last year of the century no great increase took place; but in the year 1800 we observe a very rapid rise, caused, no doubt, by the increased demand in consequence of the machinery invented and perfected about 1785. The first notice we have of the import of cotton from India is in the year 1783, when 114,133 lbs. are mentioned as among the imports of cotton from thence, (v. E. I. C.'s papers, p. xiv.) In the year 1788 we find the Court of Directors of the East India Company writing for cotton from India, thus, " we have, in compliance with the wishes of the manufacturers, come to a resolution of importing 500,000 lbs.

weight of Broach and Surat cotton, or cotton of the produce of Bengal, of a similar quality."* The result was the import of 422,207 lbs. in the year 1790, together with some valuable reports on the cotton of India, which we have already noticed. The above cotton, on being brought to sale, "produced only from $7\frac{7}{8}d.$ to $10\frac{1}{2}d.$ per lb." "It is evident, therefore, notwithstanding the flattering allurements held out by the British manufacturer, that the article will by no means answer."

In the year 1809, at the period of the American Non-intercourse Act, the Court again wrote to the Governor in Council at Bombay, in consequence of the urgency of the demand in England for cotton-wool, as "it is to our territorial possessions in Asia that the hopes of the manufacturing classes are principally directed. It will, no doubt, become a very pleasing duty to our Government to use their utmost efforts that these hopes may not be disappointed." In consequence of these instructions, about 30 millions of pounds weight of cotton-wool were sent from India, but of which only 1,250,000 were used by the British manufacturers, and 3,250,000 exported to the continent of Europe, making together somewhat less than 5 millions. The remaining $24\frac{1}{2}$ millions remained on hand, and without any demand, when the Court determined, that it would not be consistent with commercial policy "to persevere in the importation of Indian cotton-wool into England, if the British manufacturers continued to manifest so adverse a disposition to the use of it."

This unfavorable result, probably, prevented for a time the further import of cotton from India, for even during the period of the American war (1812 to 1814), when the price of American cotton became high, little cotton was imported into this country. But after the peace, a general revival of trade took place, and a great increase of the imports of cotton, as from 60 to 90 millions of pounds in 1816. In 1817 to 1819, when excessive speculation prevailed, and prices remained high, large quantities of cotton, that is, 86,000,000 of pounds in 1818, were imported from India into this country; a larger quantity than at that time came from America, even with the assistance of 17 millions of pounds exported from Calcutta to America, for the purpose of mixing with American cotton, previous to re-exporting it to Europe.

* 2,000,000 of pounds are mentioned as having found their way to this country, in 1789, from India, through Flanders and Denmark.—(*E. I. C.'s Papers*, p. v.)

The failures which took place in Calcutta in 1820, in consequence of this over speculation, are stated by Mr. Bruce to have been the first check experienced by the cotton growers of Bundlecund: at all events, the exports from Calcutta to this country amounted only to about 2,000,000 of pounds in the year 1822. The Indian trade did not recover itself even for the year of hazardous speculation (1825), in cotton and everything else: luckily perhaps, followed as it was by a commercial panic. About this time the exports from Bombay became considerable (v. E. I. C.'s Papers, p. 132), probably in consequence of the settled state of the interior. The exports from India generally began gradually to increase, but the price of cotton having sunk to under 6*d.* a pound in 1829, the imports of Indian cotton fell from 80,422 bales in that year to 35,212 bales in 1830. But as prices began to rise in 1829, so we find the imports beginning to increase, and amounting in 1832 to 109,285 bales. But as the rise in price in 1830 was immediately succeeded by a fall, so the imports began to diminish, and amounted, in 1834, to only 88,122 bales. But in the year 1832, a gradual rise took place in the price of American cotton, and continued to increase until the year 1836, when the average price of Upland cotton was 10½*d.* This rise, it is said, was caused by the operations of the bankers of the United States, for the diagram does not show at that time any falling off in the imports of American cotton; they were, in fact, nearly the same in 1836 as in 1835. Such a rise of price could not but be felt in India, and the imports of its cotton greatly increased, reaching in 1836 to 219,157 bales. The aggregate increase of the imports of cotton in the year 1836 amounting to 110,000 bales, were due almost entirely to India, as 100,000 bales of Indian cotton were imported in excess of what had been received in the year 1835. The transit duties were at this time abolished in the Bengal Presidency, and in the next year in the Bombay, but not till 1844 in the Madras Presidency. The effects of this measure might have been expected to have been felt in the increased exports of Indian cotton, but 1837 was a period of great commercial distress, and the price of the raw material fell one third, to the great injury of the exporters. The imports in 1838 amounted only to 108,879 bales. The slight increase of price which took place in that year gave an impulse to the exports from India, which continued to be in increasing quantities, but would, probably, soon have decreased, had it not been for the seizure of opium in 1839, and the consequent Chinese war. This prevented the exports of Indian cotton to China; and, therefore, that which had been brought from the interior was forwarded on to this country, augmenting the imports to nearly 275,000 bales, that is higher than they had been in 1818, or indeed in any previous year; but here we have large imports with low prices, and an exception to what we have hitherto found to be the case, that is, small imports with such prices.

The depreciation of 1840 was caused by a combination of great distress in the manufacturing districts, with the occurrence of the then largest crop of American cotton. Distress, and the closing of mills, with failures, continued through 1841; but Indian cottons were largely consumed, and in some instances machinery, it was said, was adapted to their use. They were also much employed for mixing with American cotton. In the year 1842, peace was concluded with China, manufactures were reviving, with a still larger crop of American cotton. The increasing prosperity of manufacturers continued to 1845, when the largest American crop occurred. Prices became lower than they had ever been, and the average of that of Upland American cotton sunk to $4\frac{1}{4}d.$ per lb., and that of Indian to $3\frac{1}{4}d.$, much of it being sold as low as $2\frac{1}{2}d.$, which was less than it cost the exporters in India. Hence the enormous falling off in the imports of Indian cotton: these amounted to only 94,643 bales in 1846, the year which the Bombay Committee have particularly referred to. This was also the recommencement of difficulties for manufacturers, because the crop of American cotton had fallen short by 600,000 bales, as we have already noticed (p. 16.) This, however, caused an increase of price in the autumn of the year, which stimulated the markets at Bombay, and raised up the imports in 1847 to upwards of 220,000 bales, and still higher in the following year. Though a diminution again took place in 1849, to the extent of 45,493 bales, the rise in price which ensued from the failure of last year's American crop will probably carry the imports as high as they were in 1836, and perhaps as high as in 1841, though the export trade to China now exists to divert some of the cotton from this country.

One favorable result has ensued from the of late rather frequent, though fitful, demands of the English market; this is, that Indian cotton is looked to more frequently than heretofore as a resource in case of necessity, and brokers, merchants, and spinners include it in their calculations. In the present year we find the Manchester press writing to the same effect: "If spinners continue to act cautiously, looking at the augmented stock of cotton in Liverpool, and heavy supplies at hand, especially from the East Indies, a considerable concession in prices of cotton must shortly ensue. To show the effect of the high prices ruling here, we may mention that about 600 bales of cotton have already arrived at Liverpool from Oporto, and that, by the last advices, it appears upwards of 70,000 bales are on their way from the East Indies."—(*Times, Feb.* 27, 1850, *from a Manchester Paper.*) Indeed, the imports up to the present time have greatly increased, as appears from the following statement, for which we are indebted to the Messrs. Tetley:—

COTTON WOOL *imported into Great Britain from the East Indies, from January* 1 *to May* 23, 1850.

	Bombay.	Madras.	Total.
To Liverpool	73,850	1290	75,140
London	31,320	6540	37,860
Glasgow and Hull . . .	11,000	—	11,000
	116,170	7830	124,000

Against 30,000 in the same period in 1849.

The only method upon which any reliance can be placed for getting rid of this hopeless dependence on the American market, is to improve the condition and, if possible, the quality, of Indian cotton; substituting in its place, whenever this is feasible, superior kinds, diminishing at the same time every expense that is possible, whether in carriage, in packing, or in shipping; improving old ports, and establishing new ones. The transit and export duties having been abolished in the East India Company's territories, those in the native states should be controlled, as their produce has the advantage of passing securely and free of interruption throughout the British territories. The land-rent or tax, as it is called, may require modification in a few districts, from the fall in prices of almost all produce; as some say that land-rent must in this country, from the fall in the price of corn; but the author cannot learn from those practically acquainted with the subject, that this rent, amounting as it does, in the majority of places fitted for cotton culture, to from 1*s.* 6*d.* to 2*s.* 6*d.* an acre, interferes with the proper culture of cotton.

TABLE

Of the Aggregate Imports of Cotton into Great Britain, of the Quantities received from the United States and India respectively, with the Prices of the two kinds.

Years.	Aggregate Imports into Great Britain.	Imports from United States.	Imports from India.	PRICE of other than East Indian Cotton at Liverpool.	PRICE of Surat Cotton at Liverpool.
	lbs.	lbs.	lbs.	Pence per lb.	Pence per lb.
1697	1,976,359	.....	.....	.....	.....
1701	1,985,868	.....	.....	.....	.....
1701 to 1705 (average.)	1,170,881	.....	.....	.....	.....
1710	715,008	.....	.....	.....	.....
1720	1,972,805	.....	.....	.....	.....
1730	1,545,472	.....	.....	.....	.....
1741	1,645,031	.....	.....	.....	.....
1751	2,976,610	.....	.....	.....	.....
1764	3,870,392	.....	.....	.....	.....
1770	.....	2000*	.....	.....	.....
1771 to 1775 (average.)	4,764,589	.....	.....	.....	.....
1776 to 1780 (average.)	6,766,613	.....	.....	.....	.....
1781	5,198,778	.....	.....	.....	.....
				West Indian.	
1782	11,828,039	.....	.....	20 to 42	.....
1783	9,735,663	.....	114,133	13 to 36	.....
1784	11,482,083	.....	11,440	12 to 25	.....
1785	18,400,384	.....	99,455	14 to 28	.....
1786	19,475,020	.....	.....	22 to 42	.....
1787	23,250,268	.....	.....	19 to 34	.....
1788	20,467,436	.....	.....	14 to 33	.....
1789	32,576,023	.....	4,973	12 to 22	.....
1790	31,447,605	.....	422,207	12 to 21	8 to 10
1791	28,706,675	1/1000	3,351	13 to 30	8 to 15
1792	34,907,497	1/128	.....	20 to 30	11 to 16
				Uplands.	
1793	19,040,929	1/223	729,634	13 to 22	10 to 16
1794	24,358,567	1/110 (1791–1799: Ratio of Imports from U. S. of the total Imports into England.)	239,245	12 to 18	9 to 11½
1795	26,401,340	1/25	197,412	15 to 27	11 to 22
1796	32,126,357	1/11	609,850	12 to 29	11 to 22
1797	23,354,371	1/11	912,844	12 to 37	10 to 23
1798	31,880,641	1/8	1,752,784	22 to 45	20 to 26
1799	43,379,278	1/8	6,712,622	17 to 60	11 to 29
1800	56,010,732	16,000,000	6,629,822	16 to 36	10 to 18
1801	56,004,305	19,000,000	4,098,256	17 to 38	14 to 18
1802	60,345,600	23,500,000	2,679,483	12 to 38	10 to 18
1803	53,812,284	27,750,000	3,182,960	8 to 15	9 to 14
1804	61,867,329	25,750,000	1,166,355	10 to 18	8 to 15
1805	59,682,406	32,500,000	694,050	14 to 19	12 to 17

* See note on the opposite page.

Years.	Aggregate Imports into Great Britain.	Imports from United States.	Imports from India.	PRICE of other than East Indian Cotton at Liverpool.	PRICE of Surat Cotton at Liverpool.
	lbs.	lbs.	lbs.	Pence per lb.	Pence per lb.
1806	58,176,283	24,250,000	2,725,450	15 to 21½	12 to 17
1807	74,925,306	53,250,000	3,993,150	15½ to 19	15
1808	43,605,982	8,000,000	4,729,200	15½ to 36	14 to 25½
1809	92,812,282	13,500,000	12,517,400	14 to 34	11 to 26
1810	132,488,935	36,000,000	27,783,700	14½ to 22½	12½ to 19
1811	91,576,535	46,750,000	5,126,100	12¼ to 16	10½ to 13
1812	63,025,936	26,000,000	915,950	13 to 23½	12 to 16
1813	50,966,000	War between	497,350	21 to 30	15½ to 20
1814	60,060,239	England and U.S.	4,725,000	23 to 37	18 to 25
1815	99,306,343	45,666,000	8,505,000	18 to 25½	14½ to 21
1816	93,920,055	57,750,000	10,850,000	15 to 21	14 to 18½
1817	124,912,968	51,000,000	40,294,250	16¼ to 23¼	14½ to 20
1818	177,282,158	58,333,000	86,555,000	16½ to 22	7 to 20½
1819	149,739,820	57,750,000	62,405,000	10 to 19¾	5¾ to 14½
1820	151,672,655	89,999,174	20,294,400	8 to 13¾	6¾ to 12
1821	132,536,620	93,470,745	10,626,000	7 to 11½	6½ to 9¼
1822	142,837,628	101,031,766	6,742,050	5¾ to 11	5½ to 8½
1823	191,402,503	142,532,112	13,487,250	6¼ to 10¾	5¼ to 8½
1824	149,380,122	92,187,662	17,796,100	7 to 10½	5½ to 8
1825	228,005,291	139,908,699	21,175,700	6 to 19½	5½ to 16
1826	177,607,401	130,858,203	22,644,300	5¼ to 8¾	4½ to 7
1827	272,448,909	216,924,812	25,742,150	4⅛ to 7¾	3⅞ to 6½
1828	227,760,642	151,752.289	29,670,200	5 to 7⅜	3½ to 5½
1829	222,767,411	157,187,396	28,147,700	4⅝ to 7	2⅞ to 5½
1830	263,961,452	210,885,358	12.324,200	5⅜ to 7⅞	3 to 6
1831	288,674,853	219,333,628	26,828,900	4¾ to 7¼	3½ to 5¾
1832	286,832,525	219,756,753	38,249,750	5 to 8	3½ to 5½
1833	303,656,837	237,506,758	32,755,164	6½ to 12½	4¼ to 8¾
1834	326,875,425	269,203,075	32,920,865	8½ to 10½	5¼ to 7¾
1835	363,702,963	284,455,812	41,474,909	9⅝ to 12½	6⅝ to 8¾
1836	406,959,057	289.615,692	75,746,926	7⅝ to 11	5½ to 8½
1837	407,286,783	320,351,716	51,577,141	7 to 8¾	4¼ to 6
1838	507,850,577	431,437,888	40,229,495	6¾ to 9	5½ to 6½
1839	389,396,559	311,597,798	47,170,640	5¾ to 7¾	4¾ to 6¼
1840	592,488,010	487,856,504	77,010,917	5¼ to 7	4 to 5
1841	487,992,355	358,214,964	97,368,312	4⅝ to 6¾	3 to 5
1842	531,750,128	405,325,600	96,555,186	4 to 6	3¼ to 4½
1843	674,196,992	558,735,600	68,820,570	4⅜ to 6	3⅛ to 4⅛
1844	646,111,304	517,218,622	88,639,608	3¾ to 4⅝	4 to 4¼
1845	721,979,953	626,650,412	58,437,426	3½ to 4½	2½ to 3⅜
1846	442,759,336	382,526,000	33,711,420	4⅛ to 7	3½ to 5
1847	474,707,615	364,599,291	83,934,614	6 to 4⅛	5 to 2¾
1848	713,020,161	600,247,488	84,101,961	3½ to 5½	2⅝ to 3¾
1849	775,469,008	. . . . .	. . . . . .	5⅝ to 8	3¾ to 5

* See p. 13 for the earliest shipments to Liverpool.—The aggregate imports and those from India up to 1833 are taken from the East India Company's Papers, p. xiv, and from other published papers after that date. For all the imports from 1846 to 1849, the author is indebted to G. R. Porter, Esq., of the Board of Trade, as well as for the column of imports from the United States up to 1830. The prices are taken from Mr. Chapman's table. Those from which the averages in the Diagram are given, were taken from Brokers' circulars.

Improvement of Cotton from India.

Whether we take a cursory or a careful view of the details of the cotton trade, as given in the above table, or of the same facts as represented in the diagram, it is evident that, as far as India is concerned, the question is one of price. Of the imports we have seen, that whenever the prices of American cotton are high, the quantities of Indian cotton sent to our markets are large; and this not in a small per centage, but to the extent of doubling and nearly trebling itself in a single year. This the author was first fully aware of when preparing the above diagram, as stated in his paper on this subject, read before the Statistical Section of the British Association, at Oxford, 28th June, 1847.* But the fact was, of course, well known to commercial men, especially of late years, though it does not appear in the representations of Chambers of Commerce. Mr. Turner, President of the Commercial Association of Manchester, not less distinguished by his knowledge and judgment than by his position, stated, before the Cotton Committee (Q. 900)—"There is no difficulty, at any time, in getting a supply of common Surat cotton, when it will sell in Liverpool at from $3\frac{3}{4}$*d.* to 4*d.* a pound; the falling off is only when it is worth from $2\frac{1}{2}$*d.* to 3*d.* a pound." From the statements of different parties in the various cotton districts of India, we have seen that cotton can be laid down at Liverpool, all expenses included, for $3\frac{1}{2}$*d.* a pound. The Bombay Cotton Committee state, as already referred to, that the advance of price, in the autumn of 1846, "was quite sufficient to leave considerable profit to the exporter, with some benefit to the cotton trade also. We may suppose that advance to have been $\frac{1}{2}$*d.* per pound upon a price of $3\frac{1}{2}$*d.*, or 15 per cent." Hence it is evident, that cotton may be imported into this country when the price is $3\frac{1}{2}$*d.* a pound, and profitably when it is

* This has been printed in the Report of the Cotton Committee of the House of Commons, 1848, together with the above diagram, and another, which the author prepared at the suggestion of the then Chairman of the East India Company, H. St. George Tucker, Esq., who has himself, for many years, paid great attention to the subject. In this diagram are shown the exports of cotton from the three Presidencies to Great Britain and China respectively, from 1796 to 1846.

anything above that. But if it is desired to increase the quantities, a rise in price or profits to be shared between the exporter and the grower, is necessary, as both complain that low rates do not afford sufficient encouragement. This might be done by getting rid of some of the middlemen, and dealing more directly with the growers in the districts: thus ensuring a better and cleaner article, which would command a higher price in Liverpool. The Indian cotton has of late averaged about $\frac{3}{4}d.$ to $1d.$ below the Uplands American cotton. From the table given in by Mr. Bazley (v. p. 24), we see that the spinner can afford to give $3\frac{1}{2}d.$ a pound for Indian, when American cotton is $4\frac{1}{8}d.$ But as the latter has been sold for even lower prices, it becomes an important point to ascertain how often this has occurred. Mr. Turner, when asked (Q. 870), "Will you state how often, within the last 20 years, the average price of cotton has been at $3\frac{1}{2}d.$ in the Liverpool market?" replied, "Not more than once: $3\frac{1}{2}d.$ is an extreme case; by that I mean the ordinary Uplands cotton."

872. "Take the years from 1843 to 1846, before the crop fell off very greatly, would *4d.* be about the average price of the cotton of which we have been speaking? I think so; about *4d.*

873. "It has been stated here, that the Indian cotton could be landed at Liverpool at $3\frac{1}{2}d.$; under such circumstances, the average American cotton being *4d.*, and the Indian cotton being produced at Liverpool at $3\frac{1}{2}d.$, would that drive it out of the market? A. 874. I think that at $3\frac{1}{2}d.$ it would be used." But, in answer to Q. 864, Mr. Turner said, "that the inferior description of Indian cotton, he thought, would be driven out of the market."

The Bombay Cotton Committee, in their report, state that, "as it is evident that no influence or efforts exercised in India can affect the prices of Lancashire, so is it apparent, that the only effectual way by which we can attain the same end, namely, add 15 per cent. to the difference between the cost and the sale price, is by reducing the first cost here in a corresponding degree." Indian efforts may not be able to affect Lancashire prices, but they may do what is equally advantageous; and that is, secure better prices for their produce, by improving its state and quality. All unnecessary expenses ought, of course, to be diminished; such as those caused by the cotton passing through so many hands, or such extra ones as are incurred in the transit. The removal of the latter would be beneficial to other kinds of produce, as well as to cotton. Reduction in price without any improvement is not likely to be advantageous to the culture, for American prices would still rule those of India, and the demand remain, as it has been, only casual, and not extend to the cultivator. For on him depends any extension of the culture, or improvement in the quality; and he distrusts his own countrymen, with whom alone he usually deals. Any diminution of expense, in particular directions, might increase the profits of the exporter, and thus afford him encouragement; but the prices of Indian cotton would still bear the same relative difference to those of American cotton. It is doubtful whether any great cheapening of Indian cotton would be beneficial to the country, though it might enable manufacturers here to use more of it for coarse fabrics, and, perhaps, undersell the Indian weaver in the little that is still left to him. Indian cotton, in its present state, will never be used as a substitute for American, except when the latter is scarce and dear; and, therefore, it will only continue, as heretofore, to be ordered occasionally, and the merchant in India will be able only to purchase such cotton as the native dealers bring to market, and that in the state of adulteration, in producing which they are such adepts. It is hopeless, therefore, to expect that India can in this way contend successfully against America, even in checking the prices of its cotton.

From the preceding facts and opinions, it is very evident that there is always a great demand for cotton, and that none of good quality will be rejected; and, as it is the interest of the manufacturer to be supplied from as many sources as possible, he will gladly purchase that of India at all times, if of good quality, if it were only to afford the natives the means of purchasing English manufactures. The only method, therefore, which seems open to India to secure a steady, and, at the same time, a profitable trade, is to improve the condition and quality of the produce, so as to make it the interest of the manufacturer to select, instead of, as he now does, studiously rejecting Indian cotton, except when the American is scarce and dear. Then indeed his now periodic zeal is unbounded in favour of the improvement of the natives of India. Mr. Turner, who has uniformly taken great interest in this subject, replied to a question by Mr. Cornwall Lewis (Q. 881)—"Your opinion appears to be, that any prospect of increasing the quantity of cotton imported from India into England would be derived from the substitution of a better quality in India for the native cotton?—To ensure a regular increase, I think that the other will be a fluctuating one, according to the price of American cotton. I wish the quality to be improved, to compete with the American cotton in the market." And again, in answer to Q. 855: "I should like to state, that I think there would be an increase, provided they improved the quality. I do not think that there will be a very great increase in the importations of Indian cotton, if the quality remains of an inferior description, as hitherto. But if, by improving the culture, we can increase the price, without at the same time increasing the cost, or rather decreasing the cost, because they will have a much greater quantity from the same acreage, I think, then, that India, with its cheap labour, will, at all times, be able to compete with the slave labour of America."

Experiments, it is well known, have, for a series of years, been undertaken by the East India Company, for the improvement of the cotton of India; and it is also well known, with but partial success, or at least, that the success which may have been obtained has never had any permanent effect in improving the cotton from India. For this, various reasons have been assigned; some not true, others insufficient. Some, little acquainted with the country or the people of India, have said—If the country is capable of producing good cotton, why is it not done, as it must be for the benefit of the people to do what others are so anxious for and would readily purchase at advanced prices. But it is forgotten that India is not peopled by Anglo-Saxons, nor by any race who resemble them in energy and indomitable perseverance. Others, acquainted with the country and people, but unacquainted with the principles and the practice of the arts of culture, state that India is incapable of producing better cotton, as has been proved by the numerous failures to do so, both by the Government and by individuals. But they have omitted to show that the culture adopted was suited to the soil and climate, or that it was incapable of the necessary modifications. Others, considering themselves supported by the principles of political economy, assert that India is incapable of contending with America, because it is a thickly-peopled and highly-taxed country; while in America, land is abundant and taxes light. To this it has been replied, by those practically acquainted with the details of the subject, that the expenses of culture in India are not more than from 6 to 9 rupees, while in America they are equal to 60 rupees an acre; also, that there is abundance of land fitted for cotton culture, to be had in India for eighteen-pence an acre of land-tax or rent, and that the culture might enter beneficially into the rotation series, and without displacing an acre now employed in growing food. All, they likewise state, that is required, is a regular demand and remunerative prices, and that merchants have only to establish agents in the districts, to deal directly with the cultivator and encourage him by better prices, by which means they would receive better cotton in a clean state, which would insure a better price and a greater demand for it in Europe.

Before proceeding to the details of these several experiments, at different times and in different parts of India, we will take a general view, in a tabular form, of the

MEASURES ADOPTED AT DIFFERENT PERIODS TO IMPROVE THE CULTURE OF COTTON IN INDIA.

1788. The Court of Directors called the attention of the Indian Government to the cultivation of cotton in India, "with a view to affording every encouragement to its growth and improvement." 500,000 lbs. weight of cotton were ordered to be sent. Reports were called for from the Collectors of districts.

1789. Screws for compressing cotton were at this time established, both by the Company and by individuals.

1790. Cotton (422,207 lbs., v. p. 76) received from India. Ahmood cotton-seed directed to be sent to Bengal. Reports of culture at Bombay, Benares, and Dacca received; also from Collectors of Bengal and Behar. Dr. Anderson employed in distributing cotton-seeds from the Mauritius and from Malta throughout the Peninsula of India.

1794. A machine sent out for cleaning cotton from seed and other impurities.

1797. A plantation, under Mr. M. Brown, established at Randatarra, in Malabar, chiefly for spices, but Mauritius and Nankeen cottons were grown in 1801, and the produce sent to this country.

1799. Nagpore cotton-seed directed to be tried in the Circars, and a bounty offered to growers.

— Dr. Roxburgh, Superintendent of the Botanical Garden, Calcutta, grew and described eight species of Gossypium.

1802-3. Reports received on the cotton trade of Bombay and of the Gangetic Doab.

1809. Cotton ordered from India. 30,000,000 lbs. received in the following year, v. p. 17 and 76.

1810. Samples of Georgian and Grenada cottons sent out; also seeds of West Indian and of American cottons. Directions sent out for the culture of cotton, prepared by Mr. R. Hunt and by the African Society.

1811. Bourbon seed procured and distributed to Collectors of Surat and Broach, with directions for cultivation.

1813. Mr. B. Metcalfe, a cleaner of cotton from Georgia and New Orleans, sent to Tinnivelly with saw-gins.

— Mr. Bruce directed to send cotton-seed from Persia to India. Seed from Bourbon and Seychelles Island procured.

1814. Two or three hundred bales of the best and cleanest *Toomil* cotton directed to be sent annually.

1816. Collector at Caranja cultivates Bourbon cotton there.

— Drawback allowed "of the whole internal and sea duties" on cotton exported to Great Britain.

— Two improved gins sent to Bombay, one for cleaning black-seed, the other for green-seed cotton.

1817-19. Mr. Assistant-Surgeon Gilder succeeds in cultivating Bourbon cotton at Kaira.

— Cotton culture attempted in Circars by Commercial Residents, &c.

— The Court suggest, that in addition to Caranja and Salsette, Malwan should be tried.

1818. Satisfactory report from Malwan. Pernambuco seed asked for. Mr. Hughes successfully cultivates Bourbon cotton at Tinnivelly. Mr. Heath, having obtained instructions from Mr. Hughes, succeeds in Coimbatore. Memoir from Mr. Randall, Commercial Resident in Ceded districts, proposing rewards for growing Brazil cotton in districts of Madras Presidency.

— Four Cotton Farms of 400 acres directed to be established at Tinnivelly, Coimbatore, Masulipatam, and Vizagapatam.

1819. Considerable success by Mr. Heath in Coimbatore. The cotton approved of in England, and 500 bales of 300 lbs. each, sent to China, sold well there.

1823. Barbadoes and Brazil cotton grown by Lady Hastings at Tittyghur, near Barrackpore.

1826. The Author attempted culture of the Bourbon, Nurma, and common Indian cottons in the Botanic Garden, Saharunpore.

1828. Attention again called to the subject of cotton culture by Lord Ellenborough, the President of the Indian Board, "in different and distant parts of India," and in an excellent paper by H. St. George Tucker, Esq., a member of the Court of Directors.

1829. The Court direct attention to the growth of new and better species; send out machines for cleaning cotton; send out seeds of Upland Georgia and of New Orleans cotton; also Sea Island, Pernambuco, and Demerara cotton-seed, with accounts of methods of cultivation; five of Whitney's saw-gins sent out to India, with twelve more made up in England, and metallic work for twelve sets to be made up in India.

— A quantity of Surat cotton (500 bales) also ordered to be sent, of the best quality, and well cleaned.

— Rewards to be offered both to Ryots and to Wakarias for clean picking and cleaning.

— The Agricultural Society of India had an allowance of £1000 a year, exclusive of rent, until 1833, to attempt the culture of cotton. 20,000 rupees allowed for premiums for Cotton and Tobacco.

— Dec. 31.—Bombay Government report establishing a farm in Guzerat, under Mr. Finney; another in Dharwar, &c. under Dr. Lush; another in Salsette. Land offered for cultivation of cotton.

1830. 300 bales of Toomil cotton sent, and 25 bales from Broach Farm.

1831. Partial success at Cotton Farm established at Akra, near Calcutta.

— Buswunt Sing, of Ahmednuggur, encouraged to grow cotton.

1832. The Court do not approve of bounty, but direct that land appropriated to the growth of cotton, sugar, &c., should not be subject to a higher assessment. 3000 to 4000 bales ordered to be sent, if procurable, at 115 rupees the candy.

— Disposal of cotton grown in the experimental farm of Guzerat, for 152 to 156 rupees per candy.

1833. Reports from Collectors of Cuddapah, Guntoor, Arcot, Salem, and Coimbatore.

— Farm subsidiary to that at Danda in Guzerat established, to be cultivated by Ryots.

— Farm established at Segee Hullee, in Bedere district, under Dr. Lush. White-seeded perennial (New Orleans?) succeeded; also the Pernambuco and Egyptian. Agency for the purchase of cotton from natives who had been instructed in picking it clean. Screws and packing-sheds at Dharwar, Noulgond, and Gudduck. Natives had the option of paying their rents in kind, or receiving a remunerating price. Foreign cotton-seeds also tried in Dharwar, Poona, and the Concan.

1834. Egyptian cotton-seed and Egyptian cleaning-machine applied for and supplied.

— Machine for cleaning cotton in Brazil applied for.

— The Author publishes an essay on the cultivation of cotton in India, in his 'Illustrations of Himalayan Botany,' p. 84 to 101.

1836. Guzerat and Southern Mahratta Farms broken up.

— Report of the proceedings of the East India Company in regard to the production of cotton-wool, published.

1837. Dr. Wight publishes an essay on the cotton culture of the Peninsula.

1839. The Court of Directors propose undertaking a more complete experiment than any heretofore, by procuring planters from America.

— An excellent Minute by the late Earl of Auckland on this subject, with Reports from Madras and Bombay, giving an account of the results of former experiments, as well as proposals for the present one.

— Dr. Wight publishes figures, &c. of cotton plants, in his 'Illustrations of Indian Botany.'

1840. Mr. Elphinstone, Collector of Rutnagerry, succeeds in cultivating both Sea Island and Bourbon cotton.

— Capt. Bayles returned with ten planters from Cotton States of North America, bringing with him seeds and saw-gins, ploughs and hoes, with model of a gin-house. A hand saw-gin was prepared at Liverpool. The Author drew up a Report on the results hitherto obtained, and on the objects of the present experiment, v. 'Productive Resources of India,' p. 312 to 355.

— The Chairman, Deputy-Chairman, and several of the Directors proceed to Liverpool, to witness the working of the American saw-gins, v. 'Productive Resources,' p. 349.

— Three planters, assigned to Bombay, were sent to Broach, but shortly left India.

1841. Three planters, sent to Madras, were first stationed at Tinnivelly, then at Coimbatore.

— Four planters, sent to Calcutta, were stationed in the Doab and Bundlecund.

— Dr. Burns appointed to the charge of the experiments in Broach.

1842. Dr. Wight succeeded Captain Hughes in the charge of the cotton experiments in Coimbatore, and still continues in charge.

— An engineer sent to each of the three Presidencies, to repair and put up machinery.

— Mr. Shaw, the Collector, cultivates New Orleans' cotton in Dharwar. Mr. Hadow, Assistant to the Collector, cultivates Bourbon cotton in Dharwar.

— Mr. Mercer having been burnt out of his farm in Bundlecund, was transferred to Bombay, and stationed at Dharwar, where he was joined by Mr. Hawley, who afterwards went to Broach.

— After two seasons, the planters despair of success in the Doab.

— Mr. Finnie explores the North-West provinces for suitable sites.

1843. Mr. Blount sent to Gorruckpore, but not succeeding, went to Bombay.

— Mr. Finnie establishes a model farm near Agra, but fails.

— Mr. Price, an American planter, employed to introduce American cotton into Bengal, has had no success; is now endeavouring to improve the culture of Indian cotton.

— Mr. Wroughton, Collector of Coimbatore, succeeds in growing New Orleans cotton.

1844. Mr. Terry began cultivation in Rungpore, but soon left from ill-health.

1845. Messrs. Simpson and Blount appointed to conduct experiments in Candeish.

— Cotton Committee appointed at Bombay to inquire into and report on causes of the decline of the Cotton Trade of India.

1847. Mr. Landon appointed to carry on the experiments in Broach, where he is now established on his own account.

— Return ordered by the House of Commons to be printed of the papers in possession of the East India Company, showing what measures have been taken since 1836 to introduce the growth of American cotton, or to encourage the production of native cotton in India.

1848. Mr. Blount having returned from America, is engaged to take charge of the culture in Dharwar.

— Report from the Select Committee of the House of Commons on the growth of cotton in India.

1849. Mr. Simpson having returned from America, is engaged to prosecute the experiments in Candeish.

— 200 cottage saw-gins, prepared under the superintendence of the Manchester Commercial Association and of Mr. Petrie, sent by the Court of Directors to the three Presidencies. Seeds and saws sent at various times during these experiments.

1850. The Indian Government offers, through the Agricultural Society of India, a reward of 5000 rupees for an improved cotton-cleaning machine.

These various measures, perseveringly carried on through a series of years, have necessarily involved the expenditure of large sums of money. Much information has been elicited, and published in the above-mentioned Return and Reports, as well as in the 'Transactions of the Agricultural Society of India,' &c. But, as it was desirable to have recent and accurate information from every part of India with respect to the cost, the carriage, and the quantity of cotton at present cultivated, or which might be cultivated in case of an increase in the demand, the Court of Directors of the East India Company, in November 1847, framed six queries, which they desired might be circulated among the Collectors of Land Revenue under the different Presidencies, as also among the Political Agents resident in such Native States as are known to produce cotton. Answers to these queries having been received from many parts of India, some of the information obtained has already been referred to, and will again be quoted in the following pages. The following are the six questions:

1. What is the price of cotton, freed from seed, at the principal mart or marts in your district?

2. At what prices does the ryot sell his cotton, cleaned or uncleaned, and with or without advances?

3. What is the expense of cleaning cotton by the churka, or foot-roller, or by any other method which may be in use?

4. What are the expenses of conveying cotton to the nearest port for shipment?

5. What is the average produce of cotton per beegah or acre?

6. What is the quantity of land under cultivation with cotton, and to what extent is it probable that the cultivation could be carried, in the event of an increased demand?

Difficulties in Improving Indian Cotton.

The first inference a reader will be apt to deduce from so numerous a series of experiments, given up and again resumed, varied in every way, and conducted in almost every part of India, and all without permanently improving the nature of the cotton from India, or the condition in which it is sent to market, will be, that there must be something physically incompatible in the soil or climate of India for the proper growth of cotton; or fiscal regulations, or the difficulties of transit, render it unprofitable. As far as we have yet proceeded in our investigation, the cultivators seem very indifferent about the improvement of their cotton, and indeed have little inducement to do anything. Those to whom they sell do not reward such efforts, and with the purchasers for the English market they seldom come in contact; while these adduce the uncertainties of the American and European markets, as placing an effectual bar against all permanent arrangements. As far as the author has been able to form an opinion, from all that has been written respecting former experiments, he thinks that sufficient attention was not always paid to the peculiarities of soil and of climate, as suitable or unsuitable to the different kinds of cotton. And in case of failure or of success, no explanations are given of whether this was owing to the mechanical or to the chemical nature of the soil, or to the more or less warm or cold, dry or moist state of the atmosphere, and also whether one kind or state of soil was not more suitable than another to particular conditions of climate, as prevailing in different and distant parts of India. It seems usually to have been forgotten, that plants are endowed with life, and, though fixed in the soil, are subjected to the atmosphere, and that their nutriment is derived from both sources. This, if supplied in too scanty or in an over-profuse degree, might in one case starve a plant into dwarfishness, or stimulate it into soft and sappy luxuriance. A check to the process of vegetable nutrition, that is, to the production of branches and leaves, being moreover necessary when a plant has arrived at maturity, in order to favour the development of the parts of fructification, or the formation of flowers and fruit. For these reasons, the author was induced, on a former occasion, to say, that we knew "too little of the details and particular results which were obtained to be able to rank them among successful investigations, or as partial or complete failures;" and also that, " In the experiments which have been instituted on the improvement of the culture, it is extraordinary to observe how little attention has been paid, or, at least, how little information is given us, respecting the attention that was paid, to all the points essential to ensure success in culture, and improvement in produce. Also, how seldom any attempts are made, or reasons given, to explain the causes of failure. We find, as was to be expected, a general want of knowledge in the practical details of culture, but, also what was not to be expected, equal inattention to, if not ignorance of, principles. The majority also appear wise only after personal experience, and paying little attention to that of their predecessors. For we find that the same course is followed, the same faults are committed, the same results are obtained and continue to be announced as new, though we have had them on record for a series of years."—(*Productive Resources of India, p.* 316.)

Some seem to think that failures may have been due to the experiments having been conducted by government officers, where the stimulus of personal interest was wanting to ensure success; but this was not found to operate as an objection in the experiments on the improvement of silk or of opium, or in the present ones on the culture of tea in the Himalayas, which from its success, promises in a few years to be of national importance. With cotton we shall see that individuals have experienced the same difficulties as those employed by Government. The success that was obtained is also sometimes objected to, as having been on so small a scale as to have been rather of the nature of garden culture than to the extent to give confidence for great farming operations. But all cotton cultivation is of the nature rather of garden than of field culture, for each individual plant requires to be attended to, as in the case of hop cultivation in this country; but the experimental farms consisted, in many instances, of some hundred acres, and were quite as large as one man could superintend.

But all the experiments did not prove failures; cotton of excellent quality was produced in several situations, and sold well, both in England and in China. Judging from subsequent experience, it ought to have been remunerative, as it sold for better prices than are now obtainable, and the expenses were not greater then than they are in the present day. A part of the success obtained, the experimentalists themselves were not aware of, that is, in foreign cottons having become so naturalised as to have been mistaken for indigenous species, whence Mr. Elphinstone called one of them *Conkanee*. Dr. Burns, again, collected seeds out of the hedges of Mr. Gilder's garden, near Kaira, from which he grew plants, and obtained cotton which was considered equal to New Orleans cotton, by merchants at Bombay. In both cases the plant proved to be naturalised Bourbon. This species is also described by Mr. Fischer and by Dr. Wight, as being quite common in Salem, Coimbatore, and other southern provinces. The Brazil cotton, moreover, is so completely naturalised in some places, as to have a native name (Deo-kupas) applied to it. Dr. Roxburgh described it as an Indian species, from having received seeds from the interior, where it had no doubt been introduced.

That difficulties are experienced by experimentalists, other than Government officers, is evident from the several failures of the Agricultural Society of India, though they subsequently attained partial success, as we shall afterwards relate. Their failures they ascribed to saltness and moisture of soil.

Colonel Skinner,* a large landholder in the west of India, describes himself as discouraged, when cultivating Upland Georgia cotton, from the result of a consignment sold in the Calcutta market, "*which was about the same as what good*

* Transactions of the Agri-Horticultural Society of India, vol. vi. p. 109.

country cotton realized." Upon this, the Cotton Committee of the Agri-Horticultural Society of India, composed of mercantile men, observe,—" Your committee regret exceedingly, that Colonel Skinner's opinion should have been advanced on such frail grounds. The Calcutta market can be no criterion—parties here are interested in keeping down the prices of staples, while in England competition soon draws out their good and bad qualities."

Mr. Bruce again, to whom we have before referred, as having been long settled in North-West India, writes,—" I have tried, at various times, the Sea Island and Upland American, the Egyptian, the Bourbon, and the Pernambuco cottons, several years on my own account, to the extent of 15 and 20 beegahs at a time; and lastly, on a scale of 400 beegahs, in partnership with two of the Calcutta mercantile houses in 1837, in the neighbourhood of Calpee, with and without irrigation, but never at a remunerative price. My last experiment of 400 beegahs happened to be made when the famine raged with so much severity in the North-Western provinces; and I attributed the drying-up of the plant, notwithstanding it had the benefit of being irrigated during the prevalence of the hot winds, to the unfavorableness of the season, (*Return*, p. 102.)* So Merwanjee Hormasjie, formerly native agent to the Commercial Resident, in reference to his endeavours to prepare and clean native cotton for the English market, says, that the first purchaser, " after laying out from 40 to 50 per cent., frequently becomes a loser by the speculation, as the price of the English market continually varies, and the article sometimes sells for less than prime cost. The cotton I have hitherto sent to England has certainly, as the Governor General has been pleased to state, in his minute of the 14th August 1839, fetched a higher price than the usual description of Surat or Broach cotton; but the expenses of preparing it for the market has almost equalled the profit. I merely mention this to show the vast importance of inducing the ryot to be more careful in gathering the kuppas in the first instance." (*Return*, p. 59.)

In addition to the difficulties of a physical nature, nothing

* Mr. Bruce has, however, been so little deterred by these failures, that he engaged to grow American cotton in the very same situations, if supplied with seed. This has been sent to him by Dr. Wight, from Coimbatore.

seems more unaccountable than the opposition thrown in the way of improvement by the natives themselves; for instance, in the experiments of 1833, when the cultivators "had the option allowed them of paying their revenue in cotton, or of receiving a fair remunerating price (about 20 per cent. above the market price) for the quantity sold to Government," no success was obtained, and the failure was attributed "to the influence of the principal merchants of Dharwar, with whom it was at first proposed to contract for the supply of cotton cleaned on the new plan," and who refused to "co-operate in what they conceived to be innovations on established usages and customs." So Mr. Shaw, when asked before the Cotton Committee (Q. 3819), whether the ryots had any reluctance to change the native for the American plant, replied, "Yes; a ryot has the greatest disinclination to every kind of innovation; it is not only that he has a disinclination to change, but it is not to the interest of the Brahmin part of society to allow of any innovation." And again (Q. 3825), they oppose "any improvements of any sort, even the introduction of a new assessment;* they opposed that in the Southern Mahratta country, where it has been carrying on for years; the great opposition was from the Brahmins." So we have lately been informed by Dr. Cleghorn, who is a careful and intelligent observer, and who is most zealous for the improvement of Indian products, that having obtained seeds of the New Orleans cotton plant from Dr. Wight, of Coimbatore, he distributed them among the villagers of Mysore. He found the Brahmins discouraging the cultivation, as it would cause the disappearance of the native plant, and that, therefore, "the evil eye" would be upon all their efforts. To ensure the truth of their prophecy, men in blanket cloaks were sent out into the fields at night, and were seen rooting up the young plants. While this page is passing through the press, we observe in *The Times*, 23d May, 1850, a letter from an engineer of the Coimbatore district, stating that the abolition even of the transit duties (which were complained of as a grievance) was objected to by the traders, because having no previous payments to make, the cultivators were enabled to take their produce to whatever market they pleased, and thus to escape from their grasp.

* This was for the purpose of making reductions and removing inequalities

Good Quality of some Native Cotton.

Our object, however, is not to dwell upon difficulties, or to depreciate Indian cotton, but rather, by pointing out the true nature of the impediments which prevent its being improved, to enlist those really interested in the subject to apply exertion in the only direction where it can be effectual, that is, in the districts where the cotton is grown. That the task is not a hopeless one, notwithstanding numerous disappointments, will be evident from the few following facts, which we somewhat anticipate events in at present relating. But without something to counteract the effects of continued failures, the subject would appear to be so discouraging, as to make the second part of our Essay appear unnecessary.

In the first place, it is desirable to show that some of the native cotton is not devoid of good qualities. In the year 1810, the Court of Directors wrote to the Bombay Government, that their Toomeel (that is, the best Broach) cotton was considered by manufacturers here to be of a desirable quality, such as will answer well as a substitute for the bowed Upland Georgia cotton. (E. I. C.'s Papers, p. 30.) That the native cotton of the above province has not lost its good character, will appear from the following Report, from Messrs. Clarke, the well known brokers of Liverpool, on 292 bales of Broach and Surat cotton, sent them last year :

Particulars as to the Working Qualities of East India Cotton, per "Gulterus," viz.;—(Jan. 1849,)

49 Bales, marked $\frac{\text{BC}}{\text{A}}$; 141 Bales, $\frac{\text{BC}}{\text{B}}$; 82 Bales, SC.
20½

The general character of the cotton by this ship is superior to any that has yet been sent from India, especially the 82 bales SC, which are quite equal in staple and fibre to good middling Boweds, and are well qualified for spinning any weft under 40's.

The marks $\frac{\text{BC}}{\text{A}}$ and $\frac{\text{BC}}{\text{B}}$ are fully equal to the best that we have seen (previous to the above mark); they work well, and are clean and fair staple, and suitable for any weft up to 24's.

Cotton like the SC will always find a market, and we should like to have 150 bales a week of such cotton at market price.

Yours, &c.,
(*Signed*) JOSEPH CLARKE & BROTHER.

The cotton of the Southern Mahratta country appears also to be naturally of good quality. Dr. Lush reported, in 1832, that the cotton cultivated in that province was "capable of maintaining a respectable footing, if properly cleaned,—in such manner as to increase its value in the market, without adding much to the cost of production." Some cotton prepared in this manner was formerly reported on by London brokers;* and some consigned to Canton was highly approved of by Chinese merchants.—(*E. I. C.'s Papers,* p. 260.)

In the year 1846 Mr. Mercer sent some Dharwar cotton to Mr. Turner, which was tried in his North Shore Mills at Liverpool. This had been cleaned by the saw-gin, but unfortunately had not been previously clean-picked. In passing through the grating of the machine, the dried leaves were ground by the saws into small fragments, which adhered with such tenacity to the fibres of cotton as not to be separable afterwards, and thus gave a speckled appearance to the yarn spun with it. This is the more unfortunate, as the cotton itself was ranked as "about the best specimen of East India cotton we ever worked. In the carding and spinning it has given unqualified satisfaction, but all these good qualities are rendered null by the impossibility of eradicating the small shell-dirt above alluded to." The cotton being therefore naturally of good quality, the precaution of clean-picking it, previous to subjecting it to the action of the saw-gin would probably render it a valuable article for some manufactures.

From Dharwar we may proceed to Tinnevelly, the most southern of the cotton districts, whence 230 bales of indigenous cotton, bought from the natives, and cleaned by Mr. Finnie, were last year received in London, and sold for the East India Company by Messrs. Tetley. But of these, 60 bales were

* Good bright colour, with a yellowish tinge, quite clean, and remarkably well got up, firm, and heavy in the hand, good sound staple, but not fine; worth 5⅝*d.* per pound.

7

sent to Manchester for the opinions of manufacturers. The cotton is thus spoken of:

"We have already noticed the arrival here, per 'Aurora,' from India, of sixty bales of native indigenous cotton, grown at Tinnevelly, and consigned to Mr. Hugh Fleming, secretary of the Manchester Commercial Association, by order of the Board of Directors of the East India Company, for sale. This cotton was purchased of the native ryot growers, and cleaned at Tinnevelly, under the superintendence of Mr. Finnie, an American cotton planter, who was sent thither to superintend the culture, picking, and cleaning of cotton. It is a fine, clean, bright cotton, and thought well of by the manufacturers. Of the 60 bales, 30 were saw-ginned (Whitney's American gin), and 30 churkaed. The latter had a little better staple than the ginned; but the whole was so clean, and of so good a colour, that the entire quantity was disposed of in two lots, one of 50, and the other of 10 bales, both at the same satisfactory price of *five-pence* per lb. This, for native cotton, is a very striking result."—(*Manchester Paper, Aug.* 1849.) Tinnivelly cotton has always been more approved of than any other Madras cotton by manufacturers.

Improved Cotton from American Seed.

India being a consumer of its indigenous cotton, and an exporter of it to China, its improvement is necessarily a subject of great importance, especially to the producers, from the regularity and extent of the demand. But as far as the manufacturers of this country are concerned, they take an interest chiefly, if not only, in the introduction into and extended culture in India of American cotton. They say that this alone is capable of supplying the place of American-grown cotton when there is a deficiency in the market, and of maintaining its position even when there is an abundant crop. We are happy to be able to prove that enough has been done to give the assurance of ultimate and very extended success in this also, if the mercantile and manufacturing community will second the efforts of the Indian Government in encouraging the actual cultivator to grow such cotton, and to collect it and to clean it in such a manner as will satisfy the spinners of Lancashire. But what has often been stated as essential must be remembered, and that is, that nothing short of the presence of European agents in the interior of the districts will have any great or permanent effect in rousing the ryot and in counteracting "the baneful influence" of the present race of middlemen, or, in supplanting the indigenous cotton, for which notwithstanding its dirty condition and inferior quality, there is always a demand for home consumption.

We have seen that in the former experiments good cotton was produced, and that American species of cotton-plant have become naturalised in the country. We may state, as an interesting fact, that when the ten American planters arrived in London, Mr. Mercer, in examining the specimens of cotton produced in the former experiments, and which are preserved in the India House, picked out some grown in the Dharwar district by Dr. Lush, and marked as that of the "white-seeded perennial," as the best of the whole, and as quite equal to New Orleans cotton. It was in the Dharwar district that Mr. Mercer himself afterwards attained the greatest success. There American cotton still continues to be extensively cultivated, being profitable both to the ryot and to the exporter, and a cotton is produced which is highly approved of by spinners and manufacturers in Manchester.

The author stated, in a report so long since as November 1845, on the occasion of the first deputation from the Commercial Association of Manchester to the India House, that "complete success (that is, good cotton, from American seed, cheaply produced by natives of India) has attended the experiment at Dharwar, in the southern Mahratta country, and here some excellent cotton was produced when the experiments were tried in 1834. The cause, no doubt, is a favorable climate, which Mr. Mercer, the American planter, says is more like the Mississippi climate than any other he has met with in India. The elevation (the whole district being above the Ghauts) modifies the climate, which also feels the influence of both monsoons or rains, so that it never becomes excessively dry, and is never inundated with excessive rains. Mr. Mercer finds the seed returning to its original Mexican character, instead of deteriorating, as in other parts of India. Here the natives, witnessing the success of cultivation in the Government farm with American cotton, have themselves adopted and are rapidly increasing it, as they find it yields a larger quantity per acre, and they get a better price, even from the native weavers, for every maund they grow.

The culture of American cotton has here been greatly increasing in quantity, from 600 acres the first year (1842) to about 15,000 acres this year (1845), when Mr. Mercer thought that not less than 1,000,000 lbs. of American cotton would be produced. This crop has now been ginned, and 40,000 rupees worth, at 66¼ rupees per candy of 784 lbs., has been bought from the ryots for transmission to this country." (*Rep.* 1845.)

"The further expenses on this cotton amounted to 17½ rupees* in conveyance, &c. to Bombay, or altogether to 83¾ rupees. Some of this cotton (100 bales) was sold at Bombay for 113 rupees a candy, and the 500 which were sent to Manchester for 6½*d.* a pound, having cost 3¾*d.* a pound, judging by 200 bales of the same cotton imported into Manchester by individuals." (*Author's Report for* 1847, v. *Return*, p. 62.)

We are informed by Mr. Shaw, the collector of the district, that in the season of 1847, 50,000 acres of land had been ploughed and made ready for sowing with New Orleans cotton-seed. But the season was, unluckily, unfavorable, from the late coming on of the rains, and the ryots were, therefore, unable to sow their seed. Discouraged by this, and also, probably, in consequence of the departure from the district of Mr. Shaw, the collector, and of Mr. Mercer, the planter, the cultivation of New Orleans cotton fell off, having been 23,000 acres in 1847, and in the season of 1848 only 3400 acres. But Mr. Blount having returned from America, and appointed to this district, the culture has again revived. The author has received from him the two following letters, showing that the culture only requires an agent on the spot, to encourage the natives in their efforts to establish it on a permanent footing:

"I have much pleasure in informing you, that the number of acres planted this year is in round numbers 15,400, against 3400 in 1848; and we have had a copious monsoon, and the expectation is, that there will be another good productive season; should such be the event, I have no doubt the crop will double itself another year. —*Dharwar*, Oct. 27, 1849."

* Carriage by bullocks to the coast, Rs. 10; expenses in bagging and packing, Rs. 3.8; expenses in shipping to Bombay, Rs. 1.8; freight to Bombay, Rs. 2.8. Total, Rs. 17.8.

The fine crop of New Orleans likely to be realised this season will, I think, induce a more extended cultivation of that variety; and I should not be surprised to see the cultivation come up, next season, to 30,000 acres. I have now completed the dispatch of the cotton purchased in 1849, for Government, and can give you the correct quantity:—New Orleans, 330 candies, which will cost, put down in Liverpool, about $3\frac{78}{100}$*d*. per pound; native cotton, 60 candies, cost, put down in Liverpool, about $3\frac{1}{2}$*d*. per pound. The cotton is superior in quality to the previous crop.

"The system I pursue, in encouraging the growth of the New Orleans cotton, is to engage the interests of all classes of cultivators and trades, in its production. Our chief difficulty is the want of the like competition for this cotton that exists for the native. If the Bombay merchants could be got to interest themselves, by making purchases in the district markets, either through an agent or through resident dealers, it would stimulate the growth of this cotton in a greater degree than any measure Government can take.—*Dharwar*, Feb. 8, 1850."

"At Coimbatore, where the climate is not altogether favorable, from occasional storms and droughts, the cultivation of American cotton has now proceeded for some years, and upon the whole with considerable success. Some of the American cotton grown there, on red soil, in 1841, when the experiments were first established, was exhibited (by the author) at Manchester, and was pronounced by some experienced manufacturers and spinners to be "quite equal to the fine qualities of the same cotton produced in the United States." Last year, Dr. Wight, the superintendent, was of opinion that "he could carry on the culture with profit." Since then, in a letter dated 25th April, 1845, in reply to some queries which were sent to him, he states, that by sowing early, that is, in July or August, instead of in September and October, as is usual in that part of India, he had obtained much larger returns per acre; also, that the natives here are gradually becoming willing to cultivate American cotton, and on the American plan, provided we will ensure them a certain market and honest prices for their produce. In this case, Dr. Wight states that there will be no difficulty in getting the natives to cultivate cotton fit for the English market to any extent; and he has also stated, that there is abundance of land in the Coimbatore, Tinnivelly, Salem, and Madura districts. This is very important, for 24 bales of American cotton, grown by Dr. Wight, and 10 bales grown by the Collector at Coimbatore, which have arrived at Liverpool, have been pronounced, by experienced brokers and spinners, to be of excellent quality, and worth $6\frac{3}{4}$*d*. a lb. It was reported to be equal to fair Orleans cotton, value $6\frac{3}{4}$*d*. at the same time, that is, the 4th Dec., 1846, at Liverpool." We annex the brokers' reports upon this cotton.

" *Valuation of* 24 *bales and* 8 *bundles cotton, ex* ' *Colonist,*' *from Madras.*

LIVERPOOL, 4th Dec., 1846.

24 bales, 6¾*d*.....Clear, bright, good cotton, fair staple, and much more free from nep than last shipment, per ' Grindley.'

8 bundles, 5¼*d*.....Clean, but high coloured, short staple.

CUNNINGHAM & HINSHAW.

P. S.—We consider the bales to be equal to fair Orleans cotton.

Value to-day, 6¾*d*.

" 14 *bales cotton, ex* ' *Sir John Beresford,*' *from Madras, 4th December,* 1846.

N. O., 1 to 10....10 bales, 6½*d*....Very clean bright cotton, but rather soft and light in staple.

11 ,, 14.... 4 ,, 5*d*.....Pretty clean, but high coloured, soft staple, and neppy.

CUNNINGHAM & HINSHAW.

P. S.—1 to 10 quite equal to fair Orleans, as regards colour and cleanliness, but wanting in hardness and weight of staple."

Dr. Wight has since stated, that this cotton could be landed in Liverpool for 3½*d*. a lb. He subsequently produced still finer specimens from New Orleans seed, by sowing earlier in the season, viz. in May, at the suggestion of the Commercial Association of Manchester. But the climate there appears too uncertain to allow of perseverance in this beneficial practice. He has since adopted irrigation to a limited extent, in order to bring forward or save a crop, as the case might be, when drought prevails; and could see nothing to prevent cotton being as important a crop in Southern India as indigo was in Bengal. In the last letter, dated 8th April last, he reports very favorably of the effects, on the minds of the ryots, of this limited degree of irrigation from the fine crop of New Orleans cotton.

OPINIONS OF SPINNERS, ETC. ON THE EXPERIMENTAL COTTON.

Considering the anxiety which has been displayed for the improved culture of cotton in India, and the difficulty which has always been experienced in inducing the natives of India to make any change in their habits, one is surprised to find a great diversity of opinion respecting a material tangible substance like cotton, of which the quantities can be measured or weighed, or the number of bales counted, and the quality of the produce compared with that of American cotton, or with ordinary Indian cotton. The author regrets to find that the

Chamber of Commerce of Manchester speak unfavorably of the experiments, though the Commercial Association of the same place think favorably of the results as far as they have yet gone. A deputation from the latter body having come to the India House for information respecting the course of the experimental culture, were, of course, supplied with whatever information the Court possessed. The author, in visiting Manchester for the purpose of acquiring information on practical points, naturally went to the same body, and considered himself safe in trusting to the opinions of those whom he had so much reason to respect, as he found Mr. Turner, the President, though engaged during the day in conducting vast establishments, devoting his evenings and leisure hours to scientific investigations; Mr. Malcolm Ross, the Vice-president, armed with the strong sense of his country; Mr. John Peel at the head of both a Manchester and a Bombay firm, with sagacity characteristic of his name; Mr. James Lees paying careful attention to the physical requirements of the plant; and the Secretary obliging and ready to procure whatever information was required. As the author had himself to acquire correct information before he could venture to advise others, and as he has also to guard himself against taking too favorable a view of any results that may have been obtained, he considers it incumbent upon him to show that he does not stand alone in his opinions even on practical points. He, therefore, begs to quote from Manchester papers accounts of the arrivals of cotton, as well as of the opinions of Manchester men at the time, on the results which have been obtained.

"The '*Quentin Leitch*,' which arrived at Liverpool on Thursday last, from Bombay, has on board nearly 700 bales of cotton, presumed to be of superior quality, and grown partly from American, and partly from native seed, but cleaned in a more careful manner than ordinary. Of this cotton we understand 500 bales belong to the East India Company, and about 200 to a mercantile firm in this town."—(*Manchester Guardian, August 28th,* 1847.)

"Since our last, ninety bales of the East India cotton, ex '*Quentin Leitch*,' consigned to Messrs. William and John Peel, have arrived in Manchester, and the 500 bales consigned to Mr. Hugh Fleming, Secretary of the Manchester Commercial Association, are on the way, by canal, from Liverpool. We are desirous to direct the attention of spinners and manufacturers to this important matter. Much, very much, depends upon the encouragement now afforded to the cultivation of cotton in India; and if it is once found there, that by improvements in its culture and cleaning, by greater facilities of transport, and by the adoption of all available means for reducing the cost of production, of land transit, and of export from India, it is becoming an article more extensively in demand in this country, and commanding a better price, we shall then give that impetus to its cultivation in our Indian empire which alone seems wanting to secure us more ample and valuable supplies of the raw material from that quarter of the world.—(*Ibid.*)

"This cotton is the produce of the Dharwar district, and was raised on the experimental farms of the East India Company. It is the first cotton imported by the East India Company that has been brought to Manchester direct, and it is desirable that the efforts of the Company should meet with such encouragement as ought to convince them that a real anxiety exists here on the subject, and that encouragement on the part of the Company to the ryots to grow cotton will be met in the same spirit here, by a constant demand and market."—(*Manchester Courier.*)

The samples of (Surat) cotton, grown in the Dharwar district, from New Orleans seed, which we stated on Saturday were to be exhibited on our Exchange, were placed there for a short time on Monday, and again during yesterday. On the latter occasion, being the market day, they attracted general attention, and created a considerable sensation amongst the spinners and manufacturers. Nor was this mere idle curiosity; for, of the whole bulk of 500 bales, from 300 to 400 were sold during the day, on 'Change, at 6½*d*. per lb.—(*Manchester Guardian, Sept. 8th,* 1847.)

"PARTICULARS AS TO THE WORKING QUALITIES OF EAST INDIA COTTON,

Per 'Quentin Leitch,' 1000 Bales, marked WL-DC.

General character of the Cotton, as to Staple, &c. } Moderate staple, rather curled, not very regular in length.

Nos. of Yarn spun.......—No. 26 mule.

		Experimental.	Common Surat.
What does it lose as compared with common Surat?	Before carding, in 332 lbs.,	21lbs.....46lb. 8oz.	in 398lbs.
	After carding... „	16lbs.....34lb. 8oz.	„

"The experimental cotton is very well suited for all Nos. of weft under 40's, works quite as well as Boweds of good middling quality, which will always regulate the price in this market.—JOSEPH CLARKE & BROTHER."

"Amidst all the turmoil and disasters we have lately been in, and are passing through, we are glad to find that the subject of the cultivation of cotton in India is not being lost sight of. We may—unless the Manchester Commercial Association shall continue its useful endeavours in the matter—find some difficulty in keeping the public mind sufficiently attentive to the consideration of the all-important subject, as we have every prospect of an abundant supply of cotton from the United States for the next twelve months; but it is not on this account any the more likely we may not discover again, before many years, the absolute necessity of being less dependent on one country for our supply, and at the time when we require the cotton, will the short-sighted policy of being content with present abundance be forced on our attention. This, we say, will inevitably occur, unless the commercial associations of this town continue to stir in the matter. We have at present to notice that 45 bales of East India cotton, grown from New Orleans seed, in the Company's farms at Coimbatore, have been imported into London per the ship *Olinda*. The cotton has been sampled in London, and found to be of superior description; the staple is good, and of a fine silky texture."—(*Manchester Courier, 4th December,* 1847.)

"This cotton is stated to be of a very good quality. In February last, the Commercial Association, through their President, Mr. James A. Turner, addressed a letter to the East India Company, suggesting that, as the improvement in the quality of the cotton grown by Dr. Wight, at Coimbatore, seemed to be greatly owing to his having sown it earlier than the time usual in India, the experiment should be tried of sowing still earlier. The Honorable Court of Directors, anxious that nothing should be neglected which might tend to promote the improvement of East Indian cotton, immediately forwarded a copy of Mr. Turner's letter to Dr. Wight, with instructions to try the experiment therein recommended. Dr. Wight did so, and by the last mail, letters have been received from him, stating with what success it has been attended.

The plants on the portion of land which he sowed in the latter part of May instead of in July, as previously, were, when he wrote (the latter end of September), drooping exceedingly; he did not, however, despair of getting a second crop, should the weather become more favorable than it then was. Samples of the early sown cotton, both of such as has duly arrived at maturity and of such as has been damaged by the drizzly weather, have been received by the Commercial Association. The first description is considered as good as New Orleans cotton; while Dr. Wight states that he expects the other will be good second-rate cotton when it has passed through the gin."—(*Manchester Guardian, 4th December*, 1847.)

"The cotton grown from New Orleans seed is of an exceedingly good description. The first lot of 16 bales realised 4*d.* per lb. The quality of the single bale of the early grown cotton has quite borne out the predictions of the Manchester Commercial Association, as to what might be effected in the improvement of the cotton crop by sowing in the latter end of May. It is decidedly the finest sample of cotton yet received from India; its colour and cleanliness are unexceptionable, and its staple is very little inferior to the New Orleans cotton received from America. 4¾*d.* per lb. has been offered for it by several spinners; but this has been declined, as it is valued by the broker at 5*d.* per lb."—(*Ibid.*, 12*th August*, 1848.)

"We understand that Mr. Hugh Fleming, Secretary of the Manchester Commercial Association, yesterday received a letter from the Secretary of the Board of Directors of the East India Company, stating that the Directors had ordered their agent at Liverpool to forward to Manchester 871 bales of cotton, the produce of the Coimbatore district, and which had arrived at Liverpool on board the ship *Ganges*, from Cochin. The letter also requested that the Association would be pleased to furnish to the East India Company any observations with respect to the quality, length of staple, &c., of the different descriptions of cotton comprised in this shipment, which an examination of them might suggest. Amongst the descriptions of cotton of which samples are contained in this shipment, we may mention some farm-grown from New Orleans seed, and also some of the Bourbon description, of the growths of 1848 and 1849; and some from New Orleans and Mexican seed, both May sown. All these samples were grown on the experimental farm, under the superintendence of Dr. Wight. There are also samples of New Orleans and Bourbon cottons, and of the Oopum kind, or the indigenous cotton of India, all purchased from the natives. Of this latter kind, one portion is gin-cleaned, another churka-cleaned and threshed, and a third cleaned at the gin-house of the Company, and afterwards threshed. This is altogether the largest consignment of cottons from the Coimbatore district ever received by the Association. It is expected that the whole of the samples will be in the market on Tuesday next; and an inspection of them will afford to those interested in the question of cotton cultivation an opportunity of judging of the kind of seed most suited for cultivation in our Indian possessions, and the season of the year when it can be most advantageously sown. It will also show the difference in the quality of the article produced on the Company's farm, under the direction of their agent, and that produced by native growers. It is gratifying to see so much interest exhibited in the subject on the part of the East India Company, and the desire which evidently exists to be guided in their operations, to some extent at least, by the opinions of those practically acquainted with the merits, for this market, of the different growths of cotton. In connexion with this subject, it may be stated that the Commercial Association have now shipped the whole of the 200 cottage saw-gins made under their superintendence for the East India Company.—(*Ibid., 21st January,* 1849.)

" *To the Editor of the Manchester Guardian.*

" Sir.—In your publication of Wednesday last, I read an account of the proceedings of the annual meeting of the Chamber of Commerce, and was extremely sorry to find expressions made use of, both in the secretary's report and in the speeches of the chairman and others, respecting the cultivation of cotton in India, which are, in my opinion, calculated to give to the public an erroneous idea of what has already been done, and is now in progress, and also to discourage the efforts of those who are now taking so deep an interest in the question.

" In the latter part of 1845, the subject of cotton cultivation in India was taken up by the Manchester Commercial Association; and, on the 28th December, a deputation was sent to confer with the Court of Directors of the East India Company. The Court promised to act upon the suggestion of the Commercial Association, and appear to have done much in fulfilment of that pledge; for, in 1846, a considerable quantity of this cotton was grown in Dharwar, by the natives, from New Orleans seed, and purchased by the Indian Government. Part of the cotton was sent to Liverpool, on account of the government, and part was sold by auction in Bombay. Of the latter, my partner in Bombay purchased, on account of my Manchester firm, 130 bales, at the price of 113rs. per candy, which arrived in Liverpool in the month of August, 1847, and was sold at 6½*d*. per lb., giving us a handsome profit on the transaction.

"Five hundred bales were shipped by the company at the same time, and consigned to the secretary of the Commercial Association, and fetched the same sum, or thereabouts. A subsequent shipment was made by the company, and fetched an equally high price in proportion to the value of American cotton at the time."

Mr. Peel after quoting a letter from his partner at Bombay, says:

"I think the above will clearly show, that it was unjust to say that 'no important progress has been made in improving the quality; that 'the natives have not derived much additional instruction,' and that 'the American planters had not succeeded in anything.'

"Since October last my partners purchased, on account of my firm here, a parcel of the New Orleans cotton, which is now on the way to this country; and, by the mail, arrived this evening, I have advice of a further purchase on account of an eminent Lancashire spinner. The quality of this cotton is now well known and appreciated in Bombay, and its value is quoted in all the prices current; on the 15th of January, the quotation was 114rs., *whilst the highest quotations for Surats were* 74rs. The return to the cultivator, upon an acre of ground, is thus doubled; for he gets 50 per cent. more weight of cotton, and an increase of 50 per cent. in value. I feel, therefore, most confident, that this will give a stimulus to the native grower, and that we shall see a rapid increase in the production, as well as a great improvement in quality.

"SWINTON PARK, *February* 21, 1848. JOHN PEEL."

At the Annual Meeting of the Commercial Association of Manchester, held at their offices, on the 20th January, 1850, the subject of Indian cotton was referred to in the following words:

"The anxious attention which has been so long devoted by the Association to the above important subject, has been in no degree relaxed during the year which has just terminated. The same active interchange of communications between the Association and the Court of Directors of the Honorable East India Company has continued to exist, and numerous communications bearing on the question have also reached the Board from private sources. Several shipments of cotton, amounting in the whole to nearly 2,400 bales, consisting both of the produce of the indigenous plant of India and of that raised from American seed, have been consigned to your Secretary for sale, and most satisfactory prices have been uniformly obtained. The 200 cottage sawgins ordered by the East India Company have been forwarded to their destination, and have, according to instructions from the Honorable Court, been pretty equally distributed throughout the Presidencies. The Association has not, however, as yet, received any report as to their arrival in India. From the spirit in which recommendations from this Board have been at all times treated by the East India Company, and the amount of activity which the latter body has of late years displayed with reference to the cultivation of cotton, your Directors viewed with surprise, not unmixed with incredulity, an announcement which appeared in the public journals on the arrival of the Overland Mail of August last, to the effect that the cotton experiments at Broach, in the Bombay presidency, and Coimbatore, in the presidency of Madras, had been, by order of the Government, entirely abandoned; it being further alleged that that course had been determined on from a despair of success, as well as on the score of unnecessary expense. This appeared the more strange as private advices from the cotton districts had led to the formation of very different conclusions. Steps were therefore instantly taken, in order to ascertain what reliance might be placed on the statements referred to; and a letter was addressed to the chairman of the East India Company, requesting to be favoured with full information on the subject. A reply was returned, dated the

17th September, stating that the Court had received no information which would lead them to apprehend that the measures in progress for improving the culture of cotton in the Broach district had been in any way interfered with: but, on the contrary, they had reason to believe that they were proceeding with a greater prospect of successful issue than at any former period. But with regard to Coimbatore, the Court had learned that, under a misapprehension of their orders, certain measures had been adopted which might have had a tendency to retard the progress made under the superintendence of Dr. Wight, in developing the capabilities of Madras for supplying cotton; that the Court, however, had lost no time in issuing the necessary instructions for placing the cotton experiments on a satisfactory footing. Your Directors have since had the gratification to learn that the Court's orders had reached Dr. Wight at the very moment that he, after surrendering his charge, was about to retire from India; and they further ascertained, that he had vigorously resumed the prosecution of his labours. The letter from which the foregoing extracts have been taken, extends to a considerable length, and has already appeared in print. To one further remark only which it contains, your Directors would call earnest attention. The Court, assuring the Association of the lively interest which they have never ceased to take in obtaining from India an ample supply of cotton fit for the requirements of English manufacturers, observe, 'that they must at the same time express their conviction that the efforts of the Indian Government will fail in producing any extensive and permanent effect, unless they are aided by the cordial co-operation of the manufacturers of this country.' In this last observation your Directors entirely coincide, and would commend it to the serious consideration of the cotton consumers of Lancashire as a body, entreating them not to allow the subject only to enlist their sympathies while suffering from an inadequate supply of the American staple, and dismiss it from their minds when supplies become abundant, and prices begin to fall. With reference to this portion of the subject, a very gratifying instance of the exercise of private enterprise, with regard to Indian cotton, may, in conclusion, be mentioned. On the 24th July last, a letter was received from a highly respectable mercantile firm of Madras, forwarding a sample of excellent cotton (valued at $5\frac{1}{4}d.$), grown in the Madura district, from American seed, being the result of an experiment made by them to induce the natives to cultivate that plant, requesting the Association to favour them with an opinion as to the quality of the sample. The firm in question had succeeded in causing 800 acres to be planted, by offering to such of the ryots as would sow their farms with American seed, a bonus of five rupees per candy over and above the current market price for Tinnivelly cotton. In consequence, however, of the failure of the usual rains, the season turned out unfavorable; but the letter intimates that it was intended to repeat the experiment during 1849, and your Directors look forward to the result with much interest. A letter has also been addressed by the Board, in reply to the communication from the Court of 17th September, containing certain further suggestions as to the steps which, in the opinion of the Association, may, with advantage, be taken by the Hon. East India Company; and a reply has been received, to the effect that a copy of the document had been forwarded to the local government."

Mr. Malcolm Ross, the Vice-president of the Association, in addressing the meeting, said, " With respect to the cultivation of cotton in India, he observed at a meeting held in this town last week, great complaints were made that the East India Company had not done their duty in this respect. He was not going to excuse that Company, or to echo the grounds of complaint which might or might not exist against them ; but it did strike him, in looking over the proceedings, as a singular fact, that some of the gentlemen who took part in them had been invited to Liverpool, to inspect the experiment made with the saw gins, and to receive the planters from America, who were to be sent out to India, to carry them into effect there. And yet during the many years that elapsed from that day to the formation of that Association, no trouble was taken by those gentlemen, who were so kindly received and so hospitably entertained by the directors of the East India Company, and who expected such great results to arise from that reception, to ascertain what the results of those experiments were; and it was a singular fact that cotton, the produce of these experiments, had lain for many months—he had almost said years*—in Liverpool, without any of those gentlemen going to inquire whether such cotton had been sent to this country or not. He thought it was a reflection upon them (and many members of that Association were of the number) not to have given to that cotton the importance which it deserved, and he could not help saying that it must have been exceedingly discouraging to the East India Company and their servants, and the planters, when they saw that, notwithstanding the great attention they had paid to the subject, those at home in England were positively indifferent about the matter."

Mr. James Lees said "He wished to be allowed to make a few remarks on the subject of cotton culture in India, and in other tropical countries, which was at the present time a subject of peculiar interest, and which still continued to hold a prominent place in the annual report of the directors. The efforts of the East India Company to introduce into India the American cotton plant, and the American cleaning machine, ought not on any account to be disparaged; for although they had not yet been attended with any great result, they had not been fruitless. Every successive failure had led to renewed exertions, and to an increased acquaintance with the subject (hear, hear); and it was a subject, though so vitally important to us, with which we had far too little acquaintance."

The Chairman (Mr. Aspinall Turner, who is also President of the Association) said "There was one subject to which he had intended to omit any reference, but as Mr. Ross had alluded to some information which he (the chairman) had before him, he would venture shortly to allude to it. He referred to a meeting which was held in that neighbourhood on one day during last week, for the purpose of taking important matters into consideration, those matters chiefly relating to the cultivation of cotton in India. It was not their business to pass an opinion, either of praise or censure, upon what took place within the walls of a body like themselves. But the proceedings of this body being reported in the public papers, they were of course within the range of their observations; and if they affected themselves, either as a body or as individuals, it might be expected, and it was even proper, that they should notice those parts of their proceedings.—He thought that by another speaker on the occasion to which he had referred,

* See note on the next page.

scarcely justice had been done to that Association, with regard to the efforts they had for some years made to lay information before the public, and to obtain accurate information for that purpose from India. He alluded to the speech made by Mr. Henry Ashworth. He had the speech reported before him; and, with great deference to Mr. Ashworth, and without wishing to express the slightest censure upon him, he (the chairman) would suggest that Mr. Ashworth had scarcely done that Association justice, when he said that nothing was done until the year 1847, 'when the Company themselves, or the people here,'—meaning, he (the chairman) presumed, the Commercial Association,—' set something in motion which had the effect of raking together a few garden plots, which raised a little better cotton.' He would just explain this point. In 1845 they had an interview with the East India Company on this important subject, and they found, to their surprise, that comparatively large quantities* of cotton had been from time to time sent to this country, the produce partly of the farms of the East India Company, and partly the produce of the field-culture of the ryots—cleaned in the government machines, and consigned to this country for sale. Who was to blame he knew not, and he had no wish to inquire: but certain it was that large quantities of such cotton were warehoused in Liverpool, and sold, like any other cotton in the place, without any particular remark or comment upon them. Some entered into consumption; but people only knew that they were using good India cotton; other portions were sold for export; but little notice was taken of the circumstance. They might flatter themselves unduly, but he hoped that since the formation of that Association they had paid more

* The shipments of experimental cotton were no less than thirty-five in number, previous to 1847. The quantities varied from a few to upwards of 300 bales, as will be noticed under the heads of the several experimental farms. Information respecting the consignments from the year 1841 to the year 1846, with the opinions of Liverpool brokers, may be seen in the "Return relative to Measures taken since 1836, for promoting the Cultivation of Cotton in India," at pp. 341, 345, 347, 349, 370, 377, 398, 448, 456, 462, 471, 499, 505, 512, and 528. It is to be regretted that the sales of Indian experimental cotton at Liverpool did not attract any notice at Manchester; especially as Messrs. Holinshead of Liverpool say: "19 Sept. 1845; The cotton we consider was worth more than it was sold for, if a spinner could have been found to test its merits."—"They are least inclined to try experiments in prosperous times." American cotton was cheap from 1841 to 1846.

minute attention to this matter; and on ascertaining this fact at the India House, they suggested to the Company that it would be much better if this cotton were sent direct to Manchester, in order that the observations and opinions of the trade might be expressed upon it, and distinctly known, and that these reports and opinions might be sent to India, in order that the growers of the cotton and the agents of the Company might know where they had succeeded and where failed. The first result of that conversation was the consignment of the produce, not of 'a few garden plots,' but of the produce of the field culture of a large number of ryots, purchased by the agents of the East India Company from the ryots, and cleaned in the government machine; and the 'scraping together' was a thousand bales of cotton. (Hear, hear.) It was sent direct to Manchester, and very properly the name of the agent to whom it was consigned (Mr. Hugh Fleming) was announced; very properly also—for he did not know any more important subject that could go into the Manchester Exchange—the committee were asked if the Association might place those samples upon one of the tables in the Exchange, in order that country and town spinners, and the trade generally, might have an opportunity, in the most easy way, of knowing the fact that a thousand bales of cotton grown by the East Indian ryots, from American seed, was then in the market. That was the simple fact. If the Association had done wrong to the public, or to the Committee of the Manchester Exchange, they were prepared to ask their pardon; but they were not aware that they had done so. Mr. Ashworth went on to say, 'and what a fuss was made of its arrival:' certainly they did wish to make the fact known. 'The name of the ship by which it arrived was announced.' It was so: the cotton arrived by the 'Quentin Leitch.' 'Nothing less would do, crowded though the Exchange was at that time, but that they must make way for stalls for these samples of cotton to be shown in the Exchange.' 'We had heard no more about it;' that was, he supposed, no more cotton came after that was received. But the Company followed up the system and they had since had nine other arrivals. The 'Olinda' (from Cochin) brought 45 bales;* the 'Pemberton' (from Bombay),

* 60 other bales sold in London.

616; the 'Argyra,' 483; the 'Gulterus' (from Bombay), 623; the 'Ganges,' 871; the 'Aurora,' 60;* the 'Brahmin,' 630; the 'George Buckham,' 644; and the 'Anne Cropper,' 53: making a total of 5025 bales. All this quantity of cotton, of improved quality, had been grown, not on the Company's model farms so much—not in 'garden plots' at all—but it was the produce of the field culture of the poor Indians, cleaned by the government machines. It was brought and exhibited in Manchester, and he did think that some credit was due even for that small amount of success which the East India Company had attained; and he did not think that any blame was due to the committee for the 'fuss' they made about it. These 5,025 bales of improved cotton had been brought into the town through the instrumentality of the East India Company, but they had told the Association that they did not wish to be merchants, but merely to increase the import of this kind of cotton, and they had suggested over and over again, that the merchants and spinners of Manchester should do what they could to assist in this object. He could speak for himself, for Mr. Peel, and for three or four other firms, whom he did not wish to drag before the public, who had acted upon that suggestion. He knew that he should be speaking very much within compass if he said that another 5,000 bales—[Mr. Peel: Much more;]—or a very much larger quantity of this improved cotton had been brought into Manchester, not only by the merchants, but by many spinners who had given orders; and he believed that if Mr. Ashworth had consulted them, he would have found that a great number of the members of the Chamber of Commerce had imported it for their own use. Besides this, it had been extensively bought up by the native manufacturers themselves in India, because they had found it to be so superior to the indigenous cotton of the country. They had been eager competitors for it, and therefore we in Manchester had not derived all the supply of this cotton which had been grown. But never mind who got it if it was grown, for if the growth of it went on increasing, we should in time get it. Mr. Ashworth (continued the chairman,) is an old friend of mine, and I was exceedingly sorry to observe the way in which he spoke of us. I would just suggest to him, that the friendly

* 170 other bales sold in London.

garb, and the principles of peace, are as much belied by sneering and contemptuous language, as when they are manifested by a more manly and open mode of warfare."—(Applause.) (*Manchester Guardian*, 23d Jan., 1850.)

The foregoing facts, respecting quality and price, afford sufficient proofs that India is capable, in many parts, of producing good and serviceable cotton, and at a rate sufficiently cheap to contend even against the large returns of American farming. But, to judge more accurately of the bearings of the whole question, it is necessary to consider the cotton from India not only as it is, but what it may become, not only in small but in largely increasing quantities, and of improved quality. This will lead us to principles of culture, and to details as connected with soil and climate, and these as suitable to different species of cotton plant. We must inquire, also, whether the principles of culture, as applicable to cotton, have been judiciously applied to practice in India, what are the results which have been obtained, and what others may be hoped for without adding greatly to the expense of cultivation. Also, whether by adopting a higher style of farming, or by having recourse to draining in some situations and irrigation in others, we may not succeed in producing a very superior article, or obtain a much larger quantity of cotton from the same breadth of land, and thus be able to repay the outlay, either by high prices or by increased quantities. Such questions will naturally occupy us in the Second Part of our Essay, where details respecting the different cotton districts, as well as the several experiments, will be treated of, and show us that the difficulties which have been experienced have been more frequently of a physical than of a fiscal nature.

CULTIVATION OF COTTON.

§ 1. Early History of Cotton.

Before proceeding to consider the principles which should guide us in the Culture of Cotton, or determine the practical rules most worthy of observance in different situations, it is necessary to fix with precision on the species or variety of plant which we intend to cultivate, and understand exactly the nature of the part of the plant which we wish to obtain, whether in a natural or improved state. In determining the identity or difference of species of cultivated plants, some assistance may be derived from their history. With respect to the cotton plant, we have satisfactory proof, that one kind at least was known in India, and that another existed in America when first discovered by Columbus. The probability therefore is, that these two at least are distinct species, as is the case with the majority of plants found in the old and new world.

India being one of the earliest civilized countries, and having an ancient literature still in existence, it is interesting to discover the period when cotton is first mentioned, either as a natural product, or as used in the art of weaving. The earliest notice which we know of this substance is in that most ancient digest of law, the Institutes of Manu, written 800 years before the Christian æra. There cotton is mentioned so often, and in such a way, as to indicate that it must have been long in familiar use by the natives of the country. Professor Wilson has been good enough to inform the author, that cotton and cotton-cloth are mentioned by the Sanscrit names *kurpasa* and *kurpasum*, and cotton seeds as *kurpas-asthi*. The common name *kupas*, indicating cotton with the seed, is no doubt derived from the Sanscrit name, and is in common use all over India, and may even be heard occasionally in Manchester. In Book ii, p. 44, of Manu, cotton is mentioned in a manner to indicate the esteem in which it was held, for it is said, that " the sacrificial thread of a Brahmin must be made of cotton, so as to be put on over his head, in three strings ;

that of a Cshatriya, of *sana** thread only; that of a Vaisya, of woollen thread. In Book viii, p. 397, we have evidence of the minute attention paid by the Hindoos to the mechanical arts, and of the antiquity of the process of starching, for it is directed, " Let a weaver who has received ten palas of cotton-thread, give them back increased of eleven by the rice-water, and the like used in weaving: he who does otherwise shall pay a fine of twelve panas." Fines are directed to be levied for stealing cotton in other passages, as viii, p. 326, and xi, p. 169.

In addition to the above, Professor Wilson has referred me to a still earlier notice of the process of starching, which he says " boasts of a still higher antiquity, for, in the first book of the 'Rig Veda,' Hymn 105, v. 8, occurs the following expression, 'cares consume me Satakratu, although thy worshipper, as a rat gnaws a weaver's threads;'—and the Scholiast explains the rat's temptation to be the starch in which the threads had been steeped to improve their tenacity. This passage dates in all probability at least fifteen centuries before the Christian era." Cotton was most likely the material starched.

The next earliest notice which we have is in the Bible, though cotton, it is sometimes stated, is not mentioned in the sacred volume. But in the Book of Esther the word *karpas* occurs in chap. i, v. 6, in the account of the hangings in the court of the Persian palace at Shushan, on the occasion of the great feast given by Ahasuerus, where " were white, *green*, and blue hangings, fastened with cords of fine linen and purple to silver rings and pillars of marble." The word corresponding to *green* is in the Hebrew *karpas*, and is rendered in the Septuagint and Vulgate by the word *carbasinus*. It seems to mean cotton-cloth, or calico, formed into curtains, which were white and blue. Such may be seen throughout India in the present day, but padded with cotton, and used as a substitute for doors and window-shutters, and known by the name of purdahs. The colours are usually either blue and white or red and white. They may be seen in the Hall of Audience of the Emperor of Delhi, which is described by Bishop Heber as " a beautiful open pavilion of white marble, richly carved, flanked by rose bushes and fountains, and some tapestry and

* Sun or sunnee, the fibre of *Crotalaria juncea*, or of *Hibiscus cannabinus*

striped curtains hanging in festoons about it."* These accounts may be compared with that of the feast given by Alexander to celebrate his nuptials, as recommended by Mr. Yates, in his learned work entitled 'Textrinum Antiquorum.'

We have seen that Herodotus was acquainted with the wool from trees, and mentions that the cuirass sent by Amasis, King of Egypt, to Sparta, was "adorned with gold and with fleeces from trees." This was probably a highly ornamented vest, padded with cotton, and such as is worn even in the present day. Both the cotton and the gold work were probably imported from India, as indigo was from Barbarike on the Indus, into Egypt. Ctesias, the contemporary of Herodotus, was acquainted with cloth made with tree-wool. Subsequent to the expedition of Alexander into India, information is more precise, for Theophrastus describes the trees, from which the Indians make cloths, as "having a leaf like that of the black mulberry, the whole plant resembling the dog-rose. They set them in the plains arranged in rows, so as to look like vines at a distance." Nearchus described the natives as having garments made with this tree-wool, "which reached to the middle of the leg, a sheet folded about the shoulders, and a turban rolled round the head:" a description which would apply to many of them in the present day.

Arrian, the author of the 'Periplus of the Erythræan Sea,' himself a merchant, and who probably lived in the first or second century of the Christian æra, is the first who mentions cotton goods as articles of commerce. He describes Arab traders as bringing such to Aduli, a port of the Red Sea, and that a trade was established with Patiala, Ariake, and Barygaza, which is the modern Broach. This continues now as then to be a mart for cotton, as it is expressly stated to have exported "*carpasus*, and the fine Indian cloths made with

* The author described the same Hall of Audience thus—"in the court of the king of Delhi's palace, where, on a paved mosaic terrace, rows of slender pillars support a light roof, from which hang by rings immense padded and striped curtains, rolled up, or removable at pleasure." This appeared to the author to explain the use to which were applied the rows of pillars in front of the palace in the ruins of Persepolis. (*Antiquity of Hindoo Medicine*, p. 145.) The first notice which we have of the cotton plant out of India, is in the island of Tylos, identified with Bahrein, in the Persian Gulf. It would be curious if the curtains which lately fell to pieces when discovered by Layard should prove to have been made of cotton.

it." Goods were brought there from Tagora, across high grounds, no doubt the Ghauts, which are still the great impediments to the transit of cotton. Masalia, on the east coast, is identified with modern Masulipatam, which was then, as it has continued until of late to be, famous for the manufacture and export of cotton-piece goods. The muslins of Dacca seem also to have been well known, as they are described as being superior to all others, and were called Gangitiki by the Greeks, from being produced on the banks of the Ganges.

Cotton goods, obtained by the Red Sea, were no doubt imported into Egypt, and Antony's army is described as "vix leve *carbasum* vitando sole tolerantes." From Egypt and Arabia some of these cotton goods could hardly fail to be taken into Greece and Rome. That the word *carbasus* or *carbasum,* the Greek *karpason,* signifies cotton, is evident, from its being used, by different authors, in describing the dress of the Indians: as Q. Curtius, "Corpora usque pedes *carbaso* velant;" and Lucan, in describing the Indian nations as drinking, "dulces ab arundine succos;" and staining their hair of a saffron hue, as they still do with henna or *mhendee* (Lawsonia inermis), adds, "Fluxa coloratis adstringunt *carbasa* gemmis." The earliest notice which Mr. Yates has found of the word *carbasina* is in Statius, and he infers that cotton cloths of some kind were known to the Greeks as early as 200 years before Christ. Perhaps cotton is meant, when long before Schönbein's discovery, "Exhibuit vivos *carbasus* alba focos," when the vestal virgin, upon the extinction of the flames on the altar committed to her care, threw upon the ashes a fillet of muslin from her head and saved her life by its ignition. (*Yates,* l. c., p. 343.)

But the term *linum,* or flax, was sometimes used to designate cotton, as in "capita linteis vinciunt," and *carbasus* was in later times often employed, when probably linen only was meant: we find even an historian of India (Orme) applying an incorrect term, when referring to a cotton fabric: "The rigid, clumsy fingers of an European would scarcely be able to make a piece of canvass with the instruments, which are all that an Indian employs in making a piece of *cambric,*" that is, muslin.

Carbasus is in later times frequently mentioned; sometimes as being employed for tents and for the sails of ships, though we have no proof that cotton was actually employed. Mr. Yates says, that authors may employ it as a poetical term, even when they mean to speak of linen. But as Dr. Robertson has observed, "If the use of the cotton manufactures of India had been common among the Romans, the various kinds of them would have been enumerated in the 'Law de Publicanis et Vectigalibus,' in the same manner as the different kinds of spices and precious stones. Mr. Yates, in his learned work, 'Textrinum Antiquorum,' (to which we are indebted for many of the above references,) says, that after the fourth century cotton was known by various names, which had not before been in use. Probably *Gossypium* was one of them." (Gossympinus is mentioned even by Pliny, as the name of cotton in the island of Tylos.) "Another set of names probably arose from a misapplication of the name of the silk-worm—whence comes Bambacinus, *made of cotton; Bambacinum, cotton cloth;* Bambacarius, a dealer in cotton cloth; and in Italian bambagio, bambagino, and bambasino." (*Yates*, l. c., p. 354.)

From India cotton appears to have spread into China, for it does not seem to have been used in the ninth century, as the two Arabian travellers who then visited China observe, that "the Chinese dressed not in cotton, as the Arabians did, but in silk;" and it is supposed that the cotton manufacture was not established there until the 13th century. The Chinese now possess cotton plants of their own, but we have no means of determining whether these are indigenous or introduced from India. The colour of Nankin cotton will not determine the question, as we shall afterwards see. From India, there is no doubt, the culture spread into Persia, and a little into Arabia and into Egypt, and from thence, probably, into central and western Africa. From Persia the culture extended into Syria and Asia Minor, also into Turkey in Europe, and from these into other parts of the south of Europe: so that we may find varieties of the Indian plant in all these localities.

As already mentioned, there is equally satisfactory evidence respecting the existence and employment of cotton in America at its first discovery. Columbus found it in the West India Islands. Cortes, in his conquest of Mexico, is described as receiving garments of cotton among the first presents from the natives of Yucatan, also cotton cloths to cover his huts; and from Montezuma, cotton fabrics of fine and silk-like delicacy of texture. Among the presents he sent to Charles V were garments of cotton cloth of different kinds, both white and variously coloured. Cotton was afterwards found to constitute the principal material of the clothing of the Mexicans. When Magelhaens touched at Brazil, he found the natives there acquainted with cotton, and in the habit of using it for making their beds. In the ancient Peruvian tombs, raw cotton and cotton fabrics have been discovered, of which specimens have been brought to Europe and deposited in museums. Humboldt describes cotton as being produced in the hot regions of Vera Cruz, as well as in the neighbourhood of Valladolid, in Yucatan. Martius and others have noticed cotton plants in the interior of Brazil. All these may belong to one or more species.

Besides the continents of the old and new world, we have cotton plants noticed as existing in far distant islands, as in the Galapagos, in the Sandwich Islands, in the Seychelles, in Java, Borneo, and other islands of the Indian ocean; also in the islands of the Chinese coast, extending up to Japan. It will be a question for examination, as far as materials exist, whether different species of cotton are found in these different and distant islands, or whether they have received seeds from the nearest continents. In the latter case, the plants will be identical with those found there, or differing from them only as varieties of the same species.

§ 2. Structure of the Fibre of Cotton.

In submitting to examination the filamentous substance which constitutes cotton, we find, in point of structure, that it corresponds entirely with hairs found on other parts of plants, and that it is in fact a mass of vegetable hairs, of considerable though of varying lengths, rising from the surface of the seeds, enveloping them, and assisting to fill up the cavity of the seed-vessel. It would be interesting to ascertain the functions which they perform with respect to the seed, as we might thence be led to draw some deductions as to the mode in which they might be increased in quantity or in length. But in the present state of information, the only inferences which we can draw are such as are applicable to hairs in general, or to their position on the parts of fructification, instead of on those of vegetation. Hairs are formed of cellular tissue, usually of one or more filiform elongated cells, joined end to end, formed of extremely thin and transparent membrane. When composed of only a single cell, the structure will necessarily appear continuous; but if of several cells, then a number of transverse partitions will be observed along its length. As usually examined hairs appear to consist of only a simple delicate membrane, within which may, in many cases, especially when in a young state, be seen a regular circulation of fluid, in which are suspended a number of fine granules, which proceed from and return to a particular point in the cell. Some of these cells, when examined with a higher magnifying power, are seen to be composed of two membranes, one within the other, between which fluid appears to circulate. Such hairs, when allowed to dry up, display the two sacs more distinctly, as the inner collapses more than the outer one. Such delicate organs, it is evident, must be readily influenced by the varying state either of the soil or of the atmosphere, whether with regard to heat or cold, dryness or moisture. Hairs are found on all parts of plants exposed to the air, and are absent from, or are but sparingly seen, on those growing in water. They are abundant on plants growing in dry situations, but disappear from the same species when growing in moist places, and would therefore appear to be useful in absorbing nutriment.

The filaments of cotton have been subjected to repeated examination, in consequence of the interest attached to the mummy cloth of Egypt, and of the desire to ascertain whether it was composed of cotton or of linen. Larcher, in his Notes to the Translation of Herodotus, and Forster, in his Tract 'De Bysso Antiquorum,' had asserted, "from their own examination, that the mummy cloth of Egypt was cotton," as Rouelle had done before them, and as Rosselini has done since, even after most satisfactory evidence had been adduced to prove that it was linen. Mr. Thomson, of Clitheroe, was the first to have recourse to the only satisfactory method by which the fact can be determined, that is, by the use of the microscope. He had first ascertained that other methods of judging were unworthy of confidence, as several intelligent manufacturers, on examining a collection of pieces of mummy cloth, "were of opinion, that the cloth was cotton, others that it was linen; and some, again, that there were in the collection specimens of both."

Mr. Thomson justly observes, that "the great difference in the specific gravities, as well as in the conducting power of linen and cotton, is sufficient to enable us, by careful experiments, to discriminate accurately between them. There are few individuals who have been accustomed to the use both of cotton and linen, who cannot readily distinguish, by that delicate sense of touch diffused over the white body, between the two fabrics." But this, of course, requires larger pieces than Mr. Thomson had of the several mummy cloths. The author has already observed, that cotton, from the irritation which is produced, "is not so well fitted for surgical dressings. But being a worse conductor of heat than linen, it is well suited for inner clothing, where the object is to preserve uniformity of temperature, as it will retain heat, and prevent the body being so readily affected by external heat or cold, at the same time that it condenses less freely than linen the vapour of perspiration, but absorbs it readily when it has been condensed into the form of sweat. For these reasons, probably, thick calico shirts, &c., have been introduced into the army for the use of soldiers." (Manual of Mat. Med., p. 289.) It may, in short, be considered the flannel of tropical countries, as, from its inferior conducting power, it renders the body less liable to be chilled when in a state of perspiration.

As the differences in the conducting power of small fragments of mummy cloth are not sufficient to determine whether it is linen or cotton, it occurred to Mr. Thomson to subject the filaments to microscopic examination, and he was fortunate in obtaining the assistance of the late Mr. Bauer. Mr. Thomson having transmitted to him various fibres of cotton and linen, both manufactured and in their raw state, as well as fibres of unravelled mummy cloth, in a few days received from him a letter, in which he pronounced "every specimen of mummy cloth subjected to his examination to be linen." A drawing which accompanied the letter exhibited "the fibres of both raw and unravelled cotton as flattened cylinders, twisted like a corkscrew, whilst the fibres of linen and various mummy cloths were straight and cylindrical." In a more detailed description Mr. Thomson observes, that "the filaments of cotton, when viewed through a powerful instrument, appear to be transparent glassy tubes, flattened, and twisted round their own axes. A section of the filament resembles in some degree a figure of 8, the tube, originally cylindrical, having collapsed most in the middle, forming semi-tubes on each side, which give to the fibre, when viewed in certain lights, the appearance of a flat ribbon, with a hem or border at each edge. The uniform transparency of the filament is impaired by small irregular figures, in all probability wrinkles or creases arising from the desiccation of the tube. The twisted and corkscrew form of the filament of cotton distinguishes it from all other vegetable fibres, and is characteristic of the fully ripe and mature pod, Mr. Bauer having ascertained that the fibres of the unripe seed are simple, untwisted cylindrical tubes, which never twist afterwards if separated from the plant; but when the seeds ripen, even before the capsule bursts, the cylindrical tubes collapse in the middle, and assume the form already described. This form and character the fibres retain ever after, and in that respect undergo no change through the operation of spinning, weaving, bleaching, printing, and dyeing, nor in the subsequent domestic operations of washing, &c., till the stuff is worn to rags; and then even the violent process of reducing these rags to pulp, for the purpose of making paper, effects no change in the structure of these fibres."

Cotton was next examined by Messrs. Bowerbank and Williams, and even before the publication of Mr. Thomson's paper, though his results had been obtained many years previously, and communicated to many both in this country and on the continent. Messrs. Bowerbank and Williams describe cotton-wool as consisting of a multitude of fibres, each having the appearance of a flat ribbon or tape, about the $\frac{1}{1000}$th part of an inch in width. A piece of ancient Peruvian gauze, which formed the envelope of a dried body found in a sepulchre at Guacho, in Peru, when examined, likewise exhibited the flat fibres of cotton. (Egypt. Antiq., p. 192.) Dr. Ure observed them to be substantially the same; but being tortuous, when viewed in one part they look like a ribbon, and in another like a narrow line. Dr. Lindley describes them, when immersed in water, as long weak tubes, looking like flat, narrow, transparent ribbons, with a perfectly even surface and uniform breadth. It is only occasionally that any appearance of joints is observable in these tracings, perpendicular, or nearly so, to the side of the tube. Sometimes a slight trace of fine grains is discernible in the interior, but more frequently the hairs seem empty.

Mr. E. Wilson says, "I found the fibre of cotton opaque along each border, and translucent in the centre." When immersed for some time in water, the fibre assumed a cylindrical form, which Mr. Wilson apprehends is its appearance in a fresh state. It is, then, obviously composed of tubular parenchyma, enclosed in a thin transparent cylinder. The author has been favoured with a view of Mr. Wilson's original drawings, displaying in the interior the appearance of granules. A figure is given of a fibre of cotton in his work on 'Healthy Skin.' The nature of the fibre of cotton, and its distinctness from that of flax, having been so well established by the preceding observations, as well as by others in this country, it seems hardly possible to doubt that mummy cloth is composed of flax and not of cotton. But Mr. Thomson, having found that some (as Rosselini) still doubted the correctness of his deduction, has been induced to go over the whole subject again, with the assistance of Mr. Warrington and of Mr. Cornelius Varley. The author has been favoured by Mr. Thomson with a beautiful series of engravings of the fibres of flax, of cotton, and of mummy cloth; from one of these the artist has copied the figures *a* and *c*, in Pl. 1. He has himself submitted both American and Indian cottons to examination, and found the fibre of the Sea Island cotton exactly like the beautiful drawing of Mr. Varley, Pl. 1, fig. *a*, while the Indian cottons he found more like Mr. Bauer's drawings, in Mr. Thomson's original paper,* in the series marked B. The fig. *b* is copied from the series C, which represents the fibres of some unravelled threads of manufactured cotton. Mr. Thomson, to whom the author sent genuine specimens of the Indian and American cottons out of the pods, observes, that the fibre of cotton, whether of the east or west, is essentially and characteristically the same.

* On the Mummy Cloth of Egypt, &c., from the 'Annals of Philosophy,' June, 1834, by James Thomson, F.R.S.

§ 3. Commercial Varieties of Cotton.

The different kinds of cotton which are imported and used in this country have been examined under the microscope by Dr. Ure and by Mr. E. Wilson. To their observations we are indebted for the following measurements. In examining a sample of cotton, it is usual to take a portion of it between the forefingers and thumbs, and laying the portions as they are successively drawn out back again on and parallel to the filaments from which they have been drawn out; and repeating this process several times, small tufts are formed, in which the respective lengths of staple may be observed, as represented in Plate 1. fig. *d* to *o*. For the card containing the different cottons, the author is indebted to the kindness of Mr. Fleming, Secretary of the Commercial Association of Manchester, and for the drawings on stone to Mr. Ford, the talented artist, distinguished by his labours in 'Falconer and Cautley's Fauna Sivalensis,' and in Dr. Smith's 'Zoology of Southern Africa.'

The fibres of cotton, when drawn out from the mass in which they appear entangled, display so many irregular twists as to give them a jointed appearance, and, as Mr. E. Wilson observes, "in this state they resemble a string of oval beads, pointed at each extremity, and connected by their points." The entire fibre appears to taper finely to both ends, that which is adherent to the seed being somewhat the thickest. Under the microscope the fibre is observed to be continuous, moderately twisted, flat, ribbon-like, clear, and transparent in the middle, and opaque towards each margin. The finer and more uniform the fibre, and more inclined to twist, the better is it suited for spinning into fine yarn. But if the fibres are short, broad, and formed of flimsy ribbons, they are less suited for machine spinning, though they may yet, as before mentioned, be twisted into thread by the delicate fingers of the Hindoo.

The value of cotton depends on the length, strength, and fineness, as well as on the softness and equality of the fibre. But these essential qualities are modified by colour and cleanliness, that is, freedom from knots and impurities, so that there may be less waste in spinning. Formerly colour had great influence, but now the great distinction is into long-stapled and short-stapled. The different kinds of cotton differ from each other not only in the above properties, but also in considerable differences in quality between different samples of the same kind of cotton. "The finest quality of Sea Island is sometimes worth three times as much as the common quality of the same class. The variation of quality in most of the other denominations, is from 20 to 25 per cent., and in none of them is more than 50 per cent." (*Baynes.*) These are sometimes divided into three or four qualities, as ordinary, middling, fair, and fine. At other times these are still further subdivided, as into inferior, ordinary, middling, good-middling, middling-fair, fair, good-fair, fine, or good and fine. "Except the better qualities of Sea Islands there is no sort of cotton which is now confined in its use to any peculiar or exclusive purpose. By mixing different sorts together, and by careful management in preparing the mixture for spinning, the manufacturers can now make a substitute for almost any particular kind of cotton, except the very best. It is only requisite to add, that the long-stapled cottons are generally used for the twist or warp, and the short-stapled for the weft." (*Baynes*, l. c., p. 311.)

Sea Island, or long-staple cotton, the most highly esteemed of the cottons, is remarkable for the length and fineness of its fibre as for its silky softness. Among white cottons it is distinguished by a slight yellowish tinge of colour. This kind sells from eighteen-pence to two shillings, and has sold as high as five and seven shillings a pound. The quantity is limited, from the peculiarity of physical circumstances required for its production. The fibres are equable, about $1\frac{1}{2}$ inches in length, and examined under the microscope, about $\frac{1}{2000}$th of an inch in diameter, formed of flattened cylinders transparent in the middle, opaque towards the margin, and more or less twisted, as represented in Pl. 1, fig. *a* and *d*. Dr. Ure has observed some kinds crimped transversely with irregular bandages, and some with flimsy ribbons and warts which adhere to the sides of the filaments, called neps by spinners. Mr. Wilson describes the Sea Island as thick and narrow, but looking the finest of all as seen with the naked eye. This kind is employed for spinning the finest yarns.

Uplands, or short-staple cotton, under which names are

now usually included the produce of the interior of Georgia and Carolina, as well as of Alabama, Mississipi, Louisiana, and Tennessee. It used to be, and is sometimes still called *Bowed*, from the cotton of Georgia having formerly been cleaned with the Indian cotton-bow. Though shorter in the staple and unequal, this is white in colour, much esteemed, and forms the bulk of the cotton of commerce. The staple is 1 inch to $1\frac{1}{4}$ inches in length. The best kinds are fit for spinning as high as No. 50, some higher; the shorter kinds are worked up into No. 30 and other coarser yarns; but mixed with good Egyptian or with Pernambuco cotton, even these can be spun into higher numbers. Under the microscope, the fibres appear less twisted than others, some as cylindric fibres with many twists, of the width of about $\frac{1}{1400}$th of an inch; thin and broad, Pl. 1, fig. *i*, New Orleans; fig. *j*, Mobile; fig. *k*, Uplands.

EGYPTIAN.—The best Egyptian cotton ranks next to Sea Island in quality and length of staple, though it is not usually so well cleaned. It was only about the year 1821 that the Pasha began the cultivation, by importing seed from America and the Mediterranean and from Brazil. These different kinds may, therefore, be met with in cultivation there, though the Sea Island yields the best kind of cotton called *Maho*, which is used here like that kind for the finest yarns. It has a staple of $1\frac{1}{4}$ to $1\frac{2}{3}$ inches in length, from $\frac{1}{1500}$th to $\frac{1}{2000}$th of an inch in breadth, uniform, spiro-cylindrical, thin and broad Pl. 1, fig. *e*. Some excellent cotton has been sent from Port Natal; that from the Island of Bourbon used formerly to be much esteemed. Some has also come from the west coast of Africa.

WEST INDIAN.—The West Indies supplied England with the largest quantity of cotton in the 18th century; but the cultivation was neglected when sugar became more profitable, and the imports have greatly fallen off, (v. p. 10.) But the cotton is long-stapled, silky, and might be produced of a quality equal to Sea Island. Bourbon cotton is the same species that is cultivated in the West Indies. The cotton of Porto Rico was at one time considered to be the best; that of St. Domingo has been spun into No. 100 yarn; and some of the finest cotton ever grown was in Tobago by Mr. Robly, between 1789 and 1792. The cottons of Barbadoes, Guadaloupe, and Jamaica were also highly esteemed. Bryan

Edwards ('Hist. of the West Indies,' 1793) mentions a green-seeded cotton, from which the cotton can only be separated by hand. Inferior kinds, or shorter-stapled cottons, may, therefore, be imported from these islands. Dr. Ure describes the St. Domingo cotton as composed of narrow twisted ribbons, from $\frac{1}{1000}$th to $\frac{1}{1200}$th of an inch, with a few flattened cylinders and some spiry fibres.

South American Cottons.—In the year 1780 Mr. Bryan Edwards states, that "the finest grained and most perfectly cleaned cotton which was brought to the English market was, he believed, that of the Dutch plantations of Berbice, Demerara, and Surinam, and of the Island of Cayenne;" and that these cottons sold at that time for 2*s*. a pound. The first importations of cotton are stated to have first taken place from Maranham in the year 1781. The Pernambuco was soon afterwards sent, of so fine and superior a quality as to be highly esteemed, and its price ranked next to the Sea Island. The staple is long and fine, generally well cleaned, glossy, some with a yellowish tinge; spins into a stout yarn, and is esteemed by hosiers. It continues to be imported from all these places, as well as from Bahia, Maceio, Para, and Ceara, also from Peru; inferior qualities from Carthagena. The fibre is in length about $1\frac{6}{10}$ to $1\frac{1}{5}$ of an inch; is cylindrico-spiral, about $\frac{1}{1500}$th to $\frac{1}{2000}$th of an inch in diameter; some with a few twisted ribbons and warty excrescences on the sides of the filaments, Pl. 1, fig. *f*, Tufts of Pernambuco; *g*, of Maranham; *h*, of Bahia cotton.

East Indian Cotton.—Considerable though varying quantities of cotton, we have seen are imported from India. It varies a great deal as obtained from different districts; is esteemed for its colour, though all is short-stapled, and generally sent in a dirty state to market. In those of this country it is known by the name of Surats, Madras, and Bengal, while the name *Surats* is often used as a general term for Indian cottons. We have seen that some of this cotton is of good quality and fit for general purposes (v. p. 96); while the great mass is only bought when American cotton is dear. The cottons of Surat, of Broach, and of Berar are all included under the name of *Surats*, forming the kinds which are most esteemed here. The cottons of Cutch, of Candeish, &c., are likewise exported from

Bombay, whence also we obtain the cotton of Coompta, which is produced in the Southern Mahrattaern country and in the most southern part of Berar. These are also cottons naturally of good quality. Under the head of Madras, the cottons of Salem, Coimbatore, and Tinnivelly are included, which rank higher than the cottons of Bellary, Guntoor, and the Ceded districts. Bengal cottons include those from the North-West provinces, from Bundlecund, as well as what is imported from Nagpore and Berar. The latter kinds are of the same quality as are exported from Bombay; but they are generally used up by the weavers of the upper parts of the Bengal Presidency. Some Bourbon cotton is also exported from Madras, the produce chiefly of the southern provinces of the Peninsula; though esteemed, it is inferior to the original Bourbon. The Indian cottons, under the microscope, appear less spiry; a few flattened cylinders, with many flimsy ribbons, and warty excrescences varying in diameter from $\frac{1}{600}$th to $\frac{1}{1000}$th of an inch; some are $\frac{1}{1500}$th to $\frac{1}{2000}$th of an inch. In length differing from $\frac{17}{20}$ths to $1\frac{1}{10}$th of an inch.

Mediterranean Cottons.—Much cotton is cultivated in the countries surrounding the Mediterranean sea. It is generally the produce of the Indian species of plant, though American seeds have been introduced into some other places as well as into Egypt. These are cultivated in Asia Minor, in parts of Greece and the Islands; generally known as Levant, some as Smyrna cottons. The Italian cottons are produced in Sicily, in Calabria, near Naples, and in Malta. The cottons of Sicily, of Calabria, and of Castellamare are the best, and are probably the produce of an American species. A Nankin cotton is cultivated in Malta, and used there. Most of these cottons are employed for native manufactures in the countries where they are grown, or are exported for the use of the manufacturers of the Continent. They are seldom brought to this country except when the price of cotton is very high.

Though we have noticed the appearance of the filament of cotton under the microscope, it is to be observed that the fingers of practised brokers have a delicacy of touch that enables them to judge most correctly of the fineness and length of staple, and some will pronounce, even in the dark, on the value of cotton. But the different varieties might yet be subjected with benefit to further microscopical examination to ascertain the effects of the different processes of culture, in the several soils and climates of different countries, on the length, breadth, and smoothness of the fibre. The author hopes to be able to observe some of these when he can command sufficient leisure.

The foregoing account of the several varieties of cotton may most appropriately be concluded with the following Table, of the kinds of cotton as named in commerce from the places of export, with the species of plant which probably yield them, and their prices in a cheap year 1845, and in what is now considered a dear year 1849. To these are added references to Pl. 1, where the staples are figured from *d* to *o*.

Pl. 1.	Kind of Cotton.	Sp. of Gossypium.	Prices in 1845.	Prices in 1849.
d.	Sea Island	G. Barbadense	10½*d.* to 20*d.*	9*d.* to 24*d.*
e.	Egyptian		5¼ „ 8	6 „ 9¼
	Peruvian	. . . .	4¼ „ 5¼	6 „ 6¾
f.	Pernambuco	.		
	Aracati and Ceara	G. Peruvianum	5⅜ „ 6¾	6¼ „ 7
g.	Maranham and Para		4 „ 6	6 „ 6¾
h.	Bahia and Maceio		5⅜ „ 6	6 „ 6¾
	La Guayara	. . . .	4 „ 4½	5½ „ 6
	Carthagena	. . . .	2½ „ 3¼	4⅜ „ 4¾
i.	New Orleans		3½ „ 6½	5⅝ „ 8
j.	Mobile and Alabama	G. Barbadense	3½ „ 5	5½ „ 7½
k.	Uplands		3½ „ 4¾	5½ „ 6¾
	Demerara and Berbice	. . . .	. . . .	5¼ „ 8
	West India	. . . .	4 „ 5	5½ „ 6¾
	Smyrna	. . . .	. . . .	5 „ 5¼
l.	Prime Surats			
m.	Common Surats	G. Indicum	2⅜ „ 3¾	3¾ „ 5
n.	Madras		2½ „ 3¾	4 „ 5
o.	Bengal		2½ „ 3	2⅞ „ 3⅛

§ 4. The Genus and Species of Gossypium.

In pursuing our inquiry into the principles which should guide us in the Cultivation of Cotton, not in one, but in all the countries where this valuable substance is now produced, some facts require, in the first instance, to be determined respecting the plant, its soil, climate, and culture. Every one will admit the importance of ascertaining whether there be one or more species of cotton plant, and if the latter, whether the cotton of commerce is yielded by one or several of these species. The determination of this point will naturally lead to an inquiry into the places where they are indigenous, and

Pl. I

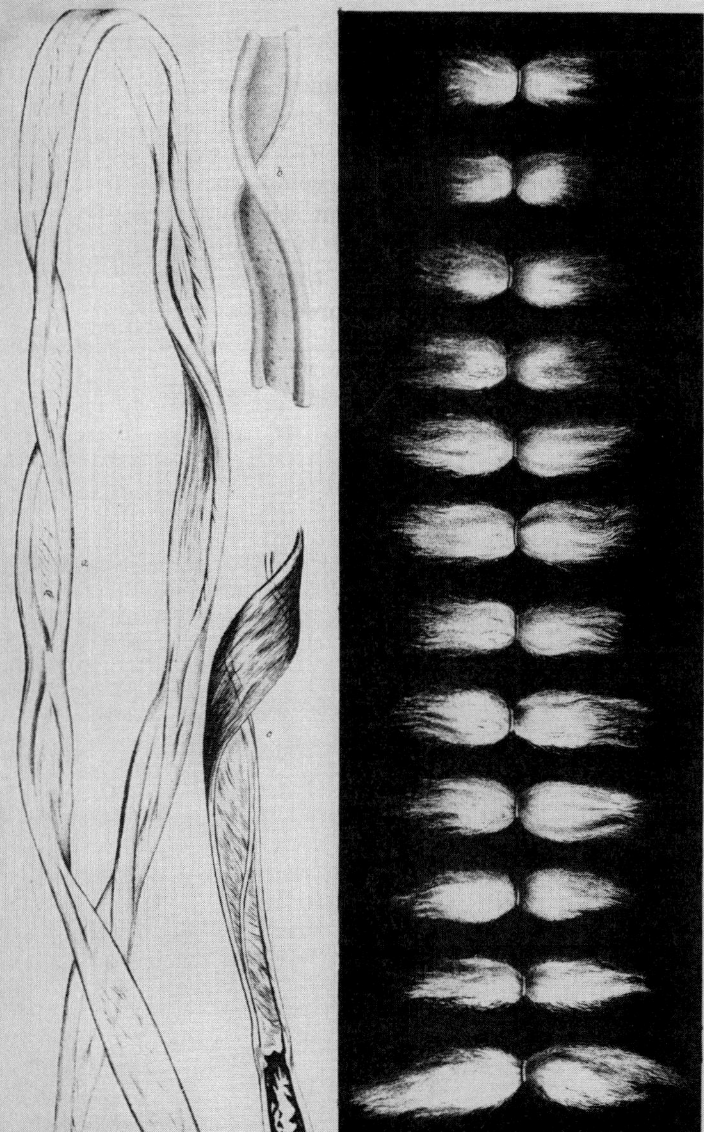

Bird & George, Lithographers 54, Hatton Garden.

into the soil and climate of these localities, as well as of those where the several species are successfully cultivated. If possible, it is in many cases desirable to ascertain, whether a vegetable product is yielded in the largest quantity and finest quality by a plant in a wild or in a cultivated state. In the case of cotton, we believe, it will be sufficient to take the cultivated plant as our principal guide. With this it will be requisite to ascertain the peculiarities of soil, of climate, and of culture which suit the different species, and enable them to yield not only a large quantity of cotton-wool, but also such as is suitable in length, strength, and fineness of fibre, or staple, as it is commonly called. We must further inquire, whether the same kind of soil and culture is suitable to each particular species, and whether due attention is paid to the selection of soils for the cultivation of cotton according to differences of climate, in order to suit the one to the other. We shall also have to determine whether soil, or climate, or culture is most influential in altering the nature of the product, and also whether increased quantity of produce is accompanied with any deterioration of its quality, or whether we may not increase our return and improve its quality, by one and the same process of culture. It will also be important to ascertain whether the different species are apt to deteriorate when introduced into new situations, either from physical differences in localities, or from accidental hybridization. The last point will naturally suggest the possibility of producing by such means new varieties suited to particular situations. We can then describe such results as have already been obtained by this process.

In attempting to ascertain the number of distinct species of the genus Gossypium, the author has, on a former occasion, stated, that there are great and, in some respects, insurmountable difficulties. Botanists appear to him injudiciously to neglect cultivated plants, and apply their correct observation and precise descriptions generally to such as are considered to be new species. Cultivators, on the contrary, deal in loose descriptions, and call their plants by provincial names or apply new ones of their own, to the exclusion of any notice of the names in use among botanists; so that it is impossible for others to ascertain to what species their otherwise valuable observations refer. Many of the cultivated cottons having been produced by plants or seeds which were introduced from one country into another, must necessarily be varieties of the same species however much they may vary, from the effects of soil, of climate, or of culture. From the endless diversities in these, a multitude of changes are produced in the appearances of plants, so as to render it difficult on first seeing one in a state of cultivation, to determine whether it is a distinct species, or only a variety of some well-known one. But these differences of soil and of climate do exist in nature, and the seeds of plants are carried by winds or by birds over great distances, and they often germinate in situations differing much in physical characteristics from the site from whence they came. So from such causes, or from natural hybridization, occasional varieties of a plant may be, and no doubt are, produced in a wild state.

The only mode in which we can satisfactorily determine whether a plant is a variety or a species, is to sow its seeds in a variety of situations, or the seeds of different varieties in the same soil, and subject them to similar treatment, so as to get rid of adventitious circumstances and of the characters dependent upon them, and thus enable a plant to return to its natural state. Cultivated plants afford numerous instances on an extensive scale of the effects of soil, of climate, and of culture in modifying the habits and characters of plants, and are favorable instead of objectionable subjects for investigation to the philosophical botanist, who wishes duly to appreciate the full influence of physical agents in modifying botanical characters. This is more than all necessary in the present day, when there is so general a disposition to form species on every trifling modification of character.

With regard to cotton, there is no doubt, that species have been formed from imperfect specimens, indifferent drawings, and frequently from insufficient characters, and these liable to change. Swartz and others have observed, that the several species varied in the size of parts, in the division of leaves, in the number of glands, in hairiness, in having the leaflets of the exterior calyx more or less divided, in the capsules having three or four cells, in the colour of both the seeds and the wool, as well as in the adherence and tenacity of the latter; so that from the difficulty of distinguishing the several species, Swartz thought that they might easily be believed to be only varieties of one species ('Illustr. of Him. Botany,' p. 97). So that "some botanists," as Dr. Wight observes, "seem to attach no value to characters taken either from the colour or quality of the wool or the seed, or the absence or presence of a coating of short hair or down, with which the seed of some sorts are clothed; neither to the forms of the foliage, or to the native country, or clothing or habit of the plants, whether glabrous or hairy, arboreous or annual;" and he does not hesitate to consider the Bourbon, the short and the long-stapled cottons of America, to be varieties of only a single species.

Many may be surprised to find the short-staple, or Upland Georgian, considered to be the same species as the Sea Island cotton. But if we look to the plants only, there is nothing of a permanent nature by which we can distinguish the one from the other. The seeds, indeed, differ to a very considerable extent, the Sea Island having a clean black seed without any adhering short hairs, fuzz, as they are called by the planters. While that of the short-staple, or Upland Georgian, which is the same as that from Mississipi or Alabama seed, is large and whitish-coloured, in consequence of a dense covering of the above short hairs or down. It may appear improbable to those unaccustomed to watch such changes, that so great a variation should be caused by the arts of culture or the influence of physical agents: but there can be no doubt of the fact. Mr. Spalding, an American planter, writes "that the same cotton-seed planted in one cotton-field will give a black and naked seed, which planted in another, different in soil and situation, will be prone to run into large cotton, with long bolls and with seeds tufted at the ends with fuzz." The same thing has been experienced in India with some of the American cottons which have been introduced there, and which have lost this fuzz, and been converted into clean black seeds. The author questioned the American planters when in this country respecting their experience on this change of character. They said that they always found it to be the case if they continued to cultivate from the same seed for a series of years. They were chiefly accustomed to the New Orleans or Mississipi seed, which they stated was originally imported from Mexico, and they were obliged occasionally to procure fresh seed from that country, as the large gray-seed of the

New Orleans cotton was apt to degenerate, as they expressed it, into the black-seed, or that of the Sea Island cotton. This, of course, much surprised the author to hear, as it was a change from a short-staple into a long-staple, or from an inferior into a superior kind of cotton, the seed appearing, as it lost its short wooliness, to be enabled to produce a longer and a finer stapled cotton. But the Mississipi planters value this less, because they say that the plant becomes less productive, and that they preferred the profit derivable from the quantity of produce per acre, to that which might be obtained from the fineness of cotton, or the length of its staple.

§ 5. The Genus Gossypium.

The genus Gossypium, so named from what is said by Pliny to have been the name of the cotton-plant, is distinguished by having a double calyx, or, in other words, a simple calyx supported externally by three leaf-like bracts forming an involucel, a three to five-celled capsule with seeds immersed in the wool-like substance, so well known by the name of cotton.

The species of this genus are either annual or perennial, often shrubby, one of them arboreous, natives of the hot parts of Asia and America, probably, also, of Africa. The leaves are alternate, with long foot-stalks, cordate at the base, three to five lobed, sometimes undivided at end of branches, often, as well as the bracts and young branches, covered with blackish gland-like spots and hairs; often with glands near the base of the nerves on the under surface; stipules two, lanceolate or cordate at the base of the petiole; flower-stalk terminal, axillary or opposite to the leaves; usually single-flowered; flowers large, showy, and hibiscus-like.

Each flower is supported externally by three bracts, which are broad, cordate, united at the base, entire, toothed or deeply cut; the calyx is cup-shaped, nearly entire, or obscurely five-toothed. Corol of five petals, inserted below the pistil; unequally obovate, united by the claws to the staminal tube, convolute in æstivation, staminal tube arched and dilated over the ovary, columnar above; filaments free in the upper part, simple or forked, bearing kidney-shaped anthers. Ovary sessile; superior, three to five celled; ovules numerous, in two rows, inserted in the centre angle of the cells, ascending; style terminal, equalling or exceeding the stamens in length, three to five furrowed. Stigmas three to five, club-shaped. Capsule roundish or ovoid, often pointed, thick, leathery, three to five celled, three to five valved; dehiscence loculicidal at the apex; valves with the partitions in their middle. Seeds numerous, ovate, angled, with a spongy coating, covered with a thick layer more or less long and fine, of wool-like fibres or cotton; often with an under-layer of short hairs or down. Embryo curved within mucilaginous albumen. Cotyledons leaf-like, folded up, dotted with black spots; radicle inferior.

§ 6. The Species of Gossypium.

The species of Gossypium are extremely uncertain in number. Linnæus admitted five species in 1762, Lamarck described eight species, and four more are described by Poiret in the 'Suppl. to the Encyclopédie Méthodique.' De Candolle enumerated thirteen in the year 1824. Two others had been previously described by Dr. Roxburgh, though not published. Eight other names of species with specific characters, and one without a name, are brought together in Walper's 'Repertorium.' So that at least twenty-four species are considered as distinct in the most recent systematic works. If we refer to cultivators, we find Dr. Von Rohr describing twenty-nine species or varieties, Badier eighteen, and Mr. Bennet mentions that he knew more than one hundred kinds, and that they appeared to him never ending. The celebrated De Candolle, however, when enumerating the several species, stated, that all were uncertain, and that no genus required more the labours of a monographist who could describe them from living specimens.

Of botanists who instead of increasing, have wished rather to reduce the number of species, we may first mention Dr. Buchanan Hamilton, who following Von Rohr, employed the seeds to furnish specific characters, and, according as they were black or white, reduced all the forms to one or other of two species distinguished by that mark. All the Indian cottons, as observed by Dr. Wight, and the gray-seeded American cottons being included under the species *G. album*, while the black-seeded cottons, including the West Indian, Sea Island, and Brazil cottons, were all placed under *G. nigrum*. The author agrees with Dr. Wight, in considering that the character on which this division is established cannot be depended upon, for we have abundant evidence, that the seed may change from gray to black, and *vice versâ*. Messrs. Wight and Arnott, however, in the 'Prodromus of the Flora of the Indian Peninsula,' admitted only the above two species. Dr. Lush and Mons. Jacquemont also reduced them to two species; but the author cannot think that either possessed materials sufficient to settle the many disputed points involved in the question, requiring not only the examination of living plants growing in different situations, but also the comparison of a number of dried specimens from different parts of the world. The author attempted in his 'Illustr. of Himal. Botany,' p. 98, to determine some of these points, but avowedly with little confidence in some of the results, from the want of authentic specimens. He relied chiefly on the observations of Dr. Roxburgh, who states that he had studied the subject for thirty years, and on "those of Dr. Swartz, who has described with great care ('Observ. Bot.,' p. 265) the species of cotton which he found cultivated in the West Indies." The author enumerated the same number of species as Dr. Roxburgh, that is eight, though his *G. vitifolium* was suppressed, and *G. micranthum* added. He thought that there were one or two more in the herbaria which he had examined, those of the British Museum and of the Linnean Society, as well as Dr. Lindley's and his own private collection. Dr. Wight was of opinion that the list like that of De Candolle would probably be found to be in excess. The author adopted two of the species on the authority of others; that is, *G. obtusifolium* of Roxburgh, from Ceylon; and *G. micranthum* of Cavanilles, from Persia, and which that author described from a plant which flowered in the *Jardin des Plantes* in Paris.

G. religiosum was admitted with great doubt, it being stated, that "the distinguishing characteristic of what is at present considered such, is the bearing *tawny* instead of *white* cotton; but there is considerable difficulty in ascertaining whether one or more species have such, or whether the colour is sufficiently permanent to allow of its being depended on as a specific character." The author thinks that it is not.

G. hirsutum was adopted, as Swartz, Roxburgh, and Cavanilles had all described it; but the author was unable to refer to any genuine specimen of the plant, and stated, that "it would appear, from the character of the seed, to be the *green-seeded, short-staple*, or *Upland cotton* of the Americans." He was not prepared then, as now, to consider it only a variety, as well as the Sea Island cotton, of *G. barbadense*, or what is called Bourbon cotton in India, from having been brought from that island, where it had been introduced from the West Indies.

Dr. Wight, after his return to India in 1833, cultivated several of these Gossypiums in the neighbourhood of Madras, and acknowledged in his 'Illustr. of Ind. Bot.,' p. 57, 1840, "three species as certain, viz., the old *Gossypium herbaceum*, with palmately-lobed leaves, whether an annual or a tree of indefinite duration; secondly, the American forms with simply lobed or angled leaves, equally leaving duration out of question, *G. barbadense;* and thirdly, the forms with the seed adherent in form of a cone, *G. acuminatum,* comprehending the various forms known under the names of Pernambuco, Peruvian, Bahia, and Ava cotton." The author agrees with Dr. Wight, in considering *G. barbadense* as including Bourbon, West Indian, Sea Island, Uplands, New Orleans, Mexican, and some other cultivated cottons. *G. acuminatum,* as including Pernambuco, Brazil, and Peruvian cotton. *G. herbaceum,* or, as the author would prefer Lamarck's name, *G. indicum,* as embracing the several varieties of indigenous cottons cultivated in India. But he cannot consider *G. arboreum* as being a variety of the same species, as it retains all its distinct characters in every situation in which he has seen or heard of it. Having received specimens of *G. obtusifolium,* Roxb., from Scinde, collected there by Dr. Stocks, he believes this also to be a distinct species, though not one of the cultivated ones. And he believes that there are at least two other distinct species in different herbaria, as will be mentioned at the conclusion of the following enumeration. He has been enabled, through the liberality of Sir William Hooker, Director of the Royal Botanic Garden, Kew, to have access, for a considerable time, to the extensive collection of the different species of Gossypium in his most splendid herbarium. The author has thus been enabled to form a much more decided opinion on some points than he would otherwise have had it in his power to do. Having carefully, some months since, considered the characters of the several species, examined specimens of the cultivated varieties, and referred these to what he considered to be their true species, both in his own and Sir W. Hooker's herbarium; the author lately went over the whole again, in company with an Indian botanist, Dr. Cleghorn, and on referring to his notes, found that he had come to exactly the same conclusions as he had done previously. The following appear to be the species and varieties of the cultivated plants:

Gossypium indicum, Lamarck, Pl. 11, is the same species as the *G. herbaceum* of Linnæus; and as the latter, though the older name, is not very applicable to Indian cotton, we prefer adopting that of Lamarck, which is, moreover, only a translation of the name *Kootn hindee,* often applied to the Indian cotton-plant by other Asiatics. It is herbaceous, stem more or less branched, about 1½ to 2 feet high in temperate climates; hard and wood-like and bi-triennial, 4 to 6 feet high, in its native and other warm countries; but it may be cultivated as an annual, germinating and ripening its seed within a period of from four to eight months, while some varieties seem to require nearly a year. The young parts are velvety, often hairy, in the upper part sometimes of a reddish colour, frequently marked with black spots. Leaves hairy, palmate, 3 generally 5-lobed; in herbaceous varieties, lobes broad and rounded with a little point; in those which are woody, sublanceolate and acute, with or without glands on the under surface of the mid-rib. Stipules falcate-lanceolate. Petioles long, usually hispid and dotted. Flowers axillary, generally solitary towards the extremities of the branches, petals of a lively yellow colour, with a purple spot near the claw. Segments of the exterior Calyx or involucel, D.C. cordate at the base, margin dentate, sometimes entire. Capsules ovate, pointed, 3 or 4 celled. Seeds free, about five in number, clothed with firmly-adhering, grayish down, under the short-staple white wool.—*Xylon s. Gossypium antiquorum.*—*G. herbaceum.* Linn. sp. Pl. 3, p. 355. Lamarck Encycl. 2, p. 133. Cav. Diss. 6, p. 310, t. 164, f. 2. Willd. 3, p. 803. Roxb. Fl. Ind. 3, p. 184, D.C. Prod. 1, p. 456. Royle, Illustr. of Himal. Bot., t. 23, f. 1. This and its varieties are by far the most generally cultivated in India. Dr. Roxburgh particularly distinguishes three varieties:

"DACCA COTTON may be reckoned the first variety, or deviation from the last-mentioned common sort, v. Pl. 111, fig. 1.

"*G. herbaceum* is in general cultivation all over Bengal and Coromandel. It is reared about Dacca, and furnishes that exceedingly fine cotton-wool employed in manufacturing the very delicate, beautiful muslins of that place. The Dacca variety differs from the common *G. herbaceum* in the following respects:

"1st. In the plant being more erect, with fewer branches, and the lobes of the leaves more pointed.

"2d. In the whole plant being tinged of a reddish colour, even the petioles, and nerves of the leaves, and being less pubescent.

"3d. In having the peduncles which support the flowers longer, and the exterior margins of the petals tinged with red.

"4th. In the staple of the cotton being longer, much finer, and softer.

"These are the most obvious disagreements, but whether they will prove permanent I cannot say at present. The most intelligent people of that country (Dacca) think the great difference lies in the spinning, and allow little for the influence of the soil." (*Flor. Ind.*, vol. iii, p. 184.)

But several varieties of cotton used to be known in Dacca.

Mr. Bebb mentions 1st, the *Photie*, most valuable in quality and considerable in quantity, an annual yielding the finest cotton, "of astonishing beauty and fineness," The seed requires to be preserved with care. It is sown in October or November, and in April or May. The first yielding a crop in April, and the second in October. The plant is described as being "from 20 to 30 inches in height, to be of a very tender nature, and to yield only one crop;" but "to produce from five to ten maunds of 80 sicca weight, and to sell in the Mofussil (that is, the country) at seldom less than 4 or 5 rupees per maund," v. *E. I. C.'s Papers*, p. 342.

In the Hurriaul district, Mr. Taylor describes,—1st, the Dessy, or indigenous cotton, as consisting of four different kinds. (l. c. p. 339.)

2d. The *Byratty*, or *Bairati kupas*, growing to the height of from 3 to 4½ feet, sown in October and November, and producing in March on an average about five maunds per beegah, but grown only in small quantity in the districts to the north-west of Dacca. The capsule is described as being large; the fibre shorter and less firm than that of the Dessy. It was produced in Momensi (an Mymensing?) Pergunnah, of which Seerpore is the head.

Mr. Tucker describes the staple of the bairati kupas as being extremely fine, silky, and strong; but very short, and adhering most tenaciously to the seed. He mentions having long since sent some of its seeds to Bermuda.

Mr. Taylor says, "the finest fibres of kupas are those which adhere firmly to the seed, and from which they can be separated only by a machine. From this superior part of the kupas, the spinners who make the finest thread carefully remove, by means of a fine comb, all the loose and coarse fibres." This account is not very intelligible, but it proves that the weavers of Bengal paid great attention to the selection and preparation of the yarn for their fine muslins.

3d. *Bhoga* is a kind of cotton produced in the hills near Chilmarry, to the eastward of Dacca, or the Currybarry hills, north of the Burrampooter, where about 20,000 maunds of this cotton were annually grown, and exported into the plains. The capsule is described as being larger than that of even the Byratty. The fibre short and coarse. Little care was bestowed on the culture. The old plants being cut down, were burnt, and the ashes used as manure. The seeds were sown in March or April; in May or June the ground was weeded, and the produce gathered in October. It was used at Dacca for coarse cloths, and for the stripes of others. The fibre was coarse, but swelled much in bleaching.

In Sir W. Hooker's Herbarium, there is a specimen of a cotton-plant from Assam, which very closely resembles that figured by Dr. Roxburgh as the cotton-plant of Dacca; but the bracts, though large and leaf-like, are cordate and acute, either entire or slightly toothed, and not deeply cut or laciniate, as in Dr. Roxburgh's plant, of which a portion is figured in Pl. iii, f. 1.

Mr. Duncan mentions at Benares, 1st, the *Rarreah* or *Buroweh*, as the best produced, and giving one fourth of *ruée*, or clean cotton; always cultivated by itself; sown in August, and the crop reaped in March or April; requiring a good rich soil, and to be near some means of irrigation, as it must be regularly attended to, and watered. 2d, *Munnoah* or *Jettooee*, inferior to the former, yielding one eighth of clean cotton; but cultivated with other crops. It requires nearly a year to bring it to maturity; but it will grow up well in an indifferent soil.

The variety cultivated about Cawnpore and in the Gangetic Doab is figured in the author's Illustrations of 'Himal. Bot.,' tab. 23, fig. 1, from a drawing in General Hardwicke's collection. Specimens collected by Dr. Thomson at Moradabad, and marked as cultivated, may be seen in Sir W. Hooker's Herbarium, named *G. arboreum*, with lanceolate segments of the lobed leaves, and rather silky cotton. The cotton-plants of the Northern Doab are usually from 3 to 4 feet high, woody, very hairy, with lanceolate-shaped lobes; the cotton short in staple, and coarse. The cotton-plants on the banks of the Jumna are from 1½ to 2 feet high, with few lateral branches, but with deep penetrating roots. Lobe of the leaves narrow, lanceolate, and the plant said to resemble the triennial cotton of the Peninsula. The cotton is short in staple and woolly. But much finer cotton is grown further in the interior, and to the westward, and which by degrees approaches the cotton of Berar.

"BERAR COTTON, I call the second variety. It is in cultivation over the Berar country; and it is from thence imported into the Circars, or Northern Provinces, by Sada, Balawansa, &c. to Yourma-goodum, in the Musulipatam district. With this cotton the fine Madras, more properly, Northern Circar long cloth is made.

"It differs from the above-mentioned two sorts in the following respects:

"1st. In growing to a greater size; in being more permanent, or living longer; and in having smooth and straight branches.

"2d. In having the leaflets of the exterior calyx more deeply divided, and the wool of a finer quality, than in the first variety." (*Flor. Ind.*, vol. iii, p. 185.)

The fine fabrics of Chunderee are made from the Berar cotton, which is imported from Indore. Dr. Irvine, then settled at Gwalior, stated, that the name Nurma is applied by the Mussulmen to the cotton used at Chunderee, but that is not produced there; its real name, from time immemorial, is *Berari,* and that it is imported as required from Cholae Muhaisore, beyond Indore on the Nerbuddah, where it is regularly cultivated. Mr. Mercer, who travelled through Berar, and paid particular attention to the nature of the cotton which he found there, describes the Oomerowtee cotton as being fine, silky, and of a staple quite equal to the middling qualities of short-staple American cotton. He did not observe any great difference in the plants, but ascribed the superiority to soil, climate, and culture. We have not had an opportunity of examining any plants from Central India. The beautiful drawing in Col. Sykes's collection, from which we have taken Plate 11, as a representative of the Indian cotton plant, was taken from a Deccan plant, and, therefore, probably does not differ much from that of Berar. The bracts are deeply divided, as described by Dr. Roxburgh, and there are small supplementary lobes between the larger lobes of the leaves. The specimens in Col. Sykes's collection, of dried plants of *Schwet-kupas,* have the lobes broader and more obtuse, with the bracts less divided.

The cotton of Guzerat is described by Mr. Vaupell as of different kinds. In the eastern districts of the province, namely, Jumbooseer, Ahmode, Broach, and Surat, the cotton grown and known by the native name of *Kanum* or *Lalliah,* is of a superior description. Broach, or Surat cotton, is a term comprehensively, and often indiscriminately, used to denote the finer sorts; the cotton of these, when ripe on the plant, hangs pendent from the pods, which shrivel and dry up. The plant rises to the height of three or four feet, sending out several diverging and pod-bearing branches. It thrives best in the black cotton soil of the province, which contains a considerable admixture of sand.

In the districts to the west of the gulf of Cambay, comprising Ihallowar, the Kattiwar Peninsula, and Cutch, a variety called *Wagriah* is cultivated, especially about Dhollera, Bhownuggur, &c. This is an annual, attains a height of two, or two and a half feet, in a single upright tapering stem. The flowers are yellow. The capsules instead of opening, remain shut up, with only a small opening at the apex, and require some force to extract the seed-cotton from the cells. The wool, therefore, remains confined within the capsules, and is then gathered, in which state it is termed *Kalliah.* It is of an inferior and more woolly staple, about three fourths of an inch long, and better adapted for coarse manufactures.

In the peninsula of India there are at least two distinct varieties of the common Indian cotton, one called *Oopum,* the other *Nadum.* These Dr. Wight describes as differing from the New Orleans plant, especially in taking deeper root, and as being slower in their progress towards maturity. The *Oopum* is an annual which grows on the black or richest and highest assessed land. It is said to be called *Oopum-purthee,* literally *sea-breeze cotton,* from opening its bolls after the setting-in of the sea-breeze. The staple comes nearer that of the American Upland than does any other Peninsular cotton. The *Nadum* is a triennial plant, which grows on the red or inferior soil; but it is a poor bearer, and is cleaned with greater difficulty. Its cotton is frequently mixed with that of the Oopum, and thus depreciates its value.

Pl. II

GOSSYPIUM INDICUM.

Ford & George, Lithographers, 54 Hatton Garden.

There is a specimen from Dr. Wight, No. 176, in Sir W. Hooker's Herbarium, and one from Surat, collected by Captain Giberne, resembling it very closely.

The Oopum is well figured by Dr. Wight in his 'Icones,' tab. 198; the leaves are 3 to 5 lobed; lobes broad, lanceolate; bracts serrate; capsules four-celled The native names are, Tamool, *Vanparatee*, Telinga, *Puttee*. In Dr. Rottler's Herbarium, there are three varieties marked *G. herbaceum*, one with a tall, slender stem, short branches, and small three-lobed leaves; another marked *Uppu parutti*, "caule suffruticoso hirsuto, fol. 3-5 lobis, uniglandulosis, *lobis obtusis*, mucronatis;" and a third, distinguished from the last only by "*lobis acutis*." Besides these, there is a distinct variety much more hairy in every part. The lobes of the leaves lanceolate, pointed; bracts cordate, acute, entire, or tri-dentate at the apex. This is considered to be a distinct species and called *G. hirsutum*, with a variety also so named, but with broad-lobed leaves and tawny-coloured cotton.

The specimens in Sir W. Hooker's Herbarium marked *G. religiosum*, with tawny-coloured cotton, would appear from their locality to belong to this variety; but the two vary, one having broad, and the other lanceolate-lobed leaves; the stipules narrow, falcate; the former with tawny-coloured cotton, the latter with yellow flowers, with a dark stain at the base of the claws; bracts coarsely serrated.

"CHINA COTTON," Dr. Roxburgh calls, "the third variety. It has lately been introduced into Bengal from China, where it is cultivated, and its wool reckoned 25 per cent. better than that of Surat. It differs from the former sorts,

"1st. In being much smaller, with but very few, short, weak branches.

"2d. In being, so far as my experience yet goes, annual.

"3d. In having the leaflets of the exterior calyx entire, or nearly so." (*Flor. Ind.*, vol. iii, p. 185.)

The specimen in *Herb. Hook.* from Mr. Fortune is less hairy than most Indian specimens, though clothed with a number of short hairs. Mr. Fortune states in a note with some specimens that he sent to Dr. Lindley from China, that the white-coloured and the nankeen-coloured cotton are yielded by the same species and even by the same plant, and that the two kinds are separated by the Chinese.

Besides India and China, this species is cultivated in Persia, Syria, Asia Minor, and the islands of the Mediterranean, as well as in the north of Africa and the south of Europe. The kind yielding the nankeen-coloured cotton in Malta, is probably a variety. Specimens have been brought by Mr. Wilkinson from Egypt; "wild cotton from the oases" appears also to be a variety, as well as *gotun bilade*, of the same collection, deposited in the British Museum. So also the specimens collected by Kotschy in Upper Egypt, and by Schimper in the Abyssinian province of Tigre.

G. punctatum, of the 'Flore de Sénégambie,' 1, p. 62, is described by Guillemen and Perrottet as a perennial very nearly allied to *G. herbaceum*, growing naturally upon the banks of the Senegal, and in the country between it and the Gambia; also as cultivated by all the people of Africa. The authors describe it, "lana gossypinâ niveâ seminibus valde adhærenti," and as "coton qui adhère fortement aux graines, et d'une grande finesse et d'une blancheur éclatante." The author would also with Dr. Wight refer here *G. micranthum* and *G. eglandulosum* of Cavanilles, and would inquire whether *G. prostratum*, found in Guinea, is a variety of this, or more closely allied to Dr. Roxburgh's *G. obtusifolium*. The author believes, that some of the more hairy varieties of Indian cotton have been considered to be the true *G. hirsutum;* but Linnæus stated this to be a native of America.

G. obtusifolium, Roxb., shrubby, very ramous. Leaves small, with three, rarely five, obtuse, ovate, entire lobes. Stipules falcate. The exterior calyx with entire divisions. Capsules ovate, cells three-seeded. Seeds free, and clothed with firmly-adhering, short greenish-gray down, under a small portion of ash-coloured wool. A native of Ceylon, but not cultivated. Flowers during the rains and cold season in the Botanic Garden at Calcutta. ('Roxb. Fl. Indica,' vol. iii, p. 183; 'Ic. ined.' 1495; 'Royle, Illustr. Himal. Botany,' p. 98.) Dr. Stocks, an excellent observer and botanist, has sent specimens of this species to the author, collected in Scinde, described by him as "found everywhere on limestone in Scinde, perfectly wild, and where it could not have been cultivated." The specimens resemble *G. obtusifolium*, Roxb., Ic. ined. 1495, very closely; but differ in the obtuse lobes of the leaves being slightly mucronate, in the bracts being deeply laciniate, instead of perfectly entire. In both, the capsules are small, roundish, pointed, and few-seeded; but in the Scinde specimen the cotton is somewhat tawny-coloured. Can this be the original of the different cultivated varieties of the common Indian cotton?

Gossypium arboreum is thus described in the author's 'Illust. Himal. Botany:' "*G. arboreum.* Stem arboreous, 15 to 20 feet, sometimes shrubby, young parts hairy, tinged of a reddish colour. Leaves palmate, 3 or 5 lobed, hairy, dotted with blackish spots, of a dark green colour, lobes elongated, lanceolate, sometimes mucronate, sinus obtuse, glands one, sometimes three. Stipules awl-shaped. Flowers solitary, with short peduncles, red, with a yellowish tinge near the claws. Leaflets of the exterior calyx cordate-ovate, entire, sometimes dentate. Capsule ovate-pointed, 3 or 4 celled, four to five seeds, covered with a greenish-coloured fur, enveloped in a fine silky yellowish-white wool.—*Xylon arboreum auctorum. Gossypium arboreum gotnem segiar* (i. e. the large cotton) Prosp. Alp. Exot. t. 38. *G. herbaceum vel Xylon maderaspatense rubicundo flore pentaphyllæum.* Pluk. Alm. 172, t. 188, f. 3. *G. arboreum, cotn el sadjar.* Forsk. Ægypt. p. 70. *An G. rubrum.* Forsk., p. 116. Willd. 3, p. 804. Lamarck Encycl. 2, p. 135. Cav. Diss. 6, p. 310, t. 165. Roxb. Fl. Ind., p. iii, 183. D.C. Prod. 1, p. 456. Dr. Roxburgh was of opinion, that *Cadu pariti* of Rheede, *Hort. Mal.* 1, p. 55, t. 31, is not this plant; but observes, it may be *G. religiosum of Gærtner*, 2, p. 246, t. 134, f. 1. It is marked *G. religiosum* in Heyne's Herbarium. I was informed by Huree Sing, the head-gardener in the H. C.'s Botanic Garden at Saharunpore, that the cotton of this plant was never used for making any of the lower garments, but only for turbans for the head, as it was sacred to their deities. Some legend of this kind may have reached Linnæus, though the name is now applied to a different species.* *G. arboreum* is found in the island of Celebes, in Arabia, Egypt, and in India; in the latter it is called *nurma-barree*, and is generally found in the clumps of trees which surround temples, or the abodes of Fuqueers."

G. arboreum, in 'Herb. Hook.' from Bengal, Surat, Madras. *G. rubicundum*, Roxb., Ic. ined. 1496, is only a variety. The author published a figure in 'Himal. Bot.' from General Hardwicke's drawings; and, as he has mentioned, it is cultivated near villages, in clumps of shrubbery, and in sides of, but never in fields, though he himself did attempt the cultivation in this manner, but found it a poor bearer, though the cotton was fine and silky. Dr. Stocks has sent him specimens from Scinde. There are specimens in Rottler's Herbarium from the Peninsula, both with white and with tawny-coloured cotton. There is also a specimen marked both *G. hirsutum* and *G. palmatum*, but which appears to be only a young plant of *G. arboreum*.

---

* Dr. Cleghorn has lately informed the author, that it is called *Deo kupas*, or the sacred cotton, in Mysore.

Dr. Burns employed it for hybridising with the American cottons, so as to obtain a variety better suited than either to India.

The Nurmah cotton is mentioned by Mr. Duncan as "one of the kinds in the Benares district, though not sown in the fields, but generally round gardens, near ponds, &c. It rises to the height of 8 and 10 feet, and when in flower is remarkably handsome. It is also very productive, and frequently continues to yield cotton during a period of four or five years; but it is generally cultivated more for ornament than use."—*E. I. C.'s Papers*, p. 360.

Mr. Vaupell mentions it as a shrub met with in the neighbourhood of large towns in the eastern districts of Guzerat, in spots most favorable for irrigation. Its wool is the finest of any,—of a beautiful silky staple, upwards of an inch in length, and only used in the manufacture of the finest muslins. It is but sparingly cultivated.

The Nurmah is particularly mentioned at p. 100 of 'Return,' as a very fine silky cotton, sent from Khorassan, and stated to be well known in Malwa. Mr. Bruce mentions, (p. 101,) that he found in 1808 a few plants of the Nurmah cotton at Calpee, in the gardens belonging to the Jaloun Rajah. That it had been sown before 1804 or 1805, to supply the Rajah's household with the brahminical thread. The cotton was beautifully soft, and of a good colour. Mr. Bruce supposes that it was the kind cultivated at Chunderee for the beautiful muslins of that place. But Captain Abbott, when written to on the subject, stated that it was a bush lasting 10 or 12 years; not, as far as he could learn, cultivated for manufactures in Nimar or Malwa.

Gossypium barbadense: perennial, stem shrubby, 6-12 feet in height, glabrous; some varieties studded like the leaf-stalks, with tuberculous points. Leaves, the upper sometimes undivided, cordate and acute, or tridentate, usually three—the lower five-lobed, lobes ovate, acute, angles obtuse, smooth on the upper, often pubescent on the under surface, with one to three glands; stipules awl-shaped. Leaflets of the exterior calyx large, deeply laciniate. Flowers yellow; capsule ovate, acute, smooth, three to four, sometimes five-celled. Seeds eight to twelve, free, oblong, black, and without any other pubescence than the long, fine, easily-separable white wool, but in some of the varieties, and apparently, in its original Mexican form, covered with closely adhering down. Swartz, Obs. Bot., p. 266. Roxb. Fl. Ind. 3, p. 187. *G. vitifolium* Cav. Diss. 6, p. 311, tab. 166. *G. barbadense*, Roxb., Ic. ined. 1499. *G. fuscum*, Roxb. Ic. ined. 1497. The wood-cuts given by Dr. Ure, in his Cotton Manufacture, vol. i, p. 60, of the Sea Island Cotton, from Mr. Seabrook, of Edisto Island, and of the short-staple or green-seed cotton, from Mr. Spalding, of Sapelo Island, near Darien, do not differ essentially from each other nor from this. Bot. Register. Wight, Illust. of Ind. Bot. 84, Pl. 28 A.

G. barbadense was named by Linnæus, in the first edition of his Species Plantarum, 1753, and taken from Plukenet Almagest., 172, t. 188, f. 1, and stated to be a native of the Island of Barbadoes. In India it is known by the name of Bourbon Cotton, having been introduced into the Peninsula of India from that island and the Isle of France, or Mauritius, at least as early as the year 1790. In an account of the 'Culture of Cotton in the Island of Bourbon,' it is stated, "the cultivation of this valuable plant in this country is of recent date, and has only been followed since the years 1788 and 1789." (*E. I. C.'s Papers*, p. 385.) Swartz states, that the plant described by him under this name, is more extensively cultivated than any other kind in the West Indies. The Americans, we know, received the seed with which they commenced the culture of Sea Island Cotton in 1785, from Anguilla, one of the Bahamas. The planters of New Orleans Cotton* of the present day renew their seed, when it deteriorates, from Mexico, or from the Gulf Hills in Mississippi, every fourth or fifth year. Humboldt states, that cotton, celebrated for its fineness and whiteness, is produced in the hot coast, Tierra caliente, of Vera Cruz, and also of excellent quality in the vicinity of Valladolid, in the province of Yucatan. In both situations there must be considerable heat, but, from the vicinity of the sea, the atmosphere must always be loaded with much aqueous vapour.

The author has formerly stated ('Illust. Himal. Bot.,' p. 100), that he coincided with Sir J. Smith in considering "*G. barbadense* of Swartz and Roxburgh as the same plant as the *G. vitifolium* of Cavanilles, described by the latter from a specimen in Commerson's Herbarium, collected in the Isle of France. It is singular, that the latter author, when describing all the species which he could procure of Gossypium, mentions *G. barbadense* as a plant unknown to him. Swartz, in describing the West Indian species, omits all mention of *G. vitifolium*, but his information, that his *G. barbadense* is the species most cultivated in the West Indies, is important, as showing that from it, probably, some of the most valuable of the cultivated varieties of cotton have been obtained."

Taking the smooth and shining stem and leaves, the latter deeply lobed or obtusely angled, and the seeds distinct from each other, usually black in the Sea Island and Bourbon varieties, covered only with the easily-separable long wool, we find this plant cultivated in a variety of places; as, in addition to the West Indies, in the Sea Islands of Georgia and of Carolina, also in Egypt and in India, in the form of Bourbon cotton. We now have abundant proof, that the blackness of the seed is not a character to be depended upon, as it becomes covered, in the course of cultivation, with the short down or fuzz, while the Mexican seed loses this, and becomes smooth and black. There are no other trust-worthy characters by which the Bourbon can be distinguished from the Sea Island or the Upland cotton-plant. Dr. Wight, who has had the opportunity of growing them all from seed, has figured and described them as varieties of *G. barbadense*. The figures 2, 3, 4, in Pl. iii, are copied from his 'Illust. of Indian Bot.,' Pl. 28, *a. b. c.* In Rottler's Herb. there are specimens both with white and with tawny-coloured cotton, from the Peninsula, the latter marked *G. religiosum*. Of the former it is observed, "Nullam video differentiam inter hoc

---

* The great esteem in which New Orleans cotton is held at Liverpool, is evident from the following extract from an American paper: "*New Orleans Cotton.*—The preference continued to be shown to this description at Liverpool is the more remarkable, as it is well known this season, that a larger proportion than usual of the heavy receipt at New Orleans has been made up of Georgia, Florida, and South Alabama growth, which has found its way there for the benefit of a clearance from that port, the staple of much of which is doubtless as good as the average of the favoured growth of Louisiana and Mississippi, but which experience has demonstrated will not sell as well at Liverpool under its proper name. Shippers thus find it their account in paying the additional freight to New Orleans, with the host of small charges thereon, for the benefit to be derived from the classification of it abroad as New Orleans cotton." (*Times*, Aug. 7, 1848, from *New York Commercial Intelligencer* July 25, 1848.)

et *G. religiosum* nisi quod lana nivea. Varietas *G. religiosi* esse videtur." (The *G. fuscum* Roxb. Ic. ined. 1497, is a similar variety.) There are also specimens, in Rottler's Herbarium, of "Cotton from Mauritius," which is named *G. Mauritianum.* The leaves five-lobed, hairy, as well as the young stems and petioles, the cotton tawny-coloured. There are specimens of this species in the British Museum, as cultivated in Egypt, one of them from Sir G. Wilkinson, and one from Bové in Dr. Lindley's Herbarium. The author has himself received specimens from Mr. Grant, late of the India House, collected by him near the Nile, in flower on the 16th Feb. He has also received specimens from the West Indies, as of the cotton cultivated there. Sir W. Hooker has them from Jamaica. *G. jamaicense* and *oligospernum*, of Macfadyn, described as growing in Jamaica, can only be varieties of this species. In Sir W. Hooker's Herb., there are specimens under the name of *G. vitifolium*, from Dr. Wallich as *G. nigrium*, from Dr. Wight as *G. religiosum*, from Surat, also from the west coast of Africa (*marked G. punctatum*) and from Crete, where the plant has no doubt been introduced. Prof. Tenore, in a paper on the cotton of Castellamare, which is known to be of a superior quality, states, that the seeds were introduced by the French, from Calabria, which alone, of all the places in Italy, produces cotton of the same quality; also, that the species is quite distinct from *G. herbaceum*, and that it corresponds in character with the "Xylon præstantissimum semine virescente," which is the American *G. hirsutum*. The author's specimens were grown in the botanic garden at Saharunpore. This species seems also to be distributed in the Pacific Ocean, as Dr. Lindley has specimens from Owhyhee and Sir W. Hooker from Tahiti.

The *Bourbon Cotton* is so named from having been grown in the Isle of Bourbon, where it is supposed to have been introduced by the French from the West Indies. Its seeds were early distributed by Dr. Anderson throughout the Peninsula. Dr. Wight, Mr. Fischer, and others, state that its cultivation is now common in many of the southern districts. Dr. Roxburgh early ascertained, that it succeeded better on the Coromandel coast than in Bengal. On its introduction into Guzerat, it is described as growing into a large shrub, spreading its branches, laden with cotton, to a great distance, attaining full vigour only after a period of eighteen months, but lasting for a series of years. Mr. Gilders, in 1818, succeeded in cultivating Bourbon cotton in the eastern districts of Kaira, between the Suburmutty and the Myhee, in light sandy soil, (l. c., p. 67.) Mr. Hale, at the same time, sent a satisfactory report of the cultivation of Bourbon cotton in Malwan. Both these localities are interesting, as plants have continued to be raised apparently from the original seed, and have become so naturalised as to have been taken for indigenous species. That found by Mr Elphinston in the Concan was by him called Conkanee, and the cotton highly valued by the merchants at Bombay, as was that grown from seed collected by Dr. Burns, in the hedges of Mr. Gilders's garden. This variety is every where treated as a biennial.

Sea Island Cotton.—When formerly treating of this subject, the author stated, from the specimens which he had then seen of the cotton cultivated in Egypt, that it was a variety of this species, and he inferred it as probable, that because the Sea Island cotton would be found to belong to the same when the cultivation was commenced in Egypt, seed would most likely be introduced from the then best known sources. This has been fully confirmed by subsequent information, as has been already detailed. Dr. Wight says, "The other two varieties of *G. barbadense* here figured (that is, in his 'Illustr. of Indian Botany,' 28, *a*, *b*, *c*), the long and short-stapled kinds, or

"Sea Islands" and "Uplands" as they are called, are derived from the same stock as the Bourbon." The Sea Island variety has succeeded in some parts of India, as under Mr. Elphinston's care in the maritime district of Rutnagherry.

Of the *Egyptian cotton*, Dr. Wight says, "which in that country partakes largely of the valuable properties of this kind, is supposed to have been derived from the Sea Island stock; however, judging from some that I had sown in my garden, it has either got mixed with the short-stapled sort, or is in course of transition into it. The latter I suspect rather to be the case; but whether or not, it is most certain that, from a quantity of Egyptian seed sown in Madras, both kinds were produced, and having the distinctive characters of each strongly marked." In Mr. Gleddon's 'Memoir on the Cotton of Egypt,' the kinds cultivated are said to be *Billaidee* (that is, foreign), *Jamulwa*, *Nankin*, and *Soudan*.

"Respecting the origin of the *Uplands variety*," Dr. Wight stated, in 1840, "and the period of its introduction into North America, I am not so well informed;* but I have no hesitation in considering it another variety of *G. barbadense*, from which, in fact, it scarcely differs, except in the much greater size of the pods, the shorter and stronger staple of its wool, the usually five-lobed leaves, and the seeds more or less clothed with down. This last is a mark of very minor importance, as it is now known, a single generation may change the character of the seed from smooth to downy. Those of the Bourbon cotton are generally described as black and smooth, yet I have scarcely ever met with one that was not more or less downy, and often not less than the American green-seed." In the 'Proc. of the Agric. Soc. of India' for May 1844, it is reported of some cotton cultivated from acclimated American seed at Garden Reach, near Calcutta, "that the cotton-wool of the third descent from New Orleans† seed *actually verged upon a long-stapled cotton*, with the characteristics of the latter in a freeness from the wool of the seed, and the seed of a black or dark colour." The author supposed, when formerly determining these species, that the *G. hirsutum* of Linnæus taken from Plukenet was the *green-seeded, short-staple*, or *Upland cotton* of the Americans, especially as Swartz mentions it as cultivated in Jamaica and other West India Islands, and Roxburgh that it had been lately introduced from America into India, where the cotton was much admired by the natives. *G. hirsutum* is usually described as "ramulis petiolisque hirsutis," young parts very hairy, also the under surface of the leaves and the seeds as thickly covered with green down under the long white wool. There are specimens in Sir W. Hooker's Herbarium from Louisiana, from Drs. Wight and Shuter from the Peninsula of India, also from Requien and from Gouan grown in France, marked *G. hirsutum*, all which, except in being more hairy, closely resemble specimens of *G. barbadense*. The author has now no doubt of the

---

* A short-staple cotton was grown in the United States in small quantities long previous to the time usually supposed, as will appear from the following extracts:—"Short-staple cotton was certainly grown in Virginia, in a limited way, at least 130 years before the Revolution."—"In 1736, as far north as Lat. 39°, cotton was cultivated as a garden plant near Gaston, on the eastern shore of the Chesapeake Bay." "The first Provincial Congress in Carolina recommended cotton culture." (Macgregor's 'Commercial Statistics,' p. 452.) Mr. Jefferson in his 'Notes on Virginia,' writes in 1781, that the articles of cotton which they had manufactured would bear comparison with those of Europe, and Mr. Maddison, in 1786, remarked, "that the United States would one day become a great cotton-producing country."

Pl. III.

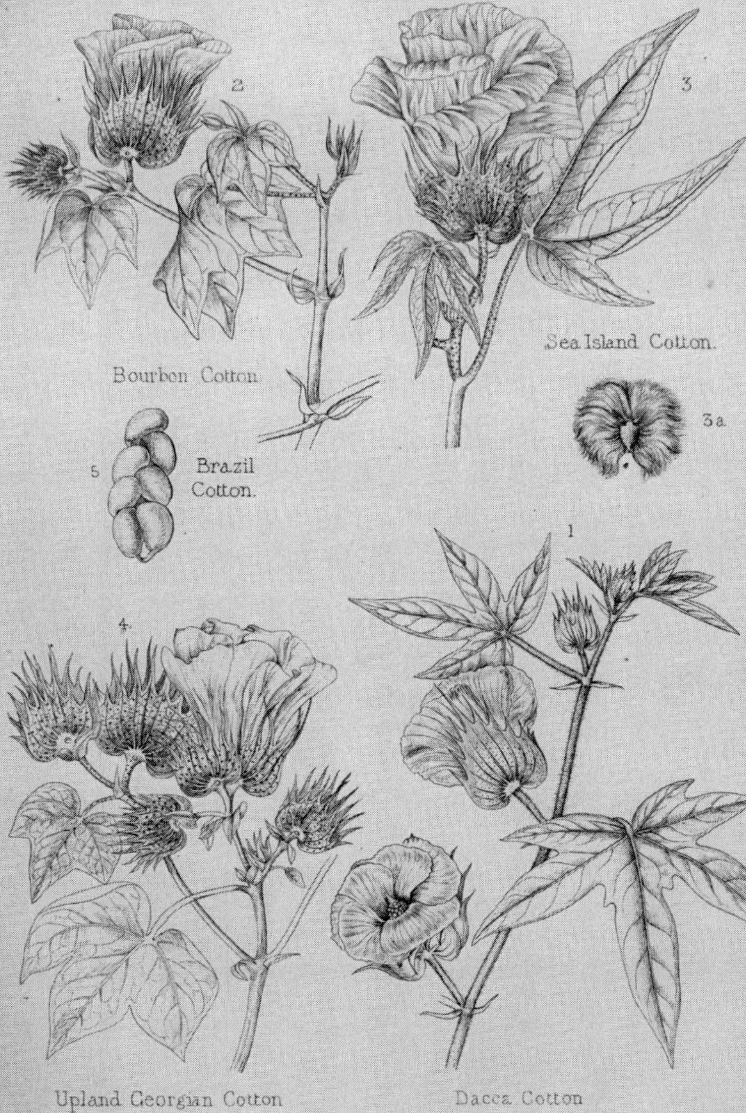

Ford & George, Lithographers, 54, Hatton Garden.

Sea Island, *Upland*, and *Bourbon* being all varieties of one species, proving how great is the influence of soil and climate in producing such changes, and encouraging us to study their respective habits, so as, if possible, to trace each to its true cause. We may thus be enabled to show, that if such changes take place in one country, we may be able to induce or prevent similar ones in another, by a due selection of sites, and by paying attention to the culture required for each variety, according to variations of soil and climate.

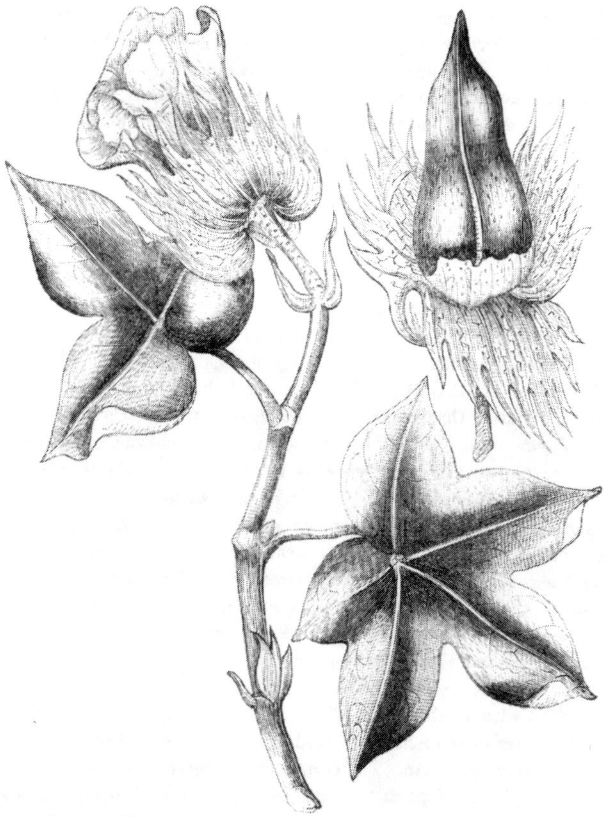

IV. G. peruvianum, or Brazil cotton.
Seeds, Plate iii., fig. 6.

G. PERUVIANUM, Cav., perennial, sub-arboreous, growing to ten or fifteen feet in height. Leaves, the lower and sometimes the upper ones entire, usually large, from three to five-lobed. Lobes oblong, tapering, very acute; the upper surface glabrous, the lower with scattered stellate pubescence, and one to three conspicuous glands. Stipules long, linear, and very acute, sometimes broad and dentate at apex. Bracts or exterior calyx large, dotted externally, broad, cordate, and auriculate, deeply laciniate, with a gland-like depression at base. The flowers large, yellow; the lobes convolutely imbricate; capsules long and large, ovoid at base, much pointed or acuminate at apex. Seeds, eight to ten, adhering firmly to each other, so as to form a cone-like mass, black, and free of every pubescence, except the long white wool, which is easily removed.—Cavanilles, Diss. 6, p. 113, tab. 168. Willd. Spec., Pl. 3, p. 806. D. C. Prod., i, p. 457. *G. acuminatum*, Roxburgh, Fl. Ind., iii, p. 186. Royle, Illustr. of Himal. Bot., p. 100. Wight, Illustr. of Indian Bot., t. xxvii. *G. vitifolium*, Roxb. Ic. ined. 1498; haud Fl. Ind. *G. brasiliense*, Macf. Fl. Jamaica, 1, 72, can only be this species.

This species, remarkable for its seeds adhering together in the form of a cone, includes the cottons of Pernambuco, Brazil, Bahia, and Peru. There are specimens in Sir W. Hooker's Herbarium from Guayaquil, Peru, Oahee, Buenos Ayres, St. Vincent, and East Florida. Dr. Roxburgh thought it was a native of the mountains to the north and westward of Bengal, but that it was never cultivated. He gave it the name of *G. acuminatum*, from the pointed character probably both of its leaves and capsules. The seeds had, however, been so frequently introduced into India, it is most probable that Dr. Roxburgh received specimens or seeds of some of the acclimatised plants. In Dr. Rottler's Herbarium it is named *G. vitifolium*, a name which is applied in Dr. Roxburgh's unpublished drawings to what must be this species. It has become perfectly naturalised in many parts of India. Mr. Randall (E. I. C.'s Papers, p. 90) describes it thus, "Brazil, or *kidney* cotton, is a tree which grows from ten to twelve feet in height, and which produces an immense number of pods, having the finest wool enveloped about conglomerated seeds;" and he states, that it succeeds well in moist situations, and that he had counted as many as 1000 pods upon a large plant. In Col. Sykes's collection there are specimens from Poona, where he states it is called *Deokupas*, and that Brahmins' sacerdotal threads are made with its cotton. Mr. Elphinston states, that plants are established in the Conkan, where also it is called *Deokupas*. Mr. Vaupell, in his account of the cottons of Guzerat, mentions having found several cotton plants growing in the enclosure of a temple at Sidhpoor, on the banks of the Surwati river. The seeds seemed to have been brought from a distance, and it was known by the name of the *Heergoonda-kupas*. Mr. Vaupell sowed some of the seeds on Bandera Hill near Bombay, and obtained plants which he, considering them to be a new species, named *G. imbricatum*, from the imbricate arrangement of the seeds; but it is no doubt only the acclimated cotton plant of Brazil. Respecting this kind of cotton, Koster says, in his account of Brazil, that "The districts which are chosen for the purpose, and universally allowed to be the best adapted for its growth, are far removed from the sea coast, arid, and oftentimes very scantily supplied with fresh water. The opinion is very general, that the cotton-plant will not thrive in the neighbourhood of the coast, and that frequent changes of weather are injurious to it, &c. The cotton-plant requires, that a great portion of the year should be dry; for if much rain falls when the seed is open, the wool is lost. The soil which is preferred for its culture is a deep red earth, with veins of yellow occasionally running through it: this becomes extremely hard after a long interval without rain. The cotton plantations are yearly receding further into the interior."

G. religiosum of Linnæus seems to be distinguished from other species only by having tawny-coloured cotton; but we have seen, that both the common Indian cotton, the Chinese cotton, the arboreous species, and *G. barbadense*, (*G. fuscum* Roxb. Ic. ined. 1497,) all occasionally produce *nankeen*-coloured cotton: and that, therefore, it cannot be considered as characteristic. The author supposes that the name was applied originally to *G. arboreum*, as that is called *Deo-kupas* in the Peninsula of India, whence Linnæus early received both specimens and information from some of his earliest pupils.

G. vitifolium is also only another name for varieties of *G. barbadense;* but the author believes, that the name is also applied even to specimens of the Brazil or Peruvian cotton, *G. peruvianum* (G. *acuminatum* of Roxburgh), as St. Hilaire, Gaudichaud, and Martius all mention *G. vitifolium* as cultivated in Brazil and the East, together with *G. herbaceum* and *G. barbadense.* Dr. Roxburgh's unpublished drawing, No. 1498, also named *G. vitifolium,* in no respect differs from his *G. acuminatum;* though the plant described by him in Fl. Ind., iii, p. 186, seems to be only a variety of *G. barbadense.*

The other species which appear to the author deserving of notice, are the following, though he is not aware that they yield any of the cottons of commerce:

G. racemosum, Poir. Suppl. 2, p. 370; D. C. sp. 13, said to yield the cotton of Porto-Rico, seems to be distinct, as its peduncles support two or three flowers, each with a pedicel. A specimen in Sir W. Hooker's Herb. agrees with the description, and was collected by Sleeman from Paccare. *G. tomentosum,* of Nuttal MSS., from the Sandwich Isles, appears distinct. *G. purpurascens,* Poir. Suppl. 11, p. 369, seems to be only a variety of *G. barbadense;* but the specimens in Herb. Hooker do not correspond with each other. One collected by Dr. Gardner in moist shady places near Crato, may be a variety of *G. barbadense.* The other from the Galapagos, with entire leaves, may be a variety of *G. peruvianum.* In Herb. Hooker there is a specimen with entire, cordate, acuminate leaves, from Magdalena Bay, Lower California, and is probably the plant referred to by Mr. Bentham, in 'Botany of Belcher's Voyage of the Sulphur.' Other species, which are mentioned as *G. latifolium, G. javanicum,* do not present sufficient characters to distinguish them from others of which they are most likely only varieties.

While this sheet is passing through the press, the author has received the following observations from Dr. Cleghorn, to whom he had shown, a short time previously, all the specimens of Gossypium in Sir W. Hooker's and his own Herbarium. Dr. Cleghorn writes from Edinburgh, 5th of July 1850, that he had "brought together all the Asiatic and American species of Gossypium to be found in the University collection (which comprises the Herbaria of Hamilton, Countess of Dalhousie, &c. with additions from Wight and Campbell)." "The collection is large enough to illustrate the fact that there has been an *excessive confusion and multiplication of species.* I believe all the specimens in the Herbarium at the University may be referred to:

1. *G. acuminatum,* Roxb. (The above *G. peruvianum.*)
2. *G. herbaceum,* Linn. (The above *G. indicum.*)
3. *G. arboreum,* Linn.
4. *G. barbadense,* Linn.

Of the first there is no good specimen; of No. 2 there are a great variety, bearing I know not how many names, such as, *Gossypium nigrum, G. nigrum læve, G. vitifolium, G. indicum, G. viridescens, G. rubicundum.* All of these appear to me manifestly the indigenous *G. herbaceum,* or country *kupas,* of the Peninsular ryots."

The result of our investigation of the species of the genus Gossypium is, that there are at least four distinct species which may be easily distinguished, and that the great mass, probably the whole of the cotton of commerce, is yielded by three of these species and their varieties. Whatever other species there may be, have been referred to above, as far as materials are available. But it is unnecessary for our present purpose to notice them in detail.

Gossypium indicum, Lamarck, *G. herbaceum*, Linn., tab. i and tab. ii, fig. 1, including under it various perennial and herbaceous varieties, yields the different kinds of Indian cotton, probably also much of the cotton of China. It extends from Arabia and Persia into Syria and Asia Minor, and along both shores of the Mediterranean. It is probable, that some of the African cottons are only varieties of this species; and there is no doubt, that seed has been taken from Smyrna and other places to America, and we might, therefore, meet with varieties of it even in the new world, though the kinds cultivated there belong to entirely different species.

G. arboreum is a species found in many parts of India, in gardens and clumps of trees, near temples, &c., but never cultivated in fields. It is commonly called *Nurma*, but in Mysore *Deo-kupas*. It is distinguished by its arboreous habit, thicker dark-green leaves, lobes with blunt angles, red flowers and silky cotton, which is preferred for making the sacerdotal thread of the Brahmins. It has been employed within the last few years for hybridising, in order, if possible, to obtain a variety which would produce good cotton and be well suited to India.

G. barbadense, Linn., or Barbadoes cotton, was early introduced from the West Indies into the Mauritius and the Isle of Bourbon, and from thence into the Peninsula of India, where its cotton was at one time called *Maurice*, but now Bourbon cotton. This variety has been established in many parts of India. The Sea Island, New Orleans, and Upland Georgian cotton are all varieties of this species, which seems to be a native of Mexico. Pl. iii, figs. 2, 3, 4, the seed fig. 5.

G. peruvianum, Cav., *G. acuminatum*, Roxb., distinguished especially by its black seeds adhering firmly to each other, yields the cotton of Brazil, Pernambuco, Maranham, Peru, &c. It has been long introduced into India, where it is in many places completely established, though grown only in small quantities, or as single plants near villages. Pl. iv & iii, fig. 6.

Having examined into the several plants which yield the cottons of commerce, and ascertained the exact nature of the substance which is called cotton, and then enumerated the principal commercial varieties, we may now proceed to treat of their culture.

§ 7. Chemical Analysis of Cotton and of Cotton-Seed.

Before determining on the soil which would, *à priori*, appear best suited for the production of the cotton-plant and its wool, we should refer to the chemical analysis of the ashes of an entire plant, so as to be certain about what it takes up from the soil: but, unfortunately, no such analysis, as far as we know, has yet been made. We know that, like all other vegetable matter, the cotton-plant must contain carbon, with oxygen, hydrogen, and nitrogen; all of which it may, and probably does, obtain from the atmosphere. The seeds secrete a good deal of oil, for which an excess of hydrogen will be required. We are glad to be able to refer to an analysis of the ashes of cotton-wool by Dr. Ure. This experienced chemist states, having slowly burned 2000 grains of clean Sea Island cotton in a silver basin, and then thoroughly incinerated the residuum at a red heat, so as to consume every particle of charcoal, a light gray ash was obtained, which, upon an average of six similar experiments, weighed 19 grains, being nearly one per cent. of the cotton-wool.

One hundred parts of these ashes yielded:

1. Matter soluble in water, 62 parts consisting of	
Carbonate of potash	44·8
Muriate of potash	9·9
Sulphate of potash	7·3
2. Matter insoluble in water:	
Phosphate of lime	9·9
Carbonate of lime	10·6
Phosphate of magnesia	8·4
Peroxide of iron	3·0
Alumina, water, and loss	5·0
	100·0

In addition to the above analysis of Sea Island Cotton, the author is indebted to Mr. Landon, lately in charge of the cotton experiments in Broach, and now settled there on his own account, for the following analyses of New Orleans cotton and seed, made by an American chemist in New Orleans, in the year 1843. The analysis of the cotton-seed is interesting, not only on its own account, but also as proving how valuable it must be as a manure to cotton-fields, as a great portion of the inorganic matter, forming a component of, and taken away by, the cotton, is returned to the soil.

"*Results of an Analysis of Cotton-Wool and Cotton-Seed, made in New Orleans in December* 1843.

1st Analysis.—Cotton-Wool.

One hundred parts of cotton-wool, on being heated in a platina crucible, lost 85·89 parts. The residuum, on being ignited under a muffle till the whole of the carbon was consumed, lost 12·735, and left a white ash which weighed nearly 1 per cent., or 0·937; of this ash nearly 44·00 was soluble in water. Its constituents were as follows:—

Carbonate of potassa (with a trace of soda)	44·29
Phosphate of lime (with a trace of magnesia)	25·34
Carbonate of lime	8·97
Ditto magnesia	6·75
Silica	4·12
Sulphate of potassa	2·90
Alumina	1·40
Chloride of potassium, Do. magnesium, Sulphate of lime, Phosphate of potassa, Oxide of iron (a trace) and loss	6·23
	100·00

Supposing the carbonic acid in the above-mentioned salts to have been derived during the incineration of the cotton, the following will more certainly express the important mineral ingredients abstracted by the cotton from the soil for every 100 parts of its ash:

Potassa	31·05
Lime	17·09
Magnesia	3·24
Phosphoric acid	12·32
Sulphuric acid	1·20
	64·90

So that for every 10,000 lbs. of cotton-wool, about 60 lbs. of the above-mentioned ingredients are abstracted from the soil, in the proportion indicated by the following figures, omitting the fractions:

Potassa	31 lbs.
Lime	12 "
Magnesia	3 "
Phosphoric acid	12 "
Sulphuric acid	1 "

2d ANALYSIS.—COTTON-SEED.

One hundred parts, heated as before, lost 77·387, and the residuum, after being burned under a muffle, left 3·936 parts of a perfectly white ash, the composition of which was as follows:

Phosphate of lime (with traces of magnesia)		61·34
Ditto potassa (traces of soda)		31·73
Sulphate of potassa		2·65
Silica		1·68
Carbonate of lime		47
Ditto magnesia		27
Chloride of potassium		25
Carbonate of potassa	and loss	1·63
Sulphate of lime		
Sulphate of magnesia		
Alumina, and oxides of iron and manganese		
		100·00

A comparison of the above table with that afforded by the cotton-wool, will show a great dissimilarity between the two.

The ash of the cotton-seed is four-fold that of the fibre, while the former has also three times as much phosphoric acid as the latter, as will appear on presenting the analysis in a form corresponding with the second table under cotton-wool.

Phosphoric acid	45·35
Lime	29·79
Potassa	19·40
Sulphuric acid	1·16
	95·70"

The information afforded by these analyses is interesting, and would be still more so, if it referred to the ashes of entire plants, instead of to the ashes of cotton and cotton-seed only. It is to be hoped, that planters will carefully dry entire specimens of the plants of different kinds of cotton, and place them in the hands of chemists, taking care, at the same time, to ascertain the loss sustained, by weighing the plants both before and after the process of drying; or, if they are sufficiently careful, they might burn the plants when dry, taking care that no additions are made, and then submit the ashes, carefully preserved in glass stoppered bottles, to a scientific chemist.

The chemical characteristics of cotton, as detailed in Dr. Thomson's 'Vegetable Chemistry,' may be here enumerated, to give a more complete view of the subject. It is well known that cotton is insoluble in water, alcohol, ether, oils, and in all vegetable acids. Chlorine gas bleaches cotton: diluted alkaline leys have no perceptible action on it; but the strong alkalis dissolve it when assisted by heat. Sulphuric acid chars it. Nitric acid, in certain proportions, converts it into colladone, or the gun-cotton of Schönbein, and, when assisted by heat, into oxalic acid. When distilled, it yields a great portion of acidulous water, and a small quantity of oil, but no ammonia. The ashes were known to Neumann to contain some potash. Cotton has a strong affinity for alumina; hence this earth is used to fix colours in cotton; the cloth being dipped in a strong solution of alum, or acetate of alumina, and afterwards dyed. Several of the metallic oxides of iron and of tin combine readily with cotton; so also tannin. Hence the infusion of galls and of other astringent substances are often used as mordants for cotton.

The seeds have frequently been employed in countries where the cotton is grown, to form pectoral emulsions. This is in consequence of the oil which they contain along with mucilaginous and saccharine principles. Being, therefore, nutritious, and not repugnant in taste, the seeds are universally employed in India for feeding cattle. An oil also is expressed from them, and this is used as a lamp-oil.

Attention has been turned of late years to the oil of cotton-seed, and an apparatus has been constructed to free the seeds of the short down or fuzz, before subjecting them to pressure in the oil-press.*

The oil is of a brownish colour with a slight tinge of green, and is compared by Messrs. Miller and Arthur to "oil expressed from partially-scorched linseed;" they "think that it would not come into general use as a burning oil, unless very much under the price of linseed oil. It will not suit the purposes of machinery or of leather-dressing; but we entertain no doubt, that large quantities of it would be purchased by parties who, like ourselves, boil and refine oils." (*Transactions of Highland Society*, March 1850.) It might be useful in wool-dressing.

Dr. Anderson, chemist to the Highland Society, had sent to him by Mr. Robert Burn, some of the refuse cake obtained

* The author has been consulted about the method adopted in America for getting rid of the down from the black-seeded cotton, as it was supposed that this must have been effected by some mechanical means!

after the expression of the oil. Dr. Anderson thus describes it (l. c., p. 263):

"The cake has a brown colour, and contains large fragments of the husk of the seed. It is very brittle, and breaks down much more readily than linseed oil-cake. Moistened with water, it appears to be much less mucilaginous than that substance. Its taste is not unpleasant. In its analysis I have pursued the method usually employed for linseed-cake, determining simply those constituents upon which its feeding-value is believed to depend.

Water	11·19
Oil	9·08
Sugar	10·70
Albuminous compounds (nitrogen = 3·95)	24·69
Ash	5·64

The ash contains

Silica	1·32
Phosphates	2·19
Excess of Phosphoric acid	0·15

By comparing these results with those of linseed-cake, I find that this substance possesses very considerable feeding properties. The quantity of oil contained in linseed-cake varies from 9 to 11, and is sometimes even as high as 12 per cent., and the quantity of nitrogen is about 4·5 per cent. These are the most important constituents of an oil-cake, and those by which its value is to be mainly determined; and the analysis, although it fixes the value of cotton-cake below that of oil-cake, shows it to be sufficiently high to make it a substance of very great importance to the farmer."

§ 8. Analysis of Cotton Soils.

In inquiring into the nature of the soils best suited to the culture of cotton, we have first to determine whether we should take the soil of the wild or that of the cultivated plant as our standard. There is no doubt, that, in cultivating a new plant, it is of the first importance to obtain accurate and detailed information respecting the site, soil, and climate in which it is found growing naturally: as, for instance, if we could obtain and attempt to grow any of the valuable Cinchonas, or the Myrrh tree or Rosewood, in new situations. But with a well-cultivated plant, the case is different. In the first place, we are unacquainted with the wild state of many of our most extensively cultivated plants, and no one need search for wild Wheat before he commences cultivating that most valuable and now generally diffused cereal; because, in fact, success has given much, if not all, the information for which we are obliged to seek in the case of a new plant. Culture, moreover, is calculated to favour the secretion of some, and to promote the formation of other products of plants: as, to cite familiar instances, is the case with the carrot and the lettuce, neither of which should we take in their wild state as guides in cultivation, unless we wished to employ them as medicines. In the case of cotton, the product is a natural one; but we have only vague information respecting the plants in a wild state, and no proof of the quality of the staple, nor of the quantity in which this is produced; both of which are most important considerations for the planter, who looks to profit. We shall, therefore, take the soils of cotton fields where that staple is already produced, as examples which it is desirable to imitate or to avoid, though not neglecting any information obtainable from the state of the same plants in a wild state, because these often give us hints respecting their powers of existence under different circumstances.

Sea Island cotton is cultivated on a range of islands lying along the coast of South Carolina and of Georgia, from 32° 30′ to 30° of N. lat. These islands are described as having been the abode of a tribe of red Indians, who were fishermen rather than hunters; and that the accumulation of oysters, clambs, and other shells mingled with bones and pottery, is astonishingly great, and these have become intimately mixed with the sandy soil and decayed vegetables into a peculiar loam, of a light and fertile nature.

Mr. Piddington, of Calcutta, having received some of this Sea Island cotton-soil (No. 1), describes it, when dry, as appearing like a mixture of fine dark-gray sand and charcoal dust, with fragments of shells, wood, both dry and charred, twigs, leaves, and even the shells of cotton seeds; but the label sent with it stated, "In order to view this soil as it is, wet it, as though a shower of rain had fallen upon it." Upon sifting nine ounces of this soil, eight ounces passed through muslin, as fine sand mixed with dark charcoal-looking dust. The remaining ounce was coarse sand, with fragments of shells and vegetable rubbish. Upon burning some of the dark-coloured powder in a glass tube, acrid and highly disagreeable smoke was evolved, such as characterises the peats and lignites. From this Mr. Piddington considers it to be lignite or peaty matter, in the state of very fine powder, of which a portion is readily taken up by cold water. Another specimen (No. 2,) of Sea Island cotton-soil, of a uniform brown colour, was also analysed.

On analysis, 100 parts of the fine sifted part of these soils yielded :

	No. 1.	No. 2.
Saline matter, muriate of lime and soda, but no potass	0·20	0·60
Vegetable matter, mostly lignite or peaty powder, with a little water	3·20	5·00
Iron (protoxide)	1·00	1·30
Lime (carbonate)	2·75	4·00
Alumina	0·20	0·63
Silex	92·00	88·02
	99·35	99·55
Water and loss	·65	·45
	100	100

Uplands Georgian cotton received its name from being cultivated in the interior of that state. From the sea-coast to the interior, for a considerable breadth, the country is level, and the soil a sandy loam. Beyond these plains stretch the hilly undulating tracts, which have a deep black loamy soil. Analyses of these soils have been made both by Mr. Piddington and by Professor E. Solly. The former obtained some Upland cotton soil, from what was stated to be one of the best estates. It was a light, fawn-coloured, sandy soil, with coarse particles of silex, of felspar, and of shells, some peaty, much divided vegetable matter, but without any saline matter. Analysis yielded :

Extractive matter, but no saline	0·10
Vegetable matter, peat or lignite	4·60
Iron, protoxide	1·25
Alumina	1·00
Lime, carbonate of	2·90
Silex, coarse grains	89·35
	99·20
Water and loss	·80
	100·00

Professor E. Solly analysed the soils of four Georgian cotton farms, obtained by Lord Palmerston from Mr. Consul Molyneux. One plantation was much elevated, the land of a deep chocolate colour, and yielding from 1000 to 1500 lbs. of seed-cotton to the acre; a second was said to produce the best cotton in the state of Georgia; a third was situated in a limestone region, "which invariably grows a good product;" a fourth was a specimen of poor land, and the quality of its cotton is what is termed "deficient in staple." Mr. Solly observes, that these were all of a similar nature, their difference being merely in the relative quantity of their constituents; the structure of all was light, porous and friable, of such a nature as to possess a considerable retentive power for water, and yet, from its openness, to allow of sufficient degree of drainage. They consist mostly of sand, the poorest of little else. They also all contain alumina, oxide of iron, and manganese, but with hardly any lime. The organic matters consist either of decayed portions of plants, &c., or very finely divided and soluble matter; these in the soils vary from 4 to 8 per cent., and in the subsoils from 1 to 1½ to 4 per cent. The soils also contain traces of saline matter.

Cotton culture, it is well known, extended from Georgia into South Carolina, west into the hilly country, and into all the southern states, that is, into the alluvial plains of the Alabama and Mississippi. The soil here is a rich fertile alluvium, of a blackish colour, no doubt containing much organic matter; but we have seen no analysis of it.

The soil of these regions is described by planters, without referring to their chemical analyses, as extending, from the sea coast to one hundred miles into the interior, as a level tract, consisting of sandy loam, covered with pine (*pine-barrens*), a mixture of sand 8 to 10 inches deep, with clay and loam. Beyond this plain, undulating hills stretch backwards, till they unite with the Apalachian chain. These waving tracts are described as among the pleasantest and finest in the United States, especially on the river Savannah and its western and north-western branches, where the soil is a deep black loam. Mr. Spalding states, "that the short-stapled cotton is of a better quality when raised near the sea than at a great distance from it, and it thrives most luxuriantly in alluvial soils, a little impregnated with salt, as in some of the districts of Louisiana. There the soils, which are deeply tinged with red, and well seasoned with salt, between the waters of the Arkansa and the Red river, give forth the most abundant crops of the best quality of that description of cotton." (Ure, l. c., p. 115.) But the red soil of the interior of Georgia is said to give a tinge to the wool grown upon it, and that the gray soil produces a finer crop. Mr. Spalding further says, that several varieties of the short staple cotton "grow well and perfect their fruit all the way from the southern borders of Virginia to the south-western streams of the Mississippi, and in every soil, whether clay, loam, or sand, provided the waters be kept well drained from the surface of the land." (Ure, l. c., pp. 115-16.) Mr. Seabrook considers a light sand to be the best soil for the Sea Island cotton-plant; but that, "for high and loose sandy soils, salt, mud, and green marsh grass, or rushes, are now commonly put under the sward on which the bed is to be made several weeks or months before seed-time. For low close lands, fresh cotton-seed, pine-straw, marsh rushes, or any substance rotted in the cow-house, may be used;" though "on the Mississippi, the growers of cotton think, that new land does not produce so fine a quality of cotton as that which has previously borne two crops of grain." Excess of food, Mr. Seabrook observes, "produces a large and luxuriant stalk, but renders the fruit scanty."

Mr. Piddington also analysed some cotton soil of the best description from the Mauritius. This consisted of saline, and extractive, with vegetable matter, protoxide of iron, and of carbonate of lime, as much as 40·85 per cent., with a trace of magnesia, alumina, and silex. Some soil from Singapore, in which good cotton had been grown, was found to resemble the peaty soil of the Sea Island cotton, with only a trace of iron, no alumina, and little carbonate of lime or saline matter. The Egyptian soil, in which excellent cotton is cultivated, is described to be of a sandy nature, but enriched by the deposits of the Nile.

In contrast with these soils, it is desirable to compare those in which cotton is cultivated in India. Of these, one is distinguished by the name of the " Black Cotton Soil," in which native cotton is much cultivated, and which seems to extend, with very little variation, from Bundlecund nearly to the south of the Peninsula. Mr. Piddington describes the soil when dry as a dark brown heavy clay, interspersed with soft nodules of *kunkur* (or calcareous concretion, containing from 50 to 80 per cent. of carbonate of lime, some magnesia, iron, and alumina), which forms with water a tenacious clay, that dries into tough lumps. This, indeed, is the characteristic of the black cotton soil, which forms a tenacious mud in the rains, and dries into a hard black clay, crossed by innumerable deep fissures and cracks in the hot winds. It differs from the American soils, in displaying no trace, when heated, of any lignite or peaty matters; the lime is in larger proportion, and the silex in the state of a fine powder. Mr. Piddington's analysis corresponds very nearly with one given by Dr. Spry. Professor E. Solly obtained 9 per cent. of carbonate of lime in a specimen of black cotton soil sent by Capt. Newbold, which he examined.

	Bundlecund.	Coimbatore.
Vegetable matter	2·00	2·30
Saline	0·33	trace
Iron protoxide and extractive	7·75	4·00
Lime, carbonate of	11·90	7·50
Magnesia	trace	trace
Alumina	3·10	2·80
Silex	74· 0	82·80
	99· 0	99·40
Water and loss	1· 0	·60
	100· 0	100·00

The *red* soil of India, which is produced by the disintegration of granitic rocks, and in which American cotton has been usually found to succeed better than in the black soil, differs from this, especially in the iron being in the state of *peroxide*, or red oxide. It may be described as a coarse yellowish red soil, intermixed with small fragments of *kunkur*, of silex, felspar, and aluminous earth. The fine parts consisted of about one half, and on analysis yielded:

Extractive and saline matter	0·20
Vegetable matter	0·15
Iron peroxide, with some carbonate	2·88
Carbonate of lime	19·50
Magnesia	0·15
Alumina	2.00
Silex	74·00
	98·88
Loss	1·12
	100·

Mr. Piddington, having given the results of his analyses in a tabular form, they are here republished from the *Transactions of the Agricultural Society of India*, vol. vi, p. 216.

Tabular View, with Notes, of the Analyses of Cotton-Soils. By H. Piddington, Esq.

No.	COTTON SOILS.	Vegetable matter.	Saline, and extractive, *geine?*	Iron.		Carbonate lime.	Magnesia.	Alumina.	Silex.	Water and loss.	Price of best Cottons in Liverpool.	REMARKS.
				Protox.	Deutox.							
	AMERICAN.										*d.*	
1	Georgia Sea Island . . .	3·20	0·20	1·0	—	2·75	—	0·20	92·00	0·85	24	Vegetable matter peat or lignite; partly soluble in cold water. Silex in coarse grains.
2	*Supposed Georgia* Sea Island	5·00	0·60	1·30	—	4·00	—	0·63	88·02	0·45	24	Ditto.
3	Upland Georgia	4·60	0·10	1·25	—	2·90	—	1·00	89·35	0·75	12	Vegetable matter peat or lignite, but nothing soluble in cold water. No saline matters.
	INDIAN.											
4	Bundlecund	2·00	0·33	—	7·75	11·90	trace	3·10	74·0	1·00	5	No peat or lignite. Nothing soluble in cold water. Silex in fine powder. *Kunkur* in the gravel.
5	Coimbatore	2·30	traces	4·00	—	7·50	trace	2·80	82·80	0·60	5	Gravel mostly silex, with some felspar, but no *kunkur*.
6	Bourbon-seed cotton (Tinnevelly?)	0·15	0·20	—	2·88	19·50	0·15	2·00	74·00	1·12	10	Gravel almost wholly *kunkur*. Some carbonate of iron. Half the soil of gravel.
7	MAURITIUS	1·75	0·30	9·15	—	40·85	trace	2·50	43·60	1·85	12?	Silex mostly coarse-grained. Gravel mostly calcareous.
	SINGAPORE.											
8	Best soil	9·15	0·60	—	0·25	1·25	—	—	88·20	0·55	9	Vegetable matter mostly peaty, and very soluble.
9	Inferior soil	1·00	—	—	0·71	0·07	—	—	98·85	—	4	Vegetable matter peaty.

With respect to the practical inferences deducible from the chemical analyses, we may first quote the opinion of Mr. Piddington, that carbonate of lime was essential to good cotton soil. Subsequently he observed, that the American, the Mauritius, and the best Singapore soil contain a considerable per centage of vegetable matter, and some part of it easily soluble in cold water, while the Indian soils contain very little vegetable matter, and this wholly insoluble in water; but that the best contain a far larger proportion of carbonate of lime, and, some of them, their iron in a different state from the others. The lime, though not indispensable, he supposes, may be highly useful; but he ascribes greater value to the presence of vegetable matter. For in a soil in Bengal, which contained but exceeding minute portions of lime and carbonaceous matter, he cultivated cotton, worth from 9*d.* to 11*d.* per lb., as an experiment, for seven or eight years, during which he had always good and often abundant crops. This effect he ascribes to the plants having been constantly manured with the black, peaty earth, so abundant in the jheels (pieces of water) of India, and of which an average good specimen contains 26 per cent. of vegetable matter, and 15 per cent. of carbonate of lime, yielded chiefly by the small shells contained in the above deposits.

Dr. Ure, referring to his own results, long since remarked, that the chemical analysis of cotton-wool throws "considerable light on the predilection of the cotton-plant for the neighbourhood of the sea, as this supplies plentifully the saline substances requisite to the perfect development and constitution of its woolly fruit, and that it enables us to infer, that the compost or manure best fitted for cotton plantations should contain neutro-saline matter, with alkaline, calcareous, and magnesian bases, and that the presence of magnesia deserves notice, as it indicates marine food. But with respect to the absence of soda salts from the ashes of cotton, he observes, "Here, as in many other examples, the vegetative powers of the roots seem to eliminate potash from the stone detritus of the soil, which replaces the soda in the sea salts. For otherwise we should have found salts with a basis of soda, instead of potash salts in the ashes of the cotton." But as only the cotton was submitted to examination, it is quite possible, that the soda-salts, if such are necessary to the plant, might be detected in the stem, branches, or leaves; that is, in the parts of vegetation.

The American chemist observes, that the ashes of cotton-seed are fourfold that of the fibre, and that the former contains three times as much phosphoric acid as the latter. In respect to the phosphoric acid and the lime, the quantity of both these substances is greater in the American analysis than in that of Dr. Ure. Whether this may be owing to different kinds of wool having been employed, or to differences in the soils in which they have been grown, can only be known when the analyses have been repeated by chemists with different kinds of cotton. The subject is well worthy the attention of Mr. Assist.-Surgeon Meyen, of the Madras Medical Service, who has made so admirable an analysis of the mineral constituents of the flax-plant, and of the soils in which the plant had been grown. (*Journal of the Chemical Society.*)

Prof. E. Solly, as the result of his analyses, remarks, "that the goodness of the soils from Georgia depended, probably, far more on the mechanical structure than on the chemical composition, and that the presence of lime or any other substance would appear of far less importance than that the soil should be, not too rich, but of a light and porous character, so that the delicate fibres of the roots might penetrate easily in all directions." This opinion is probably not far from the truth wherever the climate is most suitable to the cultivation of cotton.

Dr. Wight, after practical experience of some years, states, that were it is in his power to choose, he prefers "a deep dark coloured light almost sandy loam, and if it has been long out of cultivation so much the better." The black cotton soil in which so much of the cotton of India is grown, and which is generally considered the best for the purpose, is remarkable for its power of retaining moisture; while of the red soil he says, "again I am informed that in some parts of the country, for example, in the Vizagapatam district, the finest cotton crops, both as to quantity and quality, are raised on red soils, and the redder the better for the purpose." But the suitableness of these several soils must be considered in connexion with climate.

In endeavouring to draw practical inferences from the composition of soils, it is first of all necessary to observe that, though no one will dispute the paramount importance of the chemical constituents, yet these may be considered in some respects to be only of comparative value, since it is equally necessary to attend to the mechanical state of the soil, and to both in connexion with the climate of particular localities. The mechanical state of a soil, its greater or less degree of porosity or of tenacity, enabling the roots to spread with more or less facility, so as to fix the plant steadily in the earth, at the same time that they supply it with a large portion of its nutriment, is necessarily of great importance. But as a considerable portion of the food of plants is supplied by the air, its different states and due supply require also to be attended to, in addition to climate. No chemical composition or mechanical state will compensate for unsuitableness of climate. We all know that our oaks are as little likely to flourish within the tropics as South American palms in our meadows, and no one expects that our rich variety of orchids would flourish, if, supplying them with every requisite of site, of soil, of culture, and even of temperature, we denied them a moist atmosphere. And yet a few years only have elapsed since it was considered a rarity to flower these air-plants; and also since mountain rice was attempted to be cultivated here in the open air, because it came from a cool climate, and was said to be cultivated without irrigation. But it was forgotten that, during the season of cultivation in its native mountains, rain falls almost every day, and the air is in a state of continual moisture. So, also, in the culture of cotton, a certain state of the soil, both with respect to its chemical composition and its mechanical state, may be well suited to one situation, and yet not be desirable in another, chiefly from a difference in the condition of the atmosphere. For instance, a certain degree of porosity of the soil may retain and bring just enough of water within reach of the roots, and yet if the atmosphere became more damp, the soil may require to be made drier by drainage. Again, if in another situation the air is more dry, and evaporation necessarily greater, both from the surface of the earth and from that of the leaves, a soil more retentive of moisture will be more suitable than one which is more open, and which thus allows moisture to escape, not only by evaporation but by drainage. These varieties may be observed not only in the soil and climate of different localities, but even in the same locality at different seasons of the year, especially in a country like India, which, in the language of meteorologists, has a climate in many parts of great extremes. As plants obtain from the ground their water, holding in solution saline and earthy particles, and are dependent upon the air for the elements of organic matter, it is evidently essential to pay equal attention to both, for it is difficult, nay impossible in most cases, to say whether the soil or the climate has the most influence upon successful cultivation, and it is nearly as useless, to use the words of Mr. J. S. Mill, as "attempting to decide which half of a pair of scissors has most to do in the act of cutting, or which of the factors 5 and 6 contributes most to the production of thirty." *

§ 9. Climate of Cotton Districts.

In inquiring into the climate best suited to the Cultivation of Cotton, we must remember that we have to pay attention not only to the air, but also to the vapour. These may be considered in some respects as forming two distinct atmospheres; the one uniform in quantity and in the proportion of its ingredients, but ever varying in temperature; while the vapour varies not only in this respect, but in the quantity in which it is present, and also in its point of deposition, when alone it becomes perceptible as moisture. Cotton is cultivated in so great a variety of countries, that we cannot but expect it to be capable of flourishing in considerable diversities of climate. Thus the rich alluvial lands of the Mississippi differ not only in soil, but also in temperature and dryness, from the sandy fields of Georgia. In dryness both must differ from the uniformity of moisture which prevails in the islands where Sea Island cotton is produced. Some grows naturally in the hot parts of Mexico, and much is cultivated in the moist parts of Guiana and of Brazil. Humboldt has seen it at 9000 feet of elevation

* The subject of the physical requirements of the cotton plant and its culture, were treated of by the author, in a series of articles in the *Gardener's Chronicle*, at the request of its distinguished editor. They are here republished, with additions.

in the Equinoctial Andes, and at 5500 feet in Mexico. But here different species may perhaps be included, as we know that the species yielding Pernambuco cotton is cultivated in many parts of South America. In the Old World we find cotton growing in the interior both of Africa and of India, where there must be considerable dryness of climate. It is cultivated successfully in Egypt, and also of late near Port Natal, but in the former only by the aid of irrigation. It is produced in various islands of the Indian Ocean, in many parts of China, and in almost every part of the Continent of India. From thence it may be said to extend into Persia and Asia Minor, and from thence to the southern parts of Europe, including the islands of the Mediterranean, whence our English manufacturers received their earliest supplies of cotton.

Within these limits, extending from the equator to 40° of latitude, we know that there are considerable diversities of climate; but the summer temperature of many of these localities does not differ so much as might be expected from their latitudes. The temperature of tropical regions is known to be modified by the greater moisture, while that of the interior of continents, even in high latitudes, is increased by the greater clearness of sky, which is dependent on the comparative absence of moisture. This cause tends to increase even the cold of winter, from the more free radiation which takes place at night in a cloudless atmosphere. Humboldt has remarked, that Gossypium barbadense, hirsutum, and religiosum have their favorite climate, from 0° to 34° of latitude, where the annual mean temperature is from 82° to 68°, but that G. herbaceum is successfully cultivated in the temperate zone, where, with a mean summer heat of 73° to 75°, that of winter is not less than 46° or 48°.

In taking, however, a general survey of the localities where cotton is chiefly cultivated, we cannot but observe, that many of them are in islands, and others in the vicinity of the sea. This is certainly the case with the districts where the finest cottons are produced, and the largest returns per acre obtained. It has frequently been stated, that the beneficial effects of such localities are chiefly due to the presence of salt in the soil, or to its being carried up in the spray, which is transported by winds into the interior. Koster, in his 'Travels in Brazil,' states, on the contrary, that "the districts which are universally allowed to be the best adapted for the growth of cotton, are far removed from the sea-coast, arid, and oftentimes very scantily supplied with water. Also, that the opinion is very general, that the cotton-plant will not thrive in the neighbourhood of the coast, and also that plantations were yearly receding further into the interior, the soil preferred being a deep red earth, which becomes extremely hard after a long interval without rain." Something must, no doubt, be owing to the species which is cultivated, and something to the climate of the plantation being more or less moist. Thus Spix and Martius, in their 'Travels,' state "that the cotton-tree cultivated at Rio (G. barbadense, L., sometimes, but more rarely the G. herbaceum,* L.) thrives very well, but is said not to furnish such durable materials as that in the higher and drier districts of Minos Novos."

Vicinity to the sea has, however, other peculiarities besides the facility of affording saline ingredients to the soil or to the atmosphere. It participates, to a certain degree, in the peculiarities of an insular climate; that is, in greater uniformity of temperature than is found in places further in the interior, and in a greater freedom of circulation of air from the usually alternating land and sea breezes. There is also greater equability of moisture, for air passing over the surface of the sea necessarily takes up a large proportion of water. This it does not immediately deposit on the coast, unless this is backed by hills, because it usually becomes a little warmed by the heated land, and is then capable of taking up a little more moisture. But as it does reach the coast in a comparatively moist state, it necessarily rather checks than favours excessive evaporation, and thus does not force the foliage exposed to its influence to give up an undue quantity of moisture. This, however, is necessarily the case whenever a dry current of air passes over the surface of leaves. To the influence of moisture, therefore, we must ascribe the more luxuriant vegetation of some sea coasts, as, for instance, that of the south of Devonshire, and of many tropical islands and coasts. With respect to cotton, the author, in his 'Illust. of Himal. Botany,' observed, that so

* Under these names are probably included varieties of *G. Barbadense* and *G. Peruvianum*, as defined in this work.

few meteorological registers give the dryness and moisture of a climate, as well as its temperature, that he was unable to draw any just conclusions, but that "an insular climate, though comparatively moist, may be useful from the equability of temperature, the freedom of atmospheric circulation which promotes evaporation, as much as from mere vicinity to the sea."

§ 10. Climate of North American Cotton Districts.

In inquiring more particularly into the climate best suited to the American Cotton-plant, not only in its native country, but in the countries where its culture is most successfully conducted, we must remember what both Baron Humboldt and Professor Dove have pointed out, that while Europe has a true insular or sea climate both in winter and summer, North America inclines to a continental climate in winter and to a sea climate in summer; that is, has a cold winter with a cool summer. But northern and central Asia have a true continental climate both in winter and summer, or a cold winter and a hot summer. Notwithstanding this, we must also recollect, that though each locality may participate in the characteristic climate of its continent, yet that all places near the coast will have more or less of an insular climate, while those in the interior have such as are of a continental nature, though in varying degrees.

The different kinds of cotton cultivated in the United States of America appear in the present day, and as far as we have been able to procure satisfactory information, to be varieties of one species, that is, that the Georgian is the Sea Island carried into the interior; the Sea Island itself was originally introduced from Anguilla, one of the West India Islands. The New Orleans does not differ specifically from the Sea Island cotton, and is admitted by the planters of the southern states of America to be identical with the plant of Mexico, from whence indeed they import their finest seeds. It is probable, that it was from the neighbouring coast of Mexico that the indigenous cotton of that country was introduced into the West Indies, and from thence it was taken to the Island of Bourbon. Hence we may account for Gossypium Barbadense being identical in species with both the New Orleans and Sea

Island cottons as well as with Bourbon cotton, as is evident from the coloured representations given of these three varieties by Dr. Wight.

The Mexican plant is not a native of the temperate regions of that country, but of the Tierras Calientes, or hot districts. It is produced, for instance, in the neighbourhood of Vera Cruz, and is described as growing spontaneously near Valladolid, a town situated on the great plain of the peninsula of Yucatan, described by Humboldt as one of the warmest regions in equinoctial America. Mr. Stephens states, that the spontaneous growth of cotton around that town had led to the erection of a cotton factory in the place. Mr. Norman, in his 'Rambles in Yucatan,' says: "The cotton plantations, or rather the districts where the material is raised that is consumed in the manufactory in this city, are to the north, and known as the Tizemen district. The same spot is seldom cultivated for two successive seasons. After the crop is gathered, the ground is suffered to be overrun with weeds and brushwood; which, when years have elapsed, are cut down and burned, and the field is replanted." This rude method of culture is adduced only to show how little attention is paid to the plant in its native country. But as it is desirable to know something precise respecting the climate of one at least of its native districts, we take from Professor Dove the following notice of the means of observations made at Vera Cruz for 13 years. This town, situated on the coast in N. lat. 19·12, and W. long. 96·9, has a mean temperature of 77°·02, with a difference of only 12°·42 between the hottest and coldest months: thus—

Jan.	Feb.	March.	April.	May.	June.	July.	Aug.	Sept.	Oct.	Nov.	Dec.
69·98	71·60	73·40	72·17	80·48	81·86	81·50	82·40	80·96	78·44	75·38	71·06

The Mexican cotton has been introduced into Texas as well as into Louisiana and Alabama. In the southern parts of Texas, where the climate is described as being very congenial, "the plant does not require to be renewed more frequently than once in three or four years to yield a crop superior in quality and quantity to the annual planting of Louisiana." Mr. Kennedy informs us, in his work on Texas, that cotton planting commences there in February, and picking begins at an earlier, and continues for a longer period than in the United States; also, that the average return on the acre is considerably greater in Texas than in the States, and the expense of cultivation considerably less, in consequence not only of the greater richness of the soil, but also of the superior mildness of the climate. The cotton is, moreover, of a superior quality, and that "planters of acknowledged veracity stated that it is not uncommon to pick 4000lbs. of seed-cotton from an acre of ground." But, in connexion with this statement, we must not forget that Mr. Spalding, himself an American cotton planter, says, "The besetting sin of agricultural statements is their exaggeration."

Mr. Featherstonhaugh, after crossing into northern Texas, in about lat. 33° 40′, from the United States, observes, that he had never seen the cotton-plant growing in greater perfection before; for in the cotton districts he had passed through, the plant was a low dwarfed bush, not exceeding two feet in height, but here the bushes were five feet high, often bearing 300 bolls, and yielding from 1500 to 2500 lbs. of seed-cotton to the acre. This gives from 25 to 30 per cent. in weight of raw marketable cotton. He states, that it is considered a fair crop if one bale of 450 lbs. to the acre of such cotton is produced. The most successful cultivation of cotton in the United States is in Louisiana, Mississippi, and Alabama. In the southern parts of these states—as, for instance, in the latitudes of New Orleans and of Mobile, there is little frost, and the winter is considered mild, with considerable heat in summer, but this is tempered to a great extent by the pleasant and salutary effects of the sea breeze, which sets in from the Gulph of Mexico for a great part of the day. There are heavy dews at night, and frequent showers occur both in spring and during the summer. In the interior and more northern parts of these states (which are in some parts elevated from 500 to 1000 feet above the level of the sea), frost is expected in October, and continues till near April, sometimes it occurs even in May, so as to injure, though it does not then destroy, the cotton-plant. The heat of summer is considerable, but still tempered by the influence of the Gulf of Mexico, and of the numerous great rivers, as well as by dews and occasional showers of rain. The cultivation of cotton is commenced about the beginning of April, when the land is still saturated with the winter rains, and difficulty is sometimes experienced in getting the land sufficiently dry;

otherwise a good shower of rain is essential when cotton is first sown, and it is desirable also to have occasional showers during the planting, ploughing, and hoeing seasons. The bolls of cotton begin to open about the middle of July, and continue doing so until the frosts come on in the middle or end of October. The yield is about 400 lbs. of clean cotton to the acre.

In order to have a precise idea of the climates of the most favorable cotton districts, and for the advantage of comparing them with that of other countries into which it may be wished to introduce the American cotton, we select, from Professor Dove's Tables, as published by the British Association, the following mean temperatures of places in Texas, Louisiana, Mississippi, and Alabama, as indicated by their initial letters.

Mean Temperatures.

	Lat. N.	Lon. W.	Jan.	Feb.	March.	April.	May.	June.	July.	Aug.	Sept.	Oct.	Nov.	Dec.	Mean of Year.
1. Galveston, T.	29°18′	95°1′	60·3	62·5	75·0	73·2	83·5	86·5	88·2	88·5	87·1	64·2	60·1	59·4	74·03
2. New Orleans, L.	29·58	90·7	56·75	58·39	66·58	72·41	77·26	81·18	82·22	82·12	79·42	69·71	58·71	52·26	69·80
3. Mobile, A.	30·12	87·59	56·40	57·37	65·64	70·00	76·36	82·17	82·41	82·73	78·94	69·97	61·50	55·50	69·92
4. Baton Rouge, L.	30·26	91·18	52·37	51·86	61·55	68·99	76·58	82·9	80·1	82·04	76·58	66·84	62·47	55·89	68·15
5. Jackson, L.	30·51	91·1	47·6	49·4	56·6	65·4	70·8	78·7	81·7	79·9	75·1	67·4	50·	48·4	64·23
6. Houston, T.	31·54	95·56	65·2	60·5	68·7	72·7	85·5	80·1	84·2	81·4	83·5	72·3	62·3	60·0	73·00
7. Natchez, M.	31·34	91·25	50·13	50·89	62·2	69·93	72·72	80·62	81·78	80·13	74·99	64·58	55·23	49·09	66·10
8. Vicksburg, M.	32·24	91·6	51·40	53·72	63·99	74·01	76·84	80·65	82·48	80·11	76·40	64·92	55·26	50·91	67·56

To compare with these, we shall further adduce, from the same Tables, the mean temperatures of places on the Atlantic coast, as in Florida, Georgia, and Carolina, as well as in the interior of the last two.

	Lat. N.	Lon. W.	Jan.	Feb.	March.	April.	May.	June.	July.	Aug.	Sept.	Oct.	Nov.	Dec.	Year.
9. St. Augustine, F.	29°50′	81°27′	60·73	64·97	67·55	70·06	76·89	81·41	82·81	82·67	80·16	73·83	63·55	60·92	72·13
10. Savannah, G.	32·5	81·10	52·15	53·74	61·19	67·36	73·14	77·89	82·23	82·09	75·96	66·92	57·20	50·50	66·70
11. Charleston, C.	32·47	79·57	49·61	52·80	58·34	63·20	75·19	78·85	80·70	80·15	74·3	66·7	58·6	51·8	65·91
12. Fort Johnston, C.	34·0	78·5	51·42	52·19	60·52	65·28	73·70	78·98	81·57	80·39	76·32	69·11	60·13	53·83	66·96
13. Columbia, C.	34·0	80·58	37·7	42·9	47·3	62·2	67·3	72·4	76·1	76·5	66·3	53·2	43·7	39·5	57·09
14. Augusta, G.	33·28	81·54	45·69	47·63	53·66	62·34	69·38	77·72	79·47	75·95	72·96	60·35	54·23	43·45	61·90

The climate of Georgia is somewhat warmer than that of Carolina, but the low flat country of both is moist and unhealthy. The spring is commonly rainy, the heat of summer is considerable, but relieved by the gentle winds which blow almost daily from the sea. The winds change from S. E. to S. W. about the end of July, but are variable, from storms of thunder and lightning, and the heavy rains of July and August. The cold weather seldom commences until about the beginning of December, and terminates in March, but the winter is usually mild, and snow seldom falls near the sea, and soon melts away. The hilly parts 200 miles from the sea are agreeable and favorable to health. The winter is colder; snow falls to the depth of five or six inches. Though the above tables are sufficient to give a general idea of the climates, it would be desirable for agricultural purposes to have also the maxima and minima; for a night of frost may destroy plants, as great heat with drought will be equally injurious from drying them up. Cotton is sown in April; picking commences in July or August, and continues till November, and, on the coast, sometimes even to December. The Sea Island cotton plant yields about 125 lbs. or 130 lbs. of clean-ginned cotton per English acre. Of the short staple cotton, Mr. Spalding states, that in the hill country, from the Mississippi to the Carolinas, not more than 500 lbs. of seed-cotton, or 150 lbs. of clean cotton, can be obtained to the English acre. (*Ure*, i, p. 115.) The short-staple cotton is cultivated all the way from the southern borders of Virginia to the south-western streams of the Mississippi. The mean quantity over all is given by Mr. Spalding at 125 lbs. of both Sea Island cotton-wool and of the short-stapled wool to an English acre, but the amount of labour is much greater for the former than for the latter. (*Ure, Cotton Manufacture*, i, p. 116.)

In comparing the climate of the above cotton regions with that of other countries, it is necessary to remember the peculiarity of American climate, with which this subject was commenced, and also how much the best cotton districts are influenced by the Gulf of Mexico or the Atlantic ocean. The climate to the west of the Alleghany mountains is considered more mild than that under the same parallels in the Atlantic states, and by some even to the extent of 3° of latitude. This has been explained as caused by the warm air of the Gulf of Mexico being driven up the basin of the Mississippi and that of the Ohio. The direction of the valley being north and south no doubt favours the course of the southern winds, while the valleys of the Atlantic states being transverse, oppose any such transmission, also the migration of plants. The majority of the places of which the mean temperatures have been adduced being on the sea coast, necessarily participate to some extent in the peculiarities of insular climate; that is, of seasons moderately contrasted. But still the difference between the hottest and the coldest month of the year is much greater than at Vera Cruz, that is, than 12°; being at Mobile, Galveston, and New Orleans, 27°·23, 29°·10, and 29°·96, respectively. But in the interior, at Natchez and at Vicksburg, the differences are greater, being 32°·69 and 31°·57. On the Atlantic states the differences are nearly as great as those on the south coast, being 31°·73 at Savannah, and 31°·09 at Charleston, while in the interior the differences are much greater, being 36°·02 at Augusta, and 38°·10 at Columbia.

In addition to the foregoing, it is desirable to notice some of the general features of the climate both of the Gulf and of the Atlantic states, as it will then be readily seen how much it is modified by the vicinity to the sea and by the configuration of the coast.

MISSISSIPPI.—Near the gulf of Mexico the climate resembles that of the lower parts of Louisiana; the winter is mild, the summer warm, but tempered by the constant prevalence of the sea-breeze from the Gulf of Mexico, together with the elevation of the surface. In sickly seasons the inhabitants remove to the high banks of the bay of St. Louis.

ALABAMA.—In the low southern parts of this country the heat is very great. The climate of the inland and upper parts resembles that of Georgia, and may be considered remarkably mild. Frost commences in October, and continues sometimes as late as the 20th of May, so as to injure, but not to destroy, the cotton in the more elevated parts. During summer, westerly winds are found to prevail. Those from the S.E. are the sure harbingers of rain. At Mobile, from nine in the morning till evening, the pleasant and salutary effects of the sea-breeze are felt. The rich verdure of the earth, with the copious dews that fall during the night, and the elevation of the soil (which, in the upland parts, is from 600 to 1000 feet above the sea), produce a beneficial effect on the climate.

LOUISIANA.—The climate varies in different parts. From the sea to Point Coupée it seldom snows, nor does it ever freeze, except in the months of December and January, and when the wind is from the N. or N.W. There is less heat and more moisture than in similar latitudes on the eastern continent, and the climate is generally very mild. In winter the thermometer seldom falls more than two degrees below the freezing point. At Natchez, the greatest degree of cold observed was 17°. In December 1800 the thermometer sunk to 12° near New Orleans, and snow fell for the first time during 20 years. In January 1811 the thermometer sunk from 78° to 10°, and the Mississippi was completely frozen over.

GEORGIA.—All the flat country is described as being moist and unhealthy, especially the rice swamps, and the climate as somewhat warmer than that of South Carolina. The winter is the most pleasant season of the year, and the thermometer usually ranges from 40° to 66°, though sometimes a considerable degree of cold has prevailed; but snow is uncommon, and frosts have been experienced even as late as April. A strong N.E. wind will occasionally blight a promising field of cotton, as insects will sometimes destroy it. The spring is commonly rainy, the summer inconstant, with a temperature of from 76° to 90° from June to September. "The atmosphere feels springy and enlivening, being refreshed by gentle winds which blow almost daily from the sea-shore." About the 20th of July the summer rains set in, often with storms of thunder and lightning, and though not tropical in their violence, are often so heavy as to deluge the fields. About the end of July or beginning of August, the wind usually changes its direction from the S.E. to S.W. The month of August is described as being the period of most solicitude to the cotton-grower, as heavy rains at that time sometimes cause the plant to part with its fruit and even its leaves. The autumn is usually fine and clear; about the 20th of October frosts are expected; but do not often come on before the end of the month. The hilly tracts, distant 200 miles from the coast, enjoy an agreeable climate which is favorable to health. The winter is colder; snow sometimes falls to the depth of five or six inches; the summer is not so hot, and the winds of autumn are less violent; and the cotton being less exposed, is allowed to hang longer, so as to become perfectly ripe.

South Carolina.—The winter is described as being mild; and the difference between the mildest and severest winter as about 17°, often with heavy frosts, but with a hot sun during the day; snow seldom falls near the sea. The winter may be considered to terminate in March, when snow and heavy rains usually occur; but April and May are commonly dry months. In the low country the heat of summer is intense: but the climate is liable to sudden changes of temperature when it is damp with fogs and heavy dews. June, July, and August are usually the wettest months, and the rains consist of heavy bursts and frequent showers, which are liable to occur in spring, summer, and autumn. November is usually fine, when frosts come on, but sometimes not until December. The average quantity of rain for ten years was 49·3 inches. The largest quantity 83·4, and the least 36·6, in any one year. In the upper country frost commences earlier and continues longer; but the weather is not so variable. In winter the cold is considerable, but does not last very long. The climate of the Santee Hills, which are situated about 80 or 90 miles from the coast, is of the same nature.

In connection with the climate of the cotton districts of the United States, it is desirable to take some notice of the climate where another species, the Brazil or Kidney Cotton, is cultivated. We are fortunately able to refer to the observations of Dr. Loudon, at Pernambuco, by which it will be seen, that the quantity of rain which falls is considerable, and that the air must always be in a moist state. As Koster states, that the cotton succeeds better from 50 to 150 leagues in the interior; the climate may still be a moist one, though drier than that on the coast.

Meteorological Observations, made during the year 1842, *in the City of the Recipe de Pernambuco, by the late John Loudon,* M.D.

MONTHS.	Temperature by the Thermometer of Fahrenheit.			Saussure's hygrometer at midday.		Quantity of rain, in English inches.	Number of days and nights in which it rained.	
	Maxm.	Minm.	Mean.	Maxm.	Minm.		Days.	Nights.
January	86·00	72·00	79·59	—	—	6·09	20	—
February	86·00	73·00	81·19	—	—	2·01	3	—
March	87·00	72·00	81·80	—	—	8·23	5	20
April	84·00	73·00	78·30	—	—	25·24	17	19
May	83·00	71·00	78·22	—	—	16·21	15	21
June	82·00	70·00	76·44	—	—	25·26	20	20
July	82·00	67·00	75·38	—	—	16·11	17	19
August	81·00	69·00	75·03	96·00	75·00	3·15	7	11
September	85·00	70·00	76·33	98·00	80·00	1·04	4	6
October	87·00	70·00	81·06	99·00	70·00	1·13	2	5
November	87·00	73·00	82·93	97·50	85·00	0·29	5	—
December	88·00	74·00	81·09	100·00	87·05	1·31	9	5
Medium	84·23	71·10	79·00	98·01	77·05	109·27	124	130

—(*Commercial Tariffs, &c.*, Part xxi, 1847, by John Macgregor, Esq.)

Excellent cotton, we have seen, is cultivated in Egypt and at a distance from the sea; but it is only after the Nile has inundated the country that it is sown, and then it is grown by the aid of constant irrigation, as related by Lieut. Waghorn and by Mr. Mercer.

Cotton has also been lately produced of very good quality at Natal, nearly at the southern extremity of Africa. Along the sea the coast is low, and in some parts swampy; the land within ten miles is considered most favorable for the cultivation of cotton, probably "from the constant moisture of the atmosphere and warmth of the climate," though it no doubt may be grown further in the interior. The hills which begin to rise within a few miles of the sea, must be useful in retaining, in a moist state, the climate and the intervening lands. The country beyond is described as being more favorable for grazing purposes. Mr. Bazley lately mentioned at a meeting at Manchester, that cotton grown on the Natal coast was worth from 14*d*. down to 7*d*. per lb.; the greatest part of it was worth about 9*d*. per lb. Mr. Bergtheil said that it would be profitable to grow it when it sold in Natal for 2½*d*. or 3*d*. per lb., and that he believed there was sufficient moisture in the ground from rain to grow the cotton. Some of the cotton (yellow in colour) was from indigenous seed, and some was "grown from American, and from Sea Island seed." Mr. Johnston, the Abyssinian traveller, before proceeding to Natal, was supplied with some cotton seed from the India House. The author agreed with him, that the cultivation might be successfully undertaken there, as the moisture seemed sufficient. One of the first made cottage saw-gins was also taken there by a colonist.

Various attempts have been made to obtain cotton from the west coast of Africa, and the superior American cottons have often been introduced there. The author has seen some very good specimens of cotton from Liberia, and samples from Dahomey, and others lately obtained from the Gold Coast have been highly approved of, being the produce of the green-seed and kidney-seed cottons. The climate is favorable, but a population is required who are willing to cultivate cotton.

A very interesting set of experiments in crossing one cotton with another was made by Dr. Thompson at Sydney and in the neighbourhood of Moreton Bay, which we shall afterwards notice. Dr. Lang particularly called the attention of the Cotton Committee to the tract of country from 26° to 30° of s. latitude, as being well fitted for cotton culture. But as our object is to draw inferences respecting climate from examining that of places where cotton is successfully grown, this does not afford us any additional information.

Some cotton has, however, been grown by Messrs. Dickson at Bolwarra, near West Maitland, from seeds obtained from the government gardens at Sydney. One kind was a white, and the other a drab-coloured cotton, both with the seeds adhering strongly to the cotton, and both of good quality. The plants were, when young, attacked by a grub, but many recovered from this, grew steadily, and became 3½ feet to 5 feet high, branching bushy plants, bearing on an average about thirty pods; and it was remarked, that the hot winds of the season, when the experiment was made, did not seem to injure the plants. But cotton-plants are able to bear a good deal of heat when they have not been previously exposed to much moisture; and, as the experiment was made in rich alluvial land, they were, no doubt, able to draw sufficient nutriment from the soil.

Temperature, as we have seen, is only one of the elements

of climate, and though a very important one, is yet unable of itself to do any thing towards the growth of a plant, unless water be within the reach of its roots to dissolve and carry into the vegetable cells and vessels the elements of nutrition. It must itself be decomposed, in contact with air, not too dry nor yet too damp, but containing its due proportion of oxygen and of carbonic acid gas, and illumined by the light of the sun. There is no doubt that cotton-plants may exist through a long range both of temperature and of moisture and of dryness of the atmosphere, but it is equally certain, that they will never attain healthy vigour of growth unless there is a due supply of moisture in a moderately warm or rather hot atmosphere. Though the degree of heat may be measured with a thermometer, moisture is not always indicated by the rain gauge, for rain may fall, run off the surface, or drain through the soil, and the earth and the atmosphere both be left in a parched state, even during the season of growth. The moisture can only be measured by the Hygrometer, and, imperfect as the majority of such instruments are, their information from many situations would be invaluable, as we might then be more sure of drawing correct inferences. Because, though we might not be able to calculate correctly the exact quantity of moisture contained in the atmosphere, we could see whether this was in a state of saturation, or was capable of taking up a still further quantity, and thus in the one case checking and in the other favouring evaporation from the soil, and from the surface of plants. To the comparative moisture of the air on the sea-coast, and in places within the reach of the moist sea air, must chiefly be ascribed the preference of the cotton-plant for such situations, or at least for its successful culture in so many islands and along so many coasts. But to this it may be objected, that a long-stapled cotton is successfully grown in the dry climate of Egypt: there, however, copious irrigation produces the same beneficial effects in a warm dry atmosphere. Excess of moisture in a warm climate may, however, prove as injurious as its deficiency, for then the parts of vegetation may be altogether stimulated, or be in a state of continual growth, when plenty of branches and of leaves are produced, but few flowers and very little cotton. In European climates the influence of a wet spring and summer may be seen in the luxuriant growth of many vegetables, with a deficient supply of fruits; or in a fine crop of turnips, with a short one of corn.

For these reasons we can account for the American planters destined for India, when in England, objecting to irrigation, as they did in conversations with the author, when he mentioned its occasional necessity in some parts of India, as in 30° of N. lat., for which the planters had a preference. The author communicated the substance of these conversations to Dr. Spry, Secretary of the Agri-Horticultural Society of India, who having published the letter (a private one) in the proceedings of that body for August, 1840, enables the contents to be referred to:

"Dr. Royle writes, with reference to their thinking 30° of lat. essential, that he had tried to undeceive them in this respect, and read them the accounts of the culture in Guzerat, Surat, Dharwar, and Tinnivelly, Ganjam, and Vizagapatam, in Dr. Wight's excellent paper on the subject. Moisture is decidedly objected to, the climate and soil cannot be too dry after the plant has once taken hold." So Mr. Mercer, a most intelligent planter, in passing through Egypt, wrote to the author, 25th Oct., 1840, that he had seen some of the cotton in cultivation near Cairo, in a farm of the Pasha's, the only one at present in the country, for the Nile had spread itself over all its banks. The kinds cultivated were the black-seeded Egyptian and a green-seed American. "The cotton was planted in ridges, something in the American manner, but closer. Instead of working it with the plough and hoe, it was irrigated every ten days, by complete flooding." Mr. Mercer observes, that "as it was beginning to flower, it seemed suffering from watering at that advanced stage and from its closeness, yet there was a fair show of top bols, and a promise of a tolerable crop. Nothing but the dry atmosphere of this country could ever enable cotton to stand such gorges of water." So Mr. Blount, another of the planters, observes, after experiencing the effects of an Indian climate, "it will no doubt appear strange, that we should complain of the dryness of the season, as we have always asserted, that cotton does not require a great deal of rain." (*Return*, p. 148.)

But it must be remembered, that the planters who went to India had all been cultivators in the Gulf States, where water is in many places near the surface, the soil usually in a moist state after the passing away of winter, and the climate frequently refreshed by showers, even by storms; also that the air is always loaded with moisture, as it passes from the Gulf of Mexico up the valleys of the Mississippi and Alabama. But in India the planters had to experience the effects of excessive drought, in two very dry seasons, and they had to modify their practice and their opinions to the climate in which they were settled, as we have seen in the quotation from Mr. Blount. Mr. Allen reports, in 1842, that "the planters, one and all, think the climate of Bundlecund too dry." Mr. Mercer says, "This country is too dry, and we will find it so in comparison with the valley of the Mississippi. All India is dry: not that there is not more rain falls during the year in some parts of India than falls in the same time in Mississippi, yet the large quantity that does actually fall there is scattered throughout the year, and falls frequently at times when most injurious, that is, when the crop is making and maturing." (*Report*, p. 138.) Mr. Terry says, "If we could get three and a half months of moist damp weather, with frequent light showers, and dews at night, and the sun not quite so hot after the rains are over as it is here, there will be no doubt of success in such a climate and season." (*Rep.* p. 139.) So Mr. Finnie: "The cotton-plant requires a warm moist climate; it will not luxuriate in hot winds alone, nor will it live in a low swampy situation. It will bear a great deal of rain if the land is high, so that the water will run off; it will also bear a considerable drought, if in good land and properly cultivated, and if the atmosphere is humid only during the night." (*Rep.* p. 181.) In the same manner Mr. Simpson, stationed in the southern part of India, reports that a genial, moist, moderately warm climate suits cotton best. (*Rep.* p. 332.) Dr. Wight's first impressions (10th Jan., 1842) were, that "the air of Coimbatore was too dry, and he suggested the propriety of removing the experiment in part from the inland to a coast situation." In the same manner, Dr. Gibson, when consulted on the subject, writes in 1839 (*Rep.* p. 61), "that cotton is a delicate plant in regard to its choice of weather: too much rain is decidedly hurtful to the indigenous kind, and again, a long interval of sunny weather stunts its growth." (p. 61.) "With respect to the production of exotic species in the interior, such as the Bourbon or Egyptian, the New Orleans

DIAGRAM OF THE CLIMATE OF INDIA,

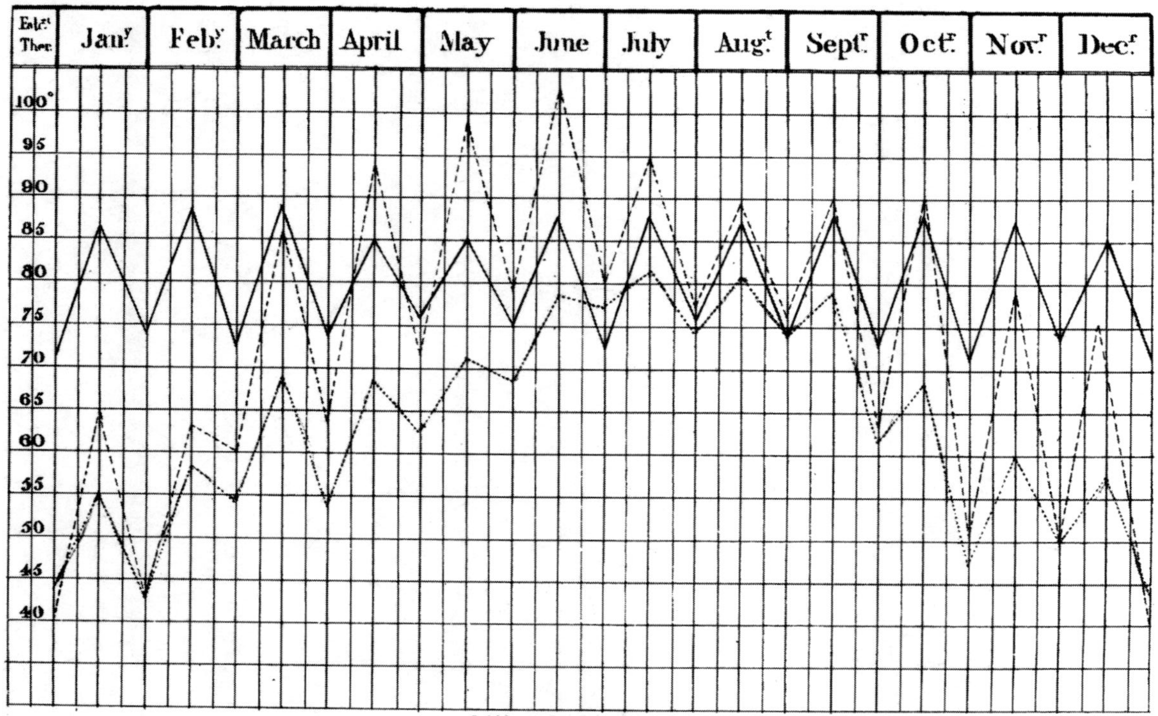

Ford & George, Lithographers, 54 Hatton Garden

and Pernambuco," he was of "opinion that the result of the experiments tried by himself and others have shown that they will not succeed except within the influence of the sea air;" also, that he had "a small plantation of New Orleans cotton at Nurgore, which might be said to be within the Ghaut range, the whole of the pods of which were blighted, owing, probably, to the peculiar misty moisture of the Ghauts, so very different from a healthy sea moisture." From these various statements, from different and very distant parts of India, it is evident that the difficulties of climate are very considerable, and, as these difficulties are not the same in all parts of India, it will be preferable to give the details of climate with the account of the experiments on culture in the different presidencies; but still it is desirable to take a general view of the extremes of climate to which the cotton-plant may be subjected, and which occur in different parts of the Indian Empire, as from Sincapore to Saharunpore.

The seasons of India are, over a great part of the country, divided into the cold weather, hot weather, and rains, names which sufficiently indicate the particular characteristics of each. If we take an equatorial climate, like that of Sincapore, as a standard of comparison, we shall observe a very great difference between it and that of a north-western situation in the plains of India, such as Saharunpore in 30° of N. latitude, the first being remarkable for uniformity, and the latter for a great range both of the dry- and wet-bulb thermometer. Plants which live throughout the year in the open air at Sincapore will, in most cases, suffer from both the cold and the heat of Saharunpore, though they may flourish in the rainy season almost as well in the one as the other. This will perhaps be better illustrated by a reference to the accompanying diagram, which was given as a part of the author's evidence before the Cotton Committee of the House of Commons, and published in their Report, 17th July, 1848.

The black line indicates the regularity of an equatorial climate at Sincapore.

The yellow line indicates the rise and fall of the thermometer at Saharunpore, in 30° of north latitude.

The blue or dotted line indicates the range of the wet-bulb thermometer at Saharunpore, showing the state of dryness and moisture of the air throughout the year.

Between the equability of Sincapore and the extremes of Saharunpore, there are many gradations of climate, more or less suitable for the cultivation of cotton. In the north-west of India, a rapid rise of temperature takes place in March, accompanied with dryness, and continues increasing until the middle of June, when the rains come on. After this, there is considerable uniformity of temperature, until their cessation about the middle of September, when considerable alternations of heat and cold, as well as of dryness, are observed. This dryness is indicated whenever there is much difference between the dry- and the wet-bulb thermometers; but the nearer they approach each other, as may be observed during the rainy season, so much greater is the moisture of the atmosphere. Before their accession, there is great dryness with heat, rendering culture difficult, if not impossible, without irrigation; so at the end of the rainy season, plants, accustomed to its equability, will suffer from the great changes of heat and of dryness, though they may, perhaps, be preserved by the aid of irrigation.

In the Peninsula of India the climate is different, inasmuch as it is greatly influenced by the two monsoons: the north-east monsoon, which blows chiefly on the eastern coast; and the south-west monsoon, which is chiefly felt in Malabar and the western parts of the country. In some parts the advantages of both monsoons are enjoyed; but in others, the change from the moisture of the rains to the heat and dryness which succeed them, is nearly as conspicuous as at Saharunpore, and plants will equally suffer from the transition. But this will be better illustrated in noticing the experimental culture of cotton in the several parts of India.

Such being the extremes of temperature and of dryness, and such the shortness of the several seasons during which the plant may be made to grow—as, for instance, during the hot and dry weather from March to June, or during the steaming moisture of the rainy season, followed, at first, by a hot and moist, and then by a cold and dry autumn, which is itself succeeded by a bracing winter—a plant must be hardy to sustain uninjured such extreme and sudden vicissitudes. But all India is not identical in climate. In some parts the accession of the rains is earlier, their termination more gradual, and the cold of winter less, or the country enjoys the advantages of a double monsoon; so that there is a longer period of growth. As the American cotton plant is stated, in the above extracts, to require moisture, and to have suffered from the great dryness of the Indian climate, it is desirable first to select the soils and climates which seem most likely to afford the required desiderata. But, having exhausted these, the next point of consideration is, to inquire whether it is not possible to modify the climate of particular localities, for a time at least, so as to suit it to the American cotton plant. This is not, probably, so visionary as at first sight may appear. Nature modifies tropical climates, where the sun is most powerful, by continual showers or by the vicinity of the sea. Where a soil and climate are moist, man has considerable power in modifying it to a certain extent, by opening the country to the influence of winds, clearing away jungle, cutting down forests, and getting rid of superfluous water, either by surface or by sub-soil draining; and it is well known, that the climate of many countries has been greatly modified by such means. In an extremely dry state of soil and climate, we might produce a contrary set of effects by reversing the order of procedure. Thus by entirely flooding any particular tract of country, we might at once convert a dry into a moist climate, and substitute continued evaporation of water for absorption and subsequent radiation of dry heat. In both cases, the heat which is transmitted by the solar rays is again given off from the surface of the earth; but in the one case, in combination with water, and in the other, as rays of heat. Similar effects, though less in degree, may be produced by other operations, as by covering a country with grass-land, with under-shrubs, or with trees. In the latter cases, any excessive drying-up will be impeded, if not prevented, by the coating of grass as well as by the umbrageous covering of trees. Whatever evaporation does take place will be augmented by the transpiration of water from the leaves of trees, which their roots have pumped up from below the surface of the earth. Such methods will not, however, answer when the object is to clear the ground for a new cultivation. But hedges, belts of shrubbery or of forest, may be employed to intersect and enclose tracts of land, which may be copiously irrigated, and a comparatively moist atmosphere be produced and maintained for some time, even in the midst of surrounding aridity. The raising of water, therefore, from wells or from the beds of rivers, by wheels, windmills, or by machinery of any kind; flooding the banks of rivers, or damming them across so as to raise the level of the water, and allow it to run over the neighbouring country, or intersecting this with canals of irrigation, are among the most important works for improving the resources of a country where drought is experienced, and they are as beneficial as draining is in a wet and cold country like England. Such considerations, however, belong rather to the department of culture than to that of climate.

§ 11. Principles of Culture.

Cotton, we have seen, is cultivated in the rich alluvium of the Mississippi, and in the sandy plains of Georgia; also in the low islands which skirt its coasts, and in the hilly tracts which form its background. We find it in the chain of islands which form the barrier between the Atlantic Ocean and the Gulf of Mexico; also in the hot parts and the mountains of the latter country, and at still greater elevations in the Equinoctial Andes, v. p. 169. It is also cultivated in different parts of Africa, and the same species in such widely separated countries as Egypt and the coast of Natal. In every part of India we find some kind of cotton, both near the coast and far in the interior; on the table-land of the Peninsula, and on the mountains of its north-west frontier, at elevations of between 4000 and 5000 feet. From India we have seen that its culture has extended to other countries of Asia, and even to the southern parts of Europe.

The first subject which suggests itself for inquiry, in connection with so wide a field of distribution, is, whether temperature is of so little consequence as to allow of the production of cotton in such very different places. But, as has before been remarked, the summer temperature of many of the countries mentioned is not so different as might be inferred from their wide diversity of position. Temperature, moreover, is modified in many of the places by the moisture of the atmosphere, either from vicinity to the sea, or from the presence of water from some other source. But it may also be asked, whether the soil is not very different in the various localities which have been indicated. This is no doubt the case; but it has also been proved, that cotton can be grown in widely varying soils, if care be taken to modify the culture so as to suit it to these and to the climates of the different countries. If such be the case, nothing would appear more important than to study the principles which should guide us in such a course, that is, understand the reasons why changes are made in the details of culture; for the practice must differ, if it is to suit the peculiarities of soil and of climate in different localities.

It is much to be regretted, that it should seem so distasteful to the planter abroad, and until very lately to the farmer and gardener at home, to make themselves acquainted with the reasons why things require to be done in one way rather than another, when they wish to succeed in the culture of any particular plant. The subject is, no doubt, one of considerable difficulty, and the reasons assigned are in some cases conjectural; while it is usually a safe course to follow the practice of successful cultivators. Few think it necessary to inquire how these first ascertained the proper method of cultivating any particular plant in a new locality. It may be inferred generally, as can be proved to have been the case in many instances, that some man more energetic than his neighbours in character, and at the same time fertile in expedients, made a series of experiments. Many of these no doubt failed; but of them we usually hear nothing, while others succeeded and formed the basis of future practice. This has by degrees been varied, so that a certain method of culture has been found suitable for the production of certain crops in particular localities: the cultivator, in many cases, being unaware of any reasons why one mode had succeeded with him and another failed. If the most successful farmer of one place removes to another country or to a distant district of the same country, he is surprised to find that he fails in a culture, which he thought he understood better than others; and that, in fact, he is beaten in his own calling by the common cultivators of the country. But these, in fact, follow the practice of those who, like himself, have succeeded, though perhaps only partially, in these localities; while he the stranger tries to introduce practices which may be suitable only to a very different set of circumstances, that is, of soil and of climate. But still the culture, in the locality in question, may be susceptible of great, and perhaps easily effected, improvement, if the right means were adopted. What these are can only be certainly ascertained by experiment. But we may be much assisted in the course which we should adopt, by understanding how the different parts and products of plants are affected by the processes of culture, varied as these necessarily must be according to differences in soil and seasons; for the growth of plants and the functions which they perform depend upon the chemical constituents and physical conditions of the soil and atmosphere, as well as upon their state of moisture or dryness, and upon the stimuli of heat, light, and perhaps of electricity. It would hardly seem necessary to call attention to these subjects, if it were not for their unaccountable neglect in English education, so that though a large class are connected with, and others dependent on, the arts of culture, few or none think of making themselves acquainted, with even the general principles of the sciences which treat of and explain the phenomena of vegetable and animal life.

Yet the earth, with its variety of soils and stores of mineral treasure; the air in which we live and breathe, with its striking contrasts of climate; the vegetable and animal kingdoms, with their endless diversities of external form and curious fitness of internal structure, affording food and materials for the arts and manufactures of the whole human race, and everywhere displaying the design and goodness of the all-wise and beneficent Creator, would seem to afford as interesting objects of study as any that are now pursued. This more especially as the mind may be trained to correct observation and careful discrimination, as well as in the power of methodical arrangement, at the same time that the study of the functions of organic life would teach us how health may be best preserved, and the products of the vegetable and animal kingdoms both increased and improved. The author having formerly drawn attention to this subject, when treating expressly of the subject of education, will take the opportunity of quoting one passage,* as showing that he is not

* "As one of the objects of all education is to train the intellect, we must not lose sight of some of the advantages attendant on a careful attention to such pursuits as those of natural history. Among these, we may enumerate the culture of the habit of observation—that of distinguishing and defining, nearly similar objects—as well as learning to arrange, in a methodical manner, an immense number of distinct subjects. The latter is, of itself, of no small importance; it has been successfully accomplished, and its principles are of extensive application."

Mr. John Mill, a profound thinker of the day, in his recently published work, entitled '*A System of Logic; or a Connected View of the Principles of Evidence and the Methods of Scientific Investigation*,' says:

"Although the scientific arrangements of organic nature afford, as yet, the only complete example of the true principles of rational classification, whether as to the formation of groups or of series, those principles are applicable to all cases in which singular in his opinions. The distinguished De Candolle indeed went to the length of stating, "that all the errors in vogue in the world respecting the social and natural sciences depend upon our having accustomed youth to the more positive sciences, and not sufficiently to those where we must weigh so great a number of contradictory arguments. The logic of these studies is more difficult, perhaps, but it is more applicable than that of the affirmative sciences to the ordinary business of life."

If the study of the principles of the sciences connected with vegetation enables us so to modify culture, as to suit it to the varying soil and climates of the different countries in which a plant can be cultivated; nothing would appear more important to a planter than that he should acquire some knowledge of principles which will form safe guides to his practice. Before proceeding, therefore, to treat of the details of culture, we may take some notice of the parts of plants and the functions they perform, as well as of how they are affected by the different vital stimuli we have cursorily enumerated, though it would be preferable to study writings expressly devoted to these subjects. The author would particularly recommend Lindley's 'Theory of Horticulture;' and, in conjunction with it, any elementary work, as Lindley's 'Elements,' or Balfour's 'Manual of Botany.' But as these may not at once be procurable by the planter in the colonies, the author thinks it desirable to give an abstract view of the subject of such works.

Plants, it is well known, are living bodies composed of cells and tubes, usually fixed to the soil, and dependent upon it and upon the atmosphere, for their means of nutriment. Possessed of the powers of growth, and of forming within their cellular tissue a variety of products, plants must necessarily be able to absorb as well as to digest the various materials which they receive from without.

mankind are called upon to bring the various parts of any extensive subject into mental co-ordination. They are as much to the point when objects are to be classed for purposes of art or business, as for those of science., The proper arrangement, for example, of a code of laws, depends upon the same scientific conditions as the classifications in natural history; nor could there be a better preparatory discipline for that important function than the study of the principles of a natural arrangement, not only in the abstract, but in their actual application to the class of phenomena, for which they were first elaborated, and which are still the best school for learning their use." (*Essay on Medical Education*, p. 21, 1842.)

If we enclose a plant within a glass case, and place it in the light, we may soon observe that a quantity of vapour is exhaled, because we see it condensing into a watery fluid. If we examine the air in which the plant has been confined, we shall find that a considerable change has taken place in its chemical constituents. Processes analogous to the perspiration and respiration of animals must, therefore, have been performed by the plant. If a piece of its wood, or the entire plant, is burned in a covered-up vessel, we shall find that a large portion of it remains in the form of a black mass, so well known as charcoal. This shows that much of it was composed of carbon as it is called by chemists, and which the plant must have obtained from the soil or the atmosphere. If the plant be further analysed by the chemist, it is found to be composed of several elementary substances variously combined with each other; some, as oxygen, hydrogen, nitrogen, and carbon, are called *organic elements*, because of these the substance of the tissues is chiefly formed, and they are dissipated when the plant is burnt under full exposure to the air. Others are called *inorganic* elements, and generally remain among the ashes of the plant when it is burnt. These are generally combined with oxygen and acids, and are the source of the potash, soda, lime, silica, iron, and other substances found in the ashes of plants.

If we take a full grown plant and examine its different parts, we may readily divide it into *root*, *stem* with *branches* and *leaves*. These parts are especially adapted for fixing the plant to the soil, for elevating it into the atmosphere, and for enabling it to obtain its food as well as for converting this into its own substance. They are often named the parts of vegetation, and are contra-distinguished from those of fructification. These consist of the *flowers* and *fruit*, of which the especial object is the formation and maturation of the *seed*, which is intended for the continued propagation of the *species*. It is not calculated for transmitting any peculiarities which may distinguish the individual, called by practical men a *variety*. This is propagated by cuttings, grafting, &c., and then care must be taken that the local influence of physical agents be really the same as those which favoured the production of peculiarities in the parent plant.

The SEED composed of the embryo plant, often accompanied by a substance called albumen, all enclosed in a seed covering. The embryo itself consists of seed-leaves, or cotyledons, and of the *plumule* and *radicle*, with the collum or point of union between the two. When perfectly ripe the seed usually contains a large proportion of starch (a principle which abounds in carbon), oils or fatty matters, compounds containing nitrogen, such as caseine and vegetable albumen, with some saline matters and woody fibre. According to its composition, a seed may require to be sown immediately it is ripe, or it may, in many cases, remain unchanged for ages, or until circumstances are favorable for its growth and development.

The circumstances favorable for germination, as it is called, are—1, a certain quantity of moisture; that is, the presence of water, which, as is well known, is composed of oxygen and hydrogen; 2, a certain degree of heat, which varies for different seeds from a little above the freezing point to a temperature of 80° or 90°; 3, air, which consists of one fifth of oxygen and of four fifths of nitrogen gas.—Seeds must not be exposed to the influence of light, for this prevents some of the chemical changes which are essential to favorable germination. Moisture being absorbed into the interior of the seed causes it to swell; some of the dry parts become softened and even dissolved in the water which is absorbed, and thus some sap is formed. Heat, at the same time, stimulates the vital principle, and the whole internal organisation is set in motion, and considerable changes take place in the sensible properties and nature of the constituents of the seed; for instance, in the albumen or perisperm, when this is present, as in the cocoa-nut or cereal grains; or in the cotyledons of the embryo when there is no perisperm, as in peas, beans, and cotton-seed.

The change which takes place in the seed during germination consists chiefly in the conversion of the dry, tasteless, and, insoluble starch, into a soluble and sweetish substance, that is sugar, which thus becomes fit for the nourishment of the young plant. This then begins to grow and burst its integuments, pushing its radicle downwards into the ground, and its plumule, or young stem and leaves, upwards into the air. The conversion of starch into sugar, during germination, may be seen on a large scale in the process of malting grain. Chemists have ascertained, that the change consists in the conversion of the starch into dextrine and grape sugar: they suppose, by the influence of a nitrogenous compound, which they have called *diastase,* and which is developed during the process of germination. At this time, it has also been observed, that oxygen gas is absorbed, and carbonic acid gas evolved; the latter, from the combination of the oxygen of the air with the carbon of the seed-starch; some heat is likewise generated. It is probable, also, that some oxygen is obtained from the water which is absorbed, and of which the hydrogen becomes fixed. Hence we see the necessity of the seed not being sown too deep in the ground, as then air does not get access to it. On the other hand, if sown too near the surface, the seed is apt to become dried up, and to suffer from too much light, which, as we shall see in the functions of leaves, favours the extrication, but not the absorption, of oxygen gas. Therefore, seeds are usually sown, according to size, just under the surface, from half an inch to two inches below it.

Roots, besides serving to fix the plants, are useful in absorbing nutriment from without, through their delicate extremities. These are called *spongioles* or *spongelets,* and are composed of loose cellular tissue, which is constantly renewed, as the several divisions of the roots grow by additions to their extremities. By this means, roots are able to force their way round obstructions, and to insinuate themselves into crevices, and to pass on from place to place as fast as the food, in contact with them, is consumed; and thus "plants, though not locomotive like animals, do perpetually shift their mouths in search of fresh pasturage, although their bodies remain stationary." The roots may be composed of cellular tissue, or of this with vascular bundles; but in ligneous plants, the woody fibres descend from the young wood of the stem into the roots, whence the fluids which are admitted by imbibition or endosmose, are readily conveyed into every part of the plant. But the root itself is sometimes a reservoir of nutritious matter, such as gum and starch-like substances, upon which the young stem of the year may feed. Roots, moreover, give off certain excretions, both of organic and of inorganic matter, by a process of exosmose. Hence it was supposed, that the necessity of a rotation of crops depended on these excretions being injurious to the plant which had produced them. But it is now considered, that plants rather suffer from the absence in the soil of certain ingredients which they require, and that the advantages of a rotation depend upon time being allowed for some of these being supplied by a further disintegration of the constituents of the soil; as, for instance, of felspar or mica, which would yield potash, &c. The same crop, we know, may be grown successfully for many years in rich and well-manured land.

The minute fibrils of the root die away, and are constantly renewed, so as, in some respects, to resemble deciduous leaves; and it is generally thought, that the quantity of roots is in proportion to the number of leaves. The function of the roots being to supply nourishment, and the spongioles, from their hygrometric state, being ready to absorb whatever of a suitable nature comes within their reach, it seems very probable that this may be so, especially as Dr. Lindley states, that the "force of absorption is always proportioned to the quantity of food that a plant requires: when the sap is consumed rapidly by the leaves, as in the spring, the roots are in rapid action also; but as the summer advances, and leaves require a smaller quantity of food, the roots become more and more torpid." (*Theory*, p. 17.)* But if we examine the roots of water plants, or of those growing in moist and shady situations, we shall find that they are much less developed than those of plants growing in dry and open places; so in "plants whose perspiring powers are feeble, the roots are small." But if we look at the roots of plants growing in Ward's cases, and exposed to bright light, or to those in moist hothouses, we shall find that they are short in comparison to the luxuriance of the foliage. This is also the case with plants growing in moist and shady situations, or during the rainy season in hot or tropical countries, even though the plants may have grown vigorously and are luxuriant; and this notwithstanding that the formation of roots is favoured by moisture and darkness. The cause seems to be,

* "Powerful as the absorbing action of roots is found to be, these organs have little or no power of selecting their food; but they appear, in most cases, to take up whatever is presented to them in a sufficiently attenuated form," and therefore they will absorb poison as readily as nutritious food, provided its molecules are minute enough and soluble. It is curious, that the substances which are poisonous to man are also those generally detrimental to plants.

that when roots are readily supplied with nutriment they do not travel farther than is necessary in search of it, even though the demand upon them must be considerable, if we are to judge by the size of the foliage or the rapidity of its growth, and allow that perspiration is diminished. Such plants, however, are extremely liable to suffer on any diminution of the moisture of the soil or of the atmosphere, while the temperature continues undiminished; as evaporation and perspiration from the plant being increased at the same time that the supply of moisture to the roots is cut off, the plants will necessarily flag, and drop their flowers and fruit; the more so, as the roots, from their shortness and superficial position, are apt to have their delicate spongioles injured by the heat and drying-up of the ground.

The STEM supports the leaves and flowers, generally elevating them into the air and exposing them to the light; but it sometimes creeps on the surface, as in ferns; at other times remaining under the ground, as in the ginger and arrow-root plants, when it is called a rhizome or root-stock. The stem conveys the nutriment which it receives from the roots to the leaves, and in return receives from them various secretions. It varies much in form and size, and though at first cellular, afterwards becomes vascular and woody, and is, moreover, distinguished by its internal structure in different classes of plants. Thus some are called exogenous, as the stems of European trees, in consequence of growing by additions to the outer surface of their wood; others endogenous, as palms and grasses, from the additions to their substance being made at first by the curving inwards of the vascular and woody bundles, which afterwards converge outwards. In tree-ferns, the stem is formed by the extension of its point, and by the growing together of the bases of the leaves.

Several distinct parts may, moreover, be distinguished in the stem; as the *pith* occupying the centre, and composed of cellular tissue, which stores nutriment for the young leaf-buds, and from the large space it occupies in young parts, greatly extends the surface exposed to the air. It is surrounded by the *medullary sheath*, or circle of spiral vessels with woody fibres intermixed, between which pass horizontally, projections of compressed cellular tissue, the *silver grain* of carpenters, which thus form a communication between the pith and the bark, or the centre and the circumference. They are called *medullary,** though the name of *cellular rays* would be equally appropriate. The vessels of the medullary sheath are continued into the leaf-buds and into the veins of the leaves, and are considered to convey air, and some oxygen gas, "liberated by the decomposition of carbonic acid or of water."

The Wood formed of concentric zones lies immediately on the outside of, and surrounds, the medullary sheath. It is formed of bundles of porous vessels in the inner, and of ligneous tubes on the outer side, with the medullary rays crossing them transversely. A single concentric layer of wood is formed every year, and surrounds that which preceded it. The age of a tree, therefore, in ordinary cases, may be ascertained by counting the several rings of wood. But in tropical countries there are exceptions to this rule, in consequence of many trees enjoying a double season of growth. These woody layers may very often be seen to be of different colours and densities. The internal and oldest layers being usually hard and dark coloured, form the *heart-wood* or *duramen;* while the outer layers, which are whitish in colour and soft in texture, constitute the *sap-wood* or *alburnum.* The tubes and fibres of this, when first formed, are pervious, and form the channel by which the fluids absorbed by the roots pass up the stem and into the leaves. The elaborated juices of the plant, on the contrary, descend from the leaves by the inner bark, and partly pass afterwards across the alburnum, by the medullary rays, into the interior layers of wood. The tubes and fibres hence become by degrees thickened and converted into heart-wood through which no fluids can afterwards pass, nor does any further thickening take place.

On the outside of the alburnum, and under the *liber* or inner bark, there is to be seen, especially in spring, a layer of viscid semi-fluid matter, which is called *Cambium.* In this, cells of the elementary form are observed, of which some are the

* The word medullary, derived from *medulla*, the pith, is differently applied in the two names adduced; as in *medullary* sheath, which, being composed of vessels and woody fibres, forms a sheath to the medulla; while, in *medullary* rays, it signifies that these rays are composed of medulla or cellular tissue.

continuation of the medullary rays, and others are afterwards changed into the vessels or tubes of the woody tissue.

The BARK is, like the wood, formed of concentric layers, but placed on the outside of it. It consists of two very distinct parts; inasmuch as the inner part is composed of woody and cellular matter, with some laticiferous tissue intermixed, while the external part consists only of cellular tissue covered by epidermis. The latter is the rind or cortical covering, and is very conspicuous in the cork-tree; and the former is the *liber*, or inner bark, which is particularly useful as yielding fibre, remarkable in some cases for its toughness, from its elongated woody fibre being thickened by deposits in the interior, as in the case of the lime-tree, the lace bark-tree, species of Grewia, &c. These differ from the layers of wood in growing by additions made to their inner faces. From the additions made to the woody circles on their outside, and to the layers of bark, there is necessarily a constant distension going on, which eventually causes the bark to crack and peel off in some trees. The function of the bark, besides protecting the young wood and layer of cambium, is to transmit downwards even to the root the elaborated juices of the plant, and to pass it horizontally towards the interior of the stem. But much of these descending juices becomes deposited in the cells of the bark itself, whence we see it so frequently employed in medicine and the arts. Thus we see the stem of exogens is cellular in the centre and on the outside, that is, in the pith and outer bark, and it is fibrous and vascular in the medullary sheath, wood, and inner bark. These parts are connected together horizontally by the medullary rays.

Endogenous stems, as those of palms, do not display the distinctions into pith, wood, bark, and medullary rays. They consist of a mass of cellular tissue through which bundles of vascular tubes and woody fibres are distributed, and the whole covered by a false bark composed of cellular and woody tissue. But this cannot, like bark, be separated from the stem. These vascular bundles are at a distance from each other near the centre, but are closely pressed against one another towards the circumference, in consequence of the vascular bundles of the centre pushing outwards those which had been formed in previous years. Mohl has shown, that the vascular bundles connected with the leaves are first directed towards the centre, and that they afterwards slope outwards, so that at last they intermix with the fibres of the false bark, where they lose their vascular character. Hence the outer part of a palm-tree is far more dense and hard than the centre, and is the part from which the best planks of wood are obtained. We need not notice other kinds of stems.

As the formation of wood depends entirely upon the functions of the leaves being properly performed, it is evident that these must have sufficient space allowed for air and light to have free access. Otherwise, as we may observe in trees planted too close to each other, that they become tall but remain thin, or drawn up, as it is called; the leaves fall off, and the roots are found to be short and the wood soft. Trees, therefore, which are expected to yield good timber must be planted at proper distances, so that pruning may be unnecessary; though softer-wooded trees may sometimes be intermixed; but these must be thinned out as the others grow up and spread. The specific rules must necessarily vary according to the nature of the tree and the soil and climate.

The stem is, also, distinguished by producing buds; some of these are *leaf-buds*, others are *flower-buds*. The former consist of rudimentary leaves, some in the state of scales, others in that of small, undeveloped, variously-formed leaves, which surround a growing point. The flower-buds also consist of rudimentary leaves, which afterwards assume the appearance of flowers and floral envelopes, but they surround a fixed point. Though these parts appear so distinct from each other, nothing is more common than for *leaf-buds* to be converted into *flower-buds*, and we may often observe flower-buds partly converted into leaves. Leaf-buds are formed either at the end or sides of branches, in the angle between the leaf and stem; but they may be produced from other parts where there is cellular tissue: they are then called adventitious. These facts are of importance, inasmuch as they enable the scientific cultivator to adopt such measures as may favour the production of flower-buds, and diminish the tendency to form leaf-buds, or *vice versâ*; for instance, checking the formation of *terminal* buds is well known to favour the production of lateral buds.

The Leaf, so well known as forming the green clothing of

plants, is usually distinguished into the broad and expanded part, called the *lamina*, limb or blade, and into the narrow stalk, called *petiole* or foot-stalk, by which the limb is connected with the branch or stem. This leaf-stalk, often supported by two stipules or leaf-like bodies at the base, is composed of one or more bundles of vascular, with some woody tissue, covered by compressed cellular tissue, the former a continuation of the medullary sheath, and the latter of the bark. The leaf itself is considered an expansion of the bark, and is composed of cellular tissue traversed by veins which are formed by the continuation of the vascular bundles of the leaf-stalk, themselves derived from the sheath surrounding the pith and from the inner bark. They are arranged in two layers; of these, as has been well observed, "one is superior, and arises from the neighbourhood of the pith; the other inferior, and arises from the liber; the former maintains a connection between the wood and leaf, the latter establishes a communication with the bark. As sap, or ascending fluid, rises through the wood, and principally the alburnum, afterwards through the liber, it follows from what has been stated, that a leaf is an organ of which the upper system of veins is in communication with the ascending, and the lower system with the descending current of sap." There are also, at least, two layers of cellular tissue, differing from each other in the arrangement of their cells, the stratum of the upper surface being composed of oblong cells closely packed together, and perpendicular to the plane of the leaf. On the under surface, the cells are parallel with this plane, often irregularly and more loosely arranged, with spaces, or intercellular cavities, which are exactly opposite stomata or breathing pores. Both surfaces are covered with thin transparent skin, which is called *epidermis*. This also differs on the two surfaces, being in the upper surface usually smooth and shining, often dense, while on the under surface it is soft, of a pale green, and more easily separated, at the same time that it is pierced by innumerable pores which are called stomata. Sometimes when leaves grow vertically, or when the edge is turned upwards, this arrangement of the cells and pores is the same on both surfaces. So when leaves float on the surface of water, the upper surface is alone furnished with stomata. Submerged leaves are without fibro-vascular tissue, and their cells are irregularly disposed, sometimes elongated, often with cavities filled with air, probably useful in floating the leaf. They are without epidermis and stomata, but have a layer of compact cells on their surface. It has also been observed, that these stomata are largest and most abundant in plants which inhabit damp and shady places, while those growing in dry situations have a thick epidermis and but few stomata. But their size, in some cases, makes up for deficiency in numbers. Thus *Crinum amabile*, inhabiting damp situations in India, has about 40,000 of these stomata on a square inch of its epidermis, and *Aloe* and *Mesembryanthemum*, natives of the dry rocks of the Cape of Good Hope, have respectively 45,000 and 70,000; but 10,000 of the *Crinum*, from their large size, are equal to 70,000 of the *Mesembryanthemum*. The *Crinum* and *Aloe* have them equally numerous on both surfaces, while the lime, lilac, holly, and cherry-laurel have none on the upper, but great numbers on the under surface of their leaves.

The structure of the leaf being such as to form a thin stratum and a large surface, it follows that if the sap of the plant passes into its cells, it must be exposed in thin films to the action of heat, light, and air, and a portion will necessarily be affected by the ordinary influence of simple physical laws; that is, watery fluid, exposed to a dry and warm air, will necessarily evaporate. In a very moist state of the atmosphere, some pure water will be deposited on the leaf, and a portion will probably pass into the interior of the cells by simple imbibition or endosmose. The exposure to light and air of the sap, that is, watery fluid holding organic matter in solution, or if only suspended, in a state of minute subdivision, will favour the chemical combinations and decompositions, and all this independent of the effects produced by the vital actions of the plant. All these different effects do, in fact, take place in the leaves of plants. Observation will readily show, that a considerable quantity of fluid is exhaled from the surface of plants. A sun-flower, three feet high, has been observed to give off daily, twenty ounces of fluid; other plants also do so in considerable quantities. This process of exhalation is assisted by a thin, and impeded by a thick, epidermis and the number and size of stomata, and is at all times increased by heat. Hence the general effect of vegetation and of extensive forests is to keep up the moisture of a climate, by constantly pouring into the atmosphere a quantity of fluid pumped up by the roots from below, at the same time that they impede evaporation from the surface of the ground. The effects will be beneficial or injurious to men and animals, according to the nature of the climate.

The aeration of the sap and the transpiration of gases, such as oxygen and carbonic acid, is supposed to take place chiefly through the stomata, and is mainly influenced by the presence or absence of light, as it has been observed, that plants in bright light exhale oxygen, while in darkness they give off a small portion of carbonic acid gas. Plants enclosed in air containing a much larger proportion than natural of carbonic acid gas, and exposed to the light of the sun, are found to purify the air by removing the carbon and increasing the proportion of oxygen. This they are supposed to do by first absorbing the carbonic acid gas, and then decomposing it with the aid of light, assimilating the carbon and exhaling the oxygen. Hence it is inferred, that plants generally absorb carbonic acid by their leaves and green parts from the air, as well as receive it dissolved in water by their roots. During darkness, this process is not only suspended, but actually reversed, some oxygen being absorbed, and a little carbonic acid exhaled; Liebig supposes by simple exosmose, as the plant, in the absence of light, is unable to decompose it. Others conceive that this carbonic acid is produced by the combination of the oxygen of the air with the carbon of the plant. This process, no doubt, takes place with fungi and parts of the plant which are not green, such as roots, and likewise during the processes of germination, of fertilization of the seed, and of maturation of the fruit. But the great proportion of the carbonic acid which is decomposed by plants must be obtained either from the air or from the soil; either dissolved in water, or in combination with ammonia, &c., in the form of carbonates; or how else could plants obtain the large quantity of carbon which forms nearly one half of their substance? The oxygen which is both evolved and fixed by plants is, no doubt, derived from the decomposition of this carbonic acid, as also probably in part from the water of which the hydrogen is assimilated. The nitrogen, therefore, alone remains to be accounted for. It has been inferred, that this is obtained either direct from the atmosphere, of which it forms nearly 80 per cent., or through the means of ammonia. This is a compound of one part of nitrogen with three of hydrogen, and as it is always being formed from the decomposition of vegetable and animal matters, it then rises into the atmosphere. From thence it is washed down by rain, and taken up by the roots is carried into every part of a plant.

By others it is inferred, that ammonia is formed in the earth itself by the combination of the nitrogen of the atmosphere with the hydrogen of decomposing substances; and that uniting with different vegetable acids, it is carried into plants, and there decomposed. Hence the great importance, in the case of manures, of having it combined with such acids as do not form with it volatile salts, such as nitrates and muriates. This is called *fixing* the ammonia. In this way may be derived all the nitrogen which forms a constituent of the albumen, caseine, gluten, &c., found in the juices of plants. The chief part, therefore, of the food of plants may be obtained from the atmosphere, that is, the water, carbonic acid, and ammonia: whence we can account for many living suspended in the air. But the same acid and alkali are also obtained, dissolved in water, by plants from the soil, either in combination with each other, or with some other of the acids and alkalis which are absorbed. But some of both are also formed by plants. In this way we account for the phosphates, sulphates, and the potash, soda, lime, &c., found in plants. The water forms not only the medium by which these are conveyed into plants, but is itself assimilated into their tissue. Hence it is essential, that plants for their healthy growth should not only have a due supply of water and be exposed to the influence of the air, but that they should be able to obtain from the soil the saline and earthy ingredients, which, from the constancy of their presence and regularity of their proportions, seem essential to their healthy existence. We also see how requisite it is that plants perform their functions in a due exposure to light, which alone enables them to carry on the several decompositions and assimilations. It appears from the careful experiments of Dr. Daubeny and of Mr. Hunt, that the largest amount of chemical power is possessed by the blue rays of the spectrum.

With these few elementary substances may be formed the other products which plants contain, in addition to their great mass of water and carbon. The combinations of hydrogen and carbon will form the class of oily substances; and oxygen with carbon, oxalic acid. Oxygen, hydrogen, and carbon form the cellulose of which vegetable tissue is chiefly composed; likewise gum, sugar, and starch; while a further proportion of oxygen will form many of the acids. Such substances as albumen, fibrin, caseine, and gluten, require not only nitrogen in addition to the other three elementary substances, but that these should form a basis called proteine, combined with different proportions of sulphur and of phosphorus.

Thus the nutriment absorbed by the roots is conveyed up the stem, and exposed in the leaves to the influences of heat, air, and light. The exhalation which takes place, as well as the subsequent thickening of the sap and its conversion into the juices of the plant, will in different ways favour endosmose and the movement of fluids, and promote the circulation of the sap generally. Leaves, besides exhaling, and probably also absorbing gaseous and watery fluids, thus elaborate the secretions of the plant: on the due performance of their functions, therefore, depends the healthy growth of plants.

The Organs of Reproduction consist of the floral envelopes and of what are considered the essential parts of the flower, that is, the stamens and pistils, which form the sexes, and reproduce seeds for the propagation of the species. As observed above, these organs are modifications of those of vegetation, and are composed, like the leaf, of cellular and of fibro-vascular tissue. They may sometimes be seen converted into leaves. The *floral envelopes* consist of the *calyx* and of the *corolla;* the former is external, and composed of one or of several pieces which are called sepals. These are usually green in colour from their cells containing chlorophylle; like leaves they contain vascular and woody tissue, and have stomata on their outside like the under surface of leaves, and like them give off oxygen in the light. The *corol* is internal, its divisions are called petals, and are usually delicate in texture, variously coloured, from the cells being filled with colouring matter. The vessels are thin and some of them are spiral. The calyx and corol form what is alone considered the flower by the generality of people, and are useful in protecting the stamens and pistil. The latter differs from the former in absorbing oxygen, exhaling carbonic acid gas, and in converting starch granules into saccharine matter. This, it has been supposed, may be useful in the process of fertilization. During this change some heat is produced, as may readily be observed in large flowers, as those of the species of Arum. Within the corol stands the circle of *stamens*, with the *pistil* in the centre. The essential part of the stamen is the *anther*, which contains the fine powdery matter called *pollen* necessary for the fecundation of the ovule contained in the *pistil*. This consists of two very distinct parts :—1. The *stigma*, a cellular body, on which a viscid secretion is produced, and to which the pollen being applied, fecundation subsequently takes place. 2. The *ovary*, or *germen*, within which are contained the *ovules*, with the embryo of the young plant. These, after the period of flowering, become the *seeds* contained within the changed ovary or *fruit*. Seeds thus produced will propagate whatever is typical of the species; but none of the peculiar characteristics of the individual which may have been the result of soil, climate, or culture.

It has already been observed, that flower-buds and leaf-buds are mutually convertible the one into the other. In the *Nymphæa*, or water-lily, and in the *Nelumbium* of India, we may readily observe the gradual change from the green colour and leaf-like appearance of the outside of the sepal to the coloured petal and the narrow stamen. So, on the contrary, we may see even the interior parts of the flower, as of a rose, converted into leaf-like bodies, and sometimes even into a branch with leaves: satisfactorily proving that the different parts are capable of being metamorphosed into one another; and allowing us to infer, that these changes can be effected by the arts of culture.

Further, with regard to flowering, it is well known that different kinds of plants produce their flowers at different periods of their growth. Annuals, for instance, within a few months after germination; biennials in the second year of their existence; perennials not until several years have elapsed and allowed them to arrive at maturity in order to produce flowers.

But in all of these the period of flowering may be more or less hastened or retarded, according to the position of the plant and the natural influence of physical agents, or by a due modification of the processes of culture. The fact being, that a plant seems to require some stoppage in its growth, in order to accumulate sap or matter fitted for the production of flowers. In many plants, we may observe a change in the sensible and chemical properties of leaves, and in some the disappearance of stores of starch taking place immediately the flower-stalk shoots up. We may also observe, especially in countries like India where the climate is more regular than in England, that when a tree has flowered and borne fruit very copiously one year, that a much smaller crop is produced in the succeeding season. A plant growing in a dry, warm situation, where it is well exposed to light and air, though checked in growth, attains maturity more readily and flowers both earlier and more copiously than another plant, otherwise similar but growing in a rich soil and more shaded situation. This may send out its roots, collect abundant nutriment, and be forced into a luxuriant growth of leaves and branches, but will produce comparatively few flowers. Dr. Lindley, whose great experience makes his opinions particularly valuable, has well observed, "Whatever produces excessive vigour in plants is favorable to the formation of leaf-buds, while on the other hand, such circumstances as tend to diminish luxuriance and to check rapid vegetation, without affecting the health of the individual, are more favorable to the production of flower-buds than of leaf-buds." (*Theory*, p. 65.)

The ovules contained in the ovary being fertilized by the application of the pollen prepared by the anther of the same flower, or the same on a similar plant of the same species, one is naturally led to inquire, whether the ovules of one may not be fertilized with the pollen of another species of plant. The plants called *hybrids* are, in fact, so produced, and the term of *cross-bred* is applied to plants produced by the same process practised on varieties of the same species. These partake usually of the characteristics of both parents, as may be seen in many of the cultivated varieties both of garden flowers and of kitchen vegetables. They are particularly valuable as producing fertile seed, while hybrids are usually sterile and, therefore, do not produce fertile seed. The question is interesting even as respects the improvement of the culture of cotton in India, as endeavours have been made to produce a hybrid between an American and Indian species of Gossypium, but the success has as yet been inconsiderable.

The ovule being fertilized, the next consideration is to secure the ripening of the fruit, including, of course, the seed. But before we proceed, it is necessary to notice a distinction among *fruits*, and that is, that some are called *inferior*, others *superior*, or, in other words, *adherent* and *free*. The latter are so called from the pistil not forming any attachment to the floral envelopes, and as these remain below and are entirely distinct from the pistil, the latter is called superior. While the *fruit* which is called *inferior* and also *adherent*, is so called from the lower part of the floral envelopes and the pistil growing together, so that the former appear above the latter. This kind of fruit having more points of attachment to the plant, will be better supplied with nutriment, and less likely to suffer and drop off, than a superior fruit, like that of the cotton plant, from the influence of such causes as cold, wet, or a hot and dry atmosphere.

The fruit, like the leaf and the calyx, while in a green state, will decompose carbonic acid, fixing the carbon and exhaling oxygen; but its chief business is to elaborate matter for its own use, and to protect and nourish the seed. It obtains food from the nearest parts; a portion from the atmosphere, but the greater part from the leaves, consuming the chief portion of what it receives in the essential purposes of the seed, and becoming itself usually dry and leathery; but in other cases it retains a large part of the aqueous portions, and becomes succulent in nature. The leaves, therefore, ought not to be at too great a distance, nor ought the fruit to be too crowded, for the same quantity of nutriment will then be divided among a larger number, while if the leaves are too thick, the fruit is deprived of the beneficial influence of air and light. Without the latter, the fruit will remain green and sour, while exposure to bright light with heat produces sweetness and richness of flavour; it is supposed from a more free decomposition of carbonic acid gas, of which the carbon is useful in converting starch into sugar, the oxygen, of which acids contain an excess, being exhaled. A necessary process in the ripening of fruit is, that it should be able to get rid readily of the water which forms so large a part of the sappy juice which it receives from the leaves. Though much water is sometimes supplied to fruit just when it begins to swell, in order to enlarge its size, yet it is absolutely necessary that the supply should be diminished, in order to favour and hasten the process of ripening; for the more aqueous the nutriment, the longer time will the fruit require to get rid of the watery particles.

As the *seed* obtains its nutriment from the fruit, its healthy condition is dependent upon that of the fruit. It has, however, much to do, in order to store up, in a dry state, the gum, starch, and oily substances which are required as food for the young plant when it begins to germinate. The seed of cotton has, however, more to do than many others, as it has also to elaborate the cotton with which its whole surface is covered. It is more than probable, that if we require this to be long and silk-like, the process of ripening should not be hurried, nor interrupted by changes in climate, either from too much wet or from excessive dryness. Seeds if kept dry, it is well known, may be preserved for a long time in a fit state for germinating; but it has been observed, that oily seeds are the first to spoil, some of them requiring to be sown almost immediately after they are collected. Hence we can account for cotton-seed spoiling so frequently as we find recorded in the different experiments which have been made for the cultivation of cotton. It is not enough, however, merely to collect and keep dry such seed as may be ripened; for the produce, as has been ascertained, depends upon the goodness of the seeds, and also, in some respects, upon our not continuing to cultivate with the same seed in the same place, but to introduce seed of the same kind, even if not superior in quality, from a distance. Hence the constant interchange of seeds among skilful gardeners and farmers. The Indigo planters of Bengal, no doubt, keep up the vigour of their plants by importing their seed from the north-west provinces of India. It is also desirable, if we are very solicitous about the produce in general, to select "the plumpest and heaviest seeds;" but even this is not to be done indiscriminately, for they are suitable only when "the greatest vigour is required in the seedling;" otherwise "feeble or less perfectly formed seeds" may be preferable, "when it is desirable to check natural luxuriance." (*Lindley's Theory*, p. 80.) For this reason probably old melon seed is preferred to new, because the plants should not be too luxuriant in the small space in which they are usually cultivated. So also the natives of Bengal, where the soil is rich and the climate warm and moist, prefer old cotton-seed to new, drying it, and then hanging it up in jars in the smoke of their fires. Being careful observers, they have no doubt ascertained, that their plants required to be checked rather than stimulated in their growth.

Having in this cursory manner noticed the different parts of plants and the functions which they perform, we may proceed to a very general consideration of the effects on them of the different vital stimuli upon which the phenomena of vegetation so entirely depend. Every one is familiar with the fact, that the plants of different climates require very different proportions of these several stimuli, for the due elaboration of their sap, as well as for the healthy growth of their foliage and flowers. When we wish to cultivate the plants of these different countries, we provide a hot-house for some, a green-house for many, and plant others in the open air. But it is not sufficient to attend to temperature only. The Orchids, or air-plants as they used to be called, never flourished until they were supplied with a considerable degree of atmospheric moisture; and now they flower in our hot-houses even more luxuriantly than in their native groves and forests. Cactuses, Aloes, Euphorbias, and similar plants delight, on the contrary, in a warm, dry atmosphere, with a little moisture before the period of flowering. As the temperature of all countries, except of strictly tropical islands, varies much between morning and mid-day, as well as between different seasons of the year, it is evident that plants which live throughout the year in such situations must be able to bear considerable vicissitudes of temperature; while those which are peculiar to particular seasons, will only have to bear the extremes of that season of the year. The species of cotton plant being cultivable both as annuals and as perennials, will come under both categories, and must be able to bear considerable vicissitudes of temperature, if we consider the great range of latitude over which the plants are now distributed. But being naturally plants of a warm climate, they suffer more from cold than from excessive heat.

When *heat occurs with dryness,* plants being unable to obtain the materials for growth, necessarily become dwarfed. Heat will first expand the air contained within the cellular tissue, and then cause the evaporation of fluid from the surface of the plants. The emptying of one cell will favour the infiltration into it of fluid from the neighbouring cells, and thus set the whole in motion, and ultimately promote the absorption of moisture by the roots. If the supply of nutriment be small, the process will take place slowly and growth be much impeded. But if temperature be higher than is necessary for the plant, it may over-stimulate it, and if occurring with dryness, then the loss by evaporation and by transpiration from the surface will be greater than can be supplied by the roots. The leaves and branches will be observed to droop, and though high temperature with dryness, usually occurring with excess of light, favours the secretions of plants, yet a still higher degree will not only dry but turn them of a brownish colour and burn them up. Temperature is usually considered only with reference to the atmosphere; but that of the earth is of equal importance, as by it the roots of plants are chiefly affected, and on it depend the rules respecting bottom-heat in their artificial cultivation.

If *high temperature* coexists *with moisture* either *of the soil* or of the atmosphere, or of both, then a different set of phenomena will be observed. A certain degree of moisture in the soil is essential. What that degree is, may vary for different plants. We know that a friable yet loosely aggregated state of the soil, in which moisture is retained by capillary attraction, and all above that quantity which is superfluous, easily drained off, is the state most favorable for its gradual suction by the delicate fibrils of the root. But if the soil be overloaded with water, the temperature will remain low, and air will not have access to the roots; the quantity which is absorbed by the radicles may be larger than is absolutely required by the plant, and its structure, therefore, becomes more succulent than is healthy. Leaves may be produced in abundance and be tender, but they may also be sickly and yellowish in colour; the shoots weak and wandlike, and instead of flowering and preparing to bear fruit, apt to rot off. But during the period of growth, a larger quantity of fluid nutriment may be supplied than is afterwards found necessary, unless, in some cases, it is wished to effect the swelling of fruit.

Excessive *moisture* and richness *of the soil,* especially if coexisting *with a moist state of the atmosphere* and suitable temperature, will produce a rapid growth of the leaves and other herbaceous parts. But, from the obstruction to evaporation and transpiration, there will be imperfect decomposition of the fluids, and consequently less elaboration of the secretions and of new organised matter, and hence a diminution in the number of flowers and the quality of the fruit and seed. But the same state of the soil in a drier and warmer climate, which favours evaporation and the due elaboration of the vegetable secretions, might suit the growth of the parts of vegetation, and yet favour the production of flowers. The presence of air, we have seen, is essential to plants, and a certain degree of motion in the air is also favorable, as it promotes evaporation, and apparently the motion of fluids; for Mr. Knight ascertained, that wood was increased in the parts subject to be moved by the wind. By planting close we prevent the access of air, impede ventilation as well as evaporation from the leaves, and the drying up of the soil, and thus increase moisture and the effects which it is calculated to produce. In such a situation, plants shoot up in search of light, grow soft and slender, are weak and watery, and being unable to decompose carbonic acid so rapidly as it is absorbed, they do not harden their wood, nor store up secretions for the production of flowers and fruit. When the object is to encourage the growth of vegetable fibre, and to preserve it in a soft and pliable state, as in the cultivation of flax and of hemp, plants are sown thick. So young plantations of trees planted close to save space, shoot up straight and tall, but require to be thinned out to prevent the whole from becoming weak and pole-like. In open planting, we lose space and expose the plants to the influences of light and heat, as well as to the drying effects of free ventilation, which will act both upon the soil and upon the leaves. This may be beneficial in a moist soil and damp climate, in checking the production of leaves and favouring that of flowers; but excess of dryness we know will stunt the growth of plants even when it does not completely wither and destroy them. In such a situation we might, by surface or subsoil irrigation, supply the roots with sufficient moisture to keep up transpiration from the leaves, and enable them to perform all their functions even in very dry air. The advantages to plants of protection are considerable, if we take care to avoid too great closeness and consequent stagnation of air; for it is useful in cutting off gusts and currents of wind. When placed above plants, it shades them from the effects of direct solar heat in the day, and at night from the cooling effects of radiation from the earth.

We have hitherto considered the effects of excess of moisture or of dryness as coexisting with heat in a warm climate, as is that of the cotton plant. But in many of the places where it is now cultivated, equally great injury is experienced from the prevalence of a damp soil and moist atmosphere with *cold and frosts*, either late in spring or early in autumn. Dr. Lindley, who has paid great attention to the effects of cold in producing injury to plants, has observed that if the temperature to which a growing plant is exposed is just reduced to that point within which it will continue to live, and is brought, by the absence of a sufficient exciting cause, into a state not unlike the effect of over-excitement, "it absorbs food from the earth and air, but it cannot assimilate it; its tissue grows, but is not solidified by the incorporation of assimilated matter; aqueous particles accumulate in the interior; a general yellowness ensues, partly from the want of a sufficient power of decomposing carbonic acid, and partly from inability to decompose the water collected in the interior." But when a plant is frozen, "fluids contained within the cells of tissue are congealed, their sides are lacerated, the air they contain is expelled, and cold air admitted; the interior of the tubes which convey fluids becomes obstructed by the thickening of their sides, while the different secretions are decomposed and destroyed." (*Theory*, pp. 86-7, and *Hortic. Trans.*) Hence the culture of cotton is prevented by late frosts and wet cold weather in spring, and a crop may be completely destroyed by an early frost in autumn in the United States.

Excess of light is often experienced at the same time with great heat, and its powerful effects will be readily acknowledged if we observe the unnatural appearance of plants excluded from its influence, as those grown in a dark room, or such as are purposely blanched, as Lettuce and Celery. Therefore, as open planting is essential in moist situations, so a closer approximation and shade may be useful in a poorer soil and drier atmosphere, by covering the surface, and enabling the soil to retain much of the moisture which would otherwise evaporate. As the effects produced on the soil depend so much on the climate, it is evident that the selection of the soils required for particular purposes must depend not only upon the culture for which we require it, but on the climate and the season in which we intend to make use of it.

The operations of culture, moreover, must necessarily vary at different periods of a plant's age. Thus, though it requires water during its growth, this should be diminished at the period of maturity, though it may again be supplied when the plant is in full flower, or we wish to favour the swelling of fruit. Dr. Wight has well observed, "Every annual passes through its various stages of germination, growth, and maturation, or perfecting its seed, in a single year. We may conventionally call the seasons in which these stages are completed, the spring, summer, and autumn of the plant, without reference to the so-called natural seasons of the year. Moisture in moderation is required to excite germination, in somewhat greater excess to promote assimilation and growth, and dry and warm weather properly to mature the seed."

In this manner, therefore, the comparative dryness of summer gives a check to the growth of the parts of vegetation, when the plant forms flower-buds, bursts into flower, and begins to ripen its fruit or seed. An increased supply of nutriment is then often required to enable this to become abundant and large in size. Gardeners frequently favour the tendency to flower by transplanting, which checks the growth of a plant; also by starving it, by exposing it to the influence of dry air, to heat, and to the light of the sun; so likewise by stopping or topping, that is, by pinching off the ends of the growing shoots, and by other methods of pruning which favour the production of lateral and fruit-bearing shoots, leaving, of course, sufficient leaves to carry on their necessary functions. Every one knows that to ripen fruit, or to enable it to become of a fine flavour, a plant cannot be grown in a thicket of its own species, or in one of other plants, nor must it be shaded by a superabundance of its own leaves, as these will deprive the fruit of the genial influence of the sun and air, not only upon the fruit but upon the leaves themselves. Of these a due proportion is essential for healthy growth; but a superabundance draws off sap, and prevents its being properly matured for the uses of the plant and fruit.

Many of the practical details necessary for the culture of different plants and the production of fine fruits, can only be accurately ascertained by carefully conducted experiments. But the course of these may be rightly pointed out by a study of the functions of plants, and the influence on them of physical agents. In a new situation, for instance, including some change of soil and of climate, it is impossible for merely a practical farmer or gardener to say at once what should be the precise mode of cultivation, in order to obtain success in producing a good crop of either the parts of vegetation or of fructification. But if in addition to his practical knowledge he is acquainted with the principles which should guide him, he will at once see the direction in which he should proceed. But the best practice, or the details for successful culture, can only be ascertained after numerous tentative experiments and probably some failures. Principles should, therefore, be combined with practice in the improvement of any culture; for all that is to be done by blind empiricism has long since been attained by our predecessors. It is by studying the principles of science and applying them to practice, that gardeners have attained the marvellous results of the present day. A course in which they have been followed by many farmers, who are astonishing their brethren by the almost incredible returns which they obtain from their fields, and extort the admiration of the public at the improved breeds and fine appearance of their herds and flocks: the result of a judicious application of the principles of physiological science to the breeding and feeding of animals.

The object in the cultivation of cotton is to obtain as large a quantity as possible of cotton-wool, with staple of moderate length and strength, of a good colour and in a clean state, and some of it very long, fine, and silky. As cotton is an appendage of the seed, the principles which should guide us in the cultivation of the plant are, after a certain period, those which favour the production of the parts of fructification instead of those of vegetation. Its production must depend upon whatever favours or impedes the production of fruit, and though the healthy growth of the stem, branches, and leaves is necessary for the fair production of fruit, yet it is quite possible, as we have stated, that the growth of the parts of vegetation may be over-vigorous as well as too stunted. For we may repeat, that at a particular period of the growth of a plant, the parts of vegetation and those of fructification may be considered as antagonistic, and that a check is required in the growth of branches and leaves, in order to favour the production of flowers; as we may have the most luxuriant vegetation without even the appearance of fruit, or fine foliage and little or no cotton-wool.

The American culture of cotton in the best localities consists especially in deep ploughing, in the careful selection of seed, in sowing in lines on ridges, keeping the plants wide apart, throwing the earth up about the lower parts of their stems, extreme care in the destruction of weeds by frequent ploughing and hoeing between the ridges. With these is sometimes combined topping or pruning. The cotton as it ripens is at once carefully picked, dried, and freed of its seed.

The Indian culture, on the contrary, in most parts of the country is as different as the produce is inferior; the seed being sown broadcast, often with three or four other crops, the plants closely crowded together, and weeds allowed to grow unrestrained. The wool, moreover, is allowed to hang long after it is ripe, or to mix with the dirt on the ground. But in some parts of India, as in Broach, the Southern Mahratta country, and in Berar, cotton is sown by itself in drills, as in the time of Alexander's expedition, is carefully weeded, a rotation of crops strictly attended to, and the produce, as might be anticipated, holds the first place among the cottons of India. It would hold a higher place among those of the world, if the cultivator would pick and clean his cotton as carefully as he grows it, or the middleman would allow it to come into the market even in as clean a state as he gets it from the cultivator.

We shall proceed now to detail the best method of culture, as adopted in the Gulf States, where the largest returns per acre are obtained, adding in notes any peculiarities of culture which are practised in other countries.

§ 12. Culture of Cotton in the United States.

In proceeding to consider in detail the culture of American Cotton, we may safely consider the Sea Island, New Orleans, and Georgian Cottons to be varieties of one species, that known to botanists as *Gossypium barbadense;* for the Mexican cotton has been traced to the Tierras Calientes of Vera Cruz and of Yucatan; from thence we may suppose it was early introduced into the West Indies. The first cultivators of Sea Island cotton trace their plant to the Bahamas, and the Bahama seed is said to have been obtained from Anguilla, one of the Caribbee Islands. We have already shown that there is reason for believing, that the Sea Island, and the best Egyptian, the West Indian, and the Bourbon, the New Orleans, and the Georgian Upland, are all varieties of one species, the above *Gossypium barbadense.* That some of these are perennial and others annual in habit is no valid objection, for we know in many cultivated plants, that varieties which originated in accident, or were the result of a designed culture, have become permanent in character if similarly cultivated. It appears, indeed, that " any tendency which is once given to a plant may be carried on from generation to generation, by a careful attention to the stoppage of all disposition to depart from the new character."

So with cotton itself, the Indian species, which is annual in the south of Europe, produces varieties which are perennial in its native country. The cotton cultivated in the West Indies was perennial, and we have seen that the Mexican plant introduced into Texas survives for three or four years. Mr. Spalding states, that he has known the Sea Island cotton " in warm alluvial lands to survive for five years." But both this, the New Orleans, and the Georgian Upland cotton, are all cultivated as annuals. So in India we find New Orleans cotton is usually cultivated as an annual, but occasionally as a perennial. Mr. Price, the American cotton planter employed in Bengal, speaks of the plant as taking a few months longer before bearing, and says, " it is a triennial plant here, not an annual, as in the United States." But Mr. Spalding observes, that " where the plant grows so large, it yields no return of cotton-wool to the cultivator," and also that "the Sea Island cotton was very subject to this overgrowth when first introduced into Georgia." Even now in newly cleared lands it is apt to run into long shoots, in consequence of which planters in the first year take a crop of Indian corn.

In noticing the details of culture, we must keep these facts in mind, also that the winter of the Southern States leaves the soil in a moist and cold state, and that it is followed by frequent falls of rain in the spring as well as in the summer, and this in a climate which we have seen is upon the whole a moist one, and where, consequently, some difficulty is experienced in having the soil sufficiently dry for ploughing and for sowing. "Fortunately," Mr. Spalding says, "Tull's ridge husbandry became known to the colonists, and was adopted for the Sea Island cotton with great success." It may also be observed, that the cultivation of cotton in the United States is more of the nature of garden than of field culture; meaning by the first,—culture, in which attention may be and is paid to plants individually, while in the latter it is adapted to the species or variety, and each plant takes its chance among the mass. Mr. Spalding considers a rotation of crops essential, or rather that an intermediate crop of grain should be reaped, and all root crops be avoided.

For the cultivation of cotton the ground is well ploughed and cast into ridges, which are about 10 inches in height, but vary in being from 5 to 6 or 7 feet apart, according to the richness of the soil, or the kind of cotton to be cultivated. In poorer soils the ridges are narrower, so that the plants which do not grow so large may yet be able to cover the ground. The ridges allow superfluous moisture to be carried off by the water-furrow, which in low situations is made into a trench. The soil is allowed to settle for a few days before sowing, as the young plants take root more vigorously than when they spring up in freshly ploughed and loose earth. Sometimes the ground is manured by running a deep furrow, early in the spring, between the old rows of cotton stalks, which are beaten down into it by women and children, who follow the ploughman; or well rotted cotton-seed is added as a manure, and well covered up by forming a slight ridge over it. When the ground is quite prepared, a one-horse drill makes a slight furrow, from $1\frac{1}{2}$

to 2 inches deep, along the centre of the ridge. The sower follows and drops in the seeds pretty thickly. These are immediately covered by a light harrow, which also smooths the ridge. Sometimes five or six seeds are dropped into holes, which are made at intervals of about 15 inches, on the top of the ridge. In favorable weather the plants make their appearance in five or six days, and are thinned out as soon as they put forth the third or fourth leaf. This operation is performed by scraping out with the hoe all the superfluous plants and weeds, leaving three or four together, with spaces of 12 or 14 inches between them. When the plants are sufficiently established, they are reduced to a single one, and care is taken to remove every particle of grass or weed. A light furrow is then run with a one-horse plough within 5 or 6 inches of the plants, turning the earth inwards towards the roots, and even drawing it around them with the hoe, in order to supply the place of that previously removed by scraping. Hoeing and ploughing are frequently repeated, so as to keep the ground free from weeds, and this is considered essential towards obtaining a good crop. The above processes, besides loosening the soil and keeping it clean, must assist in drying it, at the same time that they prevent much lateral extension of the roots.

The cotton plant is one of those having a tap root, which, according to the dryness or moisture of the season, will penetrate from two to three feet in the former, and perhaps not more than a foot in the latter. The plant may be fine-looking in a moist season, when there are only short roots; but in a dry season, the roots penetrate deeply, obtain a supply of moisture from a greater extent, and are necessarily better able to bear drought and the vicissitudes of seasons. The cotton being sown towards the end of March or as late as the middle of April, attains, in about six weeks or two months, what the planters call a "good stand," that is, plants well-grown, and at intervals proportioned to the richness of the land. About the beginning of June the weather becomes hot and the air dry; this checks the upward growth of the plant, while the root continues to penetrate deeper, and has thus to supply a smaller bush and less wood at the very time when there is a tendency to the production of flowers. But when the parts of vegetation have grown freely, in consequence of a moist season, the roots being easily supplied, spread little, and will be found small in proportion to the size of the plant. Here the hopes of the planter cannot fail to be disappointed when drought comes on. Though in the other case he has often been surprised with a good crop when the appearance of the plant above ground did not seem to him to give much promise. Topping or pinching off an inch or two of the top of the plant is not always necessary, but is useful when there is a tendency to the production of wood and leaves, to the detriment of flowers and bolls.*

When all the operations have been completed, the plant is

*NOTES ON THE CULTIVATION OF COTTON BY MR. MERCER AND OTHERS.

"The Hon. the President, in submitting the following communication from the pen of Mr. Mercer, one of the American cotton planters, informed the meeting that it had been drawn up at the request of the Right Hon. the Governor-General:

"The best season for sowing, I think, would be after the heavy rains of the s. w. monsoons are past. Much water would be likely to injure the fresh-planted seed, and also the young plants.

"The ground should be prepared by being well broken up with the plough, and cast into ridges eight or ten inches high, and six or seven feet apart—say, six feet for Sea Island. After the ground has been prepared in this matter, if it is allowed to settle for a few days previous to sowing, the young plants are likely to take root more vigorously, than if they sprang up in the freshly-ploughed and loose earth.

"In planting, one hand with a hoe should make, on the top of the ridge, holes about an inch and a half in depth, and sixteen or eighteen inches apart; another should follow and drop into each hole five or six seeds, and a third coming after should cover them lightly, taking care to leave the ground perfectly smooth.

"When the plants are up and begin to put forth the third leaf, they should be thinned to two stalks. In doing this the hoe should be used to scrape away from the remaining plants any grass or weeds that may have sprung up in the meantime. In a week or ten days they will be mature enough to risk thinning again, when they should be reduced to one stalk, and the hoe used as before to remove any interlopers. At this stage the plough should be used, and a light furrow turned with it towards the cotton, taking care not to run it so close as to cover any of the plants; the hoe should follow the plough, and draw the mould around the roots sufficient to replace what had been removed by the previous scrapings, but not any more. When this is done, the spaces between the rows should be ploughed afresh to destroy the grass, and this operation should be repeated as often as they become foul, still using the hoe to keep the spaces between the plants on the ridge clean; the hoe should be so set as to scrape and not to dig or chop. It is the most essential feature in this cultivation, to keep the ground free from all extraneous vegetation while the plants are growing.

"Topping is important only when it is disposed to produce wood and leaves to the detriment of flowers and pods. When this is the case, to take off an inch or two of two or three months old, and from two to three feet high; but at other times it attains a height of four or five feet. The plants flower in about eighty days after the seed has been sown.

the top after it has fairly commenced podding—say about the beginning of the fourth month after planting—will materially assist that operation.

"The cotton should be gathered or picked as the pods burst, not leaving it exposed to dews or sun; if it is even dried under cover, it will advantage its glossiness of appearance. The picker should be provided with a bag about the size of a pillow-slip, suspended to his side by a strap across his shoulder, in which to thrust the cotton as he picks it, taking care to keep it free from trashy leaves or dirt of any kind; he should grasp the cotton with his thumb and three forefingers, and avoid as much as possible drawing away any of the pod or outer leafy covering.

"Sea Island cotton is always cleaned in America by the roller-gin, the saw-gin is never used."—(*Proc. of the Agri. Hortic. Soc. of India.* 1841.)

Cultivation in the West Indies.—Though the culture of cotton in the West Indies has almost ceased, from the greater profits obtained from sugar, the successful opposition of the United States, in consequence of the large returns obtained from their careful cultivation of cotton, yet it is desirable to notice any peculiarities of culture, though this seems never to have been conducted with much care.

In the West Indies, they used, in land which had not been cleared, to fell and set fire to the trees, and dig holes for sowing the seeds. These were in straight lines and placed in a quincunx form, about fifteen to eighteen inches deep and about a foot wide, and as wide at the bottom as at the top. They were then filled up again lightly to the *level* of the soil. The distance of the rows varied; in level and fertile districts the intervals were larger than in poor and mountainous situations. The sowing may be performed in any one of the six months from November to April inclusive. The seeds were then sown, about twelve in number, at equal distances asunder, and then lightly covered to the depth of half an inch or an inch with mould. They sprang up in three or four days when the weather had been showery; and when the shoots were three or four inches out of the ground, all, with the exception of three or four to each hole, were pulled up by hand. The ground was then carefully weeded, and the operation repeated as frequently as might be required. At the end of the third month, or earlier, all the young plants, except one, were drawn from each hole. When this had attained a height of eighteen or twenty-four inches, it was usual to pinch off its top, which was found to favour the formation of lateral branches, as in other places where the growth is luxuriant.

In Guiana, where the kidney cotton (*Gossypium peruvianum*) is, no doubt, chiefly cultivated, the plants do not produce a full crop before the second year of their growth, but remain productive for four or five years. Fresh plants or seeds are introduced into the field, as the old plants appear to become deficient. Pruning takes place in the second year of their growth, and is commenced some time between April and July. The whole produce is most commonly gathered in by April; the following month is considered to be the fittest for pruning, which will occupy the whole strength of the plantation during four or five weeks. It is advisable to keep the height of the plants about four feet; but this will, of course, depend on circumstances. Careful weeding is essential and thorough hoeing, at

In 1849 they did not flower until the 15th of June, and this year not until from the 5th to the 10th July, which was twenty to twenty-five days later than usual. From the fall of

least three times between the pruning and the gathering of the crop. The blossoms generally appear about the end of July or beginning of August, after which the pods form a regular succession. Some cotton may be ready for picking in September, but principally after the middle of October, and the crop is not all got in until the end of December, forming what is called the first crop. After this time the planters look for more or less rain during two or three weeks, which causes the trees to vegetate luxuriantly and to put forth their blossoms anew, so that by the end of February the picking of cotton may be recommenced. The second crop generally lasts until the middle of April. Weeding must be carefully attended to, as in the first year. (*Porter's Tropical Agriculturist.*)

In the *Directions for the Culture of Cotton in Africa*, issued by the African Society, and which were, no doubt, obtained from the best sources of information, it is stated, that no plant requires so little rain as cotton. "The sowing is recommended to take place in the early part of the rainy season, or the operation may be deferred till the rains are within a month or two of their termination, with a view to guard against over-luxuriant vegetation, whereby the plants might exhaust their strength in branches and leaves, and to avoid the injurious consequences of rain at the time the blossoms are appearing." The instructions for cultivation are generally the same as have been given above. With regard to pruning, it is recommended that an inch or more be broken or cut off the "end of each shoot, which makes the stems spread and throw out a greater number of branches; and this operation, if the plants are very luxuriant, will require to be performed a second, or even a third time, with a knife, on the stem and branches."

The plant should be cut down every year, within three or four inches of the ground. The time for doing this, which must be in the rainy season (?) ought to be regulated by the same circumstances which regulate the planting of the seed at first. But every fourth or fifth year the plants ought to be grubbed out, and their places supplied with plants grown from fresh seed brought from a distance.

Culture of Cotton in the Islands of France and Bourbon.—The cultivation of cotton, it is stated (*E. I. Papers*, p. 385), "has only been followed since the year 1788 and 1789. Towards the year 1796 the plant began to degenerate, and a greater quantity of cotton was produced of a yellow than a white colour, owing, it is said, to the puncture of an insect. At present (1811) this culture is little attended to, owing to the great quantity of yellow cotton which it is necessary to separate carefully from the white." Cotton seems to thrive best in warm low grounds, and within a league or a league and a quarter of the sea-shore. "This preference is not to be attributed to the vicinity of the sea, but rather to the difference of climate and temperature, which varies according to the degree of elevation;" for it does not succeed on the sides exposed to the influence of the trade-winds, "because in all this part the rains are too frequent." "Flat, free, and too rich soils, particularly those which retain humidity, have been found little suited to this culture. The shrub flourishes luxuriantly; the leaves and pods become formed; the former are large and of a dark green, but the tree produces little fruit." (Loc. cit., p. 387.) In the driest part of the island leeward, they plant the cotton-tree about the month of November, the flower to the ripening of the pod is another period of from six to eight weeks; but it may be shorter, and has sometimes extended to three months, and hence may be as early as the middle of July, though picking usually begins about the middle of August, and from that to the 1st of September. The extent of the crop that can be collected will depend upon the

and may do so as late as January; but in the parts where rain is more plentiful, they can sow all the year round. The seeds are sown in lines; a slight blow of a pickaxe is sufficient to make the hole where they are to be deposited, and these holes may be seven to nine feet, or six feet by five asunder, and the seeds, when sown nine or ten in each hole, should be covered with about half an inch of earth. Some plant maize between the rows of cotton-trees. "The slight damage which the shrub experiences, and the smallness of the first crop, are amply made up by the return in maize." Any places where the seeds have failed must be resown. When the plants are three inches high, the number in each hole must be reduced to "two or three of the strongest plants, near which the earth should be opened and a little heaped up around each shoot," and subsequently to one plant, care being taken to keep the ground clear and free from weeds, at least until the plants are six months old.

At *Bourbon*, about the month of April, the cotton-tree begins to shed its leaves. This fall precedes the blossoming, fifty days after which the gathering begins. The blossoming varies from a month to a month and a half; but in general the earlier it takes place, the more abundant is the crop.

If the cotton-tree has been planted in November or December, it bears in six or eight months; if in winter, it is more backward, and only produces in May or June. Until that time it requires nothing more than clearing from weeds. Its greatest produce is when the plant is eighteen months or two years old. It is gathered between the months of June, August, and September. It has been known to produce a few pods in October and November, and some trees have sometimes after the great crop, given a small one in the month of May following; but at this period, as after September, it is a mere gleaning.

At the Isle of France, opinions are much divided as to the advantage or necessity of pruning the cotton-trees every year; as by some they are only pruned every third or fourth year, and some never cut the plants at all. One advantage of pruning is stated to be, that the planter is enabled to grow maize between the rows of cotton. Some advise that the plants should be renewed after the third year, by planting in the rows usually intended for maize.

But the necessity or advantage of pruning, or of renewing, must depend upon the peculiarities of soil and climate, and the luxuriance of the plant and its fruitfulness.

In the Isle of France, the inhabitants encourage in their plantations the growth of the plant called *esquine*, and in Bourbon they have the saying, "No esquine, no cotton." Its roots do not strike deep, not above an inch, and, therefore, cannot hurt those of the cotton; nor is there anything in its flower or seed which can adhere to the wool. It smothers all other weeds, covers the soil, and protects it from the heat of the sun; is also useful in protecting the wool from the dust, by receiving it when it falls. They have also "the custom in the isle of Bourbon of planting peas in the cotton-grounds (*Dolichos utilis ?*) which afford the same advantages as the esquine, and, moreover, a pulse useful in domestic economy."

earliness or lateness of the frost. This is expected about the 20th of October, but sometimes does not come until the 10th of December; and in some of the warm districts picking has gone on even until Christmas. The plant usually requires about seven months for germination, growth, flowering, and full maturation of its fruit.

The foregoing account has been drawn up from the different published accounts of the culture in America, with the aid of the relations of the planters who have visited this country and India. Dr. Wight, who has had great practice in experimental culture, considers the principles of the American system to be about the nearest approach to perfection yet promulgated; but to suit it to the Indian climate, he proposes several modifications, such as deep ploughing in the first instance, to promote the free absorption of moisture and the ready diffusion of the roots through the earth, closer sowing and more hoeing, to keep the ground clear, instead of repeated ploughing and hoeing. For open planting favours free ventilation, and by exposing the turned-up soil to heat, light, and air, equally promotes evaporation and drying up. Frequent ploughing between the rows will also have the effect of checking growth by cutting off any lateral radicles, though the cotton plant has comparatively few such. The planters of India, in a drier soil and climate, place their rows of plants much nearer to each other, or sow thick and broad-cast, often with other crops. This may be detrimental to the cotton in one way, but may be useful in shading the ground and preventing excessive dryness. The ridges appear not only superfluous but injurious in a dry climate; for being raised, and forming a comparatively thin stratum of earth, they must be heated and even baked by the powerful sun of India, and the tender radicles of the plant proportionately injured. Any rain which falls will also run off too rapidly by the water-furrow on each side of the row of plants, which though beneficial in a moist, will be detrimental in a dry climate.

But such terms as moisture and dryness are so entirely comparative, that in one country we hear the cotton plant described as one requiring moisture, and in another we find it stated, that no plant requires so little. The fact being, that the plant can bear both great heat and considerable want of water, provided it is growing in a not over-dry atmosphere. But great differences may be observed in this respect even in the different seasons of the same country and climate. A good cotton soil being deep and light, permeable both by roots and rain, and a suitable climate one that is moderately warm and genially moist, poor lands will produce fine crops in a wet season, and rich lands and river bottoms by retaining moisture in a dry season. Even the depth of sowing will depend upon the season and situation; thus, two inches may be deep enough in early spring when the ground is moist and cold, and four inches not too deep later in the season, when the surface is dry and heated. The distance at which the rows are kept must depend upon the extent to which plants are likely to spread, so that the ground be well covered and shaded. Therefore, according to the richness of the soil should be the distance of plants, being not more than four feet in the Santee Hills of Georgia, and eight feet apart on the Mississippi.

Seasons also differ so much from one another, that the culture which is suitable in one year may not prove so the very next year in the same place; but to such difficulties all culture is liable. The season of 1842-43 was, in the cotton districts of the United States, a very rainy one; the stalk has been described to the author as growing, in some instances, to twelve feet in height, and looking at the same time so luxuriant, that those who allowed themselves to be deceived by appearances, estimated the crop at 3,000,000 of bales. The root was found, notwithstanding the great length of stalk, to be only about six inches in length, and the production of cotton amounted only to 1,700,000 bales, while in the previous year, which enjoyed a favorable dry season, the crop amounted to 2,500,000 bales. Similar disappointments and surprises have occurred in India. Dr. Wight mentions his having one season 100 acres of noble-looking plants loaded with fruit, so that he expected to realise not less than 1000 pounds of cotton per acre; but a diminution of moisture took place, thousands and tens of thousands of bolls never opened, and only 40,000 pounds were realised, though a second crop was afterwards obtained: while from a field of cotton in black soil, of which the plants at one time looked almost withered up, he obtained a fair crop. The general complaint in India, however, is that the crops are destroyed by excessive drought at unseasonable times.

Having seen how carefully the Americans cultivate their cotton, we may be the less surprised at the large crops which the Mississippi planters obtain, being about a bale or 400 lbs. of clean cotton from an acre of ground, while those at a distance from the river, on higher ground, and in the interior of the Atlantic states, do not, on an average, get more than 250, perhaps only 200 lbs., this being about the quantity obtained by the cultivators of Sea Island cotton, though their expenses are much greater. Notwithstanding the large returns, the best planters are not satisfied with continuing to cultivate from the same seed, but interchange with one another, or every four or five years obtain seed grown on the Gulf Hills of Mississippi, or import fresh seed from Mexico. But it may happen that seeds producing the most strong-growing plants may not be the most suitable in a rich soil, while in a dry one they may require to be assisted by rubbing up with mud, or soaking in water. From the richness of the soil, the planters of the Gulf States are enabled to continue to cultivate in the same fields without the necessity of rotation, and give as manure only the leaves and ashes of the burnt stalks. Others continue to cultivate in the same fields from year to year, with the simple change of the drill into the furrow and back again, with only the above manure and cotton-seed (v. p. 161), until the ground seems tired of growing cotton, when a crop of some grain is taken. But a rotation of crops, in which cotton is cultivated only every second or third year, is found the most advantageous course in poorer soils and less favorable climates.

The above may be considered as the general features of cotton culture in the United States. In Guiana, where the climate is both hotter and moister, and the land chiefly an alluvial mud, this is divided into beds, which are slightly elevated in the middle, and which are surrounded by drains, emptying themselves into trenches. By these the redundant moisture is readily carried off, and its lodgment prevented round the roots of the cotton, which is so injurious to its growth. Topping or pruning is here more frequently practised, and may be useful from the moisture and warmth of the climate, but may depend perhaps as much upon another species being that commonly cultivated. (See also the note, p. 220.)

The climates hitherto mentioned, in which cotton has been successfully cultivated, being all more or less moist, means are necessary to get rid of superfluous moisture. It appears curious that the same cotton should be successfully cultivated in Egypt, which is remarkable for being a dry climate. But there moisture is supplied artificially. Lieutenant Waghorn some years since described the cultivation of the foreign cotton in Egypt as consisting of four or five seeds being sown at every eighteen inches, in trenches about five feet apart, though only one plant of each group, and that the most healthy, is afterwards left. The soil must be a rich and not a sandy one, situated either near the banks of the Nile or some canal near it, where there is water the whole year. It must be watered every three or four days when it first begins to sprout, and afterwards every ten days. The crop is gathered from June to January (v. p. 183).

The Chinese have an admirable mode of overcoming the dryness of a soil. It is thus described: "When the Chinese cultivators wish to appropriate to the production of cotton land which is poor and approaching to sterility, they keep the field covered with water during the winter, which practice proves, they say, an admirable preparation for this kind of plant. They maintain that this inundation is as sure a means of amelioration to poor and dry lands, as draining is to such as have been subjected to a lengthened inundation." "The herbaceous cotton, which is the species principally cultivated in China, is usually raised in land of a medium quality, which is sandy and rather dry than otherwise." But they also "allow the cotton shrub to remain on the ground during three years, and in the fourth year root it out, and plant the land with grain." (*Porter*, l. c., p. 29.)

The natives of India raise excellent crops of wheat, &c., on lands which have been inundated during the long-continued rains. But as the season when the inundations run off just precedes the accession of the cold weather, it is not, in most parts of the country, favorable for the culture of cotton. In some of these, they obviate the shortness of the favorable season by irrigating both before and after the rainy season; and they used to cultivate the best cotton in the Benares district (v. p. 141), where the climate is excessively hot and dry before the accession of the rains, only in the vicinity of water. Knowing its occasional necessity, the author recommended the subject of irrigation to the planters who were proceeding to the North-Western provinces (v. p. 183). But as the methods of raising water are all too expensive for the cotton crop, he referred, in a paper which he read before the Natural History Section of the British Association at Manchester, in 1842, to "the great canal which has been sanctioned by the Court of Directors to be made through the centre of the Doab, and which is to be 500 miles in length, and will afford water for irrigating five miles on both sides, as (under Providence) it will render famine impossible, so it will make the cultivation of cotton easy and independent of dry seasons." The author has as yet seen no reason to change his opinion; but believes that cotton may, by means of irrigation, be cultivated in places which he did not then contemplate, such as Scinde and the Punjab, in both of which the facilities for irrigation will soon be very considerable.

In connection with the directions for cultivating the cotton plant as an annual, it is desirable to notice in detail the method of treating it as a perennial. Mr. Hughes, of Tinnivelly, in the Peninsula of India, long distinguished for growing both excellent cotton and senna, gave, in the year 1819, the following as his method of growing Bourbon cotton, to Mr. Heath, at that time commercial resident at Salem and Coimbatore, and who had received instructions from the Board of Trade of Madras to attempt to introduce the cultivation of Bourbon cotton into the above districts.

On the Cultivation of Cotton, as a Perennial.—Mr. Hughes stated, "That the Bourbon cotton demands, in India, a mode of treatment similar to that of America; and arranged his observations on its culture under the heads of *Soil, Climate, Culture, Pruning,* and *Cleaning,* attention to all of which he considered to be equally essential for attaining success.

"1. With regard to *Soil,* he stated that the red and brown loams, or indeed any siliceous or calcareous soil, fertile in a moderate degree, was the most suitable and fruitful. That no very rich, heavy, retentive, stiff soils, should ever be selected;

for though the plants might be luxuriant, they have more tendency to produce redundance of wood and leaf, than of fruit-buds, besides harbouring insects. What is commonly known in many parts of India, under the denomination of *black cotton soil*, was to be entirely avoided for the Bourbon cotton.

"2. With regard to *Climate*, he was of opinion, that the vicinity of the sea, or situations to which the influence of the sea-air extends, were on every account to be preferred. A dry soil and a dry atmosphere, from March to May, and from July to September, seem almost essential to the good quality of the wool, as well as to the productiveness of the plant. The free admission of sun, the freest circulation of air, and of light winds, are of the greatest benefit to a perfect culture.

"3. Mr. Hughes ascertained that the plant will last a great number of years, and that it does not fall off if well and properly managed. The seed should be sown, or the young plants be set, in straight rows, eight feet apart; the rows, also, should be regularly eight feet asunder. The facility for ploughing and hoeing, and the advantage of a free circulation of air being so great, he particularly insisted on this being attended to, especially as he knew that too close planting was a common mistake. If the seed can be got into the ground in September, the young plant may be able to resist the continued wet of a heavy monsoon; but little is gained by sowing in October, November, and December, unless the land is very high, dry, and free from weeds. The clear intervals of these months, especially of the early part of October, answer well for transplanting; and the first week of January very well, in general, both for sowing and transplanting.

"4. *Pruning* was practised twice in the year, the first and principal, as soon as the heavy rains have passed away, that is, from the 15th to the 31st of December, when the shrub is cut down, generally to two feet high and two feet wide, only the firm wood being left with the strong white and brown bark. In the fine days of January, the plantation is ploughed thoroughly three or four times. In less than two months the whole is again in the finest foliage and full blossom, and continues in full bearing all the months of March, April, and May. A good many pods still remain in June; early in which month a second pruning is practised of the long, straggling, twisted, soft shoots with diminutive pods. Good produce is yielded from July to September, unless the plants receive damage in these months from rain.

"5. Great importance is attached to the process of *Cleaning*. The cotton should never be picked but when in a mature state; and even then it requires to be thoroughly dried, and carefully preserved from dirt or sand getting into the wool. Before being sent to the mill, all the decayed, damaged, and immature parts of the pods are first separated, when about a tenth of the whole is rejected. After being a little exposed to the sun, the wool is separated in the usual way; but women are always present to clean it by hand as soon as it comes from the mill, that is, they search rather than pull the wool, and about five per cent. is rejected during this process.

"With regard to the extent of produce, Mr. Hughes stated that some of his dependents did not get more than fifty pounds of cotton from the acre. He himself was well content with one hundred pounds per acre, of fine clean cotton, which he calculated cost him about twelve pence a pound, and which was sold in London, in 1817, for 2*s*. 1⅜*d*. to 2*s*. 1⅞*d*."

Mr. Heath, in addressing the foregoing to the Royal Asiatic Society, stated, "That his experience differed from that of Mr. Hughes, with respect to the influence of vicinity to the sea, as he found the cotton came to perfection at a distance of one hundred and fifty miles from the sea. He could also produce it at a cheaper rate, by availing himself more extensively of the services of the natives, whom he found most trustworthy, and fully to be relied on. He made an abridgment of Mr. Hughes's paper, which he had translated into Tamul, and given to every farmer, who agreed to make trial of the new seed. He, moreover, employed a person to go round, inspect, and report on the progress of the cultivation. At the proper seasons for pruning, Mr. Heath himself went round and showed how the operation should be performed.

"He made his experiments on the Bourbon cotton in a very light soil, formed from the disintegration of granitic rocks, especially when mixed with *kunkar*, or calcareous tufa. This kind of soil is more abundant than any other in the districts on the Coromandel coast, south of Madras, and he entertains no doubt that the Bourbon cotton-plant might be successfully cultivated wherever this kind of soil occurs. In introducing this cultivation, he had to encounter the usual difficulties consequent on the introduction of any novelty in agriculture; but these gave way to perseverance. At the end of four years, Mr. Heath had the satisfaction of seeing the experiment completely successful, as in the season 1823-24 he procured from the district of Coimbatore five hundred bales of clean Bourbon cotton, of three hundred pounds each; and the natives were, at that time, well satisfied that the cultivation of this was more profitable to them than that of the common cotton of the country.

As the methods of *gathering the crop* may be nearly the same wherever it is cultivated, they may be treated of together. Immediately the cotton is ripe, the capsules or pods burst, the cotton is exposed to view or hangs down, and should be gathered as it ripens, though the Uplands may be allowed to remain unpicked for a longer period than the Sea Island. Cotton should be gathered as soon as the capsules burst, and should not be allowed to hang in the sun, or be exposed to the dews of night. Women and children are much employed, for the labour is light, and they are well qualified to perform it. They are usually provided with two bags suspended from their shoulders, in order to keep separate the clean from the dirty or discoloured specimens which they may collect. Care must be taken to lay hold with the thumb and fingers only of the locks of cotton including the seeds, without any dried leaves or bracts, as the admixture very much deteriorates the value of cotton. Any that has become so mixed, or has fallen on the ground, must be kept apart in one of the bags, taking care that the clean specimens in the other do not become dirtied as the picker passes along the bushes. Some planters do not allow the fallen locks to be gathered until after the clean cotton has been removed from the field. The process is repeated as the cotton becomes ripe, with intervals of from five to ten days, according to the nature of the crop. The quantity collected by each picker is weighed, and it is found that a good hand will pick from 90 to 100 lbs. of seed cotton per day, some say more; while of Sea Island cotton not more than 25 or 50 lbs. can be collected in the same time. The cotton having been conveyed on carts to the homestead, is spread out on tiles or wooden scaffolds, usually in the sun for two or three days, taking care to avoid wet or dew. If dried under shade the glossiness of its appearance is said to be improved. When the cotton has become dry, it is not liable to heat, nor the oil to ooze out and discolour the cotton, while the seed has become hard enough to allow of the cotton being separated from it. But before being submitted to this process, the best kinds are carefully inspected and sorted, when any discoloured cotton, motes, leaves, or other impurities are carefully picked out, usually by women seated on benches with wire-frames or slit-tables before them. The seed cotton, as examined in small parcels, is then thrown into baskets, after which it is again dried in the sun a short time, whence it is removed, and then taken to be ginned, as will be afterwards described.

We have not alluded to the *disasters* which attend cotton culture arising from "rains, winds, and worms;" also that a single night's frost in spring "will ruin the whole prospect, and require a renewal of the labours;" and after long-continued drought "the whole plant puts on the appearance of having been scorched by fire." Some at least of these drawbacks must be looked for when the culture is tried in other countries. The casualties to which cotton is subject in America would seem sufficient to check its extension; yet we find that it continues to be extensively cultivated. Failures, therefore, in other situations ought not to operate as permanent obstacles, until it has been satisfactorily ascertained by competent judges that the difficulties are such that they cannot be profitably overcome, nor any modification of culture made to suit the peculiarities of soil and climate. An American author has stated that no crop is more precarious, "in its first stage it is attacked by the grub; it is devoured by bugs in the second, and by caterpillars in the third; it is often withered by the wind in its infancy, and by the blight in mature age; and when the grower is about to reap the golden harvest, an equinoctial gale, or a few saturating showers, deprive him at once of the fruit of his labours." In short, some of these disasters are dependent on the uncertainties of climate, and others on the devastations of insects. The former are usually distinguished by the name of blast or blight, though the effects are very different in kind. Sometimes they arise from over-vigorous vegetation, caused by excess of moisture in the soil or air, and in some respects correspond with those of a plethoric state in animals; at other times, the wet being lodged about the roots, these rot, and the plants necessarily droop and perish. Sometimes the blight depends upon the exhaustion of vegetation, consequent on dryness of the soil produced by long-continued drought, or occurring with drying winds. The leaves become brownish, and the whole plant puts on the appearance of having been scorched by fire; the blossoms do not develope but droop, and the pods within become blackish and drop. Notwithstanding this destruction, the plant is not always killed; but by pruning or cutting back, and a change of weather taking place, fresh leaves, flowers, and fruit will be produced, and a partial crop realized. Unfortunately when in this sickly state, the plant is sometimes attacked by its other great scourge—insects.

Considering of how great importance the culture of cotton is to America, we might expect that the *Insects* which attack the cotton plant would have been accurately observed and carefully described; but this does not appear to have been the case, so far as the author has been able to learn even from the most distinguished entomologists. The insects are mentioned by planters by the name of Army-worm and Boll-worm, of Bug, Cut-worm, and Chenille; but whether these are all generically and specifically distinct, or whether the same insect has different names in different localities, the author has been unable to ascertain, and has, therefore, placed in a note such information as he has been able to procure. The army-worm and chenille* are, no doubt,

* The *Chenille* is, no doubt, the larva of a lepidopterous insect, and the ravages which it has committed are almost incredible. As they consume the leaves, they in a very short time denude of foliage every stalk in a field. The cotton plant is subject to the attacks of this caterpillar in Guiana, and in the Bahamas it has sometimes destroyed two thirds of a crop, and is particularly distinguished by a fragrant smell being perceived, even at a hundred yards, when it is feeding on the leaves of the cotton. It is described as being "about an inch or an inch and a half long, its back and sides of a glossy black; a single line of white runs down the whole length of the back at its middle, and dull white lines are seen at each side of the single line, and running in a direction parallel to it. The belly is of a whitish-yellow colour, and is covered with a soft downy hair intermixed with bristles which are short and black." (*Porter's Tropical Agriculturist*, p. 24.) Either this or another caterpillar forms the *Army-worm* of the United States, which congregates in such swarms upon the cotton plant in some seasons, as to destroy a large portion of the very extensive American crop.

The caterpillar of the cotton-moth, or *Noctua xylina*, as it is called by Mr. Seabrook, attacked the cotton in Georgia in 1793, seven years afterwards in South Carolina, and has since then frequently repeated its desolating attacks.

The August full moon is the time when the caterpillar makes its appearance. It the larva of a moth, and the boll-worm is some kind of beetle. An accurate knowledge of the natural history of some of these animals might lead, in some cases at least, to rational methods of prevention. But such subjects are neglected; for the public seem to consider everything minute as trifling, and the planters whatever is scientific as useless.

Various remedies have been suggested against these animals, but apparently with little benefit, from the extent of their field of operation. But as shelter and weeds favour their production, open planting and careful weeding, besides being useful to the plants, will tend to impede the progress of the insects by giving free access to the wind, to birds, and to poultry, as

is the offspring of a small brown moth resembling the candle-moth, which deposits its eggs upon the leaf of the *Gossypium* always a night or two before the full or new moon. They hatch a few hours after they are deposited, and are so small at first as to be hardly discernible to the naked eye; they do little or no damage during the first nine or ten days of their life, like the silk-worms eating but little in their infancy; but a few days before they complete their growth they become so excessively voracious as to destroy an entire plantation in a few hours. Mr. Spalding has seen 400 acres of cotton of a promising aspect, which four days thereafter did not possess a green leaf or scarcely a solitary pod upon a plant. (*Ure's Cotton*, vol. i, p. 106.)

Planters also mention the *Cut-worm*, or grub, which prevails in the month of April, and destroys the young plant, either above or below the ground, just as it has come up, when whole fields require to be replanted.

Besides these, we find both red and black bugs mentioned, and a *Cotton-Bug* is described as destroying whole fields of cotton in Jamaica. Whether this name is intended to indicate a species of *Cimex*, or is only a general name for some kind of coleopterous insect, it is difficult to say. In Georgia "it is described as a winged insect with a long proboscis, with which it pierces the green pods, extracting the juices of the seed, and leaving the capsules blighted and hard, and the cotton stained of a deep yellow or red colour. Another is mentioned by the old name of *Apate monachus*. Its larva eating with a revolving motion, penetrates to the wood and pith, and by arresting the ascent of the sap, either destroys the plant, or renders it comparatively barren. This is probably the same as the *Boll*, or *Bore-worm*, which Mr. Turner thinks is probably the larva of a coleopterous insect, perhaps a *Curculio*, which feeds upon the pods and seeds of the cotton, and prevents them from ripening.

In a letter, with which I have been favoured while this sheet is passing through the press, Mr. Turner writes: "I do not know where you will find a description of *Noctua xylina*. 'Noctua' is a very old genus of moths, which it has been found needful by modern entomologists to break up into a vast number of sub-genera; and several of the specific names under the genus Noctua have been adopted as the names of the sub-genera. *Xylina* is one of these. There are a great number of species, and the larvæ, doubtless, of all, prey upon the leaves of some particular plant. The Cotton-plant has the benefit of one of them, it seems." "I do not know *Apate monachus*."

well as to labourers to pick off infected leaves or to cut out whole branches. Fumigating with sulphur under temporary covers placed over the plants; sprinkling them with lime, and filling up the holes made by the borers, have all been recommended. The moths might probably be destroyed in considerable numbers, if oil-lamps floating in vessels of water, and placed in the open rows, were lighted at night in different parts of a field. The moths would fly towards the lights and be destroyed in myriads, and the method might perhaps be adopted, in some cases, with great benefit, as it is in the vineyards of France.

Mr. Turner suggests, "that, among the preventatives used to abate the evil, a plan might be adopted which is used by moth-collectors in this neighbourhood (that is, Manchester), viz. depositing with a brush a little liquid mixture of sugar and rum, diluted to about the consistence of treacle, on several places, such as the stems of trees, or on railings. The same might be done in the neighbourhood of the cotton plantations. About dusk, when the moths are flying, they will congregate in great numbers to sip the nectar, are then quite stupefied, and may easily be caught or destroyed, by which means the depositing of myriads of eggs might be prevented. When the eggs *have* been deposited on the leaves, the young family of caterpillars confine themselves for a day or two after being hatched to the single leaf on which they emerged from the eggs; and their presence may be detected by the number of *pin-holes* which they perforate in their first attempts to eat. A little attention in picking off these leaves, just at the hatching season, would save the whole plant. In a few days, the creatures disperse themselves over the whole plant. Gardeners in this neighbourhood adopt the plan with success to save their gooseberry crop."

In concluding the subject of the culture of cotton in America, it is important to ascertain the *expense* at which it can be produced, so as to yield a profit to the planter and to the merchant who transports it to the place of consumption. On the first establishment of the cotton experiments in India in 1840, the author made inquiries respecting the expenses of culture in America, and found that a cotton-planter had first to purchase his land, and then to pay for having it cleared. If the land had been cleared by some other planter, then he had to pay a higher price for it, while in the other case time was required to make it available for a cotton crop. He had also to purchase slaves, cattle, agricultural implements, as well as saw-gins, and to erect gin-houses in addition to the ordinary farm-buildings.

The annual expenses consist, besides the interest of the money expended and of the deterioration of property, of the pay of overseers and of incidental expenses, of food and medicines for his slaves and cattle, though the greatest portion of the food is, of course, raised on the farm.

The author, in his report written in 1847, stated, "Though the price of land may, therefore, be small in the first instance, the subsequent and annual expenses are so considerable, that the planter, even with enormous returns per acre, as, for instance, from 300 lbs. to 600 lbs. of clean cotton, is yet unable to produce it at a lower cost than about 3*d.* a lb. (6 cents.) This accords very nearly with the evidence of Mr. Joshua Bates, of the house of Baring and Co., and also with what I recently learnt at Manchester, that cotton could not, on an average, be produced under 3*d.* a lb., and this without profit to the owner of the property, or the expenses to Liverpool, and from that to the mills at Manchester, &c. The diminution in the imports of cotton from America during the present year, is considered to have been occasioned chiefly by restricted cultivation in the United States, in consequence of the low prices of 1846, when fair New Orleans cotton sold at Liverpool for 3¾*d.* a lb." (*House of Commons' Return*, p. 66.) Mr. Porter, in the 'Tropical Agriculturist,' states the cost of cotton to be 2½*d.* a lb., and Mr. Woodbury, in his 'Tables,' stated, "Where rich lands and labour were low, as in Mississippi and Alabama a few years ago, two cents (one penny) per lb. for cotton in the seed, or eight cents when cleaned, would pay expenses. It is supposed to be a profitable crop in the South-Western States at ten cents per lb." But the produce per acre in the old States of the Atlantic is not half what it is in the Southern States, though the expenses are at least equal; no increase has taken place in the quantity of cotton produced or exported for many years, as may be seen in the table at p. 14.

The expenses in cultivating cotton in the West Indies were considered to be much greater than the above, probably from the smaller production per acre, and less efficient superintendence. Mr. Edwards stated them formerly at 7½*d.* a lb. It is understood that at present they require in the West Indies 6*d.* a lb. for the cotton to pay. But there seems no reason why they should not be able to increase the returns, by suiting the culture to the peculiarities of soil and climate; and as cotton of excellent quality can be produced, there seems no reason why the culture should not be remunerative, if the difficult question of sufficient labour can be satisfactorily settled.

In Egypt, also, the expenses are said to be considerable, but the large quantity per acre which is now obtained, and the high quality of the cotton produced, enables it to pay. When in lower latitudes, the quantity obtained per acre was small; but when the culture was removed to the Delta, and cultivated with care, under European superintendence, cotton has been produced abundantly, and of a quality superior to the great mass of American cotton.* In consequence, no doubt, of the fall in price, and the profits of sugar cultivation, the supply from the West Indies has almost entirely ceased, as well as that from the Mediterranean; while in the Brazils no great increase has taken place, apparently from the apathy of the inhabitants, as good prices have always been realized whenever their cotton has been clean, and the expenses of cultivation do not appear to be so great as in the United States.

India alone, notwithstanding its alleged deficiencies and high taxation with well known small returns per acre, has been able to meet each fall in price in America, with a still lower rate for Indian cotton; and notwithstanding the want of

* We have understood, that the expenses of cultivating twenty acres of land, and sending the cotton produce, properly cleaned and packed, to the market, amount to about £100 sterling. These expenses consist of miri, or the government land-tax, and the proportion of poll-tax; of wear and tear of cattle and of implements, as well as of fodder for cattle; labour for ploughing, watering, &c.; for picking, ginning, and for packing the cotton; and then sending it to Alexandria. The returns vary from three to seven cantons per acre, and a canton is equal to about 97 lbs. English, that is, from near 300 to 600 lbs. of clean cotton per acre, which is as large as the American returns. This result is obtained by careful cultivation, by the aid of irrigation in 30° of north latitude, in what is considered a dry climate, but where there is probably a free circulation of air, and this somewhat moistened, within the Delta, by the vicinity of the sea and the free irrigation. The course is not beyond imitation in Scinde, the Punjab, and in the dry parts of India, as we shall afterwards point out.

a regular demand in this country, is enabled to export from its surplus production 100,000 to 250,000 bales, whenever a deficiency occurs in the markets of Europe, and could as easily send 1,000,000 bales, if the people knew how to do justice to themselves and to their country. It seems also the only country where a planter or mercantile agent has nothing more to do but to require that a certain quantity should be grown for him, and it will be grown by the native planters without any further exertion on his part, except looking that it is carefully picked, and then kept clean. If he wishes to get it at the cheapest rate, he has only to follow the fashion of the country and make advances, when the crop will be delivered to him at a certain rate. In other countries, he would have to pay labourers or feed slaves, before he could realize any returns. The country, therefore, is well worthy to be the subject of culture, and of experiments to ascertain whether the quality of its produce cannot be improved. We may, therefore, now proceed to treat of the—

§ 13. Experimental Culture of Cotton in India.

In the foregoing pages we have endeavoured to extract some principles as applicable to the successful culture of American Cotton. The chemical constituents of the soil did not, upon the whole, appear to be of greater importance than its physical state. A high degree of summer temperature seemed essential, with, at the same time, considerable though not excessive moisture. The practices of agriculture seemed indeed to be varied chiefly in reference to the more or less moist state of the atmosphere. The quantity of cotton required by our manufacturers being so immense, it is not extraordinary that they should wish to be supplied from a variety of sources. India has generally been looked to as the country most likely to supply a greatly increased quantity in a short space of time; chiefly because it already produces largely not only for the consumption of its millions of inhabitants, but also for export both to this country and to China. But the quality of Indian cotton not being generally approved of by our spinners, it has been thought that careful culture might improve its nature, and also that where one species was so extensively cultivated, another might be successfully introduced: especially as the country is so frequently described as including every variety of soil and climate.

It would be extraordinary if no attempts had been made to attain so desirable an object, as the production of an article greatly in demand in Europe and which would appear to be of benefit to the country producing it as an article of export. On inquiry, however, we have seen that a vast number of experiments have been made by the East India Company for a long series of years, indeed from the year 1788 to the present period, and in spite of failures enough to have deterred most other governments, they have persevered in what appeared a hopeless undertaking. These experiments commenced with inquiries, were followed up with the distribution of seeds to cultivators, and the establishment of Government farms; the despatch of planters from America for growing the cotton in India, as well as of machines for cleaning it, and of presses for packing it. These were followed by a repetition of the same measures at successive times and in new localities; and, if we except some very recent ones, all without any great effects having been permanently produced. The efforts of the Government have been aided by the co-operation of Agricultural Societies, as well as of individuals in different parts of India, and all with no better success, and this in a country where the same efforts have established the manufacture of indigo and of sugar, and improved the preparation of silk and the collection of opium.

But the Indian Government seems never to have entirely abandoned the subject (v. pp. 86-88), notwithstanding the numerous failures, though it is hardly fair to call them all such, because good cotton was produced, and we have no reason to think at a greater expense than has since been found to be necessary. In some of the situations, moreover, the exotic plants have continued to grow and to produce good cotton, in the very places where they had years before been introduced. It has been said, that previous experiments had proved that the country was unable to grow good cotton, and there is no doubt that nothing can be grown successfully in an unfavorable climate, and as little in an unsuitable soil. But India presents great diversity of soil, from the rich and moist alluvial delta of the Ganges to the dry and sandy plains of North-Western India; with, in Central India, an abundance of what is emphatically called Black Cotton Soil, and in the Peninsula, an addition of much of the red granitic soil which has been found favorable to the growth of American cotton. The climate also of many parts did not appear unsuitable to an improved, as it already supported an inferior cotton. Others objected that the Government having already made numerous experiments, it was the business of individuals to carry out the culture, if it was likely to be profitable, especially as no permanent good could accrue from it if it was in any way to be forced. But the Government overruled all objections, and were prepared to entertain a fresh project, no doubt considering the peculiar circumstances of India, and probably also that the information formerly obtained was imperfect, and the inferences deduced inconclusive. For, nowhere do we find that the physical conditions of the question were accurately studied, nor that the processes of culture were carefully adapted to the varying soils and climates of the different parts of India. The subject, moreover, is of importance enough in itself to justify excess of zeal rather than over-caution. For if we can in any way improve the quality of Indian-grown cotton at the same time that we increase its quantity, we enable the Indian agriculturist to obtain a portion of the millions now paid by England to America, and in addition to facilitating the payment of his rent and other expenses, we increase his means of comfort and of comparative wealth, as well as enable him to supply himself with the luxuries of his own and of other countries, including among these some of the manufactured goods of Great Britain. Every step, therefore, that is taken for the benefit of the ryot of India, has an indirect and beneficial influence upon the large portion of our population, now connected in various ways with the cotton manufacture, by not only increasing but regulating the supply of the raw material, which is thus not only of local but of national importance.

In the year 1838, the Chamber of Commerce of Manchester addressed the Court of Directors of the East India Company, in order to induce them to devise and adopt such measures as might appear to them most conducive to the extension of the agricultural resources of India, and particularly for the improvement of the quality, and the extension of the cultivation of cotton. In March of that year, the Court informed the Indian Government that they had adopted measures for obtaining from America the services of properly qualified individuals to proceed to India for the purpose of instructing and superintending the natives in the cultivation of cotton, and of teaching them the proper mode of cleaning it by machinery. Captain Bayles, of the Madras Army, who had paid attention to this subject in India, was deputed to America, and returned to England in June 1840, bringing with him ten experienced planters from the Southern States, also large quantities of cotton-seed of the best kinds; American ploughs and hoes for growing the cotton according to their own methods; gins for cleaning it, and presses for packing it when cleaned. The planters, in addition to their stipulated salaries, were promised gratuities proportioned to their success. An engineer was subsequently sent to each Presidency, in order to set up and keep in order the different parts of the machinery of the gins and screw-presses, as well as to instruct the native artificers how properly to repair the several tools. If we refer to the observations of the press of that time, or to the proceedings of the Agricultural Societies of India, the project was thought very favorably of, and likely to be productive of good results. American editors of the period pronounced it a "gigantic enterprise" and an "extraordinary project," and described it as "a combined influence of the British interests against the Southern interests of the United States." And yet we find that able paper, the 'Bombay Times,' of the 25th July, 1850, stating that, "perhaps no experiment, undertaken solely with the view of benefiting a country, has ever met with so many enemies and opponents."

Of the planters, three sailed immediately for Bombay and three for Madras; the four for Bengal were retained to accompany Captain Bayles by the Overland Route; the subsequent distribution of all being left to be settled by the local Governments. Advantage was taken of the opportunity of the Bengal planters being in England for them to visit brokers, spinners, and manufacturers in this country, in order that they might become acquainted with the various wants which required to be supplied. The author accompanied the planters in their first visit to Manchester and Liverpool, and afterwards returned to witness the trials with the American saw-gins in cleaning cotton at Liverpool, as will be subsequently related.

§ 14. Experimental Culture in Bengal.

India is so vast a country, and its different parts vary so much from each other, that it will be difficult to make any observations which are equally applicable to all; we shall, therefore, divide our inquiry into these experiments, and our observations on them, into certain great divisions of the country, where there is some general similarity of soil and of climate, without paying any great attention to a chronological order. First of all we shall notice the province of Bengal, not that it is peculiarly a cotton country, or that its cotton is of a superior quality, though Dacca, one of its districts, was long celebrated for its muslins. We must premise, however, that the province of Bengal has nothing to do with what is commonly called Bengal cotton, which is produced, as we have seen, entirely in the distant and dry north-west provinces, and exported from Calcutta, the capital of Bengal. But we select Bengal because it affords the requisite temperature, is near the sea, and is conspicuous for moisture of climate. Numerous experiments, moreover, on the culture of cotton have been made within its limits by individuals, by the Agricultural Society of India, and by two of the American planters. A notice of its climate may prove interesting to horticulturists, as the Botanic Garden of Calcutta, from which so many plants are received in this country, is situated in and is under the influence of the climate of Bengal.*

* Calcutta, the capital of Bengal, in lat. 22° 23′ N., and long. 88° 28′ E., and situated only a little above the level of the tides, has a mean temperature of about 78°.

Jan.	Feb.	March.	April.	May.	June.	July.	Aug.	Sept.	Oct.	Nov.	Dec.
66·2	69·8	80·0	85·4	85·7	83·7	81·8	82·0	82·8	79·2	74·2	66·6

The thermometer ranges from about 45° to 75° in the cold season, when a dry wind blows from the N.E. in the day; but at night there is a dampness with cold. In the hot season, or from the beginning of March to the middle of June, the temperature rises gradually from 80° to about 90°—95° in the shade, and reaches to 100°—110° in the sun and air. Though no rains fall, the wind blowing from the S.W. is loaded with moisture in its course over the Bay of Bengal. In the rainy season the temperature is high and equable, but the Orchid house-like climate is oppressive, from

The province of Bengal, now divided into several districts, lies between 21° and 27° of N. latitude, and is about 350 miles in length, with an average breadth of about 300 miles. It is throughout a flat champaign country, bounded to the S. by the Bay of Bengal, and the dense forests, intersected by numerous rivers, called the Sunderbunds. The northern frontier, which runs westward from Assam, is formed by a belt of from 10 to 20 miles in breadth of a tall grass and tree jungle, which runs along the foot of the lower Himalayas. On the east it is bounded by the Cossya hills and other low ranges in Tipperah and Chittagong, while the west is confined by the low hills which stretch from Rajmahl towards Birbhoom and the Jungle Mehals. This wide expanse of plain is intersected by the mighty Ganges, the wide spreading Burrampooter, and by numerous other navigable streams, which, however, often change their course, washing away an estate in one place, covering another with sand, and leaving some intermediate part a stagnant marsh. These rivers, moreover, overflow their banks about the month of August, and inundate the country to a great extent. In autumn they drain off, but as the agriculturist wishes to retain a supply of moisture, embankments are made to retain the water even over extensive fields. Besides these, there are numerous tanks and jeels, *i. e.* "shallow lakes or deep morasses," so that everything tends to increase the moisture of the climate. But the effects of a raging sun with drought are occasionally felt, when the natives describe "the earth as iron and the sky brass."

The seasons are divided, as over a great part of India, into three: that is, the hot, the rainy, and the cold. The hot weather begins with March, and steadily increases until the rains come on, early in June. But occasional storms, with rain, occur, which relieve the intensity of the heat. During the first two months of the rains, the falls are incessant, but during the two following months intermissions are frequent. On an average, 60 inches of rain are said to fall in Calcutta. Prinsep gave 59·83 as the average for three years. If the rains cease early in September, intense heat is experienced, men become sickly, and plants languish. As the weather becomes

the combination of heat with moisture, and still more exhausting when, towards the latter half, the wind veers to the S.E.

colder, the moisture which is evaporated during the day is deposited during the night, and fogs obscure the sun till late in the morning. The cold being combined with moisture is felt as severe, but not invigorating, and though the thermometer does not fall to the freezing point, ice is obtained by exposing shallow vessels to the effects of the free radiation which takes place in the more open parts. In the more eastern districts showers are more frequent during the dry months of the year, but the moisture of the climate is still greater, and increased by the exuberant vegetation and clumps of trees in even the cultivated parts, while on the frontiers this is still more the case; the dense forests and jungle of grass, often twenty feet high, not only add aqueous vapour to that already in the atmosphere, but prevent the free evaporation of water from the undrained surface.

In such a climate we may expect that wild animals will abound and insect life be rife. The farmer, indeed, complains that tigers and leopards carry off his cattle, wild hogs crunch his sugar-cane, and birds destroy his seed when sown, and his grain when in the ear. But from the peculiarity of climate he can easily obtain two crops off the same field, one being rice or other cereal, the other some one of the numerous millets, pulses, or oil-seeds. He also cultivates the sugar-cane, indigo, mulberry, tobacco, safflower, &c.; but prides himself especially on his clumps of mangoes and of bamboos, or his plantations of cocoa-nut, areca, or wild date, the last valuable only as yielding sugar, while the bassia affords saccharine matter in its flowers for an intoxicating liquor, and a valuable oil in its seeds. In such a climate the culture of a plant like American cotton, which requires heat and moisture, does not appear to be impracticable.

In proceeding to notice the Culture of American Cotton in Bengal, the first thing to determine is the proper time for sowing the seed. In such a climate as we have described, with a high annual temperature, very little if any frost, and a fair share of moisture even in the driest months, it is evidently possible to propagate a variety of plants throughout the year. Thus rice may be sown in March and April, and again in June and July, the first being reaped from August to October, and the second from November to January, in different parts of the province. In the northern parts of the district, wheat, barley, peas, and other summer crops of Europe are sown in October, and reaped in January and February.

In the distribution of the planters it would, no doubt, have been desirable to have spread those allotted to the Bengal presidency over as wide a surface as possible, as we might then have had the results of simultaneous experiments over a greater diversity of soil and climate; and it was originally intended that one of the planters should have been stationed in Bengal, one about Ghazeepore, and the others in Bundlecund and its neighbourhood. But as the planters at the several presidencies naturally wished to be together at first, their wishes were acceded to; and it was only after they had all tried Bundlecund and the Doab near Calpee, that one went further north-west, and established a model-farm near Agra; one went to the south-east to Goruckpore; and a third, still further, in the same direction, to Rungpore. An additional planter was engaged for Bengal, and stationed at Dacca; so that, though not simultaneously, we have to refer to the results of eight farms in different parts of a line of about 800 miles in length.

In order to inform the planters of what had already been attempted for the improvement of cotton culture in India, the author drew up and printed a summary of the various experiments which had at different times been made by the Government and individuals, and suggested the several points which appeared most deserving of attention; first, in a general point of view, and then with reference to the different presidencies, such as climate, soil, and the modifications which the culture might require in India. He referred to the parts of India suited to the culture of cotton, both on the red and black soils of India, and stated, that he had no doubt that the picking, cleaning, and packing, that is, all the mechanical parts of the operation, would be perfectly performed. The author also suggested that the practical men from America should be put in communication with scientific men in India, who had paid some attention to the arts of culture; as, for instance, Dr. Wight in the peninsula of India, Dr. Gibson in the Bombay and Dr. Falconer in the Bengal Presidency, who, it was thought, would not only serve as the media of communication between the Government and the natives of India, with whose language and habits the planters would necessarily be unacquainted, but that they would also be capable of supplying the principles which should guide the planters in modifying their practice, so as to suit it to new soils and climates. It was thought that by such a union only could any good results be obtained in the present day, and after the numerous experiments which had previously been made. He also suggested, that though the American plant appeared most eligible, yet it was desirable, in a small farm, to try every variety of cotton, in order to ascertain whether one kind was not better suited than another to the different parts of India; while, in another farm, as large as the planter could conveniently superintend, it was proposed to cultivate that which was found most suitable to each particular locality. It was also suggested that the native assistants should be taught the best methods of culture, and that as soon as this had been ascertained, the ryots should be induced to adopt these as well as the culture of the best kinds of cotton; also, that this might be much assisted by instructions for culture being prepared in the native languages, and distributed among the ryots. It was also proposed, that the planters should be furnished with good specimens of cotton for comparison with what they might grow, and that their own specimens should be reported on by cotton-brokers at the presidencies and in this country; also that all the cotton cultivated should be sent for sale to the markets of Liverpool and London. It was likewise recommended that reports should be made on the progress of the monthly operations as well as on the results obtained at the end of each season.

The earliest account which we have of the cultivation of cotton in Bengal, is that given by Mr. Bebb, then of Dacca, in reply to the desire expressed by the East India Directors in 1788, for information on this subject. He describes that cultivated in Bengal, and in the days when Dacca was famous for its muslins, known by the name of *photee*, "as the finest cotton in the known world, producing cloth of astonishing beauty and fineness." The plant is further stated to be an annual, of which two crops are obtained in the year, one being sown in October or November, and its crop gathered in April, while the other is sown in April or May, and the crop collected in

September. The April crop is the most esteemed, and bears a higher price, but is liable to failure from long drought or from violent storms, moderate showers being very beneficial to it. The inferiority in the September crop is probably owing, Mr. Bebb thinks, "to the vegetation from April to September being more rapid and less substantial." The cultivation appears to have been carefully conducted, and the price from $5\frac{1}{2}$ to $6\frac{1}{2}$ rupees. He states that experiments were then making to ascertain whether it would retain its excellent qualities when cultivated in other parts of Bengal. Dr. Roxburgh, who was appointed to the Calcutta Botanic Garden in 1793, early paid attention to the cotton plant of Dacca, which he considered to be only a variety of Gossypium herbaceum, and states that "the most intelligent people of Dacca think the great difference lies in the spinning, and allow little for the influence of soil." Mr. Lamb, long resident at Dacca, writing in 1831, says that the cotton crop is not in favour with the farmers, more especially as the price had fallen from 5 to $3\frac{1}{2}$ rupees the maund within a few years. It is, moreover, an uncertain crop, being liable to injury from insects, from rain and hail, and from inundations.

The cultivation of American cotton seems to have been early attempted, for Dr. Roxburgh describes the Bourbon cotton as having been introduced about twenty years, and says that it succeeds better in the more elevated, drier, and less fertile soil of Coromandel than in Bengal, where the plant grows to a great size, yields less cotton, and the cultivation is very generally relinquished. The Agricultural Society of India state, that their attention had been directed to the cultivation of cotton ever since 1820, but that distinct measures of operation were taken in 1829. At the close of that year, the Bengal Government placed at the disposal of the Society 20,000 rupees for premiums, but this was all lost by the failure of an agency house. They also authorised a farm to be established, for which the annual sum of 10,000 rupees (£1000), exclusive of rent, was allowed, and 4500 rupees for building and stock for the first year. In June 1830, Upland Georgia, Sea Island, and Demerara cotton seed, together with a saw-gin for cleaning cotton, were received from the Court of Directors, and made over to the Society, together with Captain Basil Hall's account of the culture of cotton in America. A farm, amounting to 500 beegahs, was taken at Akra, a place eight miles south from Calcutta, and active measures were commenced on 14th October, 1830. A sub-committee was formed, two of whom were to visit the farm twice a week, and M. de Verinne was selected to be its superintendent out of 45 candidates. The experiments were vigorously prosecuted until June 1833, about which time the lease expired, and the Society determined upon discontinuing the experiments, which had generally had an unfavorable issue.

The Committee ascribe the failure to bad seed, to their positive ignorance respecting the proper season for sowing, to the land (which had been forced upon the Society by circumstances rather than been selected by them) being wholly unsuited to the growth of cotton, being *too rich* in most places, and *too salt* in others. This has been shown:—1. By the rapidity and luxuriance of vegetation, producing abundance of wood, leaf, and flower, but little cotton. 2. By an almost unceasing process of blossoming, thereby exhausting the plant before it had attained maturity, and consequently deteriorating the staple in the ratio of the excessive bearing. 3. By the general result of short produce, an invariable sign of too rich and moist a soil. 4. They also ascribe the failure to an improper mode of planting; the native broadcast plan being unsuited to the American cotton plants, which, besides requiring to be planted at a distance from each other, should have the soil dug to the depth of at least 18 inches, in order to allow the exceedingly delicate tap-root to penetrate freely.

A part of the failure was also ascribed to hail-storms, which, however, the Committee observe, "may possibly be the means of leading to the discovery of a mode of culture better adapted to foreign cotton." Their superintendent says, "the culture of the last season, 1832-3, shows a more favorable result, as 60 maunds of clean cotton, and 180 maunds of cotton-seed, were gathered at the farm, from December 1832 to May 1833," chiefly from 90 beegahs of Upland Georgia cotton, sown the previous season, "the stumps of which only were left after the severe hail-storms of the 25th and 26th March 1832; these stumps threw out fresh shoots during the rainy season of that year, were partially pruned, and well hoed up at the conclusion of the rains, and yielded, from December to May, 12,963 lbs. of cotton, including seed, making an average per beegah (120 square feet) of 144 lbs., which, after having been separated from the seed, gave 40½ lbs. of clean cotton, and 103½ lbs. of seed."

On this the Committee inquire, whether this description of cotton might not be more successfully cultivated as a perennial plant, under a course of treatment similar to that which Mr. Bruce describes as followed in Persia, where, after the goats and sheep have been allowed to browse freely upon the plants (after crop), the peasantry are permitted to complete the work of spoliation by breaking off the remaining branches to the root. Thus the hail-storms destroyed the crop of 1831-2, but they were the means of providing a tolerable crop in 1832-3.

M. de Verinne was so well satisfied with his accidental success, as to be led to calculate, that the culture would be profitable if carried on on a large scale. The Committee, after making considerable deductions from his estimate, concur in his idea, and give 30 per cent. as the probable rate of profit. It is to be regretted, that the Committee, having had practical experience, and apparently such just views of the causes of failure, did not prosecute their experiments for a few years longer on a small scale, as five acres would have answered as well as 500 for determining many of the unsettled points of soil and of culture, in so warm and moist a climate.

Our limits will not allow us to enter into the details of the experiment, which is still proceeding, to grow American cotton in Dacca. This district was selected as formerly famous for its muslins, as well as for its cotton, which is still highly esteemed. Mr. Dunbar, the highly intelligent commissioner, thinks there is nothing "to which the soil of the district is so well suited as cotton." Mr. Price, a planter practically acquainted with the culture of cotton in America, was appointed, in the year 1843, to conduct the experiment. He seems to have been indefatigable in his endeavours to visit very frequently every part of the district, but, like almost every one else in India, appears to have been unacquainted with (at least he does not refer to) the labours of his predecessors.

Mr. Price induced some indigo planters and several Zumeendars to grow the American cotton on their farms. The

Government authorised advances to be made to ryots willing to cultivate, and engaged to purchase all that they grew. A farm was directed to be established under Mr. Price's personal superintendence. But failure seems to have attended nearly all his experiments. Yet, as the American plant in some situations grew and bore flowers and fruit, not for a short time only, but for months together, we cannot help thinking, that there was something in the soils selected, or in the methods of culture adopted, unsuitable to so moist and warm a climate as that of Dacca. New Orleans and Bourbon seed were sown both at the conclusion of the rainy season, and with the first showers in February and March, again in May and June, and, indeed, in every month of the year. Various complaints were made; that the seed did not vegetate, that the ground was too moist or inundated, that the weather was too dry for the young plants, &c. In some situations the plants did grow freely, but were utterly destroyed by insects. Unfortunately, there seems hardly a period of the year which is free from insects. In one year, it is stated, that all the American cotton planted subsequent to the 1st October suffered from caterpillars; in December we read of a gray grub; and in May that every boll contained a small red worm; also, that in June they were destroyed by insects, and a second time in August and September by innumerable small green insects. Such devastation can only be remedied by studying the natural history of the several insects, and applying appropriate remedies, if such be practicable. The indigenous cotton being harder and more hairy, is less attacked by insects. Some of these insects may be avoided by changing the period of sowing, and others by pruning down the plant; for one of the difficulties of the culture is, no doubt, over-luxuriance from a warm and moist climate. The plants, as might be expected, grow well in the rainy season. In one year there was a cessation of rain in July, when the leaves looked withered, and as if blighted. Again, in the middle of November in another season, the coldness of the nights withered the leaves and made them fall, and prevented the bolls opening; but the plant "re-leafed itself," though the second leaves were smaller than the first. We read nowhere else of a check to vegetation. Some plants which were four feet high in May, and bearing abundantly, were destroyed by gales of wind; but they quite recovered themselves, and were bearing again, by the 26th of August, for the second time. In December, the same plants, when just a year old, had been in bearing for five months, and they long continued to bear, with the exception of two or three short intervals of about three weeks at each time. Mr. Price animadverts on the length of time the New Orleans plant requires, and hopes "it will soon repay the few months longer it takes before bearing in this country;" and observes, "it is a triennial plant here, not an annual, as in the United States." The Bourbon cotton, Mr. Price found running too much to wood, and was afraid it would require to be checked by pruning. In September he cut it down to three feet; by the end of the month it threw out new branches, and it was hoped it would bear in the dry season, though this was a system he had never seen tried in America. Subsequently, it is reported to be better suited to the eastern parts of Bengal than any other foreign cotton.

Notwithstanding the apparent over-luxuriance, and the absence of any check to growth, we find rich soils especially selected, and manure thought essential. This may be the case; but in so moist and warm a climate, cotton might more easily be grown in a more sandy and poorer soil, exposed to the influence of the sea-breeze, as near Luckypore, or in the sea islands of Hattea and Sundeep. In the interior drainage is necessary, and poorer soils, which the roots could easily permeate, but which yet are not wholly free from moisture and nourishment, would seem to suit the American cotton plant better than the rich soils selected. The plant should be checked in its growth by pruning, so as to make it come into bearing at the most appropriate season. Mr. Price, however, seems to despair of success with the exotic, and was, therefore, trying to improve some of the native cottons. Those of Broach, of Omerawatty, and, perhaps, of Bundlecund, seem most desirable. He seems to think, that the exotic cottons would succeed better on the Tipperah hills, where a coarse cotton is already grown, than on the plains. "On the hills the rain speedily runs off, yet not until it has given sufficient moisture to the soil, which he believes to be eminently adapted to the cultivation of cotton, and yet unfavorable to the growth of those weeds which are so troublesome on the plains." The experiment might be tried on these hills, as also in poorer districts, but more exposed to the equalising effects of the sea-breeze, and where probably insect life would be less rife.

The foregoing account is reprinted from that published in the year 1848 (v. p. 168), in order to compare with it such results as have been since obtained. The difficulties with the exotic American appeared then to be those of over-luxuriance complicated with the depredations of insects. Mr. Price had, therefore, commenced the cultivation of some cotton from native Patna seed, and as he found that the stiff lands of the northern parts of the district did not seem to suit the cotton so well as he expected that the *chur* lands (containing a good deal of sand) would do, he proposed to change the farm from Toke to near Bukhtabullee. On visiting the former in December, he writes, that "he found the cotton suffering much from the extreme stiffness of the land, so much so, that on examination the roots appeared to be perfectly earth-bound, and which, I have no doubt, was the cause of the cotton having the same unhealthy appearance, at this season last year, when it should have been in full bearing. This evil we will not have to contend with in the *chur* land, which is of a free soil and easily cultivated at all seasons of the year." With respect to the plants in this chur land, he says, that the plants grown from Patna-seed, both by himself and by the ryots, looked healthy, had escaped the attacks of caterpillars, and seemed to be preferred by the natives to their own. In September, Mr. Price reports, that they "look promising wherever uninjured by trespass of stock," and "promise to become a profitable crop;" and that "the natives had never seen cotton equal to it in the district." In October, that "in one place in particular I found it eight and ten feet high, and bearing until the weight of the bolls were nearly overcoming the strength of the plants." In November, he sowed twenty-five beegahs with both Bourbon and American (that is, acclimated New Orleans) seed; the rest being reserved for the May sowing, which Mr. Price thinks is the best time, as the October sowing only comes to perfection in the commencement of the rains, and is little better than a lost crop. In the month of December he reports, that "the labourers are employed in weeding and scraping the mould round the young plants, which are now looking very healthy, and in growth equal to any plants I ever saw in America of the same age."

Having passed safely through the cold nights of January, with no other detriment than the stoppage of their growth during the time, Mr. Price reports in February, that "they continue to stand the dry weather, and are now in a very healthy growing state." "The season continued very dry, and there was no rain until the 11th of May, while they were employed in sowing Bourbon seed, and afterwards in planting suckers of plantain (Musa), in order to form a shelter to protect the young cotton plants from high winds." The seeds vegetated well, but a fresh set of disasters were now experienced. "The rains, when they came on, were heavy, and washed away the soil; and the labourers were, therefore, employed in *moulding* the November plant, which notwithstanding the heavy rains, with little or no sunshine, still looked healthy." But the rains continued so incessant, that from the 21st to the 25th of July the farm became inundated with a foot of water, so also did most of the chur land round about. Upon this Mr. Price observes, that "the young plants will all require replanting, and that, therefore, May and June sowings will not answer in the chur land, on account of the plant not having sufficient time to attain either size or strength to survive through a long inundation." This receded early in September, but increased again on the 15th of the month. On the conclusion of these rains, the people were employed in sowing Bourbon, American, Patna, fine Dacca, and a little of the Tipperah Hill cotton-seeds. The natives seemed inclined to cultivate cotton, as they had taken advances for about 500 beegahs of land; but "it is difficult to get the ryots to cultivate cotton land as they should do. This appears to arise from the common crops of this country requiring so little attention after the seed is planted." The first planted field on the farm which stood the inundation so well, yielded about ten maunds of cotton; but not one fourth of the bolls opened, probably owing to the cold nights. But in February Mr. Price reported to Mr. Dunbar, that the cotton prospects had never been so favorable since the experiment had been begun. In April, 1849, a heavy hail-storm occurred from which many of the plants had suffered;

but it was supposed probable that most of them would recover. Reports to a later date have not yet been received.

Bengal not being properly a cotton country (v. p. 39), we may appear to have paid too much attention to the difficulties which have attended the experimental culture. But this is far from being a disadvantage, for we may frequently learn more from a series of difficulties than from a smooth and unruffled course. The culture has frequently appeared to be on the eve of success, when some fresh disaster has involved the abandonment of the last-adopted measures with the devising of a new set of operations, and yet without any considerable result, though more than 30,000 rupees have been spent on the experiment. Yet cotton used to be successfully cultivated in the district; and Mr. Price says, that even now the natives in some parts "get a fair proportion of cotton when they plant it singly; but this is seldom done." The culture was formerly conducted by the natives with considerable care, for they first selected a suitable, that is, a light sandy soil, observed rotation of crops, planted in rows eighteen inches apart, ridged the earth up to the roots of the plants, weeded them well, and forced them to grow to a height of four or five feet. The natives of the present day seem also desirous of cultivating cotton, and have taken advances, and grown it to some extent; and Mr. Dunbar, the Commissioner, gives it as his opinion that such a cultivation of raw material is required for the benefit of the district, of which the manufactures have been declining since 1789. The exports from Dacca to Europe amounted in 1789 to 12 lacs of rupees worth. In the year 1813, they did not exceed $3\frac{1}{2}$ lacs, and in 1817 ceased entirely. As the prosperity of Dacca, as connected with the cotton manufacture, has passed away, it can only be benefited at present by providing raw materials for other manufactures. Indigo and safflower have already been introduced, and sunpat (a substitute for hemp and flax) has been taken up; but as Mr. Dunbar says, "there would appear to be no article of indigenous growth to which the soil of the district is so well suited as cotton." The district is, moreover, in other respects favorable for the culture, as the permanent settlement has prevailed ever since the time of the Marquis Cornwallis, and, therefore, the alleged annual revisions of the rent cannot operate as an impediment to the culture. The Cotton Committee of the Agricultural Society of India did not consider the amount of the tax to be a hinderance, as it averaged about a rupee per beegah, and the profits they allowed might amount to about 30 per cent. (see above). The want of roads also cannot prevent the extension of the culture, for water-carriage is near every farm, and Calcutta, the port of export, may be reached within a few days. But the great difficulties are those of soil and of climate, and the ascertaining the best localities, including the sea-islands, for the culture of the kinds of cotton best suited to the different soils of the district; also the modifications in culture required; for instance, the best season for sowing the seed; the distance at which the plants should be kept, with or without some other crop in the case of great distances being found the most profitable; the advantages of pruning, &c. Some of these questions might be determined in a cultivation of an acre quite as well as on a larger extent, for as before mentioned,—cotton is more of the nature of garden than of a field culture. Some of the experiments might be conducted by the Agricultural Society in the Botanic Garden of Calcutta, and they could not have a better assistant than Mr. Scott, the Head-Gardener, who after the charge of the great conservatory at Chatsworth, and there growing the *Victora regia*, would not find it a difficult problem to ascertain the physical wants and most suitable culture of the different kinds of cotton plant in the rich soil and moist climate of Bengal.

In attempting, however, to cultivate cotton in such localities, it is desirable to know whether it is likely to be of sufficiently good quality to come into competition with good cotton from other parts of the world. Mr. Price expresses his surprise at the unfavorable accounts which had been received from England of the quality of the cotton which he had grown, for a gentleman in Dacca, whom he had supplied with samples, sent three of them to Liverpool, where the Bourbon was valued at 6*d.*, the New Orleans at 5½*d.*, and the native at 5*d.*, but the time is not mentioned.

Messrs. Willis and Earle, of Calcutta, to whom some cotton had been intrusted for the purpose of being packed and shipped to England, report that the "Upland Georgia," grown at Akra, realized at Liverpool (when no particular activity prevailed) from $6\frac{5}{8}d.$ to $7\frac{1}{2}d.$ per lb., averaging about 7*d.* per lb., which price corresponds with that assumed by M. de Verinne in his estimate; and further, that "the date of their advice being in March 1834, cotton has greatly risen since then in England, and they assume the value of such cotton now (July, 1835) at 9*d.* per lb." A portion of this cotton was packed and forwarded to the Court of Directors, but was allowed to be *four* years in the country before it was despatched, and about five years old when reported upon by brokers. It was valued by them, the Upland Georgia at $7\frac{1}{2}d.$ to $8\frac{1}{2}d.$, the price of Fair Upland being at the same time 10*d.* to 11*d.* The Sea Island was estimated at 12*d.* per lb. if well got up, stained Sea Island being at the same time in Liverpool market worth $12\frac{3}{4}d.$ per lb. Mr. Patrick, of the Fort Gloucester Cotton Mills, to whom 2400 lbs. of Upland Georgia seed cotton and 1800 lbs. of Sea Island seed cotton produced at Akra were sent for report and experiment in 1833, states 21st September, 1835, "I have often and carefully examined it, and have no hesitation in saying, that the quality of the Upland Georgia grown at Akra is fully equal, if not superior, to the best cotton of the same description grown in America." Further, "This cotton I have carefully watched through the various stages of cleaning, carding, roving, spinning, &c., and have no hesitation in characterising it as equal to the very best *Upland Georgia cotton;* its staple is fully as long, and I would say stronger and better adapted for mule-spinning than any I have imported direct from America;" and adds, "My own opinion with regard to the cultivation of Upland Georgia cotton in India, judging from what I have seen of it when tried under great disadvantages, is, that if judiciously prosecuted, it would ultimately be crowned with the fullest success."

On receiving the report on the samples sent to the Court of Directors, with a letter from the Court, dated 11th July, 1837, the Cotton Committee of the Agricultural Society again met and reported, "They are constrained to admit, that degeneracy, to a certain extent, has taken place in all descriptions of cotton cultivated at Akra." This they ascribe partly to the causes already enumerated (v. p. 246), but partly also to the Sea Island cotton sample having been made up from different sowings, "and that from these sowings the produce was picked in April, but the greater part in July and August (the very heart of the rains) which satisfactorily accounts for its being much stained." But they are much more confident of the probable success likely to attend the extensive cultivation of Upland Georgia cotton; and "although perhaps there are not, within the delta of the Ganges, many provinces in which this description can be profitably cultivated, there are many *without* the delta where the introduction of the Upland Georgia would, in all probability, be attended with eminent success."

Mr. G. Prinsep, a member of the Committee, objected to the "opinions expressed as to the future, and the inferences drawn from the supposed causes of failure at Akra," as he had known no instance of success with the Sea Island or Bourbon cottons." But the Georgia seed he considered to be "an acquisition, and having partially succeeded everywhere, likely to do very well in some of our various climates." (*Trans. Agric. Soc.*, vol. v, p. 181.) The 'Transactions' of the Society, however, contain some notices which it is desirable to refer to; for instance, Mr. Piddington (vol. vi, p. 219) states, that he had in 1823 brought from Singapore some Bourbon cotton-seed, which he had cultivated for seven or eight years in small quantities. "At the end of this time, during which I had always good and often abundant crops, it was found, on sending samples of the first and last year to Mr. Finlay, of the Gloucester Mills, that the cotton had not in the least degenerated, and was worth from 9*d.* to 11*d.* per lb." Again, Dr. Huffnagle, an American gentleman resident near Calcutta, sent a sample bale of the second year's crop, from plants grown at Cossipore from seed imported by the Society in 1836, which the Committee pronounce, "that it is one of the finest specimens that has been submitted to the Society," and remark, "this is the second example in the present report (the other was in Upper India) of the *second* year's crop being better than the first, thereby leaving good ground for hope, that under proper management, the Upland Georgia cotton will become a valuable staple in India. (Vol. vi, p. 109.)

Experiment in Rungpore.—In addition to the experiments near Calcutta and in Dacca, we may refer to another in the northern part of Bengal, that is, near Rungpore. Mr. Rehling, of Bhetgarra, wrote in 1844 to the Agricultural Society of

India, and sent some cotton which he had grown from New Orleans seed distributed by the Society, and which had been acclimated at the Government farm at Coimbatore. The cotton was considered in Calcutta to be good, soft, tolerably strong, and of fair colour, but the staple rather short. The grower, however, stated that he knew nothing of cotton, but that the district appeared to him remarkably well adapted to its culture, some of the plants on the high lands literally groaning under the weight of the bolls, which, however, are subject to the puncture of worms. These cause the bolls to fall off, and the cotton to be injured in colour and quality. Rungpore, Mr. Rehling considers one of the richest and best cultivated districts in Bengal; the soil retains its moisture the whole year round, except during the months of March and April, which are generally relieved by refreshing showers. Irrigation is entirely unknown to the ryots, who otherwise pay a great deal of attention to their cultivation.

Mr. Terry, an American planter, who had had charge of a cotton farm in the Doab, wished afterwards to attempt the culture in a moister soil and climate, such as those of Rungpore. The Revenue Board observe, that more cotton is grown in Dinagepore than in Rungpore. Mr. Terry reached the latter district in the summer of 1844, and on the 2d of October, he reports having visited several parts of the district. The soils he describes as consisting of a black clay with a black sand; in many places, black low land, in others, *keara* or high light soil, and in some parts there are sandy plains. The natives grow more or less of a perennial cotton about their houses and yards. The plants grow large, eight or ten feet high, become full of bolls, so as to be propped up with bamboos. Though the bolls are small, the cotton-wool is very fine. At Meetapoku, four miles south of Rungpore, the annual plant is cultivated with the indigo, and some with their capsicum and ginger. In the first, the cotton has little chance until the indigo is cut in June and July. The capsicum and ginger being planted more apart and the weeds kept down, the cotton plants grow six or seven feet high and are very full of bolls, which are larger than in the perennial kind, though the wool is coarser and shorter.

At the village of Muckeranpur, Mr. Terry found two or three ryots growing the Mexican cotton from seed distributed

17

by the Agricultural Society. This had been placed at their disposal by the Government in March 1841, and distributed immediately afterwards over all parts of the country. Mr. H. Bonnevie, a planter resident in the district, had "induced them to plant it by reducing their rent two rupees, and now they have got it, they find it more profitable than the indigenous cotton. Half a beegah of plants three years old afforded the ryot cotton enough to clothe himself and family, five or six in number." When Mr. Terry saw these plants, a good deal of cotton had been collected from them, and they yet had a good many bolls on them. One ryot grew the plant as an annual, and found it producing six months out of the twelve. Mr. W. Jackson afterwards saw the same ryot, Khodadel, who had made himself a chudder, or coarse cloth, from the Mexican cotton which he had grown. This was ascertained to be worth twelve annas, when a similar chudder from the native cotton was not worth above eight annas. The thread also is stronger and more valuable.

A proof that the produce was considered superior is, that his Mundal wished to raise his rent by one half, but this Mr. Jackson took care to prevent. He stated, that the insect destroyed ten out of sixteen pods, and that it attacked the Mexican much more than the common country cotton. He had sown in May, which he thought the best season; that sown in October will not, in his opinion, answer; but of this Mr. Jackson was not satisfied. A member of the Cotton Committee considered that the sowing should take place in Bengal in August and September, not later, so that the cotton might be gathered in the dry months; when there will be also less chance of the bolls being injured by the red-worm and of the wool being discoloured. Mr. Jackson sent some of the damaged pods to the Agricultural Society, requesting some information respecting the natural history of the insect. He himself described the injury as caused by some fly depositing its eggs in the pod, and the production of small caterpillars of a brown colour. He inquires "whether it might not be possible to keep off the fly by some application to the pod, or to time the sowing so as to bring the plant into bearing at a season when the insect does not lay its eggs." As Mr. Terry considered that a rich sandy soil was best suited to the Mexican cotton,

Mr. Jackson directed that some of the Mexican cotton-seed should be sown in the lighter and drier, though less rich parts of the district to the eastward and northward of Rungpore.

The author has thought it desirable to be more minute in his account of the experiments in Rungpore than their extent would warrant, because the testimony of two resident planters and of an American stranger, as well as of the civilians of the district, all concur in giving a favorable account of its capabilities. The chief difficulty seems to be the damage caused by insects. This might possibly be obviated if the nature and habits of the insects were a little understood. Mr. Dick, the Collector, was disposed to give every assistance in his power to carry out the experiment, and Mr. Welby Jackson, the Commissioner, took the warmest interest in its success. He recommended that small advances should be made to the ryots of the district for the cultivation of American cotton, and the produce purchased from them and cleaned.*

The 'Transactions of the Agricultural Society of India' which we have frequently quoted, contain numerous notices of other experiments in different parts of the lower provinces, with reports on the cotton that had been produced; but space cannot be spared for their further investigation, though it would be interesting to examine into the peculiarities of some localities, such as of Assam, where that most zealous of public officers, Major Jenkins, presides.

Some of the desiderata, such as sufficient moisture and a free circulation of air, might be secured as well in the sea-islands of the Bay of Bengal as on the hilly tracts which bound the province on its eastern frontier. Experiments in the vicinity of the sea-coast are fewer than might be expected. The Tenasserim coast was at one time thought to be very favorable for the growth of cotton; but it was afterwards considered to be less so, because the plants, though luxuriant, produced little cotton. But this would appear to be completely within the control of the arts of culture properly applied.

* Mr. Terry was unfortunately taken ill. He was just recovering from a severe attack of fever in December, and had another illness in January; and as he thought the climate of Rungpore would not suit him, he left the station and returned to America.

On the Cuttack side, we can refer to a notice which would seem to prove that the climate is favorable for the growth of American cotton. Mr. J. Weeks, who describes himself as having had practical experience for several years with various kinds of cotton (*Trans. Agric. Soc.*, vol. ii, p. 132), recommends the cultivation of Bourbon cotton as being likely to be a profitable culture in that district. He states, that half a beegah of land contained 320 plants from which he made nine pieces of cloth, each one yard wide and twelve in length, making a total of 108 yards. The land of his garden he describes as being sandy and inferior, but this is probably in its favour in that climate. He further says, "I believe there is no difference between the Bourbon cotton and that which is denominated Sea Island, and I never saw plants more hardy or require less care. Putting the seed into the ground (which should be well turned up) at the commencement of the rains is the principal part of the labour; in eighty-five days the plants will be in flower, and cotton may be gathered nine months in the year, and the plants will continue eight or ten years. I should observe, that at the commencement of the rains of each year, I take the shears and clip the plants down to about four feet; their average at the close of the rains will be about seven feet. I have frequently transplanted them during the rains, when in full leaf and bud, and saved the gathering." The suitableness of this and of other districts along the far-extended coast, we shall consider in connection with the Madras Presidency.

We may conclude with a notice of the cotton of the hilly regions which bound the province of Bengal to the eastward.

As early as 1788 we find Mr. Taylor (*E. I. Papers*, p. 343) referring to the Bhoga cotton of the Currybarry hills. In the year 1832 Captain Bogle, at that time in charge of the hilly tract of the Goalparah district N. E. of Rungpore, applied to the Agricultural Society for a quantity of cotton-seed to be distributed among the Garrows who inhabit these hills, and who, he stated, "are mainly dependent for subsistence on the means of barter which the growth of cotton amongst their hills enables them to carry on with their neighbours in the plains below; who again export it to the adjoining districts of Assam,

Rungpore, Dinagepore, Mymunsing, Dacca, &c." "To the comfort of these barbarous people, the production of such cotton as will meet with a ready market is of vital importance." Mr. Willis, of Calcutta, who examined the specimen of cotton sent by Captain Bogle, describes it as extremely coarse and short in the fibre, but strong, and the small seed abundantly covered with wool. Mr. Terry, in 1844, again called attention to the cotton grown on the Bootan or Garrow Hills, of which he states some thousands of maunds are annually imported into Rungpore. He also describes the wool as being coarse and short, though the bolls were larger than Mr. Terry had ever seen anywhere else in the world. He inquires whether the same soil would not grow the Mexican cotton equally well. But the difficulty would probably be to induce the natives to take much care in the culture or collection, without the presence of some European to guide and instruct them.

Mr. Price, when engaged in his experiments, mentions that the Rajah of the Tipperah Hills to the east of Dacca, whence cotton is likewise taken to the plains, was anxious to cultivate both native and American cotton of improved kinds. It is probable that both would succeed, if the natives could be induced to prepare their soil with care, and not allow the cotton to be injured by weeds or by the other crops. Mr. Price having had an opportunity of visiting two or three of their small settlements, gives the following account, which corresponds with that of Mr. Taylor, of the cultivation of cotton in the Tipperah Hills, in the neighbourhood of Commilla.* He found them picking their cotton on the 18th of November:

* "The system of cultivation pursued by the natives on the hills is very simple, that part of the country being overgrown with a small kind of bamboo, it is cut down in the months of February and March, and allowed to remain until dry, when it is burned off the land, which leaves it quite clean and ready for planting, besides giving them the advantage of the ashes as manure; and as soon as the rains commence, they open small holes with the hoe at irregular distances from each other, but generally from twelve to eighteen inches apart, into which they drop a few cotton-seeds with the seed of any other mixed crop that they wish to cultivate with it, such as rice, chillies, &c., &c., and cover them lightly with mould. This is all the cultivation they give, unless the jungle has grown too quickly, in case of which it is simply cut down. From all the information I could obtain from them, I understand they get about five maunds of cotton to the beegah in a favorable season, in addition to which their crops mixed with it are equal to about one maund of cotton. This should pay them well for their cultivation, but unfortunately they can only cultivate for one or two years in succession the same land. This appears to be

In all these moist situations, the great point would appear to be to secure a sandy permeable soil, probably laid out in ridges, which, sufficiently moist could yet be easily drained. Open and distant planting, with frequent hoeing and weeding, would secure cleanliness and a free circulation of air. With these should be conjoined a careful determination of the proper time of sowing, and occasional pruning to check over-luxuriance. We shall now proceed to consider the effects of a dry climate on the culture of cotton, as exemplified in the experiments made in the north-western provinces of India.

§ 15. Experimental Culture in North-Western India.

In the above account of the attempted culture of American cotton in Bengal, we have stated that the faults appeared to be those of over-luxuriance in a rich soil, combined with a moist and tepid climate. But even when Dacca was most famous for its muslins, much cotton, we have seen (p. 41), was imported by the Ganges. Mr. Taylor stated, in 1788, that the first importations took place in 1783, previously to which Dacca had been supplied from Surat. In 1799, we learn that the weavers of Bengal depended upon the importations from the north-west for seven-eighths of the cotton which they required. In 1802, of the 450,000 maunds (of 96 lbs.) imported, 180,000 were obtained from the Deccan or Nagpore, and 270,000 from Calpee, the produce chiefly of the district of Etawah, and of Bundlecund, and of the vicinity of Jaloun and Jhansee, and of other Mahratta states immediately to the westward of the Jumna. These cottons were required for the manufacturers of Benares, of Behar, and of Bengal.

When the nature of the different cottons was less understood than at present, and the effects of soil and of climate in

occasioned by the quick descent of the hills, and the surface of the land being composed in a great measure of reddish sand, so that when exposed to heavy rains the surface is washed off, and only the red clay left, of which the strata immediately under the surface consists. They are, therefore, obliged to be constantly changing their place of abode, which must not only be a great inconvenience, but also a loss to them, although they do not complain of it as any particular hardship. The kind of cotton they plant is called the *Bogah;* it is rather short in staple, but strong, and from the large size of the bolls, they are enabled to pick it clean, which is a great matter, and very difficult to do with the small Bengallee kinds."

modifying the length and the fineness of the staple of cotton were almost unknown, it is not surprising that what was found suitable for one kind of cotton should be considered as good for another, and that the localities which were found favorable for the growth of the Indian species should have been considered equally so for the culture of the American plant. Induced, no doubt, by such views, and strengthened by the results of some experiments with this species, the Agricultural Society of India, the author, and General Briggs, all recommended the banks of the Jumna in Bundlecund and in the Ganges-Doab, as suitable sites for the cotton experiments commenced in 1840.

Before proceeding to detail the results of these experiments in North-Western India, it is necessary to take a general view of the physical features of the country included within this term, and within which are included the great divisions of Benares, Allahabad, Agra, Rohilcund, Kumaon, Meerut, and Delhi. The first is bounded on the south-east by the province of Behar, which intervenes between it and Bengal. With the exception of the hilly province of Kumaon, these may be considered as forming the north-western part of the great Gangetic valley, which stretches in a direction parallel with the great Himalayan mountains, from about 20 miles to the westward of the Jumna river to the Bay of Bengal, a distance of about twelve hundred miles from N.W. to S.E. This great alluvial valley, or rather plain, varies in breadth from 80 to 200 miles, being at least of the latter breadth at Agra, and not more than the former at Monghir, while near Delhi it is about 100 miles: the contraction at both places being evidently caused by the projection eastward of ramifications from the great central mountain mass of India. The elevation of this great plain varies in different parts from the level of the sea to about 1000 feet at Saharunpore, which is within nine miles of the eastern bank of the Jumna. But so gradual is the slope, that not a hillock is to be seen on the eastern side of the Ganges, which is everywhere a slow and winding river. If perpendiculars be raised at the latitudes of Saharunpore, Delhi, Benares, and Calcutta, and the ascertained heights 1000, 800, 328, and 50 feet of these places be laid off on them, a straight line will nearly pass through all the points.*

* *Vide* the author's Introduction to the 'Illustrations of Himalayan Botany,' p. x.

We may now take some notice of the climate, in order to contrast it with that of Bengal, as well as of the cotton districts of America. In the first place, after a mild winter, there is a short spring in February, when several plants known in Europe come into flower, as the Apple, Pear, Peach, and Plum, together with the Chinese Loquat, the Strawberry, Poppy, Flax, &c. In March the Mango flowers, also the Melia and other Indian trees; Strawberries are ripe, and shortly afterwards the Peach. In April, a great rise in temperature takes place, and goes on increasing throughout May, and to the middle of June, with an unclouded sky, a blazing sun, and a parching hot wind. The maximum of temperature —ranging from 100° to 110° in the shade, but in the sun to 120° and 130°—is now attained. From the 15th to the 20th of June the rains come on and often fall in torrents, usually continuing until the middle of September. The quantity varies in the most northern parts from 20 to 40 inches in different years. A reduction of temperature takes place, but it is still high, though more equable. The Mango ripens at the accession of the rains, and Rice is cultivated, which forms, with other grains, the *khureef* (or wet season) crop. In October the sky is clear, the sun bright and powerful, and evaporation from the surface of the ground and of plants abundant. But during the clear nights radiation is free, the nights become cool, and a copious dew is usually deposited. The cold increases until about the middle of January; but the weather is, upon the whole, mild and pleasant, with occasional frosts and a few showers about Christmas. The climate is well calculated for the culture of wheat, barley, and other European produce, which constitute the (dry or) *rubbee* crop, as it is called. We adduce, in the form of a note, the mean of the thermometer for a few places, and instead of Delhi give that of a place on the Delhi canal, 10 miles to the north of that capital.*

The portion of the great Gangetic valley, to which the name

*	Lat. N.	Long. E.	Height above sea.	January.	February.	March.	April.
Benares . . .	25° 18′	82° 56′	300 ft.	62·56	72·49	79·07	89·91
Cawnpore . . .	26 29	80 22	500 „	63· 8	69· 5	72·15	88·55
Surouli, 10 miles N. of Delhi . .	28 41	77 13	800 „	51·43	59·29	67·22	75·03
Saharunpore . .	29 57	77 32	1000 „	52· 5	63·25	68·	79·
Deyra Doon . .	30 15	78 5	2350 „	52· 8	59· 5	67·	73·

of the North-Western Provinces is now applied, consists of the above great divisions, divided into thirty-two districts, and contains 71,985 square statute miles, with a population of 23,199,668 souls. The extreme distance, from Goruckpore, on the south-east, to Hissar, on the north-west, is nearly 700 miles. The perpetual settlement extends to the province of Benares, with the exception of the districts of Goruckpore and Azimghur; but the revenue settlement of the north-western provinces, being for twenty and thirty years, cannot throw any impediments in the way of cultivation, if it does so anywhere. The demand of Government on account of land revenue is, on the total area, at the rate of 14a. 8p., but, on the total cultivation, at the rate of 1r. 12a. 11p. per acre; but it varies in different districts, from 1r. 0a. 3p. in Goruckpore, to 2r. 13a. 8p. in Cawnpore.*

The best introduction to the experimental culture in these north-western provinces will be the letter from the Secretary to the Board of Revenue of the North-Western Provinces, which gives an abstract view of the contents of the Reports, referring to the statistics of the culture of cotton in these provinces, in reply to the queries circulated by order of the Court of Directors, in 1847:

From William Muir, Esq., *Secretary to the Sudder Board of Revenue N. W. Provinces; to* C. Allen, Esq., *Officiating Secretary to Government, in the N. W. Provinces.*

Dated the 27th February, 1849.

Sir,—Copies of the order of Government, No. 529, of 12th February, 1848, having been forwarded to all the Commissioners of Divisions in the North Western Provinces, the Sudder Board of Revenue N. W.

* A writer in the '*Calcutta Review*,' in contrasting the central parts, that is, the Doab, with the eastern parts of this territory, observes: "Wheat, sugar, and rice are less extensively raised; but cotton, as a valuable article of produce, in some degree supplies their place."

May.	June.	July.	August.	September.	October.	November.	December.	Mean of year.
94·35	90·28	85·71	85·72	85·99	81·49	72·13	63·45	80·26
96· 5	91·23	86·65	87· 4	85·03	78·95	75·25	67· 5	80·21
82·53	87·75	88·61	88·90	77·83	72·32	60·26	49·35	71·70
86· 5	89·	86·75	85·25	78·	74·	64·75	56· 5	73·58
81·	86·	83·	81·	78· 5	73· 5	57·	56· 5	70·65

Provinces, have received, in return, the reports herewith submitted, showing the cost of cultivating, cleaning, and exporting cotton, and the extent to which the cultivation may be increased.

2d. Excepting Saugur, the reports of which division were forwarded to government direct, a general statement, exhibiting the information supplied from all the districts of these provinces, has been prepared in this office, and accompanies the separate returns. The board direct me to offer also the following general observations for the consideration of his honour the Lieut.-Governor:

Area Cultivated.—3d. The area cultivated for cotton, is reported at 1,002,040 acres, which may, it is estimated, be extended to 1,689,662 acres; but this includes territory which affords no supplies for Europe: the exports being derived from a tract which extends no higher, within the Doab, than Allyghur, but on the south-western side, or the right bank of the Jumna, includes districts of the Allahabad, Agra, and Delhie divisions, as far as Rohtuck, which contain important marts. Exportation is also spoken of as taking place from Rohilcund, but it seems to be limited to the western portion of Budaon, and to the mart of Chundouse, in Moradabad; and as the article produced is of inferior quality, Rohilcund may be left altogether out of the account. The more northern and western districts, in the plains, in which cotton is grown, generally require it for their own consumption, or for places in their vicinity, or when there is a surplus, it is exported to the states westward. The hill-districts on the north produce little or none; and with respect to the remaining division of Benares, however well situated it is, as respects exportation, and whatever may in future be effected in realization of the Commissioner's expectations, various prejudices have hitherto operated against its natural advantages, so that the quantity it at present yields is insignificant.

4th. The more productive of the exporting districts* have 829,753 acres under cultivation, which, it is stated, may be extended to 1,474,801 acres; and if the Benares division be added, the extension will be from 834,669 to 1,493,040. Whether any further addition

	Acres.	Acres.
* Rohtuck	14,552	18,750
Gurgaon	29,617	35,418
Allyghur	69,050	69,050
Moradabad	50,000	100,000
Budaon	34,091	79,489
Agra division	283,156	504,881
Allahabad ditto	349,287	667,213
Total	829,753	1,474,801

should or should not be made, is a question. The district officers consider the soil itself unsuited to the cultivation, but the commissioner seems to doubt the fact, as respects Zilluh Goruckpore. (See below for his observations in the account of the experiment at Goruckpore.)

5th. Several documents which accompanied the Commissioner's report offer important information, as respects Goruckpore. But whilst the Commissioner agrees with the collectors of the other districts, as to the unsuitable nature of the soil, it may be found that this difficulty has no real foundation. On this point, the board beg to direct attention to the following remark of Mr. Pearson, deputy collector, at Calpee :—

Paragraph 7, *Extract of Letter No.* 50, *dated* 9*th June*, 1848.

"As, however, no kind of land is unsuitable for the purpose, except such as is low, or exposed to inundation, there can be little doubt, that if an increased demand should raise the price of the article, a much greater extent of land might be devoted to its production."

6th. The opinion of Mr. Bruce, uncovenanted deputy collector at Cawnpore, whose experience is known to the home authorities, may also be thought worthy of special notice. He observes, that under certain conditions and encouragements, he would undertake to produce as much good merchantable cotton as may be required, and not to cost, when landed in England, more than 3½*d.* per lb. In his opinion, there is no difficulty whatever, as to the means of extending the cultivation.

Price in Marts.—7th. The price of cotton at the principal exporting marts, varies from 5r. 15a. 3p. in Gorgaon, to 10r. 6a. 5p., the rate for the ordinary maund of the best description, in Furruckabad. The average of all these marts is a little above 8 rupees.* The average price of cleaned cotton realized by the ryot, is 7r. 14a.; or, when he receives advances, 6r. 11a. But the system of making advances is not general, though it apparently reduces the cost from 3 per cent. in some districts to 10 in others. When the East India Company's investments were provided, purchases were not, it seems, made by advances, and there is no encouragement offered to have recourse to that method now.

8th. The price of the uncleaned cotton with the seeds, as sold by the ryot, varies from 2r. to 2r. 8a. per maund.

Mode and Cost of Cleaning.—9th. The churkee is the instrument

* N.B. This, at 1*s.* 10*d.* per rupee, is at the rate of 2·1*d.* per lb. for cleaned, not uncleaned cotton.

invariably employed by the natives to free the staple from seed, after which, remaining impurities are separated by the bow (dhunnee), though the latter process does not appear to be resorted to for cotton shipped to Europe. The practice very generally is, to give the seed, or a portion of it, as remuneration for cleaning, but where money is given, it ranges from 6 annas per maund to above a rupee ; the weight of the cleaned article being understood, and the usual proportion being a maund of clean cotton to 3 maunds of seed, that is 4 maunds of cotton with the seed, yield 1 maund of clean staple. This item of charge may, perhaps, be reduced by the introduction of the machine in the improved form recently given to it by European inventions.

Cost of Transport.—10th. Very different estimates have been given of the cost of transport to Calcutta, the only port for shipment. Thus the Budaon return fixes it at 10a. 10p., and that of Furruckabad, at only 8a. 4p. But the mere carriage forms only a proportion of the actual charge, and therefore such estimates as 2r. 14a. 10p. (Kurrah *via* Calpee), are given from some of the districts. The greatest part of the exported cotton changes boats at Mirzapore; the charge from which place is uniformly given, at 1r. 4a. per maund, including every item, thus :—

	r.	a.	p.
Boat-hire and churrundar (servant in charge)	0	7	6
Insurance	0	4	0
Insurance Office peon (guard)	0	0	9
Pilotage, &c.	0	1	0
Agent's commission	0	0	9
Hundeaon (premium on drafts)	0	5	6
	1	4	0

This sum has, of course, to be added to that of such returns as give the charges only to Mirzapore.

As examples of the charges previously incurred, the information supplied by officers at some of the greater marts is here given.

	r.	a.	p.
From Cawnpore to Mirzapore, including every charge	1	0	0
From Agra to Mirzapore (duty added to the return)	1	0	0
From Humeerpore, average of different marts (ditto)	1	1	7
From Bunda, carriage and duty	0	14	3
From Culpee, all charges included, cotton previously brought from Kurrah, bears a further charge of 6a. 7p.	1	4	3
From Allahabad to ditto, carriage, insurance, and duty	0	9	7

The following charges are included, taking Calpee as the instance :

	r.	a.	p.
Brokerage	0	0	3
Weighing and porterage	0	0	3
Packing and thread	0	0	3
Porterage to Ghat	0	0	3
Commission of agent	0	0	9
Boat-hire and churrundar (servant in charge) . . .	0	4	0
Government duty and Darkhaust nuvees . . .	0	9	9
Hundeaon	0	1	6
Insurance and Peon	0	1	9
Gomashtah and Peon	0	1	6
	1	4	3

The cost is somewhat increased to the trader in cotton grown on the right bank of the Jumna, as he has in most instances to pay the duty before his despatch reaches the Ghaut; which has the effect of multiplying the number of his transactions, and taking a part of his capital out of his hands for a period not required in the other cases.

The cost then to Calcutta may be reckoned:

	r.	a.	p.
Price in mart per maund	8	0	0
Charges to Mirzapore	0	15	7
Ditto from Mirzapore to Calcutta	1	4	0
	10	3	7

This gives a cost in Calcutta, taking the maund at 80 tolas, and the rupee at 1*s.* 10*d.*, of 2·733 pence per pound.

11th. The Board cannot but observe, that in most of the discussions in England, touching both cotton and sugar, there appears a silent assumption, that the produce of both these articles must be sent to England, and that there is little or no sale for either in this country.

At the time when the Company's investments were provided, and afterwards when large shipments were made to China, the price of cotton in the Agra market used to be, from 12 to 15 rupees per maund, and though there can be no doubt whatever, that there would be a rapid extension of cultivation of cotton were the demand to increase, the price would so much rise by the export as considerably to check the latter.

By the occupation of more land for cotton also, some grain production must be abandoned. The rise in the price of grains would tend to diminish the comparative profit of extending cotton culture.

12th. The information supplied by the local officers in regard to weights and measurements, gives throughout the *area* of land in acres; the *maund* is always one of 40 seers; and the *seer* is usually one of 80 tolahs. The exceptions in the latter case are the following:

Mozuffurnuggur	92 tolahs	15 per cent.
Moradabad	100 „	25 „
Bareilly, 125 lbs. troy		
Furruckabad	96 „	20 „
Etawah	102 „	27½ „
Cawnpore	97 „	21¼ „
Futtehpore	96 „	20 „
Humeerpore	96 „	20 „
Allahabad	100 „	25 „
Calpee	96 „	20 „

13th. The cost of the article and the rate of charges must in these cases be correspondingly reduced. In Allahabad, a further allowance is made of 7 per cent. being given on the punseree (5 seers) weight, as for a wholesale transaction. But whether this allowance is made elsewhere on cotton does not appear.

I have the honour to be, &c.,

(Signed) W. MUIR, *Secretary*.

§ 16. Experimental Culture in Goruckpore.

Having seen the effects of culture both in the southern and the northern parts of the province of Bengal, and that these were of the nature of over-luxuriance, as might be expected in a moist and warm soil and climate, we may next proceed to observe the results which have been obtained in the more northern and interior parts of the Presidency, which are drier but also warmer than might be expected from their latitude. Passing over Behar, we may briefly notice the Benares division, though not a cotton country, because a part of it seems adapted for this culture. Though the district was formerly famous for the coarse kinds of cotton manufacture, pp. 41 to 43, yet much of the raw material was imported both from the north-west and from central India. But still some cotton was cultivated, and one kind more carefully than the others, and with the aid of irrigation, p. 141. In reply to the queries circulated by order of the Court of Directors, very full answers were sent by the Commissioners and Collectors of the north-west provinces. From these we have already quoted some valuable and recent information on the state of the cotton trade in India, and shall now extract some notices respecting the culture. Mr. Reade, the Commissioner, states that "in his division the culture of cotton is little more than nominal. It is most commonly mixed with other crops; it is nowhere carefully tended; in many places it is an object of superstitious aversion, and often when the plant contrives to struggle to maturity, it is left, after being stripped of a portion of its bolls, enough to supply present domestic purposes, to be devoured by cattle." The quantity of land occupied by cotton it is difficult to estimate, being as it is mixed up with other crops, and "planted along the skirts of fields;" but probably about 25,000 acres in the whole division. Mr. Reade states, that "the average produce of the better sorts is 50 per cent. less than that of the inferior kinds. In a beegah of 3136 square yards, the estimated produce of the former is 80 lbs., and 150 lbs. of the latter, two thirds of the former, and four fifths of the latter, being seed." The kinds named *munnuea* and *rarhea* continue to be cultivated as in the time of Mr. Duncan (v. p. 141), though not to a greater extent than 3000 acres in the Benares district, though there must be a considerable demand notwithstanding the large import of English yarn. The Government demand for revenue amounts on the total area to 1r., 5a., 9p., per acre, and on the total cultivation to 1r., 12a., 6p. The Ganges gives easy communication both up and down the country (vide '*Memoir on the Statistics of the North Western Provinces of the Bengal Presidency*:' compiled from official documents by A. Shakespear, B.C.S.)

Though Mr. Reade agrees with the several Collectors of the districts of Benares, Azimghur, Jaunpore, Mirzapore, and Ghazeepore, that these districts are not cotton-producing countries, and are not likely to become so from the apparent unsuitableness of soil and climate; he is of opinion that the district of Goruckpore, especially in its eastern parts, is well suited to the culture. And Mr. Cooke, a gentleman described as "one of the most practical agriculturists in the district," and as also acquainted with Bundlecund, is of opinion that it might be made to compete with other districts; also, that the ryots would grow cotton with encouragement and the prospect of a ready market. But as 3,627,000 lbs. of cotton are imported into the district, of which 60,000 lbs. are afterwards exported into Nepal, it is evident that a good deal more cotton than that produced on the 15,000 acres at present in cultivation would be sold if it was grown; but it is probable, as mentioned by Mr. Reade, that the cultivation of the poppy is more profitable, as is also that of the sugar-cane. Cotton is usually grown with other crops; yet Mr. Cooke says whole fields may be seen unmixed with any other crop, principally on elevated soils which are free from deposits of water. Three kinds of cotton are known: 1, *Koktee*, a Nankeen cotton, sown in February and plucked in September and October; 2, *Nurma* (probably *G. arboreum*), a perennial usually planted in strips along sides of fields and gardens; and 3, *Desee*, the common Indian cotton. The district appeared to the author favorable for the cultivation of cotton, and, therefore, in a letter dated 12th Dec., 1842, addressed to J. C. Melvill, Esq. (v. '*H. of C.'s Return*,' p. 81), he mentioned that Mr. Sym, who had had a large grant of land made to him, had stated that "they never required to irrigate their land, and that their crops never failed from want of rain," and "promised that any planter should be made most welcome on any part of his grant of land." As the situation appeared desirable in other respects, independent of this information, the author suggested that the district of Goruckpore should be pointed out to the Indian Government as an eligible site for one of the American planters, if everything proved as desirable as it seemed to be (l. c., p. 83). But the same district had been selected for a fresh experiment by one of the planters before the above letter could have reached India, though Mr. Blount objected to the forest-land.

The American planters, when settled in the Doab and in Bundlecund, sighed for Rohilkund and Goruckpore, as well as for Dacca and Jubbulpore, while Mr. Terry wished for Rungpore. The effects of the moist climate of the latter, and of Dacca, we have already seen, and now proceed to state the results of American culture in a medium situation and climate, as found at Goruckpore. Mr. Blount on arrival at this place, in January, 1843, writes, "I do not hesitate to state as my opinion, that the character of the rainy season and moist climate of this district will prove highly favorable to the production of the American plant;" and "I think this one of the most favorable districts that could be selected for carrying out the object of Government." So Mr. Reade, the Collector of the district, writes at the same time: "The humidity of the atmosphere, the absence of hot winds, the abundant and lasting dews, the rich vegetable mould, the undulating surface of the country, and the invariably plenteous supply of rain, enable me to anticipate success." A glimmering of success, he states, would make the culture popular and extensive, and he adduces the sugar-cane, of which not less than 150,000 acres were in cultivation, though seven years ago there were not 10,000 acres in all Goruckpore. "Indian superstition vanished at the sight of success," (*Cotton Papers*, p. 214.) Mr. Blount was, on the 16th February, authorised to establish a farm of 118 acres, and directed to be supplied with all the requisites.

But the first accounts we hear are, that up to the 1st of August the season had been a most unpropitious one, and that Mr. Blount had been unable to plant his cotton until late in the season, and that, of the native cotton sown, the greater portion had not then come up; while Mr. Reade writes, that "the pest of this place is countless cattle, whose pertinacity and agility in overcoming fences is proportionate to their cupidity of Mr. Blount's cotton plants." On the 30th of September, we regret to find Mr. Blount reporting "that the American cotton plant is an entire failure at this farm." He is unable to assign any other cause for this failure than that it appears entirely unsuited to the climate of the country, being forced to maturity at too early an age. The plants, though only three months old (when they should be in full vigour), appear entirely exhausted. They "were green and flourishing up to the 15th inst., at which time the fruit commenced falling without being touched by the worm;" others, on the best soil of the farm, produced young fruit plentifully, which was immediately attacked by a small caterpillar, which eat into both flowers and fruit—every pod touched by them immediately fell off. "All the first foliage has dried and dropped off; the plants are now putting out a few sickly shoots from the top bud, which may produce cotton, but such a result is scarcely to be hoped for."

Notwithstanding these unfavorable appearances, Mr. Blount reports, on the 1st of December, that "after the rains of the 11th September the plants began throwing out new shoots, and the major part of these continued to improve up to the present time, and have now more blossoms on them, and quite as good a prospect as at any time during the season;" and he inquires, " Has the American cotton plant elsewhere ever manifested such a remarkable example of premature decay and complete resuscitation ?"

The experiment was repeated in the season of 1844, and Mr. Blount reports, on the 1st October, " a total failure of the experiment," though the season had " been quite different from that of 1843; in that year there was rather a scarcity of rain; this season has been a very wet one, the old plants pruned promised to yield a most prolific crop, but the fruit has dropped off before arriving at maturity; this has not only been the case with the American, but with every other description of cotton on this farm," with the exception of the kinds indigenous in the district. But on the 18th December he reports, that though " the plants during the month of September had been entirely stripped of foliage and fruit by worms," yet " during the month of October it put forth new shoots and flowered again, and in a great measure had recovered from the damage sustained from worms and insects," and that the plants will yield a very fair produce; a quantity of cupas (cotton with the seed) is already collected, and I think, from the quantity of pods yet on the plants, that 30 or 40 maunds will be collected during this and the next month; while of a small portion, planted on a spot freshly cleared from jungle, he says, on the 8th of January, " The American is, without doubt, the best I have seen since I have been in the country; the plants are weighed down with the fruit, and the pods are quite as large as they attain in the United States. If I can secure this field from thefts, I think it will yield 300 or 400 lbs. of cupas per acre."

It is to be regretted, that Mr. Blount's engagement having nearly expired, the experiment was not repeated, with his improved information; for it appears to have been prematurely considered to be an entire failure, as neither the soil nor the culture best suited to the climate, nor the causes of failure, had been ascertained. A horticulturist here might as reasonably conclude that fuchsias could not be successfully flowered, because full-grown buds fall off in such numbers, when plants are removed from a greenhouse to a warm and dry room. Though Mr. Blount does not mention the fact, we have no doubt that the shedding of the leaves, and the falling of the bolls, will be found to be connected with the change of climate which takes place at the conclusion of the rains. That is, from heat and excessive moisture, with a cloudy sky, to a bright and powerful sunshine with great evaporation, and then to comparative cool and clear weather, with much dew. It was at this time that the plants were found to revive and bear a crop, though they were supposed to have been exhausted. A little irrigation, as practised in many places by the natives, would make the transition probably more easy. Mr. Blount's exertions and zeal were undoubted, for Mr. Reade states, "It is due to him from me that I should observe, if industry and attention could have insured success, he would have succeeded."

Mr. Blount, however, proposed that in future the experiment should be conducted in a different manner, that is, that it should be changed from a *Neej* to a zemindary or ryot-war system, by giving advances to the natives for cultivating, with an agreement on their part to pursue the system of cultivation pointed out by the planter, and also secure to Government a repayment of the advances either in produce or money. The planter might still as heretofore have a small model-farm, but of not more than 40 or 50 beegahs; this would give land enough for the trial of every description of foreign and indigenous cotton, and would allow the planter time for superintending and instructing the ryots in the American mode of cultivation.

Mr. Reade, on a subsequent occasion (16th August, 1848) in reference to the failure, observes that the experiment was confined to a single spot, a piece of available Government land, and to American processes of agriculture, and thought with Mr. Blount that the ryot-war system of cultivation was best adapted for securing the extension and improvement of cotton cultivation, and that it was more likely to succeed in the eastern than in the central parts of the district.

It appears to the author that the farm, or *neej* cultivation, is only the first step of an agricultural experiment, made for the express purpose of ascertaining whether a new plant is suited to a district, and what are the modifications of culture with which it should be treated. These having been determined, and the culture likely to be profitable, the earliest opportunity should be taken to induce the ryots to take up the cultivation on their own account, as without their co-operation no extensive or permanent effect can be produced.

In considering the capabilities of the north-western provinces, and their suitableness for the growth of cotton fitted for the manufacturers of Europe, it is desirable to ascertain the quantity of cotton which a certain area of land is capable of producing, as upon that will ultimately depend the profitable nature of the culture; also what probability there was of a successful issue to the experimental culture of foreign cotton, which had been ordered to be instituted.

Taking the most southern of these localities, Benares, we find Mr. Duncan, in 1788, stating that the best kind of native cotton, called rarreah, was sown by itself in the month of August, in a good rich soil, a little elevated and near a well. About the beginning of December the ryots begin to water it once in every four or five days, and continue doing so till the capsules are ripe in March or April. Mr. Vincent, in 1831, stated that in the district of Allahabad, which begins about 50 miles to the west of Benares, the ryots sow their cotton immediately after the first heavy showers in June or July; irrigation is seldom necessary, and never before the end of September. Some prefer sowing in May, and irrigating until the rains set in. The return is about 300 lbs. of seed cotton to the beegah of 160 feet square, and the crop is not so subject to failure as the grain crop in general. Mr. Bruce, then of Calpee, on the s.w. bank of the Jumna, and about the same latitude as Cawnpore, gave an account, in 1836, of the different kinds of soil in Bundlecund, and stated that, in the best black soils, upwards of 700 lbs. are obtained from the beegah of 18,225 square feet; but, on the average, about half that quantity. The cotton is invariably sown at the beginning of the rains, and begins to be collected about September or October. He also states, that very often the crops cultivated with the cotton more than pay for the land-rent and labour of the whole cultivation. As these statements refer to native cotton, we must add that, previous to this period, American cotton had been cultivated still further to the north by the author at Saharunpore, and by Colonel Colvin in several villages along the Delhi canal. The Georgian cotton had, moreover, been cultivated both at Allahabad and at Delhi, also in the Deyra Doon. The difficulties experienced in the last-mentioned locality were those of over-luxuriance, owing, probably, to the moisture of the soil and climate in that Himalayan valley during the season of cultivation.

In the recent reports of the Collectors of districts, there is much information respecting the productiveness of the soil of different parts of India; some of this we shall now extract, as we proceed up the Doab, but keeping chiefly to its eastern side, and then noticing Rohilcund. The discrepancies are considerable, and the proportion of seed to cotton requires to be carefully ascertained, as it is usually considered to be one fourth; but many of the Collectors state it to be one third, to which Mr. Bell's experiments in these regions, to be afterwards mentioned, give some probability.

The production of cotton in the district of Allahabad is described by the Collector as being extremely small (27,689 acres), and he says that hardly any is exported; but the quantity produced per beegah seems to be large, as in the tracts on the left bank of the Ganges it is stated to amount to 3 and 5 maunds, in the Doab to $1\frac{1}{2}$ and 3 maunds, and on the right bank of the Jumna to 3, 4, and 5 maunds.

In the Futtehpore district, a little above Allahabad, the produce is said to amount to 3 maunds, 11 chetaks per acre.

In the Cawnpore district, 3 maunds of kupas per beegah, or 6 per acre, that is, one maund of clean cotton, and 2 maunds of Bennoula or seed are obtained. If we take the cotton to be one fourth of the seed, the quantity will be 123 lbs. per acre, but if one third, then 164 lbs. Mr. Bruce (a good practical authority) mentions 2 maunds, 8 seers, or about 180 lbs. per acre.

In Mynpooree it is stated by the Collector, that the average produce of cotton per pucca beegah may be taken at 7 maunds, or something less than 13 maunds per acre, that is, of course, cotton with the seed, or about 250 lbs. of clean cotton.

The district of Allygurh is described as well suited to the culture of cotton, though at present only 69,050 beegahs are under culture, a portion for home consumption, and the remainder for export to Mirzapore. But if a steady demand was established, the cultivation would be greatly extended, as cotton, in an average rainy season, is a remunerating crop; but the produce is stated to be only 3 maunds, 13 seers, 7 chetaks, per acre, of which about from one third to one fourth may be clean cotton. This district is the highest mentioned by Mr. Muir, in his letter, as likely to supply cotton for export.

But the able report of Mr. Pidcock, the Commissioner of Rohilcund, takes so comprehensive a view of the reports of the several Collectors of his division, comparing their details, and showing both the facilities and difficulties of the culture, that it is desirable to present it entire, especially as it will afford data, though from a non-exporting cotton country, for comparison with others which are considered especially adapted for the purpose.

From HENRY PIDCOCK, *Esq., Commissioner of Rohilkund; to the Sudder Board of Revenue, N. W. P., Agra.*

Dated the 29th September, 1848.

GENTLEMEN,—The despatch of the Honorable the Court of Directors, No. 14, dated 10th November last, received, with your Board's docket, No. 63, dated 18th February, and the memorandum regarding the cultivation of cotton in India having been forwarded to the collectors of this division, I have the honour herewith to transmit their replies to the queries proposed by the Court.

I. What is the price of cotton freed from seeds, at the principal mart or marts in your district?

The average price of such cotton, soon after it has been gathered, may be safely estimated at 2*d.* per pound avoirdupois, for the whole division of Rohilkund.

In the Bijnour return it is set down at 11lbs. per rupee.

Moradabad ditto, at 10½ rupees per maund of 100 sicca weight to the seer.

In the Budaon return, at 5 seers of 80 tolas each per rupee.

Bareilly ditto, at 10 rupees per maund of 125 lbs. troy.

Shajehanpore 10r. 13a. 9p. per maund of 111r. to the seer weight.

The highest price is estimated at 2¼*d.* per pound in Shajehanpore; the lowest at 1⅔*d.* per pound in Moradabad.

At Chundowsee, Zillah Moradabad, it would naturally be cheaper, that being the great cotton mart in this division; and it is exported thence to Bareilly and Shajehanpore by land.

At the present time the best cotton of last year is selling in the city of Bareilly at the rate of $3\frac{1}{2}$ seers of 100 sicca weight per rupee. A month hence, when the new cotton has been brought to market, the best will sell for four seers per rupee, or $2\frac{1}{4}$*d.* per pound avoirdupois. But the best is impure, and apparently unfitted for the English market.

II. At what price does the ryot sell his cotton, cleaned or uncleaned, and with or without advances?

In the Bijnour district, the ryot is said to sell his cotton, cleaned or uncleaned, at the rate of 12 lbs. per rupee, or $1\frac{5}{8}$*d.* per pound. This is not, I think, the case. The seed pays for the cost of cleaning.

In the Moradabad district, the ryot sells his cotton uncleaned. If the price of cleaned cotton be 7r. 8a. per maund, cotton with the seed in it would fetch 2r. 8a. per maund, or 1*s.* 3*d.* only. No advances are now taken by assamees. The ryot prices of cotton have not been given.

In the Budaon district the ryot seldom takes advances. He sells his uncleaned cotton at the rate of 20 seers, his cleaned cotton at 5 seers 80 sicca weight per rupee.

In the Bareilly district the ryot sells his cotton, if not freed from the seed, at 2r. 8a. per maund; but he usually sells it, when cleaned, at a rate varying little from the city current price. He takes no advances.

In the Shajehanpore district, on the contrary, the ryot is said never to sell his cotton in a cleaned state, but always raw. The price may be estimated at 2r. 8a. 6p. per maund. No advances are taken by the cultivator.

It appears by these returns that the cotton is generally sold by the producer, with the seed in it. His price varies but little from the current rates at the time existing in the chief marts. The reason assigned for its being sold in its raw state is the want of leisure; the season at which the cotton ripens being a very busy one for the cultivator. He seldom takes advances, because he grows chiefly for the consumption of his own family, and because, under the existing revenue system, he has time to dispose of this produce before he is called upon to pay rent.

III. What is the expense of cleaning cotton by the churka, or foot roller, or by any other method which may be in use?

In the Bijnour district it is said to be 2r. 2a. per 100 lbs. avoirdupois, or nearly one halfpenny per pound.

In the Moradabad district, one rupee per maund of 100rs. per seer= 103 lbs., or somewhat less than one farthing per pound. Out of one maund of raw cotton, from 12 to 15 seers of cleaned cotton are procured.

In the Budaon district, one rupee for five maunds is the charge stated. The cleaned cotton is about one-fourth of the produce with the seed in it.

In the Bareilly district, cotton seed is given in return for labour. If in grain, nine or ten pies per day, and one anna per day, if four seers of cotton be cleaned.

In Shajehanpore, the cotton cleaner using his own churkee gets all the seed he extracts, and a quantity of coarse grain, equal in weight to the cotton cleaned. If the churkee belongs to the owner of the cotton the cleaner only gets the cotton seed.

The cost of cleaning may be said to vary from one farthing to one halfpenny per pound avoirdupois. The churkee is the only machine used for separating the seed from the cotton. It is a rude contrivance, but it costs little, can be made and mended by the most ignorant carpenter; and in the hands of the most unskilful, the young and the old of either sex, effectually separates the seed, although it does not free the cotton from impurities.

IV. What are the expenses of conveying cotton to the nearest port for shipment?

The information on this head is imperfect, as regards the Bijnour return. Those from Bareilly and Shajehanpore contain none. The collector of Moradabad calculates altogether that the charge of conveying cotton from his largest mart, Chundousee, to Calcutta, the nearest port, for shipment, a distance by water of at least 1200 miles, would be about 13r. 5a. per cent. on the value of the cotton shipped. The Budaon calculation would not differ much from this, if insurance be added.

V. What is the average produce of cotton per beegah, or acre?

The beegah varies much in each district; the acre has, therefore, been used in this calculation.

The returns from the different districts vary very much; and so indeed do the several subdivisions of each district. The Bijnour return appears to have been prepared with much care. In it the highest and the lowest average, and the general average produce of clean cotton per acre, in each Pergunnah is given. The highest is Pergunnah Nujababad, 357 lbs. avoirdupois; the lowest is Ufzulgurh Rehur, 58 lbs.; the general average of the district is 162 lbs. per acre.

The Moradabad return gives an average of		247 lbs. per acre.	
Budaon	,,	,,	360 ,,
Bareilly	,,	,,	128 ,,
Shajehanpore		,,	241 ,,

The average for the whole division is 227 lbs. per acre. This is greatly in excess of Dr. Royle's estimate of Indian cotton produce, which he considers not to average more than 100 lbs. per acre. I think it may have been somewhat overrated; and I feel disposed to accept the Bijnour average of 162 lbs. per acre, in preference to the general one deduced above.

VI. What is the quantity of land under cultivation with cotton; and to what extent is it probable that the cultivation could be carried, in the event of an increased demand?

	Quantity of land now under cotton cultivation.	How far it could be extended.
Bijnour . . .	19,039 acres.	— —
Moradabad . . .	50,000 ,,	— —
Budaon . . .	34,091 ,,	As far as 45,398 acres.
Bareilly . . .	29,711 ,,	— —
Shajehanpore . .	7,160 ,,	As far as 11,733 acres.

The collectors of Bijnour, Moradabad, and Bareilly, state that the quantity of land in their districts adapted for rearing cotton is very great; and if a remunerating price could be obtained for the article, that is, if its cultivation were more profitable than that of any other produce, it could be grown to almost any extent.

3d. The result of the inquiries instituted proves that the average price of cotton freed from seed, at the principal marts in this division, shortly after the crop has been gathered, is *2d.* per pound avoirdupois; and that the ryot himself sells it at this rate, or perhaps a trifle cheaper.

4th. The cost of packing and of conveying the article to Calcutta, which is the nearest port, for shipment, has not been accurately ascertained. It is never so conveyed; and therefore the returns from Moradabad and Budaon on this head can only be considered an approximation. Information on this point can be much better obtained at Agra and Calpee, or at other large marts on the Jumna and Ganges. I think it will be found that 1*d.* per pound will cover all expenses to Calcutta, and will leave a reasonable profit in the hands of the exporter.

5th. This would raise the price of the cotton of this province to 3*d.* per pound in Calcutta; and this appears to be the price below which it cannot be sold in America. This, too, has for a series of years been its price at Bombay. I am not aware what the charge of freight from Calcutta or

Bombay to Liverpool would be, but it would certainly exceed the charge from America to Liverpool.

6th. It may, therefore, be safely assumed, that the actual cost of the cotton of this province will, on its reaching Liverpool, exceed that of American cotton. Nor does there appear to be any possibility of decreasing this cost; on the contrary, the export of cotton from this province in any large quantity would immediately raise its price; and so would all improvements in the culture of the plant, and the clean picking of the cotton.

7th. The cause of this high cost of production is to be traced chiefly to the high price paid as rent for good cotton land. In the Bijnour district it is excessively high. For the whole of this division it cannot be estimated at less than four rupees per acre. Assuming the average produce per acre to be 162 lbs., and the market price of the article to be 2*d.* per pound, it will be seen that one-half of the said price is composed of rent.

8th. Nor is this high rent the result of the Government assessment. However moderate the demand of Government may be; nay, even if the land be rent-free, the rent charged to the ryot for good cotton land would be much the same.

9th. The soil of Rohilkund appears to me to be well adapted to the production of cotton; this is proved by its vigorous growth; and if a remuneratory local price, say 3*d.* per pound, could be obtained, its cultivation might be greatly extended. At present the total produce cannot be said to exceed the demand of the people of the province. A considerable quantity is imported from the country westward of the Ganges to Chundowsee, whence it is taken by land carriage to the eastward, to Shajehanpore and Oude.

10th. The following Table shows that only one twenty-sixth part of the cultivated area of this division is grown with cotton; and that the average produce available for each inhabitant is only five pounds avoirdupois. This must barely suffice for the wants of the people.

DISTRICT.	Area of district in acres.	Cultivated area in acres.	Extent of cotton cultivation in acres.	Cotton produce in lbs., calculated at 162 lbs. per acre.	Population.	Quantity of cotton produce to each person.
Bijnour . . .	1,218,561	503,083	19,039	3,084,318	620,546	5 lbs.
Moradabad . .	1,899,065	675,862	50,000	8,100,000	997,362	8 "
Budaon . . .	1,515,764	829,323	34,091	5,522,742	825,712	6¾ "
Bareilly . . .	1,880,163	949,879	29,711	4,813,182	1,143,657	4¼ "
Shajehanpore .	1,589,308	674,645	7,160	1,159,920	812,588	1⅓ "
Total . . .	8,102,861	3,632,792	140,001	22,680,162	4,399,865	5 lbs.

11th. The cotton now grown in Rohilkund is inferior in quality and staple, and is so full of impurities as greatly to deteriorate its value, and to render it unfit for the English manufacturer.

12th. The chief cause of the inferiority of the cotton of this province, is to be found in the bad quality of the seed sown. The same has been sown from time immemorial in the same village. It may, originally, have been good; but it is in the nature of all seeds to deteriorate, if constantly reproduced in the same locality, unless great care be taken to prevent the process by attention to cultivation. This is not done. The seed originally bad, is sown broad-cast, in a soil that is rarely manured, and in this province never irrigated. The plants come up most irregularly, generally so closely packed together, as to interfere with their lateral growth; and occasionally, a patch of several yards may be seen without a single plant, the seed having been washed away by the rains. In the same field, too, are sown inferior grains, such as oord, tilh, urhur, &c. The fields are weeded, and the soil loosened about the roots of the plant, but not hoed. Such is the process of cultivating the plant.

13th. The second drawback upon the cotton of this province, is to be found in the impurities it contains. These are almost all attributable to carelessness in gathering. In America, each cotton gatherer is provided with three pockets. Into No. 1, is put the very best and purest cotton; into No. 2, that of second quality; into No. 3, the worst of all. In this country, the good, the inferior, and the refuse, which falls to the ground and is attacked by insects and animals, are all put indiscriminately into one common bag, and all thereby contract so many of the dry friable particles of the leaves of the plant, as to render their separation from the cotton a matter of great difficulty and expense. The American precaution is extremely simple, could readily be introduced, and would soon be appreciated by the natives when they found that it secured to them a higher price for their produce.

14th. In conclusion, I would strongly recommend that each collector of this division be supplied with a quantity of the best cotton seed from Central India. I would prefer the indigenous to foreign seed. That done, the rest may be left to nature and the ryot. Without this first necessary, improvement in the quality and staple of the cotton of this province is hopeless.

I have, &c.,

(Signed) HENRY PIDCOCK, *Commissioner.*

Mr. Pidcock's observations certainly make it appear that it

is improbable that cotton can be sent with profit to Europe. It may be so as the distance is great; but the returns being large and the Government demand small, it does not seem impossible. If the cotton as grown was kept clean, that of itself would increase the profits, for the expenses of transit would be the same, but would be paid upon a pure article for which a better price would be given, as the consumer, taught by experience, never gives the full price which the cotton itself is worth, but the price of cotton with a quarter to one eighth of dirt and refuse. Mr. Pidcock objects to the rough estimate formed by the author of 100 lbs. of clean cotton, as the average produce per acre in India. The author will be happy to find that he has made an erroneous estimate; and he believes that he has done so, especially if those sent in by the able Revenue officers of the north-western provinces are correct. But he has seen some elaborate statements from cotton-producing districts of other parts of India, where the production of cotton per acre is made much lower than in the author's estimate. The truth can only be ascertained by the careful observation of competent observers in various localities of the different provinces of India.

The system alluded to in Mr. Pidcock's* letter, of a higher rent being charged according to the nature of the crop, is one that is contrary to all the regulations of the Indian government, but which it will be extremely difficult to prevent if the people choose so to arrange it among themselves. The Government demand amounts to 1r. 15a. per acre on the total cultivation, and has no reference to the nature of the crop cultivated; but

* The same practice is thus referred to in the letter of R. K. Dick, Esq., Collector of Bijnour, dated 12th August, 1848, addressed to H. Pidcock, Esq.:

"There is abundance of land adapted to the growth of the country cotton; but the system of Buttae tenures, which so generally prevails, acts as a check on the extension of the cultivation. Under that system, the rent paid varies with the crop, and is very high on cotton. The most prevalent nominal rate is 4*s.* 8*d.* per beegah; but, as the size of the beegah varies in every pergunnah, the actual rent also differs. The ryot, therefore, does not find it profitable to grow cotton, except in the best lands. He is obliged, in many places, by custom, to plant a certain quantity, but he reluctantly exceeds the prescribed amount. Moreover, the crop depends upon being carefully cleared from weeds early in the season; and, at the same time, the extensive sugar crops grown in this district, and the rice also, require the same process. The supply of labour does not equal the demand at that particular season; and therefore the cultivator finds it better to give up the cotton crop, and use the land, that ought to produce cotton, for rubbee (that is, for the cold weather crops)."

the Zemeendar who underlets it takes a higher rent, and in some places varies this according to the nature of the crop.

An able writer in the 'Calcutta Review' on the "*Revision of the Settlement of the North-Western Provinces,*" in contrasting the territories lying to the eastward of the Ganges with those within the Doab, says, "There is no longer the same moisture in the soil or climate, nor the same spontaneous fertility." To this it is perhaps that we may ascribe the large returns quoted by Mr. Pidcock, and certainly as we proceed westward the fertility seems less and less conspicuous, especially in reference to the culture of cotton, though the districts are peculiarly considered to be producers of cotton. The same writer observes, "It is not till the visitor reaches the arid plains to the west of the Jumna, from Etawah to Hissar, on the extreme verge of the British territory, that vegetation really languishes." The reports of the Collectors on the western side of the Doab, and those of the western bank of the Jumna, give a much smaller return of cotton per acre than we should have expected from districts so long famous for producing and exporting cotton.

Thus near Banda the produce per acre is said to be 1 maund, 1 seer, 1 chetak; at Seonda, a little above 2 maunds; and at Terohan, 2 maunds, 10 seers, that is, about 174 lbs. per acre, and in some villages, only from 11 to 20 seers per acre.

Mr. Cooke (v. p. 271), in answer to the question respecting the average produce of cotton per acre, says, "In Bundlecund, the average produce of cotton with the seeds is about 8 maunds per beegah, or about 10 or 11 maunds per acre. Cotton-wool separated from the seeds will, therefore, be $\frac{1}{3}$ ($\frac{1}{4}$?) that quantity."

In the district of Humeerpore, the report from five different pergunnahs gives an average of 33 seers, 9 chetaks per acre; (?) in one, 15 seers is given as the average; and in three others, 10 to 45 seers as the produce per beegah. In that of Humeerpore, 35 seers per beegah is given as the produce of cotton in a good season. The quantity of land under cotton cultivation is stated to be 80,000 beegahs, but that 200,000 more might be brought under the same culture, if a demand existed.

In the Calpee district, the beegah contains 2025 square yards; 2 beegahs and 6 biswahs are reckoned to a statute acre. The average return is 1 maund, 18 seers, per acre, or 118 lbs.

In the district of Etawah, on the western bank of the Jumna, returns from seven pergunnahs give 2 maunds, 11 seers, 7 chetaks, as the average produce of cotton with the seed, and 30 seers, $5\frac{3}{4}$ chetaks, as that of clean cotton per beegah.

In the district of Muttra, "the average produce of cleaned cotton per acre is 2 maunds and 8 seers," or about 180 lbs.

In the Agra district, "one acre of land produces 1 maund and 15 seers of cotton," or avoirdupois weight, 3 quarters, 29 lbs. 2 oz. 4 drachms.

From Delhi, the most north-western of the divisions, the reports are interesting from the country lying between 27° and 30° of N. latitude, and forming the arid tracts on the western bank of the Jumna, and yet where, with the aid of irrigation from the Delhi Canal, the cultivation of cotton is carried on not only for the consumption of the people, but for export to the countries both to the north and north-east, or into the Punjab and Pattiala, and westward into the Bikaneer territories. In the Rohtuck district, "the average of good and bad seasons may be about $1\frac{3}{4}$ maund." At Hissar, the returns are stated to be 2 maunds, $10\frac{2}{3}$ seers, of cleaned cotton per acre. The collector of Delhi district states, that "in the northern pergunnah the average produce of clean cotton, per acre of 4840 square yards, is said to be 1 maund, 11 seers, 8 chetaks, or 103 lbs. In the southern pergunnah, the average produce per acre is 34 seers, 14 chetaks, or 69 lbs. The average of the two pergunnahs is 1 maund, 3 seers, 3 chetaks, or 86 lbs.; but I consider this to be below the mark. The averages have been framed upon the statements of the zemeendars themselves and the village accountants, who are ever prone to underrate the amount of produce." Mr. John Lawrence, afterwards so conspicuous for his services in the Punjab, was in 1845 employed in making a census of this district, which the officiating Collector of 1847 believed "was as accurate as could be expected." This is an important fact; for we shall afterwards have to refer to his comparison of the cultivation in the Delhi district with that in the Jullundur Doab. Sir Theophilus Metcalfe, Commissioner of the Delhi division, has embodied the information transmitted by the Collectors to the several queries in the following tabular statement:—

Statistics of the Culture and Prices of Cotton in the Delhi Division.

DISTRICT.	Price of cotton, freed from seed, at the principal marts in the district.	Price at which the ryot sells his cotton, cleaned or uncleaned, and with or without advances, per maund.				Expense of cleaning cotton by the churkee, per maund.	Expense of conveying cotton to the nearest port for shipment, per maund.	Average produce of cotton per acre.		Quantity of land under cultivation with cotton, and extent to which it is probable cultivation could be carried, in the event of increased demands.	
		With advances.		Without advances.							
		Cleaned.	Uncleaned.	Cleaned.	Uncleaned.			Cleaned.	Uncleaned.	Under cultivation.	Probable extent of cultivation.
	r. a. p.	r. a. p.	r. a. p.	r. a. p.	r. a. p.	r. a. p.	r. a. p.	m. s. c.	m. s. c.	Acres.	Acres.
Bhutteeanah . . .	—	—	—	—	—	—	—	—	—	—	—
Paneeput . . .	5 15 8	5 4 7	1 14 0	5 13 11	1 14 9	0 6 0	—	—	8 34 2	14,820	16,703
Hissar	6 13 0	—	1 10 7	6 5 4	2 1 11	0 8 0	2 2 0	—	5 35 3	9,271	11,271
Delhi	6 2 5	—	—	6 1 6	2 0 0	0 8 0	2 12 0	1 3 1	—	3,321	6,642
Rohtuck	6 8 5	5 9 10	—	6 12 0	—	0 7 0	2 7 0	2 32 0	4 29 5	14,552	18,750
Goorgaon . . .	5 14 2	5 8 0	1 7 9	5 13 1	1 15 5	1 2 11	2 12 3	1 23 0	6 32 14	29,617	35,418
	6 4 4	5 7 6	1 10 5	6 2 9	2 0 0	0 9 7	3 5 9	1 19 6	6 22 14	71,582	87,535

The maund, seer, rupee, and beegah used in these calculations are respectively valued at: maund, 40 seers; seer, 80 Co.'s rs.; beegah, 3025; rupee, Co.'s rs.

Delhi Commissioner's Office;
June 28th, 1848.

(Signed) T. METCALFE,
Commissioner.

§ 17. Experimental Culture in the Doab and Bundlecund.

The Governor-General, Lord Auckland, directed that the experiment should be first tried near Calpee, in four separate farms, within communicating distance of each other; but owing to the difficulty of obtaining suitable villages, Mr. Finnie alone was settled on the Doab banks of the Jumna, and the three others on the other side; Mr. Mercer furthest in the interior, and about 20 miles from that river at Raath, which is nearly south of Calpee, and not very far from Jaloun so long famous for its cotton. Captain Bayles fixed himself at Humeerpore, to be in a centrical situation.* The planters have furnished reports of their proceedings, some of them very short, and others lengthy. All (writing in November of their first year) complain of the lateness of the season (April and May) before they were settled in their farms; also of the smallness of the bullocks which were first supplied them. But they thought favorably of the land. Mr. Finnie writes, "I think, from the appearance of the land, that cotton can be produced in abundance;" and Mr. Mercer, "There is no question that the soil of this part of the country is excellently suited for cotton." But in the season they were singularly unfortunate; the rainy season, which usually continues for three months, not having extended altogether beyond six weeks. With Mr. Finnie the first shower fell on the 24th of June, but he had no rain from the 23d of August to the 10th of September. Mr. Mercer had a sprinkle of rain on the 9th of June, but no proper rains until the 24th of July, though it had been raining for a fortnight all round him, but then the country became flooded. During August, and till the 7th and 8th of September, the rain was almost incessant, but on the 11th the weather became clear. "The sun looked down with the fiercest glare, and a hot dry wind, almost like that of June, sprang up from the west." The surface of the earth became hard and baked, the leaves began to wither as if scorched by fire, and the

* Mr. Finnie, in the village of Kotra Muckrundpore, which is in the Doab, and near the banks of the Jumna; Mr. Terry was placed in the village of Chuack; Mr. Blount at Soomeirpore; and Mr. Mercer, as above mentioned, at Raath.

bolls or young capsules began falling in showers. Of these, Mr. Mercer says, "I never saw a greater abundance or more healthy-looking on plants of the same size." After the 1st of October the weather became a little cooler at night, and after the 10th the air somewhat damper. The unblighted leaves of the cotton assumed a lively look, and the plant afterwards began to revive, and though slowly, to put forth fresh leaves. Mr. Mercer adds, "if I can get a rain, I yet have hopes of finding a very fair return from what I have planted;" also that "the cotton has sustained its character, being its first year in a foreign land, as a hardy drought-enduring plant, in having survived such weather at all; and I am most satisfied now, that with anything like the season described as usual in this country, that is, rains followed by heavy dews and cool nights, that the most abundant crops of cotton can be produced."

Mr. Finnie justly observes: "this country requires more rain than the southern states of America. The season at home would have been called dry, but still the cotton crops would have been fine;" there "we are anxious to get the ground dry enough to plough after the winter breaks up," but "here we wish to get it wet, to cool the atmosphere and send forth vegetation;" and again, "here we plant in a hot-bed." He also says, "The grand characteristic of this country appears to be —a flood, a drought; the latter greatly predominating,—we plant in low land to avoid the drought, and then comes a flood and drowns all the cotton; we plant upon high land to avoid the flood, and a drought prevails which blasts the cotton." We have seen Mr. Price, in Dacca, complaining of the length of time which the American plant takes to come to maturity. In the Doab it follows a very different course. Mr. Finnie states, in one place, that the cotton which was planted on the 25th of June commenced opening on the 23d of September; that planted on the 28th of June on the 26th of September, and that he picked some on the 28th of September. But in his journal he states, that he first picked on the 8th of August, which was from twenty to twenty-five days sooner than it blossoms on the Mississippi, and concludes by stating, "It is with the greatest pleasure, however, that I receive the fine produce of the few beegahs I planted early in the season." Both planters, however, complain of the destruction of their cotton by insects.

Captain Bayles, as the result of the whole, states, "We have this year laboured under very great disadvantages; the only thing that has been fully established is the superiority of the American over the native mode of cultivation; for fields of native cotton, planted in the same villages, and in the same soil, have produced almost nothing, and are now almost dried up, whereas the cotton (native seed) planted by the Americans is still green and bearing fruit."

In the foregoing pages we have given the result of the experiments made by the American planters in north-western India during the first year of their being in that country. We see that, though they laboured under some disadvantages, and the season was unusually dry, yet that the American method of cultivation seemed very superior to that pursued by the natives, for even the Indian cotton, as planted by the Americans, continued green and was bearing fruit, when that planted by the natives produced nothing, and was dried up. Of this we have several testimonies independent of the accounts given by the planters. Thus, Mr. Lowther, the Commissioner of the district, writes in Feb. 1842: "I have great pleasure in reporting, that while the indigenous cotton in the vicinity of the farms and other parts of the country had altogether failed, or suffered so much from the drought as barely to yield a return to the cultivator, the plant on the farms without the aid of irrigation was superior to any I have seen in the best of seasons. The Mexican cotton was somewhat stunted, but the pods were full and healthy, and the produce exceeding fine." So Mr. Fraser, another Commissioner, writes, "I could not have imagined that a little care and cultivation would have made such a complete change;—it afforded a most gratifying contrast with its numerous healthy shoots and plentiful produce, to the miserable dried-up dwarf cotton immediately adjoining it and in the same soil." Mr. Finnie, in Nov. 1841, wrote still more confidently: "I unhesitatingly avow, that from all that I have seen this season, even this *unfortunate* and very *unfavorable* season, that the American, and even the native cotton, cultivated upon our plan, will form a profitable investment." "It will not require one tenth of the capital that it would require in the United

States." With regard to the native method of culture, and the care they bestow on their cotton, he says, "as sure as they plant and do the little work they do in their own fields, so sure will it fail to produce well. Cotton will not grow and produce well, in this or any other country, if committed to the Hindoo gods, without proper cultivation." (*Proc. Agric. Soc.*) Mr. Willis, of Calcutta, on examining specimens of the cotton which had been produced, refers "to the fair and really encouraging prospects held out by good exertion and attention being paid to the further trial and improvement of the indigenous plant."

Captain Bayles having represented that the American planters, far from being disheartened, were confident that they could succeed not only in introducing the Mexican seed, but in improving the indigenous cotton, so as to make it a marketable and profitable cotton, the Agra Government authorised whatever was thought requisite for insuring the success of the experiment. (*Return*, pp. 113 and 116.) But neither land nor money, nor the zeal of men, nor the labour of cattle will suffice, unless the elements are favorable; and the planters were singularly unfortunate in the particular seasons during which they made their experiments, though it is doubtful whether the climate in general is ever suitable to the successful culture of American cotton, without the aid of such artificial irrigation as may be supplied by a canal. Mr. Allen, who succeeded Captain Bayles, reports, on the 19th of August, that 1008 acres of land were under cotton culture on the part of Government, but "the beginning of the season was decidedly favorable, though rather late; between the 7th and 25th of July ten inches of rain fell, and the planters began to complain that there was too much, for the red soils became a mass of mud, in which it was impossible to work, and the low lands were flooded. Since the 25th of July we have had no rain, and the plants are consequently beginning to droop for want of moisture; the season is certainly now unfavorable." Of the planters themselves, Mr. Mercer states his conviction that Bundlecund "is, and always will prove too dry and uncertain ever to produce cotton to advantage." Moreover, "the seasons in this part of India are too short, even if they were more favorable, for after the rains end, and no other than the recommencement of this dry west wind ever can be expected, which will always inevitably cut short our crops, and deteriorate their quality."

Mr. Finnie says, "the grand characteristic of this country appears to be—a flood, a drought; the latter greatly predominating." Mr. Blount observes, with both candour and good sense, "it will, no doubt, appear strange that we should complain of the dryness of the season, as we have always asserted that cotton does not require a great deal of rain. Last year there was no rain after the 26th August, and this season bids fair to be like the last, as it has now been twenty-five days since we have had rain. If such are the average seasons of Bundlecund, you will at once perceive that the rains are not sufficient, nor can planting operations be commenced early enough to ensure a good crop of cotton. There is no doubt but that cotton will grow in this part of Bundlecund, and yield a small produce, but we must have a far more favorable season than I have yet seen, to expect more than one maund of 'seed cotton' from the best lands."

These letters, embodying the opinions of three of the planters on the subject of the unsuitableness of Bundlecund to the growth of cotton, particularly of American cotton, were forwarded by Mr. Allen, with an intimation that "they think that Rohilkund or Goruckpore may answer. The planters seem to me to think more of climate than of soil, or rather I should say that they find it more difficult to find a favorable climate in India than a favorable soil." Subsequent to this, Mr. Finnie was directed to make a tour through the Doab to ascertain its capabilities more to the north and east, while Mr. Blount proceeded to the south and east, through Goruckpore and the adjoining districts. Mr. Mercer, who had been transferred to Bombay, was to report *en route* on the capabilities of the country in the Sangur and Nerbudda territories, through which he would pass." Mr. Finnie having perambulated a great portion of north-west India, applied for permission to establish a model farm at Agra. This being granted, he arrived there in April, 1843. It was also arranged, "that the ryots should be encouraged to cultivate cotton on their own lands, according to Mr. Finnie's directions, receiving from the planter seed, ploughs, and such advances (of money) as might be absolutely necessary." "But the model farm was a complete failure." Want of rain, when most required, and a superabundance afterwards, are stated by Mr. Finnie to have "combined to ruin a great portion of the cultivation, whilst that which was produced was injured by insects, and suffered from the depredations of the natives." Cotton-cleaning machinery, under an English engineer, Mr. Frost, was also established at this place; though this we need not notice further at present. (*v. House of Commons' Return.*)

We have experienced some difficulty in tracing the cotton of the different seasons to the sales in this country; 360 bales, by the ships 'Amwell,' and 476 bales by the 'Monarch,' arrived here in May, 1847, and were sold in London in the following month, that by the former at $3\frac{3}{8}$*d.* to $4\frac{5}{8}$*d.*, and that by the 'Monarch' at $4\frac{1}{8}$*d.* to $4\frac{5}{8}$*d.*

Though we reserve our final observations on these experiments, it is evident that neither in Dacca nor in the Doab is there any want of heat for the American cotton plant. But in Dacca, from excess of moisture, there was over-luxuriance, while in the Doab, from a deficient or irregular supply of water, there was extreme dryness, and the plants were burned up. This can be counteracted apparently only by a supply of moisture from wells, rivers, or canals, either for early sowing before the rains come on, or at their conclusion, to make up for the increased evaporation until the weather becomes cooler.

Having stated our conviction that the climate of Bundlecund and of the Doab is too dry for the culture of American cotton without the aid of artificial irrigation; we find that Dr. Irvine, then of Gwalior, was of the same opinion, for he advises, "that about two waterings ought to be given early in the season, before the rains are heavy, and three copious waterings after the rains cease, at proper intervals. Under this treatment, I venture to say that there will be no obstacle found to the successful culture of American cotton, of the common though most superior species." (*Return*, p. 113.)

That it was not unreasonable to expect that American cotton might be cultivated in some of the above localities, may be inferred from what has been done, both previous to and since the above experiments in still more northern situations. The author, when Superintendent of the Botanic Garden at Saharunpore, in 30° degrees of N. lat., endeavoured to improve the culture of cotton, and as he had the advantage of a cut from the Doab Canal, which passed through the Garden, the only difficulty he experienced was from over-luxuriance, though he planted in lines five feet apart and pruned. As the Bourbon was the only exotic then procurable, the kinds he tried were two: (1 and 2), indigenous varieties; 3, the Bourbon; and 4, the arboreous species or tree-cotton (v. p. 144.) Specimens of the cotton produced were submitted to G. Saunders, Esq., at that time Commercial Resident at Calpee, and accustomed to inspect cotton for the Company's investment. In a letter dated Mussooree, 29th of July, 1829, Mr. Saunders writes, "I have just had the pleasure to receive four samples of cotton which you sent me through Col. Fielding. Nos. 1 and 2 are of very excellent fibre and beautifully cleaned, but like the cotton generally of this country defective in staple, and, therefore, difficult to be spun into thread by machinery. No. 3 is better in this respect, and shows the advantage that might be gained by introducing good foreign seed for cultivation in this country. No. 4 is, I think, on the whole the best description of cotton, the fibre and staple being both good. It appears to be indigenous; if so, I wonder that the tree has not been more generally cultivated."

Col. Colvin, of the Bengal Engineers, at that time Superintendent of the Delhi Canal, wrote in 1834 (v. '*Trans. Agric. Soc.*,' vol. ii, p. 96), that he had obtained about a dozen seeds of the Upland Georgia and Sea Island cotton. Of the former six vegetated and ripened their pods. From these he obtained seeds, which he sowed in various places along the canal, all of which thrived well; the weight produced, he says, was at least equal, if not superior, to that of the native cotton; the quality certainly so. Of some more seed, which he subsequently received, he says, "the green, or Upland Georgia, has vegetated freely everywhere, and is now growing not in one or two, but probably in one hundred villages."

Mr. Smith, Collector of Delhi, addressed the Agricultural Society on the culture of Exotic cottons in the Delhi district, and thought some situation between Muttra and Delhi was more favorable for experiment than the neighbourhood of Agra, as "cotton cultivation prevails to a much greater extent than in the vicinity of Agra." Mr. Smith had himself cultivated Egyptian, Upland Georgian, Sea Island, and Nankeen, and found the first and the last gave the largest returns, and the Upland Georgian the most scanty; but this he ascribed to accident, as on ordinary occasions it gives very nearly as heavy a crop as the Egyptian. The Sea Island and Nankeen were most injured by insects. The Nankeen, though not valued in England, is esteemed in some parts of India, and has sold well in Lucnow. Col. Skinner's experience has already been given at page 93.

Col. Cautley, the successor of Col. Colvin, and now engaged in constructing the great Ganges Canal, has been anxious like his predecessor to introduce the culture of cotton along the Canal. In a letter dated the 16th of April, 1850, to the author, he observes, "On my way from Suez to Bombay, at the end of 1847, in the 'Atalanta,' I made Mr. Blount's acquaintance. He gave me a few seeds of what he called the Mastodon cotton (a large variety of New Orleans); these seeds were planted in my garden at Roorkee, and the muster (sample) that I now send is from these plants after the second year, *i. e.* this is the produce of the second year's bearing. The ground in which the seeds were planted is not what is called cotton-land; on the contrary, it is light coloured. It is, in fact, land at the foot of the Bangur, or high land, on which Roorkee stands." Lately (14th of August), when passing through Manchester, the author was accidentally present at a meeting of the Commercial Association, when the subject of cotton culture in India was under discussion. He took the opportunity of exhibiting this cotton to the meeting, and it was pronounced by Mr. Brown, the experienced broker of that cotton-capital, to be of excellent quality, and worth at that time $8\frac{1}{4}d.$ per lb.

§ 18. Experimental Culture at Agra.

Notwithstanding these failures, and the departure of the American planters as well as of the English engineer, the Lieutenant-Governor of the North-Western Provinces, the Hon. J. Thomason, determined upon making a fresh experiment, according to the proposal of Mr. Hamilton Bell, "a gentleman of superior education, great intelligence, and the highest respectability, long resident in this neighbourhood (Agra), engaged in commercial and agricultural pursuits, and possessed of great local knowledge and influence." (*House of Commons' Return*, p. 260.) Mr. Bell was at first inclined to doubt how far it would be practicable to produce a cotton which would be able to contend successfully with the American cotton in the English market, as he did not find the New Orleans kind suited to the climate. He, therefore, felt persuaded that the indigenous cotton must be depended upon; and tried every variety of seed that he found appreciated in the great bazaars, and stated that "a safe rate to the grower" would be 8 rupees per maund, which is not quite $4\frac{1}{2}$ cents per lb." But he subsequently mentions that, under advances, it might be obtained for 7 rupees a maund. "The transaction, to be remunerative to the merchant, could only be done by cultivating, cleaning, packing, and despatching the cotton on a sufficient scale to prevent disproportionate charges," such as 10,000 beegahs. The author in reporting (Oct. 1847) on this plan, observed that "the best method" for improving the indigenous cottons "would appear to be, to select the districts where the best cottons were already produced for the first experiments," and that "the next best method is to introduce good seed into districts where inferior cottons are produced, in order that this may be supplanted by a superior article, hoping that the quality of the imported seed may be retained in the new situation, when this has the advantage of more careful culture; otherwise, it does not follow that the new seed will give an improved produce beyond the first year. This method Mr. Bell has, from his local situation, been compelled to adopt. It has the important characteristic, that failure would not deter from other attempts in more favorable situations; yet success, under adverse circumstances of soil or climate, would greatly stimulate exertion in all other situations." (*House of Commons' Report*, p. 69.) Mr. Bell found that the best cotton in north-west India was produced in the countries lying to the westward of the Jumna, whence the author observed in the 'Report,' l. c., p. 68:

"The cotton of Bundlecund has long been celebrated in India, but with it has probably often been confounded the cotton of Central India, which used formerly to find its way to the Ganges, but is now chiefly conveyed to Bombay." "But Bundlecund itself is, no doubt, well suited to the cultivation of cotton, as it has always been supposed to be, and Mr. Mercer and Mr. Frost, as I have recently learnt, both consider the district as most favorable for the improved culture of cotton. Mr. Mercer would, no doubt, have succeeded in improving it, had he not been burnt out of his farm during the disturbances in that district in 1841. The cotton of Jaloun and Jhansi was formerly most celebrated, and Mr. Bell now finds that the cotton of Baugcheenee, a district on the south of the Chumbul near Dholpore, and therefore probably very similar in soil and climate to Jaloun and Jhansi, which are not very distant, is that which is at present most in repute. This Baugcheenee cotton is that which Mr. Bell, after numerous experiments on all the varieties of seed which he was able to procure, found to be the best for cultivation in the Doab, and it is sufficiently esteemed by the natives to be able to command a higher price in the local markets. Mr. Bell states, 'that a small parcel of the latter cotton, which came into this market, was instantly taken at about 7½ per cent. higher than the rates paid for the other best reputed cottons.' The quality was, moreover, highly approved of at Liverpool, for nine bales sent by Mr. Bell to Messrs. Nicol, Duckworth, and Co., are reported as 'pretty clean, but rather seedy, fair colour, staple fair length,' and valued at 4⅛*d*. per lb. on the 6th February, 1846, when fair qualities of Bowed Georgia were selling for 3¾*d*., and the same quality of New Orleans cotton for 4¾*d*. The samples of this cotton sent this year to the India House, and which I sent to Mr. Turner, were pronounced by him as saleable at 5*d*. per lb., though the staple was short, provided the cotton in bulk should prove as clean as the samples I sent him. Mr. Tetley, the cotton broker of London, who has been so long employed by the East India Company, values these cottons, supposing the bulk to be equal to the samples in point of cleanness, at from 6*d*. to 6¼*d*. per lb., the same price as middling to fair American."

Mr. Bell having been unable the first year to obtain seed enough of the Baugcheenee to distribute among the ryots, was induced to send people to the districts producing the best cotton, in order to buy it up, and have it carefully cleaned and packed: the seed being distributed for cultivation.

The cotton grown by Mr. Bell's ryots, and cleaned with the Government's saw-gins under his superintendence, was shipped at Calcutta, in October, 1847, 749 bales by the 'Surat,' and 622 bales by the 'Guisachin,' and was sold at Liverpool by Messrs. Rathbone, in July, August, September, and October, at a time when, unfortunately for the experiment, in consequence of the general depression of trade, the prices of every kind of cotton were low, indeed, never had been so low except in 1844-45; and at the latter period of the sales, a large supply of new cotton was expected from the United States. The cotton by the 'Guisachin' was sold, 160 bales at from $2\frac{5}{8}$*d.* to $2\frac{7}{8}$*d.*, and 456 bales at 3*d.* per lb., and the cotton by the 'Surat' at the same rates. Of this cotton only 186 bales were sold for export, and the remainder to numerous buyers, chiefly manufacturers. Messrs. Rathbone mention, that at the same time they were selling ordinary New Orleans at $3\frac{1}{4}$*d.* and $3\frac{1}{8}$*d*,, and middling Orleans at $3\frac{3}{4}$*d.*, which, in September, 1847, had been selling at $6\frac{7}{8}$*d.* The fall in other kinds had, therefore, been relatively as great.

It was to this cotton that Mr. Bazley referred in his evidence before the Cotton Committee, as being at that time, March 1848, in Liverpool from Agra, and which though well cleaned, he considered unsuited for our manufactures. (Qs. 746 and 747.) Mr. Turner, who had seen the cotton about the same time, observed that the bulk was not so clean as the samples which had been previously sent, and that the whole was better suited for export than for home manufactures.

Mr. Bell's zeal was, however, unflagging, and when cultivating the Baugcheenee, he was at the same time trying other kinds of cotton, of which he sent samples to the India House, with the following notices respecting them:

1. *Sophur*. From a place so called on the confines of the Gwalior territory, near to Kotah. The cotton he considered superior to the Baugcheenee, perfectly hardy, coming quickly to maturity, fully as productive, and one which had greatly attracted the attention of cultivators. "In several very carefully conducted experiments, I have ascertained that the kupas yields the very large proportion of $35\frac{1}{2}$ per cent. of clean cotton."

2. *Hybrid*, between Baugcheenee and Chundehree cotton, much the same as the above.

3. *Coimbatore-seed,* that is, acclimated New Orleans. It will hardly succeed in these districts, from the degree of irrigation it demands, its comparatively limited produce, and the diminished relative proportion of cotton in the kupas: the means of several trials varying but little, being only 25¾ per cent. Its fineness and staple are, however, attractive.

4. *Hybrid* between Bombay and Baugcheenee; cotton much the same as No. 2.

5. Cotton from *Bombay-seed,* resembles Chundehree cotton. It is fine, but the plant extremely tardy in arriving at maturity, "exuberantly productive of cotton bolls;" but these small, and the relative proportion of cotton and seed is discouraging, the former giving in my trials only 25 per cent. of the kupas.

6. *Jeypore.* This has attracted most regard from the native cultivators. "It is by far the most productive, the plants being large and covered with bolls, larger a good deal than the Sophur or Baugcheenee, and double those of the Desee (that is, the indigenous) cotton." The staple seems longer than other descriptions, but it is equally harsh to the feel as the *desee.* "The mean relation of cotton to (seed in the) kupas is 38¾ per cent., but some trials gave me 40 per cent."

7. *Nundpore,* a variety of Baugcheenee, but the produce of the villages of Nundpore, Bindwas, Debee, and Deoghur, has the highest reputation. This probably arises from the deep black soil there prevailing, but is partially attributed to the careful selection of seed for cultivation.* "That the cotton is superior is undeniable; for struck by the remarks, I sent at some expense a man to Nundpore to get some seed, and used it for my *neej* (farm) cultivation. The produce is undoubtedly better than in other Baugcheenee, which is fully equal to the general Gwalior descriptions so named, and its ratio of cotton to (seed in the) kupas is remarkable, being no less in my trials than 38 per cent."

8. *Omeghur,* a variety produced on Mr. Bell's farm, which

* "The women, in seeding the cotton by the churka, are accustomed whenever a large boll comes into their hand, to throw it aside into a basket placed for the purpose, and the same process is pursued when the basket's contents are freed from the seed. In this way, the very finest bolls produce the seed, and they thus account for their superior cotton."

flowered early, was fairly productive and fine. Cotton $33\frac{1}{3}$ per cent. in the kupas.

9. A white-flowered variety from Jeypore seed.

Samples of these cottons having been sent to the India House, were forwarded by the author to Manchester, and were submitted by Mr. H. Fleming "to many spinners and brokers of high standing, both at Manchester and at Liverpool, and the following may be considered as the result of their examinations:

"Nos. 1, 2, 4, 6, 7, 8, and 9. All these samples are very clean and of good colour, but so coarse and short in staple as to be next to worthless for spinning purposes; present value $3\frac{1}{2}$*d.* to 4*d.* per lb.

"Nos. 3 and 5 are the only cottons thought worthy of much attention as approaching more nearly to the American species, and likely to be extensively used. A slight difference of opinion exists as to their relative value, some persons preferring the latter to the former. All, however, agree that they far surpass the other samples. They are clean and bright, and of fair length as to staple, and may be worth to-day from $4\frac{1}{2}$*d.* to $4\frac{3}{4}$*d.* per lb. Mr. Turner at the same time writes of No. 3, that is the cotton from Coimbatore-seed, that he would willingly give 5*d.* per lb. for 1000 bales of such cotton."

As the manufacturers did not approve of the cotton generally, the experiment was discontinued after the second year. We have entered more into the details of this experiment than may be thought necessary from the inferior quality of the mass of the cotton, as far as its application to spinning purposes is concerned. But there were several buyers for it, and the price, notwithstanding the low rates for New Orleans cotton, was still as high as could be expected for the shortest stapled of all the Indian cottons. Mr. Bell calculated that if the cotton sold at 4*d.* per lb., it would yield a profit after freight and all expenses both in this country and India had been paid. This price might probably have been obtained for it at any period since 1848, and something above it in the present season, if the above relative proportion was maintained between it and New Orleans cotton; and we know there is always a greater demand for the Indian when the American cotton is dear. But it is interesting to observe how numerous are the varieties of cotton, and how practicable it seems to produce others suitable to different soils and climates. Some of these, however, are so remarkable for the large quantity of cotton to seed, that one almost suspects some mistake. The American cotton, moreover, though growing in an unsuitable soil and climate, is considered very low in its proportion of cotton. Though these peculiarities are worthy of further investigation, we do not advocate the culture of such cotton for the English market, because it would appear equally easy in some situations to cultivate kinds, such as the acclimated New Orleans, which would at all times command a ready sale and bring higher prices, and not be more expensive to cultivate, when irrigation is facilitated by the opening of the great Ganges canal.

§ 19. Culture in the Jullundur Doab.

The places we have enumerated may appear to some too high in latitude, and too distant from the sea to prove profitable sites for cotton cultivation. But we find the people engage in the cultivation of their own accord, if not for export, at least for home consumption, and, therefore, it is important, as far as the country is concerned, to ascertain what is most suitable for culture, and how this may be made most suitable to the country. Though the above may be considered too far north, others have thought that the culture of cotton might be carried still further north, that is, into the Sikh territories beyond the Sutledge. That the country produced cotton was first made known to Lieutenant Baird Smith, of the Bengal Engineers, by his being directed, on the eve of a general action, to "take a company of sappers, and clear that low thick *brushwood* in front of the line"—the brushwood in question being "a capital crop of the cotton plant!" When the Jullundur Doab was first acquired, information was in some way communicated that it was well suited for cotton, and that much was cultivated in the country. Directions were immediately sent by the Court of Directors for its capabilities to be investigated and reported on.

A valuable report was shortly after obtained from Mr. J. Lawrence, and Messrs. Vansittart and Cust, and Dr. Sill. By these it appears, that in the Jullundur Doab, cotton occupies only $2\frac{1}{2}$ per cent. of the whole cultivation, and it is, therefore, little entitled to the character of a cotton country. It does not grow enough for home consumption, and the merchants of Jullundur, as well as of the other towns, import considerable quantities from near Delhi and from Rohtuck, in carts, a distance of about 200 miles, and of course at considerable expense. Near Jullundur, the soil is light and sandy, mixed with *kunkur*, water is 10 to 15, sometimes 40 feet below the surface, the Persian wheel being employed to bring it up. At Hoshyarpore, it is nearer the surface and the soil moist. Cotton is sown both in March, and towards the end of June after the first fall of rain. It is usually cultivated on unirrigated land, because sugar-cane is more profitable wherever there is a command of irrigation. The best is produced on the high lands where irrigation is impracticable. It is sown broad-cast, that which is sown early is gathered in October to December; that sown in July a month or six weeks later. The climate seems suitable, for it is described as growing 9 or even 12 feet high in irrigated land; but it is mentioned as not producing lateral branches. The returns per acre are much larger than are obtained in other parts of India, for Mr. Vansittart states that an acre yields 692 lbs. of seed cotton; and Dr. Sill that irrigated land yields 207, and unirrigated land 168 lbs. of cleaned cotton. But notwithstanding these comparatively high returns, the culture was not considered profitable, and sugar-cane, tobacco, poppy, and garden-stuff, all yielded a higher rent. Mr. J. Lawrence had taken some pains to ascertain the different items of expense in cultivating cotton, also in comparing these with the same culture in two districts of the Delhi territory, for which he was particularly well qualified, having formerly been in charge of a district (vide p. 286). We, therefore, republish his tabular statement, as useful for comparison with other places, and also as showing the advantages of irrigation in a dry climate, as is also experienced in Egypt. The most remarkable thing in the statement is the great produce per acre, which is far beyond what is usually stated to be obtainable in India, and yet the profits are not greater than in other places.

Statement, showing the Cost of an Acre of Cotton Cultivation in the Delhi and Jullundur Districts.

DISTRICTS.	Description of soil.	Expenses of One Acre of Cotton Cultivation.									Quantity produced.			Value of produce.			Net profit.
		Land rent.	Ploughing.	Manure.	Seed.	Weeding.	Water.	Collecting.	Cleaning.	Total.	Cotton.	Seed.	Total.	Cotton.	Seed.	Total.	
		r. a. p.	r. a. p.	r. a. p.	r. a. p.	r. a. p.	r. a. p.	r. a. p.	r. a. p.	r. a. p.				r. a. p.	r. a. p.	r. a. p.	r. a. p.
Near Delhi*	Best soil, irrigated from canals.	6 6 4	4 0 0	6 6 5	0 4 10 for 19lbs.	3 13 2	1 0 0	7 10 4	10 12 9	40 5 10	384	1152	1536	28 12 9	14 6 5	43 3 2	2 13 4†
	Second-rate, irrigated from canals.	4 12 9	3 3 2	3 3 2	0 4 10	3 12 2	1 0 0	5 1 7	7 3 2	28 9 10	256	768	1024	19 3 2	9 9 7	28 12 9	0 2 11
	First kind, unirrigated soil.	4 12 9	4 0 0	2 2 2	0 4 10	3 13 2	—	5 11 10	8 1 7	28 14 4	288	864	1152	21 9 6	10 12 9	32 6 3	3 7 4
	Second-rate, ditto.	3 9 7	3 3 2	1 9 7	0 4 10	3 13 2	—	4 7 4	6 4 9	23 4 5	224	672	896	16 12 9	8 6 4	25 3 1	1 14 8
Pulwul* Southern Division, Delhi Territory.	First-rate, unirrigated land.	4 12 9	5 9 7	3 3 2	0 9 7 for 38lbs.	3 9 7	—	3 3 2	4 3 2	25 3 0	342	682	1024	23 7 6	6 13 2	30 4 8	5 1 8‡
	Second-rate, ditto.	3 9 7	4 6 5	2 6 5	0 9 7	3 0 0	—	2 6 5	3 3 2	19 9 7	256	512	768	17 9 7	5 2 0	22 11 7	3 2 0
Rahoon, Zillah, Jullundur.	Best, unirrigated land.	5 3 4	2 9 0	1 4 0	0 5 1	2 9 0	—	3 13 6	4 12 10	20 8 9	154	460	614	19 3 2	4 12 10	24 0 0	3 7 3§
	Second-rate, ditto.	3 3 10	2 9 0	0 10 3	0 5 1	2 9 0	—	2 9 2	3 3 2	15 1 6	102	306	408	12 12 10	3 3 10	16 0 8	0 15 2

* The Government demand for Land Revenue amounts, per acre, to 15a. 1p. on the whole area, and to 1r. 15a. on the total cultivation.

† The expenses appear great; but, as the people cultivate their own land, the expenses shown in the fourth, seventh, and ninth columns are hardly felt, as the family perform it themselves.

‡ The remarks on the expenses of cultivation, made on the return for Delhi, is equally applicable here. The expense of seed is very much greater in this return; but the Tehsuldar remarks, that, for the seed, he took its price at the time of sowing, and, for the value of produce, its price at harvest, and that the difference is 36 per cent. The soil of Pulwul is superior to that of Delhi, but I do not understand why double the quantity of seed is used. Formerly it was the practice in Pulwul, that the cleaner took the seed as his wages, and the cultivator the cotton. Seed has now risen in price, and cotton fallen. A fixed sum, therefore, is now paid for the operation. Clean cotton varies from 20 to 12lbs. for the rupee.

§ Average price of uncleaned cotton, 32lbs. for the rupee. The cultivators, when selling it, usually dispose of uncleaned; but when cleaning it, give the seed to the cleaner, as the wages of labour. The soil here being very light and easily ploughed, accounts for the moderate expense of ploughing. It is usual, about Rahoon, to grow cotton in succession to a wheat crop.

(Signed) J. LAWRENCE, *Commissioner and Superintendent.*

The figures of the foregoing table being derived from the information of the native officers of the different districts, can be considered only as approximations. Allowing that the expenses are made to appear high and the profits small, as stated in the notes, yet the return of cotton per acre, even in the worst soil, is large; and that in the best irrigated land nearly as great as in the good cotton-lands of America. Allowing even for some exaggeration, we cannot believe that the native authorities would err so much on the side of excess as to make the statement worthless for comparison. We may at all events take them as evidences of the great benefit of irrigation in the dry soil and climate of North-Western India, and of which the benefit will be as certainly experienced in the Punjab, whenever the means are afforded for fully employing it. Indeed, we believe it will be easier, as it will be more certain, to cultivate cotton in a country like the Punjab, where the sun is sufficiently powerful, by means of canal irrigation, than in parts of India where the rains are abundant, partly on account of the uncertainty of their accession, but still more from the absence of those alternations of moisture and dryness referred to at p. 185, "as interfering with the healthy growth of the cotton-plant, which requires more than three months for its full growth and for maturing its fruit, and which after having grown in the tepid moisture of the rainy season, is unable to bear the dryness which occurs at their cessation." The rains are not altogether absent from the Punjab; Mr. Elphinstone long since remarked, that "the south-west monsoon which deluges India with rain for three or four months in the year, extends in a north-west direction into which it is forced by the Himalayas, even until it meets with the Hindoo Coosh. Then the clouds, exhausted of their rain, are barely able to water the mountains without much affecting the plains of Affghanistan. In the north of the Punjab, near the hills, the rains exceed those at Delhi; but in the south of the Punjab, distant both from the sea and the hills, very little rain falls." In the plains of the Punjab, as near Lahore, these rains occur only as occasional showers, or as heavy falls about midsummer; but they do not produce that continually moist and muggy state of the atmosphere which is so characteristic of the rainy season in most parts of India. The plains of the Punjab are described as sterile merely from the want of water. The rivers though numerous have such high banks that their waters can be made little use of for the purposes of irrigation. But canals might, with comparative ease, be formed down the centre of the several Doabs, and bring the water either from the foot of the mountains, or from the upper parts of the rivers, as has been recommended by Lieut. Baird Smith.* Some canals, the author believes, are now in course of survey, if not under execution, by the orders of the Earl of Dalhousie and the sanction of the Court of Directors. In a very few years, therefore, it will be possible to cultivate cotton if it should be profitable to do so.

From the statement in p. 302, of the cotton-plants at present cultivated broad-cast with irrigation, growing 9 or 12 feet high but without lateral branches, it would appear that the difficulties are those of over-luxuriance rather than of stunted growth, as we might reasonably expect in so dry a climate. The introduction of American seed, sowing in lines, perhaps wider planting, and topping, might produce as large, and perhaps as profitable crops as in Egypt. Though the distance is great, the expense of conveyance down the canals and the Indus would not be so great as from Central India either to Calcutta or to Bombay.

Canals of Irrigation.—The effects likely to be produced and the benefits which accrue from the construction of canals, are well exemplified in those which have already been formed, and which Lieut. Baird Smith fitly describes by stating, that "Indian canals of irrigation are essentially artificial rivers." "Wherever the canal now extends, the richest cultivation covers the lands." "The average rate at which water is supplied amounts to about one rupee, or two shillings, per acre," allowing the great advantage to the ryots of employing their bullocks either in ploughing or in their carts. "The Western Jumna Canal is nearly four times as large as that on the eastern bank of the river, and with its branches, of large dimensions, has a course of about 430 miles in length." "During the great famine of 1837, when the crops failed everywhere else from want of water, the canal districts were safe and flourishing." It was along this canal that Col. Colvin (p. 294) spread the American cotton seed, and it is by

* *Agricultural Resources of the Punjab*, &c. By Lieut. Baird Smith, B. E.

means of the water supplied by it that the cultivation of cotton can be carried on in the otherwise arid tracts of the districts to the westward of Delhi, which are referred to in the above table. The Eastern Jumna or Doab Canal, as it is sometimes called, leaves the Jumna under the Siwalic, or Sub-Himalayan range, and, after flowing about 145 miles, rejoins it near Delhi. "Its subordinate channels, each a small canal with its complement of masonry works, exceed at this time 490 miles in length, and are extending annually. Not less than 2000 miles of village water-courses spread their waters over the adjoining fields." It was in consequence of a cut from this canal which passed through the Saharunpore Botanic Garden, that the author was enabled to cultivate cotton without any difficulty, and it is from near its banks that Col. Cautley lately sent the cotton mentioned at p. 295. The greatest work of irrigation, projected by Col. Proby Cautley, and now in course of execution, is the Great Ganges Canal, which will have a discharge of 6750 cubic feet of water per second. Its total length, navigable throughout, will be 898 miles, and it will furnish the means of irrigating a tract of country between the rivers Ganges and Jumna, having an area of 5,400,000 acres.* When completed, this canal will give considerable facilities for the cultivation of cotton, in addition to all the other crops. With its aid, cotton may be sown and brought forward before the rains come on; and if it can be used immediately after

* "The works," as Lieut. Baird Smith says, "are advancing with great energy, and to his honour be it stated, that even during the enormous financial pressure of the late campaign, the Governor-General of India, Lord Dalhousie, would admit of no check being given to an undertaking calculated to promote so materially the best interests at once of the Government and the people." (Loc. cit., p. 13.)

"The magnitude of the undertaking, and the difficulties attending it may be judged from the fact, that a volume of water discharging 6750 feet per second, has to be conveyed over the bed of a mountain-torrent, by an embankment and aqueduct 2¼ miles in length. This noble work will run along the high central land of the Doab, throwing off branches along the ridges which separate the smaller streams, and will thus afford water to most of the worst sandy tracts, hitherto entirely destitute of irrigation. From Hurdwar down to Futtehpúr it would immensely increase the produce of the country, while it will for evermore relieve the intense anxiety now occasioned by any signs of a failure of rain. Whatever may be the state of the seasons, sufficient food will always be grown for the subsistence of the people and cattle, and sufficient land will remain in cultivation to afford them employment."—(*Calcutta Review*, Dec. 1849.)

the rains cease, a crop of cotton may certainly be secured from injury during the change of climate which then takes place.

That the cultivation of American cotton in these districts, even after the failures we have recorded, is not impracticable with the aid of irrigation, appears from the facts which we have related at p. 294. In addition to these, we may refer to the letter of Mr. Bruce, dated 31st of July, 1848, to the Agri-Hortic. Soc. of India, the object of which, he says, is to attract "the notice of the Government as well as of the associations and manufacturers in England," "and to make it known that there is one in India who is willing to undertake to procure for them as much real good merchantable cotton, either American or indigenous, as they may require—after the second year, if it be American, and immediately, if it be indigenous—and not to cost them, when landed in England—the former, more than about an average of 4*d.* or 4½*d.* per lb., and the latter 3*d.* or 3½*d.* per lb. In December, 1844, I offered to have 1000 beegahs of the American cotton cultivated in Bundlecund at my own private expense, to show the Government of the North-western Provinces, provided I was supplied with 125 maunds of seed from some of its experimental farms there existing and removed to Calpee, the practicability of the successful introduction even of the American cottons. My object was simply to prove, at my own cost, the feasibility of the thing, through the agency of the landed proprietors as cultivators of the soil. The result of my experiment of 1000 beegahs, I had sanguine hopes, would have shown not only the uncertainty, but the expensiveness of the *Neej*, or home cultivation system, unsuccessfully adopted at the Government experimental farms. In conclusion, permit me to beg the favour of your endeavouring to procure for me 125 maunds of good American cotton-seed, to enable me to commence operations in May and June, 1849." The Society agreed to place a portion of the stock of seed which had just then been received from the United States at Mr. Bruce's disposal, and addressed Dr. Wight to inquire whether he could supply some of the acclimated American cotton-seed from the government farm at Coimbatore. On the 17th of January, 1849, Mr. Bruce applied to the Indian Government for American cotton-seed, as Dr. Wight was ready to send 3000 or 4000 lbs. of such seed.

The above communication is extremely satisfactory, in consequence of Mr. Bruce's local experience and his own previous failures in cultivating cotton (v. p. 94). But we do not perceive how the Neej, or home cultivation, has anything to do with the failure, as in this Government pay the expenses and bear all losses in case of failure, and the ryots derive the advantage of the example in cases of success. The two seasons in which the experiment was made were unfortunate either in the deficiency or the irregularity of the fall of rain (v. p. 288). That the mode of culture was suitable we have the independent testimony of eye-witnesses (v. p. 290). R. Lowther, Esq., Commissioner of the Allahabad division, in a letter dated 12th of September, 1846, writes in reference to these very failures, "Nothing could more satisfactorily establish the fertility of the soil, under careful and scientific management, than the result of the first season's operations; the cotton-fields were the admiration of the people who travelled from considerable distances to see them. The season was below an average, for in many parts, including the farm on the bank of the Jumna in the Cawnpore district, the fields of native cotton either partially or wholly failed: yet the adjoining American plant was not only very healthy, but produced an abundant crop. The succeeding seasons were still more adverse, the planters became dispirited, and in the absence of the stimulus imparted to them through the energy of the late Captain Bayles, they became dissatisfied and disheartened, and requested they might be removed to a climate better suited to the experiment." With the aid of irrigation from the Ganges Canal, good culture would be almost sure of producing good crops in the Doab.

We continue to believe, not only that good culture with irrigation in these dry climates will produce good crops of American cotton, but also that when the irrigation is general, the climate of localities, especially if these are enclosed within hedges, will be sufficiently modified to favour the lengthening of the staple of the indigenous cotton, and render this less harsh, also to allow of the successful cultivation of the better varieties of Indian cotton. The cotton so cultivated can hardly fail to be of good quality, since spinners here were ready (p. 390) to purchase two of the kinds of cotton grown by Mr. Bell, but which, he wrote, he found a difficulty in cultivating from their requiring too much irrigation.

We proceed now to consider the peculiarities of Central India, so long famous for the production of good cotton.

Central India.

We have seen in the experiments in Bengal proper that failure seems to have been chiefly owing to over-luxuriance in a rich soil, and moist, warm climate; while in the North-Western provinces failure was due to dryness combined with heat: still, in the former, we thought that success might be attained by selecting poorer soils and the more open situations, attending, at the same time, to drainage and pruning; also to the best times for sowing and to the destruction of insects. In the more northern parts of the province, such as Rungpore, success seems easily attainable, as the American cotton plants which had been introduced, and cultivated even by the natives, required to be propped, to prevent the branches breaking down from the weight of produce. In the hotter and drier parts of the north-western provinces, we believe that deeper ploughing and closer planting, with the aid of irrigation, in some cases before the rains, and in others after their cessation, would secure a crop of American cotton, even where experiments have failed.

In our account of the experimental culture in the north-western provinces, we stated that even when Dacca was most famous for its cotton manufactures, Bengal depended much upon the import of raw cotton from Surat, and upon that which reached Bengal by the Ganges. Some of this was cultivated in the Gangetic Doab and some in Bundlecund, but a portion reached the Ganges from Central India, or, as it was commonly called, the Deccan.

We now know that this central region forms a somewhat triangular but irregular surfaced table-land, supported on the south-east and west by prolongations of the Indian ghauts, and on the north by the ranges of mountains which stretch entirely across India from the Ganges to Guzerat. Of the rivers of this region, some, as the Nerbudda and Tapty flowing to the west, fall into the Gulf of Cambay; the Soane and others join the Ganges on the east, while the Godavery and Mahanuddy, meandering to the south-west, flow into the Bay of Bengal. It is curious that the cotton of this region has long traversed the country in these three directions. That carried to the east used to be shipped at Allahabad, but of late chiefly at Calpee and Mirzapore, for transit down the Ganges. The western stream of this commerce has greatly increased, and the cotton is now well known at Bombay by the name of the Oomrowtee, while that to the S. E. has nearly ceased, because the calico manufactures of the Coast and Circars have been superseded by the more cheaply manufactured goods of Manchester.

§ 20. Culture in the Saugur and Nerbudda Territories.

The Saugur and Nerbudda territories, situated chiefly on the table-land of Central India, have already been referred to (p. 50), as stretching westward and southward from Bundlecund, and lying between Scindia's territories and Malwah on the north, and Nagpore and Berar on the south. Some excellent cotton is said to be produced at Hirdeenuggur, which is near Saugur (v. p. 53), and that of Nursingpore is also esteemed in the present day. Mr. Mercer found cotton cultivated more carefully in the Maheer valley and Nursingpore, than he had seen further to the eastward (v. p. 51); "a portion of the tract being named Bhanwar Garh, the cotton of this part universally bears that name in the market." The soil consists chiefly of the black cotton soil. "It has been observed, that this basaltic soil yields almost every description of crop. In all those parts where water does not lodge during the rains, cotton is produced in it of very good quality, though inferior to that of Berar, and also to that raised immediately on the banks of the Nerbudda and of the rivers flowing into it. ('*Bengal and Agra Directory*,' 2d series, p. 325.)

The climate of Jubbulpore is described as being cooler than that of the north-western provinces, and it has been observed, that it is only just before the rains set in, that anything like great heat is experienced; 29° Fahr. is given as the lowest, and 114° as the highest temperature. The rains usually commence on or about the 10th of June, and cease about the autumnal equinox; the greatest quantity of rain usually falls in July and August, and that at Saugur varies from 34 to 46 inches in the year. The prevailing winds are westerly, varying a few points in the rains, to south, and in the hot winds, as much to the north. Heavy hail-storms occasionally occur in February and March.

Mr. Mercer, when at Jubbulpore, observes, that he learned from Mr. Macleod 'the following favorable facts in regard to the climate of this region. The hot winds blow here very mild, and not longer than two months at the extreme point. The rains are never later than the 15th of June, and are always abundant.' Again, when at Hoshungabad, in the Nerbudda valley, he states, 'It appears on all hands here that a scarcity of rain is what never occurs, and that the greatest cause of failure in the cotton crops is the superabundance of it." "Though grain crops are the staple crops of the valley," Mr. Mercer further observes, "grain is often a perfect drug;" he found it selling in the bazars at the rate of 100 lbs. for a shilling; but cotton is the most important in all the villages bordering the rivers where the land is raviny, and it is the crop of all others, probably hemp excepted, that produces the most ready sale." "The natives consider no land suited for cotton unless the water runs quickly and thoroughly off. For this reason, it is only sown in the broken country near and among the ravines." He observed "much rich but level land left uncultivated," whence he infers, that as cotton is not there, as in Bundlecund, "one of the riff-raff crops," the ryots would certainly fall into "a plan of cultivation (the American) which would make the very lands they now reject the most productive."

Col. Sleeman, in charge of these districts, writes, "In the Nerbudda valley, cotton is grown only upon lands from which the rain-waters flow off quickly, and these are to be found only on the banks of rivers and sides of hills. The richness of the soil in such situations soon flows off as the surface is turned in tillage. As far as I have seen, the hills in the country from the valley of the Nerbudda to Baitool and Nagpore, on the way to Hingunghat and Oomrowtee, are all either composed of decomposing basalt or lava, or are covered with strata of it, and the soil formed from it is inexhaustible. In the valley of the Nerbudda, the level lands only are composed from the debris of such rocks, which cap the sandstone hills on either side; upon these level lands the cotton is not grown." Mr. Mercer says with respect to culture at Nursingpore, "The cultivators here say, I think with much reason, that much rain is nearly as injurious as too little; as they never stir the soil about its roots, and the position of the plant is not raised at all above the general level of the field, much rain only cakes the earth over its roots and smothers it. The abundant moisture, accordingly, instead of stimulating its growth, as it would with better cultivation, only retards." The returns seem to be small; Mr. Mercer calculates about 50 lbs. to the acre. The natives say they plant *urhur,* that is, *Cytisus Cajan,* or pigeon-pea, with the cotton, that if the cotton fail, they may still have something from the land. Mr. Mercer says, "It is quite probable that our cultivation would take with them in that sense, as it admits a half rubbee crop being sown between the rows." ('*Return,*' p. 217.)

The quantity of cotton per beegah does not appear large: in reply to the queries circulated by the Court of Directors, the average is stated to be 32 seers in the Saugur district. It is stated to be in Jubbulpore 60 seers per beegah; but if the season has been unfavorable, the average produce will be 40 seers; 30 seers at Nursingpore, 50 seers at Sreenuggur, 60 seers at Choomputta, and 30 seers at Shahpoor per beegah, and that 100 beegahs are equal to 75 English acres. These statements being derived from native authorities, can be considered only as approximations, as many of the European officers observe, that the bias of the natives is to give a low estimate of the returns of farming. The leases of the lands are for a period of twenty years, and the Government demand on account of revenue, amounts to from 5 anas 3 pie, to 1 rupee 12 anas 10 pie per acre.

We have been unable to ascertain satisfactorily whether these territories are well suited to the culture of American cotton, though there is little doubt of the western parts being so. Some attempts have, however, been made to cultivate different kinds of cotton.*

Mr. Ommaney, Political Agent at Saugur, furnished the

* Dr. Spilsbury, in '*Trans. Agric. Soc.*,' describes Jubbulpore as "situated about 5 miles from the Nerbudda, and it may be considered as almost the eastern extremity of that very fertile tract of country called the valley of the Nerbudda, because from it to Omerkuntuk, the source of the river, the country is little more than a series of wild, mountainous, jungly tracts, with small villages intervening. Cotton is extensively cultivated on the banks of all the rivers and nullahs north, and about which

Agricultural Society of India with the following details connected with the experiment then going on at Saugur on the productive qualities of foreign and native cottons:

	Quantity of land.	Quantity sown.	Produce of Cotton.	Seeds.	Cotton cleaned.
	acre.	lbs.	lbs.	lbs.	lbs.
Tinnivelly . . .	1½	unknown	186½	142	46
Upland Georgia .	4 biswas	7	44	30	14
Chunderi sown very late and had not a fair chance . .	11 biswas	6	24	18	6
Nankeen	unknown	not stated	9½	7	2¼

By this statement the superiority in the productive qualities of the Upland Georgia in the Saugur soils, Mr. Ommaney considers to be clearly established.

D. Macleod, Esq., at that time (August, 1839) in charge of the Saugur district, in acknowledging a consignment of foreign cotton-seed, stated, that he considered it was the prevalence of black basalt, where this is of a sufficiently friable character, that renders the Saugur country, Nursingpore, and especially Berar so pre-eminently a cotton country. The vigour with which cotton thrives in it is astonishing. All the cotton that Mr. Macleod had sown the year before was left standing, and there were besides the Pernambuco and Egyptian varieties in their third year. Sufficient cotton had been procured to make one or two bales, and more was expected in the following year, as there were upwards of ten beegahs in cotton cultivation. Mr. Macleod further writes, "that all the country people state, that unless the cotton-seed be sown on the surface and in land not worked up, it all runs to leaf and stalks, yielding little flower." Some of the cotton planted in the gardens close to the water-courses had yielded a crop, and flourished with a vigour far exceeding all the rest.

nodules of kunkur are spread over the land, and, as a general rule, I should say that the cultivation of this plant is not usual in the poor decomposed trap soil. It is a great mart for cotton, so that from the end of March to June, the whole road from this to Mirzapore is covered with hackeries (carts) and droves of buffaloes and bullocks." He also says that at Omerkuntuk it rains every three or four days. The Mahadeo hills are some 1500 feet higher and as thickly clothed, and it does not rain so there—the one is all sandstone and trap—here (20 miles west of Omerkuntuk) all capped with laterite.

The district of Nimaur is frequently mentioned in the '*Cotton Return*,' p. 199, as growing what is considered the finest cotton in these regions, as with it are made the famed muslins of Chunderhee, a district noted as well for this manufacture as for its frequently disturbed state.

Nimaur lies between 21° 28′ and 22° 25′ N. lat., and long. 74° 48′ and 76° 45′. It is, therefore, east of Broach, and much nearer the Bombay than the Bengal Presidency; but it may be considered, in one respect, as the extreme west of the Nerbudda valley. The general appearance of the country is that of an undulating valley, intersected in various directions by low rocky ranges mostly clothed with jungle. It is bounded on the north by the Vindhya range, elevated above Nimar from 1600 to 1700 feet, and separating it from the table-land of Malwa, to the south by the Satpoora range, dividing it from Candeish. "To the west its confines are very rugged and mountainous, hemmed in by the prongs of the two principal ranges which unite about Burwanee, the Nerbudda flowing between." From the number of rivers, its valley-like character, and the heavy masses of vegetation with which much of the land is covered, there can be no doubt, that the climate must, upon the whole, be moist and equable. It is curious that famous as it is for the production of cotton of a fine quality, no Brahmins take their food in cotton clothes; either silk or woollen fabrics must be worn when they eat.

The cotton named Mohalee is of a superior description, and is that used for fine cloths. "It formerly formed a staple article of trade with the manufacturers of Chundehree muslins, for which purpose it sold at higher rates, but is now little grown, owing to the decrease of that branch of commerce."

Col. Sleeman, the Commissioner of the Saugur and Nerbudda territories, writes, "By experiments tried, at my suggestion, in the Chundehree district by Capt. Blake, it is found that the Berareea cotton used in the fine cloths made at Chundehree deteriorates rapidly from year to year, when removed to that district from Nimaur, where it is produced in perfection. The causes I have not yet discovered. I suppose it is the finest cotton known and the dearest. It is worthy of remark, that the manufacturers cannot use this cotton unless it is brought from Nimaur to Chundehree, a distance of some hundred miles, before the seed is removed from it. It requires to be used immediately that the seed is removed, or the thread is not fit for the finest quality of cloth."

Countries to the North of the Nerbudda.—To the northward of the Nerbudda, there are vast tracts which might be noticed with those of which we are now treating, though much of these are not especially adapted to cotton cultivation. Thus, Scindia's territories extend over six degrees of latitude; but the provinces are extremely irregular in their outline, and intersect and are intersected by those of other powers in every direction. The portion to the northward of 25° of N. lat. is very productive when there is a plentiful supply of rain; but being subject to irregularities in this first essential of fertility in these otherwise dry and treeless regions, it is not particularly eligible for the culture of cotton, though irrigation would, no doubt, produce the same beneficial effects as still further north. Indeed, Colonels Hall and Dixon, by their judicious management, and by providing a due supply of water for irrigation, have converted the barren and predatory country of Mharwara, on the edge of the desert, into a fruitful agricultural district.

The southern portion of Scindia's territories, with soil consisting of a deep black loam extremely retentive of moisture, with generally regular and very copious rains, is probably as fertile as any other part of Central India. They are, indeed, identical in many parts with the Saugur and Nerbudda territories by which they are intersected, and they are equally well suited for the culture of cotton. Chundehree is famous for the manufacture of muslins for which the native princes give from 80 to 100 rupees for a piece of the finest kind, being about ten times the price for which equally fine-looking specimens of Scotch or Manchester manufactures may be bought. But these do not wash nor wear so well. The cotton, as we have stated, is imported from the distant district of Nimaur. The weavers are Mahomedans (*momeen julahee*) and work in underground workshops, in order to procure a uniform degree of moisture in the air, and prevent their yarn becoming too dry.

Malwa, lying between 22° and 25° of N. lat., forms a tableland which is elevated about 2000 feet, having a very abrupt descent to the south, but a gradual slope towards the north. The soil is rich, and the climate mild and moderately moist, so as to be well suited to the cultivation of cotton, as was long since pointed out by Sir John Malcolm; but the poppy being as easily cultivated, and its opium more readily exported, yielding at the same time considerable profits, has chiefly engaged the attention of agriculturists. We may now proceed to notice the countries to the southward of the Nerbudda.

Countries South of the Nerbudda.—Before noticing the territories of the Rajah of Nagpore, we may notice an extensive tract of country which lies to the eastward, and is now known as the South-West frontier of Bengal, extending from Mirzapore and Benares, on the north, to Ganjam, on the south. Hazareebagh stands on the road between Calcutta and Benares, on an elevated table-land. Chota (small) Nagpore is an extensive zemindary of this Agency, consisting of undulating table-land of about 3000 feet elevation. In the district of Sirgoojah there is also an elevated tract of table-land called Mynpat, and in Sumbuhlpore, which is the most southern of all, there are extensive plains, some parts of which are well cultivated, but the climate is pestiferous. The climate of Hazareebagh is healthy, that of Chota Nagpore cooler and healthy, and well suited as well as the soil for the culture of coffee. The soil of Sirgoojah is singularly rich, and so well supplied with moisture, that even the tops of the hills are marshy. The soil of Chota Nagpore is in many parts of a reddish colour, and extremely productive, especially of cotton. From the goodness of the soil and the moisture of the climate, with the variety of surface, there is a probability that the American species of cotton would succeed if properly cultivated. A few experiments have been made on the culture of American cotton in these regions, and they have been rather favorable. A native gentleman, Baboo Raj Kissen Mookerjee, to whose zeal the Cotton Committee of the Agricultural Society bear ample testimony, attempted to grow foreign cotton at Hazareebagh from seed which they had sent him. They observe upon it, that it is the first specimen of a foreign cotton grown by a native gentleman, and that the quality was so superior as to have been supposed by the Committee to have been the produce of Sea Island seed, whereas it was that of Egyptian seed, and estimated by them as worth in England from 1*s.* 4*d.* to 1*s.* 6*d.* per lb. in July, 1838. Other notices mention that the cotton grown at Hazareebagh is very long and soft in staple. Col. Ouseley made some attempts to grow the American cotton at Chota Nagpore, but some difficulty was experienced, and his attention was afterwards directed to the cultivation of coffee, in which he succeeded admirably. A recent notice from a resident planter gives some account of the effects of the soil and climate in producing plants nine and ten feet high, without the aid of manure. Here, therefore, open planting, on ridges, and whatever checks over-luxuriance, would probably be useful.

Nagpore and Berar.—The tracts of country most favorable to the growth of cotton belong chiefly to the Nizam of Hyderabad and to the Rajah of Nagpore. The valley of Berar is considered the most suitable, though much excellent cotton is also produced in the Nagpore country, and is that known by the name of Hinghat cotton. The quantity which could be cultivated is so much greater than what is now produced, that it becomes both interesting and important to ascertain what are the peculiarities of soil and of climate which cause it to produce this superior cotton, and to inquire whether these are such as to render it probable that American cotton could also be produced in the same regions. Before proceeding, it cannot but strike some of our readers, that the fact of good cotton being produced at a distance of 300 or 400 miles from the sea, militates against the theory of a saline atmosphere being necessary to the production of good cotton, and also apparently against our inference that a certain degree of atmospheric moisture is essential. For it may be supposed, that the dryness of the air will be greater in proportion to distance from the coast, especially as we have seen that drought was the chief cause of failure with American cotton in the Doab and Bundlecund. But this apparent exception only confirms the rule which we have deduced: and which is also confirmed by American cotton being grown in the dry climate of Egypt only by the aid of irrigation.

The range of mountains which form the northern boundary of the tract in question seems to arrest the air loaded with vapour from southern regions, and to cause its deposition on their sides, and thus the countries in their vicinity are kept in a moister state than would otherwise be the case. Instead of theory, it is more satisfactory for our present purpose to refer to the observations of one of the American planters, who on being transferred from Bengal, marched across the country in question from Mirzapore to Bombay, and made it his special object to observe its fitness for the growth of cotton. Mr. Mercer first examined this cotton at Mirzapore, and thought it better than fair American. During his progress he met with immense droves of bullocks laden with the cotton of Oomrowtee and with that from Hingunghat. The latter he describes as "like all the Nagpore cotton he had seen, of fair length and fineness, colour excellent, and, if a little better cleaned, would certainly equal good Mobile or Upland Georgian. It has none of the harshness so common to the cottons of the north-western provinces." This indicates moisture of climate. In the Nerbudda valley, Mr. Mercer states (p. 311) that they complain of excess of moisture. It is probably moderate in the valleys of Berar.

§ 21. Culture of Cotton in the Nagpore Territories.

The extensive tracts of country subject to the Rajah of Nagpore occupy that part of Central India which forms a part of ancient Berar, and extends from 18° 40′ to 20° 40′ of N. lat., and from 78° 20′ to 83° of E. long. The average length and breadth is considered to be about 300 miles, and the area was computed by the late Col. Blacker to be about 70,000 square miles. This territory is bounded on the north by the Saugur and Nerbudda districts; on the west, by the Wurda and Wyne Gunga rivers, which separate it from the Nizam's territories, which bound those of Nagpore also on the south-west to the south-east, where there are many uncivilized tribes. On the east, the Mahanuddy forms the boundary in many parts, and there lie the districts of Sirgoojah and Sumbhulpore, with ranges of hills and tracts of forest-land. The general aspect of the country is irregularly mountainous and woody. But in the vicinity of Nagpore, between the Wurda and Wyne Gunga rivers, as well as in Chuteesgur, there are extensive plains which are calculated to be elevated about 1100 feet above the level of the sea. To the north, the

Puchmaree Hills rise to an elevation of 4200 feet. The soil in the open country and valleys of the hilly parts is almost invariably black loam, which when moist is muddy, and when dry cracks in all directions. In the hilly parts of the country, and in some parts of Chuteesgurh, the soil is red. The rivers are mostly navigable in the rains, and a few during a part of the cold weather. Many parts of the country, especially to the south and east, are covered with long grass and dense and unhealthy jungles. There is, therefore, probably considerable moisture of climate, though the quantity of rain which falls is not considerable, having amounted to 36¾ inches on an average of five years at the Residency. Tanks are numerous, formed chiefly by throwing an embankment faced with masonry across the gorge of any valley favorably situated, by which the water falling or flowing into the valley is collected. Many parts of this are highly cultivated and extremely fertile, producing both wheat and rice, sugar-cane and cotton.

The climate is naturally divided into three seasons, viz. the hot, rainy, and cold. The hot season extends from the middle of March to about the 10th of June, the greatest intensity of heat occurring from the latter end of April till the first fall of rain, which it is said almost invariably occurs about the 4th of June. The temperature, even in the house, is as high as from 96° to 104° Fahr. from 12 o'clock to 4 p.m., but exposed outside, the thermometer has been observed to rise to 140°. After the first showers of the rainy season, there is generally an interval of some days of fine weather before the monsoon is regularly established. The greatest quantity "of rain falls in August and September, the average for the year being 40 inches; but in the year 1838, it was less than 22 inches."

"The coldest season commences about the 20th of October, and continues till the middle of March. During this period there is a considerable diurnal range of temperature, which is often found to be prejudicial to those who are weak in constitution. There are usually heavy dews, which are highly beneficial for agricultural purposes, and in the early part of the season fogs prevail, more particularly along the ravines and nullahs, where moisture exists to a greater extent than in the open plains. The lowest temperature observed outside at sunrise has been 36° Fahr., and the highest 110°, from noon to 3 p.m., but lower temperatures must occur at the surface of the ground, as hoar frost is occasionally seen, and thin pellicles of ice on small pools, from the free radiation which occurs on clear nights." (*Madras Medical Reports.*)

The author has been unable to find any detailed account of the culture of cotton in Nagpore, and he has not seen any answers to the queries circulated by the Court of Directors in 1847. There is no doubt that much of the soil is suitable and the climate favorable, and we know that there are two principal cotton-marts within the Nagpore territories. Major Wilkinson has stated that the cotton brought to the Hingunghat market is grown in districts which lie to the south-west of Nagpore, while that taken to Arvee is grown in districts westward of Nagpore, both tracts being different parts of the valley of the Wurda. Lieut. Munro, of H.M. 39th Regt., himself a good observer and naturalist, mentions the banks of the Wurda as the parts which are chiefly cultivated with cotton at present; but that in making a tour with the Resident through the province of Chuteesgurh, he had seen many places apparently well adapted for the cultivation of cotton. We have seen that Nagpore cotton is esteemed at Mirzapore, and that the portion taken westward passes at Bombay as Oomrowtee. Mr. Mercer, when at Oomrowtee, was informed by native merchants, that they ascribed the superiority of the Nagpore cotton to the "very superior land in that district," also to "care in growing and gathering." Mr. Macleod, then in charge of the Saugur and Nerbudda territories, says (v. '*Trans. Agric. Soc.*,' vol. vii, p. 143), "In Berar (the Nagpore country) the black basalt soil yields two crops of cotton a year; the rubbee, or spring harvest, being the most esteemed." Mr. Mercer's observation, that the cotton is devoid of the harshness which characterises the cotton of North-western India, and that it is of fair length and fineness, sufficiently indicate the suitableness, indeed, the moderate moisture of the climate, for we do not find that cotton ever attains these qualities unless in a moist equable climate. It was proposed at one time to establish some saw-gins in the great cotton marts; but these would be of little real benefit as we shall afterwards see, unless the cotton has first been cleanly picked.

The distance of Nagpore in the interior is perhaps unfavorable; but the road to Mirzapore being available for carts, it only requires that those within the Nagpore territories should be made so, for if the journey is commenced on bullocks, it will probably be so continued notwithstanding all its inconveniences. A branch from the proposed Great Railway of the Bengal Presidency would easily convey the coal, corn, and cotton of the Nerbudda valley and of the Nagpore territories to the banks of the Ganges. It may also be a question whether the Mahanuddy cannot be made available, by some improved methods of river navigation, for the conveyance of the produce of these central regions to the Bay of Bengal.

In conclusion, it may be stated, that it would be extremely important to ascertain whether many parts of the country are not well suited for the growth of American cotton, which is so much more esteemed than that of India by Lancashire spinners. But the indigenous cotton itself is, no doubt, susceptible of improvement, as both soil and climate are favorable to its growth. Improved culture would, therefore, have every advantage. The cotton could certainly be sent in a better state to market. His Highness the Rajah of Nagpore might probably be induced to institute such a course of useful investigation, and to employ one of the planters, when relieved from his engagements with the Indian Government.

§ 22. Culture of Cotton in the Territories of the Nizam.

The Hyderabad territories, or those of the Nizam, which include a part of the ancient province so often referred to as Berar, extend between 15° and 21° 30′ of N. latitude, and 75° and 81° 30′ of E. longitude; bounded on the east by Nagpore, and on the north by Meiwar and a part of Candeish, on the west by the Bombay territories, and on the south by the Ceded Districts, that is, by Bellary, Kurnool, Guntoor. Their average length is estimated at 320 miles, and their breadth about 270. The general surface of the country is irregularly hilly, being elevated from 1800 to 2000 feet above the level of the sea, with bare rocky hills of granite common throughout all parts of the province, in some places pervaded by dykes of basalt. The soil, in general, between the granitic hills is extremely fertile, and when capable of being irrigated, as on the alluvial banks of the rivers, produces rich crops of rice, &c. Dr. Voysey says the only parts of the country which are entitled to the name of plains, are those in the neighbourhood of the rivers. The outline of the basaltic trap hills is smooth and rather flattened. They are covered with long grass to their summits, and their course is usually the same with that of the granite they cover. The lakes and tanks are innumerable, all are artificial, and are found only in the granitic and sandstone country. They are usually formed by uniting two projecting points of low hills. "They are less frequent in the sandstone country, and the unirrigated cultivation is accordingly more abundant." Tanks are rarely seen in the basaltic trap.

The fertility of the soil which composes the cultivated districts of the granitic parts of this province, depends greatly on the facility with which the rock of which they are formed becomes decomposed. The soil is siliceous, and "it may be said, that usually the spontaneous fertility is in the inverse ratio of height above the level of the sea."

A garden soil (sp. gr. 1·70) at Secunderabad contained the following ingredients in 480 grains:

Water of absorption	10	grs.
Stones consisting of quartz and felspar	255	"
Vegetable fibre	2	"
Siliceous sand	154	"
	421	"

The country is described as being generally thinly wooded, without any jungles of any great extent, and no forest-trees except in the northern parts and the little known north-eastern districts, where there is the Nirmul jungle. This is about 40 miles in breadth. But extensive clumps of wild date and of palmyra trees are to be found everywhere: both of these yield toddy and sugar.

The rivers are numerous and add greatly to the fertility of the valleys through which they flow. The Poorna flows through the rich valley of Berar, and unites with the Taptee. The Wurda runs along the western boundary and joins the Godavery. The Pyne Gungah takes its rise in the north-western part of the country, and flowing eastward joins the

Wurda. The Godavery, the most considerable river of southern India, takes its rise in the mountainous parts of Aurungabad, and flowing eastward and south-eastward, falls into the Bay of Bengal. The Kistnah also rises in the western ghauts, takes a directly easterly course, is joined by the Beema and Toombuddra, as well as by other small streams, and enters the sea at Masulipatam. These rivers require to be noticed, as it is in the valleys through which they flow that the most favorable sites for cotton culture are found.

The city of Hyderabad is elevated 1672 feet; the observations on climate have been chiefly made at the cantonment of Secunderabad, which is ten miles to the north. "The south-west monsoon commences generally at Secunderabad in the beginning of June, and continues, at intervals, till about the middle of October. During November and December the sky is frequently cloudy, and sometimes in the north-east monsoon a considerable quantity of rain falls. From the beginning of January to the end of May, the sky is generally clear and the weather dry. Dews are not unfrequent in January and the early part of February; and in some years, light showers of rain occur during these months. The annual fall of rain is estimated at thirty-two inches; but in years when the monsoon fails, it does not amount to half that quantity."

Major Oliphant, one of the Directors of the East India Company, and well acquainted with the Nizam's territories, has favoured the author with the following notice of the climate of Hyderabad, which, he says, is decidedly a dry one. "The rains usually commence about the 4th of June, during which month they are in most years light. In July more rain falls, chiefly in the night, alternating with fine days; it is rare to have more than two days' consecutive rain. August continues a pleasant month with rain at nights; September also. October is a drier month; but there is no dry hot weather till April. Sometimes there is rain in the end of December, being a portion of the N.E. monsoon. December and January are decidedly cold, and the climate delicious. March, April, and May are steady, hot, and dry months. Plenty of dew in the cold season. Wet fogs often occur in February and March. All about Hydrabad Proper the soil is red, except in the beds of tanks where the alluvial deposits take place. The cotton districts are in Berar."

At Bolarum, which is five miles further north and twelve miles from Hyderabad, the annual fall of rain is from 25 to 30 inches, occurring principally between June and October, though 4 or 5 inches have been known to fall in December during the north-east monsoon.

Jaulnah, which is near Aurangabad, is distant about 270 miles north-west from Hyderabad, and in a direct line not more than 210 miles from the sea on the western coast. The surrounding country is hilly, the soil black cotton ground, interspersed with patches of red ground. The climate from March to June is hot; but the mornings are comparatively cool, the prevailing winds being westerly, the rainy season continues from July to October. The average fall is 32 inches. From November to February the weather is cool and dry, the temperature ranging from 40° to 80°, with occasional ice on the ground and copious dews.

Capt. Reynolds, well acquainted with the valley of Berar (v. '*H. of C.'s Report,*' p. 413), describes it (p. 37) "as bounded on the north by the Vyndhia range, which divides it from Bhopal and the Nerbudda provinces; on the south by the Hingolie and Aurungabad districts of the Nizam's country; on the east by the Nagpore state, and on the south by Candeish, and as peculiarly suitable to the cultivation of cotton. It is very well watered by a branch of the Taptee river, running from east to west, with numerous tributary streamlets from the north and south."

Again, he states, that the "portion of the country denominated the Berar valley, which consists of an alluvial soil of great depth, is more intersected with rivers than, I suppose, any part of India, Bengal proper excepted; the ramifications of the streams in this valley are most astonishing. There is no part of India so well irrigated, and it is admirably adapted for the cultivation of cotton and dry grains." Also, that "it is a dead flat from the banks of the Wurda, between Oomrowtee and Nagpore, all the way down to the range of the mountains that divide the Nizam's territories from Candeish." On ascending the ghaut at Lakunwara, on the road between Oomrowtee and Aurungabad, "we get into a comparatively hard stratum of soil."

He also states (p. 413), that the space of country included between the river Pynegunga and the river Godavery consists, almost the whole of it, of an alluvial soil, and is adapted to the cultivation of cotton.

With regard to cultivation he states, that "the rice cultivation is dependent entirely upon the quantity of rain you have during the rainy season;" but there is this advantage in dry cultivation, that after the seed is once in the ground, the dew is quite sufficient to mature the crop without any rain whatsoever, so that you find the dry cultivated tracts in a state of the greatest prosperity, while you see the wet, or rice cultivation, starving for want of water."

Mr. Mercer, in passing through the north-western parts of the valley of Berar, states with respect to soils, "There seem to be three kinds of soil devoted to cotton in Berar: the black *regar*, or basaltic soil; the ranker, or gray kunkery (nodular limestone) land, and a brown kunkery soil. The produce of the black land stands first in the Oomrowtee market. The ranker produces a small plant and a harsh weak staple. The brown soil produces the finest-looking plants, apparently a larger produce than either of the others, and the staple is scarcely inferior to that from the black land. All these soils seem to me of a mellower nature than soils of a similar description in Bundlecund." "There is no irrigation used for cotton, nor manuring, except when it is accidental, by the bringing in a piece of ground used as an encampment by the passing Brinjarras (carriers), or by the villagers as a herding-place for their cattle; when this does happen, the superiority of the cotton is very remarkable."

Mr. Mercer's published journal concludes at Baitool, but he subsequently visited Oomrowtee, in the Berar valley, for in a memorandum dated Lackenwara, Feb., 1843, he states, that between Ellichpoor and Oomrowtee he found that cotton formed one-half of the whole cultivation, and that the merchants at the latter place accounted for the superiority of the cotton of Hingunghat by the care in gathering and cleaning, and the very superior land in that district. "The cotton is planted without admixture of other crops, and is sown in rows of a cubit or a little less in width, thinned to a single stalk in a place. There is nothing, however, like ridging; and the same complaint I heard in the valley of the Nerbuddah, of too much rain, is also made here. From the omission of that one single process, the crop is at the mercy of every shower that falls." In the picking, housing, and cleaning, everything requires to be improved.

From these statements of those well acquainted with the country and with the culture of cotton, there can be no doubt, that both the soil and climate of many parts, though not of the whole of the Nizam's territories, are well suited to this cultivation. The cotton which is already produced, is described as fine and soft, and though unequal, of pretty good length of staple. The specimens sent to the author by Mr. Mercer bear out this character, and have been approved of by spinners in this country; but the mass of the cotton exported is much too dirty to command the full price that the cotton itself is worth. If the ryots could be taught to pick it clean and to keep it so, its value would be greatly enhanced. But of this there is not much probability at present. The revenue system as practised in the Nizam's territories, and so well described by Capt. Reynolds (v. '*H. of C.'s Report,*' p. 414) as existing in his time, is not calculated to give encouragement to the cultivator, and the country does not appear in a better state in the present day. The ryots usually sell their cotton in the state of kupas, that is, cotton with the seed, to the agents of the Marwaree firms established in Oomrowtee and other cotton marts. These middlemen have not hitherto shown themselves disposed to make their profits depend upon the purity of the cotton which they sell.

Many parts of the Nizam's territories must be suited for the culture of American cotton; but there are considerable difficulties in cultivating it in the black cotton soil, indeed, it has usually failed in that soil, especially when there has been much moisture in a wet season; but, again, in a dry season the soil has retained moisture, when plants in a more porous soil have been burned up, as will be more particularly related under the head of the "Experimental Culture at Coimbatore in the Madras Presidency." Any improvement in culture so as to suit it to the soil and climate, or the introduction of new species, is not likely to be successfully undertaken unless under the special superintendence of a competent planter, as has been already mentioned under the head of "Nagpore."

The mode of carriage, that on bullocks, is moreover unfavorable to the preservation of the cotton in a clean state, from the daily necessity of unloading and throwing the packages down; whatever may be the nature or condition of the soil. Capt. Reynolds has stated, that there will always be considerable difficulty in making a good road in the Berar valley itself, from the peculiar nature of the black basaltic soil, and the numerous rivers. But as the travelling is chiefly during the dry weather months, the irregularities (*oonchas neechas*) of the surface might be removed at a comparatively small expense, so as to enable carts to travel with facility. Capt. Reynolds, indeed, himself says, that "he drove his carriage nearly the whole of the distance from Jubbulpore to Bombay. ('*Report*,' p. 417.) The road (about 400 miles) from Jubbulpore to Mirzapore he describes as excellent, and that from Nagpore to Jubbulpore (about 350 miles) made at the expense of the Indian Government, and metalled throughout, as "a most magnificent undertaking." The military roads which connect the Madras Presidency with Nagpore and the Nizam's territories, are stated in the '*Madras Medical Reports*' to be in excellent order; but the communications on the westward, or between Berar and Bombay, are described as being imperfect, and therefore requiring the employment of bullocks. Mr. Fenwick, however, who is settled at Khamgaum, states (v. p. 59), that the use of carts was increasing, and that perhaps a third or more of the cotton from Khamgaum is now carried on carts.

Capt. Reynolds has, however, called attention to the route taken by the Brinjarras being dependent, in a great measure, on the agreements made with those who farm the transit duties from the Nizam. He adds, "You would suppose that the cotton would naturally take the route indicated by the main-road, but that is a mistake;—the route is not dependent upon your having made a carriage-road, but upon the route defined by the hoondakars who have contracted for the duties, and unless you do away with your transit duties, your roads are of no use whatsoever." ('*Report*,' p. 418.) According, therefore, to the terms offered by the contractor being satisfactory or otherwise, produce may be carried by the direct road, or it "eventually arrives at Bombay by a circuitous route." The Brinjarras, or carriers, will never allow themselves to be restricted to time; they confine themselves to the road, because they are obliged to adopt roads that the hoondakars have previously established.

It is probable that some part of the cotton, as well as other produce of this interior tract, might be conveyed down the Godavery, as was done in the time of the Messrs. Palmer, but this would require, in the first instance at least, the energy of European agency and some improvement in the mode of river navigation.

But it is in the direction of Central India from Bombay that the railway projected by Mr. Chapman is to come, and it will greatly facilitate the transit of cotton as of everything else. Mr. Chapman has stated, that "cotton of good quality for English use is to be had in Berar (in Central India, 300 or 400 miles from Bombay) at about 1½*d.* per lb., ranging of late years from 1¼*d.* to 1⅞*d.*" The Bombay Cotton Committee "estimate the total cost and loss of carrying cotton from the interior to Bombay at 1*d.* per lb.; by railway, they would not be more than one third of a penny."

"With a railway, the cost of cotton from these countries landed in England would be made up, on an average of years, as follows:

"Price in Berar*	1·5
Transit duties in the native states	0·1
Conveyance per rail, at 2¾*d.* per ton per mile	0·37
Screwing and shipping charges in Bombay, at 6½ Company's rupees per candy of 784 lbs.	0·2
Freight to England, at £3 per ton of 50 cubic feet	0·52
Pence per lb.	2·69"

This, as Mr. Chapman says, may be considered to be about 2¾*d.* per lb. without profit. But it is improbable that the price would remain so low if the cotton was found fit for the English manufacturer, and especially if any were presented to him in a cleaner state, or at all improved in staple. The

* "16 Hyderabad rupees, or 15 Company's rupees, per load of 240 lbs., is a current price in Berar."

railway would not only facilitate the transit of cotton to the coast, but that of agents into the interior, who would purchase up the cotton and sell it for what it was worth at the prices of the day, which must, for some time at least, depend upon the crop of American cotton and the state of the manufacturing interests in general. The prices in Dharwar, even for cotton from American seed, were about 55 rupees the kandee only a year or two since. This year, the native dealers are giving 100 rupees for the same quantity to sell again at Bombay, as will be more particularly related under the head of "Dharwar."

§ 23. Culture in Shorapore.

Capt. Meadows Taylor (pp. 55—59), to whose valuable report on the state of the cotton trade of Shorapore (not Sholapore) we have already alluded does not, in reply to the queries, give a very favorable view of the culture or cleaning of the cotton of that province, nor of its being carried on to any great extent; but the soil is varied, and the climate appears favorable. There is little doubt, therefore, that much good cotton might be produced in addition to what is already grown, either for home consumption or for export. Capt. Taylor states, that the ryot does not usually get advances for his cotton, but sells it in small quantities to itinerant merchants after he has himself cleaned the cotton, reserving the seed for the feeding of his cattle. By keeping the cotton in his own possession he is able to take advantage of the market, and in many cases also to dispose of it after it has been spun into yarn by his family. By this means he realizes a much higher rate of profit.

Capt. Taylor, in addition to giving an account of the present state of the cotton trade in Shorapore, has given a notice of his attempts to introduce the culture of American cotton into the province where he is stationed on special duty. We have made the following extracts from his report, by which it may be seen, that though the quantity of cotton produced per beegah is not so large as we have seen stated in the reports of the North-West provinces, yet it is larger than is admitted in some of the districts we have to mention, which are specially considered to be cotton-yielding districts. This indicates a favorable state of the soil or climate, perhaps of both. The success which has attended Capt. Taylor's last experiments, bids fair to introduce the American cotton as a permanent product of the province of Shorapore. This will greatly benefit the ryots, for they seem to have the trade at present in their own hands, and will be ready to take advantage of the example of the neighbouring district of Dharwar. The following are the reply and experiments referred to:

"QUESTION. What is the average produce of cotton per beegah or acre?

"REPLY. An average good crop of cotton per beegah or acre from a clean field of 30 beegahs, the size of the beegah being 3864 square yards, is estimated with seed at six candies of 240 seers per candy, or 1440 seers, or 48 seers = 98 lbs. per beegah. A lesser crop would be 5 candies or 1200 seers, 40 seers per beegah. An inferior crop, 3 candies or 720 seers, 24 seers per beegah. A very poor crop, 2 candies or 480 seers, 12⅔ seers per beegah.

"The above would give an average of four candies at least on each 30 beegah field, and on all descriptions of soil, 32 seers or 64 lbs. per beegah, and as the cotton crop is usually a good one, I do not think, in a series of years, that the average would be under five gross candies per field of 30 beegahs, or 40 seers = 80 lbs. per beegah, as the highest average taken is often exceeded in favorable seasons and in fertile roads. The above estimate is taken from several, obtained from different cotton districts of the Sumusthan, principality of Shorapore.

"*Quality of Cotton.*—I have frequently examined the quality of cotton in various localities of the Sumusthan, and have observed considerable difference in it. That grown upon the ordinary régur, or black soil, which is connected with trap rocks or boulders, is of a rough, strong, but short staple. That again which is grown on lands in which limestone measures prevail, is much superior, being longer in staple and of a softer quality, and as the limestone tract is of great extent comparatively with the other, I should estimate that the produce of the latter would be at least as five to two of the former. No classification is, however, made by the dealers or merchants, who are probably unaware that any general difference exists.

"The cotton grown is entirely of the native indigenous kind, and the same objections to it as to short staple, and in breaking of the dry leaves about the seed pod into the cotton, as well as of the thin shell of the pod itself at the time of gathering, exists here as elsewhere where the same description of produce prevails, and which has been found so difficult to eradicate in the various cleaning processes resorted to in England.

"I have made several attempts to introduce into the Sumusthan the Bourbon and New Orleans seed which has succeeded so well in the Southern Mahratta country, and made trials of both in limestone and trap black soils, but hitherto without success to any extent. The cotton succeeded very fairly upon the limestone soils, and when sown at the usual time of sowing there, that is, about August. Last year, however, there was a total failure of the crop on the land where the American cotton was sown, which has induced me, with a new supply of seed from Dharwar, to try it again this season, upon a different principle.

"Thus I have tried small portions, both of Bourbon and New Orleans cotton, in red gravelly soil, sowing them at the very commencement of the monsoon, and the result was more complete than I could have supposed. The plants grew to a height of upwards of six feet, the branches spreading laterally about three feet from the stem, they were vigorous and healthy; the branches weighed down by the weight of the pods and leaves, and the produce, both in amount and in quality of staple, far surpassed any that had been grown in black soils, and a later period of the monsoon. I beg to transmit with this report a sample of the cotton thus produced. I have carefully sown all the seed of the Bourbon cotton, and this with the New Orleans received from Dharwar, is now being sown, under my own superintendence, on red and mixed soils which I have selected. The amount of cultivation will probably be 100 beegahs, which will afford a fair proof of the adaptation of the cottons to the red soil, which has never hitherto been tried here for cotton. Should this trial be successful, I should not despair of being able gradually to introduce the cultivation of both kinds of cotton among the ryots, upon the red soils which now bear produce of an inferior quality and value."

The author has no doubt that the last-mentioned experiment has continued to succeed, as he was informed in the beginning of the year by Mr. Blount, the planter in charge of the experiments in Dharwar, that he had sent two gins to Shorapore, to clean the American cotton which Capt. Taylor had grown.

§ 24. Culture in the Bombay Presidency.

The Bombay Presidency derives its name from its capital, which is situated on an island of the same name. This island, formed by the union of several smaller isles, is itself now united by a causeway with Salsette, and thence with the mainland: so that cotton is imported both by sea and by the Sion causeway. Surat, about 150 miles further to the north, the original capital, became superseded from the difficulties of its position. But its name still designates Indian cotton in general. Bombay is distant 965 miles from Delhi, 770 from Madras, and 1300 from Calcutta, and is situated in lat. 18° 55′, and long. 72° 54′. The Presidency extends both to the north and south, in the former direction being bounded by a part of Marwar, and in the south by the Portuguese territory of Goa and by Malabar, and above the ghauts by Mysore and a part of the ceded districts. On the east lie the Nizam's dominions.

If we consider the physical aspect of this Presidency, it is especially distinguished by the western ghauts running along its whole length and dividing it into two very distinct tracts, that is, the low country which lies between the sea and the mountain range, distinguished, in its southern parts, by the names of North and South Concan, divided into the collectorates of Rutnagherry and Tannah. The northern part, known as Guzerat, is formed into the collectorates of Surat, Broach, Kaira, and Ahmedabad, with some tracts (a part of Kattywar) on the west of the Gulf of Cambay, included in the collectorate of Ahmedabad. The country above the ghauts is usually known by the general name of the Deccan or Dukhun, and includes the collectorates, proceeding from north to south, of Candeish, Ahmednuggur, Poona, Shorapore, Belgaum, and Dharwar, the two latter usually spoken of under the name of the Southern Mahratta country.

Experiments have been made to cultivate improved kinds of cotton in different parts of the Bombay Presidency at various periods, as enumerated in the tabular statement, pp. 86 to 90. As at Randatarra, then in this Presidency, in 1797; in Broach and Guzerat, in 1811; at Malwan, at Caranja, Salsette, and at Kaira, in 1817 to 1819.—Cotton farms were established at

Salsette and in Guzerat, in 1829 and 1833.—Sea Island cotton was cultivated by Mr. Elphinstone at Rutnagherry, in 1840. In that year the present set of experiments were commenced, and continued until the year 1849 in Broach.

In the country above the ghauts experiments have also been tried at different times, as in Dharwar in 1829 to 1836, and again in 1842 to the present time, and also by Dr. Gibson and Dr. Johnson in different parts of the Deccan, in Belgaum in 1845, and in Candeish in 1845, in both of which collectorates, as well as in Dharwar, the experiments are still in progress.

Having just treated of the countries of Central India which are situated on the same table-land as the Deccan collectorates, it will be preferable to treat of the course and results of the experimental culture in these regions, before we descend to the country below the ghauts.

The territories comprising the collectorates included in the Deccan, or Dukhun, have been examined by Col. Sykes, now one of the Directors of the East India Company, then Statistical Reporter to the Bombay Presidency, and described in the '*Reports of the British Association for* 1837.' "They lie upon that elevated plateau which has an abrupt termination on the western side of India, in what are usually denominated the Ghats, but which plateau gradually declines, occasionally by a succession of low steps, as is seen in the courses of rivers to the Coromandel Coast, except in Khandesh (*Khind* meaning a gap or trench, and *Desh* a country), where the river Tapty disembogues to the westward, from the peculiar configuration of the narrow valley in which this collectorate lies. The general level of the main plateau of Dukhun is about 2000 feet high near the Ghats, and scarcely exceeds 1000 feet in the eastern limits of the collectorates. The whole territory is mountainous near to the Ghats, and has numerous valleys, some of these narrow and tortuous, others broad, open, and flat. At from thirty to fifty miles eastward from the Ghats, most of the mountain spurs which produce the valleys terminate, and the country becomes open and tolerably level for considerable distances, with an occasional step down to the eastward; the country, in fact, being made up of beds of trap, the beds extending the further to the eastward, the lower they are in the series."

"There is much forest and underwood and jungle along the line of the Ghats; but to the eastward, the country is open and there is a want of wood; parts of Khandesh and Dharwar are exceptions to this description. The western tracts along the Ghats are called the *Mawuls*, in contradistinction to the open country, which is called the *Desh* or *Des*."

The Colonel further describes the climate of the Ghats and the Desh as having distinct features: "The tract along the line of the former has a lower mean temperature, much more moisture, greater prevalence of westerly winds, a more limited range of the thermometer, but a greater prevalence of fogs before, during, and after the rains, but not in the winter months, and, finally, is characterised by the absence of hot winds. The Desh, on the contrary, has the air excessively dry in the hot months, a great diurnal and annual range of the thermometer, a comparatively small fall of rain in the monsoon, the frequent occurrence of hot winds, and the rareness of fogs." These well-defined characteristics we shall find have considerable influence on the culture of cotton, especially of the American kinds.

With respect to temperature, it is low in the early part of March, but rises suddenly after the middle of that month; the latter end of March, and April and May are the hottest periods of the year, from the position of a nearly vertical sun, the intensity of whose influence is but slightly modified by the occasionally cloudy weather. The temperature falls in June on the accession of the rainy season, and continues nearly stationary until the end of September. It then rises in October (in consequence of the cessation of the rains), less suddenly than in March; falls again at the end of the month, and continues to do so until its annual minimum in December or January. The temperature, as observed by Col. Sykes, was, in 1827, on the 28th of March, 96° 8′, and the minimum 48° on the 12th of December at sunrise, the range between these extremes being 48° 8′. "In 1828 the maximum occurred on the 7th of May, being 101°, and the minimum was 56°, the range, therefore, 45°; but for a very short time the thermometer rose on the 7th of May, between 2 and 3 o'clock, to 105°; this was the more remarkable as I was then encamped on the edge of the Ghats, at the source of the Beema river, at an elevation of 3090 feet above the level of the sea." The mean temperature of the year at Poona is stated to be 77° 7′; at Ahmednuggur, at an elevation of 1900 feet above the sea, as ascertained by Dr. Walker, 78°; Col. Sykes, living in tents and moving about the country, made it 77° 93′. He observes, that the mean temperature of places on the table-land of the continent of India is much higher than the calculated mean temperatures of the *same* places agreeably to Mayer's formula.

With respect to moisture, the Colonel further observes, that a remarkable feature in the climate of Dukhun is the small quantity of aqueous vapour generally suspended in the air, compared with the proximate climate of Bombay and the Coast, or even of the hilly tracts of the Ghats. There is a gradual increase of moisture from the most dry month, February, until June and July. After this the moisture remains nearly stationary until the beginning of October, when it diminishes somewhat rapidly and regularly until February. "The greatest monthly range of the dewing point was in October, 30°, and the smallest range, 7°, was in July and August." Another instance, but which is characteristic of India, of the difference of moisture between the rainy season and the period at its conclusion. A plant, therefore, which has flourished during the equability of temperature and moisture of the rainy season, will probably be unable to bear the sudden rise in temperature and the increase in dryness, which occur at its conclusion, as we have already explained in the diagram at p. 184. The daily range of the thermometer is very considerable in some months, as in December, but comparatively small in the months of June, July, August, and September (v. *Diagram*, p. 184).

"In Dukhun the rains are light, uncertain, and in all years barely sufficient for the wants of the husbandman, and a slight failure occasions much distress. They usually commence at the end of May, with some heavy thunder-showers from E. to S.E., but they do not set in regularly until the first ten days in June, and continue until the end of September, from the W. to the S.W., and break up with thunder-storms from the E. to the S.E. before the middle of October. During the remaining months of the year, an accidental shower or two may fall from the Coromandel monsoon; and the further the distance eastward from Poona, the greater the chance of showers in the cold months. The mean fall of rain at Bombay for the years 1826-7-8 was 93·62 inches, and at Poona 26·926 inches, or 28¾ per cent. only of the fall in Bombay."

The fall of rain varies, as is well known, in different seasons, and is the chief cause of the difference in the productiveness of the crops of good and bad years. A copious and regular fall of rain being as essential in hot countries for the production of good crops, as a fine summer is in high latitudes for the production of wheat. But, in the Bombay Presidency especially, there are very great differences in the quantity of rain which falls at places not very remote from each other. This has been very clearly shown, in a tabular form, by Col. Sykes, in his paper "On Meteorological Observations, taken in India at various Heights" ('*Phil. Trans.*,' 1850), where he has also shown, that, in the small island of Bombay (seven miles by two miles) the quantities of rain vary much within short distances, as indicated by nine rain-gauges (l. c., p. 352). The following table is particularly interesting, in giving the quantity of rain both on the low lands of the coast and on the table land of the Deccan, both of which have been the sites of experiments on the culture of cotton.

Sea-coast of Konkun.		Konkun, somewhat inland.		Western Ghâts.		Western Ghâts, East branch.
Bombay, sea-level.	Rutnagherry, 150 feet.	Tanna, sea-level.	Dapoolee, 900 feet.	Kundalla, 1740 feet, 1833 and 1835.	Mahabuleshwur, 4500 feet.	Paunchgunnee, 4000 feet, 1835, 1842, and 1843.
68·73	114·55	106·16	134·96	141·59	254·84	50·69

DECCAN.							
Sattarah, 2320 feet.	Kolapoor, 1847.	Poona, 1842 feet.	Nassick.	Belgaum, 2000 feet.	Dharwar.	Ahmednugger, 1900 feet.	Shorapore, 1847.
39·20	30·74	19·02	26·72	40·90	38·81	21·83	32·16

"From the crest of the Ghâts the supply of rain decreases towards the sea-coast westward, but decreases in an infinitely greater ratio eastward, on the plateau of the Deccan. Along the coast the supply of rain diminishes with the increase in latitude."

Dr. Murray, stationed for many years at the Sanatarium on

the Mahabuleshwur Hills, has observed: "The prodigious influence of the Ghâts in modifying the amount of the s. w. monsoon rain, is perhaps nowhere more strikingly shown than in the N. W. parts of the Sattarah territory. If we draw a line nearly straight from west to east, from Mahabuleshwur, on the summit of the Ghâts, to Phultun, a distance of little more than forty miles, we shall find, at the commencement of the line, a rain-fall of 240 inches, at an altitude of 4500 feet; 180 inches at Sindola, *a mile distant,* and elevated 4600 feet; 50 inches at Paunchgunnee, at a further distance of eleven miles and an elevation of 4000 feet; 25 inches at Wye, four miles further east, and 2300 feet in height above the sea; while, at the extremity of the line, at Phultun, thirty miles from Sattarah, and about the same level as Wye, the quantity is reduced to 7 or 8 inches."

On this, Col. Sykes remarks: "Dr. Murray must have meant during the s. w. monsoon, as he had previously represented the fall of rain at Phultun at 24·18 inches in 1848, in 1847 at 24·04 inches, and in 1846 at 18·09 inches. Some inches of these amounts, however, are attributable to the Madras monsoon, which commences in October, when the Malabar coast monsoon terminates, and Phultun, from its easterly position, gets an uncertain sprinkling from the Madras side."

If it has thus been shown necessary to determine the quantity of rain in a district only from observations in a number of places, it is equally necessary to ascertain the state of moisture in the air in the same manner, for here local influences affect the rate of evaporation and the state of atmospheric moisture quite as much as the fall of rain. Col. Sykes, in referring to his former paper "On the Meteorology of the Deccan," observes: "Speaking of dew, I said, in the year 1828, 'At Marheh, in the Pergunnah of Mohol, garden produce (which is usually irrigated during the day-time) was covered with a copious dew every morning; the lands bordering the gardens for forty or fifty yards around were slightly sprinkled with it, *but there was not a vestige of it* in the fields constituting the rising ground north and south of the tract of garden land.' Hence I inferred, that 'aqueous vapour had been taken up by the action of the sun during the day, *suspended over the spot,* and deposited by the lower temperature at night as dew upon the land, in proportion to the supply obtained by day.' My tents were within 200 yards of the fields where I observed these phenomena, but from the 11th to the 30th of January, 1828, there was not any deposition of dew about them, excepting on the 13th of January. In consequence of these observations I was induced to remark particularly the localities of dew at Poona and in its neighbourhood. In September and October I found that when there was not a trace of dew in the cantonment, there would be a deposition on the fields of standing grain half a mile distant, and when there was not any dew either in the cantonment or in the fields, it would yet be found on the banks of running rivulets and on the banks of the Mota Mola River; but with respect to the rivulets, '*fifteen or twenty feet from the water were the limits of the deposition.*' I gave numerous other instances of the local deposition of dew proximate to irrigated lands, or in the neighbourhood of water, indicating the suspension of vapours over the localities, in complete analogy with what occurs to the wet bulb thermometer when the air is calm."

When a thermometer with its bulb kept wetted is employed to ascertain the dryness or moisture of the air, it is obvious, as has been frequently observed, that while the air is in a tranquil state, the vapour which is formed will remain suspended near the wet surface, and prevent, for a time at least, the formation of further vapour; hence agitation of the air is necessary to remove that which surrounds the wet bulb. So in the case of evaporation generally, this, it is well known, is in proportion not only to the surface exposed and the temperature of the air, but depends also on the prevalence of currents of air, which are useful both by removing the vapour as it is formed, and by supplying fresh quantities of air into which more vapour may expand. These facts are particularly applicable to the effects produced by irrigation, for not only is the earth watered, but the air is moistened. Plants, moreover, nourished by their roots, transpire by their leaves a portion of the water which they have absorbed, and thus add to the moisture of the air of the locality. If the place is open and low, or sheltered by walls, or strips of plantation, the moistened air will be partially retained within the sheltered parts, radiation taking place, dews will fall, and the climate be rendered suitable for the growth of plants which will not flourish in more exposed situations: because there the fresh currents of air are ever abstracting fresh quantities of moisture from the leaves, and thus obstructing growth in the very soil and air where the supply of nutriment is small. But in an over-moist soil and atmosphere, currents of air are useful in drying the surface of the earth, and in promoting healthy evaporation from the leaves. Draining, therefore, and open planting are not more useful in Louisiana and Bengal, than irrigation and moderate shelter are in Egypt, the Deccan, or in North-Western India. Nothing can be more important, therefore, for the development of the resources of a country where the supply of rain-water is deficient or irregular, than the extension of works of irrigation, such as have been and now are carrying out in North-Western India, and as have been constructed with much benefit in Tanjore, and are now constructing on the Godavery river in the Madras Presidency. The supply of water on the table-land of the Deccan is small; but the necessity is greater of preserving that which falls, either in tanks or by damming up some rivers and using underground water-courses, as is practised in the dry climates of the Punjab and of Affghanistan.

§ 25. Experimental Culture in the Deccan generally.

It has already been stated, that a fresh series of experiments to improve the culture of cotton were ordered by the Court of Directors to be undertaken in the year 1829. The first that were instituted in consequence of these instructions in the Southern Mahratta country, were placed under the superintendence of the late Dr. Lush, then Superintendent of the Botanical Gardens in that Presidency. He established an experimental farm at Segeehullee, near Gurruck in the Beedee Talooka in the Dharwar collectorate. Mr. Shaw, lately collector of Dharwar, has since observed, that "the cotton cultivation was the least of all the Talookas in the two collectorates of Dharwar or Belgaum, and which, from its situation on the summits of the Ghauts, was most unlikely to be adapted for the growth of cotton." The objects contemplated were the introduction of new species of cotton, and improvement in the cultivating and cleaning of the indigenous species. An "agency was also established in connection with this farm for the purchase of cotton direct from the ryots, and several powerful presses were erected at Dharwar, Noulgoond, and Gudduck, for the packing and pressing of the cotton so purchased."

The kinds of cotton-seed which were sent out by the Court of Directors were Sea Island, Upland Georgian, Louisiana, and New Orleans, tried both as annuals and perennials. Besides these, a white-seeded perennial from the Dapooree Botanic Garden, together with Bourbon, Seychelles, Egyptian, and Pernambuco were sown, also the Broach, Jumbooser, and Nurmah indigenous kinds. The seeds, Dr. Lush says, were in many cases old and worm-eaten, and did not vegetate. But the soil was considered by him to be best adapted for the culture of the white-seeded perennial (New Orleans?), the Pernambuco, and the Egyptian cotton. "The green-seeded American cotton sown here has put on the appearance of black seed mixed with white and green." With regard to staple Dr. Lush observes, "that the naturalised Pernambuco and the Egyptian, all foreign cotton, of long staple, have become short." Of some Egyptian seed sown in 1834, he says, "It has borne a good crop the first year; the quantity of cotton by weight in proportion to the seed is double that of ordinary cottons, and of three specimens grown in Bagulcote in the year 1834, two of them were declared superior by a committee of merchants in Bombay to any Broach cotton in the market." Nothing, however, can upon the whole be more unfavorable than Dr. Lush's account of his experiments; and Mr. Baber, the principal collector, reported, that after five years "no natives, not even those in the vicinity of the farms, had embarked in the cultivation of any of the foregoing cottons." The Bombay Government, therefore, abolished the farm and agency in 1836. The quality, however, of some of the cottons produced was as good as was required, for a committee of native merchants who examined (in Jan. 1834) some bales of the white-seeded perennial and Upland American cotton grown on the Seegeehullee farm, pronounced the cotton to be "of superior quality, staple good, worth about 180 rupees per Surat candy, and fit for the English market." Mr. Mercer, on his first arrival in England from America, picked out samples of the white-seeded perennial cotton, from among the collection of specimens of experimental cottons preserved in the India House, as quite equal to good New Orleans cotton. By brokers in this country it had been pronounced of good quality, and worth 9½*d.* per lb. Messrs. Ritchie, Stewart, and Co., who examined some of the Dharwar-grown cotton in 1834, observed that a large proportion of the Koompta, or Dharwar cotton, received in Bombay in 1833, although of a coarse staple and dirty, was of a more valuable description than the sample of white-seeded perennial. "On account of its length of staple, it (the Koompta) was preferred to Dhollerah Toomil cotton by their Manchester and Glasgow friends, and sold by the latter at an advance of 1*d.* per lb."* These observations on the good quality of some of this Coompta cotton have been confirmed by more recent information.

In connection with these original experiments in the Southern Mahratta country, may be noticed others which were instituted in other parts of the Deccan. Dr. Gibson says, with respect to the production of exotic species of cotton in the interior, he is of opinion, that the results of the experiments tried by himself and others have shown that they will not succeed, except in places within the influence of the sea air. The opinion that the black soil of the Deccan is well suited to the production of cotton, he "considers has been too hastily formed—he has always observed that the plants present a stunted and poor appearance, and he doubts whether, in the end, it will be found as profitable as a grain crop." "In the alluvial soils of the province, the plant flourishes well and yields a good return, but such soils are limited in extent, and are more profitably employed in raising valuable garden produce." We have already quoted Dr. Gibson's opinion about the necessity of a moist climate, and that the alternations of dryness and wet are injurious to the culture of cotton: an average fall of rain of between forty and fifty inches he considers most favorable. Lieut. Wingate observes, that the soil in some parts of the eastern districts of the Poonah zillah, and more generally in

* Vide '*House of Commons Return*,' pp. 70—73, and '*E. I. Company's Papers on Cotton, Wool, Silk, and Indigo*,' p. 264, and pp. 275—279. The author regrets that he is unable to quote from Dr. Lush's pamphlet, having lost the volume in which it was bound up with some other papers on the same subject.

the Sholapore collectorate, is adapted to the cotton plant, but the climate he thinks unfavorable to it. This, however, he considers as of little importance, as the demand for grain to supply the great marts of Poonah and Sholapore will always render it more advantageous to the cultivator in the former zillah to turn his attention to the production of that commodity, and, in the latter collectorate, the scantiness and uncertainty of the annual rains occasion a scarcity of fodder, which requires almost an exclusive cultivation of *joaree* (*Sorghum vulgare*), one of the large millets, approaching Indian corn in its principal characteristics.

"The collector of Candeish reports (in 1849), that the only direct measures, as far as he is aware, which have ever been attempted in that province for the extension and improvement of cotton, have been a purchase made in 1832 of the produce to the amount of 20,000 rupees, by which a temporary stimulus to prices was given,—no permanent benefit was attained; and an occasional distribution of foreign seeds, from which nothing satisfactory resulted."

In the year 1836, in order to encourage the cultivation of cotton in the zillahs of Poona (these including the sub-collectorates of Sholapore and of Ahmednuggur), the Bombay Government were induced to issue a proclamation, declaring that all lands, whether irrigated or unirrigated, on which cotton is cultivated, shall be entirely free from the land-tax, and that no assessment whatever shall be levied thereon during five years, or until the 30th of April, 1842. The Government of India having disapproved of these proceedings, referred the matter to the Court of Directors, who also disapproved of them. The proclamation was withdrawn, and cancelled in June 1838. The Court "considered it just as contrary to the principles upon which they wished their land assessment to be regulated to give a bounty upon the production of cotton, as to put a higher assessment upon it." (See Mr. Prideaux's evidence, '*House of Commons Report*,' pp. 23 & 44); but it was at the same time ordered, that "The rights of the individuals to whom the faith of Government has been pledged, and who have either established a claim to, or have received, a remission of assessment, previously to the revocation of the notices, must not, of course, be interfered with." The proclamation, during the two years it was in force, had very little effect, and was not likely ever to have had much. Indeed we do not learn that those who had obtained grants, and whose rights were directed not to be interfered with, ever obtained good or profitable crops. The climate in fact is too dry for the successful culture of either indigenous or of American cotton; for even when Government have not only remitted the rent, but paid all the expenses of an experiment, they have been unable to produce any effect in an unsuitable climate.

§ 26. Experimental Culture in the Dharwar District.

Of the several collectorates into which the British portion of the Deccan is divided, we shall notice only those which seem suitable to the culture of cotton of a superior quality, and of these Dharwar demands the first notice, not only from the extent and success which have attended the culture, but also because it is the nearest to, and therefore forms the most easy transition from, Shorapore, which we have just noticed. Dharwar forms that part of the Southern Mahratta country, which is bounded on the north by the Kolapoor territory and the Kristna river; on the east by the Nizam's dominions; on the south by Mysore and the Toomboodra river, and on the west by Soonda and the Syhadree ghauts. Of this district Col. Sykes says, "Viewing Dharwar, whether with respect to its numerous towns and well-peopled villages, the comparative density of its population, the size of its farms, the quantity of land in cultivation, the amount of its revenues, the lightness with which they press supposing they were raised as a poll-tax, the indications of manufacturing industry (so languishing elsewhere), in the number of its weavers, and its superior means of school instruction, it is unquestionably the finest of the British possessions in Dukhun."

The author, on a former occasion, observed, that "the position of Dharwar does not at first appear very favorable, from its situation on the table land, elevated probably there about 2000 feet: but we have been unable to ascertain its exact height, nor have we been able to learn that any register of the weather has been kept there, either by the experimentalists or by any other person. Though the soil does not seem better than that of many other parts of the Peninsula or of Central India, there are certain advantages of climate, which have facilitated the cultivation of American cotton, in addition to the energy of the collector, Mr. Shaw, and the judicious management of the planter, Mr. Mercer. Dharwar being situated, in a direct line, about 40 miles from the western Ghauts, and 70 from the sea, enjoys some of the advantages of a maritime climate, especially in a greater degree of, and a more uniform state of, atmospheric moisture. The Ghauts, it is well-known, rise abruptly on their western face from the comparatively narrow slip of land which intervenes between them and the sea. The monsoon expends itself in a great measure on this mountain range, so that the fall of rain (which, in the interior, is not 30 inches at many places) along the coast varies from 120 to 150 inches, and, on the Mahabhuleshwar hills, has extended to 250 and even to 350 inches in the year. But places above and in the vicinity of the Ghauts experience some of the effects of the monsoon. Dr. T. Christie has related, that, in two different years, much rain fell at Dharwar in July and August, while none fell fifteen miles to the eastward. Mr. Mercer has described the climate as being mild and pleasant, especially when the effects of the sea breeze are experienced in the afternoon."

Mr. Blount, the American planter, mentioned at pp. 272—275, and who arrived at Dharwar in the beginning of the year 1848, has, on application, favoured the author with the following account of the climate of that year and of 1849:

"Dharwar is, indeed, for India a mild and moist climate; in the shade our warmest days are about 85° morning, and evening 75°, from November to March, mornings 60° to 70°, and mid-day 76° to 80°, *the two seasons I have been here.* March is warm, but the heat is nothing to compare with the northern districts; a healthy man may be out all day without danger. On April 1st, 1848 and 1849, thunder-storms set in, and were more or less frequent from that time till July, when the regular monsoon commences. The warmest days are just before one of these storms, but do not extend over any long period. The monsoon sets in light, or I may say, we only get what water the clouds bring over the ghats, and it falls more like a Scotch mist than a rain; but now and then there are heavy showers. This kind of weather continues during August and July. In August the cotton is generally planted. In September a break in the weather occurs until the middle and end of the month, when there are two or three heavy falls, followed by misty rain, until the middle of October, when the rains cease (but in 1849 the heaviest rain fell in the early part of November), with the exception of a light shower in January."

Nothing (v. p. 340) could well appear more discouraging than any further attempt to grow American cotton in the elevated parts of the Deccan; but A. M. Shaw, Esq., Collector of Dharwar at the time when the experiments were resumed in the year 1840, was of opinion, that the soil and climate of the Southern Mahratta country would be found favorable to its growth. He writes in the year 1842, "I would respectfully submit, that perhaps the climate of no part of Western India approaches so near the climate of the cotton districts of the United States, as the Southern Mahratta country. I would submit, also, that it has become an established rule, that cotton should be grown only on black soil; this I believe to be an error, and that the very best soil for the culture of cotton is a partially damp red soil." In the season of 1841-42, Mr. Shaw having obtained some of the Mexican cotton seed, which had been sent out by the Court of Directors, tried to cultivate it in the Hooblee Talooka, in ten acres of land selected for the purpose. Notwithstanding some adverse circumstances which attended the experiment, the produce was found to be much superior to that of the native cotton cultivated by the ryots during the same season, as well in respect to quantity as to quality. Difficulty was experienced in separating the cotton from its seed, and some differences of opinion were at first entertained respecting the exact proportion of cotton to the seed; but the hopes of success in the culture were even at that time very promising. Mr. Mercer, who on the retirement of the American planters destined for Bombay,* had been transferred from the Bengal to the Bombay Presidency, and arrived at Dharwar in April, 1843, reported on the 1st of May, "I have much satisfaction in saying, in regard to your fields of Mexican cotton near Dharwar and Hooblee, that the individual plants of each are equal to the best I have seen of that description of

* See the account of the experimental culture in Broach.

cotton in India. They are quite as well grown and healthy, and judging from the number and size of the bolls now on the plants, as also from the old shells from which the cotton has been picked, I think they have the advantage of any that I have seen." Some of this cotton having been sent to Bombay, the Chamber of Commerce of that place reported on the 9th of June, 1843, that the cotton was of fair quality but of rather irregular staple, and that it would bring about 10 or 15 rupees per candy more than the best Broach cotton in the market.

Mr. Mercer, on his arrival at Bombay, was appointed to conduct the experimental culture of cotton in the Dharwar district. He reported after his arrival there, that having examined the neighbourhood of Hooblee, a town celebrated as a cotton-mart, he had selected the adjoining village of Khooseghul as a site for the experiments, "the soil there being excellent, and the climate favorable." He commenced operations in planting from the 8th of June to the end of August; the natives not planting until the middle or end of September. The cotton came up, grew slowly, but much was destroyed by insects. He took 220 acres into cultivation, half with American seed obtained from Coimbatore, and half with Broach and other native cottons, and about 10 acres with Abyssinian seed brought by the late Sir W. Harris. The natives had been induced by Mr. Shaw to cultivate some, and Mr. Hillier, a German missionary, some more, so that there were altogether 425 acres under cultivation. The land Mr. Mercer describes as red near the hills, but in the plains all black; and that his farm was in the plains, with but little red soil. After a little experience, he complains that at his farm, which is 17 miles from Dharwar, the rains of the west monsoon are very slight. On the 24th of September he wrote to the author, that the climate at Dharwar, previous to the setting-in of the monsoon, struck him as resembling that of Mississippi. It was warm but not excessively hot, it then rained frequently and heavily. During the south-west monsoon the rain reached him in slight and occasional showers, though it was pouring in torrents within six miles. There was a constant gale of wind blowing to which he attributed the slow growth and unhappy looks of the cotton: for in sheltered situations it grew well. "On the 4th of July the violent s.w. wind ceased, and almost immediately the cotton began to recover, and new leaves showed themselves in the places where the old ones were shrivelled. Yesterday and the day before we had rain such as fell previous to the monsoon in April and May last. It is calm and hot, but not more so than at home (*i. e.*, in Louisiana in August). It is expected that this sort of rain will continue throughout October and during the continuance of the N.E. monsoon." "The cotton continues to improve rapidly, and now looks far more like American cotton than any that I have before seen in India;" and "There is hardly a question, if I am not disappointed in my crop, that the ryots will soon entirely adopt the American cotton, for they seem very much interested about it." In March and April of the following year, he wrote, that he felt satisfied he should succeed in his endeavours to introduce the culture of American cotton in one large portion of the Presidency, and that profitably to the ryots, even above any other unirrigated crop they can put into the ground. "The ryots having planted New Orleans cotton on their own account, in picking their crops had already gathered so much per acre, and are getting so much more per maund for it than for the country cotton, that the question whether they would continue to plant was set at rest." "Every seed produced this year will be planted next, and ten times as many if I had them to distribute." The seed, moreover, seemed to improve, as that which Mr. Mercer had received from Coimbatore, when grown in Dharwar, "looked almost as well as fresh seed from America." The bolls also were described as growing large, yielding fine cotton and a good deal from each boll. The picking also was easier with it than with native cotton. "The proportion of cotton to seed is in almost every instance one third, and never more than a very small fraction under." The natives who had picked and had had their cotton ginned were quite delighted with it, as some sold it at an advance, above the market price of country cotton, that is, at 11 annas per maund of 28 lbs., or nearly 50 per cent. more. Others preferred keeping it unless they got still higher prices, as it was worth more to them, from its being so clean and fine, for spinning into thread for the use of the native weavers.

Even in the first season Mr. Mercer made the saw-gins useful, by substituting straps for cog-wheels, and by using hand instead of cattle labour. He found that he could obtain from 300 to 320 lbs. of clean cotton, with 12 coolies paid 2 annas a day, 6 being at work while 6 others were resting. With regard to culture, Mr. Mercer doubted whether it would be profitable, on account of the small returns per acre, for Europeans to cultivate it on speculation; but this he thought of little consequence, as the natives could certainly grow it at a profit, and would while there was any one to purchase it. "Though the quantity per acre has been small, the quality has been equal to the best ever produced here, and the quantity has been quite sufficient to pay the growers more than they ever reaped before from their land." He further states, that "I have bought all the seed from the produce of the ryots' fields of New Orleans, and I have now enough for something more than 2500 acres."

Respecting this next season, Mr. Mercer wrote to the author on the 22d of October, 1844, that "the quantity of land which was actually under cultivation with New Orleans cotton by the ryots, was not much less than 3000 (it turned out to be 2749) acres." He also observes, "That which was left standing of last year's crop is flourishing," and promises "to yield a pretty large crop," though in this Mr. Mercer was afterwards disappointed. Mr. Mercer refers to some of the cotton shedding every leaf after the heavy rains of last October. "This year several fields have done the same. One on the farm established at Gudduck under Mr. Hawley, of about 30 acres, looks just now like dry sticks, though the roots seem healthy and the stalks are full of sap, and are just beginning to shoot into new leaf-buds." Mr. Mercer was unable to account for the fact in either year, though he had also observed in the present season, that the plants were infected with numerous grasshopper-like insects. This shedding of the leaf we have elsewhere supposed to be connected with the alternations of dryness and of moisture, which so frequently occur between the changes of the seasons. Mr. Mercer continues: "Mr. Hawley, an American planter, having been transferred from Broach to Dharwar, had, in this second year, also, an experimental farm at Gudduck, in the Dummul Talooka. The field I have mentioned, at the Gurruck Farm, was as fine cotton as I ever saw of its age, about three feet high, and beautifully developed. The prospect of making a crop was very cheerless from this time till the setting in of the sea breezes, in the latter end of December. It is now generally much brighter; and, as we are sure of their benign visitation at that season, I am most confident that the out-turn will be largely increased." Early in November, there were forwarded to Vingorla, for transmission to Bombay, 3817 pounds of Broach, mixed Broach, Coimbatore, New Orleans, and Abyssinian, the growth of the Khooseghul farm in the year 1843. All these were valued nearly the same by the Bombay Chamber of Commerce, from 80 to 85 rupees per candy; but the mixed Broach at from 95 to 100 per candy. (*Summary*, p. 61.*)

This cotton was shipped to England in the 'Earl of Eglinton,' with some Broach experimental cotton. Both were sold at Liverpool on the 24th of November, 1845, for $3\frac{1}{4}$*d.*, and no distinction was made in the price, which is much to be regretted, as this, no doubt, had considerable effect in modifying operations in India; for it was observed, that "account sales showed no advantage in favour of New Orleans cotton." (*Summary*, pp. 15-17.) But, of the Dharwar cotton it was remarked: "Well cleaned and good staple, frail, weak, and uneven, valued at 85 and 90 rupees per candy, and at 80 by the Bombay Chamber of Commerce." A part of the cotton was shipped in the 'John Moore,' and sold at Liverpool on the same day, for the same price. "This cotton, and that by the 'John Moore,' ranked in the Liverpool market as fully equal to American of the same price (*Return*, p. 526)." The cotton which was bought by Mr. Mercer from the ryots, and ginned by him, was shipped in the 'Lucinda,' and sold at Liverpool, in January and February, 1846, also for $3\frac{3}{4}$*d.* per pound. Mr. Mansfield, who was acting as Collector of the district when the account of these sales arrived, observed: "The price obtained for it, $3\frac{3}{4}$*d.* per pound, would have enabled a merchant in Bombay to have given one hundred (100) per candy; while the quoted price, in Bombay, of Coompta cotton, had not exceeded 75 rupees during the two previous years. Thus, there appeared a difference in favour of the New Orleans cotton of 25 rupees per candy,

* The author here quotes from 'Summary of Proceedings connected with the Government Cotton Experiments in the Southern Mahratta Country, under the Bombay Presidency, from 1830 to 1848.' Bombay, 1849.

which, after deducting the cost of cleaning, packing, and carriage, was nearly 50 per cent. increase in the value of the raw article." (*Summary*, p. 19.)

At the end of the year 1844, Mr. Shaw was obliged to proceed to the Cape of Good Hope, on account of his health. As his energy commenced, there is no doubt his countenance favoured, the extension of the culture of American cotton. The Dharwar experiment was, however, particularly fortunate in Mr. Goldsmid having been appointed to act as collector, and in Mr. Mansfield being the assistant collector, as both took the warmest interest in the success of the experimental culture. Those who are acquainted with the natives of India, know how much their notice and appreciation of a novelty in culture depends upon the countenance given to it by the civil authorities.

In the month of July, 1844, Mr. Mercer proposed to the Hon. the Governor of Bombay, that the Khooseghul farm should only be kept as a neez farm, and that Mr. Hawley should be deputed to another part of the district, to superintend the distribution of seed, &c. Mr. Shaw being in Bombay, in 1844, proposed the abolition of the farms, and Mr. Mercer, in January, 1845, in modification of his first suggestion, proposed to give up the two small farms at Khooseghul and at Gudduck, and to cultivate small patches of New Orleans cotton in different districts of the country, by contract with the ryots. The farms were accordingly abolished shortly afterwards. Mr. Goldsmid remarked, that a farm was not necessary in his district for securing a supply of seed for distribution among the ryots. This step having been gained, one of the great uses of a farm had been attained, and there is one objection to retaining it,—that the planter's attention is necessarily confined too much to one place, and cultivators are apt to ascribe "the superiority of a crop grown by Government to the expenses incurred being more than the returns would enable a person, cultivating for profit, to bear." In making this proposition, Mr. Mercer, moreover, stated that the tillage on the Government farms and the ryots' lands is nearly one and the same. It has already been observed, that, in many parts of Central, and in most parts of Western India, cotton is sown by itself in drills, and the ground is well ploughed and carefully weeded. The ridge system is not practised, and is probably not necessary in a comparatively dry climate and poor soil; but the natives consider a rotation of crops essential for cotton. Mr. Shaw says: "No ryot ever plants cotton two successive years in the same land." This does not seem to have been attended to in the Khooseghul farm. To this cause, and to the attacks of insects probably, we must ascribe the difference of return in the Khooseghul farm, which was the first established, in the two seasons in which it was under cultivation with cotton, and of which Mr. Mercer has given the two following tabular statements:

Khooseghul Farm—1843-44.

Description of Cotton.	Acres.	Seed cotton.	Clean cotton.	Average of clean cotton per acre.	
		lbs.	lbs.	lbs.	oz.
New Orleans	80	13,676	4371	54	10½
Broach	66	6889½	2117	32	0⅔
Coimbatore	16	3673½	875	54	11
Abyssinian	11	362	89	8	1½
Bourbon	10	10	—	—	
Sea Island	3	Had yielded nothing at the date of report.			

1844-45.

Description of cotton.	Acres.	Clean cotton.	Average per acre.
New Orleans	150	1725 lbs.	11½ lbs.
Broach	16	1010 „	63½ „
Bourbon	10	220 „	22 „
Abyssinian	11	118 „	10·727

Gudduck—1844-45.

New Orleans Country . .	146	13,821 „	94·664
Broach	22	2721 „	123·681

On the abolition of the farms in 1845, the contract system was established for one season,—that of 1845-46. The object of this "was to extend the cultivation of the New Orleans cotton; to familiarise the natives everywhere with it; and, by making them the instruments of its cultivation, before they were prepared to incur any risk in the experiment, to enable them to compare the quality and quantity of its produce with that of the native cotton grown in their own fields."

The season, however, was not so favorable. "The rains,"

Mr. Mercer wrote, "have been very partial almost everywhere. The consequence is, that of seed for 17,000 acres, only about 11,176 have been planted." In some of the Talooks, where it was planted rather early, and the rains were moderate, the crops were superior to the best of the previous year, besides coming in much earlier. "Last year we made nothing of the flowers of October and November, as they were all blighted by insects; but this year they have turned out well, and the cotton is very good indeed, and promises to yield a fair return." He expected 159 lbs. of seed cotton per acre, and to be able to make a profit on the entire outlay. "We pay the ryots 2 rupees per acre for cultivating, and the rent of the land 1 rupee. The further expense of the cotton conveyed to the gin-house would make it amount to 3½ rupees per acre for 159 lbs. of seed cotton, or for 53 lbs. of clean cotton, making the cost about 1 anna per lb.; but, if the value of the seed be deducted, which sold for 13½ lbs. per anna, it will not cost us much over a penny a pound to produce New Orleans cotton." The produce of the district, it was calculated, would amount to 1200 or 1500 bales.

As it was physically impossible for Messrs. Mercer and Hawley to superintend the buying of all this cotton from the ryots, grown by them in different parts of the district, "Mr. Mercer contracted with the native dealers to go round and purchase the cotton from the ryots; and, for their trouble, allowed them one anna per maund (of 26 pounds), which he deducted from the price sanctioned by Government to be paid for the cotton, namely, twelve (12) annas, but which, nevertheless, left to the ryots a very good price for their produce." (*Summary*, p. 77.)

"Mr. Mercer also made over to these traders most of the saw-gins with which to clean the cotton, giving them for the expense of cleaning, the same price as it would have cost Government had it been cleaned under Mr. Mercer's own superintendence; and the native dealers bought the cotton from the cultivators, and ginned it, paying all the expenses of the same, having the sole management of it; and except that they have not the ownership of the gins, and are dependent on Government to purchase the clean cotton, have the whole thing in their own hands." About 40,000 rupees' worth was thus obtained from the native dealers, at a cost of 66¼ rupees per candy of clean cotton. The seeds they sell again to the ryots.

Mr. Mercer wrote to the author on the 14th of September, 1846, that the crop of New Orleans cotton had nearly all been sown, and though the quantity could not be exactly ascertained, it was calculated that about 30,000 acres were in cultivation. "In the Dharwar Talooka the cultivation is double that of last year; but the greatest increase has taken place in the Eastern and Southern Talookas." Mr. Mercer further stated, that "we have not pressed, nor, indeed, encouraged more extended cultivation, as we have not sufficient means for cleaning the whole of the expected crop. Thirteen hand saw-gins were in use last year, twenty-nine will probably be ready this year; but these are not enough to gin a crop of 30,000 acres. Each will gin 300 lbs. of cotton-wool (rooi) from 900 lbs. of kupas, or cotton in the seed, at a cost of 1r. 4a. per day."

Mr. Mansfield, Acting Collector of Dharwar, on the 9th of May, 1846, in taking a review of the progress of the experimental culture observed that, "The New Orleans cotton having been cultivated to such an extent throughout the Dharwar collectorate its qualities were well understood by the ryots, and he gave it as his opinion, that there would be no further necessity for Government planting any more on its own account, especially as the ryots were perfectly willing to plant it to any extent, provided the sale of the produce was guaranteed to them by the Government;" and concluded by observing, "I think Government should purchase for one year longer, and encourage the growth of the cotton as much as possible, by guaranteeing the sale of the produce at fifty-five (55) rupees, as recommended by Mr. Mercer; and if at the expiration of next season the merchants at Bombay do not come forward and aid the Government in creating a demand, I really do not see any advantage to be obtained by Government in fostering the production of an article that has not a marketable value."*

* The author concluded one of his reports in reference to this period in the following words:—

"It would appear, therefore, that nothing but encouragement on the spot is required to give great and permanent extension to the culture of improved cotton in India, accompanied with improved communication with the coast. But the first point is

Having thus far succeeded in diffusing the culture of American cotton in the Dharwar district, Mr. Mercer was appointed in November, 1846, to the district of Broach, in succession to Dr. Burn, but a few months afterwards he took his departure for Europe previous to returning to America. Judging from the united testimony of the several civil officers who had been in charge of the Dharwar district, the Bombay Government "was

not easily effected, because the most suitable localities for culture are at a distance from the seats of Government, that is, the capitals of Calcutta, Madras, and Bombay, where European merchants are chiefly established. The cultivators are therefore in the hands of middlemen, who are more interested in getting cheap than in buying good cotton, as requiring less outlay and yielding equal profit; indeed, Col. Skinner long since stated, that it was no use growing good cotton, as the merchants would not give a better price for it.

"The whole object could be simply and easily effected if merchants interested in the improvement and extension of the cotton culture would themselves engage in the business of purchasing cotton from the ryots, either with or without advances, having it cleaned with the saw-gin, either their own or with those belonging to Government. The sale of the cotton seed for sowing or for food for cattle, and in improved culture even for manure, would pay for the expense of cleaning, and yield the cleaner a profit at the same time. If the same parties would export it to this country, a further profit would be derived, and security obtained for the cotton not being tampered with between the farm and the factory.

"That such measures would have considerable effect is very evident from answers to five questions which I last year sent to Mr. Mercer, then in charge of the cotton plantations in Dharwar, now superintendent of cotton plantations in Broach. These questions were sent to assist in the establishment of a cotton company which was at that time contemplated here.

"J. FORBES ROYLE, M.D."

EAST INDIA HOUSE, *February*, 1847.

FIVE QUESTIONS SENT TO AND ANSWERED BY MR. MERCER, IN APRIL, 1845.

Question 1.—At what price is cotton to be purchased at your nearest mart?

Answer.—Cotton may be bought at Hooble at 40 rupees per candy of 7 cwt. (or for 784 lbs.), which is not quite 1¼*d.* per lb.

Question 2.—At what price do you think cotton may be purchased from the cultivator, either with or without previous advances?

Answer.—Without advances it cannot be obtained from the ryots at much less than the market price, and difficult to obtain in large quantities. With advances it can be had at a reduction of 20 to 25 per cent., and any quantity to the extent of 6 or 7 lacs of rupees' worth.

Question 3.—What is the cost of cleaning cotton by the native process and by the American gins?

Answer.—The cost of cleaning by the foot-roller, the only method in use here, is, at the lowest, 6¼ rupees per candy. The cost for the same quantity by the of opinion, that great success must be held to have attended his endeavours, and that he deserved credit and encouragement for his zeal and perseverance, as well as for the judicious measures adopted by him in order to interest the natives of the districts in the experiments, to accustom them to the use of the saw-gin, and to induce them to cultivate foreign cotton instead of the indigenous plant."

Before pursuing to a later period the progress of the culture in this district, it is necessary to follow the cotton which had been produced, to the markets of Bombay and England in order that we may learn the opinions of merchants and spinners on its quality, and thus obtain correct notions of its value. The cottons cultivated by Mr. Mercer in the year 1843 have already been noticed. Some of that grown by the ryots in the same year was sent by Mr. Shaw, the Collector of Dharwar, to Bombay, and was submitted by the Government

saw-gin is now 4 to 4½ rupees; it will be less when the machines are better understood.

Question 4.—What are the expenses of the conveyance of cotton?

Answer.—The charges on a candy of 7 cwt. to Bombay are about—

	r.	a.
Carriage by bullocks or cart to the coast	10	,,
Duty at the coast (abolished if exported to England) .	3	,,
Cooly and boat-hire at the coast	1	,,
Pay to native clerk for shipping to Bombay	,,	8
Freight to Bombay	2	8
Cost of bagging and packing	3	8
	20	8
Or without the duty	17	8

Question 5.—What measures would you recommend a company to adopt for the purchase, cleaning, and conveyance of cotton to port of shipment?

Answer.—1st. The investment of a large amount of capital in saw-gins. 2d. The employment of proper persons for establishing them throughout the district, and for purchasing cotton direct from the ryots, by making liberal advances to them yearly after their crops are sown. European mechanics would be required to look after the working, repairing, &c. of the machines; and a set of sharp young men, who would not be too lazy to learn the native language, to look after the business of advances, &c.

With 5 or 6 lacs of rupees' capital a company might, with such a plan, monopolize nearly the whole cotton crop of the Southern Mahratta country, benefit the cultivators, and make immense profits. As to the method of conveying the cotton to the port of shipment, I know of none better than the one now practised, unless Government or companies make roads.

to the Chamber of Commerce. Of the three kinds sent, New Orleans and native cleaned by the saw-gin, and native cleaned by the Broach churka, the Chamber, on the 13th of June, 1844, gave it as their opinion, "The New Orleans cotton is considered a fine sample, but of short staple, apparently cut by the gin, and weak and uneven. It is valued at 115 to 120 rupees per candy. The sample of native cotton cleaned by the saw-gin is considered superior to the New Orleans in every respect, and to any native cotton yet produced in the Bombay market. That cleaned by the churka is also of excellent quality, well cleaned, and nearly equal to the ginned sample. It is valued at 10 to 15 rupees per candy above the best Broach cotton in the market, or 118 to 122 rupees per candy." (*Summary*, p. 69.) We shall see that on a subsequent occasion the merchants supported their opinions by giving as high and even higher prices for the native than they did for the American cotton, though their opinions were not supported by the spinners of Manchester.

The cotton grown by the ryots on the contract system in the season of 1844, and which amounted to 195 dokras (bags) weighing 20,438 lbs., was shipped in 59½ bales, per 'Lucinda' to Liverpool, and arrived there in December, 1845. It was sold in the beginning of the year 1846 for 3¾*d.*

The remainder of the cotton (135 bags) cultivated in the Government Farms in 1844-45, together with 507 bags of New Orleans cotton purchased from the ryots, and grown by them in the same season, arrived in Bombay in February and March, 1845. These were repacked at Bombay into 205 bales, amounting in all to 71,321 lbs. gross weight, and shipped in the 'Clarendon,' together with 31 bales and some half bales and bundles of cotton from Candeish and Rutnagherry, which will be afterwards noticed.

Of the above cotton, 153 bales purchased from the ryots were valued by Messrs. Cunningham and Hinshaw at 6*d.* per lb. 20 bales were sold on the 10th and 11th of December, 1846, for 6¼*d.* per lb., and 133 bales for 6*d.* per lb. on the 24th of that month. The 29 bales from the Government Farms were valued at 6¼*d.*, and 9 bales bought from the ryots at 6½*d.* per lb. These were sold in February for 6*d.* and 6¼*d.* per lb. All the cotton was pronounced pretty long and good in staple, but rather light and tender in comparison with American cotton. That from the Government Farms was distinguished as being rather longer and closer than that grown by the ryots. The results may be considered, on the whole, very satisfactory.

Cotton of the growth of 1845-46 has attracted much more attention than any other, in consequence of 500 bales of it having been sold in Bombay, and 1000 bales directly to spinners in Manchester.

"Mr. Mansfield, Acting Collector of Dharwar, on the 1st of December, 1846, recommended that the New Orleans cotton purchased by Government be sold at the Presidency, where he was of opinion that the result would be such as to preclude the necessity of Government purchasing any more cotton." (*Summary*, p. 26.) The natives of the district seemed also desirous that some of the cotton should be sold at Bombay, and the Government only hesitated, because they had been unable to make up the quantity of American and of good and clean native cotton, which the Court of Directors had required to be sent to this country for three years. On the 8th of June, 1846, the Hon. Mr. Willoughby, a Member of Council, recommended in a minute, that a letter be at once addressed to the Chamber of Commerce and the firms noted in the margin,* who do not belong to the Chamber, embodying the principal facts recorded in these proceedings, and calling their attention to the circumstance, that "unless a demand is created for the New Orleans cotton grown in the Southern Mahratta country, the experiment, now so promising, must fail, and with it the chance of this part of India being ever able to compete with America in the growth of its staple product." The communication, however, was not made until the 28th of January, 1847, when the cotton from Dharwar had arrived in Bombay.

The Chamber of Commerce, in their reply of the 9th of February, 1847, concurred generally in the opinions expressed by the Government, recommended that a large portion of the Dharwar cotton should be sold in Bombay, and the rest consigned to England. But they observed, that in the then

* Messrs. Forbes and Co., Messrs. Remington and Co., and Messrs. Leckie and Co.

state of the European agency in operation in this country, it would be considered out of the sphere of most, if not all, merchants in Bombay, "to occupy the field which Government has been doing," as respects the ryots, involving, as it would do, the maintenance of establishments in the interior. "For the present, therefore, the only support which English merchants could contemplate affording, must, the Chamber added, be limited to the purchase of the cotton when brought to the Presidency to market, and which they were prepared to do." (*Summary*, p. 87.) Messrs. Leckie and Co., in their reply, concurred in the desirableness of a portion of the above cotton being sold in Bombay, as should the result of such sale prove satisfactory, the attention of the whole mercantile community, both European and native, would be attracted to this cotton, and the best chance of providing a regular market for it be thereby afforded. They at the same time expressed their fears that it would not "be in the power of the English merchants of Bombay to take the place of Government, as direct purchasers from the ryots, owing to the difficulty of procuring trustworthy agents on the spot, and also to the circumstance of such operations being foreign to the usual scope of English mercantile business." (*Summary*, p. 87.)

The Government accordingly sanctioned the sale by auction of 500 bales of the saw-ginned cotton then awaiting despatch to Liverpool. They were accordingly sold, and the following statement was published of the sale:

No. of Bales.	Description of Cotton.	Names of Purchasers.	Rate per Surat candy r.	a.	p.
14	New Orleans, from Belgaum . .	Messrs. Bates and Co. . . .	120	0	0
12	Broach cotton, the produce of Belgaum	„ Lancaster and Co. . .	125	0	0
67	Khandesh cotton, the produce of Dhurrumgaum . . .	„ Peel, Cassels, and Co. .	107	0	0
58	Ditto ditto	„ Lancaster and Co. . .	124	0	0
42	Ditto, the produce of Julgaum .	Ditto	132	0	0
307	Dharwar (New Orleans) cotton, the produce of that Collectorate	„ Higginson and Cardwell	113	0	0
500		Average Rs.	120	2	8

At the date on which the above cotton was sold, the market price of the best cotton was:

	r.	a.	p.	
For Surat	100	0	0	per candy.
„ Compta	85	0	0	„
„ Oomrawuttee	87	0	3	„
Average Rs. . . .	90	10	8	

which left a very large margin, viz. 29r. 8a. per candy, or nearly 40 per cent. in favour of the experimental cotton."

Of the above cottons, the largest quantity was supplied from the Dharwar district, while that from Belgaum, which was also from New Orleans seed, sold for 7 rupees a candy more, but the quantity was small. A note from Mr. Mercer, which the author received with the notice of the sales, stated that the 1000 packages (307 bales) of the Dharwar cotton bought by Higginson, Cardwell, and Co. were judged of by the sample dockras which had been slightly damaged. When the whole were unpacked at the screws, the purchasers said they considered it better cotton than any of the other lots." The remarkable point of the sale is, that though 67 bales of the Candeish cotton sold for 6 rupees per candy less, yet 58 bales of the same cotton sold for 13 rupees more, than the Dharwar cotton; while the Julgaum indigenous cotton cleaned by Mr. Blount, fetched no less than 19 rupees per candy more than the American cotton. When these cottons, however, reached England, a very different value was placed upon them. The American cotton, as we have already seen at p. 108, in Mr. Peel's letter, "was sold at 6½*d*. per lb., giving us a handsome profit on the transaction;" while "the Candeish cotton was with difficulty sold in Liverpool at about 3½*d*. per lb." It is necessary in the purchase of cotton, as in other matters, to remember the adage, "*Nimium ne crede colori.*"

Messrs. Mercer and Blount having arrived in England on their way to America, were anxious to communicate with the spinners and manufacturers of Manchester, in order to learn their opinions respecting the experimental cotton, and also to communicate their own views respecting the mode in which the trade should in future be carried on, in order to secure both its stability and extension. In conformity to the wishes of both gentlemen, the author accompanied them to Manchester, and was present at a special meeting of the Commercial Association of that town, holden the 14th of July, 1847, and of which a full report was given in the Manchester papers of the week. Mr. Turner, President of the Association, after an interview with the Chairman and Deputy-Chairman of the Court of Directors of the East India Company, had, in order to ascertain for himself the difficulties and facilities of the undertaking, sent an unlimited order to Mr. Mercer then in India, to procure for him a quantity of the best cotton grown in India from American seed, and also a quantity of native-grown cotton prepared in the most approved manner. By a very singular coincidence, on the morning that Mr. Mercer arrived in Manchester, the cotton which he had purchased in Dharwar, and directed to be shipped at Bombay, was received at the warehouse of Mr. Turner; but by some mistake the bales of native cotton did not at that time come to hand. As we are unable to afford space for a detailed account, we adopt the following abstract of the proceedings from the '*Manchester Guardian*,' of the 17th of July, 1847:

"A perusal of the report of the proceedings will show, that it requires only judicious enconragement from the merchants of this country, to place the trade in cotton between India and England on a footing as extensive, and, as regards quality, as acceptable, as that which is now carried on with the United States of America.

"Mr. Mercer states that, hitherto, no adequate encouragement has been held out for the exportation of a better class of cotton; and hence, nearly all the best produce of the indigenous plant of the country is consumed by the natives, who, being on the spot, have the choice of what is offered for sale, and are willing to give a rather higher price than the dealers who purchase for export, and who are most anxious to obtain the article at a low price. The natives use cotton to an extent of which no accurate estimate has yet been formed, and it only requires better prices to be given on the spot where it is grown, by the British merchant or his agent, to enable him to command almost unlimited supplies of the better article. In an experimental parcel, ordered by Mr. Turner, the cost at Dharwar was 10 annas per maund, while the ordinary class of cotton shipped to England from India was then selling at 8 annas; the difference (2 annas, or about ⅛*d.* per lb.) having enabled Mr. Turner to command cotton worth 1*d.* to 1¼*d.* per lb. more than the great mass of that which was purchased by the dealers for exportation.

"Mr. Mercer is of opinion, that it is indispensable to the success of this trade, that local buying agents, of known character, and with sufficient means, should be established, say at Dharwar, Candeish, and Guzerat; that they should be at liberty to conduct their negociations with the native cultivators with as much freedom as possible; and that they must have a knowledge of the language, and be in a position to command the confidence of those with whom they have dealings.

"The result of Mr. Turner's experiment is most valuable. The cotton purchased for him by Mr. Mercer cost him, delivered in Liverpool last week, exactly 3⅝*d.*

per lb.; and it was valued at 6*d.* to 6¼*d.* per lb. at the meeting of the association on Wednesday. In this transaction, Mr. Mercer charged no buying commission, which is the only additional charge necessary to be calculated upon in future transactions. Independent of this extraordinary difference between cost and value, we would direct attention to the results obtained on the carding and spinning of the cotton, as compared with a given weight of similar quality of American Orleans cotton; the result being a saving of about 2 per cent. in its ultimate production of yarn, in favour of the Indian cotton from Orleans seed."

ORDINARY ORLEANS, WORTH 6⅜D. IN LIVERPOOL.

Cotton, 50 lb.	lb.	oz.		lb.	oz.
When willowed	47	8	loss	2	8
When blown and lapped . . .	45	6	„	2	2
When carded and spun	41	4	„	4	2

50 lbs. of cotton produced 41 lbs. 4 oz. of yarn.—Loss 17½ per cent.

INDIA, ORLEANS SEED.

Cotton, 50 lb.	lb.	oz.		lb.	oz.
When willowed	48	12	loss	1	4
When blown and lapped . . .	47	1	„	1	11
When carded and spun . . .	42	8	„	4	9

50 lb. of cotton produced 42 lbs. 8 oz. of yarn.—Loss 15 per cent.

A more decided proof was, however, required of the value of this cotton, and of the capability of India for supplying it in large quantities, and this was afforded by the arrival of the remaining 1000 bales of the growth of the Dharwar district in the seasons 1845-46. This was shipped in the 'Quentin Leitch' from Bombay on the 7th of April, 1847; arrived at Liverpool on the 26th of August. The Commercial Association of Manchester having, in consequence of the little attention that previous consignments had attracted, represented to the Court of Directors that it would be much better if some of the experimental cotton was sent directly to Manchester, in order that the observations of the trade might be expressed upon it and distinctly known, the Court immediately ordered that one half of the cotton which had arrived should be sent to Manchester, and the other half sold at Liverpool. Subsequently the whole was ordered to be sent to Manchester, a course which has been followed with all the subsequent arrivals of cotton, much to the benefit of the experimental culture, from the zeal with which the business has been managed by the Commercial Association and their Secretary, combined with the publicity given to their proceedings by the Manchester press.

The sensation produced in Manchester, on the arrival of this cotton, has been already referred to at pp. 103-4 and 113-14. We have now only to give the prices at which it was sold. The first 314 bales were sold in the beginning of September for 6½*d.*, the next 30 on the 17th for 6¼*d.*, and 127 more on the 30th for 5⅝*d.*, and the remainder a month later for 4¾*d.* But during all this time there was a rapid fall in the price of American cotton, so that the next 500 bales sold only for 4¼*d.* and 4½*d.* per lb. Mr. Fleming, in his letter dated 2d December, 1847, reporting the sales, observes, "The prices obtained for the last lots sold are 2*d.* per lb. below those of September. It is, nevertheless, the full market value, good New Orleans cotton having reached the same level. I have sold this week about 200 bales of those last sent to me at 4½d."

Though the sales are the best criteria of value, we may append two reports on the nature of the cotton out of the numbers which have been sent to the India House.

LIVERPOOL; *3d March,* 1848.

DEAR SIR,—On the subject of the Dharwar cotton, to which you have called our attention, we have to remark, that ever since we disposed of the parcel imported last year, which you were pleased to put under our care for sale, we have had repeated inquiries from the parties who were purchasers at that time, if we had any more of it on hand, and latterly the parties have betrayed an increased anxiety to know if any was coming forward; indeed, we have no hesitation in saying, that we should have no difficulty in disposing of it, and at a full and fair competing price with what is now obtained for the middling class of Upland cotton, usually termed Bowed, and grown in the Atlantic States, the value of which to day is 4⅝*d.* per lb., and which is generally used for wefts, for which the Dharwar cotton is more especially adapted. Many of our spinners have been unwilling to adopt this cotton, not from the fear of it not answering, but because it has not yet come forward in that quantity so as to ensure them a constant supply of it.

Yours very truly,

(Signed) WM. CLARE & SONS.

JOHN PEEL, Esq., *Manchester.*

STALYBRIDGE; *25th April,* 1848.

We, the undersigned, having bought and used about one hundred and fifty bales of the East India cotton, grown from American seed, and imported by the Honorable East India Company last year, have much pleasure in stating, that we consider the cotton superior in every respect to the ordinary Surat cotton grown in the same country from the native seed. Its cleanliness, alone, will always recommend it in preference to Surat cotton, inasmuch as the dirty state in which the latter is imported causes great uncertainty in the loss in working, and spinners always prefer working a cotton of which they can calculate the loss in the operation of working, to a cotton in which there is so much uncertainty. The staple is also superior to the common Surat, both in length and fineness, and these are the two main characteristics of good cotton; but in both these respects we feel bound to say, that the new cotton does not, yet, equal the cotton of American growth. For some purposes, the colour of the new cotton would be objectionable; but for others, the rich brown colour is a great recommendation, so that in this respect the grower need not trouble himself. We have no hesitation in saying, that cotton of the same quality as that imported last year by the Company, will always enter largely into competition with American cotton, and will mostly command a price equal to *ordinary* American of the Liverpool *classification*.

For JAMES HALL & SON'S Trustees,

JOHN BATES.

HUGH FLEMING, Esq., *Manchester*.

Having thus followed up this important experiment to so successful a stage, we may pursue its history up to the present time, more briefly, though it will be of little use doing so without entering into some of the details.

The American planters having returned for a time at least, to their own country, the Dharwar district was left, during the year 1847, without their superintendence. But during their absence, Mr. Channing was deputed from Belgaum to Dharwar. Mr. Shaw, having at this time returned from the Cape of Good Hope, did not approve of the Government purchasing cotton from the ryots, especially in consequence of "everything being done by, and being in the hands of Government agents." But the system had been changed by degrees, and apparently with consideration and judgment. The farms of 1843-44 and of 1844-45 had been changed for the contract system for one year, 1845-46. Cultivation by the ryots largely increased. In 1846-47, the contract system was not renewed, and the largely increased cultivation (22,329 acres) was wholly in the hands of the ryots; but Government was virtually pledged to purchase the crop." (*Summary*, p. 27.) "In the first instance, parties were engaged to go round to the ryots, and purchase their cotton from them at the rate of 10 annas per maund of 28 lbs., when the indigenous cotton was selling for 8 annas per maund. This, although done to protect the interest of the cultivators, was the cause of much imposition and unfair dealing towards them. In 1847-48, the whole crop was purchased without interference by native dealers (Government did not purchase until the crop was cleaned, and then from the dealers); but, as there were but few gins owned by the local dealers, and none working on government account, there was no check on the gin-owners, and the ryots were as much or more imposed on than in the previous season. The ostensible price paid, 11 annas per maund, was fair; but there was a general complaint on the part of the ryots, of false weight and other impositions. This season I have heard no complaint of the kind, and it is to be hoped the unfair dealing above referred to has ceased." (*Blount, in reply to Queries.*)

The season of 1847-48 was very unfavorable to the growth of cotton, both American and native. Mr. Shaw, who was again obliged to leave India, and reached England in March, stated, in his evidence (3d April, 1848) before the Cotton Committee, that 60,000 acres had been prepared by the ryots, and would have been sown with New Orleans cotton, if the rains had not totally failed in the Dharwar district, up even to the month of October. This affected both the native and the New Orleans cotton. Mr. Shaw particularly mentioned, that, in the western parts of the Collectorate of Dharwar, or those nearest the Ghauts and the coast, they get the early rains of the south-west monsoon, so that sowing takes place in August, and might be earlier; but, in the easterly parts of the district, they feel the effects of the north-east monsoon, and are able to sow as late as December. In consequence, therefore, of the failure of the early rains, no increase in cultivation took place; but Mr. Shaw thought, that about 25,000 acres of land were cultivated with New Orleans cotton. The cotton of this season was shipped in the 'Brahmin,' which sailed from Bombay on the 19th of March, 1849. The 227 bales were sold on the 6th of September, for 5*d.* per lb., and 26 bales, marked $\frac{DC}{2}$, for $4\frac{3}{4}d.$; the remainder of the crop, consisting of 20 half-bales, shipped in the 'George Buchan,' was sold at Manchester, on the 10th of April, for $4\frac{5}{8}d.$ per lb.

Mr. Blount, having returned from his short visit, proceeded immediately to India, and reached Dharwar in the beginning of the year 1849, but not early enough to get clean-picked native cotton. He immediately applied himself, in conjunction with the able assistance of Mr. Frost the engineer, who had been again sent out to India by the Court of Directors, to have the saw-gins put in order, which, from "fair wear and tear, the imperfect original construction of some of the gins, and from ill-usage, had become unserviceable." Of the seventeen which Mr. Frost was able to remake in time for cleaning the crop, fifteen were sold to native dealers. He at this time commenced constructing small gins of six saws, which will be afterwards mentioned. Mr. Blount describes the results of the season, 1848-49, in the following extracts from a letter, addressed to the author, from Dharwar, 17th Dec., 1848:

"When I was in England, from what had been said and written about Dharwar American cotton, I was under the impression that the cultivation of that plant was progressively on the increase, and that it was so highly appreciated by the ryots, that no fears were to be entertained of a diminution of its culture. These views, I think, were entertained by others, as well as by myself. As a means of testing how far these views were correct, the influence or interference heretofore brought to bear in inducing the ryot to plant was discontinued, and the cultivation left with the ryot, to plant or not, as he thought proper, and to confine our operations to the furnishing of gins for cleaning, and the purchase from the local dealers of the cotton required for shipment to England on Government account; and as there were several native competitors for this cotton, the competition for it, it was thought, would be a sufficient stimulant to ensure its increased production. It now appears, however, that we have taken away the props rather prematurely; and I expect it will be necessary again to resort to a system of contracts, which, however, should be avoided, if possible, as it leads the people to expect too much of Government, or rather to think, that nothing can be done without direct interference. It certainly does not look well on paper to say, I have only 3400 acres to show against 23,000 last year. It is a much larger falling off than I expected; yet I am not discouraged by it.

"This year, no interference, more than persuasion, has been used: the few who have planted the New Orleans have done so from their own conviction of its superiority. We have had a beautiful monsoon; the crop is now looking fine, and I hope will turn out as well as it promises. Many of those who had left planting, express their wish that they had done so again, instead of planting native. I expect the cultivation of it next year will be as great or greater than it has ever been. Two or three successive good crops will ensure the permanency of New Orleans cotton in this district. There are several circumstances operating in our favour: one of the most material is, that, consequent on the decline in the price of cotton abroad, the local dealers can no longer pay a high price for dirty native cotton, having suffered severely from their last year's purchases. The consequence is, that they will not advance the ryot money on native cotton, but do so willingly for American. Should this state of affairs continue, it must force the growth of New Orleans cotton. Most of the crop of last year will reach the Bombay market through the legitimate channels of trade. Only about 160 candies have been bought on Government account, and I am sorry to say it is not good. The pods last year were very faulty (prematurely ripe from drought), and the cotton stained from heavy rains while in the fields."

Inquiry having been made by the Bombay Government into the causes of the falling off of the crop of New Orleans cotton; partly in consequence of its having been described as "a delicate, uncertain, capricious-bearing plant;" and partly because the ryots complained of too much interference having been exercised in inducing them to cultivate this cotton, it is desirable to notice the correspondence, as an instance of the kind of difficulties which are to be encountered in a country like India. The failure of the crop of 1847-48, from the deficiency of rain, seems to have been the main cause of the falling off of 1848-49. The New Orleans cotton is generally sown earlier than the native, and, if the rains are late in coming on, as was the case in 1847, the sowing will not take place, but something else be substituted for it. Mr. Bell, who had been appointed Collector of the district, and to whom the subject had been referred for investigation, reported, that "the general opinion was, that the crop had failed during the season of 1847 only from the want of rain." It was, in fact, the climate which was capricious, and not the plant. With regard to the annoyance alleged to have been experienced by the ryots, Mr. Bell observed:

"In all extensive operations connected with efforts to improve the products of this country, in which it is necessary to employ the district and village authorities, there is great danger to be apprehended from injudicious zeal; and this, I fear, has been exercised in some districts, to the annoyance of the cultivators of the New Orleans cotton. In the early stage of the experiment, it was doubtless necessary to instruct the ryots in the process of cultivation of this new product; but this necessity no longer exists. It has been found, by the experience of several years, that the climate and soil are adapted to the growth of the cotton in question; the ryots fully understand the mode of cultivating it, and its superior quality and value cannot, I should think, in the ordinary course of things, fail to result in its becoming a staple product of the province. There seems no necessity for Government to endeavour to extend the cultivating it by measures which must be attended with some degree of vexation to the people; and therefore I would urgently recommend, that, for the present, all interference be withdrawn, and the proceedings of the Cotton Experiment Department be, for the most part, restricted to the supply and repair of saw-gins, without which the New Orleans cotton cannot be separated from its seed."

"Mr. Bell was informed in reply, that the Government (that of Bombay) considered his remarks and suggestions, relative to the extent to which it should interfere in furthering the cultivation of New Orleans cotton, to be judicious; but it was, at the same time observed, that care must be taken that the officers of Government did not interpret the 'withdrawing of interference' into a change in the views of their superiors as to the desirableness of encouraging and extending the cultivation of the New Orleans variety, and that such an impression could not be too carefully guarded against after a year of failure." (*Summary*, p. 101.)

The crop of 1848, Mr. Blount wrote, 15th August, 1849, was a fine one, averaging, it is supposed, about 280 lbs. of kupas per acre. It produced, in every instance, equally as much per acre as the native, and in some instances much better. The price paid for it to the grower is 10 and 11 annas for 28 lbs. of kupas, from 3 to 4 annas above the price paid for the native cotton,—a difference in value which must, in the end, upset all prejudice.

In a subsequent letter, dated 15th August, 1849: "The cotton not yet being weighed, I cannot inform you of the exact quantity to be forwarded. The New Orleans will be about 300 candies, or 600 bales, and its cost, laid down in Liverpool, will not exceed $3\frac{1}{2}d.$ per lb., and the native cotton, $3\frac{1}{4}d.$ per lb." On the 8th of February, 1850, Mr. Blount wrote, that the exact quantity was 330 candies, which will cost, put down in Liverpool, about $3\frac{78}{100}d.$ per lb.; and native cotton, 60 candies, which will cost $3\frac{1}{2}d.$ per lb. The cotton is superior in quality to the previous crop.

This cotton has unfortunately not yet arrived in this country. No less than 1504 bales of cotton were shipped in the 'India,' which sailed from Bombay in the month of April, 1850; but a mutiny having occurred on board the ship, she was obliged to put into the Cape of Good Hope, and was consequently delayed.

The favorable season of 1848, having produced a good crop, had also produced a change in the opinions of the cultivators. Mr. Blount wrote to the author on the 15th of August, 1849: "Our planting season has only just commenced, and the cotton will all be sown, if we have favorable weather, by the end of the month. The feeling of the cultivators appears now to be as much in favour as it was against this cotton twelve months ago. In every part that I have heard from, the planting will greatly exceed the previous year." "There will be over 12,000 acres planted, and we have not seed to plant much in excess of that quantity. In this district, all interference with the ryot in planting has ceased, except in making it convenient for him to get his supply of seed at a liberal price, and in buying a portion of the cotton, not at a forced price, but at a fair market value. Both of these measures should continue for one or two years longer, but afterwards be gently dropt, and the production and the market left to their natural channels. The construction of the gins, it may, however, be necessary to continue a while longer, until native mechanics will undertake it." "Competition is what is most needed; for, strange to say, the natives yet scarcely believe that Bombay affords a regular market for this cotton."

On the 27th of October, Mr. Blount writes: "I have now definite information that the number of acres planted this year is, in round numbers, 15,400, against 3400 in 1848. We have had a copious monsoon, and the expectation is, that there will be another good productive season. Should such be the event, I have no doubt the crop will double itself another year."

The season continued favorable throughout, and an average produce was secured of nine maunds, or 252 lbs., per acre of kupas or seed cotton, and the whole produce of the district was estimated at between 1400 and 1500 Bombay candies, or from 2800 to 3000 bales. Of these, about one half was to be forwarded, about the beginning of this year, to this country, on account of the Government, with about 250 candies or 500 bales of native cotton.

Mr. Bell, the Collector of Dharwar, writes to Government, on the 11th of January, 1850: "In other districts, however, where the American plant has succeeded excellently for two seasons, the plant is in high favour, and I have little doubt that the cultivation of it will increase considerably, and that eventually the American cotton will displace the indigenous plant; but it must never be forgotten, that the cotton crop is not sufficiently remunerative to the cultivator, to supersede the cultivation of other crops, indispensable for food for man and beast, to an extent which will sensibly contribute to supply the home market.

"The great—indeed, the one—desideratum, now, in order to secure such success as is attainable, is co-operation with the efforts of Government on the part of the Bombay merchants. The traders of the country have not capital to embark largely in the purchase of cotton for the Bombay and home markets, and few are able to aid in the encouragement of the cultivation of the American cotton, by agreeing beforehand to purchase it. This the Bombay merchants alone can do; and, so long as they stand aloof, and are deterred by imaginary difficulties of communication or of transport to the coast, and of obtaining efficient agency, the progress made under the influence of the Experimental Department must be comparatively slow and uncertain."

According to private letters, received by the late mails, it would appear, that the monsoon of 1850 had not, up to the middle of August, been so favorable for cotton as that of last year, as there had been a scarcity of rain in some parts of the Dharwar district. The planting, however, was reported to be going on extensively, and a very large increase was expected in the cultivation of cotton there, probably not less than 30,000 acres of New Orleans Cotton.

The *Manchester Guardian* of the 9th of October, 1850, says, under the head—

"COTTON CULTURE IN INDIA.—By the last overland mail we have files of newspapers to the latest dates, and we see, with some surprise, that of late there have been many absurd articles in the Indian journals, condemnatory of the efforts to introduce a more extended cultivation of the New Orleans variety of cotton in India, and asserting it to have been, in all instances, a partial, if not even a complete and utter failure. These articles, which have doubtless been inserted with a view to be copied into English journals at home, are calculated, if believed, to produce a very erroneous impression here, as to the real result of the experiments hitherto made, in various parts of India, with the culture of cotton from the New Orleans seed. Private letters from India, which we have seen, so far from confirming these unfounded statements, give a very satisfactory and encouraging account of the progress made in the introduction of the American, and especially of the Orleans cotton, into Indian cultivation. One gentleman, well acquainted with the Dharwar district, writes by this mail:

'No district in India is perhaps *everywhere* suitable for the production of New Orleans cotton; but there are localities where it grows equally as well as the indigenous plant. In this part of India (the South Mahratta country) there are large tracts of country, in which it is found to answer. In Dharwar, a large portion of the district is favorable to its production; and, of the average quantity of land planted with cotton in the district (241,000 acres), I venture to predict, that, in a few years, one half will be devoted to the growth of New Orleans cotton.

'What we stand most in need of is, a few European agents, resident in the district, engaged in cotton purchases. The trade is altogether at present in the hands of the natives, and there is an entire want of emulation amongst them, in supplying a good article, rather than a bad one. The Manchester people should insist on having clean cotton; for no steps that government can take will remedy the evil, so long as Bombay affords a market for dirty cotton. Instead of complaints, let the spinners and merchants put their shoulders to the wheel, and make the native dealers feel as well as see their interest, in having cotton free of trash and dirt. In this way the ryots will soon be induced to pay more attention to gathering and cleaning it.'"

The editor of the *Guardian* upon this observes:

"This suggestion for creating a local demand for good clean cotton is not now made for the first time. Indeed, residents in India are pretty well agreed, that it is the one great desideratum towards a steadily increasing supply of cotton of good quality from our eastern possessions. But, as we have more than once had occasion to show, the spinners here have been, and are still 'putting their shoulders to the wheel.' We have adverted on several occasions to the satisfactory results which have attended the experiments in growing and cleaning cotton by Mr. David Lees, who has been honorably called 'The Indian commissioner of the Manchester Commercial Association.' We have also, from time to time, noticed the orders which have been sent out to Bombay, from Manchester spinners and manufacturers. We know that the President of the Association just named, Mr. James Aspinall Turner, has not only sent out orders for the kupas, or seed cotton, to be bought in the district by an agent, who, after getting it saw-ginned, is to send it down to Bombay in a clean state, ready for shipment, but that Mr. Turner has also personally urged upon a number of spinners here the propriety of sending out similar orders. He has gone further, and has afforded these gentlemen the means of getting such orders executed in India, in the same way as his own. Several spinners have agreed to avail themselves of his offers; some have ordered twenty bales, some fifty, some a hundred bales: in several cases without any limit as to price, in others with a fair limit. Of course, the object of these gentlemen is not to enter into a regular cotton-buying transaction, but rather to create that which is so much needed in India,—a demand, at fair prices, for the improved cotton, especially for that grown from New Orleans seed, and carefully cleaned,—a demand, not so much at the port of shipment, as in the districts where the cotton is grown. In this way, the demand will act directly as a powerful stimulus to the native grower; and it is but a reasonable anticipation to say, that the result must tend largely to improve the quality, and to increase the quantity, of the best varieties of cotton, the production of British India." (*Guardian*, Oct. 9, 1850.)

But, on the 23d of October, the same paper has the following article, showing the great demand which had at last taken place in the district itself for the American cotton:

"NATIVE DEMAND IN INDIA FOR NEW ORLEANS COTTON, FOR SEED.—We have already noticed the fact, that Mr. James Aspinall Turner, the President of the Manchester Commercial Association, and several other cotton manufacturers of Manchester and the neighbourhood, had sent out orders to India, to purchase cotton grown there from New Orleans seed, of course with no view to immediate profit, but solely from a desire, by causing a demand for it in the interior of the country, to encourage the native growers to extend the cultivation of this desirable variety of cotton. By the overland mail, however, Mr. Turner has received a letter, informing him that, in all probability, neither his commission, nor any of the others sent out with the same object, will be executed; and that for a reason which is considerably more satisfactory and gratifying, than even the due fulfilment of the orders. It seems, that the native dealers have been very eagerly competing with the Government in the purchase of the New Orleans seed cotton; and that, in the interior of the district of Dharwar, they are giving very high prices for it,—as much as 100 rupees the candy. In consequence of this large and growing demand, it is believed that all that has been grown this season has been cleared off. This is an exceedingly favorable feature in the cotton culture of India; showing, as it does, that, without the interference of Government, or the exertions of persons in this country, going out of the regular course of their business,—a practice which could not be expected to continue long,—a demand is rapidly springing up, indeed, has already arisen, in a natural and ordinary way, and which is therefore likely to be lasting, and which must cause a very considerable extension in the cultivation of that description of cotton, which is most needed to supply the wants of our manufacturers at home."

Culture. Having detailed the progress of the experiments, we may notice some particulars of the culture adopted, and which we can do with considerable precision from Mr. Blount's replies to fifty-one queries, circulated at the desire of the Hon. Mr. Willoughby. To these we have occasionally added Mr. Channing's replies to the same inquiries from Belgaum. Rotation is observed both with the grain and cotton crops. Mr. Channing states, that mixed soil, or the black well impregnated with sand, is best suited to New Orleans cotton. The seeds are rubbed up in cow-dung (and red earth, sometimes with ashes, C.) to prevent their sticking together, and to allow them to drop freely through the drill; "This is formed of a hollow bamboo with a funnel at top. It is attached by a rope so as to move a little in the rear of the plough, one person feeds the drill, and one draws the plough." Sowing takes place in August (Aug. to October, C.); but Mr. Blount thinks it would be advantageous to do so earlier, though it is hopeless to get the ryots to sow cotton until they have got their grain crops in the ground. Mr. Blount is of opinion, that the New Orleans requires somewhat more moisture; yet, in a good or a bad year, they both flourished, or both failed. Mr. Channing says, the New Orleans does not require more moisture than the native, but requires it at a different time; that is, when about a month old. But both planters are in districts under the influence of the two monsoons.

The picking of cotton commences in February (picking of early sown New Orleans from end of December, C.), and is usually completed in the month of April, when heavy storms occur and cause great damage. The methods of culture adopted are exactly the same for American and for native cotton. New Orleans looks healthier, and yields a better return if planted on the western side of a field of *Juwaree*, and is thus well sheltered from east winds.

Topping or pruning, though by stopping upward growth it strengthens and increases the productiveness of the plants, is not practised, nor, indeed, does it seem necessary in the soil and climate. Mr. Blount considers it preferable to allow the plants plenty of room, and to pull some up where they are too thick, in order to enable them to throw out lateral branches. Manuring is never employed for cotton, though it is both for the Juwaree and Bajree crops *Sorghum vulgare* and *Panicum italicum*. It is probable that the effect of a little would be beneficial. Mr. Channing says, the best crops are produced on fields which had produced wheat the previous year, and for which the fields had been manured. Manure applied direct makes the plants grow rank and to wither. Neither is irrigation employed, though it would, no doubt, be useful if water (from the tanks) was abundant, and not required for the rice or sugar-cane crops (B). Mr. Channing suggests the damming up of different parts of the rivers Gulpurba, Malpurba, so also of the Krishna and other streams. Having tried irrigation on a small scale, the crop of cotton was increased both in quality and quantity, but it was too expensive when the water had to be raised out of wells.

The plants of New Orleans Cotton, in good lands, are from three to four feet in height, but sometimes not more than six inches. Mr. Channing had planted New Orleans, Georgian, and Sea Island cottons in 1846, which had grown to nine feet; that of the first year was invariably destroyed by small red insects, with a peculiar strong smell, and the plants were attacked by *muddia*, or honey blight.

The other portion of the plants was regularly pruned and cropped to within two feet of the ground in June each year. They threw out good sound lateral branches, and yielded a good crop of cotton in November, December, and January.

Expense and Returns.—The expense of cultivating either American or native cotton is the same; the only difference is in the cost of seed and picking. The American seed is cheaper, because less esteemed by natives for feeding their cattle; the native seed being two annas, the former is sold for one and a half annas per maund of 28 lbs., but its picking costs a little more.

	American.			Native.		
	r.	a.	p.	r.	a.	p.
Land rent, per acre, say average . .	1	0	0	1	0	0
Ploughing, weeding, ploughing between plants .	2	0	0	2	0	0
Gathering the kupas	0	8	0	0	6	0
Seed for planting	0	1	0	0	1	4
	3	9	0	3	7	4

Mr. Channing gives the expense of culture in Belgaum at 1r. 8a. per acre. The land rent there varies from 3r. to 1r.; but, as the revenue survey had commenced, it was expected that no dry land would be above 1r. 12a. per acre.

Mr. Blount calculates the average returns per acre of each kind of cotton to be about 8 maunds of 28 lbs., or 224 lbs. Mr. Channing says 7 maunds and even 13 maunds of New Orleans, and 4 to 5, sometimes 10, maunds of indigenous; but he adds, he had never found two people agree, nor seen two fields alike. Mr. Blount mentions, that the maximum obtained by some ryots of Bunkapore was stated to be 16 maunds of American, and 12 maunds of native cotton. The produce of an acre (8 maunds) of native cotton, when at the lowest price, or 7r., amounts to 3r. 8a., if clean picked, to 4r.; while American cotton was worth 5r. 8a. The seed of the native cotton sells for one fourth of the price of the wool. Mr. Shaw observes on Mr. Blount's account of the returns, that he apprehended that the produce of New Orleans cotton was greater upon all occasions than the native cotton in the Dharwar district, and in about the some degree as that given by Mr. Blount as the relative maximum proportion, and that its yield, again, in clean wool, was also larger than that of native cotton.

With regard to the proportion of wool to seed, Mr. Blount states, that "it is estimated that 2352 lbs. of New Orleans seed-cotton will make one candy of 784 lbs., or 33$\frac{1}{3}$ per cent. wool; while 3136 lbs. of native cotton will give one candy of 784 lbs., or 25 per cent. wool. Mr. Channing says, that, out of 100 lbs. of New Orleans seed cotton, 33 of wool and 67 of seed may be obtained; but more commonly, 30 of wool and 70 of seed. 60 maunds of seed sold at 12 maunds for the rupee = 5 rupees, will more than cover the expenses of cleaning. The native cotton gives 84 maunds of seed, which, at 8 maunds for the rupee, brings 10r. 8a.

In connection with these statements respecting expenses and returns by Messrs. Blount and Channing, it is desirable to notice those originally made by Mr. Shaw as well as by Mr. Mercer.

Mr. Shaw, shortly after his first experiments, made the following calculations: "An acre, therefore, of the New Orleans cultivation, being 364 lbs. of seeded cotton, would, at 26 lbs.

per maund, give 14 maunds, which, at 13 annas per maund, would realize 11r. 6a. per acre, and, deducting the expense of 4r. 4a. 6p. as the price of cultivation, would leave a profit of 7r. 1a. 6p. per acre to the cultivator.

"The native cotton, on the same calculation, would give per acre 234 lbs. of seeded cotton, which, at 26 lbs. per maund, would be 9 maunds, which, at 10a. per maund, would yield a profit on the acre of 1r. 14a. 4p."

Mr. Mercer, in a memorandum, dated the 9th of July, 1844, stated: "The smallest average of the New Orleans, planted by ryots last year, was 48¾ lbs. of *rooee,* or clean cotton.

"The largest amount ever obtained from native cotton has been 30 lbs.; that is, in the southern Mahratta country. The average of New Orleans this year may be fairly expected to be much larger, not less than 60 lbs.; for the fields planted last year were not hardly an average of the cotton lands; and, for the want of sufficient seed, the stand of plants in the ground was in most cases very defective. The amount of seed supplied last year, per acre, was 8 lbs.; this year there has been 10 lbs." (Mr. Mercer must surely mean 50 lbs. of native cotton.)

The value of 50 lbs. of New Orleans cotton, at 3r. per maund of 26 lbs., is 5r. 12a. 3p. The expense of cultivation, 3r., consisting of 1r. for land rent; planting and preparing to plant, 4a.; planting, 4a; thinning and weeding first time—once ploughing and twice working with coontee, 12a.; gathering, 7a.; total, land rent 1r., cultivation 2r., leaving 2r. 12a. 3p. as profit to the ryot. "This is, taking an average per acre, within a quarter of a pound of the lowest produce last year, under all disadvantages."

The yield of native cotton he stated, at the same time, to be only 150 lbs. of seeded cotton, or 37 lbs. of clean cotton per acre, which was then worth 2r. 9a. 5p., at 35r. per candy of 784 lbs.—rent and expense of cultivation 2r. 0a. 5p., leaving 1r. 0a. 5p. profit.

The returns in Mr. Shaw's statement are greater; but so also are the expenses, and therefore it is a question for future inquirers, whether higher farming would not give better returns; indeed, Mr. Shaw stated, in a letter, dated 23d December, 1844, that "it was calculated from the yield of a piece of ground cultivated with New Orleans cotton, cultivated in the

Collector's garden, that the best spots in the district will produce 2600 lbs. of seeded cotton per acre."

The value of the New Orleans cotton has been sufficiently demonstrated by the sales, but we may give some additional opinions. Messrs. King, of Bombay, in a letter dated 18th of September, 1847, in addition to the report of Mr. Turner and of Mr. North, give the report of another of their friends, who compared the Dharwar cotton valued in July 1847 at $6\frac{1}{4}d$, with some New Orleans which had cost $7\frac{5}{10}d.$, a difference in value of 17 per cent., whilst the yarn spun from it was not more than 5 per cent. better. The Messrs. King remark: "We consider the foregoing report very satisfactory: it shows that in staple, in colour, and in cleanness, the Dharwar cotton from New Orleans seed must have been good, or otherwise our correspondent would have remarked on the defect."

"It also shows, that saw-ginned cotton grown in this country from New Orleans seed may be used with advantage in England, in the place of American cotton, whereas the common cotton of this country cannot be used as a substitute for American."

"We may remark, that the Dharwar cotton was valued in Liverpool at $6\frac{1}{4}d.$ per lb., when the very finest Bombay cotton was only worth $5\frac{3}{4}d.$ per lb.; and the average run of the qualities shipped from here $4\frac{1}{2}d.$ to $4\frac{7}{8}d.$ per lb."

Mr. Turner writes to Messrs. King, in a letter dated the 5th of April, that "It would even be a national misfortune, if the authorities at the India House in London, or in India itself, should take any steps which might tend to discourage the growth in India of the American seed cotton."

The price of the cotton, we may observe, has gradually increased, though this of course is in a great measure dependent on the fluctuations of the English market, but something may also be safely ascribed to the improvement in quality and character of the produce. Mr. Mercer gave forty rupees per candy of 784 lbs., as the price of the indigenous cotton. By paying two annas more for a maund of 28 lbs., he was enabled to get a better article, and which was hardly dearer than the other, because the proportion of wool to seed was greater. The American cotton was then sold for fifty-five rupees the candy, and afterwards, in 1848, for seventy-five rupees, and now we hear of the native dealers themselves giving 100 rupees the candy for it, to sell again at Bombay.

The quantity of cotton which had been raised for government amounted to 1145 candies, and 1601 for private individuals. The cotton, up to the end of the years 1847-48, had cost 85,085r. 2a. 11p., and had sold for 105,787r. 9a. 2p.; the profit therefore amounted to 20,702r. 6a. 3p. Half the profit, Mr. Blount writes, would cover the cost of native establishments and cost of machinery. The cotton purchased in 1847, 1848, and 1849, is not included in these estimates, as the account of the sales had not then been received in India. The cultivation, which amounted in the season of 1849-50 to 15,396 acres, is probably nearly doubled in the present season, while the whole cultivation of cotton in the district amounts to 204,925 acres. Much of this, Mr. Blount thinks, will be occupied with New Orleans seed instead of with indigenous cotton; but, he observes, that in districts where there is little pasturage, any great increase of cultivation will be checked, from the necessity of growing bread stuff and *kurbee* (stalks of *Sorghum vulgare*) as provender for cattle.

The facts in favour of the New Orleans cotton make its superiority incontestible, as it generally, though not always, yields a larger quantity of seeded cotton per acre, and certainly a larger proportion of wool to seed, while it always sells in England at a much better price. The only question is, to find the situations which are suited to its culture.

Dr. Gibson from what he had seen, early entertained hopes of success in the climate of Dharwar, which he found moister than further north, and stated that the undulating part of the district was better suited than the open black plains to the eastward; he particularly adduced the success of Mr. Dickenson in a generally dry part of the Deccan with some American cotton seed forwarded by the author to Dr. Gibson; "but the plantation was sheltered and watered by a well-supplied aqueduct, so that it was in a state of continual moisture." Mr. Blount, in a recent letter, mentions that in the parts of the district to the northward of Khooseghul, and north-east of the village of Ameghery, all black plains, the American cotton is not cultivated. The parts where it is cultivated are also black plains, but they are somewhat nearer the hills, and may have more moisture; but in the general features of the country there is nothing to lead to such a belief, for there is a hill-range also on the north of Nowlgoond, as well as to the N.E. and S.E. of Ameghery, Bettighery, and Munnigul. North and south of Dharwar the country is generally hilly, but little cotton is grown. In the space included between Jugulgum and Havanoora, the New Orleans cotton is most productive, and it will do equally well over a large tract of country on each side, as well as across the Toombudra in the Madras Territory, where the cultivation has been commenced, as well as in the Nizam's territory near the British boundary, and also at Shorapore under Capt. Taylor, to whom he mentions having sent two gins to clean his last year's crop. Mr. Simpson, after considerable experience in the neighbourhood of Coimbatore, in travelling from thence to the Bombay Presidency, points out the neighbourhood of the Toombudra and of Hurryhur as apparently well suited, in point of climate, to the cultivation of American cotton. (*Return*, p. 381.) Dr. Cleghorn, mentioned at p. 95, after reading the whole of the papers in the '*H. of C.'s Return*,' coincides in this opinion, and states that it was at Hurryhur Capt. Bayles formed his opinion respecting the suitableness of the climate of India to the culture of American cotton. Writers and experimentalists must, in fact, consider a little more carefully than has hitherto been the case, that a plant is a living body which, as much as an animal, requires not only food suitable to it but in suitable quantities. For it must be grown in a field before it can be carried along a road, and no diminution of rent or of expense in culture will make it a profitable crop where the soil and climate are unfavorable.

Mr. Blount mentions that the road from Hooblee to Coompta is now being made pucka (metalled), and the nullahs (rivulets) and water-courses bridged over. "The road down the ghaut has also been made on such a level as to admit without difficulty of the passage of carts. This is a great improvement; but until the transit from Vingorla is improved, our cotton cannot reach market until after the monsoon. We can get it to Coompta, but there it must stop." This, indeed, is one of the great difficulties of the Dharwar district; as Mr. Blount, in a letter dated 23d of April, 1849, observes: "We labour under difficulties which do not apply to any other district with which I am acquainted. Our crop does not ripen until the end of March, and is not all gathered before the end of April (in the northern districts it is all gathered before the end of January, and in some places earlier), and as our coast communications close early in May (the 12th), it precludes the possibility of getting the cotton to Bombay before November after the monsoons have passed. Another thing which operates against early delivery is, that the grain crop comes on simultaneously with the cotton, and the ryots will not make deliveries of the cotton until they have secured their grain. Had we other cheap communication than by boats with Bombay, all the cotton of the district, or the bulk of it, would be out of the district by the middle of June; but we must await the advent of railroads before this takes place." The new port of Wagotun will be noticed under the head of Belgaum.

Yet, notwithstanding the difficulties of the lateness of season and the delays of transit, and more than all, the extreme smallness of the returns per acre, it is in the Dharwar district that the culture of American cotton has made the most extensive strides, and Mr. Blount looks forward to its occupying a great part of the 200,000 acres now under cultivation with indigenous cotton. This is chiefly ascribable to the climate being more suitable than that of some other districts, as the soil is described as not being superior; indeed, by Mr. Mercer, it was mentioned as being decidedly inferior to that of Bundlecund. Much is no doubt due to the judicious patronage of the civil authorities, Messrs. Shaw, Goldsmid, and Mansfield, of all of whom Dr. Gibson, an impartial witness, writes in high terms when passing on his visits of inspection to the teak forests of the coast, as well as of the planters, Messrs. Mercer and Hawley. The author would add, that the present planter, Mr. Blount, is not inferior to any in zeal and discretion. Dr. Gibson does not, however, forget the natives; in one of his early visits he writes: "The Dharwar and Belgaum ryots seem a much superior set to our Deccan men. They are enterprising and industrious." He especially mentions that they only require an extension of the system of irrigation greatly to improve their country; and again, "The Lingaits, who form the bulk of the population here, as well as in the rest of the Southern Mahratta country, seem to be a class vastly more enterprising, well affected, and peaceable, than their Mahratta neighbours, on whom instruction, attention, and expenditure, are too often thrown away, and the motives of those who afford them are totally unappreciated or wilfully misrepresented, whereas the people here seem willingly to have responded to the wishes of the European authorities who have of late years been over them, in planting trees, widening and keeping clean the roads in their villages, and in giving their houses some degree of neatness and uniformity, and in planting the enclosures round them with flowers, &c."

Notwithstanding the length to which our observations on the Dharwar district have extended, in consequence of the natives there having taken up the cultivation, a few points yet remain to be noticed,—first, the peculiarities of the indigenous cotton; and secondly, the frauds to which cotton is subjected. These may be appropriately treated of under the head of Broach, as it seems to be the head quarters of both.

§ 27. Experimental Culture in Belgaum.

Belgaum is situated on the same table-land as Dharwar, and is only 47 miles to the north-west of that station. Until recently, it was included in the Dharwar collectorate, and has much the same soil and climate.* It is not, therefore, necessary to dwell much on the details of the experimental culture, which has been carried on in that district since the year 1845 under Mr. Channing, who had been placed with Mr. Mercer in Dharwar from the beginning of the year 1843 to the end of 1844, having had some previous knowledge of farming in England. Mr. Frere, the acting collector of the district, reported, on the 14th of March, 1845, that Mr. Channing had

* The following notices of the temperature, though only for six months, will be interesting in the absence of fuller information. The quantity of rain in the table at p. 336, is stated to be 40·9 inches, or nearly the same as at Dharwar:

April	85°— 94°	70°— 76° at 7 a.m.
May	80 — 94	72 — 76 at 5 a.m.
June	73 — 89	71 — 76 at 7 a.m.
July	72 — 78	70 — 72 at 7 a.m.
August	72 — 77	69 — 71 at 7 a.m.
September	74 — 78	69 — 72 at 7 a.m.

selected the village of Negunhal, in the Sumpgaum Talooka, distant 93 miles from the coast, as best suited for the farm, and that he required about 300 acres of land for the purpose. Broach cotton seed was obtained from that district, and New Orleans seed from Dharwar. On the 15th of October, the prospects of the farm were reported as being favorable, and the crop of that grown by the natives as very promising: but, on the 4th of February, 1846, "an unsatisfactory account was given of the cotton crop at the farm, the plants continuing to throw out fresh flowers, which, however, from some cause, did not come to maturity, but fell off in great numbers, just as they were forming into bolls." (*Summary*, p. 109.) But, on the 20th of March, an improvement had taken place in the state of the cotton crop, from which a good picking was expected. (l. c., p. 110.) No reasons are assigned for this change, but it was probably connected with climate.

The quantity produced amounted to 8995 lbs.; but a large portion became injured, and some was thrown overboard during stress of weather at sea, between Vingorla and Bombay. (*Summary*, p. 112.)

Some of this cotton was sold at Bombay for 120 rupees the candy of 784 lbs., on the 20th of March, at the same time with the Dharwar cotton, which brought only 113 rupees. The Belgaum cotton amounted in quantity only to 14 bales. But, this, however, was sufficient to prove that Mr. Channing had so far succeeded well.

On the 23d of February, 1846, Mr. Channing recommended that only a small portion of the farm should be retained, and, on the 10th of December, its total abolition; and also, on the first occasion, that contracts should be entered into with the ryots, for the cultivation, on account of Government, of both American and Broach cotton. On the latter date, it was reported that there were 1300 acres of land under cultivation with New Orleans cotton, and 725¾ acres with the Broach cotton.

Of the cotton produced, 59 candies and 13 maunds of New Orleans, and 4 candies 9 maunds of Broach were obtained at an average cost of 66r. 1a. 7p. per candy.

"Samples of the New Orleans, and other varieties of cotton raised on the government farm," having been forwarded to

Bombay, "they were, on the 24th of July, 1847, submitted for the opinion of the Chamber of Commerce, whose report, dated the 31st of July, spoke in discouraging terms of all these samples, except the Broach cotton, in respect to which the Chamber made the following remark:

" *Broach.*—A very excellent sample. The staple is not so long nor so strong as the Georgian, which makes it inferior to that cotton for manufacturing purposes; still the staple is good and regular, and the cotton clean and of good colour, altogether a showy lot." (*Summary*, p. 111.)

It does not appear from this document, whether this Broach cotton is compared with the American cotton in general, or with that cultivated in Belgaum; but in either case, the opinions given at Bombay were not coincided in at Manchester, for there the Indian grown American cottons have always brought higher prices than the equally experimental indigenous cottons sold at the same time. It is to be hoped, therefore, that the culture has attained stability, and that no decrease will take place when government patronage is discontinued.

As we are unable to afford space for the details of the experimental culture for the subsequent years, we may yet give the results which have been obtained; by which it will be seen, that a gradual progress has been made, except in the year 1847, when, as in Dharwar, a falling off took place in the culture of cotton, from the unsuitableness of the season. Mr. Channing was himself detached, in 1847, into Dharwar, during the absence from India of the American planters. The entire quantity grown by the ryots, it is, however, difficult to ascertain, because much was sold to dealers from the Dharwar and other collectorates. About 3500 acres were in cultivation with New Orleans cotton, in last season, or that of 1849-50.

NEGUNHAL FARM.	Grown or purchased by Government. Candies.	lbs.	Purchased by dealers. Candies.
1845-46	5	675	—
1846-47	1	581	—
„ grown by contract	2	286	—
„ purchased from ryots	59	365	5
1847-48	26	403	26
1848-49	67	75	36
	160	2385	67

Besides these 500 bales of New Orleans cotton, some Broach cotton was grown by the natives, and indigenous cotton, to the extent of 23,317 lbs., was bought in the season 1846-47, according to the orders of government, and sent in a clean state to the presidency. The American cotton cost, according to Mr. Channing, $67\frac{1}{2}$ rupees per candy, and the native $63\frac{1}{2}$ rupees for the same quantity. The carriage of a candy of cotton from Belgaum to Vingorla amounts to $9\frac{1}{2}$ rupees, and from Vingorla to Bombay, by sea, to $1\frac{1}{2}$ rupees more, or altogether to 11 rupees. The expense of bringing the cotton from different parts of the district to Belgaum, amounts on an average to 4r. 10a. 6p.

On arrival in England, the Belgaum cotton of the crop of 1848-49, which had been shipped in the 'Brahmin,' was sold at Manchester on the 12th of October, 1849; the New Orleans for $5\frac{1}{4}$*d.*, and both the Broach and the indigenous for $4\frac{3}{8}$*d.*, Dharwar cotton having been sold on the 6th of September for 5*d.* Here, also, we observe, that the Belgaum cotton sold better than the Dharwar, proving that Mr. Channing had succeeded in the culture, and must have paid at least equal attention to the cleaning. Notwithstanding the higher prices obtained for the New Orleans cotton at Manchester, and now at Bombay, the profit to the ryot is not so clear. When he has sown and picked the New Orleans cotton for Government, "it has been a much more profitable produce. If gins are near at hand to clean the American kupas for him, the ryot will obtain nearly twenty per cent. better profit on the culture than on that of the native;" but if not, and the ryot has to sell his produce to a dealer, his profit with the American cotton will be very little; but with the native cotton itself it is small, for the dealers having combined to keep down the price of cleaned cotton generally, get it from the ryots at from forty-five to fifty rupees per candy.

The importance, therefore, of multiplying saw-gins for cleaning the New Orleans cotton, is manifest, and also of constructing them of such sizes as are suitable for purchase by the ryots. Mr. Channing long since proposed constructing a saw-gin with the aid of native workmen (v. *Return*, p. 531), and he now constructs them of twenty saws, the size he prefers, for 179 rupees. These, with bullock power, will clean forty-eight maunds of

28 lbs. a day, at the rate of about four rupees a candy, while the cost by the foot-roller amounts to from seven to eleven rupees a candy. Four gins only had been sold to natives, but as hand-gins are well suited to some parts of the district, there is no doubt that some of the smaller ones at least, will become spread about, as in the neighbouring district of Dharwar.

The roads in the Belgaum collectorate are stated by Mr. Channing to be in a bad condition, and are open only from the end of October to the beginning of June. A road having been made to Vingorla, another is being opened by the Phondaghat to the new bunder or port at Wagotun, which Mr. Channing thinks will be more convenient than Vingorla. The collector doubts whether the new port of Wagotun will supersede Vingorla, and is of opinion that a new cut should be made down the Ramghat, which he learns can be easily and effectually done. "If this were done," Mr. Reeves continues, "the new landing place at Vingorla would render the old Ramghat infinitely preferable to the new one viâ Phondaghat."

"An Old Soldier" writing in the 'Bombay Telegraph,' and who describes himself as having been employed on some of the works to which he refers, says, "Vingorla and Coompta are both open roadsteads, most dangerous from there being a rocky sea-shore, where, if bad weather occurs, it is almost impossible for a vessel to escape destruction. The setting-in of the southerly winds, bringing with them a heavy sea, closes these ports early in May, because it is most perilous for boats to remain in the offing some ten miles, and also inconvenient as well as dangerous to load the vessels at that distance from land. To obviate these inconveniences, the Bombay Government in 1847 instituted inquiries for a better port, and an excellent one was found in the natural harbour of Viziadroog; an extensive and safe one without rock or bar, and capable of receiving at all seasons vessels of from 700 to 800 tons; the river communicating with it being navigable without impediment for 12 miles inland. This port had been known for many years; but as there were no roads leading to it, it was of no use. Ten miles up this river a port named Wagotun has been established. There the stream is 400 yards broad, with a depth of three fathoms at low-water spring-tide. Wagotun is therefore the harbour for country boats, and Viziadroog the harbour for ships of large tonnage, where goods may be shipped and forwarded direct to England.

"From the town of Wagotun, rough roads have been opened into the interior, as follows: to Kolapore, 77 miles, to Belgaum, 100 miles; these roads crossing a most difficult and mountainous country. Substantial, good roads have been estimated for, and will no doubt be sanctioned; those crossing the mountains being on a slope of one in twenty. Villages have been established, forests removed, and Dhurrumsallas or Caravanserais erected at convenient distances for the use of the trade."

Roads having been made from Wagotun to Kolapore and to Belgaum, and from these places into the interior, the "Old Soldier" conceives that the whole of the districts of the Southern Mahratta country having been thrown open, the trade will be directed to Wagotun instead of to the dangerous and open roadsteads of Vingorla and Coompta. Whether he is right in this opinion, or that of Mr. Reeves is more correct, in conceiving that Vingorla would be preferred if the Ramghat was improved, it is evident that facilities have been greatly increased.

Mr. Channing, when asked what degree of encouragement is required to induce the ryots to continue to grow exotic cotton, replies: "Guarantee them a certain market for the produce by government purchasing it, until merchants or dealers come forward to do so. Let the price be known as early in the season as possible, and let it be remunerating; and have gins placed in different parts of the district, so as to be convenient to the ryot in point of distance." Mr. Reeves, the collector, writes, "All the government need now do, is to purchase samples annually to test the quality of the wool; these samples ought to be exposed for sale at Bombay, and in England. A supply of saw-gins should be kept in the collectorate, for sale to such persons as require them, and repairs should be made to the machinery, when necessary, by the superintendant, at the cost of the owners; everything else ought to be entirely left to the ryots and the mercantile community." There is no doubt, now, that any quantity of New Orleans cotton, which is at all likely to reach Bombay, will readily find a sale there at remunerating prices, as so many of the agents there have orders for this cotton from Manchester houses. The prices at which this cotton is sold, both in Bombay and England, should be made known to the cultivators, and both they and the dealers should be frequently reminded, that what is well grown, should be picked free from leaf and dirt, and carefully cleaned, or its character will soon fall to the level of indigenous cotton. Wilful adulterations should be punished by fine, and the penalty of cleaning it over again, &c.; extreme cases by confiscation, as directed by Regulation III of 1829.

Mr. Inverarity, Collector of Belgaum, in 1848, in reply to queries, states that the returns per acre are only 30 to 35 lbs. per acre, for "little attention is paid to superior cultivation, or to the eradication of noxious grasses which impoverish the soil." Good land has yielded 84 lbs. per acre in favorable seasons.

The ryot receives from 6 to 11 annas per maund of 28 lbs. for kupas, and for clean cotton from 40 to 50 rupees per candy of 784 lbs. "These prices are given without account being taken of advances, which the generality of ryots receive from local dealers, often at the ruinous interest of 36 per cent. During the last three seasons, the prices of the native cotton have ranged in the market from 50 to 60 C.'s rupees per candy of 784 lbs. The very best cotton, which is invariably purchased by Pinjarrees and weavers for home consumption, fetches as much as seventy (70) rupees per candy."

Cleaning by the foot-roller amounts from 6 rupees in the Eastern, to $6\frac{1}{2}$ and 7 rupees in Sumpgaum and Purseghur Talooks; by saw-gin to $3\frac{1}{2}$ rupees. But the loss of weight being 5 per cent., in consequence of the dirt being blown out of the cotton when it is passing through the machine, forms with the natives an objection to its use. There is no doubt, however, that they will in time learn, that the consumer will pay more than what is equivalent to his loss for clean cotton. The average expenses of conveyance may be taken at 10 rupees per candy to Coompta, and 9 rupees to Vingorla.

Before proceeding with the other experimental cultures, it is desirable briefly to notice the other districts which constitute the table-land of the Bombay Presidency.

The Collector of Sholapore states that "the price of cotton at Bursee is about 65 rupees for a candy of 784 lbs. The expense of conveying cotton from Sholapore and Bursee to Panwell,

(200 miles) is from 9 to 10 rupees per candy. About 100,000 acres are under cultivation with cotton, one half for home consumption, but more than 200,000 are suited to this culture. The production of grain, moreover, is very much in excess of the consumption. An increase, therefore, of cotton cultivation to more than double its present extent may be looked for, if sufficient inducement be held out to the ryots."

The land rent is on an average only 10 annas per acre, but it requires 19½ acres to produce a single candy of cotton.

The Collector of POONA (Mr. Courtney) writes, "that the Indapoor Talooka is the only one in his Collectorate in which cotton is grown, and that experience has shown that neither the climate nor soil of the Western Deccan is suited to the growth of this plant."

The Collector of AHMEDNUGGUR (R. Spooner, Esq.) reports, that in his district there are only 2638 acres of cotton in cultivation, that the soil does not appear suitable for its growth, that what is grown is chiefly in small patches and intended more for the use of the inhabitants than for export.

"Several attempts have been made to extend the cotton cultivation in this zillah, and in the years A.D. 1830 and A.D. 1832 large sums of money were advanced by Government free of interest.

"From inquiries it appears that the result of these experiments was the ruin of the persons to whom the money was advanced by Government, and the loss to Government of the interest of the amount so lent.

"Government also, under date the 22d of March, 1832, No. 3222, authorised Mr. Collector Townsend to enter into contracts with individuals for small quantities of cotton, so as to remove all doubts the ryots might entertain of not being able to obtain a market for their produce.

"From the inquiries which I have made, I am of opinion, that the cultivation of cotton in this zillah is not likely to increase to any considerable extent; but at the same time I beg to add, that every exertion will be made on my part to increase the cultivation of that staple."

It is curious, considering how frequently we hear of the want of roads being the cause of the deficiency in the supply of cotton, that these two districts, which have the greatest facilities in reaching the port of Panwell by the great road to Bombay by the Bhore ghaut, should be the very two of the Deccan districts which grow the smallest quantities: proving, though such proofs are not necessary to those who are sufficiently well-informed to judge correctly on such subjects, that other things besides roads and rents require to be investigated, when the true causes of a deficient supply of cotton or of any other product of the soil are attempted to be determined.

§ 28. Experimental Culture in Candeish.

The province of Candeish, more properly Khandesh, forming the most northern of the districts of the Deccan, is bounded on the north by the Satpoora or Injadree range of mountains, which are not more than 1500 feet in height, and separated from the Surat, Broach, and other maritime districts by the Western Ghauts, which, in this northern latitude, have dwindled to a much lower elevation. So that, by taking the valley of the Taptee, or crossing the hills behind Broach, Candeish and the Deccan may be entered without any very great eminences requiring to be surmounted. In point of climate, Candeish is more moist than the Deccan, but less so than Surat and other districts on the coast. It is also much more wooded than the Deccan, which assists in keeping it moist. Mr. A. Elphinston, the present collector of the district, writes that, in point of climate, it may be distinguished into two parts. All the western districts (those next the seaboard) are considered too moist for cotton, but produce the sugar-cane and grain; the eastern districts, or those adjoining Malwa and Berar, are drier, yielding cotton and indigo. Wheat, being a cold-weather crop, is common to both portions.

In the year 1845, the experimental culture of cotton was commenced in Candeish, Messrs. Blount and Simpson having completed their engagements with the Bengal and Madras governments, offered their services to that of Bombay. Mr. Blount, having arrived at Poona on the 11th of April, 1845, was directed to proceed to "the fertile province of Candeish," in order to report on the feasibility of improving the cultivation of cotton, and also on the better cleaning of that already grown. Mr. Simpson, having been engaged from the 26th of June, 1845, was at first attached to the experiment in Dharwar, but afterwards to that in Candeish. Mr. Blount, on the 24th of May (*Return*, p. 519) recommended the culture of cotton, both on a small farm and on the contract system. But, on the 8th of August we find, from a joint letter from himself and Mr. Simpson, that the season for planting cotton having passed, nothing could be done towards its culture that year. They recommended that they should be employed in setting up saw-gins in Candeish, and that they should be authorised to purchase the indigenous cotton from the ryots, and clean it for the Government, if the ryots objected to have their own cotton cleaned by the saw-gin. This they considered would be a very safe transaction. Mr. Simpson, who has a great taste for mechanics with considerable knowledge of the machinery used in the cleaning and packing of cotton, was deputed to superintend the construction of saw-gins in the gun-carriage department at Bombay. He also suggested the manufacture of gins of eight and of ten saws, and stated generally, that, before ordering saw-gins from England, it should be ascertained whether they could not be made up in India. (*Return*, p. 524.) He also proposed making up a cotton screw-press at Dhurrumgaum, with the aid only of the native mechanics of Candeish. This was authorized by the Government, at an expense of 2000 rupees.

The first efforts of the planters having been directed to the cleaning of the indigenous cotton of Candeish, it is interesting to find, that they were as successful as it was possible for them to be. For the cotton, bought from the ryots and cleaned at Julgaum and Dhurrumgaum, sold, in March, 1847, for 120r. and 130r. per candy of 784 lbs., when the Dharwar New Orleans cotton sold for 113r., and the Belgaum New Orleans cotton for 120r. (v. p. 358); and this when the cotton itself was actually inferior in quality of staple, as was proved by the low price it brought in England, in comparison with that which the American variety commanded at the same time.

In the season of 1846-47, cultivation of the New Orleans cotton was tried in Candeish, in the eastern part of the district; that is, at Dhurrumgaum and Julgaum, in the Talooks of Errendole and Nusseerabad. We have seen above, that, in the eastern parts of the province, the indigenous cotton is chiefly cultivated. It may, on this account, have been inferred, that the same part would be equally favorable to the American cotton. But this does not appear to have been the case; for Mr. Blount, when at Manchester (v. p. 360), stated that the climate of the open part of the district—that in which the experiment had been made—was too dry for the cultivation of New Orleans cotton. Mr. Simpson, in a report, dated the 6th of April, 1848, handed in to Mr. Elphinston, says, in reference to this experiment, "Whatever may be the result of future operations, this much I am fully prepared to say, that the incipient efforts made in the season of 1846-47, form insufficient data to judge one way or the other, as to whether this variety of cotton can or cannot be successfully produced in this province."—"However, taking the actual merits of the results into consideration, I am, and always have been, of opinion, that they gave grounds to hope for ultimate success. Moreover, Errendole and Nusseerabad do not constitute what is generally known to be the province of Candeish—but that he had little doubt it would succeed in the Talooks lying near to or on the banks of the Taptee river, as well as in those of 'Western Candeish,' where there is supposed to exist a more humid atmosphere, arising from the river and the heavy-timbered forests that are known to exist in that direction."

At the conclusion of the season 1846-47, Mr. Blount obtained leave to visit America with Mr. Mercer for a year, and Mr. Simpson remained to take charge of the experiment in Candeish, as well as of that in Broach. As he was of opinion, that the New Orleans cotton would succeed in some parts of Candeish, he sent circulars to the mamlutdars (revenue officers), asking them whether any of their villagers would plant some of the New Orleans cotton seed; that, if they would do so, he would supply them with seed gratis, and purchase the produce at 4r. the old Dhurrumgaum maund. Only two replies were received in the affirmative, that is, from Sowda and Pachona. The seed was consequently supplied (in small quantities, of course), and it was planted in both cases. A considerable produce was obtained. The cultivators brought in their cotton, and received for it the price agreed upon; and "were so well satisfied with the results, as to be willing and anxious to go on with its culture, on the same terms, for another year, to a much larger extent." Mr. Simpson, however, wished to visit America, on account of the failure of his health. He therefore resigned his appointment on the 4th of April, 1848, and took his departure for Europe on the 15th of that month. Fortunately, at this time, Mr. A. Elphinston, who takes the warmest interest in the culture of cotton, as we shall have to relate under the head of Rutnagherry, was appointed to the Collectorate of Candeish. When in England, he had made a point of visiting Manchester, for the purpose of seeing some of the spinners and manufacturers, and acquiring information on the subject.

Mr. Elphinston, on arrival in the district in the beginning of 1848, expressed himself as highly satisfied with Mr. Simpson's exertions, and especially with the screw-press which he had made for packing the cotton, as well as with his saw-gins, all which, as well as the experimental culture, were left in charge of his assistant, Mr. Price. "The province," he observes, "is very thinly inhabited, and there is a great deal of waste land; therefore not only could the quantity of cotton capable of being sent to England be greatly increased from the wastes now unreclaimed, but also from the land under present cultivation." In the beginning of 1849 Mr. Elphinston was anxious to obtain New Orleans cotton seed from Dharwar; but as the culture of 1847 had so much diminished there during 1848-49, he was unable to procure any, and therefore his efforts to extend the culture were delayed for a year. This was much to be regretted, as he had got the ryots of all the districts to agree to take large quantities of the seed. But some Georgian cotton seed had, at the recommendation of Mr. Shaw and others, been sent out by the Court of Directors. Mr. Elphinston also received from the author a few seeds of cotton from the West Indies, and wrote, "You were right in supposing that Nimar and the adjoining district of Candeish, and those bordering on the river Taptee, form a fine cotton-field where the American might be increased most extensively." Subsequently, April, 1849, he wrote, "Since I came here I have been extending the New Orleans cotton which thrives perfectly well, and I have no doubt of its success. The ryots now make no objections to grow it; its increase, therefore, is merely an affair of time, which I am hurrying forward as fast as I can." On the 20th of June, 1849, Mr. Elphinston wrote, that "the New Orleans cotton seed sent him from Dharwar had arrived rather late, and had got wet on the journey, and therefore a month (June) of the sowing season had been lost; but that he had also received a portion of the Georgia cotton seed which had been sent viâ England from America. The natives were so satisfied, notwithstanding last year's bad crop, at the relative superiority of the exotic kind, that they have come forward in large numbers this year to sow its seed, and if this impression remains after this year's harvest, we shall go on increasing our American sort of cotton;"—"I am confident of success." Mr. Price expected that not less than 60,000 lbs. of New Orleans cotton would be produced in the season; he was himself growing a small quantity of both New Orleans and Georgia cotton, as well as some Egyptian cotton seed which Mr. Elphinston had procured. Mr. Elphinston himself in August, 1849, found the American thriving so well, and the ryots liked it so much, that no difficulty was experienced in getting them to take any quantity of the seed for sowing. He had like Col. Cautley obtained a few seeds of the Mastodon cotton-seed from Mr. Blount, and found it after a trial of more than a year, the best kind of cotton plant that he had ever seen (and Mr. Elphinston is well acquainted with nearly every sort), as it is a vigorous, hardy plant, a good bearer, the bolls very large, and the cotton both long and strong in the staple, superior to the Uplands or the New Orleans cotton of America.

Mr. Simpson having returned from America, was re-engaged by the Court of Directors to proceed again to India, which he reached in the beginning of the year 1850, and in writing to the author on the 7th of April, expressed himself as much pleased with what had been done in extending the culture of New Orleans cotton among the ryots of the district, and that 10,000 lbs. of such cotton had been produced that season, but that he expected the crop of 1850-51 to yield at least 50,000 lbs. of clean cotton.

Mr. Simpson immediately applied himself to the construction of more gins, and hoped that the establishment will be able to manufacture 70 saw-gins of 20 saws by the 1st of November of the present year. This, in addition to the supply on hand, which is about 35, will give upwards of 100 for the collectorate by the beginning of the season, and he mentions as the most favorable symptom of the progress made in the experiment, that a Bombay house, Messrs. Ritchie, Stewart, and Co., were establishing an agent there, and had applied for as many gins as could be spared by the Government after supplying the natives. Mr. Simpson had therefore recommended to be allowed to entertain an extra-establishment, in order to manufacture as many saw-gins as possible. In consequence of this demand and that in Dharwar, the Court of Directors sent over 1500 saws in the middle of summer, and have ordered a further supply of 2000, to be sent by the same route when ready.

The author had the pleasure of hearing from Mr. Elphinston in a letter dated August, 1850, in which referring to the little American cotton grown in his district when he first arrived there, he says, "They had yearly since then sown a supply of Dharwar American cotton seed, as well as the portion given us of that which came out from America viâ England more recently. In spite of late in the season arrivals from Dharwar, and the accident of unpropitious seasons, the Dharwar American seed is becoming acclimated here, and the annual increase is about ten times the amount of the previous season. The ryots are becoming well satisfied with the American seed, both on account of its greater yield of cotton, as well as its superior quality and its commanding a higher price; therefore, I feel no hesitation in saying, that in all the eastern districts of Candeish, or in that half of the province in which cotton, indigo, and opium is grown, the American cotton seed may be considered established. In the other half of the province, sugar-cane is the chief product. I only pray that the American cotton-seed plantations now in good health may not be injured by a bad season the remainder of this monsoon, to the discouragement of the ryots and the damping of their expectations."

We have already stated, that Mr. Simpson before leaving India in 1848, had succeeded in constructing a screw-press with the aid only of native mechanics, which was perfectly efficient for its purpose. But in a country like India difficulties of various kinds have to be encountered. Mr. Elphinston writes that they "had been obliged to give up screwing the cotton bales, because the carters charged cart-hire to Bombay exactly alike whether the bales were press-screwed or not, and the operation of pressing is always repeated at the Presidency, without any regard to whether it has been screwed before or not." So with regard to the adoption of large saw-gins moved either by cattle or by steam-power. There is no doubt that Mr. Landon, whom we have to mention under the head of Broach, has made his large saw-gins most efficient, and the process of cleaning very cheap. But in a district where the cotton culture has to be established, it has been stated, that the natives would be frightened by the expense of large machinery and the necessity of erecting a suitable building for its reception, rather than encouraged by its efficiency. It is, therefore, thought that it is safer to trust to hand-gins, of which those of 20 saws clean 800 to 900 lbs. a day, at an average cost of 4 rupees 12 annas per candy of 784 lbs. Mr. Frost's saw-gins with 7 saws are also very efficient instruments, and being still cheaper, are suited to a poorer class of cultivators.

The produce of Candeish is conveyed in carts to Colset Bunder by the Thull Ghat, say a distance of 180 miles from the central station of Dhoolia, and thence a further distance of 25 miles by land or water to Bombay. The expense of carriage varies from 10 to 14 rupees per candy. Mr. Simpson, when in charge of the cotton experiments both in Broach and Candeish, travelled by a more direct route from Surat, which he considers the natural outlet of Candeish. The road passes at first over a plain of black cotton soil. The country then becomes rocky, and a low jungle with occasional quagmires is passed. After this the forest becomes dense, but the soil improved, and many rippling water-courses are met with, and some rude attempts of the Bheels at agriculture are seen. About a dozen miles beyond Nowapoor, a piece of new, but then unfinished, road was passed, which leads to the Koondybarra Ghat. This line of road passes up a defile formed by two ranges of hills running nearly due E. and W., and which seemed to present the only engineering difficulties between the sea-coast and the plains of Upper Candeish. Mr. Simpson was of opinion that if a good road was made down this ghaut, carts would easily pass down in fewer days, and that though the present distance is 145 miles, it might be reduced by adopting the best line of road, and that this would much diminish both the time and expense of conveyance. He also thought, that if screw-presses were established at Surat, cotton might be shipped from thence, instead of being sent to Bombay to be unpacked and screwed into bales. But the jungly forest is unhealthy at some periods of the year, and this may prove a greater obstacle than the hills.

There is every probability that Candeish will become one of the important cotton districts of India, favoured as it is by a soil and climate which are to a great extent suitable, and encouraged as it has been by the judicious patronage of the civil authorities, as well as by the zealous co-operation of the experimental department. These are at the same time aided by the willingness of the cultivators, and though last, not least important, is the presence of European merchants, who cannot fail to encourage improved culture and cleaning, as they too well understand their own interests not to give prices proportionate to the quality of the cotton, as that alone will enable it to attain and keep a high place in the markets of Europe. It is, therefore, desirable to give some more information respecting the statistics of the cotton trade and culture in this district. This we are fortunately able to do from the replies given by Mr. Elphinston and Mr. Simpson to the queries circulated by the Court of Directors. Though we are unable to spare space for these answers in detail, we append Mr. Elphinston's observations, as these embrace the information afforded by Mr. Simpson, in addition to his own.

Mr. Elphinston observes:

"It is difficult to say what might be the actual increase of cotton in Candeish, if there was a permanent remunerative demand; but I am sanguine it would be very great, because there is a vast quantity of land, suited to the cultivation of cotton, now cultivated with grain, as well as unreclaimed waste, which, under the above encouraging circumstances, without creating a scarcity of grain, could be converted into cotton fields. Under the like encouragement, a proportionate increase of cotton might also be expected to pass through Candeish to the seaboard, from Berar and the districts adjoining this collectorate. Mr. Simpson states his opinion, that if the price of Indian cotton be maintained in the English markets at from 4½*d.* to 5*d.* per pound, an immense increase in its culture would ensue. I am not satisfied that so high a price will ultimately be required by the cotton growers, as, when the road from Candeish to Colset Bunder (the port of embarkation to Bombay) is finished, and the cotton gins and cotton presses in the Province have become more numerous, the cotton can then be delivered in Bombay, or in England, at a less expense, and may therefore be profitably sold at lower than the hitherto prevailing prices.

"At present the ryots prefer sowing grain to cotton, because, if the price of the former is unremunerative, they can consume it in their own families; whereas the cotton is of no use to them unless it is sold; and the ryots are too poor to keep it till the price rises. This uncertainty of the ryots procuring a remunerative price for their cotton is the chief reason why they do not sow more of it. If Government could secure the ryots a permanently remunerative price for their cotton, or would authorize its agents, before the sowing season, to enter into contracts with the cotton growers, to purchase large quantities of cotton at a price remunerative to them, it would doubtless cause an increase in the annual supply.

"MEMORANDUM.

"1. Of rooee, or cotton separated from the seed, Mr. Simpson states the value in Candeish of a candy of 800 lbs. avoirdupois at 50r. = £4 11*s.* 8*d.* sterling, at the exchange 1*s.* 10*d.* per rupee. This gives the price here of a pound of clean cotton at one anna, or 1*d.* 1½*f.*

"It has, however, been ascertained, from other inquiries made here, that 50r. is the maximum price, in ordinary seasons, for clean picked cotton. The price ranges from 37r. to 50r. per candy of 784 lbs., or from £3 7*s.* 10*d.* to £4 11*s.* 8*d.*, in Candeish.

"In Bombay, in first hands, a candy of 784 lbs. is sold at from 60r. to 70r. = £5 10*s.* to £6 8*s.* 4*d.* According to my information, the *lowest* rates at which cotton can now be sold without absolute loss are stated to be as follows:

QUANTITY.	In Candeish.						In Bombay.						In England.					
	r.	a.	p.	£	s.	d.	r.	a.	p.	£	s.	d.	r.	a.	p.	£	s.	d.
1 candy of 784 pounds . .	35	0	0	3	4	2	50	0	0	4	11	8	80	0	0	7	6	8
1 pound	0	0	8½	0	0	0¾	0	0	1¼	0	0	1⅜	0	1	8	0	0	2¼

"2. Mr. Simpson states the value, in Candeish, of a candy of 1600 lbs. of kupas, or cotton in seed, at 26r., which is equal to £2 7*s.* 8*d.* This gives the value of a pound of it at a little more than

3 pies, or 1 farthing. At this rate, the price of a candy of it, consisting of 784 lbs., would be 13r. 3a. 8p., the proportionate parts of which, as estimated by Mr. Simpson in a former communication, are 27 per cent. of cotton to seed. According to the native authorities of the zillah, the relative proportion of cotton to seed is supposed to be 33 per cent., or about one third.

"3. Cost of separating the seed by the native churka or roller is as follows:

Per candy of 784 lbs.	9r. = 16*s*. 6*d*.
Per lb.	$2\frac{1}{3}$p. = 1 farthing.

"By saw-gins, as follows:

Per candy of 784 lbs.	$4\frac{1}{2}$r. = 8*s*. 3*d*.
Per lb.	$1\frac{1}{10}$p. = about $\frac{1}{2}$ farthing.

"This demonstrates the advantages of the saw-gin over the country churka, in the proportion of two to one.

"4. Cost of carriage to Colset Bunder is	12r.	per candy.
From Colset to Bombay	1	,,
	13	
Gunny bags and packing	5	,,
Price of cotton in Candeish	37 to 50	,,

(This makes 55r. at a minimum, and 68r. at a maximum, rate of purchase.) 60r., when laid down in Bombay, is equal to £6 4*s*. 8*d*. At this rate, the price of a pound of cotton laid down in Bombay is 1a. $4\frac{1}{3}$p., or $1\frac{1}{2}$*d*. in English money.

"The above, however, has been calculated at maximum rates; for carriage is sometimes procurable at from 9 to 10r. per cart. The importers of Cotton in Bombay, moreover, get an allowance for the gunny-bags, which reduces the cost to a trifling extent.

"Mr. Simpson assumes the produce of cotton, with its seed, from one beegah of land, at 200 lbs.; but the district officers' estimates average about five maunds, or 400 lbs., some of them stating as much as 800 lbs. per beegah. Much, however, depends on the fertility of the soil, mode of culture, and favorableness of the season. Mr. Simpson's estimate gives the out-turn of cotton, with its seed, per acre, at about 275 lbs.; and the average of the Mamlutdars gives 550 lbs.

6. As Mr. Simpson had not sufficient data at his command, Mr.

Elphinston supplied this deficiency by submitting a table of the present cultivation and returns of cotton, stating afterwards the amount of assumed increase that might be expected, provided there was a more extensive and permanent demand for the article.

Extent of land cultivated with cotton in 1847-48.	Candies of 784 lbs. avoirdupois of seed cotton.	Extent to which it is assumed cotton may be increased, according to the reports of the district officers, inclusive of the quantity now raised.	
		Land in beegahs.	Cotton in candies.
beegahs. pands. 173,898 2	88,723	269,847	133,085

"The beegah adverted to in the replies consists of an area of 32,400 feet, or equal to 3 roods, 39 poles, and 1 yard. An acre contains 1 beegah, 6 pands, and $17\frac{8}{100}$ viswas. 20 viswas = 1 pand, and 20 pands = 1 beegah. The maximum rate of assessment on cotton lands in this province is $2\frac{1}{2}$ rupees per beegah, the minimum rate being 4 annas.

"The maund is equal to 80 lbs. avoirdupois.

"The rupee is the Company's rupee, and has been assumed at the current rate of exchange of bills on London, viz. 1*s*. 10*d*.

"(Signed) ALEX. ELPHINSTON,
Collector."

In connection with these Deccan provinces, it is desirable to notice the capabilities of the territories of the late Raja of Sattara; but we can only afford space for the following letter from Mr. Frere giving the results of his inquiries:—

From H. B. E. Frere, Esq., *Resident at Sattara, to* A. Malet, Esq., *Chief Secretary to Government, Bombay.*

Sir,—In reply to your letter noted in the margin, I have the honour to annex an abstract of the information obtained from the districts of His late Highness the Raja of Sattara and the guaranteed Jageerdars, on the points regarding which the Honorable Court desire information, relative to the power of this country to furnish an increased supply of cotton.

It will be seen from the abstract that there is a very great variation between places within a comparatively short distance of each other. This is mainly, if not entirely, owing to the want of roads, which want prevents the natural equalization of prices.

QUESTION 1. What is the price of cotton freed from seed at the principal mart or marts in your districts?

The details of the prices at each of the principal marts I must refer to the abstract.

It will be seen that the lowest price is 1½ rupee at Akulkote, and the highest 12 rupees, 6 annas at Islampoor, between Kurar and Kolapoor, per pucka maund of 40 seers (about 95 lbs. 10 oz. Troy). The lowest average price is 2½ rupees, again at Akulkote, and the highest 11¼ in the Punt Pritty Niddy's purgunnah of Hasoor.

In every case the price will be found to depend greatly on the distance, by a tolerable road, from the nearest sea-port, or on the proximity to some cotton manufacturing town; but the nature of the road, whether it be one of the great thoroughfares of the country or not, makes a great difference. Thus omitting minute fractions and taking the ordinary or average prices (the middle of the three columns of prices), we have the following result:

	Price per maund of 40 seers. r.	a.	p.	Distance from seaport.
1. Akulcote	2	4	0	About 200 miles, as the crow flies, from any port.
2. Kurar	6	0	0	About 50 miles from Chiploon.
3. Beejapore	6	0	0	150 miles from Rajapore.
4. Phultun	6	6	0	130 miles from Panwell, by a made road; 80 miles from Mhar by one unmade.
5. Koomta	6	12	0	75 miles from Mhar.
6. Pall	7	8	0	55 miles from Chiploon.
7. Sattara	7	8	0	60 miles from Mhar.
8. Nimsor	7	8	0	65 miles from Mhar.
9. Sowluj	7	8	0	80 miles from Sungmeshwur, and the same from Rajapoor.
10. Punderpoor	7	14	0	190 miles from Panwell; 120 miles from Chiploon.
11. Oomree	7	14	0	120 miles from Rajapoor.
12. Juth	8	4	0	120 miles from Rajapoor.
13. Atparee	8	4	0	90 miles from Chiploon.
14. Ound	8	4	0	60 „ „
15. Patun	8	4	0	30 „ „
16. Mussooor	9	0	0	50 „ „
17. Khutao	9	0	0	70 „ „
18. Islampoor	9	6	0	55 miles from Rajapoor.
19. Hoosoor	11	4	0	132 „ „

The cases which at first appear exceptional are:

No. 2, Kurar, which being only 50 miles from a sea-port, might be expected to stand lower on the list. But the cause of the anomaly may be found in the decayed, poverty-stricken character of the town, the existence of over-taxation, and several hurtful monopolies, and above all in its position between two of the great lines of traffic from the interior to the sea-coast, at Chiploon and Rajapoor.

Nos. 7 and 10, Sattara and Punderpoor. The prices here are better than might be predicted from their distance from any port of shipment, partly in consequence of the demand created by local cotton manufactures, and partly of a brisk general trade.

Nos. 11 and 16. Atparee and Islampoor are both on main lines of communication between the interior and sea-coast.

Nos. 12, 14, 15, Ound, Mussoor, and Khutao, all participate in the advantages of the demand caused by the consumption of cotton at Rehmutpoor, where coarse cloths are manufactured to a considerable extent.

QUESTION 2. At what price does the ryot sell his cotton, cleaned or uncleaned, and with or without advances?

Though the ryots are generally, to a considerable extent, dependent on the advances of money-lenders for the capital wherewith to carry on their cultivation, still cotton is usually grown without any advances being made for the special purpose of securing the growth of that particular crop. The ryot receives loans from time to time, as he requires them, and generally repays them in produce; but the system, common in Candeish and Guzerat, of capitalists at a distance (say Bombay) advancing funds on condition that cotton shall be grown and delivered to their agents on certain terms, is little practised, probably because in most districts, in this territory, the possibility of growing a crop of cotton depends less on the will of the cultivator than on the season.

The ryot usually sells his cotton ready cleaned.

The details of the usual prices are given in the annexed abstract. It will be seen that the highest price is at Islampoor, 12 rupees per maund of 40 seers, the lowest at Akulkote, 1 rupee 6 annas for the same quantity. The highest average or ordinary price is at Islampoor 9 rupees, the lowest at Akulkote, 1 rupee 12 annas.

In the following table, the average prices paid by merchants, as shown in the answers to Question 1, are compared with the prices obtained by the ryots as given in Question 2.

	Mercantile price, as per answer to Question 1.				Price obtained by the ryot, as per answer to Question 2.		
	r.	a.	p.		r.	a.	p.
Islampoor	9	6	0	..	9	0	0
Nimbsor	7	8	0	..	6	12	0
Punderpoor	7	14	0	..	7	2	0
Beejapoor	6	0	0	..	5	4	0
Atparee	8	4	0	..	6	12	0
Hoosoor	11	4	0	..	6	0	0
Akulkote	2	4	0	..	1	12	0
Juth	2	12	0	..	2	12	0

QUESTION 3. What is the expense of cleaning cotton by the churka or foot-roller, or by any other method which may be in use?

The foot-roller is the implement generally used for separating the seed from the cotton, except in some parts of the Akulkote territory. The cost is stated to vary from $1\frac{1}{4}$ annas to 1 rupee 2 annas per maund.

QUESTION 4. What are the expenses of conveying cotton to the nearest port for shipment?

The following table shows the cost of conveying cotton to the nearest port from the marts specified:

	Miles.		Rupees per Pucka maund of 40 seers.		
			r.	a.	p.
Sattara to Mhar	60	..	0	10	0
Punderpoor to Chiploon	120	..	0	13	0
Kurar to Chiploon	50	..	0	10	0
Ashte to Rajapoor	60	..	0	10	0
Nimbsor to Rajapoor	80	..	1	4	0
Sowluj to Rajapoor	80	..	1	4	0
Atparee to Chiploon	90	..	2	15	3
Ound to Chiploon	60	..	2	8	6
Akulkote to Panwell	257	..	0	14	0
Juth to Rajapoor	120	..	2	4	0

The whole of the above trade, with the exception of part of that from Akulkote, is carried on by pack bullocks.

It is to be observed, that the cost of transport to the port of shipment does not depend so much on the mere distance, as on the extent of the return trade from that port to the interior.

It is to be borne in mind that the trade from the coast to the interior is, to a great extent, in salt and other articles which are almost necessaries of life, and which cannot be otherwise procured. Whenever this trade exceeds in general bulk the trade from the interior to the coast, the cost of carrying the latter is reduced below what it would otherwise be, because the supply of carriage exceeds the demand, and the owners of the bullocks prefer accepting low rates of hire to getting none at all.

For instance, suppose a place at such a distance from the port, that the natural cost of sending a bullock up or down, including all the elements of his hire, would be 1 rupee each way, or 2 rupees for the trip thither and back, and that the trade in salt and other articles, which come from the coast, was double, in bulk, that which went from the interior to the coast; it is evident that, in such a case, half the bullocks required to carry the salt, &c., up to the country must return to the coast empty, or by reducing their fares compete for the goods to be carried down. The result will, of course, be the rates of hire of carriage down to the coast will be reduced below 1 rupee, the natural cost of the trip, while the difference will be added to the price of the salt or other article of trade going from the coast to the interior.

The converse of this will take place in the case which is, I believe, in these districts much rarer, where the trade downwards to the coast exceeds in general bulk the trade going from the coast to the interior.

If this fact be borne in mind, it will explain many seeming anomalies in the cost of transport.

The extent to which this cost of transport might be reduced, if the roads were practicable for carts, is worthy of particular notice. From the most careful inquiries I can make, I believe that the use of carts would effect a reduction in the cost of transport in the proportion of 5 to 3, while the saving in time would be in the proportion of 6 to 4. That is to say, that where 5 rupees are now paid for bullock carriage, 3 rupees only would be paid for carts; and where the bullocks took six days, the carts would take but four, such at least is the estimate deduced from information given by the best informed local traders and carriers.

Question 5. What is the average produce of cotton per beegah or acre?

The produce varies, as shown in the abstract, in different districts, from half a maund to 12 maunds per beegah, the latter being, I imagine, a very rare crop. The average is estimated at from 1 to 9 maunds; but though the latter is stated, on good authority, to be the average of a few villages, I imagine the average of the whole country can seldom be taken at more than 1½ to 2 maunds.

QUESTION 6. What is the quantity of land under cultivation with cotton, and to what extent is it probable that the cultivation could be carried in the event of an increased demand?

The total number of beegahs at present under cotton cultivation throughout the country is given at 21,561½ beegahs, and the utmost extent of cultivation possible under the pressure of increased demand, is estimated at 39,018 beegahs, or about double the present quantity. This, as far as I can judge, is a low estimate.

The details of local measures are given in the abstract. In the above remarks they are reduced to the Sattara beegah of 4444 square yards, and the maund of 40 seers each weighing 76 C.'s rupees.

I have the honour to be, &c.,

(Signed) H. B. E. FRERE,

Resident at Sattara.

SATTARA DISTRICTS; 13th April, 1849.

A planter, Mr. Vary, who has for some time been employed in Dharwar and Belgaum, has been appointed to conduct a course of experiments in Sattara.

In addition to the districts which properly constitute British territory, we may notice the capabilities of the different states at which there are political agents; for instance, in Kolhapoor about 4000 begas are, and 6000 might be, cultivated. In the Southern Mahratta agency there are 45,266 in cultivation, and 70,083 acres might become so in case of a demand accompanied by remunerative prices.

Having noticed these and all the Collectorates of the Bombay Presidency situated above the Ghauts, and referred to information supplied by their several Collectors, we may give the remainder of the statistical facts in a tabular form, premising, however, that we have not attended to whether they belong to the northern or southern divisions of that Presidency, but have included those which are above the Ghauts in the first table, and, in the second table, those which are situated in the lowlands which extend from Guzerat to Canara, and which we shall afterwards proceed to notice.

Mr. Townsend, in reference to the information supplied by the several Collectors, observes:

Dated 2d Feb. 1849.

Sir,—With reference to Mr. Deputy Secretary Erskine's letter, No. 1691 of 23d March last, and to yours of 25th November (No. 7387) I have the honour to submit in tabular form the substance of the replies of the Collectors of this Division (received under dates noted in the margin) to the several questions on the subject of cotton cultivation proposed in paragraph 2 of the Honorable Court's despatch, No. 21, of 10th November, 1847, a copy of which accompanied the Government letter under reply, and trust that this statement will be found to contain the information required by his Lordship in Council, of which the following is an abstract.

QUESTIONS.	Rutnagheeree.	Poonah.	Ahmednugger.	Sholapore.	Belgaum.	Dharwar.
		lbs.	lbs.	lbs.	lbs.	lbs.
Market price of clean cotton per rupee	—	17	12	12	13 to 14	10 to 13
Ryot's price per rupee	—	80	11—12	$\frac{13}{60} \cdot \frac{16}{64}$	$\frac{15}{40} \cdot \frac{19}{74}$	10 to 64
Expense of cleaning	—	213 + seed.	$38\frac{2}{5}$	The seed is given.	120—130	284
Cost of carriage per rupee	—	80	107	78—87	78—87	80
Produce per acre	—	120—240	240	160	38—84	60
Extent of cultivation in acres	—	344-5	2638	98,260	112,000	200,000
To what extent capable of increase	—	6890	not much.	196,320	300,000	400,000

From the accompanying statement and the foregoing abstract, His Lordship in Council will observe that the Rutnagheeree Collectorate grows no cotton, and that the remaining Collectorates of this Division rank as follows with respect to this valuable product:

1st. Dharwar. 2d. Belgaum. 3d. Sholapoor. 4th. Poonah. 5th. Ahmednuggur.

The first letter from each Collector quoted in the 1st paragraph, is forwarded in original for the information of Government; the subsequent communications relate to apparent discrepancies in the statements received, and it does not appear requisite to forward them; the last reply received was from the Acting Collector of Belgaum, and is dated 23d ultimo.

The replies of the Collectors to the Honorable Court's 1st question do not very much vary: the price of clean cotton, as stated by the Poonah Collector, is less than that of the other Collectors, which is not what might have been expected; but a statement of price is necessarily only an approximation to the truth, and cannot be viewed as a certainty.

The replies to the 2d question vary pretty largely even in the same Collectorate, according to the various circumstances by which the sale is attended. This may explain the great difference between the replies of the Collectors of Poonah and Ahmednuggur on this point; a reference was made to the Collector of Ahmednuggur on this along with some other points of difference. Mr. Spooner in his reply (dated 13th of December) explains that "the cotton cultivation in that zillah is exceedingly trifling, and that, therefore, it is difficult to obtain any very satisfactory information in reply to the queries proposed."

The 3d question relates to the expense of cleaning; the replies of the Collectors of Dharwar and Belgaum differ more from each other in this respect than might have been expected, and they show how difficult it sometimes is in this country to obtain distinct and correct information on a matter of daily occurrence. The Acting Collector of Belgaum shows that the saw-gin reduces the expense, as well as the dirt of the cotton: unfortunately the traders are not yet convinced that it is good policy to clean the cotton properly. It is, however, a matter of much practical importance that the cultivators and traders should find their interest in supplying clean cotton, and this can, I submit, be effected only by the merchants at the Presidency, who by examining the cotton (as they do the opium) that they purchase, and regulating the price by the purity of the article, have it in their power to compel the country traders to supply it clean.

The replies of the Collectors to the 4th question very closely coincide, excepting that of Ahmednuggur. The nearness of Poonah to Panwell is probably counterbalanced by the greater demand for carriage at so large a station, and its consequent greater price. When at Barsee in December last, I questioned some traders, and their answers very closely tallied with the reply given to this question by the Collector of Sholapoor. I found that owing to the badness of the road between that large trading town and Poonah, bullocks were still very much used in preference to carts, as it was necessary to load the latter very lightly owing to ruts and inequalities of the ground. This must hinder the cotton trade, and render the article more expensive in transit. The same remark applies to the state of the roads between Belgaum-Dharwar and the coast, which is a matter of vital importance to the existence of the cotton trade.

As regards question the 5th, "the produce per acre," the replies of the Collectors vary considerably. Either the estimates of Poonah and Sholapoor must be too high, or those of Belgaum and Dharwar too low. The remark contained in my 6th paragraph applies to this question also. It is, however, probable that the replies of the Collectors of Belgaum and Dharwar have been given after consulting the cotton planters in their respective districts, and are, therefore, more likely to be correct than those furnished to the Collectors of other zillahs by their Mamlutdars.

The 6th and 7th answers show the present cultivation, and its possible or probable extent, the latter, of course, must depend on cotton proving a remunerating crop or otherwise: its doing so will, I submit, largely depend on its being well and cheaply cleaned, and cheaply conveyed to market: the former will be provided for, so far as Government can do it, by an abundant supply of saw-gins; the latter depends wholly on the formation of some good roads and bridges between the cotton country and the coast.

I have the honour to be, &c.,

(Signed) E. H. TOWNSEND,

Revenue Commissioner, Southern Division.

DHARWAR DISTRICTS, *Reven. Comm.'s Camp,* "Yawugul," 2d Feb. 1849.

The following statement was omitted under the head of Dharwar:—

The expense of conveying the cotton from Dharwar to Coompta, and from that by sea to Bombay, was stated by Mr. Mercer to be seventeen rupees per candy, of 784 lbs. At that time Mr. Mercer stated, that if the road was completed from Hoblee towards Coompta, laden carts might easily travel down the ghauts. This road having been finished, the expense of transit has been reduced; as Mr. Blount states, that the entire charge of conveying and landing of cotton from Dharwar to Bombay, is from twelve to thirteen rupees. The distance varies from 100 to 150 miles; and the roads throughout the district are what may be called dry weather roads; from the middle of November until the monsoon sets in, they are passable for carts. Pack bullocks are able to travel, though with some difficulty, through all seasons.

Statistics of the Cotton Trade in the Collectorates above the Ghauts.

DISTRICT.	Price of cotton freed from seed.	Price at which the ryot sells his cotton, cleaned or uncleaned, and with or without advances, per maund.				Expense of cleaning cotton.	Expense of conveying cotton to the nearest port for shipment, per maund.	Average produce of cotton per acre.		Quantity of land under cultivation with cotton, and extent to which it is probable cultivation could be carried on in the event of increased demand.	
		With advances.		Without advances.							
		Cleaned.	Uncleaned.	Cleaned.	Uncleaned.			Cleaned.	Uncleaned.	Under cultivation.	Probable extent of cultivation.
Khandeish	—	—	—	37 to 50r. per Surat candy of 784 lbs.	13r.3a.8p. per Surat candy.	9r. per candy by churka; $4\frac{1}{2}$r. per candy by saw-gin.	13r. per candy to Bombay.	268 lbs. per acre (Simpson); $1075\frac{1}{2}$ lbs. per acre.		$129,345\frac{3}{4}$ acres.	200,712 acres
Poona	4r. to $4\frac{3}{4}$r. per maund.	—	1r. to 1r. 2a. per 80 lbs.	—	1r. 3a. per 80 lbs.	6a. per maund.	1r. per 80 lbs.	Land of the 1st sort, about 3m. per acre; the 2d sort about half as much.		3445 acres.	about 6890 acres.
Ahmednuggur . . .	1r. per 6 seers, or 12 lbs.	—	—	1r. per 11 lbs.	1r. per 12 lbs.	2r. per 10 lbs.	$\frac{3}{4}$r. per 80 lbs.	240 lbs. the average.		2638 acres.	soil unsuited.
Sholapore	1r. per 12 lbs., or 65r. 5a. 4p. per candy.	1r. per 14 to 18 lbs.	1r. per 64 to 68 lbs.	1r. per 13 to 16 lbs.	1r. per 60 to 64 lbs.	The seed is given to the labourers.	9r. to 10r. per candy.	$\frac{1}{2}$m.	2m.	98,260 acres.	196,520 acres.
Belgaum	1r. per $11\frac{1}{3}$ lbs. (the *best*) 1r. per $15\frac{17}{20}$ lbs.	—	—	1r. per $15\frac{17}{23}$ to $19\frac{3}{5}$ lbs.	1r. per $40\frac{8}{11}$ to $74\frac{2}{3}$ lbs.	1r. per $120\frac{8}{13}$ to $130\frac{2}{3}$ lbs.	1r. per $78\frac{3}{5}$ lbs. to Coompta; 1r. per $87\frac{1}{5}$ lbs. to Vingoorla	35 to 84 lbs.	—	112,000 acres.	300,000 acres.
Dharwar { New Orleans cotton	1r. per 10 lbs., or 8r. per maund.	1r. per $10\frac{10}{31}$ lbs.	1r. per 40 lbs.	1r. per 10 lbs.	1r. per $37\frac{11}{17}$ lbs.	3a. 3p. per maund.	1r. (Coompta.)	$\frac{2}{3}$m. average.		200,000 acres.	400,000 acres.
Dharwar { Indigenous cotton	1r. per $13\frac{1}{3}$ lbs., or 6r. per maund.	1r. per $15\frac{5}{21}$ lbs.	1r. per 64 lbs.	1r. per $14\frac{6}{11}$ lbs.	1r. per $58\frac{2}{11}$ lbs.	3a. 3p. by saw-gin; 4a. 6p. by roller.					

Statistics of the Cotton Trade in the Collectorates below the Ghauts.

COLLECTORATES.	Price of cleaned cotton per Surat candy of 784 lbs.	Price of uncleaned cotton per Surat candy of 784 lbs.	Cost of cleaning Surat candy of 784 lbs.	Cost of carriage per Surat candy of 784 lbs.	Average produce per beegah or acre.	Cotton land in cultivation in acres of 43,560 feet.	Cotton land capable of cultivation, in acres of 43,560 feet.	Remarks.
						b. w. w.	b. w. w.	
Ahmedabad . .	From 115r. 8a. to 175r. 14a.	38r. 1a. to 52r. 8a.	By churka, about 6r. 9a.	2a. 7p. per coss.	The cotton called Lalya, from 2 maunds to 20 seers, or 280 to 70 lbs. per acre. The cotton called Wagrya, from 5 to 1 maund, or 317 to 63½ lbs. per acre.	242,750 1 1 or, in acres, 142,663.	72,742 0 0 or, in acres, 42,750.	Company's rupees—beegah equal to 25,600 square feet.
Kaira	122r. 14a. 9p. to 153r. 10a. 6p.	35r. 13a. 7p. to 61r. 7a. 5p.	7r. 10a. 11p. to 10r. 3a. 10p.	From Neriad to Dholera, 6r. 6a. 5p.; Michonda to Cambay, 7r. 6a.; Barsud to Cambay, 10r. 10a. 5p.; Matur to Dholera, 9r. 13a. 4p.	4 to 8 maunds per beegah, or 637 to 1274½ lbs. per acre.	10,022 0 10 or, in acres, 5176½.	4250 0 0 or, in acres, 2195¼.	Beegah equal to 22,500 square feet.
Broach	73r. 14a. 3p. to 77r. 0a. 9p.	21r. 3a. 8p. to 23r. 10a. 11p.	9r. 0a. 2p. to 9r. 14a. 7p.	For the whole collectorate, 14a. 5p.	40 lbs. of cotton wool per beegah, or, at ⅓ wool to ordinary kupas, about 234 lbs. per acre.	340,000 0 0 or, in acres, 174,058¾.	None, (v. Collector's letter.)	Beegah equal to 2477 square yards, 7 feet, 64 inches.
Surat	70r. to 90r.	22r. 12a. to 28r.	Clean cotton about 9r.	1r. per 12 coss. (about 18 miles.)	Beegah, 186⅔ lbs.; acre, 274½ lbs.	35,597 8 14 or, in acres, 24,202.	49,402 11 6 or, in acres, 33,588.	Beegah equal to 29,615 square feet, 9 inches.
Tannah and Rutnagherry	No cotton grown in these two Collectorates.							

§ 29. Experimental Culture in the Districts below the Ghauts.

We have already seen that the Bombay Presidency is especially distinguished by being divided by the Western Ghauts into the districts which lie above, or on the table-land, and into those which lie along the coast below the Ghauts. The Western Ghauts as they separate from their point of junction with the Eastern Ghauts at the Neilgherries, stretch northward and westward, leaving between their abrupt western face and the sea a tract of country from 30 or 40 to 50 and 60 miles in breadth. This in the southern parts is known as Canara and Malabar, and in the northern parts as the Concans and a part of Guzerat. The Concans, divided into north and south, are described as being about 35 miles in breadth, their surface diversified by steep rocky mountains intersected by ravines, and towards the Ghauts covered with thick forests, but including many fertile tracts, which produce rice and sugar-cane. Mr. Chapman, looking with the eye of a railway engineer, describes this tract as a rough country encumbered with immense mountain blocks, and traversed by smaller ridges; a very confused and broken country, some ranges run north and south, others east and west. The Ghauts themselves are not mountains as you come from the interior, except that there is a ridge on the very crest of the Ghauts, over which generally you must ascend from the eastward before you can descend the great step, "or abrupt face to the westward." That ridge in some places is broken through, and affords an occasional means of passage; "the height of these passes is somewhere about from 1800 to 2000 feet above the sea; and that elevation is gained often in the course of a mile or a mile and a half." The country gradually declines from the base of the Ghauts to the sea, and is intersected by numerous mountain streams; but "the principal river valleys do not rise very rapidly; at the foot of the Ghauts they are not 300 feet above the level of the sea." Land and sea breezes blow alternately during the day, and moderate the heat of the climate. The coast is in many places broken into small bays and harbours, sheltered in some winds, but exposed to the full force of the monsoon, when it bursts upon this coast, and is arrested by the Ghauts. Thus we may account for the large fall of rain, 120 inches in Malabar, 115 inches at Rutnagheery, and from 50 to 120 at Bombay: the quantity being less as we proceed northwards, though we have been unable to obtain any account of the fall of rain, or, indeed, of the climate in general of either Surat or Broach.

But proceeding northwards, we come to the Attaveesy, a strip of country lying between the Damaun river and the Tapty, and then to Guzerat, which occupies the eastern side of the Gulf of Cambay; as well as the western or Kattywar, of which the low parts are included within the collectorate of Ahmedabad. The eastern and north-eastern boundaries of the Attaveesy and Guzerat are formed by a succession of hilly ranges, which are offsets from the Western Ghauts, some approaching close to the sea, others being 30 miles distant, and these, with tracts of forest, separate the low country from Candeish and the Deccan. A wide and funnel-shaped opening allows a passage to the Tapty, on the left bank of which Surat is situated, while another alluvial valley gives exit to the Nerbudda, which deposits in Guzerat much of the rich soil of Central India. "The valley here is about 12 miles in breadth, and we are there met by the low hills of the Burria range, which, being scattered rather than continuous, afford a comparatively easy passage to the interior of India, and here accordingly is a great entrance from the coast to Malwa." On the right bank of the Nerbudda stands Broach, the ancient Barygaza. A third valley forms an opening from the Myhee river, which like the Tapty and Nerbuddah, has its origin far to the eastward of Guzerat, and like them flows across the province.

Besides these there are several other rivers, but these are short in their course, having their origin in the Western Ghauts, and in a part of the country "underlying hilly tracts, abounding in rich soil, highly retentive of moisture, and rendered still more so by luxuriant jungle." Eighteen miles further north than the Myhee, "we arrive at the Seree river, a tortuous, sluggish, sedgy, and deep stream, which runs past Kaira. From the Myhee to the Saburmuttee, a space of 43 miles, there are five rivers. These by their union form the Saburmuttee, which falls into the sea at the head of the Gulf of

Cambay." (*Gibson on Guzerat, in 'Trans. of Medical Society of Western India.'*)

In the southern part of this district, the Attaveesy, where the hills approach nearest to the coast, there is much reddish and yellowish soil, formed from the disintegrated lateritious rock. Beyond Durrumpore, the soil passes into the black alluvium which extends widely from the banks of the rivers, and is continuous near the sea. About Soopa and Gundavee the soil is most productive. As we approach the Tapty, the black soil predominates. But north of this river, the lateritious soil prevails in the more inland parts; but nearer the sea, the soil is chiefly black, with intermixture of clayey and sandy soils, and occasionally calcareous nodules. The bed of the Nerbudda and its immediate neighbourhood is sandy, and occasionally muddy, nowhere marshy. Beyond the north side of the river, where the banks are high and ravines frequent and deep, stretches the great alluvial plain which forms the whole of the Broach pergunnah, as well as a great part of the Korril, Sinnore, Duboy, and Jumboseer (including Ahmode), pergunnahs, and part of the Baroda district, and as far as the Myhee river. In the whole of this extent, forming a breadth of thirty-six miles, we have first in order of frequency the reddish-brown soil, very rich and fertile; second in frequency, the barren soil of sand, kunker and gravel; and third, the black soil. From Baroda towards Champaneer there is much black soil, and the vegetation is most luxuriant. About Champaneer it is a rich waste, remaining uncultivated in two thirds of its extent, and thus it continues to the Myhee river. Beyond the raviney and barren banks of the Myhee, the country is again level. About Boorsud the soil is a deep brown, very favorable for the growth of all sorts of produce. Black soil predominates in the lower levels; but the brown and grayish, or "gorat," as it is called, greatly predominates. The same occurs towards Kaira, and northwards to Morassa and Tintoee. But lower down in these districts, as by Dolka and Cambay, the black soil is by far the most common, and continues so along the sea-shore. (*Gibson*, l. c.)

With regard to climate we have been unable, as we have stated above, to find any detailed account of the temperature, the fall of rain, or of the state of moisture in the famed cotton districts of Guzerat. This we regret, because we believe that the successful culture of cotton depends much upon climate, though soil, of course, is not to be neglected. The southern parts, we may on general grounds infer, are moister than the northern, while the districts near to the Ghauts are described as being moister both in soil and climate, and in many parts covered with jungle. The Broach district we should conceive to be drier than some of the others, and that less rain falls there, because the Ghauts are represented as being lower. The monsoon, therefore, instead of expending its whole force on their western face, carries much of the air loaded with moisture into Candeish.

The extensive tracts of country stretching along the sea-coast from N. lat. 16° to 22°, must appear particularly favorable for the culture both of American and of native cotton; and this whether the opinion be correct, that considers sea air as essential to the healthy growth of cotton, or that which ascribes its utility to the uniform state of moisture. Roads, however bad, could form no impediment, where the distance to rivers or to the sea must be everywhere short, and could be travelled over in the dry weather, as the cotton can be picked and shipped before the monsoon comes on. The land-rent, or tax, would therefore remain as the only one of the alleged difficulties to the extended culture of cotton. But we find it cultivated to any extent only in a part of this tract. Moisture, however, as we have seen, may be in excess, as in Bengal, or deficient, as in the Deccan, and however easy of access may be the port of shipment, cultivators may find other produce more profitable than cotton. Should this be the case, however low may be the rent, it will not induce the farmer to give up a profitable crop for one that is less so, and for which, as far as Europe is concerned, there has been for some time (as shown in a previous part of this work) low prices, and a very fluctuating demand. But it is only by inquiring into the peculiarities of any particular district that we can ascertain the facts of the case, and be in a condition to draw legitimate conclusions.

Parts of the Bombay Presidency having long been British possessions, have also long and frequently been the site of experiments on the improvement, and cleaning, and culture of cotton. In the year 1788 it was from Broach and Surat that

500,000 lbs. weight were directed to be sent to this country, in compliance with the wishes of manufacturers. In the year 1790, an excellent account of the culture of cotton in Surat was sent by the Bombay government, and the Ahmode species of cotton was recommended to be introduced into Bengal. A cotton-cleaning machine was first sent out as early as the year 1794. As Malabar at that time formed a part of the Bombay Presidency, the first experiment to improve the culture of cotton was made at Rhaudaterra,* near Tellicherry, under the superintendence of Mr. Brown. In a letter from the Court of Directors, dated June 1, 1803, we learn that "the six bales of cotton, the produce of Rhaudaterra plantation, were of very excellent quality, and we indulge the hope that its cultivation will reimburse, with profit, the expenses of forming the Rhaudaterra plantation. The Bourbon sort sold for 2*s.* 2*d.*, and the native at 15$\frac{7}{8}$*d.* per pound." The native sort was not so much inferior to the other in quality as the difference in price would seem to point out, but was not so well cleaned from seeds and extraneous matter. But we have seen no further notices of the culture. At a subsequent period, that is in the year 1825, five bales of Manilla cotton, grown probably in the same neighbourhood, were sold at Glasgow for 10$\frac{1}{2}$*d.* per lb., when at the same time Surat cotton was selling for 6$\frac{1}{2}$*d.* per lb. The cotton was pronounced "a good quality of Manilla cotton. The staple is too short to take a high stand, it is very nice as to colour and cleanliness." There is little doubt that cotton of good quality can be grown along this coast, but we have no information respecting the quantity that is yielded per acre, as upon that depends whether it will be remunerative or not to the farmer.

F. Clementson, Esq., lately collector of Malabar, in his evidence before the Cotton Committee, stated, that "The present land assignment of Malabar is only on rice; the demand upon gardens is only upon the cocoa-nut, areca-nut, and jack-tree; the cotton cultivated in Malabar bears no land-tax, it is cultivated on the high ponum lands, the produce raised is very inconsiderable, not exceeding 100 candies, and if exported from port to port, never paid any duty; the quality is inferior, and

* Apparently the same place is called Randaterra in the H. of Commons '*Report*,' p. 528.

it is seldom or ever exported, but only used for home consumption; the tariff value was 20 rupees (£2) the candy, of 640 lbs." "The soil and climate of Malabar are not considered suitable to the cultivation of cotton; upwards of 123 to 170 inches of rain fell during the year."—(*H. of C.'s 'Report,'* pp. 385-6.) It is probable that Mr. Clementson is right in his opinion, but it is possible that the Pernambuco cotton might succeed in some of the higher and well drained parts of the district, where the soil is of little value, and the site sheltered from the violence of the monsoon.

In the year 1811 we find that the Court of Directors again assigned a sufficient quantity of Bourbon cotton-seed to the different Presidencies, with a statement of its mode of cultivation, and the nature of the soil best suited to it, though the Court were aware that the experiments previously made with the Bourbon cotton-seed in India had not been very successful; it was thought from want of knowledge of the best soil and climate.

In the year 1812 the Bombay Government, in reference to the directions which had been sent respecting the culture of cotton in Africa, Georgia, and Carolina, also in Demerara and Berbice, report that translations had been made and distributed among the ryots, especially with respect to picking the cotton clean; though the directions generally were thought little applicable to the cotton-growers of Guzerat, especially with regard to the sowing time, which is after the first fall of rain. The dry soil and climate of Guzerat were considered very favorable to the growth of the cotton plant, as it is found to grow in the most sterile districts. At Surat the seed is stated to be all of the *black kind,* that it is sown annually in drills at the distance of one foot between each plant. That three gatherings of cotton are made in one season, the first from the middle to the end of February, which yields the finest wool; the second, fifteen days later, is of inferior quality, and the third is still more so from the lower parts of the bushes. Mr. Forbes, as well as the Collector of Broach, recommended that every village should deliver a portion of good clean cotton, and that the ryots should be positively enjoined to pay every attention to the gathering of their cotton; and they mentioned that of 150 villages which then paid their revenue in cotton, only eight delivered the *thomil* or best kind. In this year the Bourbon seed which had been received was distributed among the Collectors of Surat and Broach, to sow some in each collectorate on account of the Company, and to distribute the surplus to ryots. Copies of a memoir regarding the culture at Bourbon were at the same time sent.

Reference was at the same time made to the attempts which had been made to cultivate cotton in the island of Salsette, and it was stated, that every attempt which had been made to cultivate Bourbon cotton there had failed. It was also stated, that Dr. Scott, a proprietor of land in the island, had once many acres in cotton, but after a few years had given up the cultivation. Two native proprietors of land also had both expended much money, with no better success (*E. I. C.'s Papers*, p. 48). It was mentioned that this was owing to "the native labourer, who will never yield any adequate return for his wages when employed in agricultural concerns, even with the utmost vigilance of the farmer."

In the year 1816 Bourbon cotton seed having been again sent to India, and the Collector of Coranja having failed in his endeavours to prevail on the ryots to cultivate it, undertook the experiment himself. When he forwarded a sample of the produce, it was reported to be superior in every respect to any cotton produced in the Broach pergunnah with which it had been compared.

"The cultivation of the Bourbon cotton has been also attempted in the Kaira collectorate. Of 4750 beegahs that had been sown with the seed, 2186 beegahs promised to ensure its successful introduction, notwithstanding the disinclination which the ryots manifested to undertake the experiment." But subsequently a considerable failure took place, which was attributed to an essential difference in the nature of the Guzerat and Bourbon plants, which induced Mr. Gilder to give the Bourbon cotton a further trial, during the next year, in lands which have the benefit of irrigation.

The Court of Directors, on the 9th of April, 1817, in reply to this letter regret the failure which had taken place in Kaira, attributable to the want of rain in the latter part of the season of 1815-16, and to the seed having been damaged. They approve of the further trials in Kaira and Broach, "on a soil where the facilities of irrigation might obviate the difficulty, in a season of drought, of bringing the plants to maturity." The Court further observe: "As an experiment seems to have been made with more success by the Assistant-Collector of Coranja, it occurs to us that similar experiments may with propriety be continued both in that island and Salsette, or in our recently acquired possessions of Fort Victoria and Malwan, on the slope of hills sheltered from violent winds from the sea, and also on other grounds possessing the means of artificial irrigation, and also sheltered from violent sea-winds, if such situations can be found." (*E. I. C.'s Papers*, p. 64.)

The Bourbon Cotton grown at Kaira by Mr. Gilder.—Of the various experiments which have been made on the culture of cotton, few are so satisfactory as those of Mr. Gilder, assistant-surgeon at Kaira, in 1816-17, who having observed the causes which led to the failure in the attempts to introduce the cultivation of Bourbon cotton into the western districts, considered the obstacles to be exclusively physical, and, at the same time, stated that both the soil and climate of the districts lying between the Sabermuttee and the Myhee promised a more favorable result. "The greater portion of the soil," Mr. Gilder says, "is of the light sandy nature recommended by the cultivators of the island of Bourbon, and the general division of the country into inclosures protects the plant materially from the influence of the hot winds, which are considerably milder than those on the plains to the westward. The facility, also, which this division presented for irrigation, if necessary, was an object of the greatest importance."

The spot selected by Mr. Gilder was a sandy loam, the general characteristic of the district. It afforded the means of irrigation, but these were not made use of. The seed was sown at the end of July, in 1816, after the first heavy rain, in rows, distant three feet from each other, preserving the same distance of plants in each row. Bejaree was sown by drill, at the same time with the cotton, and answered as well as the Indian corn recommended at the Isles of France and Bourbon, as affording protection to the tender plants from the heat of the sun, until the grain be ripe, by which time they have acquired sufficient vigour. The after-rains of 1816 were very scanty, and the plants remained in an apparently sickly and dwindled state, until the rains of 1817, when they shot forth so luxuriantly that it was found necessary to remove every alternate plant, leaving them thus six feet apart, though Mr. Gilder thinks eight feet would be preferable. The flowering commenced early in September, and the cotton began to ripen in November, and the gathering of the first crop was finished by the middle of January. "A second, but a very small crop, may be expected in May; opinions are divided on the island of Bourbon, whether the plant should then be cut down, or simply left to the operation of nature."

The cost of this experiment consisted of rent, and of the expenses for cultivating 27 begahs of land, with those for gathering and cleaning the cotton, and amounted to 450r. 2a. The proceeds, by sale of bejaree, value of 180 maunds of seed, and of 44½ maunds of clean cotton, amounted to 631r. 3a. But the expenses, it was said, might be reduced one fourth, if the experiment had been made on a larger scale.

This cotton it is satisfactory to trace:—Mr. Goodwin, the warehouse-keeper at Bombay, to whom the cotton was sent, says, "It is gratifying to me to have it in my power to acquaint Government that I am assured by Mr. Sollier, the supercargo of the French ship Bourbon, to whom I have shown the cotton, that it is fully equal to any produced on Bourbon, that it would fetch 2*s*. 3*d*. per lb. English, in Europe." Sent to England, this cotton was pronounced "fine, silky, even staple, of fair length, good bright colour, remarkably clean, having a small portion of broken leaf and crushed seed; the few yellow spots that appear are occasioned by oil from the crushed seed. This is deemed the best specimen that has been imported from Bombay raised from Bourbon seed." This cotton has been sold for 1*s*. 3*d*. per lb.

The Bombay Government, in the same letter, dated April 11, 1818, in which they announce Mr. Gilder's success, state that "a satisfactory report has been received from Mr. Hale, at Malwan, of an experiment made in the cultivation of Bourbon cotton at that place;" and request that a supply of the seed of the Pernambuco cotton should be procured, and sent out to India, with information of the mode observed in its cultivation, and the nature of the soil in which it is produced, as "it would enable us to ascertain the practicability of introducing its growth into this country." (*E. I. C.'s Papers*, p. 69.)

Notwithstanding this success in the experimental culture, no permanent effects seem to have been produced in the Bombay Presidency, though Bourbon cotton continued to be grown at Tinnevelly in the south, by Mr. Hughes, and to be imported into this country, where it was always sold at a higher price than any other from India.

In the year 1828, attention was again called to the subject by a letter from the Privy Council to the India Board, and a slight encouragement given to Indian cotton by the reduction of the import duty from 6 per cent. on the value, to a fixed rate of 4*d.* per cwt. Lord Ellenborough, then President of the India Board, suggested the expediency of attempting, on a small scale, the cultivation of all the finer sorts of foreign cotton in different and distant parts of India, under every different circumstance of soil and climate, and of transmitting to England, cleaned in the American manner, and with every precaution to protect them from the weather, samples of the cotton so raised, for the purpose of comparison with the cottons of other countries. A very able paper was, at this time, also written by H. St. George Tucker, Esq., a member of the Court of Directors, in which a number of propositions were made, which have since been carried into execution. Orders were subsequently sent by the Court of Directors to the Bombay Government, to establish experimental plantations for cotton, at the expense of the State, within the territories under their authority. We learn that, at this time, the cost of Broach cotton was 3¾*d.* per lb., and that the expenses to Europe brought it up to 4*d.*, and that it was worth in London not more than 4½*d.*, "against good cotton, deliverable at New York at the cost price of 5*d.* per lb., and selling in London for 6½*d.* per lb."

Several farms were accordingly established; in Guzerat, under the superintendence of Mr. Finney, an indigo planter from Bengal; in the Deccan, Candeish, and Dharwar, under Dr. Lush; and, in the island of Salsette, a few plantations were established under the Collector. Seeds of American cotton, with a "Whitney's saw-gin, were sent both to Bengal and Bombay. The objects pointed out were, the improvement of the Bhyratta kupas of Bengal, and the best kinds grown about Surat and Broach; also the cultivation of all the finer sorts of foreign cottons, in different situations as to soil, and particularly in districts bordering on the sea-coast. Native growers were directed to be incited to improvement, seed to be distributed gratis or at a low price, and rewards were to be conferred on such natives as succeeded; while Europeans were to be encouraged to make experiments in cotton culture, by securing to them land at a low rent while used for the cultivation of cotton. The general capabilities and the extent of the trade in cotton of these districts having been already referred to (p. 29), we may proceed to treat of the experiments which have been made to improve the culture and cleaning of their cotton.

The general results obtained by Dr. Lush in Dharwar have already been referred to (p. 339), and we have now only to notice those obtained in the low country during this series of experiments. In consequence of the season for sowing having passed, Mr. Finney was authorised to purchase and clean some Broach cotton. This he did so effectually, that it sold for $6\frac{1}{4}d.$ per lb., when the superior thomil cotton sent by the Commercial Resident was selling for $5\frac{1}{4}d.$; but the Government were soon afterwards deprived of his services by death, and Mr. Martin was appointed to carry on the experimental culture in Guzerat. This gentleman having been authorised in May, 1831, to cultivate cotton on the farm at Danda to the greatest possible extent, so as to produce improved specimens of cotton of various kinds, and to induce the cultivators of the country to follow his example, reported that these objects might be most speedily attained if the farmers could be induced to cultivate, or contract to do so under his directions. But he at the same time stated, "that from what he had seen of the cultivation of the cotton plant, in which so much depended upon the season and so little upon the skill of the cultivator, it appeared to him that more improvement might be looked for from a better mode of gathering the kupas than from any alteration that could be introduced in the cultivation. As all the Broach cotton sold for nearly the same price, the cultivators would not take the trouble to pick it carefully." He therefore recommended that a certain quantity of well-cleaned cotton should be purchased from each village, and that small rewards should be given. It is further observed that Mr. Martin, after the experience acquired during a residence of near eighteen months, in a letter dated 26th of October, 1831, felt no hesitation in giving it as his decided opinion, "that no improvement was to be expected from any alteration in the mode of cultivating cotton in Guzerat." He subsequently rented 2000 beegahs of his farm to natives who engaged to cultivate under his directions, retaining only a small portion in his own hands. He was further authorised to establish subsidiary farms on the western side of the Gulf of Cambay. In February, 1833, he fixed upon two spots, one near Dundooka, and the other near Rampore, where he proposed planting Egyptian and Pernambuco cotton seed. In addition to these, another farm of 500 beegahs was established near the villages of Ochaltee and Uwadur in the Broach district. The land is described as being most advantageously situated about 6 miles south of Broach, and bounded on one side by a small river. In these farms the cotton chiefly cultivated was the indigenous cotton, and the chief object was to pick it clean, and then to carefully separate the cotton from the seed. This would necessarily bring a higher price for the cotton without improving its staple: it seems to have been valued at 7¾*d.* to 8*d.* Of the small quantity of New Orleans which was cultivated, we find that it was valued at 8½*d.* to 9½*d.* per lb., when some of the Guzerat was valued only at 5*d.*, and others at 6¾*d.* to 7½*d.* in the year 1834. (v. *E. I. C.'s Papers*, pp. 274 to 280.)

These immediate results are sufficiently gratifying; but some which were unexpected, and which are comparatively unknown, are still more important, and very encouraging as regards the permanence in goodness of quality of the foreign cottons introduced into India. In March, 1839, Mr. Ewart presented some cotton to the Agricultural Society of Calcutta, which was pronounced excellent and quite equal to the best New Orleans cotton. This was cultivated by Dr. Burn at Kaira, from plants which he found in the hedgerows, near where the experiment had been conducted by Mr. Gilder in 1816. The plant appeared to Dr. Burn to be something between the Bourbon and the common Broach cotton, and he states that it requires a dry sandy soil and no irrigation, water or manure sending it all to leaves and branches. He at the same time cultivated the Egyptian, two kinds of Broach, and acclimated

Bourbon. The Bombay Chamber of Commerce, in their Report dated the 28th of January, 1841, state that this cotton was compared by competent judges to the best New Orleans, and was valued at 170 to 180 rupees, at a time when the best Surat was selling at 140 rupees. Dr. Burn informed the author, in a letter dated 29th August, 1840, that he had cultivated it for five years, that the seed was small and black, evidently Bourbon acclimated, and that as it grew in the light sandy soils, without extra care or expense, he was convinced it was worth cultivating.

In connection with this may be mentioned another instance of successful experimental culture, which is likewise mentioned by the Bombay Chamber of Commerce in the above report, and respecting which the author was first informed by Dr. Gibson, Superintendent of the H. C.'s Botanical Gardens in the Bombay Presidency. Mr. Elphinston, the principal revenue officer at Rutnagheery in the Concan, animated by the laudable desire of improving a culture which was so likely to be of benefit both to India and to this country, had for some years, at considerable expense, cultivated several kinds of cotton. Of these, Dr. Gibson wrote that he had discontinued the Brazilian species, because in his locality it required too much irrigation. His Sea Island the Bombay Chamber pronounced to be the best, and beautiful as to staple, colour, fineness, and entire freedom from impurity of any kind. Such cotton, it was stated, would be likely to produce 150 per cent. above the best Surat. The New Orleans in colour, cleanliness, and fineness, was also pronounced good, but being inferior in staple, was not considered likely to produce more than 50 per cent. above the best Surat. But a third kind is more remarkable than either of the above, as it is described to be the produce of an indigenous cotton, and which was called *Conkanee* by Mr. Elphinston. This was pronounced next in value to the Sea Island, being a very beautiful cotton in staple, colour, fineness, and cleanliness, and worth above 100 per cent. more than the best Surat.

The most remarkable fact in connection with this cotton, is, that though called indigenous, and now growing all over the Conkan, Mr. Elphinston had, by care in the cultivation and gathering, raised it to a value not only exceeding the best Broach cotton, but even surpassing that grown from New

Orleans seed. But there were strong reasons for doubting whether this was really an indigenous cotton, as there is a great resemblance between Dr. Burn's Bourbon and Mr. Elphinston's Conkanee. In fact, there is now no doubt that both originate from the same source; that is, the successive introductions of Bourbon cotton-seed into India for the several experiments which were early instituted in Bombay, as well as in other parts of India. The Bombay Chamber of Commerce justly observe, that "as a considerable quantity of different foreign seeds (and among them the Bourbon) was introduced in the year 1829, in experiments in Guzerat, Candeish, the Deccan, and Dharwar, it seems by no means improbable that Bourbon seed may have been obtained by some of the Ryots of Rutnagheery." If both this fortuitous result and that of Dr. Burn, at Kaira, be considered in conjunction with the continued cultivation of Hughes's Tinnivelly cotton, which was also originally produced from seed introduced from the Isle of Bourbon, it will be evident, as the Bombay Chamber remark, that this variety, at least, does not degenerate, and a stimulus will be given to extend its cultivation. Dr. Gibson, who afterwards saw the plant cultivated by Mr. Elphinston, wrote to the author that in habit, and form of leaf, it differed from the New Orleans, but hardly otherwise, and that it seemed to him the hardiest of all our Exotic cottons.

Mr. Elphinston has given an account of his first experiments in a letter to the Revenue Commissioner (*Return*, p. 444), and as some of his results are of importance and of more extensive application, it is necessary to notice them a little in detail. Mr. Elphinston obtained the seeds of all the different kinds of cotton, and continued his experiments, at his own expense, for four years; but when he found that the Sea Island and the Conkanee, or acclimated Bourbon, were the most highly esteemed, he cultivated these on a more extended scale, and with very favorable results as far as the quality of the cotton was concerned. But the cotton was expensive from the necessity of irrigation, and from having to intrust the whole of the management to others, as well as from the experiment having been made in a district where no cotton was grown. He observes, "Having found from experience that the cultivation of cotton, where irrigation from wells was necessary, was very expensive, I rented some land with a running stream upon it, by which much of the expense was reduced. But I have since discovered, that if the Sea Island cotton seed be sown at the very commencement of the monsoon, in any land not liable to be laid under water by the rains, irrigation may be dispensed with altogether, as the plant comes into bearing about four months after the seed is sown, retains its vitality without watering throughout the hot weather, and in this country (unnipt by the frosts of America) changes its habit from an annual to a perennial, and will last for years on the same ground without fresh sowing, merely requiring to be cut down about one-half before the monsoon. It puts forth fresh leaves and shoots as soon as the rains commence. The advantage to be obtained from irrigation with both the Sea Island and Conkanee cotton seed is, that the plants continue bearing nearly the whole year round; whereas if left to nature, they would cease to bear before the end of the cold weather." Mr. Elphinston further improved what he conceived to be one of the cottons of India, that is, the Conkanee, by crossing it with the Sea Island, but these are two varieties of the same species, *Gossypium barbadense*. (v. p. 145.)

The extent of Mr. Elphinston's experiments may be judged of by the quantity he sent to Bombay for sale, and its quality by the high prices which he obtained. The cotton was sold on the 25th of May, 1841, by the Chamber of Commerce in Bombay, and brought the following prices:

10 bales of Sea Island	at 225r. per candy.
14 " "	230 "
6 bags of stained ditto	100 "
1 bale of indigenous Conkanee	170 "

Mr. Elphinston has made the following comparison between his expenses and returns and those obtained by Mr. Gilder at Kaira:

	At Kaira.			At Rutnagheery.			Difference.			Rutnagheery exceeded that at Kaira by
	r.	a.	p.	r.	a.	p.	r.	a.	p.	r.
First year	7	7	2	26	9	8	19	2	6	275 per cent.
Second year . .	9	3	11	12	9	8	3	5	9	36 "

"The following shows the respective average difference of the expense of cultivation during the two years of the experiment:

	r.	a.	p.
Kaira	8	5	6
Rutnagheeree	19	9	8
Difference	11	4	2

The Rutnagheeree exceeding in expense the Kaira cultivation by 135 per cent.

"The respective difference of produce per beegah at Rutnagheeree, Kaira, and Broach, for one year (being the second year's growth of Bourbon), is as follows:

Rutnagheeree	178 Surat seers.
Kaira	66 "
Broach	60 "

(Signed) A. ELPHINSTON,
Collector."

Mr. Elphinston has given a detailed account of his expenses and returns, by which it appears he obtained no less than 166 lbs. per beegah, hence that $4\frac{1}{2}$ beegahs of land sufficed to raise a candy of cotton, and that though there was a loss of 100 rupees in the first year, there was a profit of 132 rupees in the second year, or a net profit of 32 rupees 9 annas. But the natives, as he observes, could cultivate much more economically than he did.

Mr. Simson, the Revenue Commissioner of the time, recommended, in consequence of Mr. Elphinston's success, that he should be allowed to make experiments on a somewhat extended scale with this cotton in the red soil, at different spots in his collectorate: "I would accordingly beg to recommend that he be permitted to expend any sum, not exceeding 10,000 rupees, at such places and in such manner as he may think best," and Mr. Simson concludes with—"too much praise cannot be given to Mr. Elphinston for his disinterested public spirit in carrying out this experiment at his own expense."

The Bombay Government accordingly sanctioned the above sum being so expended, but as this was disapproved of by the Government of India, the case was referred to the Honorable Court of Directors, who expressed themselves gratified with the public-spirited exertions which had been reported to them, and "therefore approve of your having authorised Mr. Elphinston to prosecute his experiments to a certain extent on account of Government, and of your having placed 10,000 rupees at his disposal for this purpose."

Mr. Elphinston was thus enabled to continue his experimental culture until the state of his health obliged him to return to Europe. His zeal and experience have since, as we have seen above, been of great use in Candeish. He expended only a portion of the money which was authorised. The cotton which he grew was favorably reported upon, and sold well in the Liverpool market.

For instance, the Rutnagheery cotton, which was shipped in the 'Clarendon,' was valued by Messrs. Cunningham and Hinshaw, on 12th January, 1847: 6 bales of the Rutnaghery Bourbon, called equal to fair Orleans, at $7\frac{1}{4}$*d.* to $7\frac{1}{2}$*d.*, 3 bales of the Hybrid Bourbon at $7\frac{1}{2}$*d.*, some in bundles, apparently from Sea Island seed, at 7*d.* and $7\frac{1}{4}$*d.*, others at 8*d.* and 9*d.*, and two samples were considered worth 10*d.* per lb.*

* Having accidentally omitted, under the head of Dharwar, to notice an experiment with Bourbon cotton, we may here rectify the omission. Mr. Hadow, assistant to the Collector of Dharwar, and in charge of the Noulgoond and Dummul Talookas, having procured, at his own expense, a supply of Sea Island and Bourbon cotton seed from Mr. Elphinston, obtained permission to cultivate ten acres of land with it on account of Government. (*Return*, p. 454.) Mr. Hadow hired ten acres of unoccupied black soil (the only land then available), near Guddug, but which he afterwards learned was unoccupied, because, having been incessantly cropped, it had become unproductive. One fourth of the field failed. "The plants, however, that sprung up thrived well, and continued healthy throughout the hot weather, without irrigation being had recourse to, and yielded the crop much about the same time as the indigenous shrub." Having cleaned about one half of his crop with the churka, Mr. Hadow obtained about six maunds of first-rate clean cotton from these plants, for which Mr. Hadow was offered 2r. 8a. per maund by a Parsee cotton merchant in Belgaum, but which was sold in Bombay for 4r. 8a., or 27r. for the six maunds. He expected as much more for the remainder, and 16r. for the seed, making his return 54r.; but, as his expenses had been 87r. 6a., a loss of 17r. 6a. was entailed on the first year's culture. As one fourth of the field had failed, and the expenses had been greater than if the field had been cultivated by a native, and as the yield of the Bourbon cotton is greater in the second than in the first year, while the expenses are diminished, there seems every probability that the Bourbon cotton might be profitably cultivated by natives, even in Dharwar. But here it is of less consequence, indeed, not advisable, because the New Orleans, which can be cultivated in the same land, is more productive; and, though a given quantity of New Orleans cotton

The practical results which may be deduced from these experiments are important. 1st. We may observe, that notwithstanding the 115 inches of rain which fell, irrigation was found necessary, showing that it is not the quantity of rain, but the manner in which it is diffused over a succession of months, that is most important. 2dly. Though the plants require two years to yield a profitable crop, yet in the first year some of the ordinary grains may be grown between the rows of cotton, as was done by Mr. Gilder at Kaira. 3dly. The permanence of character in the staple of the acclimated Bourbon is another important feature.

We therefore believe, that in situations where there is facility of irrigation and the soil not too rich, these varieties of the American cotton might be profitably cultivated by natives, as their methods are economical and their skill sufficient in most of the western districts, whenever they take pains not only in growing, but in picking and cleaning their cotton, and afterwards in keeping it free from adulteration.

The above fact of the permanence in character of the American species of cotton, even when introduced into what may, upon the whole, be considered an unsuitable soil and climate, has been further proved by recent experiments. Mr. Blount, for instance, observes: "The New Orleans, Georgian white and yellow, Sea Island white and yellow, Bourbon and Egyptian, will all produce for a number of years without planting, provided there is sufficiency of moisture at all seasons. This I have seen in two gardens, particularly one at the residence of the Rev. Mr. Hillier, at the village of Bettegherry, where these cotton plants have been growing for several years, round the boundaries of a Pawn (*Piper Betle*) garden; the trees have attained a large size, and the produce from them is very superior." Mr. Blount further mentions with respect to the plants from the New Orleans seed, which have been cultivated for nine years, that they are as productive now as they were

will not realize in the Bombay or Liverpool markets as large a price as the Bourbon, yet, as Mr. Shaw says, "a given quantity of land of the Orleans cultivation will produce considerably more cotton-wool than the same land would do, planted with Bourbon cotton." (*Return*, pp. 484, 489.) The cotton was valued in Bombay at about 115r. to 120r., whilst the indigenous Dharwar cotton was valued at 80r. in the same market.

the first year, and the staple quite as long, though the pods are not so large nor the staple so long as when grown in America.

§ 30. Experimental Culture in the Broach District.

Dr. Gibson, inquiring expressly into sites suitable to the growth of American cotton, says, "looking to moisture and the sea-breeze, he could find none in the Concan suitable, though he thinks there may be some on the Malabar coast, if the moisture of the air is not excessive in that tract. Proceeding northwards, the Northern Concan beyond Damaun is occupied by sugar cultivation, which cannot be displaced without loss. Further north, the flat plains towards the mouths of the Myhee and Saburmuttee, so also the Kattywar coast, where, as at Mongrole, excellent cotton is already grown, all afford favorable sites. The Surat and Broach districts have long been famous for the growth of cotton.

"Cotton is grown in the Southern Attaveesy as an occasional crop. As we approach the Tapty it is extensively cultivated, particularly in the Bralcha and Teembra districts. Between the Tapty and Nerbudda, chiefly in the Hansot pergunnah and the Broach, Korril, Duboy, and Jumbooser districts, it forms by far the most important and frequent product; crossing the Myhee, and in all the districts north, it may be said to be an occasional article rather than a staple. The species which produces the cotton in the Ahmedabad districts and in the brownish soil generally, is a triennial, a larger plant than the other. I ought to mention that the annual kind is extensively grown in the Dolka and Dundooka pergunnahs." (*Gibson*, l. c.) The climate in the southern districts, the vicinity of the sea, and the proximity of the mountainous tracts covered with jungle, tend to render it more moist, and the temperature throughout the year more equable, than is the case in other parts of Guzerat; and near the sea, the hot winds are comparatively little felt.

Farther inland, and in the immediate vicinity of the hills, the heat is greater, and in both situations, the humid and loaded atmosphere in the s.w. monsoon is often painfully felt, particularly at night. In the whole of this district, rain falls in greater quantities than to the northward. In the jungle districts to the east, the supply of rain is said never to fail in the driest seasons, and it often falls there when none is apparent in the more open districts.

In the midland districts, viz. those from the Nerbudda to the Saburmuttee, the average of the temperature throughout the year is greater than in the northern and southern districts of the province. Here we want the open sea to temper the air as it does to the southward, while the richer soil and more numerous enclosures tend to render the nights hotter than is the case in the northern division. The hot winds blow in this district from about the 10th of March to the 20th of May (varying, of course, in different years), and at this time the thermometer in a double-walled tent often rises to 115°, while in a house it may be 103°; at such seasons, the natives themselves often suffer from "*coups de soleil.*"

North of the Saburmuttee, the heat from the beginning of March to the beginning of June is more oppressive by day than in the midland and southern districts, but the nights are greatly cooler, as the lighter soil and the comparatively open country cool the air more rapidly than in the other situations. Here the violence of the hot wind is great, and more distressing, from the quantities of fine sand it carries with it. After the 20th of October, the mornings and evenings are felt refreshingly cold, and in the cold season hoar frost and ice are not uncommon, whereas in the midland districts they are rather seldom seen. (*Gibson*, l. c.)

Notwithstanding the failure of the numerous experiments which had been undertaken at various periods, we have seen that another, more comprehensive than all the former, has been going on since the year 1840. Of the ten planters who came over with Captain Bayles, three were destined for Bombay, and sailed from London in June, 1840, arrived there about the end of the rainy season, and subsequently, having been able to obtain land within five miles of Broach, were settled in that district under the superintendence of Dr. Peart. But the experiment was a failure, if that can be called a failure which had hardly had a trial. In the first place, the planters confined their experiment to the *black* soil of Broach, which only in appearance resembles the black alluvial soil of Louisiana.

This, as related in the printed accounts* of the former experiments, had always been found unsuitable to the American species of cotton. The three planters, moreover, at the end of the year 1841, gave up their engagements and returned to their own country, having been dissatisfied, as we learn from a letter from the Hon. W. B. Baring, to Milner Gibson, Esq., with the amount of their salaries, and disheartened with the failure of their crops, from which they expected to derive a part of their remuneration. Dr. Gibson, well acquainted with the country and with the results of former experiments, wrote to the author, that he had not been sanguine of success, as he was of opinion that there is more difference in the soil and climate than in the modes of cultivation. To attempt the culture of the American cotton in the old cotton soils of Broach was, to say the least of it, a folly, because it was expecting success in the teeth of repeated failures. Dr. Gibson would have tried the culture in new soils, at the head of the Gulf of Cambay and in other places, and even in the lower or Dijburna district of Broach. Even in this experiment, some American cotton seed, sown in a garden which differed in having the common sandy soil of the district, produced good cotton and a fair proportion. But only two or three bales on the whole were grown. (*Return*, p. 462.)

On the first arrival of the planters being known, the Government authorised the purchase of cotton standing in the fields, in order that the planters might superintend the processes of picking and preparing it for market.

The experiment was ordered to be immediately resumed, by one of the American planters being sent from Bombay and another from Bengal.

The Bombay Government having pointed out Dr. Burn, who so successfully grew the cotton at Kaira, and who was then on furlough in England, as well suited for the superintendence, and Dr. Burn having offered his services, he was recommended by the Court for the office. The experiments were resumed under his superintendence in July, 1842, and he

* As in the volume of Papers published by the East India Company; in General Briggs's pamphlet on the '*Culture of Cotton in India;*' and in the author's notice, which accompanied the original dispatches (v. '*Return,*' p. 28 to p. 36), and which now forms a part of his '*Productive Resources of India.*' (p. 312 to p. 355.)

continued in charge of them until October, 1846. He first applied himself to having the gins set in order, with the assistance of Mr. Hall, the mechanic and engineer who had been sent out by the Court of Directors. Dr. Burn first cleaned the cotton which had been stored between January and May, 1841, and had remained in the warehouse till July, 1842. This was cleaned by the saw-gins then set to work. A portion of the cotton having been packed in the Atlas cotton-press at Broach, Dr. Burn recommended that it should be sent to England in the same state without being re-screwed at Bombay, The consignment consisted of 178 bales of Broach cotton purchased from the ryots, with the exception of three marked Mexican cotton, one of which seems to have been raised under the superintendence of the then Collector of Surat. The cotton was shipped in the 'Mertoun,' and realized from 4*d.* to 4¼*d.* per lb.; but we have no means of comparing this with the cost, in consequence of the changes which had taken place in the management. Dr. Burn calculated in 1843, that the cotton to pay should sell in England for 4½*d.*, that is, supposing 110 rupees had been given for a candy of 784 lbs. of cleaned cotton in Broach. If we look at the diagram, p. 74, we may observe that the price of cotton was then rising. Since that time, it is well known, much lower prices only have been obtainable, and the candy of cotton has sold in Broach for 60 rupees. The exchange being 2*s.* 0½*d.* per rupee, Dr. Burn calculated that

At 110r. per candy, one pound of cotton would cost . .	3·678
Freight at £3 per ton of 50 feet	0·514
Insurance at 2 per cent.	0·070
Charges in England	0·125
	4·387

Dr. Burn was well pleased with the favorable reports given by the brokers and spinners of this country on the native cotton cleaned by the saw-gin, and this more particularly on a future occasion, when accounts of the sale of the cotton sent to this country in the 'Princess Charlotte' reached him. He writes on the 19th of April, 1845, "There is something very satisfactory in the favorable reports on our ginned cotton. That it should beat the churka-cleaned by ¼*d.* per lb., as Mr. Laird informs me is the case, proves to me that gin-machinery may be used here with profit. Of the cotton sent home in the 'Princess Charlotte,' part was ginned and part churkaed; both were alike from the same fields, and prepared with equal care; but the ginned beats the churkaed by $\frac{1}{4}d.$ per lb. The expenses of gin-work should be only a little more than one-half of those of churka-cleaned, and I am including in my estimate every charge, wear and tear of machinery, &c." At that time, Dr. Burn stated, that the cleaning by churkas was usually calculated to cost about 10 rupees per candy of 784 lbs. of clean cotton-wool, and he thinks 5 rupees would be about the net cost for gin-work for the same amount of wool; but this, of course, would depend on skill and management.

Mr. Davies, the present Collector of Broach, in reply to a query whether the saw-gin is equally well adapted to the process of cleaning the native cotton without injuring the staple, writes:—

"Looking to the operations of the Broach factory during the last eight or nine years in which the ginning of indigenous cotton according to the American process has formed an important part of each season's operations, under American gentlemen as well as under Dr. Burn, the adaptation of the gin to the native cottons cannot well be doubted. Some degree of injury to the staple is admitted; but taking into consideration the large premiums realized on the sale of native ginned cotton in the Bombay market, the general superiority of the article so prepared does not admit of a question."

The success that was obtained by Dr. Burn has been carried to a still greater extent by his successors; but his success in cultivating American cotton was not greater than that of his predecessors.

Three small farms were established, one at Umjudbagh, where there is a large house and a garden in which the gin-house has been constructed. The second in black soil at Kokurmara, three or four miles lower down the river than Broach, where Mr. Hawley was established; and the third at Kurode, which was situated up the river, and was particularly selected by the Collector, Mr. Ravenscroft, because the soil was a light alluvium. The following account from Dr. Burn is interesting, though it only gives the same unfavorable account that we have had from North-Western India.

"The Mexican seed got on famously on light alluvial soils till the middle of this month, when the plants generally sustained a blight, which shrivelled up the leaves, and then the blossoms and pods dropped off. The great heat of the sun and *dry, hot wind* seemed the only cause of this.* Now, again, with the decreasing temperature, young leaves are shooting, and we shall have a crop in the cold weather. The plants are two and three feet high on this soil, but on the *black soil* the results are similar to last year's,—plants a foot high are completely blighted. I give up all hopes of this plant, unless acclimation, by growing it from the root as a perennial for a few years, will do it good. It is too delicate under the heat of our vertical October sun. But, if we have not been fortunate with it, we have been particularly so with the two indigenous cottons,—*herbaceum* and *arboreum*. From the lateness of the season to begin operations, in June last, I could only act upon a very small scale; but, from what I see, my most sanguine hopes as to improving them by culture, are about to be realized. What we have of them is as fine as could be wished: and there is also some acclimated Bourbon thriving. About five acres of *herbaceum* were sown on the 28th of June, in black soil, drills four feet wide, no manure, in the midst of other native crops, for comparison; in short, the only difference in treatment consisted in deeper ploughing, doubling the width between the drills, extra-hoeings, and careful choice of seed from ripe, well-grown cotton. This field is now just about to come into blossom, is about three feet high all over, and the bushes of a fine uniform, regular shape and size,—the wonder and admiration of the surrounding ryots. Mr. Hawley says, we *may expect* to succeed with this cotton, and he wants 300 acres sown with it next season. He says he will be satisfied with 400 lbs. per acre. The ryots say there will be 600 or 800, if the season continues favorable. I am told that the average of the cotton crops in this zillah is 340 lbs. *per acre*, but that, on fine, fresh soil, which has been well cared for, 960 lbs. have been picked. Our soil is what has long been under culture of cotton. The cotton plant here is raised by the natives cheaper and easier than any other produce, —easier than the two common millets even!"

In another letter, Dr. Burn writes:

"The Mexican has totally different habits from the indigenous cotton. I see, from the way in which the Bourbon seed grows, that it has in a

* In another letter: "The heat of October has been tremendous: plants, three feet high, covered with blossoms and green pods, withered by the vertical rays and heat of the sun."

curious way adopted the habit of the common native cotton, by a process which enables it to succeed in standing the climate when sown on a soil that is favorable to it. The native cotton, three feet high, is thriving beautifully: nothing could be finer. We expect the quantity and quality will equal our sanguine expectations; and, when the seed has been selected, it will no doubt do well and the staple improve. *G. arboreum* is now growing splendidly, and is putting forth bud-blossoms (that is, now the great heat is over). It was sown with the Mexican, which puts forth buds when two months old, or earlier. The gin is steadily at work, and turns out daily 560 to 600 lbs. of clean cotton, equal to the work of twenty churkas. A churka will not yield more than 40 lbs. after a hard day's work, from daylight to ten o'clock."

Here we observe, that the cotton plants appeared prosperous during the rains, but that at their conclusion they withered and became burnt up, as we have observed was also the case in Goruckpore and in North-Western India. But, as was likewise observed in those places, the plants afterwards revived, for Dr. Burn subsequently wrote: "Our crops are harvesting still, and turning out well; our Mexican seed, after all, has so far come round, as to yield at the rate of lbs. (135) per acre, we have picked thus much on the average from seven acres, on light alluvial soil, and there is more to come, as the season is not yet over. This is more than I would have given it credit for in November last. The native cotton, however, has yielded us, up to this date, at the rate of lbs. (421) per acre." The crop of this season was shipped in the 'Princess Charlotte,' and sold at Liverpool on the 30th April, 1845. The Court of Directors, in transmitting the accounts of this sale, state,—"It appears, by the printed circular of Messrs. Worthington, that the highest price at which Surats have sold, during the present year, is $3\frac{3}{4}$*d.* per lb., and the lowest $2\frac{1}{4}$*d.* The prices obtained for your consignment per 'Princess Charlotte,' were $3\frac{3}{4}$*d.* per lb. for the lowest, and 4*d.* for the highest, as per margin."* Samples of the cotton of this season were submitted to the Bombay Chamber of Commerce, who reported its value to be from 8 to 10 rupees above the average of Broach cotton then in the market.

In December, 1843, Dr. Burn submitted to the Bombay Government the details of a plan of operations for the then

* 3109 lbs. at 4*d.*; 3309 lbs. at $3\frac{3}{4}$*d.*; 20,839 lbs. at $3\frac{7}{8}$*d.*

ensuing season of 1844-45, but this appears to have been intended for the culture of the indigenous cotton only, for it is observed, by the Bombay Government, "As the fact of the climate and soil of Broach not being adapted to the culture of the American cotton had been fully established, the only object with which the experiments should be conducted in that district must be to improve the cultivation and cleaning of the indigenous kind, and, for the attainment of that end, our President did not consider that any extension of the existing operations was requisite." In the beginning of April, Dr. Burn proposed giving up the Kurrode farm, and making additions to that at Kokurmara. But as farming operations had commenced in May (sowing taking place in all June) before the subject was decided, Dr. Burn again, in March 1845, proposed giving up the land at Kurrode, which was accordingly done. From this it would appear, that he either considered the soil as not so suitable, or the distance of the farm from Broach as too great. But the Bombay Government were not satisfied with the progress of the experiments at Broach, for they observe (June 25, 1845): "We beg in this place to remark, that the experiments at Broach appear to have produced no effect beyond the precincts of the farm. The ryots have neither adopted the mode of cultivation followed on the farm, nor the saw-gin as the machinery for cleaning their cotton. In vain do we sow the finest cotton, pick it in the cleanest manner, clear it of all impurities, and throw a few bales into the market, so long as the people of the country evince no interest in the undertaking, and continue satisfied with producing a dirty and inferior staple. At Dharwar, however, under the management of the American planters, we are carrying the ryots and merchants with us, new cotton is cultivated, and the gins are getting into use." ('*Return,*' p. 509.)

Mr. Davies, collector of Broach, in his replies (dated as late as November 28, 1849) to the fifty-one queries of the Hon. Mr. Willoughby, writes: "The American varieties have never so far prospered in Broach as to enable me to say which kind of soil is best adapted to their growth." And again: "The experiments pursued in Broach for improving its cotton, have hitherto contemplated three ends,—the introduction of American cotton; an improved mode of cultivating the indigenous cotton; and the introduction of superior methods of cleaning the cotton. After a fair trial, attended by a heavy outlay, the first two objects have been relinquished as unattainable, and although a partial attempt has been made in this season (1849) to resume the experiments, by introducing small parcels of New Orleans seed acclimated at Dharwar, and also of fresh Georgian seed, received from the Hon. Court of Directors, it is greatly to be apprehended that the result will only confirm the expediency of abandoning further trials of the exotic plant."

There is no doubt of the inexpediency of making further attempts to introduce an exotic plant into a soil and climate in which it has so repeatedly failed. The reasons of this failure are not stated in the official documents. But, in the letter from Dr. Burn, we have every reason to believe that the true cause is pointed out; and that it seems to be great heat accompanied with drought, which succeeds the moisture of the rainy season. In fact, the same as we have referred to in the Bengal Presidency. If this be not the cause, we are unable to discover any sufficient reason for failure in Broach and success in Dharwar, in the same kind of black soil. Broach, being bounded by the sea-coast on one side, and by a great river on another, might be supposed to be sufficiently moist, particularly as we have seen how large is the quantity of rain which falls in these maritime provinces. It is probable, as we have inferred, that Broach may be drier than some of them, because the hills which back it are lower, and as the rains commence in June and terminate in September, there is moisture for three or four months, and drought, in a great measure, for the remainder of the year, which may assist in ripening the cotton in some places, but burn it up in others.

It is probable that the rains are succeeded by a dry soil and clear, hot atmosphere, which are as unsuitable in Broach as in Bundlecund to a plant which has lived through the moisture of the rainy season. But to form correct conclusions respecting comparative experiments in the cultivation of plants, we ought to have not only a detailed account of the temperature and of the fall of rain, but also of the moisture of the atmosphere, and, if possible, of that of the soil. This it might be possible to measure by thoroughly drying small portions of the soil from certain depths at different seasons of the year, taking care to employ the same weight of soil, and then ascertain how much it loses after having been dried. If dryness of the soil should be the cause of the failure, then irrigation, as before recommended, would be the proper remedy.

In reference to this very point, Dr. Gibson wrote to the author in December, 1842:

"I continue of opinion, that in the black 'Khanum' soil of Broach, the exotic kinds will not do. In proposing, as you do, the vicinity of the Doab canal for the growth of the plant, you appear to do so on the same grounds that I do, viz. that the extent of irrigated country there must give to the atmosphere a degree of moisture essential to the proper development of these varieties. Therefore I would say, with you, that in such places there is some chance of success, provided we have a loose soil to work in."

And further, in the same letter, he contrasts his experiment, in a dry soil and climate, with another, made in a situation where an opposite state had been artificially produced:

"I now send a small specimen of cotton, raised here from excellent seed, forwarded by you, and which all vegetated. My object in enclosing this is to show what I mean by the diseased seed, and consequently discoloured staple, which, as far as I have seen, is a great drawback to cultivation here. I have spared no pains in trying different soils, &c., but my success has been uniformly none. I mentioned in my last garden report, that a beegah of good and rather productive Upland had been raised by Mr. Dickenson, of the sugar manufactory, from seed given him by me, and which you furnished to me. His success, I think, affords a proof of what I have above stated, viz. the necessity for this variety having a moist atmosphere. His plantation was in a sheltered and rather wooded garden, watered by a well-supplied aqueduct, so abundant as to allow half the garden (about sixty acres) to be in a state of continual moisture. Here, then, the moist atmosphere no doubt was the chief cause of success, and failure would, I think, be equally certain in a dryer and more exposed situation. As to treatment of the cotton plant by the American planters, it appears to me evident, that, in the first attempts they have made, they have allowed too little for the dryness of our atmosphere, and that, by their repeated drill-ploughings, they permitted the moisture necessary for the support of the plant to exhale.

"These defects of practice a little experience will correct. I also think that they should use as little as possible exotic implements, seeing that the cultivators of this country have seldom the means, and still less frequently the will, to procure them."

Mr. Davies, however, observes:

"The Broach district is probably one of the worst adapted for irrigation throughout the Presidency, owing to its geological structure. Wells are sunk through earth, sand, and clay, to a great depth, before water is obtainable, and such wells are necessarily very expensive. So little, in fact, is irrigation had recourse to, that the whole amount of irrigated land, inclusive of those growing rice in the neighbourhood of tanks, is short of half a beegah per cent. on the entire cultivation."

But Col. Grant, in his recent work, '*Cotton and Railways,*' has shown that a remedy is within reach, at the same time that he bears testimony to the beneficial effects of water on the cotton plant. In irrigating it must, however, be remembered, that excess of moisture is as injurious as its deficiency, and that, though a check is required to favour the formation of bolls and cotton, the transition must not be too sudden.

The following are extracts from Col. Grant's work:

"Nothing appears more susceptible of improvement from culture and a regular supply of water than cotton; in fact, the cotton of the common field and that of the irrigated bed can scarcely be recognised as the same plant; not only do the shrubs attain an increased size, and bear more numerous pods, but each pod is much larger, and contains a much greater quantity of fibre; indeed, our Indian kupas has all the appearance of a degenerated plant, of which the seeds have gradually diminished in size and powers of production.

"Perhaps no country offers better opportunities for applying irrigation to cotton culture on a large scale than the districts of Surat and Broach, particularly the former; or the land lying between Surat and Broach, bounded throughout its length by those two noble rivers, the Nerbudda and the Taptee, running nearly parallel to each other, at a distance of from forty to fifty miles apart; from the nature of the soils and country, offering every facility for the construction of a canal.

"Were a canal cut from the left bank of the Nerbudda, a little above the city of Broach, to the Taptee, near Surat, it would be somewhat more than forty miles in length, and would intersect throughout its course the finest possible cotton soil. The point at which the canal would leave the Nerbudda being some thirty miles from the sea—whereas it would join the Taptee about ten miles from the sea—there could be no fear of a sufficient fall throughout the canal.

"From the right bank of the same river, above fifteen miles above Broach, near the village of Shahpoona, a smaller canal, about twenty miles in length, might, it is believed, be carried to the Gulf of Cambay, by the village of Myor, near Ahmode, thus intersecting the Broach Pergunnah.

"But there are numerous small rivers throughout the districts of the Bombay Presidency, which admit of having dams thrown across them at a very moderate expense, affording a constant supply of water for the purposes of irrigation.

"India possesses the three grand requisites for the most abundant and luxuriant cultivation,—a rich soil, great heat, and great moisture. The two former are always available; but the latter is supplied during four months of the year, the remaining two thirds of the year scarcely affording any.

"One of the great advantages of irrigating from canals is the improvement effected upon the soil: the water of such canals is always turbid, and contains a large amount of soil in suspension, which is thus conveyed to the field, where it is deposited, not only by its humidity causing the plants to grow, but constantly supplying to the soil the substances withdrawn from it by cultivation." (*Grant, 'Bombay Cotton and Indian Railways,'* p. 25.)

The further charge of the experiment in Broach having been assigned to Mr. Mercer, he left Dharwar in December, 1846, and reached his new district in the beginning of the year though his stay was to be short, as he had obtained a year's leave to visit America. Mr. Simpson was then appointed to look after the experiments in Broach as well as in Candeish. Mr. Mercer at this time observed that saw-ginned cotton is improved in its market value by that process about 18 per cent., and as he thought that much of the cotton is intrinsically as good as other short-staple cottons, in fact, nearly equal to the great mass of Uplands, he considered it susceptible of improvement to the extent of at least 50 per cent., and very desirable to attempt. This, however, could be effected only by inducing the producers and dealers to bring it to the gins in a cleaner condition, and this he conceived could only be accomplished by the power of money in the district of production. This he recommended when at Manchester, but the manufacturers generally preferred the American varieties of cotton. Mr. Mercer also thought that the hand-gin could be introduced into the district, and that they could be made up as cheaply as at Dharwar, that is, for 150 rupees.

Mr. Simpson having been appointed in March, 1847, to the charge of the Broach district, applied himself, in the first instance, to the improved working of the saw-gin, in which, with the assistance of the engineer, Mr. Laidlaw, considerable improvement was made. The clean state and good quality of the cotton which was passed through the gins during this season was highly appreciated at Manchester, as we have already related at p. 96, where the Broach cotton is pronounced by the Messrs. Clarke as fully equal to the best that they had before seen, and as suitable for any weft up to 24's, while the Surat cotton was pronounced quite equal to good middling Bowed, and quite suitable for spinning any weft under 40's. This cotton unfortunately arrived at a time when prices were much depressed, and the 82 bales of Surat sold for $3\frac{1}{2}$*d.*, and the 327 bales of Broach, from Ahmode, Jumbooser, and Broach for $3\frac{1}{4}$*d.* per lb. But a bale of New Orleans cotton sold at the same time for only 3*d.* per lb.

In March, 1848, Mr. Simpson returned for a time to America, and Mr. Landon, who was well acquainted from many years' experience with the culture and commerce of cotton in the Southern States, and who had on his own account paid a visit to Bombay and Broach to make personal inquiries respecting the cotton trade, was appointed to succeed him for a limited period. Mr. Landon, after his short visit, returned to England to arrange an establishment on his own account for the purchase and cleaning of Broach cotton, in which the cotton was to be picked, handled, and cleaned in such a manner, that manufacturers would see what Broach cotton really is when supplied in the best possible state. Mr. Landon having taken the appointment in Broach until his plans were matured, arrived there on the 25th August, 1848, too late, therefore, to make any experiments in culture, though he fully intended endeavouring to find out the cause of the failure of American cotton, and whether, by any modification of culture or selection of sites, it could be successfully cultivated. Mr. Laidlaw, the engineer, he found making a few small saw-gins, that is, with four saws, which would cost about 35 rupees. The natives seemed to take no interest in these gins, and notwithstanding the repeated experiments, there was not an acre planted with American cotton, and no improvement had been made in growing or picking the native cotton. This was now more dirty than ever, and the only contention, both among ryots and dealers, seemed to be who could introduce the largest percentage of adulteration. "The first step towards improvement was picking the cotton clean." This the natives have long known how to do, though they do not choose to practise it on their own accounts. For the Broach cotton was obtained by the Commercial Resident of three different qualities, the Toomel, the Committee, and the Rasee, the first costing 4 rupees a bhar more than the last (*Williams 'on Baroche,'* p. 42), and was highly esteemed by manufacturers in this country. The second step was to abolish the village kullee or pit-system of storing the kupas, and means adopted to prevent deterioration and fraud. The third thing necessary, and which we believe would be the most effectual as it ought to insure the others, is, licensing all the presses, and appointing competent inspectors of cotton, who should have the power of detaining any ill-cleaned or adulterated cotton, and be paid by a charge on each bale. Something of this kind Mr. Landon says is done at all the cotton ports of America, where there are public weighers who charge a certain price for weighing and recording the weights. Such a plan, by establishing a system of identification and responsibility, would go far to put a stop to the commission of fraud, which is now so destructive to the cotton trade of India. The power exists of punishing fraud, and as we have seen has lately been exerted by the Collector, Mr. Davies, carrying into execution regulation 111 of 1829.

Notwithstanding the improvement which had been made in the working of the gins, Mr. Landon was enabled to carry this to so great an extent, as to make it a most efficient instrument. On the 29th April, 1849, he wrote to the author, that they had just finished ginning the kupas purchased from the current year's crop on account of Government. He had been able to work only two gins this season; but "they had ginned, in sixty-four days, 700 bhars of 689,500 lbs. of kupas, which is equal to 5387 lbs. of kupas a day by each gin, yielding 1755 lbs. of clean cotton. This unprecedented result, however, has been partly effected by a simple improvement which I made in the front part of the gins. Before I could get them worked properly, I was obliged to discharge all the old hands, and get new ones, whom I set properly to work and taught how to proceed. Of the two gins I worked here, one has saws of ten inches diameter, and the other of twelve inches, the latter of which cleaned just 20 per cent. more than the former, or just the difference of their diameters, when worked at the same speed, proving the error of using small gins." The table which is printed on the following page gives all the details, and the result is most satisfactory.

"An average out-turn of 1755 lbs. of clean cotton by each gin per diem throughout the season is, I believe, without a parallel in the history of cotton cleaning in India; nor have I heard of any having been cleaned before at the low rate of 2r. 6a. per candy. One hundred candies of the cotton from Broach were recently sold in Bombay at 94r. per candy, showing a net profit of 23r. 7a. per candy, or 33 per cent.

"I have just completed a new bale-press at Broach, at a cost of rather less than 1000r., which will pack a bale in half an hour, of two thirds of a candy, or 523 lbs."

Statement, showing the Quantity of Cotton Purchased, Ginned, and Shipped from Broach and Surat to Bombay, on Account of Government, during the Months of February, March, and April, 1849 *; the Time occupied in Ginning ; the daily Out-turn of each Gin, the Cost of Ginning both per Bhar of Kupas and per Candy of Cotton ; the Expense of Packing, and Freight and Shipping Charges each per Candy ; the Total Cost of the Cotton per Candy landed in Bombay, the Equivalent Cost per lb. in Sterling Money ; and the Yield per Cent. of Clean Cotton from* 100 *lbs. of Kupas.*

STATIONS.	Number of gins used.	No. of working days.	Pounds of kupas ginned by each gin per diem.	Out-turn of cotton from each gin per diem.	Total kupas ginned, in bhars of 985 lbs.	Total lbs. of clean cotton.	Cost of ginning per bhar.	Cost of ginning per candy of 784 lbs.	Packing charges per candy.	Freight and shipping charges to Bombay per candy.	No. of bales.	Total candies of 784 lbs.	Cost of the cotton per candy laid down in Bombay.	Cost per lb. in sterling money, landed in Bombay.	Aggregate amount of cost and charges.	Per cent. of cotton wool.
							r. a. p.	r. a. p.	r. a. p.	r. a. p.		c. lbs.	r. a. p.		r. a. p.	
Broach ..	2 gins of 60 saws.	64	5387	1755	700 bhars or 689,500 lbs.	224,711	0 15 7	2 6 0	3 0 3	3 7 3	569	286 487	70 9 0	Rather less than 2*d.* per lb.	20,272 7 5	32½%
Surat ...	4 gins of 25 saws.	15	783	227	46,987 lbs.	13,644	2 12 4	7 10 3	3 13 5	—	41	17 316	78 13 0	Not quite 2¼*d.* per lb.	1372 7 0	29%

Broach Superintendent's Office ;
May 14*th*, 1849.

(Signed) J. LANDON,
Supt. Cotton. Expt.

The Broach cotton of 1848-49, to the extent of 355 bales, was sold in the autumn of the year 1849 for $5\frac{1}{4}d.$, and some of a superior quality (34 bales) for $5\frac{1}{2}d$, the same as 37 bales of cotton from Surat, when the New Orleans from Candeish sold for $5\frac{1}{4}d.$

Culture.—Mr. Davies, in answer to the queries circulated by the Bombay Government, has given much interesting information respecting the culture of the indigenous cotton. It is sown with the drill plough, the seeds having been prepared by being rubbed on a frame of cocoa-nut fibre, then soaked in muddy water, and afterwards plunged into ashes. It is seldom sown more than once in three years on the same ground; and, though the black soil is that most commonly used, the plants raised on lighter soil are much larger, and the staple of the cotton equally good. "Lands well manured will yield double crops for two years in succession." To do so effectually costs about 5r., or 10 shillings the acre, but commonly from $2\frac{1}{2}$r. to 4r.; but is generally confined to lands planted with sugar-cane or turmeric, sweet potatoes, and garden-stuff. Fallowing and rotation of crops are usually had recourse to for cotton. The cotton is sown in all June; the picking commences after a light monsoon, about the 20th of December, and is over by the 10th of February; but, after a heavy monsoon, the pods do not burst till the middle of February, and the cotton is not all housed till the first week in April. The average cost of cultivating native cotton may be taken at 1r. 12a. on black soil, and 2r. 4a. per beegah on light soil. The Broach beegah is little more than half an acre (2477 square yards). The average produce is stated to be only 80 lbs. per acre, and the maximum 192 lbs. of clean cotton-wool. The cotton-seed is itself "a distinct and important article of commerce, and in great request for feeding milch cattle," and bears no rateable proportion to the price of wool; for, when "fodder is scarce, the price of cotton seed is greatly enhanced, while, at the same time, cotton-wool is almost unsaleable." This was the case in the season of 1848-49. Cotton seed is sold by the kulsee of 657 lbs., and its usual price about $4\frac{1}{2}$r. for the kulsee, or about 3 annas for 28 lbs. This enables the expenses of cleaning to be paid for by the sale of the seed. Thus, as given by Mr. Davies, in answer to the queries:

"The expenses of cleaning being from 10r. to 11r. per candy, are repaid by the seeds, as these sell for 12½r. to 13r. per candy, paying also for warehouse and other incidental expenses. The gins repaired by Mr. Landon clean a bhar of kupas, 870 lbs., for 2½r.

SEASON OF 1848.

	r.	a.	p.
To ginning charges of 485 bales of cotton, inclusive of native establishments (permanent) and rent of premises	1723	0	6
To packing charges on ditto	869	4	4
To shipping charges on ditto to Bombay . . .	1003	15	11
Total	3596	4	9
Deduct cotton-seed, sold on the spot	3082	4	11

SEASON OF 1849.

	r.	a.	p.
To ginning charges of 610 bales of cotton, inclusive of permanent native establishment, and rent of premises .	1455	15	9
To packing charges on ditto	927	11	4
To shipping charges on ditto to Bombay . . .	1049	14	0
Total	3433	9	1
Deduct cotton-seed sold	4005	13	10
Total of expenses on both years	7439	6	11
Ditto of sale of seed in ditto	7087	6	10"

Roads.—An important consideration being the rate of conveyance of the cotton to the coast, we may give this from Mr. Davies's answers to the 51 queries, as follows: "The cotton of Broach is conveyed entirely on carts, and the same may be said of that brought to the coast from the interior districts belonging to His Highness the Guicowar. An average of one rupee per bale, or two rupees per candy, covers the cost of conveyance from the screws to the ports throughout the Broach zillahs."* "The combined results of the seasons of 1848 and 1849 give the cost of conveying a candy of cotton from Broach to Bombay at 4 rupees 2½ annas, to which may be added 2 rupees for inland carriage, bringing the total charge per candy to 6 rupees 2½ annas for all cotton raised within the Broach zillah;" and again, "Thirty miles may be taken as the extreme distance of the Broach cotton-producing districts from the ports of export. The average distance may be taken at

* But, in answer to six queries, we learn that the expenses of land carriage in Broach are trifling, the highest rates (i. e. from the most distant villages) being only 2r. per candy or cart-load.

about fifteen miles. The communications throughout are perfect, and are always open, excepting for three months of heavy monsoon weather. The ports of Broach and Tankaria offer great natural facilities for shipment, but hitherto nothing has been done to improve them. A boat or pile-bridge at the former place, and a raised embankment along the edge of the latter, would greatly tend to the convenience of the mercantile community. Both have been recommended."

So little being required, it might probably be granted with comparative ease. Though some engineering difficulties, arising from the spread of the river in the rains, and of the nature of the tides, have been represented, there is no doubt they could be overcome by a bridge on piles or on boats removable on the accession of the monsoon, as suggested by Mr. Davies, and thus obviate the rolling of the cotton bales over the sand and mud; but it is a small part only of the dirt in Broach cotton which is thus acquired. The systematic adulteration of the cotton by the traders of that district make all other difficulties appear of little importance.

Frauds.—We have frequently mentioned the subject of the systematic adulteration of cotton by the native dealers. The subject has of late attracted much attention from the extent to which impunity has encouraged the dealers to carry it, as will be evident first from the summary of operations in Dharwar, and then from the extracts referring to Broach:—

"In regard to punishment for adulteration, it was pointed out how inoperative the law for preventing it had been in Guzerat; but in the hopes that in the Southern Mahratta country the system of adulteration had not yet been carried to the same extent as in Guzerat, Government was inclined to think, that the publication there of Regulation III of 1829, in the manner proposed by Mr. Shaw, might be productive of benefit, if its provisions were enforced, and the influence of the Collector and his native establishment were exerted in the detection of offenders. Mr. Goldsmid was therefore requested to report how many copies in Mahrattee and Canareese of this regulation would be required for distribution within his range." (*Summary*, p. 42.)

This subject was again noticed in a correspondence handed up to Government by the Revenue Commissioners, Southern

Division, on the 15th of June, 1847. With a further letter dated the 21st of July, 1847, Mr. Townsend submitted one from Mr. Shaw, the Collector of Dharwar, reporting that cotton to the value of fifty thousand (50,000) rupees had been mixed (i. e. the New Orleans and country cotton together), and recommended, as the evil had proceeded so far as to be past remedy in that season, that the Collector might be authorised to have the mixed cotton cleaned by the Government saw-gins, and that notice should be given to the ryots that mixed cotton would not be cleaned in the ensuing year by the Government gins.

Mr. Shaw intimated that the adulteration of the cotton was caused by the seed having become mixed previously to the sowing of the cotton crop in the previous season, and Mr. Channing, then Government cotton planter at Dharwar, stated, that he thought the fraud had in all probability been intentionally committed in anticipation of Government purchasing the cotton, as it had done in the previous year.

"On the 26th November, 1847, Mr. Townsend stated that he agreed with Mr. Shaw, in opinion that nothing could put a stop to the abuses which occurred in mixing and adulterating cotton, but the general and stringent administration of Regulation III of 1829; but that he was not at all convinced that another Act of the Legislature (as suggested by Mr. Shaw) is required for this purpose. New laws, however excellent, Mr. Townsend remarked, cannot wholly extinguish fraud, though if well framed and administered, they may do much to check it. Frauds in trade are, of all things, perhaps, the most difficult of cure by the Legislature; but they may be very much controlled by decision and systematic combination on the part of the mercantile community who are the purchasers of the goods. Were they to buy only from those traders whose character they knew; to test thoroughly a certain percentage of their bales, and never to have dealings a second time with a trader who once had deceived them, or endeavoured to do so, however cheap he might sell his goods, the up-country traders would fear to attempt fraud. Till the merchants at the Presidency bestir themselves, Government's labours in this respect will be in vain." (*Summary*, p. 103.)

That Guzerat has not attained its pre-eminence in the adulteration of cotton without cause, has been well known to the author for many reasons, as he has stated on various occasions; but the case has been lately proved in so decisive manner as to have attracted general attention. The '*Manchester Guardian*' of the 9th October, 1850, contains a letter, apparently from some one in India and well acquainted with the subject, who writes as follows on this subject :—

"It is, however, not a little vexatious to find, that while the East India Company have been making such efforts to secure the extension and success of this industry, so important to the welfare of the agriculture as well as the commerce of India, the cupidity of the native middlemen has been doing what it could to bring discredit upon Indian cotton. Frauds to an enormous extent have been discovered in the packing, by adulterating the cotton with mixtures of sand, stone, and rubbish. There is now little doubt, that in numerous cases, where the condition of the cotton has been complained of, the fault has been attributable rather to the fraudulent practices of the middlemen, than to the negligence of the growers. This is an old crime in India. As early as in 1829, a severe law was passed, with a view to put a stop to it. By that law, parties detected in adulterating cotton by submitting it to dew or damp, or mixing it with other material, are exposed to severe fines, confiscation of the goods, and even imprisonment. The *Bombay Times*, in reference to these discoveries, says :—

"'Information to the effect that large quantities of adulterated cotton were stored away having been received, the supplies of some of the principal dealers were inspected, and bale on bale found vitiated by the admixture of foreign substances subsequent to the making up of the bales. The disclosures were so extensive and indisputable, that the rogues were induced to confess their villany, and to admit that it was part of a long-continued system, in which they have been engaged. Betwixt 6000 and 8000 bales (8500 bags) were seized; twelve dealers were proceeded against, and six of them at once convicted, and fines imposed on them to the extent of 2850 rupees. The cotton has not on this occasion been confiscated, but directed to be a second time cleaned, the dealers being fairly warned that any attempt to ship it in its present condition would be treated as a second offence, and dealt with accordingly.'"

This having been represented in an Indian newspaper, as a great discouragement to the culture of cotton, as the cultivator is prohibited by an act of the Legislative Council from taking his produce to market, unless he will prepare it in such a manner as the Government shall please to order, the '*Bombay Times*' of the 23d November, 1850, rightly observes: "It must here be remembered, that the Act applies to cotton intentionally adulterated for fraudulent purposes, that is with the view of swindling the purchaser out of his money, by giving him dirt or water amongst the materials he pays for as cotton."

Curiously enough, the '*Manchester Guardian*' of the same date, the 23d of November, 1850, had an article on the subject, from which the following are extracts :—

"By the present mail (23d November, 1850), we learn that considerable delay in the intended shipments from Bombay will occur in consequence. On the 30th of September, a petition was presented to Lord Falkland, the Governor, by a large body of Bombay native merchants—(we hope such a document was not signed by any of the English houses),—which speaks for itself. The following are extracts from it:—

"'At present the respective agents of your petitioners have large quantities of cotton at Broach, to the value of upwards of 500,000 rupees ready for immediate shipment to this place; but John Marshall Davies, Esq., the Collector of Broach, refuses to allow them to export a single bale of it, unless the same is free from cotton seeds.

"'Your petitioners deny that they, or, to their knowledge, any of their agents, are in any way concerned in adulterating the cotton so purchased,—*and having regard to the state of the cotton market, and the present high price of cotton, your petitioners would prefer receiving the cotton in the adulterated state in which the Collector represents it to be, rather than not receive any at all, and thus become subject to actions for breaches of contract, with heavy damages in the event of any fall of price.*'"

"We have no doubt that the petitioners would rather receive their cotton adulterated, as has been proved beyond doubt, by their own agents, to the profit of their employers, the petitioners,—so long as they can continue to palm it on the houses who ship it to England as merchantable Broach cotton, such as had been contracted for. No doubt such a course would be most profitable and convenient to them. Contracts were made for delivery, when it was not thought the vigilance of Mr. Davies would discover the tricks that had been so long practised with impunity. But that gentleman, in the discharge of his duty, and the government of Bombay, in their support of one of the most efficient servants they have, have considerations of a far more important character to bear in mind, than the temporary loss to a set of men who little deserve the sympathies of any one having at heart the credit of India, and the success of cotton cultivation there. Mr. Davies will, therefore, we understand, be supported in his determination to put an end to this fraudulent practice, which imposes on the English consumer, and brings the produce of India into undeserved disrepute."

The author may observe, "parvis componere magna," that he has, during this season of high prices, had samples given him of what was naturally fair Broach cotton, but which was almost unsaleable, from the large quantity of seeds deposited in layers within cotton that must previously have been freed from its seeds.

The Messrs. Tetley, of Mincing Lane, in their circular dated 3d January, 1851, which the author received while this sheet is passing through the press, say:—

"With regard to East India cotton there has been an unusually large supply, a very seasonable addition to the general import, and yet it is lamentable to find the condition of a considerable portion of the late import from Bombay, particularly good Broach cotton, so much mixed with seed as to render it unsaleable, except at very reduced prices. The example set by the Directors of the Hon. East India Company, for producing good and clean cotton, has, as yet, had but very limited influence of any hopeful character, which is much to be regretted."

Broach being so celebrated as an Indian cotton district, and one which has of late been so frequently adduced as an instance where the land-rent or tax interferes with the production of cotton, it is extremely desirable to inquire into the facts of the case, though nothing seems more difficult than to ascertain such as are connected with the returns obtained by the farmer from his land; and it is upon these that the whole question hinges. Mr. J. M. Davies, in his reply to the inquiries of the Bombay Cotton Committee of 1846, took considerable pains to ascertain the average produce, as "the returns received from the native district revenue officers were so contradictory, and presented so many irreconcilable facts," that he could not permit them to be embodied in the statement required by the Committee. Mr. Davies premises that four or five years previous to 1847 the former system of annually settling the land revenue in the Broach Collectorate by an estimate of the gross products aided by their prices, had given way to a fixed "Beegootee," or assessment upon the measured "Beegah," intended to be so apportioned as to admit of a rotation of cotton and dry grain crops upon the same land.

As Mr. Davies was unable to command time to go through the materials recorded for the whole of the nine years antecedent to the general introduction of the Beegootee settlement (i. e. from 1834-35 to 1842-43 inclusive), he selected three years of varying average production, as well as of considerable fluctuation of prices, viz. 1837-38, 1838-39, and 1839-40. In a native account, the first is described as a good year, the second as a bad one, and the third excellent as regarded produce, but the cotton was almost unsaleable. The price in the second year was better than in either of the others, though the crop was small.

Mr. Davies says, "I took nine villages (three good, three indifferent, and three bad) of each of the five talookas comprising this collectorate, leaving out Jumbooseer as having been during three years a Beegootee-paying district, while my object was to deal first with the appraisement system." Mr. Davies obtained the following as the rates of assessment, the average produce being about 35 lbs. to the beegah, hence the number of beegahs required to produce a candy of cotton.

	Rate of assessment per beegah on land cultivated with cotton.			Average produce obtained from one beegah.	Average number of beegahs required to produce 784 lbs. of cleaned cotton.	
	r.	a.	p.		beegahs.	wurres.
1837-38	4	6	2	Kupas, 151¼ seers, equal to 47 lbs. of cleaned cotton.	16	14 or 20.
1838-39	1	8	11	Kupas, 48 seers; or cotton, 15 lbs.	52	5
1839-40	3	5	5	Kupas, 134 seers; or cotton, 41⅔ lbs.	18	16
	3) 9	4	6			
	3	1	6			

Notwithstanding the care that Mr. Davies has taken, it does not appear that the method he has adopted is devoid of all sources of error. For instance, we do not know what kind of land is included under the head of cotton land; some of it may be unsuited to produce any cotton, and this would reduce the average; nor do we know the proportion which the extent of cotton land in the good villages bears to that in the indifferent and the bad. If the breadth of land under cotton cultivation in the villages classed as good is greater than in those classed as indifferent and bad, the returns per beegah would be higher; but if the reverse, the average would be less. One district, Jumbooseer, which is well known to be one of the best, was purposely left out of consideration because it was at that time differently assessed. So also the proportion of good to bad seasons ought to be ascertained before we deduce average returns, because unless we know this, we have no means of judging of the proper number of times that we should count good or bad seasons in a series of years. Three years are evidently too few to afford data for drawing rigorous deductions, though the years selected by Mr. Davies display some of the characteristic fluctuations of the cotton trade. If we examine the diagram at p. 74, we shall see that the years selected by Mr. Davies succeeded a series of years of high prices, that is, from 1832 to 1836, when the results of profit and loss must have been very different. In the years 1837 and 1838 there was a considerable fall in prices, with a slight rise in 1839 and a greater fall in 1840, chiefly on account of the want of demand for the China market. These objections appear to the author to apply equally to the following statement; but it is only by such inquiries frequently repeated and looked at from different points of view, and extended over a greater surface and over a series of years, that we shall feel assured that our conclusions are as correct as the nature of the subject and of the country admits.

"In so extensive a cotton growing district, possessing soils of considerable variety of fertility, it may be considered difficult, perhaps, to say what should be considered an average crop of cotton to the beegah. I have, however, spared no pains to ascertain this; and, in assuming two and a half dhurrees of kupas (equal to 40 seers, or 39·199 lbs. of cotton) for all soils, and in all ordinary years, inclusive, of course, of years of partial failure, I do not think that I am far wrong. The marginal extract from Major Williams's valuable 'Statistical Memoir,'* proves that that officer estimated eight dhurrees, or 384 seers of kupas to the khomba in 1817-18, when the crops were uncommonly good. The khomba is as 187 to 100 compared with the Broach beegah, and therefore the proportion to the latter would be, under similar circumstances, 205 seers of kupas. This may be regarded, therefore, as a high average in Jumbooseer.

"On the other hand, a reference to the paper marked Accompaniment No. 1, in which the average of three villages of Oclesur Purgunna is given in three successive years, the villages being taken with reference to their respective classes in point of fertility, will show that the average of this Purgunna is not equal to that of Jumbooseer. In 1837-38, a fair year, the estimate of the village Nudhara (first class) was given at . . . . . . 228 seers.

Soorwaree, a second class village	196	"
And Awadur, a third class village	137	"
	3) 561	"
Of which the mean is . . .	187	seers.

"In 1839-40, when the produce of cotton was never probably finer, the same village, Nudhara, was rated at . . . . . . 234 seers.

Soorwaree	166	"
And Awadur	128	"
	3) 528	"
Or a mean of	176	seers.

* "The whole of the kupas or clean cotton produced in the Jumbooseer Purgunna, in the season 1817-18, was taken by the commercial department; it amounted, both from the government and alienated lands, to 7468 bhars; the price paid for it was 67¾ rupees per bhar; and therefore the sum brought by this article of the produce of the Purgunna came to 505,957 rupees. The cotton crops of that season were uncommonly good, and it may be assumed that the lands produced at the rate of eight dhurrees, or 384 lbs.. of kupas per khoomba."

While, in the intermediate year, 1838-39, a very bad one,—

Nudhara gave	86	seers.
Soorwaree	117	„
And Awadur	25	„
	3) 228	
Or only upon an average, per beegah	76	„

"Then again, while Broach and Wagra Purgunnas may be justly held to be of a higher productive standard than Oclesur, probably equalling Jumbooser, yet the Purgunna of Hansote is below them all in growing cotton; moreover, the actual returns (Khurebands) of 45 villages of every district but Jumbooseer, taken for three years together, give but 111 seers of kupas as the average produce of a beegah (see column 7 of General Statement). In adopting, then, the average of 120 seers of kupas to the beegah, I do not, I conceive, widely depart from a fair mean, not only of all soils, but of all seasons."

With reference to the appraisement and the beegootee systems, Mr. Davies observes:

"But however stringent this [the appraisement] mode of taxation may appear (and there is no denying it), it had the advantage of squaring the demands of Government with the actual circumstances of the season. The average of 45 villages, in 1837-38 (see column 5 of the General Statement), shows the average assessment, levied by the same rule, to have been 4r. 6a. 2p. per beegah; but the very next year, upon an extended surface of cotton cultivation, the assessment fell by its own working to 1r. 8a. 11p. per beegah.

"The beegotee settlement now generally adopted was doubtless intended to balance these widely differing results, and to allow the cultivator a fair reduction upon the mean itself. Thus, the mean of the three years (1837-38, 1838-39, and 1839-40), being 3r. 1a. 6p., the average of the beegotee shown below, in the same column for 1843-44, 1844-45, and 1845-46, is only 2r. 6a. 11p., being a reduction of 27 per cent."

Mr. Davies, in his replies to the six queries, states, "That the produce of a Broach beegah of cotton freed from seed, in a fair year and a fair soil, may be taken at 60 lbs., or 120 lbs. to the acre nearly. In a bad year the return would not probably exceed 20 lbs. the beegah. Assuming, however, an average year and an average soil, my inquiries do not support a higher general average than 40 lbs. of cotton wool to the Broach beegah. Dr. Royle's average estimate of less than 100 lbs. to the acre (see his present memorandum) is perhaps near enough to the truth to answer all practical purposes." This average, as we have seen, was considered much too low in the North-Western Provinces.

Mr. Davies has in another table calculated the cost of a candy of cotton in Broach, in which assuming that 20 beegahs of land are required to produce 784 lbs., or a candy of clean cotton, the land rent amounts to 48r. 10a. 4p., or taking the rupee at 22*d.*, $1\frac{1}{4}$*d.* per lb. The average cost of cultivation is stated to amount to 16r. 3a. 5p., or to $\frac{5}{8}$*d.* per lb., and the other expenses, consisting of Wakariah's profit, native agent's commission, cartage, freight, and insurance to Bombay, to 11 rupees, or to $\frac{3}{8}$*d.* per lb. Altogether the whole cost of a candy of cotton will therefore amount to 75r. 13a. 9p., or to $2\frac{1}{4}$*d.* per lb. Whence Mr. Davies states, "It may be easily gathered from this statement, that when the price of cotton is at 76 rupees per candy, it but barely pays its expenses; when it falls below that price, some parties must inevitably suffer. Those parties are, Government, the ryot, and the Wakariah. The first party, the Government, is but too frequently made to bear a portion of the ryot's loss, in either a large remission, or a heavy outstanding balance at the close of the year."

But this calculation depends entirely upon 20 beegahs being required to produce one candy of cotton, which we cannot reconcile either with the soil of Broach being suitable to the cotton plant, or with the skill of the Broach ryot, of whom Dr. Lush said, "Who will teach the Broach ryot?" nor with the reputed character of the Broach plant being so good a bearer, whence Mr. Shaw recommended its introduction into the Dharwar district; nor with the returns from other districts as sent to the Bombay Committee; nor with the replies to the queries which have been circulated by the Court of Directors, as shown in the Tables given at pp. 407-8. The following are some of the statements sent to and published by the Bombay Cotton Committee of the year 1846.

Thus, we find that in Broach 20 beegahs are required, and in Surat only 13 beegahs, to grow a candy of even better cotton; Dharwar is said to require 13 acres, but Belgaum not more than 4, producing at the rate of 196 lbs. per acre. This is probably a mistake, and as much above as some of the others are probably below average returns. Sholapore requires no less than $19\frac{1}{2}$ acres, or nearly 40 beegahs, to grow only a single candy of cotton. In the present returns, some of the great discrepancies have disappeared; but still Ahmedabad, Kaira, and Surat, all districts in the low land below the ghauts, appear to reward the agricultural labours much more bountifully than Broach does. Thus, in the Revenue Commissioner's letter, p. 404, Poonah is said to yield 120 to 240 lbs., Ahmednuggur the latter quantity, Sholapore 160 lbs., Belgaum from 38 to 84 lbs., and Dharwar only 60 lbs. per acre: Ahmedabad is stated, p. 408, to yield from 280 to 70 lbs. per acre, Kaira from 637 to 1274½ lbs., probably of seed cotton, and Surat 186⅔ lbs. per beegah, or 274½ lbs. to the acre, though this is not the proper proportion between the two measurements.

With reference to these discrepancies, we cannot do better than make use of the words of D. A. Blane, Esq., then Revenue Commissioner of the Northern Division: "With respect to the dependence to be placed upon the accuracy of the details supplied by the Collectors, several of the items of information, for instance prices, quantity of produce, cost of carriage, &c., are liable to so many qualifying influences as hardly to admit of being stated with any great precision; but due allowance being made on this account, the results exhibited may perhaps be regarded as a fair approximation to the actual state of the culture of that staple."

The Court of Directors, in reference to the subject of the assessment of Broach, and to the labours of the Bombay Cotton Committee, observed in their despatch of the 3d November, 1847:—

"As the first principle of our revenue system is to permit the ryot to cultivate what he pleases, paying the assessment fixed on the land, it is clear that if, at the present rates of assessment, the cultivation of grain is more profitable than that of cotton, it would be equally so at any lower rate, and consequently the reduction of the assessment would not have the supposed tendency of encouraging the cultivation of cotton in place of ordinary grain crops.

"In Broach we believe the case to be somewhat different; although the assessment in this district is now placed on the land, without reference to the crop which may be cultivated on it, and is so far correct in principle; yet we are aware that the rate at which it was fixed was mainly regulated by the capability of the land for the production of cotton; that rate may have been moderate when a high price could be obtained for the produce, but at the present price of cotton in the Bombay market, it appears to be considerably higher than can be maintained without materially contracting the cultivation. You state that you shall be happy when your means of undertaking the necessary surveys admit of your extending to this province the full benefit of that systematic revision of the assessment which has been prosecuted with such signal success in the Deccan, and is now in progress in the Southern Mahratta country. In the mean time, until the means of carrying out that most desirable measure are at your disposal, we would suggest for your consideration the expediency of directing a temporary reduction in the present rates of assessment; by this means moderation might be ensured, although you could not secure the equality which would be obtained by a regular survey, and much of the mischief which must inevitably follow a continued course of over-assessment may be avoided."

Mr. Davies, in his answer to one of Mr. Willoughby's queries, states, that the assessment has now (in 1849) been reduced by about half a rupee per beegah on the lands of Broach, probably in consequence of the above despatch.

If the average returns of Broach cotton lands are so small, and the assessment is proportionately so high, as they would appear to be from Mr. Davies's statements, continued loss to ryots and wakarias must follow from the very low prices which have been obtained for cotton for a series of years. Cultivation might be expected to have considerably fallen off. But this does not appear to have been the case, for though Broach is admitted to be more highly taxed than some other districts, yet it is the only one of the cotton districts in which no extension of the culture is to be expected, because it already produces the full proportion of what is advisable, according to the approved system of rotation, as is evident from the following extract from Mr. Davies's answer:

"The cotton cultivation in the Broach zillah, for the last thirteen years, is, on an average, about 260,000 beegahs, or about half that area in British acres, adding the supposed quantity of alienated lands under cotton cultivation for the same period, or (80,000) eighty thousand beegahs, the whole would amount to 340,000 beegahs, growing cotton.

"With regard to the extension of the surface under an assumed enhanced demand for cotton, I am not of opinion that any increase could take place. It is notorious that the cultivation of cotton has been pushed to its extreme limit in the Broach zillah, and I find that it bears an average proportion of 40 per cent. to the entire tillage of the district. Comparing this fact with the established hypothesis, that cotton can only be cultivated with success for one year out of three in the same ground (in other words, that it ought not to bear a greater proportion to the whole cultivation than 33 per cent.), and knowing the capabilities of the various districts, it would not appear that there is any room in Broach for the extension of cotton."

Capt. Wingate, the able Revenue Surveyor, justly observes:

"The only case, then, in which the land-tax of India can impede the extension of the cotton cultivation, is when it is in excess of the rent. But even in this case it has no tendency to injure the cotton cultivation more than any other species of cultivation. Upon land actually under tillage, the assessment, however heavy, has no tendency either to encourage or discourage the cultivation of cotton, or any other particular crop. The farmer, whether his assessment be heavy or light, will cultivate the crops which pay him best: and wherever the cotton cultivation in India has fallen off, and been succeeded by that of other crops more remunerative to the farmer, no reduction of assessment, nor indeed the abolition of the land-tax altogether, would avail to alter this state of things. The change might make cotton a profitable crop; but this would not be enough while another crop remained more profitable still, as the consideration of the farmer is not merely what will pay him, but what will pay him best."

So the late Mr. James Mill, the celebrated historian of India, and equally distinguished as a political economist, when asked by the Select Committee of the House of Commons, in 1831, whether it would be advantageous to India to abolish the assessment on land and substitute for it some other source of revenue, stated:—

"Quite the contrary; my opinion is, that a system of land-revenue, where means are taken to confine the collection to rent, and where it is not allowed to exceed the limits of a reasonable rent, is one of the most favorable circumstances in the condition of any country; because, so far as the wants of the state can be supplied from that source, such a country is untaxed."

Having entered so fully into the details of the culture and commerce of cotton in Broach, it is not necessary to do more than to notice the other collectorates, which, like Broach, are situated below the ghauts, and along the coasts of the Gulf of

Cambay, and of which the statistics are given in the table at p. 408.

The collector of Ahmedabad, in reply to the queries of the Court of Directors, states, that little cotton is grown in the *gooraroo* or white soil of the collectorate; but in the western districts, that is, Veerumgaum, Dholka, Dundooka, and Gogo, where the black soil prevails, cotton is extensively cultivated, and conveyed to the ports of Dhollera, Bhownuggur, and Gogo, on the western coast of the Gulf of Cambay. But that there is not much likelihood of any increase in the extent of land under culture.

The collector of Kaira, in addition to the information condensed in the table, states, that the produce is conveyed either to Dhollera or to Cambay; and that, in some cases, it has to pay transit duties in crossing native states.

We have already seen, that it was in the neighbourhood of Kaira that Mr. Gilder succeeded so well in cultivating Bourbon cotton when others failed; and that it was in the hedges of his farm that Dr. Burn picked cotton seeds, which, when cultivated, produced cotton which was so highly valued by the Bombay Chamber of Commerce. Dr. Gibson has long been of opinion, that the culture of American cotton should be tried in the districts at the head of the Gulf of Cambay, in the flat plains towards the source of the great river Myhee, and in the tracts of land lying between the Myhee and the river Saburmuttee. We are happy to learn, that recent information announces the appointment of a planter, Mr. Price, to the district of Ahmedabad, to institute an experiment on the culture of New Orleans cotton there. Mr. Price has been for some time Assistant-Superintendent in the Candeish district, and was in sole charge during Mr. Simpson's absence in America, and is undoubtedly well qualified to introduce the culture of American cotton, and the cleaning of cotton by the saw-gins, into a new situation. It was proposed that he should remain in Candeish until February, so as to reach his destination in March, taking with him four or six saw-gins, which are being prepared under Mr. Simpson's superintendence in Candeish. The selection of good sites for the first experiments will require Mr. Price's most careful attention, as so much of future success will depend upon the first results which are obtained. It does not appear necessary to confine the experiments to the black soil which chiefly prevails about Dhollera and Dhundooka; but the peculiarities of each, in reference to the American cotton plant, should be ascertained, and especially in a situation where irrigation might be easily made use of. Not that it is probably necessary to cultivate cotton in that way, but it would be desirable to ascertain its effects in that climate, especially immediately after the cessation of the rains, when the sudden change from a moist to a dry climate appears to be the cause why the culture of the American cotton has so frequently failed in India.

The collector of SURAT, P. Stewart, Esq., in his letter to the Bombay Committee, says:

"The cost of production of cotton to the ryots is estimated as follows, supposing 13 beegahs of average zeraet land will produce one Surat candy of clean cotton, or 784 lbs.:

	r.	a.	p.
Average Government assessment on 13 beegahs of laud .	39	0	0
Ploughing before sowing	6	8	0
Cotton seeds or kupas, 1 maund and 25 seers . .	0	12	0
Hire for sowing ditto	3	4	0
Hire for ploughing, called kulpee . . .	3	4	0
Weeding	6	8	0
Gathering the cotton	7	0	0
Digging out the roots after the gathering . .	3	4	0
Rs.	69	8	0

"Should the above land be cultivated, as is generally the case, by the ryot, by means of his own bullocks, and the ground being weeded and the cotton picked by the members of his family, of course the profits on the produce are much greater.

"Allowing that 13 beegahs of land would yield about 66 maunds of kupas, which can be sold for 81 rupees 4 annas, after deducting the foregoing amount of expense, 69 rupees 8 annas, there remains a net profit of 11 rupees 12 annas to the cultivator.

"The price paid by merchants, and the charge incurred by them for the 66 maunds of kupas, the produce of 13 beegahs, are estimated as follows:

	r.	a.	p.
Value paid for the kupas	81	4	0
Hire for separating seed from cotton . . .	10	0	0
Screwing, including ginning, pats, ropes, binding, cart-hire, dalals, brokerage, &c.	5	4	0
	96	8	0
Deducting price of kupasea or cotton seed .	17	8	0
Leaving a net sum of . . . Rs.	79	0	0

as the expense incurred by merchants for one candy of clean cotton ready to be shipped on board the boat.

"In reply to your second letter, dated 23d ultimo, on the same subject, I have the honour to state, that I cannot suggest any mode of cheapening the production of cotton in this district; the most obvious plan would be by a reduction in the assessment of the land cultivated for cotton; but this I am not prepared to recommend, as I do not consider the rates too high on the land in which it is generally produced; this description of land, when not cultivated with cotton, pays readily the assessment from the grain it produces; and it should be borne in mind, that a great reduction has already been made in the rate of assessment per beegah on land generally throughout this zillah, and that the cultivators have been relieved from many heavy payments on account of veeras and other cesses.

"I am informed that the cotton generally would produce a higher price in Bombay and the English market, and the cultivators would consequently receive a greater remuneration, were it not that they deteriorate its quality in many ways to add to its weight, such as exposing it to the night-dew, which injures its colour; and the other modes adopted by them for this purpose render it expensive and difficult to clean. If the cotton-crop could be purchased by merchants or their agents while standing, and picked and the seed separated under careful superintendence, the best results might be anticipated."

Here we observe, that the expenses of culture are nearly double of what they are in Broach, but the returns per acre are also greater, though not in a proportionate degree; but in both districts the expenses are far beyond what they are stated to be in Dharwar. The Surat cotton, we have seen, is of excellent quality, and when sent in a clean state to market is highly approved of by manufacturers; and, if so sent, would be used to a considerable extent, as the Messrs. Clark say they would readily take 150 bales a week. The present collector states, that advances are frequently made to ryots, and that the produce is exported either from Surat or from Randier. Mr. Stewart reported, that about one third more cotton is exported annually from Randier than from Surat, and recommended that a pier should be constructed at Randier, to facilitate the shipment of cotton, and also that the small pier at Surat should be widened.

Some of the Georgian cotton seed sent out by the Court of Directors in 1849 having been sent to the Surat district, Mr. Fawcett, the collector, distributed it immediately among cultivators in different directions, especially where the soil is considered well adapted for the indigenous cotton, as in the pergunnahs of Oolpar, Koorsud, and Chourassee. The seeds were sown in June and July, the plants sprung up very well, and appeared to be strong and healthy, and continued so till the month of August, when the continuance of heavy rain caused them great injury, and in some places entirely destroyed them. The surviving plants grew up to $3\frac{1}{2}$ or 3 feet in height, "flowered in the end of September, and in the following month the pods formed, but mostly fell off before coming to maturity, owing, it is believed, to the extraordinary quantity of rain." But it was probably owing to the change from extreme wet to heat and dryness. Mr. Shaw, the Revenue Commissioner, however, did not consider the experiment unfavorable, considering the heavy monsoon, and requested permission to select a cotton planter for the Surat district, in order to induce cultivators to grow exotic cotton, and to clean it with the saw-gin. Mr. Daley, Assistant-Surveyor, who has some knowledge of the saw-gin, was appointed, and directed to proceed at once to Dhurumgaum in Candeish, where the factory is established under Mr. Simpson, to gain some experience in the work he will have to perform, and then proceed to Surat with some saw-gins. The Bombay government, by orders of the 19th September, 1850, direct the Revenue Commissioners "to arrange with the several superintendents of the cotton experiments for the required number of gins being supplied without depriving the superintendent and collector of Khandeish of the number they have to make up for the use of government and the ryots, after having furnished the prescribed number to Messrs. Ritchie, Stewart, and Co."

The situation of sites will require the most careful attention, and should not be confined to one kind of soil. Though the effects of heavy monsoons are to be guarded against by providing for drainage, it seems also desirable, in some situations at least, to make arrangements for a little irrigation immediately the rains cease, in order to make the transition from the wet to the dry weather more gradual. The effects of a moderate degree of shelter should also be ascertained, as recommended by Dr. Gibson; indeed, his advice altogether on the selection of sites would be very valuable. The cotton to be produced ought to be very superior, for well-cleaned Surat cotton already bears a high character. (*Vide* p. 97.)

Proceeding southwards along the line of coast, we find the country north of Damaun, occupied by sugar cane, which is the great staple within 15 miles of the coast, so that, according to Dr. Gibson, " any attempts to introduce the exotic cottons there would be unlikely to succeed, as they must involve a large sacrifice of revenue." Much of the Northern Concan, he observes, is untried ground, and fresh water is more abundant than in the Southern Concan. He visited, in the year 1840, the flats close to the sea of various places, and found that they were too much under the influence of the elements in the monsoon season to afford a hope that the plant could thrive, or that it could even exist. He visited Rairee, 24 miles south of Malwan, and found the extensive flats liable to the same objection. The cotton experiments tried at Malwan 20 years ago with the Bourbon plant were conducted in fields of laterite, or red soil, well sheltered by trees from the violence of the monsoon. Dr. Gibson, at the time of his visit, witnessed the healthy appearance of the Sea Island and Pernambuco plants grown by Mr. Elphinston, in situations where they had escaped the blight. He inquires, whether the blight is apt to attack the plant in unsheltered situations, and may be expected as an annual visitant, dependent on the strength of the coast monsoon; or whether it is an accident peculiar to seasons in which the monsoon is more than usually continuous, as was the case in the year of Dr. Gibson's visit.

The collectors of TANNAH, and of RUTNAGHEERY report, that no cotton is grown in these districts; and it is observed, that the soil of the Southern Concan is evidently unsuitable for the production of cotton. But it is probably the climate which is most in fault.

In connection with the above districts of the Bombay presidency, we may notice the states at which there are political agents, as they also have sent information respecting the culture of cotton. In Mahee Kaunta, no cotton is grown for export. In Rewa Kaunta only about 1000 acres, which is sent from Rajpeepla to the coast. Cotton is imported into Pahlumpore from Marwar and Meywar, but chiefly from Radhunpore, where about 7500 acres of land are under cultivation. Some of these districts might cultivate more cotton, and with benefit to themselves, if the people were so inclined.

KATTYWAR is often considered as being favorably situated for the growth of cotton; and in some places, as in a village near Mongrole, excellent cotton was produced, and it has been particularly mentioned as an instance where skill was displayed in culture which resulted in the production of cotton of very superior quality. J. Williams, Esq., the political agent in 1847, stated, that about 8 lacs of land are under cultivation with cotton every other year, and that it might easily be increased 50 per cent., and some think even 100 per cent. The best lands yield about 5 maunds of cotton, but that "the average produce from a beegah agrees very nearly with that mentioned by Dr. Royle."

The province of KUTCH, or CUTCH, is stated by Lieut.-Colonel Robarts, late political agent, to produce cotton in many parts, varying according to the quantity of rain. In a good year it may average about 75,000 maunds, of which 50,000 may be exported to Bombay from various ports. The remaining 25,000 maunds will be used up in the provinces, and supply small exports of cloth made from it to Zanzibar, Muscat, &c.

"An old soldier" formerly referred to, writes, that Kattywar and Cutch might be much improved by roads, the country offering peculiar facilities for making them, and £30 or £40 per mile would suffice for making good carriage-roads.

The newly-acquired territories in SCINDE lying to the north-west of Kutch, have by some been thought well suited for the culture of cotton, and yet the sandy soil and dry climate would by others be considered as most unsuitable. In these respects, however, Scinde is not unlike Egypt, to which it has frequently been compared. We know that in the latter, good cotton is raised, but only by means of irrigation, and we know no sufficient reason why it could not be grown in the former by the same method. The subject has not been entirely neglected, though some unforeseen difficulties have occurred, as in all fresh undertakings. The government in Scinde applied to that in Bombay, in March, 1846, for a few maunds of American cotton seed, and some Mauritius sugar-cane, which the collector of Shikarpore considered it desirable to introduce into Scinde. Twenty maunds of cotton seed were accordingly obtained from the Dharwar district and forwarded to Kurrachee. The author also conceiving that, in a dry warm climate, where there was no regular rainy season, cotton might perhaps be easily cultivated by the aid of irrigation, wrote to Dr. Stocks, Conservator of

Forests, requesting him to make some experiments on the subject. His reasons were, that plants raised during the moisture of the rainy season, being unable to sustain the sudden transition from moisture to dryness, might in a climate which was sufficiently warm and not inundated by periodical rains, be raised by artificial irrigation to succeed in such a manner and at such seasons as would promote the gradual and healthy growth of the plant, together with the seasonable maturation of its fruit, and yield a profitable crop for export from a country where there are few exportable products. Dr. Stocks began the experiment with much zeal, dug a well for the purpose, and would probably have succeeded, but the water was unluckily too brackish for and injured the plant. Subsequent ill health and frequent moving about have prevented the prosecution of the experiment. But as no one is better qualified for making an experiment of the kind, it is to be hoped that he may have an opportunity of repeating it. There is no occasion, in the first instance, of its being to any great extent, for a few acres will suffice for ascertaining the physical requirements of the plant, which ought to be determined here as elsewhere, before culture on a large scale is attempted. The assistance of a Broach ryot skilled in the culture of cotton, and one who is also acquainted with the use of the saw-gin, taking with him one of Mr. Frost's improved small gins, would be of advantage in the prosecution of such an experiment, especially under one so well acquainted with the climate of Scinde, and with the physiology of vegetation.

From the survey which we have taken, it is evident that there is ample space within the limits of the Bombay presidency for growing what has long been its staple produce. But a regularity of demand and remunerative prices, are only to be ensured by improving the character of the product; first, by growing American cotton in suitable soils and climates; and secondly, by sending the indigenous product in a clean and unadulterated state into market.

It has been mentioned at p. 368, that the cotton from Dharwar of the season 1848-49 had been shipped in the 'India,' along with the cotton of other parts of the Bombay Presidency. This sheet having been detained in the press in consequence of the indisposition of the Author, he is enabled to add that the 'India' has arrived with some of the cotton damaged, which was sold at Liverpool, but the greater portion of the 1504 bales arrived at Manchester the first week in January, and created a great deal of interest. The Author is informed by letter from Mr. Fleming, dated January 28, 1851, that the New Orleans cotton by this ship, together with some by the 'Marian,' was almost all sold at prices varying from 7½*d.* to 6½*d.*, according to quality. Mr. Blount's cotton cost 3 $\frac{78}{100}$*d.*, according to his statement mentioned at p. 368.

§ 31. Cotton Culture in the Madras Presidency.

Continuing our observations on Cotton Culture in India, we have at last come to Madras, where the first experiments were made. This Presidency is somewhat of the shape of a triangle, with its base resting on Central India, and its apex terminating at Cape Comorin. It extends from 8° to 22° of N. lat., and lies between 75° and 85° of E. long. Two ranges of mountains run along its eastern and western coasts, and support between them a table land, which diminishes in elevation from south to north, and from west to east, Mysore having a medium elevation of 3000 feet, and the Ceded Districts a mean height of 1600 feet above the sea. The Eastern Ghauts rise at a distance of from 30 to 60 miles from the coast, washed by the Bay of Bengal, with the intermediate country forming an irregularly level, and generally sandy plain. The Western Ghauts rise much more abruptly, and have a much narrower space between them and the Indian Ocean. They join the Eastern ghauts at Cape Comorin, and run an uninterrupted course, except at the valley of Coimbatore, which is about sixteen miles in breadth, and has the celebrated Neilgherries for its northern wall.

The whole of the above territory, being situated within the tropics, is necessarily under the influence of great heat, especially whenever this is unrelieved by moisture. But the vicinity of a great portion of it to the sea, the elevation of the remainder, and the influence of a double monsoon, much modify the climate. The north-east monsoon, which blows chiefly on the eastern coast, commences usually in October, and continues till December, when the rains cease, and the wind becomes dry and parching. The south-west monsoon, which begins in May, continues till August or September, and is felt chiefly on the Malabar coast and western parts of the country. At other times the winds are variable, but mostly southerly from March till May; that is, from the termination of one monsoon till the commencement of the other. (*Madras Medical Reports.*)

The Mean Temperature of Madras was, for 1848—

Month	Temp.	Month	Temp.
January	75·5	July	85·3
February	77·7	August	84·6
March	80·8	September	83·7
April	83·7	October	82·02
May	86·8	November	78·9
June	87·7	December	76·3

The Fall of Rain on an Average of Twenty-two Years.

Month	Rain	Month	Rain
January	1·33	July	3.20
February	0·23	August	5·24
March	0·36	September	4·76
April	0·63	October	10·09
May	1·03	November	12·43
June	2·03	December	3·25

As the culture of cotton, like that of every other plant, is dependent in a great measure on climate, it was necessary to premise with these observations.

In a preceding part of this work (pp. 36-9) we have noticed the extent to which export of cotton is carried in the Madras Presidency, and also the dirty state in which it is sent into market. Though other districts are capable of growing good cotton, there are some especially considered as the cotton districts of the Madras Presidency. The districts to the northward and westward of Madras, that is, Nellore, Guntoor, and the Ceded Districts, (Cuddapah, Kurnool, and Bellary,) have their produce distinguished there by the name of *western* cotton, while that from the districts of Madura and Tinnivelly, Salem and Coimbatore, is known as *southern* often as Tinnivelly cotton. But some of the Bellary cotton is exported from Coompta, as that of the Coimbatore district is from the ports of Poonany and Cochin, and that of Tinnivelly from Tuticorin. With regard to the capabilities of these districts, we may notice the quantities of cotton which they used to supply before the cessation of the East India Company's trade, and that which they now supply or are capable of supplying. This we are enabled to do from some official documents prepared by order of the Madras Government, and from the replies to the queries circulated by the Court of Directors in 1847.

J. V. Stonhouse, Esq., the Accountant-General, states, that "in Tinnivelly, as in the Ceded Districts, cotton was never purchased at once, but advances appear to have been made for the provision of cotton, which when received, used to be forwarded to the Export Warehouse Keeper. The largest quantity forwarded by the Commercial Residents of the Ceded Districts and of Tinnivelly during the last twenty years of the trade was as follows:

	candies.	maunds.	lbs.
1815-16. Ceded Districts . . .	4585	7	2¾
1829-30. Tinnivelly	7302	15	10½

But it is observed, that "no cotton transactions took place in the Ceded Districts during the last ten years of the trade;" but the Export Warehouse Keeper purchased Ceded Districts' cotton at the Presidency in the years 1826-27, candies 3100, and in 1827-28, candies 472, 8 mds. With regard to the prices paid for the cotton during these twenty-five years, the same document shows that the lowest rate paid per candy in Tinnivelly was 45 rupees in 1830-31, but the rates paid during that year were 77, 45, and 88 rupees per candy. The highest rates paid during the same period were 129r. 8a. per candy in 1811-12, and 126 rupees per candy in 1821-22, but the rates paid during the year were 102, 101, 88, and 126 rupees. The lowest rate paid per candy in the Ceded Districts during the same period was 42r. 10a. 8p., and the highest 84 rupees per candy.

The six queries (*vide* p. 90) sent out by the Court of Directors in the year 1847, having been circulated in the Madras as well as in the other Presidencies, and answers having been received, of which an abstract is given by the Board of Revenue in a tabular form (v. p. 470): the Madras Government observes on the information which had been supplied:

"From the reports submitted by the Board of Revenue, the cotton growing districts are eight in number, the principal of which are the Ceded Districts, Bellary and Cuddapah, and the districts of Coimbatore and Tinnevelly.

"In Bellary the extent of land under cotton cultivation taken on an average of the last 5 years, is 260,000 acres, which the Collector states may be extended to 400,000 acres if there were "an increased demand" for the article. He alludes to the repair of the road to Coompta on the Western Coast, as likely to effect a material increase in the exports, and the Board of Revenue observe in reference thereto, that the Davamunnay Ghat, practicable for wheel carriages, and upon the line of communication between Bellary and Coompta, will be opened by the end of 1849.

"In the neighbouring district of Cuddapah there are acres 79,562 under cultivation, capable of being extended to acres 219,587, which might be applied to this culture, if "sufficient inducement was held out to the ryots," by an increased demand, and by "the introduction of a fair and equable assessment."* The wretched state of the road to Madras is also alluded to, but calls for no remark here, as the subject of improving it has already received the attention of this Government.

"In Coimbatore the average quantity of land under cotton cultivation is acres 97,830, and the Collector states that with increased demand and remunerating prices, the cultivation can be carried to any required extent. Dr. Wight's estimate, based upon a series of calculations, is considerably in excess of the Collector's statement of the extent of land actually under cultivation, but these officers would seem to agree in respect of the capabilities of the District for producing cotton. In Tinnevelly acres 122,391 are under cultivation, and in the event of an increased demand, a further extent of 15,000 acres can be brought into cultivation.

"In Madura there would appear to be altogether 60,000 acres adapted for this cultivation; in Guntoor upwards of 100,000; and in Nellore an insignificant extent; but from the peculiarities of this last (being a grazing) district it can scarcely be reckoned a cotton-growing one.

In Kurnool acres 19,581 are under cultivation, and the agent remarks

* On this expression the Government observes: "What is meant by this is not explained, but it would seem, from his Land Revenue Settlement Report for fusly 1259, to which he (the Collector) alludes, that he proposes to reduce the tax on the black cotton lands in the district which have fallen out of cultivation, as he supposed, from the high assessment prevailing on them. The statements and arguments of the Collector were taken up by the Board of Revenue, in their review of that report, and by the Government, and shown to be untenable. It is not, therefore, necessary to pursue the subject further in this place than to observe, that, if Mr. Cochrane can clearly show that the black cotton lands are assessed out of proportion to their productive powers and capabilities, it will then be deserving of the consideration of the Board, whether a reduction shall be made."

that it can be extended without inconvenience to 75,481 if a sufficient demand were created.

"The Superintendent of the Astagram Division in Mysore states that there are about 10,000 acres under cotton cultivation, that the produce is insufficient for local consumption, but were even an increased demand offered, the district could not supply cotton for export. He alludes to a circular issued some years back to allow waste land, if taken up for cotton cultivation, to be held rent free for 5 years, and states that this offer failed of success. In one other division of the same territory, viz. Chittledroog, there are 8,000 acres under cultivation for local consumption, and as much more available. In the remaining divisions the cultivation is limited, and cotton is imported from Bellary and Cuddapah.

"The average produce of cotton on an acre of land appears to vary in different districts, and even in the same district very considerably according to soil, climate, variety, and other circumstances. In Coimbatore the produce per acre is 110 lbs. of seed cotton, Tinnevelly 300 lbs., Madura 316, Kurnool 112, Cuddapah 200, Guntoor 225, Nellore 100, and in Bellary, where the greatest extent of land is applied to this cultivation, the produce is, cleaned cotton 46 lbs., or seed cotton lbs. 184. The principal Collector of Coimbatore remarks that it is difficult to afford any satisfactory information in this respect; the New Orleans sown by him for experimental purposes yielded 1200 lbs. of seed cotton per cawnie, equal to $1\frac{5}{16}$ acres, while the country produced a most scanty crop. Dr. Royle gives the average of Indian cotton at 100 lbs. per acre of clean cotton, and this he regards as 'a small return.'

"On the whole, it appears that, as relates to the Company's territories, there is no want of land suited for cotton cultivation, particularly in the four principal districts, that while the state of the internal communications which offer so much obstruction to the transit of this essential staple of India to the coast will continue to engage, as it has heretofore done, the attention of the local government, the measures of greater importance necessary to ensure the improvement and extension of the cotton culture of the country would seem to rest solely on 'an increased and certain demand and remunerating prices,' an opinion expressed by all who have heretofore written on the subject.

(The government then call attention to the suggestions which had been made), "with a view to their being brought into practical operation so far as local means and circumstances admit. There are experimental establishments at Coimbatore and Tinnevelly, under the management of officers whose aid and advice will always be available as well as the machinery and seed in their charge, and the Governor in Council will cheerfully receive and encourage every disposition which may be shown to promote this object; indeed considering the importance attached by the Manchester Commercial Association to 'careful picking' and 'effectual cleaning,' he thinks much may be accomplished by the local officers taking an active part in impressing these points on the native mind, and directing their attention to the advantages of good seed, of improved culture, and of keeping unmixed the superior and the inferior kinds of cotton produce."

Dr. Wight, in a letter dated 20th January, 1846, in reference to the capabilities of the southern provinces, stated,

"The four southern provinces of the peninsula—Coimbatore, Salem, Madura, and Tinnivelly—all cotton-growing districts, include an area of above 28,500 square miles, 4000 of which might, nay would, be annually under cotton in the event of a rise in the price of only one farthing a pound in the local markets. These 4000 square miles, a mere fraction of India, would, at the rate of 100 lbs. per acre of clean cotton, produce 256,000,000 of pounds, more than half the quantity required for home consumption by the English manufacturers, and that without in the slightest degree interfering with the production of food for their inhabitants."

The following is the Table prepared by the Board of Revenue (p. 466), from the answers to the six queries by the collectors of the several districts.

DISTRICTS.		Average price of cotton freed from seed at the principal mart or marts of the district.	Average price at which it is sold by the ryots.				Cost of cleaning.	Expense of conveyance to the nearest port of shipment, for every ten miles.	Average produce per acre.	Extent of land in acres.	
			With advances.		Without advances.					Under cultivation.	Capable of producing cotton.
			Cleaned cotton.	Uncleaned cotton.	Cleaned cotton.	Uncleaned cotton.					
		r. a. p.	r. a. p.	r. a. p.	r. a. p.	r. a. p.	r. a. p.	r. a. p.			
Nellore	Per candy Per maund	— 2 1 1	— 1 14 0	— 0 8 0	— 2 1 5	— 0 11 4	— 0 2 3 (uncleaned)	0 5 11 0 0 3½	4m. 3v. 30p. (uncleaned)	596	—
Guntoor	Per candy Per maund	29 8 0 1 7 7	26 9 0 1 5 3	6 11 0 0 5 4	28 13 3 1 7 0¾	7 8 0 0 6 0	3 2 11¼ 0 2 6¼ (uncleaned)	2 5 4½ 0 1 10½	9ms. 13 seers (uncleaned)	47,299 21	102,646 41
Cuddapah	Per candy Per maund	43 0 0 2 2 4¾	35 0 0 1 12 0	11 0 0 0 8 9½	39 0 0 1 15 2¼	12 0 0 0 9 7¼	1 10 8 0 1 4 (uncleaned)	{ 8r. 10a. by bandy 14r. 6a. by bullocks 0 6 10¾	8m. or 200lbs. (uncleaned)	79,562	219,587
Kurnool	Per maund	1 10 5	1 9 7	0 6 4	1 10 8	0 6 7	0 0 8 (uncleaned)	0 5 2½	4m. 12¼ lbs. (uncleaned)	19,581	75,481
Bellary	Per maund	1 8 9	1 5 5	—	1 7 5	—	0 3 6 (cleaned)	0 14 0 to Coompta.	46lbs. 5oz. (cleaned)	260,000	400,000
Madura	Per maund	—	—	—	—	7 0 0 per podhee of 316 3/16, or about 9a. per md. of 25 lbs.	2 7 3 per 243 lbs. of cleaned cotton, or about 4a. per md.; but this is more than met by the value of the seed.	3 0 0 3r. 4a. in rains per cart-load, or 4 bales, of 243¾ lbs. each; or 1a. 3p. per md. to Tuticorin.	316¾lbs. (uncleaned)	48,747 including Ramnaad and Shevagunga.	60,747
Coimbatore	Per candy Per maund	45 13 10 2 4 8	— —	12 6 9 0 10 0	— —	1 0 0 —	8 18 0 0 1 2½ (uncleaned)	6 8 0 0 5 2½ to Pomeroy.	110lbs. (uncleaned)	97,830	Not specified, but to a great extent.
Tinnevelly	Per candy Per maund	47r. to 50r. 2r. 5a. 7½p. to 2r. 8a. 0p.	40 0 0 2 0 0	11 0 0 0 8 9½	47 0 0 2 5 7½	12 0 0 0 9 7½	5 0 0 0 4 0 (cleaned)	6 0 0 0 4 9½	3m. (cleaned) 12m. (uncleaned)	122,391	152,391

§ 32. Experimental Culture in the Peninsula.

So long ago as 1790, Dr. Anderson (to whom the genus Andersonia is dedicated) was employed in sending Mauritius as well as brown Malta cotton-seeds to different parts of the Peninsula. Dr. Roxburgh had very early ascertained that the dry and less fertile soil of Coromandel was better suited than that of Bengal to the Bourbon cotton. In 1813, Mr. Metcalfe was sent with American cotton-cleaning machines to Tinnivelly, or wherever his services might be required. It was in this district that success was first attained in cultivating Bourbon Cotton, by Mr. Hughes, who also produced the best, or Tinnivelly senna; a result not in either case accidental, but the natural consequence of skilful culture and careful picking. In 1819, the Madras government determined on establishing four cotton farms, of 400 acres each, under the Commercial Residents of the districts of Tinnivelly, Coimbatore, Masulipatam, and Vizagapatam. Mr. Heath, who, at that time, held the above office in Salem and Coimbatore, also succeeded in cultivating cotton, by following the directions which he received from Mr. Hughes. He found that the cotton came to perfection at a distance of 150 miles from the sea, and he obtained, in the season of 1823-24, from the district of Coimbatore, 500 bales of clean Bourbon cotton. We have seen no accounts of the other farms; but it can hardly be accidental, that Vizagapatam is stated to be the district in which the largest quantity of cotton is obtained per acre, and that liberal pruning is practised there. The efforts in other places have not been altogether without results; for Capt. Hughes says, in 1842, "Difficulties and disappointments attended the introduction of the Bourbon cotton into this (the Coimbatore) district, but which is now to be seen growing in all directions." So Dr. Wight, in the same year, speaks of improving "our indigenous and the now naturalised Bourbon cotton;" also of "the Bourbon cotton of the Coimbatore and Salem districts realizing in England 9½*d.* per lb., when the country cotton of the Tinnivelly district sold for only 6*d.* or 7*d.*" The above are at the rate of about 140 and 180 rupees for 500 lbs., for which the exporter pays only about 70 and 90 rupees. "But," Mr. Sullivan observes, "these are the prices paid to the brokers; the prices paid to the growers do not exceed 40 or 50 rupees." And he agrees with Dr. Wight, that all that is wanted is "more competition among buyers, and somewhat higher prices to growers." Mr. Fischer, himself an agent for the purchase of cotton for the Madras merchants, says, that the natives only want remunerating prices to grow the Bourbon cotton. But, in justice to the exporters, we must observe, that the prices of Indian cotton, being dependent upon those of American cotton, the uncertainties are too great for them to be very liberal, unless the cotton is sent to market in a clean and unadulterated state. (v. p. 37, for frauds in Tinnivelly.)

§ 33. Experimental Culture in Coimbatore.

We have referred to these statements as having been made previous to the present experiments. In the year 1840 three American planters were sent to Madras, and despatched to Tinnivelly in January, 1841. But it was stated that the sowing season had passed; for, according to the natives, the picking should be over before the land-wind sets in, that is, before the 10th of April. The planters conceived that a more northern climate was more suitable, for "the finest cotton is produced in a temperate climate." They were, after the loss of much time, removed to Errode in the end of August, where a piece of ground within the walls, and another on the glacis of the old fort, were selected, both having a "black cotton soil;" with other plantations two miles distant having a deep reddish loamy soil. In these, American, Bourbon, and country cotton-seed were sown. One of the planters objected to the "dry soil of Errode," observing that "at Coimbatore there has been an abundance of rain, and the land, from that and other causes, is in a good condition for ploughing." This district had been recommended by Mr. Heath and by Mr. Fischer, and subsequently approved of by Dr. Wight. Two of the planters were therefore established there. American and native cotton was sown in drills, and some broad-cast, about the middle of September, both in the black cotton ground and in the ordinary red soil of the Peninsula, that in which the Bourbon cotton is found to thrive best.

As the experimental culture in Coimbatore is interesting on

account of the several physical questions which have been discussed during its continuance, we think it desirable to be rather minute in their relation, as well as in detailing the progress of opinions. Thus so early as in December, when the leaves had shrivelled and become of a copper-brown colour, Mr. H. Morris reported from Errode, "I am fully convinced we never will succeed in raising the New Orleans cotton in India;" so Mr. Simpson stated at Coimbatore, in February, "In my opinion the New Orleans cotton plant will not succeed in this part of India." The former gave as his reasons:—"First place, during the rainy season, which is the proper time for planting, we have had entirely too much rain, and so soon as the monsoons are over, unfortunately we have no rain at all;" and Mr. Simpson, that "excessive hot dry weather has been the main cause of failure;" and also the "insects, which seem to declare vengeance against the young bolls." Dr. Wight, who visited these farms in September and in January, ascribed the failure to two causes:—First, to the soil "having become so hard as to be alike impermeable to both moisture and the roots of the plants," while "the frequent ploughing and hoeing, opening the soil, and giving free exit to the little moisture it had," with "the tearing of the superficial roots, still farther tended to impoverish the plants' channels of supply." To this Mr. Simpson replied: "By ploughing deep, the soil is pulverised below the influence of the sun, and mellows the land, which allows the tap-root (12 inches or more in length) to penetrate into a moist earth, which will give support to the plants throughout a dry hot season." There is truth in both observations, and their value depends upon their proper application.—Secondly, insects perforated the stems in all directions, but especially near the surface of the ground; but "neither the Bourbon nor country cotton suffered from these attacks, protected, perhaps, by their slower growth, and harder and more woody texture." But in the *red* soil, near Errode, "the plants, instead of being very stunted in their growth, and nearly one-third dead or dying, appeared well grown, and bearing a fair crop of large bolls."

In Coimbatore the experiment was at that time less successful, the plants in the black soils having grown hardly a pound of cotton, and being generally unhealthy, while those in the red soil, though small, were generally very healthy; but the failure of the crop was mainly owing to "an insect which seems hitherto to have attacked every flower, depositing its eggs in the germen." But neither Capt. Hughes nor Dr. Wight even then despaired of success; the latter suggested some modifications of culture, to suit it to the Indian climate.

A few short weeks, however, completely changed the prospects of the experiment; up to the middle of January it was expected that not a single pound of cotton would have been gathered. "About this time a heavy fall of rain took place, which had the effect of refreshing and greatly reviving the plants; a second fall was experienced about the beginning of February, and seemed completely to renovate them." In the middle of that month they became quite healthy, full of blossom and fruit, and gave promise of a large crop of cotton. About the 6th and 8th of February, 6 lbs. of cotton were picked at Coimbatore; after that the picking continued uninterruptedly, and almost daily increased in quantity until the 13th of April, when it rose to 3500 lbs." From the irregularity of the stand of plants, the quantity per acre could not be correctly ascertained, and though in some parts at the rate of 500 or 600 lbs., the actual produce was 183 lbs.; but allowing for wastage, for bad seed, &c., 233 lbs. 14 oz. per acre; and the black soil produced a larger proportion than the red soil. These facts prove that the culture depended almost entirely upon the season, and that opinions respecting its success varied according to the falls of rain. Dr. Wight having succeeded Capt. Hughes in the middle of February, 1842, we shall conclude this subject with the results of his experience in the following years, and up to the present time.

Dr. Wight having assumed charge of the experiment in February, 1842, bore ample testimony to the zeal and discretion of his predecessor, Capt. Hughes; a testimony, as stated by the Madras Government, very honorable to both parties. The American planters, as we have seen, despaired of success before the season was half over. At that time the plants in the black soil appeared to have entirely failed, while those in the red soil were comparatively healthy. But after the falls of rain in January and February, the plants in the black soil recovered themselves and bore a comparatively good crop, while those in the red soil suffered in turn. On this Dr. Wight observes, "The sowing having commenced about the middle of September, the plants grew vigorously, probably outgrew their strength during the wet cloudy weather which continued until the beginning of November, and therefore, on the accession of clear, cloudless weather, they became sickly and began to droop. During the ten weeks this weather lasted, they appeared paralysed and almost burned up, but the soft juicy wood became matured. The subsequent rains supplied the requisite nourishment and stimulus to renewed growth and a new formation of flower-buds. Of these few failed, and therefore a tolerable crop was obtained, when the hopes of the planters revived. With regard to the different behaviour of the plants in the two soils, it would appear that the black soil during the first rains became caked and afterwards hard and impervious, and therefore the cotton plants drooped; but as some moisture was retained under the hard soil, which moreover did not allow the plants to be inundated during the second rains, they were able to bear the longer continued drought. In the red soil, the free drainage was useful during the first rains; but the plants during the second heavy rains were soaked in water from the more open nature of the soil, as the water did not drain off sufficiently quick. The natives prefer a dry climate for cotton cultivation; but Mr. Simpson has stated, that "a quiet, moist, moderately warm climate suits (American) cotton best." With regard to culture, Dr. Wight, though highly approving of the principles of the American system of culture, as tested by both theory and practice, proposed to suit it to the Indian climate, by deep ploughing in the first instance, to promote the free absorption of moisture and the ready diffusion of the roots through the earth, closer sowing, and more hoeing to keep the ground clear, in place of the repeated ploughing and hoeing of the first season.

Samples of the cotton grown both on the black and red soils having been sent by the Overland Route to the India House, were exhibited by the author at the Meeting of the Natural History Section of the British Association at Manchester in September, 1842, when some of the best judges of cotton there, pronounced "the New Orleans cotton grown on the red soil was quite equal to the fine qualities of the same cotton produced in the United States."

Dr. Wight gives the following account of the farming returns for this season: already referred to at p. 474.

Tabular Abstract of the Extent and Quantity of Produce of the Government Cotton Farms in Coimbatore, for the Season 1841-42, *as it stood on the* 1*st of May,* 1842.

Description of soil.	Description of cotton.	No. of acres.	Amount of produce.	Average per acre.
* Black soil . .	New Orleans	94	15,923	169·6
	Indian	6	1340	223·5
** Red soil . .	New Orleans	6	160	26·10
	Indian	10	4143	414·4
*** Red soil . .	New Orleans	2	125	62·8
	Indian	2	300	150·
		120	21,991	183·4
	Deduct for wastage .	26		233·14 true average.
		94		

"The average of the whole, as shown by the table, amounts to 183·4 lbs. per acre; but, deducting on account of waste and loss of land, owing to bad seed, &c., 26 acres, which is rather under than above the fair proportion, we have 233·14 lbs. per acre of seed cotton as the average produce of the Coimbatore farms. Part of this, however, perhaps about 300 lbs., is damaged, and can scarcely be considered marketable cotton."

Dr. Wight commenced the second year's operations with considerable hopes of success, but we find him regretting that his expectations had been much too sanguine. The crops seem to have been chiefly sown in September. About the beginning of April some of their fields "were covered with probably the most abundant crop ever seen in India," when the planters expected about 1000 lbs. per acre, and 600 lbs. from the other fields of seed-cotton. But a week of stormy weather, accompanied with heavy rain, "destroyed not only the cotton ready to pick," but did incalculable injury to the less advanced parts of the crop, so that not more than from 107 to 394 lbs. per acre, or, on an average of the whole, 270 lbs. of seed cotton per acre, was obtained. The information obtained was, that a wet soil was highly injurious to a ripe crop, that American cotton succeeds best in the light alluvial and red sandy soils, and is the least suited to the black soil; and generally that unsuitable soils, rather than uncongenial climate, is the main obstacle to be surmounted, though they had still to learn the effects of manuring and of alternation of crops, likewise the proper time for sowing. Dr. Wight mentions at this time that Mr. Wroughton, the Collector of Coimbatore, had a field of a light sandy-red soil, partaking of the showery weather of the south-west monsoon, sown with New Orleans cotton in July, 1842, which the planters considered the finest crop of cotton they had seen out of America. But this was injured by heavy rains in January.

In his report for 1843 and 1844, Dr. Wight has again to express great disappointment with the results, and for which, he says, he is unable satisfactorily to account, though a native cultivator early predicted that failure would take place. His reasons were that the rains were too late by six weeks. The natives like to sow early in September, and it was the middle of October before the rains permitted their doing so. Dr. Wight among other reasons, as exhaustion of the soil and late sowing, also attributes the failure to the abundance of rain which fell in a short time and stimulated an excessively rapid growth, disproportioned to the production of roots. On the commencement of the clear and bright dry weather, greater evaporation took place from the leaves than the diminutive roots could supply. Though he does not consider this quite satisfactory, it appears to us to account sufficiently for the phenomena. Plants in a moist and warm soil and atmosphere grow rapidly, but their roots being easily supplied with nutriment, do not require to travel so far in search of it, and therefore they remain short, and are unable to supply, the great evaporation which necessarily takes place from a large leafy plant when hot dry weather comes on, from so small an extent and from so near the surface of the soil.

The plants grew scarcely at all during the dry weather, and had a seared and unhealthy aspect, and of course yielded but little cotton. In April they had some heavy falls of rain, and the soil was loosened by a slight ploughing between the rows. The shrubs then began to shoot afresh, and a second and richer crop was obtained.

The American system of ridging Dr. Wight thought was injurious, from letting the water run off in dry seasons. He also thought the time of sowing unsuitable; and proposed doing so in June if the weather was favorable, as the plant will bear the heat and drought of the Indian climate well, if not too much forced at starting, and that when well advanced, it will be in the best state for benefiting by the monsoon. The crops may then be gathered in February and March, the driest months of the year. From the second crop which he had obtained, he proposed treating the New Orleans as a biennial in the same manner as the Bourbon.

Statement of the Produce of the Government Farms at Coimbatore, for the Season 1843-44.

NAMES.	Description of soil.	Description of cotton.	No. of Acres.	Amount of produce.	Average per acre.
Superintendent's Farm, Coimbatore.	Red	Bourbon	53	5678	107⅛
	Do.	New Orleans	103	11,093	103
	Black	Do.	17	7510	440
		Total	173	24,281	140⅛
Mr. Simpson's Farm, Coimbatore.	Black	New Orleans	208½	40,053	192
	Do.	Oopum	40½	11,322	279½
	Red	Bourbon	8½	1733	204
	Do.	New Orleans	38½	6289	163⅓
		Total	296	59,397	200⅝
Mr. Morris's Farm, Oodmulcotto.	Red	New Orleans	62	9016	145⅜
	Black	Do.	100	22,566	225½
	Do.	Oopum	149	52,629	353¾
		Total	311	84,211	270¾
Courchee Farm.	Alluvial	New Orleans	87	30,329	394½
	Do.	Oopum	31	3194	103
	Do.	Bourbon	11¼	2220	197
		Total	129¼	39,743	307½

Mr. Wroughton, the Collector of Coimbatore, had even at this period begun early sowing. For we learn from Dr. Wight's '*Notes on American Agriculture as practised in Coimbatore*' (*H. of C.'s Return,* p. 354), that he had sown with cotton in July, 1842, a field situated in a valley a few miles south of Coimbatore. The soil was red, light, and sandy. The situation was exposed to the showery weather of the south-west monsoon; this assisted the growth of the plants, which made great progress prior to the setting-in of the north-east monsoon. They then attained a large size, and in December were covered with a profusion of bolls; but a heavy fall of rain in January damaged much of the cotton that had been produced. Mr. Wroughton had also about this time expressed his conviction (v. *Return*, p. 374) "that all that was wanted to establish the general cultivation of American cotton among the natives here was to ensure to them remunerating prices for the article when produced." Dr. Wight, finding that the price of the *Oopum purthee*, or best indigenous cotton, varies from 10 to 14 rupees for the candy of 500 lbs., took 12 rupees as the average, and proposed giving the natives 20 rupees for the same quantity of American seed cotton, if they would cultivate it in their own fields. Notwithstanding this great increase in price, he did not contemplate that Government would sustain any loss, as he expected a larger proportion of cotton to seed from the American plant; though he calculated this only at 28, when he might have taken it at least at 30 per cent. He calculated also on the American cotton selling in England at a better price than the Indian cotton, as he shows in the table below (v. p. 482).

In his report of proceedings for 1844-45, Dr. Wight dwells especially on the great detriment of continuing to cultivate cotton in the same fields, and observes, that "their persevering adoption of the American plan of farms, and the exclusive use of American farming implements, had prevented the natives adopting the system or plant. But the experience gained has shown them that there is no mystery in the cultivation of the American cotton plant, and that their own primitive implements of agriculture are well adapted to its culture, and that their habitual rotation system is better adapted to the soils of this country, than the farming one without rotation of America.

"To place this in a clear light, it is necessary to premise, that in the cotton districts of Mississippi, land is portioned out into cotton farms, and that there the soil is so fertile, that with no other manuring than what it obtains from the ashes of the previous crop, which in spring is burned on the ground, it yields year after year, with only an occasional relief, large crops of cotton. The same plan was therefore adopted here; with what success, the following table of average produce per acre for all kind of cotton and soil, will show:

	Average per acre.				
	1842.	1843.	1844.	1845.	
Superintendent's farm, Coimbatore.	—	140⅛	125⅛	105¾	Principally American and Bourbon; soil for the most part very poor, and generally shallow and unsuitable.
Mr. Simpson's Farm, Coimbatore.	233	200⅝	72⅝	—	Principally American and some Oopum; soil generally black, but of very inferior quality.
Mr. Morris's Farm, Courchee.	—	307½	199½	136⅛	Principally American, some Bourbon and Oopum; soil alluvial but poor, being apparently exhausted by the first very luxuriant crop.
Mr. Sherman's Farm, Oodoomulcottah.	—	270¾	234	229	First and second seasons principally American; third, mostly Oopum, which accounts for the high average out-turn of the third crop; soil black, and generally of the best quality of that sort of land.

"Here it will be seen that each farm yielded a better crop the first year than the second, even though a large proportion was destroyed by a series of stormy weather while picking; and the second better than the third, notwithstanding the labour and care bestowed in preparing the ground was each successive year increased. At first we were disposed to attribute the effect to difference of season; but, on finding the third crop so much less than the second, though the season was upon the whole more favorable than the preceding, and the care bestowed on the agricultural operations, if possible, greater, the true cause became so clearly obvious, as no longer to leave a doubt on the subject."

Dr. Wight states he was further strengthened in this conclusion by the culture of a field taken up by the Collector,

Mr. Wroughton, and cultivated on the American plan entirely by natives, and which yielded a very large crop. Dr. Wight observes, "that there was nothing peculiar in the soil of that field, but the ground had not been ploughed for many years. But we believe that it was favored by climate, having a due degree of heat without any excessive moisture. The situation is partially exposed to the influence of the south-west monsoon, but which last season was light; it also participates, to a moderate extent, in the north-east monsoon, but it also was unusually light." The field was ploughed by natives in the native manner, but sown and cultivated generally according to the American method. "The picking commenced in December, and continued almost uninterruptedly until July, when the last picking was taken, and then, on summing up the proceeds of the season, it was found to amount to nearly 1100 lbs. per acre, the greater part, too, of excellent quality." But it will be desirable to refer to Mr. Wroughton's own account of his experiment, as given below.

Dr. Wight further observes, that "acting on the information derived from these two sources, I have now given up all our original farms, and we are in course of preparing new ones, the sowing of which has already commenced. Still further to establish the culture of the American plant by the natives, which they seem averse to undertake, under the impression that they may not find a ready market for their cotton at remunerating prices,—I have undertaken to purchase all they grow of fair quality, on such terms as they themselves think will fairly remunerate them."

Dr. Wight having learned, from quotations of the Liverpool market, that the prices assumed in his first calculations to represent the relative valuations of Indian-grown American cotton and native Indian cotton in the home market, do not do so fairly, found that in place of $4\frac{3}{4}$*d.* for the former and 4*d.* for the latter, they would now be more correctly represented by 5*d.* for the former (American), and $3\frac{3}{4}$*d.* for the latter (Indian). Presuming that these two sums pretty nearly represent the relative values of the two kinds of cotton, and substituting 15 for 20 rupees as the price of American seed cotton in Coimbatore, the following table will show, in a strong point of view, the advantages the merchant will derive from exerting his influence to stimulate the production of the former, while we have every reason to believe the benefit will be shared to an equal, or perhaps even greater, extent by the grower.

Statement showing the Comparative Profits in the English Market on Indian-grown American Cotton and Native Indian Cotton, costing respectively, as they come from the field in Coimbatore, 15 *rupees per Candy for the former, and* 12 *rupees for the latter.*

American seed cotton yields 28 per cent. of clean cotton, i. e. 1785 lbs. of seed cotton are required to yield 500 lbs. (one candy) of clean cotton.

	r.	a.	p.
Cost of 1785 lbs., at 15r. per candy of 500 lbs. .	53	9	0
Value of 500 lbs. of clean cotton in England, at 5*d.* per lb., is . . .	105	2	0
Value of 500 lbs. of native cotton . . .	77	15	0
Difference in favour of American cotton .	27	3	0

Native cotton seed yields $21\frac{3}{4}$ per cent. of clean cotton, i. e. 2,300 lbs. of seed cotton are required to yield 500 lbs. (one candy) of clean cotton.

	r.	a.	p.
Cost of 2300 lbs., at 12r. per candy of 500 lbs. .	55	4	0
Value of 500 lbs. of clean cotton in England, at $3\frac{3}{4}$*d.* per lb., is . . .	77	15	0

"Assuming, then, which I believe we are fully justified in doing, that on similar lands and in similar seasons the crop of the two kinds will prove simply of equal weight, the cost of production being nearly the same, the grower has a profit amounting to three rupees a candy in his crop of American cotton over what he would have from Indian, while the merchant is enabled to realise a positive profit on the capital invested in the exportation of the one, in place of, at present, barely remitting at par exchange the money invested in the other, if he can even do that, which seems doubtful.

"Thus far my deductions are based on what may also be set down as ascertained facts; to go beyond this would lead me into speculation, which I avoid, lest I should thereby be tempted to advance opinions based on insufficient data, that might tend to weaken the force of those already advanced.

(Signed) R. WIGHT, *Surgeon,*

"*Coimbatore,* 1*st September,* 1845. *Supt. Cotton Farms.*"

Dr. Wight accordingly transferred his farms from near Coimbatore to Ootacalmont. The necessity of rotation, he observes, was clearly demonstrated by a field taken in last season and sown in the end of June, which yielded a crop amounting to 361 lbs. per acre; while the adjoining fields, which had borne two successive crops, gave only $66\frac{3}{4}$. Some delay occurred in getting all the fields that were required. The first field was sown on the 22d of July, and the last in September. The produce of the first sown field (about 22 acres) has been carefully distinguished from the rest, and now amounts to 18,000 lbs. Of the remainder, the earliest sown invariably proved the most productive. Profiting by this information, he was exerting himself to get lands which he might commence ploughing with the first rains of April, as this would allow sufficient time for working and cleaning, so as to have it in a good state for sowing in June. The land which they obtained from the ryots they were "to have the use of for 15 months, in consideration of receiving, by way of compensation, a sum equal to half the government assessment. At this rate our Puttah lands for next season will cost about one rupee 12 annas per acre, while the waste lands are nominally debited to the farm at from one rupee to one and a quarter; much more might have been obtained on the same terms, had I felt certain of obtaining a sufficiency of hired labour, as it is by such I intend principally to cultivate. I give the preference under our superintendence to hired labour, though less perfect than our own, partly as being cheaper, but principally to familiarise the natives with our methods, and facilitate their adoption of them when so disposed."

Dr. Wight assumes a produce of 681 lbs. per acre. One field, the crop of which is not nearly over, has already yielded 900 lbs.; and Mr. Wroughton's last season gave 1100 lbs., making the total produce, at that rate of valuation, worth within a trifle above 615 rupees, leaving as profit for the cultivator, after allowing for extra picking, 460 rupees on 22 acres. "The facts elicited in the progress of our experiments during the last two years are most important. We learn from them, that to obtain really good crops of New Orleans cotton in this part of India, the part should enjoy a moderately humid climate, showery weather during the first two or three months of its growth, to bring it to a state of vigorous maturity, after which it will bear uninjured much drought; but if it receives a considerable check from unseasonably dry weather in the course of the first month, it does not readily recover."

"The natives who have hitherto attempted its cultivation have failed, from delaying until the setting-in of the north-east monsoon, and sowing it at the same time with the native plant, which seems to take a deeper root, and requires less rain after being once fairly started; but even in the case of the native cotton, I greatly doubt the propriety of delaying till the end of September or later, according to the season, when it could be equally well done in July or August. It is therefore my intention, in the course of the coming season, to sow both the native and Bourbon kind at the same time as the American, to ascertain whether the native practice in this tract of country is derived from actual experience, or is mere unreflecting custom, brought from the eastern talooks, where the course of the seasons has established the practice."

Mr. Wroughton having been applied to by the Madras Government for a full report on the subject of his culture of New Orleans cotton, addressed a letter dated 9th June, 1846, to J. F. Thomas, Esq., Chief Secretary to Government, from which the following are extracts:—

"In reply, I beg leave to state, that from local knowledge and tested experience, I have long considered the land situated within the influence of the south-west and north-east monsoons as best adapted for the cultivation of American cotton, and being confirmed in this belief by the result of the experiment made by me in 1842, as communicated to Government in a letter dated 10th December of that year, I was led to select ground at Ootacalmund in last year, which had remained waste for several years past, and, lying still further to the south-west of my first operations, embraced the above two desiderata; the land was tolerable, assessed at Rs. 2 10a. 4p. per cawney. This I purposely preferred, to ascertain the capability and productiveness of the least valuable land, feeling assured, if a profitable return could be secured from soil of this character, which prevails out of all proportion to the better and other more expensive kinds, that this was all that could be desired for present purposes.

"With reference to the system pursued by me during the last three years, I beg to annex an extract of a Memorandum I had occasion to draw out some months previously, and which I trust will be found to contain sufficient information regarding my efforts to grow New Orleans cotton.

"MEMORANDUM.

"In making selection of the land for the cultivation of American cotton, two points are absolutely essential. The 1st, with reference to season; and 2dly, with reference to the influence of the periodical monsoons. The native mode of culture is defective in these points. The ryots invariably sow their lands in October, and the tender plants being unable to resist the withering north-east winds, yield only a stunted shrub, and scanty produce. The plan observed by Mr. Wroughton has therefore been to take up such land as comes within the influence of the south-west and north-east monsoons, ploughing it in the months of March and April; it is then allowed to remain fallow until the end of July, when advantage is taken of any rain that may fall, and the sowing commences after one more repetition of light ploughing. This must not be done earlier than about that time, viz., the end of July. The seed germinates, and the plant struggles against the south-west winds, *gaining root without vegetating greatly;* care, however, being given not to advance too close to the former, as too much rain is equally prejudicial as too little; the process of weeding and thinning goes on intermediately, which is repeated occasionally. By this mode, the plants acquire so great a degree of hardness as to be prepared for any change, and the showers previous to the setting in of the north-east monsoon, and rains during its continuance, produce a good-sized plant about three feet high, and yielding 200 to 250 bolls.

"The only dangers which Mr. Wroughton has had reason to dread were twofold, the drought and the grate, which latter, unobserved, being permitted to make an entrance into the boll, gradually consumes it. This can be provided against by vigilance, as the attack of the insect is not made until the boll is ripe, by pulling it off, and drying it in the sun; it progresses nearly as well as it would on the tree, and the insect dies. Mr. Wroughton finds that manure should not be applied to the land in the same year it is proposed to cultivate it with cotton; and, in fact, he is very doubtful whether manure is at all requisite, repeated and deep ploughing doing all that is needful.

"The cultivation of cotton is peculiarly a family undertaking, if such an expression may be used, for the labours of the youngest child beyond infancy may be made useful. Little children are taught to pluck the cotton, which, after a little practice, they contrive to do just as well and with greater expedition than the women, whose portion of the work ought to be given to sorting it.

"With reference, therefore, to these points of insecurity to the American farmer, it becomes incumbent to contrast the cheapness of labour and the congeniality of this district with America; and Mr. Wroughton does not hesitate in stating his opinion, that, granting that the productive power of the soil may not equal America, still cotton can be produced in any given quantity at a cheaper rate, and at the same time of an equally good staple, which fact the community of Madras has had an opportunity of testing and rewarding.

"One point is only requisite to put all matters beyond a doubt, and that is, demand of a sufficiently remunerating character to attract the ryots to its growth.

"The cultivation of the cotton for many years past has been neglected exceedingly; it is rarely attempted to be produced as a single crop. Most frequently the seed is included with three or four other kinds of grain, and where it is sown alone, the land is insufficiently worked and seasoned by previous tillage. Indeed, the successful and profitable culture of cotton requires the investment of more capital and harder labour than is encouraged by local circumstances and existing prices.

"A statement of charges incurred by Mr. Wroughton for the culture of cotton is annexed, together with a memorandum of the quantity produced.

"The above remarks refer only to the lightly assessed soils, for obvious reasons, the experiment having been tested on the most economical principles, and with such success as to leave no doubt that the richer and more loamy soils under similar influence and culture will equal, if not exceed, in return, the best American soils."

"With reference to the cost of culture, I would refer you to the statement transmitted with my letter of the 25th July, 1845, to the address of the Chief Secretary. The total charges for the cultivation of 22 cawnies of land amounted to Rs. 320 6a. 8p. With a view to facilitate reference, a copy of that statement is annexed.

"I am unable to state accurately the area of miles or the extent of country on which New Orleans cotton can be grown; but I am of opinion that it can be made a certain product in almost all the villages situated within the influence of the south-west and north-east monsoons in the talooks of Pulachey, Coimbatore, Pulladum, and Chuckragherry."

Memorandum of Charges incurred for the Cultivation of Cotton at Ootacalmund, from 1st July, 1844, to June, 1845.

	r.	a.	p.
Assessment of $7\frac{1}{16}$ bullahs, or $22\frac{1}{2}\frac{3}{16}$ cawnies of cowle lands .	24	3	8
Charges for ploughing land	24	0	0
Ditto for weeding	22	11	0
Ditto for gathering produce	76	5	0
Ditto for taking out sembandoo, or unclean cotton, at Coimbatore	58	4	6
Ginning and packing	29	15	8
Value of gunnies purchased for cotton bales, &c. . .	41	13	4
Value of ropes for cotton bales, &c.	7	14	0
Hire for sewing gunny bags	4	5	0
Ditto for conveying cotton on carts	16	4	0
Pay of a coolie	12	2	0
Value of bamboo mats	1	8	0
Ditto of a large bamboo basket	1	0	0
Total	320	6	2

Memorandum, showing the Quantity of Cotton produced in the field near Ootacalmund, from 18th July, 1844, to 30th June, 1845.

	Cotton in bales.	Cotton in gunny bags.	Total in bales.	Number of pounds.	Candies.
Cotton, 1st sort	12	10	17	4250	$8\frac{1}{2}$
„ 2d „	—	10	5	1250	$2\frac{1}{2}$
„ 3d „	3	5	$5\frac{1}{2}$	1375	2
Total	15	25	$27\frac{1}{2}$	6875	$13\frac{3}{4}$
Aggregate Produce Seed Cotton	—	—	—	25,450	$50\frac{3}{4}$

From the cursory view which we have taken of Dr. Wight's experience, it is evident that there is considerable variation in the seasons at Coimbatore. This indeed seems to constitute the chief difficulty of culture in that district. But we have also seen that considerable experience was gained and modifications of culture adopted, so that each seemed all that was required to ensure complete success. But the seasons still continued to change, and that of 1846-47 is described as one of the driest that they had had. Dr. Wight mentions that not more than six and a half inches of rain had fallen during the year 1846, instead of from 26 to 30 inches, the usual average. He sowed in June and July, had a few showers in October, and was picking a small crop during November and December, that is, during the usual period of the north-east monsoon. The season continued unfavorable throughout, and having been so dry during 1846, it was followed by unseasonable rains early in 1847. This ruined the plants which had struggled through the drought. That is in February, and again in April, they were visited by heavy rains. They were looking out for an abundant second crop, but the early accession of the south-west monsoon destroyed nearly the whole of their crop. Dr. Wight observes, that during the years 1846 and 1847, the rain which fell at Coimbatore amounted to 32 inches; of these, only $6\frac{1}{4}$ fell during the first year and a quarter, and the remaining $25\frac{1}{2}$ inches in the other eight or nine months.

Experiments in early sowing.—In the beginning of 1847, a deputation of the Manchester Commercial Association had an interview with the Chairman and Deputy-Chairman of the Court of Directors, and subsequently Mr. Turner addressed a letter to the Court (v. *H. of C. Return*) on the subject of early sowing. This was transmitted by the next mail to Dr. Wight. As the object of the letter will be understood from Dr. Wight's reply, we need only extract the following testimony to the excellence of the cotton grown by him:—

"The Association availing themselves of the opportunity thus afforded them, would, in the first instance, congratulate Dr. Wight on the great superiority of his New Orleans cotton over any other of that description hitherto grown in India, and suggest that he would devote his attention exclusively to its culture; and also, that the 5000 bales which the Hon. Court of Directors have authorised and empowered him to purchase, should consist exclusively of this kind of cotton, a cotton which, for general purposes, is by far the most serviceable."

Dr. Wight's reply, dated 8th April, 1847, addressed to J. C. Melvill, Esq., Secretary of the Court of Directors, was as follows:—

Coimbatore; 8th April, 1847.

To J. C. MELVILL, Esq., *Secretary to the East India House, London.*

"SIR,—I have the honour to acknowledge the receipt of your letter of the 8th February, transmitting extract from a letter from J. A. Turner, Esq., President of the Manchester Commercial Association, to Sir J. Weir Hogg, Bart, M.P., Chairman of the Court of Directors of the East India Company, dated 5th February, 1847.

"2d. It is a source of gratification to learn that the American cotton grown on the Coimbatore farms has been found superior to any of the same description grown in India. This is no doubt partly owing to the suitable selection of the sowing season, a point which has received much consideration, but is also partly owing to local circumstances.

"3d. Our farms are situated in an extensive valley, participating in the rains of both monsoons, by which we are enabled so to regulate the time of sowing with the one, as to have the plant coming into bloom about the time when the other usually commences, which invigorates and fits it to bring its crop to maturity during the subsequent dry season.

"4th. Mr. Turner's suggestion, regarding earlier sowing, has not escaped observation and has been tried, but in a great measure failed. But supposing the case had been otherwise, it rarely happens that it could be practised, at least in this district, as the rains seldom reach us before the middle of May, and often not until June, in sufficient quantity to admit of our parched and sun-baked lands being sufficiently prepared for the reception of seed before the first week, or even the middle, of July, which is as soon as sowing should commence.

"5th. During the hot season the soil becomes so hard that the plough cannot penetrate the surface until it has been softened and loosened by copious showers. It then requires to be ploughed two or three times to clear it thoroughly before sowing, this keeps us employed from a month to six weeks, that is, until about the middle of July. This I consider the best time for sowing, as the plant, which is of rapid growth, then comes into flower, about the time the north-east monsoon commences in October.

"6th. If it is sown earlier, so that the cotton bolls are far advanced towards maturity when these rains commence, nearly the whole of the earlier part of the crop is lost, owing to the plant becoming surcharged with sap, which the cotton seems to absorb, and in place of coming to proper maturity, rots in the capsule; we have repeatedly had to regret extensive losses from this cause.

"7th. Such being the case, our object is so to adapt the sowing to the course of the seasons as to secure, as far as possible, a continuance of humid weather for the plant, so long as it is growing, and dry clear weather for maturing and harvesting the crop. If we are fortunate in enjoying an average season, our lands yield, according to the quality of the soil, from 500 to 1000, or even 1200 pounds per acre of American seed cotton. The native Indian plant is much less productive.

"8th. As suggested by Mr. Turner, I have also tried low alluvial lands, but the return proved quite disproportioned to the previous appearance, and simply from the lands being too humid, or, in other words, owing to the wet subsoil producing nearly the same effect on the crop as rainy weather on higher and drier lands.

"9th. Adverting to Mr. Turner's remark on the more silky staple of American than Indian grown cotton of the same description, I may remark that this fact is known to us, and has engaged much attention with a view to ascertain the cause and probable remedy. At first the climate was supposed to have some effect in producing the change from soft silkiness to harshness of fibre, more extended observation has led to the conclusion that soil has more to do with the change than the climate.

"10th. It is well known to the native cotton dealers, that cotton grown on black ground has a longer and softer staple than when grown on red gravelly soil, the kind on which our American cotton is principally and most successfully cultivated, especially where calcareous matter forms a prominent ingredient. Reasoning from these facts, I was induced to try low alluvial soil, as more nearly approaching to the best American soils than either our black clays or gravelly soils, and to a certain extent established the position, that the cotton produced on such soils was of excellent quality, but the crops very uncertain, as a single unseasonable shower of rain, by loading the soil with excess of moisture, was liable to deteriorate half the crop then approaching to maturity. I, however, coincide in the view taken by the Association, of the probable advantage to be derived from cultivating cotton on lands near the coast, and have long felt anxious to have a farm established there for the cultivation of American cotton. Hitherto the plan has been beset with difficulties which I have not been able to surmount; but now it is in progress, as Mr. Finnie is located in the centre of one of the best cotton districts in the south of India, within about forty miles of the sea on the east coast, and will, I trust, succeed in finding cultivation probably to within a few miles of the shore, and I am not without the hope of being able to make arrangements for the culture of a few fields between Paulghaut and the west coast. But so far as my acquaintance with that coast extends, we need scarcely expect to approach nearer than within sixty or seventy miles of the shore, there being so little land suitable for the cultivation of cotton within that limit.

"11th. I trust that in these brief notes I have yet been sufficiently explicit to satisfy both the Honorable Court and the Association, that constant attention has been given towards the careful working out, in all its branches, of this experiment, and that the results already obtained are such as to satisfy the latter that all that is now required to bring it to a most successful conclusion, is commercial encouragement by the establishment of agents, altogether distinct from government, to contract with the Ryots to cultivate American cotton for them. They are now doing so for us of their own free will, merely because they find it profitable to do so, though still apparently jealous of government interference. Dealing with merchants will remove this objection, and in the course of a few years, lead to the general introduction of the exotic, which, I believe, they are quite satisfied can be grown as easily and cheaply as their own, and much more profitably, both as regards the out-turn from equal areas of land, and the price it realizes. The present has proved one of the most unfavorable cotton seasons that has been known for many years. In this part of India the crops of native cotton having almost universally failed, while the few natives whom we succeeded in inducing to sow American cotton at the same time with ourselves, have realized very fair returns, better, indeed, than they usually obtain in good seasons from the indigenous plant. This very unlooked for result will doubtless establish its credit beyond dispute, and stimulate its extended culture.

"I have, &c.,

(Signed) ROBERT WIGHT, *Surgeon,*

"*Supt. Cotton Farms.*"

Dr. Wight, in conformity with the suggestion of the Commercial Association, determined to give early sowing a fair trial, and accordingly prepared ground and began sowing in the month of May. The experiment was made on a sufficiently large scale to afford conclusive data. It was spread over eighty acres, distributed among four farms situated within an area forty miles in extent. It is a remarkable fact, that not only had the letters, with regard to early sowing during the first monsoon, been written and the suggestion carried into execution, but the produce was actually received in this country before the end of the year 1847. At a meeting of the Commercial Association in December, 1847, Mr. Turner stated, that "They only wrote out in February, and the cotton had been sown according to their suggestion, and a sample of the first picking was then on the table, and he was happy to say, that the result had fully justified the opinion which they entertained, that the early sowing would produce a cotton very superior even to the best cotton that had been previously sent from that district." The cotton is thus described:

"This seed cotton has been produced by plants sown on the 29th of last May, and was gathered before the 8th of October. It is a portion of a crop yielded by the plants after the rains of the south-west monsoon; and Dr. Wight expects a second crop from the same plants after the rains of the north-east monsoon, which, on the 8th of October, he was expecting daily to set in. It is evidently a much whiter cotton than any hitherto grown from New Orleans seed in India; it has also that strength, clearness, and silkiness of staple, and straightness of fibre, which spinners so much valued, and which many persons have supposed the climate of India could not produce. It is, in fact, a true New Orleans cotton."

Subsequently, a bale of this May-sown cotton was received in Manchester in August, 1848, when we find it thus described, "The quality of the single bale of the early-sown cotton has quite borne out the predictions of the Manchester Commercial Association, as to what might be effected in the improvement of the cotton crop by sowing in the latter end of May. It is decidedly the finest sample of cotton yet received from India; its colour and cleanliness are unexceptionable, and its staple is very little inferior to the New Orleans cotton received from America. $4\frac{3}{4}$*d.* per lb. has been offered for it by several spinners; but this has been declined, as it is valued by the brokers at 5*d.* per lb." (*Manchester Guardian,* 12th of August, 1848.) Great results were expected, and very reasonably, from this discovery.

Dr. Wight himself, though at this time sanguine of success,

was yet aware of several difficulties that might interfere with eventual success, as he intimated in letters written in September and October. He observes first, that he had been able to sow thus early, chiefly in consequence of the site of these farms being in the gorge of a valley, which is within the influence of the rains of the autumn monsoon, which had that year been earlier than usual by about a month. Coimbatore, though it has the advantage of participating in the two monsoons, is yet too remote from the line of both to trust entirely to either for these crops. Moreover, supposing that the season was favorable for sowing in May and June and for the subsequent growth of the plant, it would be in full crop at the very time that the north-east monsoon sets in, and it would not be the first time that he had had a good crop destroyed by a heavy fall of rain. The difficulty does not consist in cultivating American cotton in India, but in selecting such a time for commencing operations, as to have the plant in full bearing at the most seasonable time for harvesting a crop.

In the beginning of 1848, Dr. Wight issued a circular, which was printed at the Government press, and circulated to all the Collectors, &c. of the Madras Presidency, and to others interested in the subject, in order to induce them to institute a number of small and simultaneous experiments in different parts of the country, to ascertain the best times and places for sowing and cultivating American cotton.

Dr. Wight mentions, that he had "been in correspondence with Mr. James Lees, of Manchester, a member of the Commercial Association of that city, who has examined the subject in all its bearings with the most elaborate care and attention."

"The natural growing season of the plant being during the summer months (May, June, and July), Mr. J. Lees affirms we ought, in bringing it to India, enjoying seasons similar to those of its native country, to conform to its native habits, and, by sowing in May, secure for it in India, as in Mexico, its natural growing season, and urges that it is only by following such a course, that we need hope for success. In a word, he insists that the proper season for sowing Mexican cotton in India is at the same time that our ryots sow their spring crops of Cholum and Cumboo; which he enforces by adducing the fact, that in Egypt, where both crops are cultivated by irrigation, the Egyptian wheel can raise water enough to irrigate three acres of cotton, but only two of Cholum; thence deducing the inference, that cotton requires less water than Cholum to perfect its crop, and consequently, that the amount of rain that in India is found sufficient for the latter (which rarely fails), ought to suffice for the former.

"By sowing at the natural time, he observes, there would not only be more certainty of crop, but other most important results would be obtained. The crop would at all times be much greater and the staple of the cotton much superior. These results would follow from a more perfect development of the plant. The observance of the natural sowing time will produce the most perfect development of which the plant is susceptible. It will then be sown at that period of the growing season, when the soil and the climate are in the most heated state, and when this heat combines with those gentle showers, which at that time occur, to promote to the utmost the rapidity and vigour of the germination of the seed, and when also, after germination has taken place, the subsequent growing season will be more prolonged and propitious than at any other period of the year."

"The experiments," Dr. Wight conceives, "may be done without trouble or expense; all that is required being to ask a few ryots in each district, when sowing their Cholum, to sow a few handfuls of Mexican cotton seed in any convenient spot in the same fields, and watch the result. In this way the correctness or otherwise of the statement regarding the relative quantities of moisture required for perfecting crops of cotton and Cholum will be established on a wide and satisfactory basis, and, if found correct, may prove the means of at once introducing the culture of the exotic cotton into many parts of the country where it has not yet been heard of. But whether these first trials fail or succeed in districts under the influence of the north-east monsoon, the experiment should be repeated in October, for the purpose of ascertaining whether it is as certain and productive during the hot as the cool season, keeping the double object in view, of confirming or refuting the opinions of the American planters, regarding the necessity of a mild climate for its successful culture."

In May, 1848, Dr. Wight writes: "We are now engaged in sowing, instead of preparing our ground to sow in June and July, hoping to house our crop before October."

In July of the same year, Dr. Wight announced, that the early sown cotton continued to advance favorably, though there had not been a shower for six weeks; and that, with fair management, two crops might be grown annually in a great part of the

Carnatic, and one everywhere. The natives prepare their lands for spring crops with the autumn rains, and those for the autumn crops with the spring ones: we now prepare our lands months before they are wanted. He had himself sowed in April and in May, when a little rain happened to fall, as their fields were all ready; and stated, that he was going to sow again with the first autumnal rains, probably in September.

Dr. Wight particularly mentions, that he was endeavouring to induce the natives to take an interest in the culture, by renting two or three fields in different localities under native overseers, who live on the spot and hire the labour which they required. By this means the surrounding cultivators are taught by actual practice, and see the superior productiveness of the American cotton, and that it is as easily cultivated as their own. Its superior value is indicated by our purchasing any that they grow, at an advance of from 30 to 50 per cent. over what they can obtain for their own. It answers better on the cheaper descriptions of land, it produces heavier crops per acre, and it yields to the gin at least from 8 to 9 per cent. more cotton to seed than native cotton, while in the English market it sells for at least a penny a pound more. A common price for native cotton is 12 rupees for a candy of 500 lbs. (though at that time it was selling for 9r. 12a.) If the American were sold for the same price, the prime cost would be under 2*d.*, while the native at the same price would be 2½*d.* gin-cleaned, churka-cleaned somewhat less. The cost of transmission to England 1¼*d.* In order to encourage the cultivation, he was giving 20 rupees for the candy, which was equivalent to about 3*d.* a pound. In his circular, he points out that native seed cotton (Purthee) cleaned by the American gin, yields between 21 and 22 per cent. of New Orleans cotton (Pungee) to seed, American between 29 and 30. When "good fair native cotton is selling in Liverpool for 4*d.*, New Orleans of the same denomination fetches from 5*d.* to 5¼*d.* (In December, 1848, they were respectively 3¼*d.* to 3½*d.*, and 4½*d.* to 4¾*d.*) These dates, I mention, as showing the advantage attending the cultivation of American cotton." Nothing else would be necessary in many parts of the world to make the culture popular.

From a letter of the 8th of December, 1848, however, we learn that the favorable prospects had not been realised, for

Dr. Wight expected only a moderate crop, nothing like what he should have had, had their sowings been delayed six weeks or even a month. In that case, the lands would have been in better condition for sowing, and the plants would have escaped much of their windy weather. "Indeed," he says, "the May sowings have all yieded very inferior crops, and it was only owing to the plants having been checked by high cold winds, and afterwards recovering themselves during the rains of October, that they have yielded any crop at all." The fields sown in June were better, and the last sown field, that in July, was by far the best of all, notwithstanding its having borne a crop of cotton in the previous year, while two fields sown in August by Mr. Wroughton will probably yield double of any of his. Dr. Wight rightly concludes, that though it was highly desirable to make the experiment, yet that the culture of this or any other plant must depend on the seasons of the country in which it is carried on, and not on rules deduced from its culture in other countries.

§ 34. Proposed Experiments on East and West Coasts of the Peninsula.

Dr. Wight had in 1847 his attention again directed to the desirableness of having some simultaneous experiments on the east and on the west coasts of the Peninsula. In Malabar, or on the western coast, the early rains of the south-west monsoon are experienced in April and May. This is fully established in June, and throughout July and August, breaking up in September. Here the sowing season is in May or early in June, as we have seen is the practice in North-West India as well as in Broach. The influence of this monsoon is experienced in the Paulghaut valley leading to Coimbatore, and earlier in the season the nearer the places are to the coast.

The Mexican cotton plant requires from six to eight weeks from the time of sowing to that of flowering, and about the same length of time from the fall of the blossom to the opening of the pods. Allowing $3\frac{1}{2}$ months for the full growth and maturation, the picking should commence towards the end of September when the rains are over, as we have seen is the case in many parts of India.

On the Coromandel coast again the case is different, August and September bearing the same relation to the north-east monsoon, that April and May bear to the south-west monsoon on the other coast. The vegetation of Dindygul, Madura, and Tinnivelly is burnt up by the scorching land-winds during May and June. Sowing might be commenced in July, but not sooner. Then partial showers commence and continue through August and September, and are often sufficient for the commencement of agricultural operations. These showers may be considered as belonging to the south-west monsoon. They are sometimes heavy and precede the monsoon, which is fully established in October, and breaks up about the middle of December.

The sowing season must, therefore, be regulated with cotton as with other things in such a climate, by the accession of the rains, being in May or early in June on the Malabar coast, and in the first half of September or at the latest in the first week in October on the Coromandel coast. If the cotton has been sown before the middle of September, the plants will be in a good state to benefit by the heavy monsoon rains. A clear growing season of about 3½ months is obtained, during which there are almost every week more or less copious falls of rain. By the end of that month, the plants will have nearly attained their full growth, and should shortly afterwards begin to yield their crop, and continue doing so for nearly three months. But every crop is liable to be destroyed by untoward seasons.

In consequence of these views, Dr. Wight proposed on the 26th of October, the establishment of two small farms, one on the east and the other on the west coast, in order to prove experimentally that the climate of the Coromandel coast was suited to the cultivation of American cotton, and that it might be successfully cultivated all along from Ganjam to near Cape Comorin. There does not seem any reason why it should not, as this is the usual period for growing cotton over a great part of India. Any local difficulties can only be ascertained by experiments if these have not been already tried.

On the 18th of October, 1847, Dr. Wight wrote that one of the Madras Agency Houses had applied for 15,000 lbs. of cotton seed for the purpose of cultivation, as they had induced a contractor to undertake the culture of 1000 acres with American cotton in the Madura district, that is, on the east coast.

Dr. Wight was at this time in hopes that some friends of his at Cochin would establish a farm of a few fields on the low grounds near the sea of the west coast, in order to ascertain the effects of such a situation, on the growth of this cotton; and he believed there was very little room for apprehension within the range of the sea-breeze, that is, anywhere within thirty miles of the coast.

But the natives, he observes, did not appear very willing to embark in the cultivation of this cotton, as few had applied to him for seed. He feared that they would do little unless the merchants at Madras direct their agents to contract with them for American cotton, as its good quality and high price were now well established at Manchester. Little was, however, to be expected, the Doctor adds, unless European settlers would come among them and give an impulse to the enterprise, and for them there was ample space in the same favorable tract of country without interfering with the necessary growth of corn.

The year 1847 was, however, very disastrous to the cotton crop in Coimbatore, as we have seen it was to those in Dharwar and Belgaum. The farms were in full bearing in the month of October when the rains commenced, when for three months they had almost incessant rain. These pickings amounted to about 1500 lbs. a day when the rains began, but ceased on their accession; and if it had not been for their early sowings, there would not have been seed enough for the following year.

In May, 1848, Dr. Wight wrote that he had just received 30 bushels of fresh Petit Gulph seed, which had arrived in excellent condition; and being an early variety, would be useful both for early and late sowing. He also stated, that he had received some New Orleans cotton, grown on the East coast, near Vipari in the Gulf of Manaar, which has much of the softness and length of staple of long-stapled cotton.

In the following October he sent two samples of cotton, grown, one from freshly-imported seed, and the other from their acclimated seed. Both were sown at the same time and in fields near each other, and both were pronounced here to be of nearly equally good quality.

He also observed, that their April sowings on the east coast had surprised him. Young plants just above ground, or only 3 or 4 inches high, exposed to the hot land-winds, passed through the ordeal unharmed, and were then in full crop. The same thing had occurred with plants sown at Coimbatore; whence he concluded that the American cotton might be cultivated in almost any part of the Peninsula.

The Petit Gulph seed, he remarks, on the 8th December, 1848, is in course of yielding an excellent crop, and therefore he calculates on having enough of fresh seed for next year, and first mentions that he had rented a field having within it the means of irrigating some Sea Island cotton which he was expecting to receive. He about the same time sent three samples of cotton: 1, grown at Chiklamoogloor; 2, grown at Cuddoor; 3, grown at Trichinopoly, with the aid of irrigation, and stated that this mode of cultivating cotton was beginning to attract attention, and that the Sea Island was prospering under similar treatment, having received three waterings in two months. He also mentions, that some Bourbon cotton planted in irrigated ground produced plants which greatly resembled Egyptian, and that some Egyptian seed sown in dry soil turned out pure Bourbon, (*v.* p. 147.) The natives, he at the same time mentions, do not approve of irrigation, as "luxuriant plants never yield a proportionate return of cotton." But this, like many other questions, is one of degree; a certain quantity of watering or of manuring is useful to a plant, and an excess of either injurious. A farmer, as a gardener, shows his skill in giving just as much of either as is sufficient in the locality, or suitable to the season.

The specimen of cotton grown at Chiklamooglour was approved of at Manchester, and valued at 4½*d.*, in July, 1849, that grown at Cudoor at a shade less. But the irrigated cotton having been injured in cleaning, and full of minute white specks (technically called *neps*), its other good qualities were lost sight of by spinners. But the author having, with the cleaned cotton, sent some with the seed, Messrs. Lees and Petrie hand-picked a portion, which was shown by Mr. Fleming on Change, along with that grown at Chiklamoogloor, or No. 1 sample, and both were pronounced equal in value. This is important with regard to the advantages of growing cotton by irrigation.

In the beginning of the year, or rather in March, 1849, Dr. Wight published a circular, which was sent to all the revenue officers and to many of his friends, as well as published in the '*Journal of the Agricultural Society of India*.'

As, in this circular, he enters minutely into many points which are of general application, we give the following extracts from it:

"The course that suggests itself to me is simple, and I believe will be found effective. We learn from the very correct meteorological tables of Madras, that the Madras mean temperature at the beginning of September is 84°, and that at the end of October it is still as high as 81°. If the sowing is effected between the middle of August and middle of September, the plant will be well grown and sufficiently strong to bear the cold weather of November and December; while there is reason to believe the cold of these months will only so far retard the maturation of the crop as to prevent its coming to perfect maturity before the middle of January, when, though the nights are cold, causing a low mean temperature, the days are bright, warm, and dry,* well suited to commencing the harvest, which will last through three or four months.

"By following this course as closely as the course of the seasons will permit, it is my firm belief, there is scarcely a field on which water does not lodge so as to become flooded after every fall of rain, in any part of the Carnatic (watered by the north-east monsoon), on which, with due attention to agricultural management, Mexican cotton may not be as successfully grown as the indigenous now is. Soils as well as seasons vary; some will be found more, some less productive; and a few, where the plant will not thrive under any treatment; but such cases do not invalidate the correctness of the general principle, as regards the fitness of our climate for its culture.

"Hitherto I have confined my remarks to the Carnatic under the influence of the north-east monsoon. I shall now say a few words bearing on those parts of India partaking more largely of the south-west one.

"I have not at hand satisfactory registers of the rain, but the following approximations may serve the purpose of enabling me to explain the general principles which ought to guide us:

* The mean temperature of January at sun-rise is 72°—at noon 81°.

	June.	July.	August.	Sept.	Oct.	Nov.	Dec.	Jan.	Feb.
Calcutta... (7 years)	11·46	12·14	16·23	7·70	4·94	0·13	0·81	0·50	0·25
Bombay... (Almanac)	22·92	25·14	19·64	12·64	1·64	—	—	—	—
Trevandrum (4 years)	16·4	8·14	4·2	5·3	14·97	12·	1·9	0·4	0·05
Colombo...	2·2	16·7	3·3	8·2	7·1	7·1	18·6	1·6	0·4

"Assuming that these are all approximations to the averages of the different stations named, it appears that the growing season would, in the first two, continue to the end of October; in Trevandrum until the end of November; in Ceylon to the end of December. From the date of sowing until the crop is in a state of maturity and picking fully established, requires from sixteen to twenty weeks. At this rate, in Bengal and Bombay advantage should be taken of occasional breaks in the weather, to sow between the middle of July and middle of August; in Trevandrum between the middle of August and middle of September; and in Ceylon in September. The weather is still warm enough to promote rapid growth, and ere the cold nights of November commenced, the plants would have attained their full size, with strength enough to bear the cold, if supported by adequate warmth and bright sunshine during the day; it being now a well-ascertained fact, that tropical plants are capable of enduring much nocturnal cold, provided they have plenty of light and heat during the day.

"These suggestions are of course to be understood as mere hints for others to work upon, as my position here prevents my acquiring accurate information on this branch of the subject.

"To adapt the American cotton plant to the course of the seasons is indispensable to success. For this purpose two methods suggest themselves:

"1st. The one already sketched,—that of employing the earlier weeks of the autumnal period as our spring, the latter ones and part of winter as our summer, and the conclusion of winter and part of spring as our autumn: or—

"2d. To render ourselves comparatively independent of the seasons by having, as in Egypt, recourse to irrigation, and thereby securing for the growing plant a rising in place of a falling range of temperature, by sowing in October or November, according to the season.

"This idea suggested itself while studying the American meteorological tables, and shortly after I succeeded in obtaining a small piece of ground, about an acre, with a well attached. It was sown at the end of January; on the 4th February the young plants began to show themselves; on the 10th March many of them were upwards of a foot high, all very healthy, and already showing abundance of 'forms,' or coming flowers, and that too with the thermometer in the shade daily above 90°, once or twice 96°, proving clearly that high temperature, when there is sufficient moisture in the soil, is not injurious to Mexican cotton.

"This experiment will, I anticipate, be only partially successful, as we may, in the ordinary course of the seasons, expect cloudy weather and rain in May, which is adverse to the perfect maturation of the crop; but already it goes far towards establishing the principle for which it was undertaken; and, had the sowing been in October, when our rains ceased, would have proved most successful, as it would now, in that case, have been in full crop.

"Fortunately this is not the only experiment of this kind in progress. While drafting this paper, I received from Captain Lawford, Civil Engineer 6th Division, a note, informing me that he had engaged in a similar experiment some months ago, in the hope of being able to show the natives of Tanjore, that cotton so cultivated would yield at least as profitable returns as rice, which he states is there hardly worth planting. He says: 'I hope you will approve of the plan of irrigating all cotton, as it will in a great measure render the crop independent of season. Since I sowed the seed received from you in October, we have had scarcely any rain; but I have a splendid crop in good soil, where the plants are four feet high and the pods very large.' This I consider a most valuable experiment, and will, I trust, find many imitators, especially in those parts of the country where the rains are scanty and uncertain. The seed was sown in November, the picking commenced about the middle of February, and now (15th March) the plants are in full growth, covered with crop in all stages, from 'forms' up to open pods.

"Up to this time, we have had no experience in this mode of cultivating cotton; but I would suggest as a precaution, that water should be rather sparingly supplied;* that little or none should be given from

* "The above field, on which picking will commence in a few days, was four times watered: once preparatory to the last sowing; once immediately after sowing; once after the first hoeing; and lastly, had one shower, of short duration, when about two months old. The ground between the rows was ploughed when about six weeks old. No more water is required. The plants are healthy and vigorous, not large, but, in proportion to their size, covered with an uncommonly abundant crop. The hottest season of the year, therefore, is clearly the best season for the cultivation of Mexican cotton

the time the picking commences, or rather, perhaps, for some time before, as the plant, when grown in rich moist soil, is apt to become too luxuriant, in which case the produce is not properly ripened. If in active and luxuriant growth, when the crop is ripening, the pod does not open at the proper time, the cotton being highly hygrometric, absorbs moisture from the enclosing capsule, and gets spoiled before it bursts. The very bright warm weather of March, April, and May, the harvest months of irrigated cotton, will do much towards counteracting this evil, but not altogether, if the plants are kept freely watered and growing.

"Having thus briefly, but I trust clearly, explained the principles which ought to guide us in the cultivation of American cotton in India, I shall, in conclusion, say a few words on the practical details which demand our attention.

"The first point relates to the choice of soil, when selection is in our power. The best crops I have yet seen have been obtained from dark brown, very light sandy loams, mixed with much kunker limestone, a kind of soil easily worked, very permeable to rain, and easily penetrated to a great depth by the roots. Red soils, having a large admixture of sand, securing for them the above properties, also answer well, and are easily cultivated. The stiffer clayey soils have not answered so well, except in seasons when we have had frequent showers, keeping them in an easily workable state, as they are liable to bake and become very hard in dry weather. The black cotton soils were a good deal tried at first, and I now think rather prematurely condemned as unsuitable for the American plant. Subsequent consideration has led me, to some extent, to doubt the justice of the verdict, and I would like to be in a more favorable position to test the correctness of the conclusion, by a second trial with our additional practical knowledge and skill.

"The second point to which I would call particular attention is, the preparation of the ground for the reception of seed. Too much care cannot be bestowed on this. The land should be well ploughed, the deeper the better, from four to six months before the time for sowing, and allowed to lie fallow. If there is rain in the interval, it should have a second ploughing, so as to keep it thoroughly open and freely exposed to the conjoint action of the air and sun, which, while it prevents excessive absorption of heat, greatly promotes fertility, and cleans the land by exposing and killing the roots of such perennial

in India, so long as a moderately humid soil can be secured. The aggregate quantity of water supplied to this field has not, I believe, exceeded two inches between the 20th of January and the 15th of April."

weeds as may be in it; lastly, it should have a final ploughing just before sowing. If sown in drills, according to the American practice, it should, while the plant is still small, be ploughed once or twice between the rows. If broad cast, this cannot be so conveniently done; the hoe must then suffice. After the third leaf has appeared, the ground is hoed and the plants thinned out to six or eight inches between them. This will leave enough to allow of considerable destruction during the subsequent ploughing. A second hoeing is always deemed necessary in both American and native practice, when the 'stand' should be further thinned, to from a foot to eighteen inches between the plants. If the growth is vigorous, not less than an average distance of eighteen inches should be allowed; otherwise, a foot may suffice. In moderately fertile and high and dry lands, from two and a half to three feet between the rows is enough; but for moist, low-lying, rich soils, five feet is not too much, as in such circumstances the bushes will still fill the ground, it being a very strong-growing plant, and, unless it has plenty of room, the crop blights. So managed, I have seen it produce from 1000 to 1100 lbs. per acre; but half of that may be considered a fair crop, which is double the amount of what, in this district, is considered a good native cotton crop, and yields, owing to the higher per centage of cotton to seed, 100 lbs. more of clean cotton. The labour and care bestowed in cultivation is greater, but the return much more than covers it, even leaving out of consideration the higher value of the article produced, which of itself would afford a compensation, supposing the quantity of seed cotton, weight for weight, was simply the same.

"The last point to which I would direct attention is, that, however promising in appearance, we have never succeeded in obtaining a really good second crop off the same bushes. I would, therefore, always rccommend the plan of cultivating the Mexican cotton plant as an annual, and never to sow the same land oftener than every third or fourth year, as it seems a very exhausting crop,

"I have the honour to be, Sir,

"Your most obedient servant,

"ROBERT WIGHT, *Surgeon,*

Superintendent Cotton Farm."

Abolition of the Experiments by the Madras Government.— A few months after this, the experimental culture of cotton and the purchase from the natives of any American cotton that they might have been induced to grow, was put a stop to by the Madras Government. In some of the newspapers of the time it was stated, that this had been done by order of the Court of Directors; but, as far as the author has been able to learn, the announcement created greater surprise in the India House than elsewhere. If we look at the papers relating to the cotton cultivation, published by order of the House of Commons, and which we have generally quoted by the name of *Return*, we may see that the authorities at Madras had for some time disapproved of the footing upon which the experiments had been placed, and had made a reference on the subject to the Court of Directors. (*Return*, pp. 384, 395-6.)

The Court, in their reply, dated 14th January, 1848, make the following observations on the three questions which had been referred to them: 1st, the remission of 50 per cent. on land cultivated with American cotton; 2d, the abolition of the Government farms; and 3d, the deputation of Mr. Finnie to this country. This last the Court did not think necessary; and, with respect to the first proposition, the Court observed, that it was—

"An obvious violation of the general principle which prescribes that the assessment shall be regulated by the capability of the land, without any reference to the particular description of produce which may be raised on it. We are of opinion, also, that it would fail of producing the expected result. The reduction of the rates would then only have the effect of forcing a factitious cultivation, which, under ordinary circumstances, could not be carried on."

The want of a ready market for the American cotton, when produced, appeared the chief difficulty. On this the Court observe:

"This difficulty is for the present removed by the permission which has been given to Dr. Wight, to purchase American cotton from the ryots on account of Government at remunerating prices. These purchases should not at present be discontinued; but we are satisfied that no satisfactory or permanent extension of the cultivation of American cotton will be attained until the persons most interested in its production shall take the matter into their own hands, by locating in the districts competent agents, empowered to purchase from the cultivators themselves such cotton as may be produced of a description suited to the wants of the manufacturers of this country."

With respect to the abolition of the farms cultivated by Government officers, the Court observed:

"We concur in your opinion of the expediency of relinquishing the Government farm at Coimbatore. We consider, that the object with which this farm was established has now been fully attained, by demonstrating that the soil and climate of that province are capable of producing cotton of a description in every respect suited to the wants of the British manufacturer."

The Madras Government was, however, directed to continue to afford its aid by distributing American seed, either gratuitously, or at a trifling charge, and the Court also authorised the cultivation of fields in different localities, in order to ascertain whether their soil and climate were suited for the production of American, or of any other kind of cotton.

The Madras Government, however, determined in June, 1849, on abolishing, not only the experimental culture of cotton in Tinnivelly and Coimbatore, but also the mercantile operations into which the experiment had lately merged; and, curiously, so much misapprehended the Court's despatch, as to state, that this had been done in pursuance of the views communicated by the Honorable Court. Dr. Wight appealed against the decision, and observed that the lands for the farms had been in his possession many months, and compensation had been paid for them up to 1st May, 1850; that they had been ploughed, also that from two thirds to three fourths of the expenses had been incurred, and which would probably be recovered by growing the crop. He also represented, that the abrupt breaking up, and that at the very commencement of the sowing season, would have a prejudicial effect, and suggested that he should be allowed to grow the crop, giving notice that it should positively be the last, as, "by this means, our present most excellent and thoroughly acclimated stock of seed will be wholly preserved," and commercial men would have sufficient notice, if they meant to take up any part of the business. But no change was made in the orders.

Experiments resumed.—The Court, in consenting to abolish the farms, did nothing more than approve of what had already been considered a step in advance in Dharwar and Belgaum, and since then in Candeish, where, notwithstanding the abolition of the farms, the planters were retained and employed in distributing seed among the ryots, and purchasing the produce, with benefit to the ryots, and with no loss to Government.* The diversities of aspect of the Madras Presidency, and the influence of the two monsoons, made experiments in single fields, in different districts, as proposed by Dr. Wight in his circular, extremely desirable. These also were authorised. However necessary it may be to get rid of the first step in the introduction of a plant, that is, growing it in a garden or Government farm until its habits are known, and a sufficient quantity of seed is being produced to allow of its being diffused through a province, it is objectionable to make a sudden stop, as calculated to produce an impression that success had become hopeless. On this occasion it was the more objectionable, as Dr. Wight, instead of confining his attention to Coimbatore, was collecting information from all parts of the Peninsula of the most suitable time for sowing, as well as respecting the effects of irrigation. It is not surprising, therefore, that the Court did not confirm the decision, but ordered the experiment under Dr. Wight to be re-established, and sent the despatches by the mail of the 7th September, *via* Bombay.

Dr. Wight, having received these counter-orders about the end of October, when he was on the point of leaving the country, found it too late for dry cultivation, and therefore engaged in experiments, to see what could be done with irrigating both Sea Island and Petit Gulf cotton. In April, 1850, he wrote, that the plants, though late sown, yet, by the aid of irrigation, had flourished, were in full pick, and yielding most excellent cotton, especially those which had been sown in well-prepared soil; but that those in inferior or imperfectly cultivated fields had made but poor progress. The natives seemed so well satisfied with the results, that they proposed cultivating cotton in their gardens, that is, in their irrigated ground. This they are able to do, because their grain crops are off the ground in August and September, and American cotton might be sown in October or even during the first half of November. Dr. Wight had again to complain of disasters, as six inches of rain

* Dr. Wight himself (*v.* p. 480, &c.) had observed that their failures at one time were due to their having adhered too much to the American farm system.

fell from the 2d to the 8th of April, and did much injury to the ripe crop of cotton. But it was expected that the new show of flowers would produce a second crop.

Dr. Wight, in February, visited Sevacassy, where Mr. Cuxton had been sent and who had sown a field with New Orleans cotton in November, which then (February) looked exceedingly healthy, and promising a very fair crop. Dr. Wight proposed sowing again at that time, in order to see how far the course of the seasons from that time onwards was favorable to the growth. The cotton so sown continued doing well when the plants were seen in April. Dr. Wight was anxious also to ascertain whether cotton would succeed as a rotation crop to tobacco, which is largely cultivated in the Tinnivelly district, and in highly manured land. It is sown in October or November, and cut in February; thus securing time to take a crop of cotton in August or September off the same land, by sowing cotton immediately the tobacco is harvested. The natives here he found skilful agriculturists.

On the 1st June, 1850, Dr. Wight forwarded two small packets of cotton, each packet containing two samples of New Orleans and one of Sea Island. Of the New Orleans cotton, one was grown in Coimbatore, and the other in Mysore, by Mr. Meppen, agent for the Mysore Commission.

The Sea Island had been raised by means of irrigation, and though the plants had not done well, though they had every advantage, yet the cotton produced was of very good quality. The author, when present at the meeting of the Commercial Association at Manchester, on the 15th August, showed this cotton, at the meeting, to Mr. Brown, the experienced broker, who, after consulting with others, pronounced the cotton to be worth 14½*d.* per pound, a very important fact, proving that, with the aid of a little irrigation, cotton, very superior to any that has been grown, may yet be produced in the Madras Presidency, when the peculiarities of different localities, and the kind of culture best suited to each have been carefully ascertained.

Quality of Coimbatore Cotton.—The excellent quality of the American cotton produced on the Coimbatore farms, as well as by Mr. Wroughton, the principal collector of the district, and even by the natives in the neighbourhood, has frequently been referred to in this work, (*v.* pp. 101-2.)

Thus, the earliest shipment by the 'Bengal Merchant,' which arrived in London in October, 1841, with cotton from Tinnivelly and Salem, sold for 4*d.* to 4½*d.*, and that from Coimbatore for 5*d.* to 5¾*d.* The 'Samarang' brought forty-eight bales, which were shipped in October, 1842, and sold here in November, 1843. Of these, eighteen bales were pronounced good, and equal to the quality of American, though scarcely so fine. Messrs. Littledale remark: "Appearance very like good New Orleans, but not equal in price, the staple not being so good." The whole was sold for 5*d.* per pound; and it was reported: "The spinner who bought these wants more."

During the year 1845, three sales took place of shipments by the 'Flowers of Ugie,' 29 bales; 'Earl of Harewood,' 132 bales; and 'John Patchett,' 52 bales. During this period, the sales of cotton were in a declining state, and "all speculation seems to have left the cotton for the share-market." The greater portion, however, sold for 3¾*d.* per lb., and eleven bales for 4¼*d.* It was of this cotton that Messrs. Hollinshed stated, that "it was worth more if a spinner could have been found to test its merits." During the month of February, New Orleans cotton was selling for 3¼*d.* to 6½*d.*; fair New Orleans at 4¾*d.* to 5*d.*; Surat at 2¼*d.* to 3¾*d.*; and Madras at 2½*d.* to 3¾*d.* In the autumn of 1846, when a rise was taking place in the price of American cotton, 17 bales, and 27 bundles per 'Grindlay,' sold 3 bales for 4½*d.*, 8 for 5*d.*, and the remainder for 6*d.* up to 6¾*d.* (v. *House of Commons Return for Brokers' Reports.*)

In December of the same year, 8 bundles were sold for 6½*d.*; and on the 24th of February following, 24 bales, which had been valued at 6¾*d.*, sold for 7*d.* a pound; and the cotton was described as clean, bright, good cotton, fair staple, and much more free from nep than last shipment per 'Grindlay.'

This cotton, as well as that by the 'Sir John Beresford,' has already been referred to at p. 101, and the brokers' reports given in full at p. 102, in which the cotton grown at Coimbatore is pronounced quite equal to fair New Orleans cotton.

In 1847, 306 bales, per 'Elizabeth Jane,' from Madras,

were sold in June, the native cotton for $5\frac{3}{4}$*d.*, and 6 bales of New Orleans in September for $6\frac{3}{4}$*d.* (*v.* Tables, p. 513.)

During the same year, the 'Olinda' brought 105 bales, which were shipped at Cochin; of these 33 were sold in London during the month of November; 33 bales for $3\frac{3}{4}$*d.*, 21 bales for $4\frac{1}{2}$*d.*, and 43 bales at Manchester for $4\frac{7}{8}$*d.*, and 2 for 5*d.* per lb. in December, 1847.

In the year 1848, the 'Argyra' brought 483 bales of cotton from Coimbatore, which had been shipped at Cochin. The price of cotton being at that time very low, the majority of this sold for 3*d.* to $3\frac{1}{4}$*d.*, 40 bales for 4*d.*, and 1 bale for $4\frac{3}{4}$*d.*

Since this period, the consignments of cotton from Coimbatore have all been sold at Manchester, and have thus become well known to spinners, as the 871 bales by the 'Ganges,' shipped at Cochin, sold in 1849; while in the present year, of 289 bales from Coimbatore, &c., shipped at Madras for London, 50 were sent to Manchester. Of these, 30 bales were Oopum or native Coimbatore cotton, and sold for $6\frac{3}{4}$*d.*; while 20 bales of New Orleans cotton from the farm sold for no less than $7\frac{1}{2}$*d.* per pound.

N. O. F. Twenty bales, grown from New Orleans seed, clean and bright in colour, moderate staple. A good and useful cotton, approaching to fine Boweds, but not equal in staple. Cotton of this quality much wanted.

O. O. Thirty bales Oopum cotton, clean and bright in colour. Staple very short and much cut.

In November, 1850, 8 bales per 'Llewellyn,' apparently grown by the Collector, Mr. Wroughton, described as clean, bright cotton, without leaf, but short in staple and weak, sold for $6\frac{3}{4}$*d.* per pound.

From these reports of brokers, and the prices at which the cotton from Coimbatore has sold, as also from the repeated testimony of the Commercial Association of Manchester to the excellence of the New Orleans cotton produced there, and of its fitness for the general purposes of the spinner, there is no doubt that the soil and climate are both suited to produce such cotton as is chiefly required by the manufacturers of this country. Though the subject has been already referred to, we may again mention the cost at which it can be produced, and the probability of its forming, in the great majority of years, a safe investment for the merchant, even if he were to encourage the cultivator by an increase of price, to pay more attention to the culture and picking of cotton, which, according to so good an authority as Mr. Wroughton (*v.* p. 486), has for many years been much neglected in the Coimbatore district.

Cost of Cotton in Coimbatore. We have already seen (p. 471), that the exporter of indigenous cotton from the Tinnivelly district or of the naturalised Bourbon from the Salem and Coimbatore districts, pays about 70 rupees for a candy of the former, and 90 rupees for a candy of the latter; each Madras candy consisting of 500 pounds. Mr. Sullivan, however, observes that these are the prices paid to the brokers; the prices paid to the growers do not exceed 40 or 50 rupees.

Dr. Wight having, in one of his official reports, entered into the details of the subject, it is desirable to quote from his carefully considered statement.

He states that, while he has been in Coimbatore, the average bazaar price has varied from 5½r. to 5¾r. per load of ten maunds at the commencement of the season, rising up to from 6r. to 6½r. towards the close. This last season, owing to the extensive failure of the crops, it has exceeded 7r. But 6r. may be taken as the average price of 10 maunds or loads, or for 250 lbs.

The expenses to the merchant consist of the cost of bringing the cotton from the field to the warehouse, and of the interest of capital between the purchase and the sale of the article.

Carriage = 4a. or 2r. on the candy of clean cotton, because 8 loads of kupas = 1 candy of clean cotton.

8 loads of *parthee* or *kupas* in the field at 5r. 4a. = 42r., carriage to market 2r. = 44r., the cost of the cotton. If these 8 loads are sold in the market at 6r. or for 48r., the merchant's profit is 4r., or 9 per cent.

But if the merchant cleans the cotton, and sells it and the seed separately, his profits will be as follows:

Cleaning by churka 4 candies of seed cotton, which yield 1 candy of cotton-wool . . .	7r.
The sale of the seed, at 5 maunds for a rupee, will bring .	12r.
Deduct from the sale of seed, 12r., the price of cleaning, 7r., = difference	5r.
This profit of 5r. on the seed must be deducted from the price of the kupas, which will make the price of clean cotton = ...	39r.

This cotton, which costs the merchant 39r., he sells for 45r., which raises his profit from 9 to 15¼ per cent.; but, as he loses interest from the time of purchasing his seed cotton to that of selling the cleaned cotton wool, Dr. Wight deducts 1r. per candy, so as to make his profit 11¼r., instead of 15¼r. per cent.

The exporter, however, does not get his cotton on these terms. He has to employ an agent or second middleman, whose commission raises the price at least 5 per cent. more, so that he has to pay 20 if not 25 per cent. more on the first cost, say 20 per cent., or 7r. 12a. 9p. on 39r., which raises the price to 46r. 12a. 9p., or 47r. This is no uncommon price for the Madras merchants to give for good cotton in the provincial markets of Coimbatore and Tinnivelly. Inferior qualities often bring from 44 to 45r.

Dr. Wight therefore assumes 45r. as the price of a candy of churka-cleaned cotton at Coimbatore. Bagging for transmission to the coast, 3r.; bandy or cart-hire to Madras, 8½r. (this is often higher); making the total 56r. 8a., as the price of a candy of cotton at Madras. This reduced to English money, is £5 13*s*., or about $2\frac{1}{16}$*d*. per lb.

Dr. Wight states, that he has allowed 25 per cent. of cotton to seed for churkaed cotton. The gins, he states, rarely average more than 21½, but the cleaning is cheaper, as being only 5r. per candy, and the ginned cotton is more free from impurities, and fetches about 6 per cent. higher prices in the English market. The thrasher also gets rid of 3 per cent. of dirt out of even clean-looking churkaed cotton.

As it is desirable to give the details of an actual transaction, we may mention that in the year 1846 Dr. Wight purchased 32 candies and 90 lbs. of churka cleaned cotton, which cost 1297r. 2a. 1p., and lost 490 lbs. (a small fraction over 3 per cent.) in passing through the thrasher, in consequence of this throwing out much of the dirt which had passed through the churka, leaving 15,600 lbs., or 52 bales, of tolerably clean cotton: thus costing (dividing the above sum by 52) 24r. 15a. 1p. per bale, or nearly 2*d.* per pound, as the prime cost of the cotton. The charges in transmitting this cotton to port, and shipping to England, including every charge except sea-insurance, amounted to 18r. 11a. 9p. per bale, or nearly 1½*d.* per pound: raising the total cost and charges, when sold in London, to within a very small fraction of 3½*d.* per pound. Dr. Wight observes, that he would never esteem such cotton, all charges included, worth more than 3½*d.* or 3¾*d.*, as the market now usually ranges, or as promising more than a par remittance, the loss of interest between the dates of purchase and sale going far towards neutralizing any profits arising from the chance events of a favorable market. He states that he was always able to obtain the best picked cotton in the market by giving from 1r. to 1½r. above the price given by the native merchants.

The cotton shipped in the year 1845, which Dr. Wight says cost in India 3½*d.*, sold in Liverpool for 3¾*d.* to 4¼*d.*, and therefore there must have been profit even at the then low prices of cotton, (*v.* p. 509.) With this we may compare the results of the shipments by the 'Elizabeth Jane,' in 1846-7, when cotton was of higher value in this country, and sold in the country for 5½*d.* and the American for 6½*d.* a pound, though both cost only 3½*d.* in India.

OOPUM COTTON.

	r.	a.	p.
Amount cost of 846 candies, 11 maunds, 13 lbs. of seed cotton, at 13r. 4a. for candy of 500 lbs. . . .	11,025	11	4
Amount of expenses incurred in cleaning, half-pressing, forwarding to Cochin, re-pressing, and shipping there in 300 bales, of 300 lbs. each	2,601	14	5
	13,627	9	9
Deduct amount realised by the sale of seed . . .	3,071	2	4
	10,556	7	5
Freight from Cochin to Liverpool on 300 bales or 90,000 lbs., at £4 7*s.* 6*d.* per ton of 1500 lbs., is £262 10*s.*, or	2,625	0	0
Total	13,181	7	5*

* This sum, reduced to English money, gives 3½*d.* per pound.

AMERICAN COTTON.

	£	s.	d.
Amount cost of 12 candies, 8 maunds, 10 lbs. of seed cotton, at 15r. 5a. 8p. per candy of 500 lbs. . . .	190	11	6
Amount of expenses incurred in cleaning, half-pressing, forwarding to Cochin, re-pressing and shipping there in 6 bales of 300 lbs. each	50	2	7
	240	14	1
Deduct amount realised by sale of seed	27	8	0
	213	6	1
Freight from Cochin to Liverpool on 6 bales, or 1800 lbs., at £4 7s. 6d. per ton of 1500 lbs, is £5 5s., or .	52	8	0
Total	265	14	1*

* This sum, reduced to English money, gives 3½d. per pound.

The per centage of wool to seed of No. 1 was 21 per cent., and the whole batch cost, in Coimbatore, when baled and ready to load, 51r. 14a. 5p. per candy.

The per centage of No. 2 was 29 per cent., and cost, when ready to load, 52r. 13a. per candy.

(Signed) R. WIGHT, *Surgeon,*
Supt. Cotton Farms.

Extract from Minutes of Evidence, taken before Select Committee on the Growth of Cotton in India, (July 17th, 1848,) *referring to the Sale of the above Cotton.*

Mr. JAMES PETRIE'S Evidence. Question 2161, page 186.

Abstract of the Profit and Loss Account of 300 *Bales (of* 300 *lbs.) of East India Cotton; being the first batch purchased by Dr. Wight at Coimbatore, from Natives, and cleaned by the Saw-gin, and shipped to Liverpool, per 'Elizabeth Jane,' from Cochin.*

	£	s.	d.
May to Dec., 1846.—Cost and Charges in India, as given by Dr. Wight, 10,781r. 7a. 6p., or	1078	2	11
June, 1847.—Charges in England: (Freight, £240), dock and town dues, cartage and porterage, warehouse rent, fire insurance, brokerage, and commission	353	5	7
	1431	8	6
To balance—profit	695	11	2
	2126	19	8

RECEIPTS.

	£	s.	d.
June 4 to June 30, 1847.—By amount realised in England, as per statement	2126	19	8

Abstract of the Profit and Loss Account of 6 Bales of East India New Orleans Cotton; being the first batch purchased by Dr. Wight in Coimbatore, from Natives, and cleaned by the Saw-gin and shipped to Liverpool, per 'Elizabeth Jane,' from Cochin.

EXPENDITURE.

	£	s.	d.
1846.—Cost and charges in India, as given by Dr. Wight, 217r. 14a. 1p., or, at 2s.	21	15	9
1847.—Charges in England: Freight, £4 16s., dock and town dues, cartage and porterage, warehouse rent, fire insurance, brokerage, commission, &c.	7	3	4
	28	19	1
To balance—profit	18	0	11
	47	0	0

RECEIPTS.

	£	s.	d.
June 4 to Sept. 4, 1847.—By amount realised in England, as per statement	47	0	0

Expenses of Cultivation.—We may now give the expenses of cultivating cotton in Coimbatore, as reported by Dr. Wight. A statement given by Mr. Petrie is very similar.

	r.	a.	r.	a.
The tax on 1 bullah of black cotton soil is =			6	0
Three ploughings, each 2r. 8a., when the ground is hard	7	8		
Two more ditto, at 1r. 4a.	2	8		
The last, for covering the seed	0	8		
			10	8
Hoeing twice (1r. to 1r. 4a.)			2	0
Seed			0	8
Picking			2	8
			21	8*

* The Indian bullah or vellum is = 3 cawnie, or $3\frac{13}{16}$ English acres.

The Black cotton ground is the more expensive, but is more profitable, in consequence of the return being more certain and larger, and the cotton of a quality that commands higher prices in the English market.

The amount of crop, when a fair one, is 4 loads or puddies of 10 maunds (250 lbs.) each, or 2 candies of seed cotton per bullah of ground. It often exceeds that quantity, but much oftener falls below. 4 candies, or 8 loads, of seed cotton = 1 candy, or 500 lbs., of clean cotton.

The purthee or seed cotton is commonly sold at from 4r. 12a. to 5r. 8a. to petty merchants who forestal the market by going and making advances in anticipation of the crop. If the ryot keeps his crop until late in the season, when prices have attained their maximum, he may get from 5r. 12a. to 6r. per puddy; but 5r. 4a. is considered an average. This will give 21 rupees as the average value of the whole crop; that is, the ryot loses half a rupee upon each bullah. In the above statement, even if the expenses may be made a little higher than is actually the case, yet it is evident that cotton is not a remunerative crop at the low prices to which it had sunk; but there is one advantage, that all the money payments are not made out of the family, (*v.* p. 485.)

The ryots give as their reason for cultivating an unprofitable crop, that it is a money crop, which enables "them to raise funds to pay for their other lands;" that it affords employment for their own families to cultivate the land; and that, being an early crop, they were enabled, in favorable seasons, to get a second crop of corn off the land for which the cotton had already paid the tax.

These statements are sufficient to show that there has been little enough encouragement for the ryot to cultivate cotton. This has, no doubt, been caused by the fluctuating demand for Indian cotton, and by the low price to which it had sunk, partly from its dirty and adulterated state, and partly from its shortness of staple in comparison with American cotton. The latter, moreover, has in many years sold at such low prices as to depreciate the Indian below its natural value, possessed, as this no doubt is, of some good qualities, and fitted as it is for some of our manufactures. Still in many years the price paid to the ryots by the local merchants has not been proportionate to the prices realised for the cotton in European markets.

Mr. Wroughton, the principal collector of Coimbatore, has stated, (*v.* p. 486), that the culture has for many years been much neglected, in consequence of its not being sufficiently remunerative. He further states that the produce of the country plant is a most scanty crop under the most favorable circumstances, and that depending entirely on the description of the soil, the fact of its being a single or combined crop, and the quantity of labour bestowed. The cost of cleaning by churka (there called *ratnum*) is also great; but he states that a greatly augmented quantity could be produced: the great difficulty is the disposal of the produce by the growers relieved from the tax and molestation of brokerage. He mentions the port of Poonany, distant 100 miles, as suitable for exporting, and that the expenses of a cart carrying 4 bales are 6r. 8a., and 8a. for crossing ferries.

Mr. Petrie, the engineer who put up and had charge of the machinery of the great gin-house, and who latterly managed the purchase of the cotton from the natives, which was cleaned and sent to this country, addressed a letter to 'The Times,' dated 27th May, from Liverpool; in this he says:

"To show at what a low price cotton can be grown in the interior of India, I may take the liberty of repeating what I have already publicly stated on former occasions, viz., that I have bought hundreds of loads of seed-cotton that had been brought a distance of 80 or 90, and even 100 miles, to the local market. The seeds, which constitute 75 per cent. of the weight of the raw material as it comes from the fields, have then been taken out of the fibre by the saw-gin; the cotton has then been screwed, put on carts, and sent a further land distance of 350 miles to the port of shipment. Burdened with all these expenses of transport, it was sent to Liverpool, and sold there for $3\frac{3}{4}$*d.* per lb., leaving to the exporter a profit of from 10 to 15 per cent."

Mr. Petrie recommends exporting from the port of Cochin, where two cotton screws have been lately established by a Bombay house. From Coimbatore to Trichoor or to Carriputnam, there is a good cart-road, requiring in some places to be repaired, along which cotton can be conveyed in 7 days, at the rate of $6\frac{1}{2}$ rupees for 3 bales of 300 lbs. each, or 156 pence for 900 lbs., or about 1*d.* for 6 lbs. Thence it is carried in large boats by the backwater in a night to Cochin, a distance of 60 miles, at a very small cost.

The above facts and statements show very clearly that there is very little inducement for the ryot to grow or to take much pains with the indigenous cotton at the prices to which it has been reduced by the native dealers, with whom alone the cultivator comes in contact. But if we inquire into the cost of some of this cotton, and at the prices at which it has been sold in England, as shown at p. 513, and in some of the subsequent tables, there seems a sufficient margin for the merchant to afford better prices to the grower. To the cultivator, the advantages of cultivating American cotton in preference to the indigenous, wherever the soil and climate are suitable, have been amply demonstrated under the head of Dharwar, where indeed the natives, as we have seen, are largely profiting by them. The same advantages have been experienced in Coimbatore, as has been shown in the preceding pages. Dr. Wight and Mr. Wroughton have both proved that the American cotton may be cultivated by the natives as cheaply as the indigenous, and that it succeeds well in the poorer lands; and that there is an immense extent of territory within the valley of Coimbatore, where the climate is suitable and less variable than farther in the interior. The returns of seed cotton are at least as great, (p. 482,) or rather, in ordinary seasons, greater. Dr. Wight at one time calculated the returns of native cotton at 100 lbs. per acre; subsequently he considered 75 lbs. per acre nearer the truth. The American should yield from 150 to 200 lbs. of clean cotton per acre, though we have seen that in some years Dr. Wight obtained only 183 lbs. of seed cotton per acre. Mr. Wroughton calculates the returns much higher, as he has himself obtained much larger returns; and the profits to the natives who cultivated the fields under his directions were very high, (*v.* p. 483.) We have no doubt that the returns would be large and the profits considerable in many parts of the tract of country especially pointed out by Mr. Wroughton, (*v.* p. 486,) allowing that the irregularities of climate may render the returns more uncertain further in the interior. But a certain advantage, respecting which there is no doubt, is, that the proportion of wool to seed is greater in the American than in the indigenous cotton to the extent of 7 to 9 per cent. Dr. Wight, in his letter, (p. 482,) assumes only 28 per cent. as the proportion of wool to seed in American cotton; but from 29 to 30 per cent. generally, and often 31 per cent., is obtained. But greater than either of these advantages is the good quality of the cotton grown in the Coimbatore district, which has been so highly appreciated at Manchester as to be considered capable of entering into competition with American cotton, being applicable to many of the same purposes, and therefore saleable even when the former is cheap. It will yield a profit probably at quite as low a price as cotton grown in America. Dr. Wight at first considered that the difference in value between American and Indian cotton in England was 5*d.* for the former, and $3\frac{3}{4}$*d.* for the latter, (*v.* p. 482;) while a candy of clean cotton of the former costs in India only 53r. 9a., and the latter 55r. 4a., even when 3r. more had been given for a candy of seed cotton for the American than for the native seed cotton. Mr. Petrie has stated that, in purchasing from the natives, they gave 2r. more for 10 maunds (each of 25 lbs.) of American cotton in seed than they did for the native; but they got 29 per cent. of clean cotton for the American, and only $21\frac{1}{2}$ for the native. The candy (500 lbs.) of American cotton thus cost $54\frac{1}{2}$r., but was worth $5\frac{1}{2}$*d.* per pound in England; while the native, which cost $52\frac{1}{2}$r., was worth only $4\frac{1}{2}$*d.* per pound. In the year 1847, the 300 bales of well-cleaned native cotton which Dr. Wight sent, sold for $5\frac{3}{4}$*d.*, while 6 bales of New Orleans cotton bought from the natives sold for $6\frac{3}{4}$*d.*, yielding an average profit of 50 per cent.: a merchant, Dr. Wight thinks, might have made 60 per cent. profit. The particulars of this transaction are given in detail in the foregoing tables, which, however, are not isolated cases of profit; for Mr. Petrie, in his evidence before the Cotton Committee, stated that in all the transactions in which he was concerned in sending well-cleaned cotton from Coimbatore to this country, "considerable profit was realised in all the cases and in every year."

Notwithstanding the advantages which Coimbatore would seem to enjoy, the natives have not been induced to take up the culture of American cotton to any extent, though they had the example of their collector to incite them; and this is usually a powerful inducement. Neither have the high prices realised in England been followed by a corresponding rise of prices in the district, as we have seen has at last been the case in Dharwar. But it is to be hoped that the Manchester orders, either through Madras or Cochin, will have the effect of inducing the native agents to encourage the ryots to cultivate that kind of cotton which is obviously so much for the advantage of all. It is to be hoped, also, that European merchants may enter more directly into the trade, as they have done in Dhawar and Candeish. A private letter, indeed, of the date of November, 1850, gives the statement that a merchant had made an offer to Government for the buildings and machinery at Coimbatore, for the purpose of carrying on the business on account of a Joint-Stock Cotton Company.

Mr. Petrie says: "The natives can produce good cotton; but what object have they in doing so, there being no discriminating market for the produce of their fields within their reach, good and bad cotton selling at almost the same price? Such being the present state of affairs, who have we to look to, to take the lead in making an effort to put the trade on a footing which its importance deserves, but Manchester?"

An Engineer well acquainted with the Coimbatore district, has, in a letter addressed to 'The Times,' and published on May 23d, 1850, remarked, that although there is abundance of land suitable to cotton culture, and although labour is so cheap in India, yet comparatively little cotton finds its way to Manchester. He inquires:

"What is the cause of this? My experience goes to prove that it is chiefly from the want of liberal purchasers inland. Grain, however coarse, supports the cultivator; he is sure of food if he has grown a field of it; but with a crop of any kind that is not eatable he cannot feel secure that he will find a purchaser to give him food or money. The difficulty rests here,—the farmers of the country have no capital, nor have they confidence in the fair dealing of the native merchants; they cannot carry their cotton to a market where good prices may be looked for, nor can they hope that any purchaser will come to them, but one who waits his chance of getting the little cotton cultivated at a price just better for the farmer than if he let it rot upon the land. Before the ryots can have capital they must have a money-payment for some produce; and while they have no certain market they cannot risk a crop of any kind to bring this money to them. The native inland trader looks only to the profit of the year; he gets as much as he is able for every pound of produce that he purchases, without apparently the power to calculate the loss which such illiberality eventually entails. Even the agents of the better class of native merchants in Bombay are little above the rest, and quite unfit to manage any trade that needs encouragement. They are natives still, and natives will not trust them.

"How often have I heard a ryot say, 'But guarantee us as sure a profit as those men have on rice who cultivate the irrigated lands, and we shall be too happy to replace our coarse dry grains with cotton.' This is the voice of the intelligent throughout the inland districts, but there are many who say, 'What is the use of cotton, since we cannot eat it, nor our children either?'

"And as regards the land-tax as a check upon its produce, as I see asserted, I stood upon a cotton-field some months ago, speaking to a ryot of my district about his farming and his neighbours. When I asked him to tell me whether the assessment of the land was more than it ought to be to bear a crop of cotton, the old man laughed and said, pointing to the shrubs around us, 'Why, ten such plants as these would pay the whole assessment of a cawny (a cawny being about an acre and a quarter); the cotton-seed for feeding cattle would more than pay it, after the cotton-wool was sold.' And you would never doubt the fact had you seen the land, and known, as I did, that all the tax, or rent, or tithe of any kind its owner paid was *eighteen pence an acre,* and at that rate land is held quite suitable for cotton throughout vast tracts of India. It cannot, therefore, be that the land-tax is any impediment to its profitable growth."

§ 35. Culture in Tinnivelly.

In another part of this work, we have seen how successful the late Mr. Hughes was in growing Bourbon cotton in the Tinnivelly district, and that, in consequence of his success, he was applied to for instructions by Mr. Heath, (*v.* p. 227.) The American planters, on their first arrival in the Madras Presidency, were sent to the Tinnivelly district, as that was considered one of the most favorable sites for their labours; but, as we have seen, they did not approve of the situation, and removed to Coimbatore. Mr. Finnie, after the completion of his period of engagement in the Bengal Presidency, transferred his services to that of Madras. (*Return*, p. 396.) It was at first intended that he should have been employed in Bellary and Cuddapah; but it was afterwards determined that he should proceed to Tinnivelly. Dr. Wight was extremely anxious to have a farm on the east coast, and proposed establishing one at Pullicarney; but Mr. Finnie, on inspection, considered the site most unsuitable, as he "found a barren waste in all the high land, and the low land is all under water during the rains." If this cannot be drained, the objection is insuperable; but the mere poverty of the soil, if it is open and permeable to the roots, would not be an objection, if there is moisture under the surface, or the climate is suitable for growing cotton during the monsoon. Mr. Finnie was instructed to proceed (31st October, 1845,) to the Tinnivelly district, parts of which were considered by Dr. Wight favorable for the culture of American cotton, (*v.* p. 490;) and Mr. Finnie was requested to make monthly reports of his proceedings. He remained in that district until the abolition of the experiment by the Madras Government in 1849.

Mr. Finnie, in his first letter, (*Return*, p. 417,) dated from Courtallum, on the Tinnivelly side of the Travancore hills, states that he is of opinion, that both the New Orleans and Sea Island will grow here: "The former, I am convinced, will succeed in the vicinity of the hills, where it gets the benefit of the south-west monsoon; and the latter on the coasts, where it has the benefit of the sea breeze. I would not confine it to the immediate coast, as the land is miserably poor, but from seven to fifteen miles inland would answer." But he thought it most desirable to turn his attention to the indigenous article, of which about 50,000 candies, of the value of about 2,511,300 rupees, that is, at about $2\frac{3}{8}$*d.* per lb., are annually exported. He wished to induce the people to plant it more regularly and alone, to cultivate it better, to enable the plant to mature its fruit more fully. The American system of gathering the produce was to be insisted upon, to prevent the deterioration which dirt and trash has upon the staple; and this he thought was all that was required to make the Tinnivelly cotton almost or quite equal to the "Upland Georgia." As Mr. Finnie did not think the gin so well suited to the natives, he intended that they should continue to separate the seeds with their churka, and that he would afterwards get rid of much of the dirt with the thrasher, which seems an instrument corresponding with the willow of a cotton factory.

The native cotton so cleaned by Mr. Finnie having been

examined by Dr. Wight, was considered by him as only equal to what in Liverpool is called good Tinnivelly; and he observes that, having sent 300 bales of the same kind of cotton from Coimbatore, in the beginning of the year 1847, it sold for $5\frac{3}{4}d.$ per pound, when some cotton from American seed sold for $6\frac{3}{4}d.$ (v. p. 513.) Samples of Mr. Finnie's cottons having been sent to Manchester, were not considered superior to what they had been for some time in the habit of receiving. Mr. Turner says, "they are very much the same as we have been in the habit of receiving for years past from Madras." The bulk of the cotton, when it arrived, sold for 5*d.* per pound, and was well spoken of, as has been already mentioned at p. 98. Since then, 10 bales of Tinnivelly cotton were sold on the 25th June, 1850, for $6\frac{1}{2}d.$ per pound.

Since then an extremely interesting experiment has been made in this very district by Mr. David Lees, a member of the Commercial Association of Manchester, who, being unfortunately in a delicate state of health and obliged to go to some warm climate, determined to visit India, as he might there, while benefiting by the warmth, acquire from personal examination some information on the subject of cotton. Mr. Lees, having determined to visit the Tinnivelly district, arrived there in December, 1849, and was most kindly received by the Collector, Mr. Bird. He first visited Punnagoody, where Mr. Hughes formerly grew some excellent cotton. After sowing some American cotton seed there, he visited the sea-coast near Trichindore, and sowed the same kind, in various quarters, at an average distance of not more than a mile from the sea.

The following are extracts of letters from Mr. Lees to his brother, Mr. J. Lees, which were read at a special meeting of the Commercial Association of Manchester, on the 15th August, 1850, giving some account of the physical features of the places where he had made his experiments :

"Waste land means, that it is land which lies uncultivated in vast tracts, the soil varying according to locality. The greater part of that near Punnagoody is a stiff red loam, which bakes very hard in the sun: the white ant builds its nest upon it. That near Trichindore, and all along the coast for a very great distance northward, is sandy, and is trodden by goats and sheep for pasturage, and by herds of wild antelopes. In some places, as at Punnagoody, it is owned by a number of villages, which receive a rent for it when cultivated, the Government also receiving a small rent. In other places, as at Trichindore, it is Sircar-land, and is owned entirely by Government." Speaking of the rent of the field, in which sample No. 4 was grown, Mr. Lees writes: "January 2d, engaged a field, with a hedge round it, from a native, at one rupee a year. It is about three acres. The Tassildar measured it and fixed the price. Government tax half a rupee a year."

"I shall in future direct the principal sowings to be made three weeks before the December solstice, instead of two to five weeks after it, as in the present experiments. The great object is to get the root well down into the moist soil before the dry and hot weather begins. There is no doubt but that at the time of planting there must be rain, or the soil must be so damp as to cause the seed to germinate. I found that the soil near Trichindore soon dried to the depth of two inches, and even much more in some cases. When the plant has once got its root a few inches below the surface, it becomes comparatively safe, and will continue growing and deepening its root. As the cotton plant is one of the perpetual producers, it is clear that it must draw from a perpetual supply; and there is no doubt but that the tap root was intended to penetrate into those portions or strata of the soil, in which the moisture is never very greatly affected. These things tend to point out the locality most favorable for its cultivation,—a flat country, nearly on a level with the sea, and with an open sandy soil. I think that the country all along the Tinnivelly coast, extending a very great distance towards Madras, is peculiarly fitted for the cultivation of the cotton plant. And there is another country, which, I believe, will produce finer cotton than Southern India, in the same latitude, and close to it,—I mean Ceylon. The northern part of that island, and the country extending south, for an immense distance, is flat and sandy, and I think would produce, were it only tried, large quantities of very valuable Mexican cotton."

Some of the cotton (Nos. 1 to 7) was grown near Trichindore, about a mile from the sea, and elevated but little above it, near to a large field of native cotton, where there are bushes about four feet high, and some of them at least eight or ten feet high. Other localities were still nearer the sea, the soil sandy and rich in shells. On digging, the water settles at four or five feet below the surface. Nos. 8, 9, and 10 were grown about four miles south of Trichindore, and three or four miles from the sea; Nos. 9 and 10 with the aid of irrigation. Other samples, as Nos. 11 to 14, were sown near Punnagoody, where Mr. Hughes formerly grew his Bourbon cotton; one of these, No. 12, with the aid of irrigation.

Mr. Brown, having been called upon to examine and report upon these samples of cotton, observes of the samples Nos. 1 to 4 inclusive, that he valued them at 8½*d.* to 9*d.* per pound. It was clear, good-stapled cotton, and very silky, fully equal to fair New Orleans cotton, if not better than any he had seen grown from New Orleans cotton seed,—decidedly better than anything we have ever had yet, both as regards staple and fineness. It is 1*d.* to 2*d.* per pound better than any we have hitherto had of the Company's cotton. These remarks apply pretty much to Nos. 5 and 6. Samples 7 and 8 are not so good as the others by a halfpenny per pound. There is not the same staple in them by a great deal. Mr. Brown would put No. 9 with Nos. 7 and 8. No. 11 is more deteriorated than any other; it is coarse; it draws harshly; it comes more like Surat: altogether there is no comparison between it and the others.

The author having been accidentally present at this meeting, (15th August, 1850,) exhibited some specimens of cotton grown by Col. Cautley 1000 miles from the sea, but in the neighbourhood of the Doab canal. This cotton was also valued at 8½*d.*, while the indigenous cotton of the district was only considered worth 6½*d.* per lb.: a striking instance of the beneficial effects of moisture in the soil and climate, due in this case, no doubt, to the extensive effects of irrigation. This may also be observed in the specimens grown by Mr. Lees; for when he goes a little into the interior, the cotton is found to be much deteriorated. The author has no doubt that much good cotton may be grown on the sites pointed out by Mr. Lees.

In consequence of the delay which has taken place in the publication of this work, the author is able to add further information from Mr. David Lees, who continues of opinion that the climate of the east coast of Southern India is suitable for the growth of the New Orleans cotton plant, and that there is sufficient extent of land available from near Madras to within 20 miles of Cape Comorin. This is evident from the following paragraphs from a report by Mr. D. Lees, read at the annual meeting of the Commercial Association of Manchester, on the 20th of January, 1851, with some comments by Mr. Turner, which we here republish:

"On the east coast of southern India, there is a great extent of land, now lying almost waste, very suitable for the culture of the New Orleans cotton plant. There is a vast tract of sandy soil, nearly on a level with the sea—a soil and locality the best adapted to the nature and habits of a plant, which is a perpetual producer, and which, consequently, requires a perpetual supply of moisture. The whole of the Trichindore talook (or revenue district) is sandy, and, with the exception of a few isolated red sandhills, is quite flat. To the south, this flat and sandy tract extends nearly to Vissiavethee, or to within twenty miles of Cape Comorin; and to the north it extends much further. Captain Horsley, the engineer of the Tinnivelly district, informs me, that he knows the land to be flat and sandy as far to the north as Ramnad, where his district ends; and, from all I can learn, the same kind of land continues nearly to Madras. I cannot state exactly what is the breadth of this flat sandy tract; but, to the north-west of Trichindore, it is more than ten miles; and I believe that, to the northwards, it greatly increases.

"The country around Trichindore may be described as uncultivated. Immense herds of antelopes roam over it; and flocks of sheep and goats, as well as herds of buffaloes and cows, are led along it for pasturage. Near the villages are some fields of dry grains,—as cotton, sown with cambu, rapeseed, sesamum, and castor-oil plant. There are also many topes of Palmyra trees (the *Borassus flabelliformis* of botanists) near the villages, and likewise near the coast; but even amongst these topes cotton could be grown, as the trees give little or no shade, and are often far apart. The soil of this sandy district contains a large amount of salt; and, in consequence, most plants serviceable to man will not flourish in it, and some will not even grow in it; yet there are a few useful plants that love such a soil,—of these the cotton plant is the chief, and the more I see the more I am convinced it will flourish in the saline, sandy soil of Trichindore.

"The government rent, or circar rent, as it is called, for land around Trichindore, is 10 annas, 7 pice the chain,—a chain containing $3\frac{7}{11}$ acres. And if such land is rented from a native, who has enclosed it to cultivate, he asks, for cotton cultivation, one toolam of cotton in every five toolams, and he pays the circar rent. On the islets at the mouth of the river, north of Trichindore, the land, though not cultivated, belongs to natives; and there the circar rent is 1r. 9a. 6p. the chain; and the owners ask for rent one half the government rent. (If, then, the rupee be called 2*s.*, and the anna, which is 1-16th of a rupee, $1\frac{1}{2}$*d.*, and the pice, which is 1-12th of an anna, 1-8th of a penny, the government rent at Trichindore will be rather less than $4\frac{1}{2}$*d.* per acre; and the government rent and owner's rent, taken together, on the islets at the mouth of the river, will be about 1*s.* $3\frac{3}{4}$*d.* per acre.

"The cost of carriage in this district is very moderate. A bandy will carry 1000 lbs. of cotton twenty miles for a rupee. (This is at the rate of about $2\frac{1}{4}$*d.* per ton per mile.)

"The rate of wages at Trichindore is as follows:

	a.	p.	about.	
A coolie man, from 18 to 50 years of age	1	2	(1¾d.)	per day.
A great boy, from 14 to 17 years of age .	0	8	(1d.)	"
A little boy of 12 years of age . . .	0	6	(¾d.)	"
The coolies and great boys, at noon, have jaggery (a coarse sugar, made from the Palmyra), and drink water—each person	0	2	(¼d.)	"
The little boys have of the same, each .	0	1	(⅛d.)	"
An old man's wages are	0	6 or 8	(¾d. or 1d.)	"
An old woman's wages are	0	6 or 8	(¾d. or 1d.)	"
And they also have jaggery	0	2	(¼d.)	"

The above are the rates of wages from August to December; but from January to July the wages of a coolie are advanced to 1 anna 5 or 6 pice (or about 2¼*d.*) per day, as in those months the people go into distant parts to reap the rice, and are also engaged in drawing toddy from the palmyra trees."

Paragraph 7 refers to the offer of the natives to cultivate New Orleans cotton. If, according to their own methods, they would sow the cotton, rape seed, cambu (*Panicum italicum*), and castor-oil, in the same field altogether, and will give their employer as much cotton as they get in the rest of the crop for 10 annas per tolam, (20½ lbs.) But if they are to cultivate it according to the American method (or Master's mind), *i. e.* sow in rows, and no other grain in the field, they would require a higher advance, and "beg that your honour would promise to purchase the England cotton from us." This Mr. Lees was quite ready to do, and goes on to report in paragraph 8:

"I have arranged with the natives to cultivate New Orleans cotton upon the following terms:—They are to sow and cultivate as I tell them. They are to receive from me, in advance, 12 rupees on every chain of land they cultivate, which sum is to be deducted when they are paid for the cotton they grow; but the repayment of it is not to be enforced if the plants do not yield cotton enough to redeem it. They are to sell me the cotton at 9 annas per toolam; and the price is not to vary, but to remain the same in every month of the year. The Tassildar said, that on these terms many natives would cultivate. Indeed, I think there will be no difficulty in getting the natives to grow the cotton, provided they can be assured of its being purchased; but this they will require, for they always say that I must promise to buy it, since they cannot eat it, as they can their grains, neither can they sell it in the bazaar. And I am sure that they will grow it for a much less price than 9 annas per toolam, when they come to know the quantity the plants will yield; yet I think the price is a fair one, considering that native cotton has this year been selling in the bazaar at Trichindore for 8 and 10 annas per toolam. Now, as a toolam of seed cotton, which weighs 20½ lbs., will most probably yield 6 lbs., or 30 per cent., of clean cotton; and as 9 annas, at 1½*d.* each, amount to 13½*d.*, I am to give 13½*d.* for 6 lbs. of clean cotton, or 2¼*d.* per lb., for the average quality of New Orleans clean cotton at

Trichindore. But I shall have to pay, in addition, the expense of the cleaning,—a charge which you will be able to calculate from the rates of wages I have sent you.

"The charges for sending cotton from Tuticorin to Liverpool are the following:

For screwing the cotton at Tuticorin, including ropes, bags, &c., 5r. (10*s.*) per candy of 500 lbs.

Godown rent (warehouse rent) 4a. (6*d.*) per bale of 300 lbs.

Shipping, in boats, to vessels in roads, 15r. (30*s.*) per 100 bales.

Freight to Liverpool, on average, £4 to £5 per ton of 50 cubic feet.

Insurance.

Home charges, including dock charges, landing charges, wharfage, brokerage, commission, &c., about ½*d.* per lb.

All the above charges together amount to 1½*d.* per lb.

"There are twelve cotton screws now at work at Tuticorin, and one screw at Chippacolum, thirteen miles to the north. These screws are employed in pressing about 30,000 bales a year of native cotton, the average quantity shipped; but they are capable, I am told, of pressing nearly 200,000 bales in a year.

"A supply of 3000 lbs. of seed, or sufficient for sowing 100 acres, has been very kindly sent me from Coimbatore, by Dr. Wight. 'The seed sent,' says Dr. Wight, 'is from the crop picked between January and April, 1850, so is very fresh, and all from what we call first-sort cotton; that is, such as has been carefully freed from all bad or injured locks. I am not quite certain, but I think that it is the tenth descent from the stock originally brought out by the planters.' A small quantity of Sea Island seed has also been sent by Dr. Wight.

"The following is a list of the present season's sowings. By myself:

At Trichindore	10 chains	or about 91 acres.
Three miles north of ditto	9 "	
At Rany-pooram	3 "	
On an islet at the mouth of the river .	3 "	

Mr. Lees, in a later communication, states that he has himself sown from 110 to 120 acres. The natives, under his supervision, had sown about 26, and the missionaries about 70 acres; or altogether, 217 acres.

"Since the 5th of November, I have been daily engaged in sowing my own lands, and also in going to see the natives sow theirs. I have finished, or shall finish to-day (November 18th), all my sowings above named; but I have still to sow the seed obtained from my old plants, as well as that sent me by the overland mail. Some of my fields are up, and the plants are putting out their first true leaves; all that are up are very healthy, and of a dark green colour. My old plants, also, are shooting forth famously.

"Whilst I was at the mission station of Meignanapooram, many natives came for seed, but they could not be supplied. And the Rev. J. Spratt, in a letter from Meignanapooram, October 15th, says: 'There are great demands for cotton seed here. I should think that you would be able to dispose of any quantity you may bring.' And the Rev. J. Tucker, in a letter from Punnivelli, October 25th, says: 'There will be no difficulty in getting the people to sow American cotton seed. I believe, that as soon as the seed can be procured, thousands of acres will be cultivated.' And, at Punnagoody, more than thirty men came, wishing to cultivate.

"When I sent the seed to the agents at Tuticorin, I stated that it was from plants cultivated for a long time at Coimbatore, on land much elevated above the sea, and that, therefore, it might possibly be degenerated, but that a supply of good seed would arrive next year, and they could have some of it. Yet even if the Coimbatore seed be degenerated, I feel sure it will here be speedily improved. That I brought from England has, in many instances, produced a larger seed than the original.

"I notice that the New Orleans plant bears flowers on the new wood, at the axil of every leaf. If it be sown at the proper time, its branches will be thickly covered with them. In less than two months from the time of sowing it begins to flower, and in rather more than three months, to yield cotton. In February next, there will be some very good cotton,—better cotton, I expect, than the samples I have already sent.

"I have myself sown from 110 to 120 acres. All my fields look very well, and so do those of the natives. My old plants are full of fine new shoots and leaves, and some of them are putting forth abundance of forms. The finest of them have always had forms and blossoms, and pods upon them, ever since they first began to produce. I expect they will be in full blossom at the end of December or beginning of January."

§ 36. Culture of Cotton in the elevated Lands of the Madras Presidency.

In our observations on the Culture of Cotton in the Bombay Presidency, we commenced with treating first of the culture in the districts above the ghauts, and then descended to those below the ghauts. On the present occasion we have reversed this order, having treated first of the culture in Coimbatore and its valley, and then of the same in the low lands of Tinnivelly. We shall conclude our notice of the different cotton districts of India with a few observations on the capabilities of the table land of Mysore, &c. for the culture of cotton, first premising, with a brief account of an accidental, but apparently a very successful, experiment in the mountainous district of Wynaad. In mentioning the coast of Malabar, (p. 413,) we stated that the fall of rain seemed too great for the healthy growth of cotton; but we observed that it was probable sheltered situations might be found where some kinds of cotton might be grown. Messrs. Parry and Co., of Madras, a few months since, sent an account of the discovery of a fine looking crop of cotton in a part of their coffee plantation on the Wynaad hills. On further inquiry, it was ascertained that they had sown some cotton seed which was distributed by the

34

Madras Government two or three years before, but which had been quite forgotten. In this situation, where the climate is moist and the soil poor and of little value, these plants had grown without further care, and, though choked up with weeds, bore a plentiful crop of what appeared very good cotton. On sending the seeds to Dr. Wight, they were pronounced to be those of Brazil cotton, or *Gossypium peruvianum*, (*v.* p. 149.) Messrs. Parry were so much encouraged by the appearance of this crop, that they engaged to go on with the cultivation if they were supplied with some seed. The Court of Directors complied with their request, and ordered some seed from South America. Mr. Ellis, one of the partners of the above firm, when he called at the India House, was shown some of the seed which had arrived, and had been sent by Messrs. Rathbone of Liverpool, to Southampton, to be sent to Madras by the mail of the 20th December, 1850. Mr. Ellis, having brought some specimens of the original cotton grown in Wynaad, it was pronounced at Manchester worth from 7*d.* to 7½*d.* per lb., and of a quality that would be very desirable, but that it bore "the characteristics of a wild cotton, being coarse and irregular in fibre; but a very little care bestowed upon it would soon remove all that is objectionable."

§ 37. Culture in Mysore.

In the preceding observations of the Madras Government, (*v.* p. 468,) it is evident that Mysore appears, upon the whole not well suited to the cultivation of cotton, and that, in fact, it is supplied from Bellary and other districts. The climate in general is too dry and windy, but still there are districts near the Western ghauts, where the climate is more moist, and the culture of American cotton likely to succeed, as is evident from the communication at p. 532. Cotton, indeed, is grown in some of the divisions, as is obvious from the accompanying table, embracing the information supplied by Capt. Onslow, Superintendent of the Nuggur division.

STATEMENT, *giving the Information required by the Queries from the Honorable Court of Directors, contained in their Despatch of the* 10*th November*, 1847, *regarding the Cultivation, &c., of Cotton in the Nuggur Division.*

TALOOKS.	Price of cotton freed from seed at the principal mart or marts, per maund.	Price at which the ryot sells his cleaned cotton per maund.		Price at which the ryot sells his uncleaned cotton per maund.		Expense of cleaning a maund of cotton.	Expense of conveying cotton to the nearest port for shipment, per maund.	Average produce of one Kristraj candy of seed.	Quantity of land under cultivation with cotton.
		With advance.	Without advance.	With advance.	Without advance.				
	r. a. p.	r. a. p.	r. a. p.	r. a. p.	r. a. p.	r. a. p.	r. a. p.	maunds.	candies. c. s.
Honally . . .	2 8 0	—	2 8 0	0 7 0	0 8 0	0 4 0	0 4 0	360	8 12 4
Hurryhur . .	1 14 0	5 0 0	5 0 0	0 7 0	0 8 0	0 5 4	0 6 2	320	41 0 0
Terrikeray . .	2 9 0	2 6 0	2 10 0	6 0 0	6 0 0	0 5 4	0 7 0	300	39 9 2
Chengherry . .	7 0 0	5 0 0	5 0 0	0 7 0	0 8 0	0 5 4	0 8 0	400	74 0 0

The maund is 48 seers; the seer weighs 24 raja rupees. The Kristnaraj candy is 160 seers; the seer measures $1\frac{3}{4}$ quart bottles.

The quantity of land is that which will hold a Kristnaraj candy of seed sown.

It is difficult to say to what extent cultivation might be carried on the extensive plains of the open Talooks, composed of great varieties of soils, many of them suitable for cotton.

The ryots of the Hurryhur and Chengherry Talooks do not clean their cotton.

The ryots of the Terrikeray Talook do not sell uncleaned cotton.

Cotton is not sold in the market towns of the Chengherry Talook; it is brought only from the ryots, and exported.

The above are the only Talooks of this division in which cotton is grown to any extent. A very trifling quantity is cultivated in the Talooks of Cuddoor, Chiccamoogloor, Shemogah, Shekarpoor, and Sorub, but only for domestic purposes,—chiefly for lamp-thread.

There is much land in the Cuddoor, Shekarpoor, and Shemogah Talooks, which from appearance seem to be suitable for cotton, where the climate seems to be suitable also. In the Mulnaad Talooks the climate and soil are not suitable.

(Signed) W. C. ONSLOW, *Superintendent.*

Captain Onslow has further instituted an experiment at Cuddoor under Mr. Meppen, a man of intelligence and observation. Dr. H. Cleghorn has informed the author that he had himself distributed American cotton seed to the ryots in the neighbourhood of Shemmogah and Cuddoor, which grew in such a manner as gave evidence of the suitableness of the climate. Cuddoor is within 60 miles of Hurryhur, also in this division, where the soil, elevation, &c., are very similar to that of Dharwar, (p. 378,) whence, indeed, we have seen the cultivation of American cotton spreading into the Madras side of the Toombudra. Mr. Meppen has given the following interesting account of his first year's experiment, in a report to Dr. Wight:

"*To* ROBERT WIGHT, Esq., *Superintendent Government Cotton Farms, Coimbatore.*

"Dear Sir,—Agreeably to promise, I have the pleasure of sending you an account of our cotton experiment at this place, and, in doing so, I have first to remark that the season was a very unfavorable one: instead of dewy nights and sunny days, we had a succession of clouded days in December, January, and February; this caused blight to the cotton, and the consequent great falling off of the anticipated crop. This being the first large experiment, it may have been, but for other circumstances, considered a bad beginning; it, however, had the good effect of proving which cotton could best stand a bad season. In many places, indigenous cotton was sown in the adjoining field to the 'New Orleans;' and the result of the two shows, that, while the latter yielded a remunerative crop, the former was a complete failure and loss to the ryot. Such convincing proof, although accidental, was the best that could be brought forward to prove to a people naturally shy of taking up any new cultivation, the superiority of the imported cotton to their own. The intention of this experiment was to teach the ryots the mode of cultivating and gathering cotton clean, and suitable for the home market, and to ascertain from actual results whether or not cotton would be a remunerative cultivation in this part of the Mysore country. Taking into consideration the season, the experiment has answered the intention beyond expectation. The ryots followed the instructious given them in every particular, and have picked their cotton very clean and fine, and have altogether taken to the cultivation in a very promising manner. The result has also proved that the cultivation is a remunerating one, and in a good season would be very profitable. The following statement shows the extent of land cultivated, the average rent of land per acre, the produce per acre, and the average height of the plants:

Quantity of land.			Rent of land.			Average rent per acre.			Quantity of produce.	Average produce per acre.	Average height of plants.
No.	acres.	sq. yds.	r.	a.	p.	r.	a.	p.	lbs.	lbs.	inches.
1	3	100	0	12	0	0	4	0	311	103	18
2	15	1930	20	7	1	1	5	4	3696	242	22
3	35	340	31	3	1½	0	14	2	3482	991	16
4	27	654	50	2	2½	1	13	6	4975	183	26
5	17	2276	35	2	0	2	0	0	3417	194	27
6	21	3400	47	4	3	2	1	9	3372	154	27
7	14	368	52	10	4	3	11	0	2352	167	28
8	15	2240	16	11	6	1	1	3	2560	165	22
9	5	1200	7	9	0	1	5	0	1036	167	18
	152	12,508	261	13	6	1	11	0	25,201	163	—

"The above statement shows an average produce, in a very bad season, of 163 lbs. kuppas or seed cotton to an acre of land paying 1 rupee 11 annas rent: this, when freed of seed, will yield 50 lbs. of cotton wool. A sample of this cotton you have already seen and pronounced 'excellent,' and equally as good in quality as that grown at the Government farms; you are therefore able to form an opinion of its value in the home market. The cotton was grown on what is called dry cultivation lands, without any manuring or irrigation; the seed was sown in August and September; the fall of rain from that time up to the 30th April last was 10 inches 49 cents, and the thermometer under shade during the same time never rose above 88 degrees. In December, January, and February, there were no less than 36 clouded days, which I found very injurious both to blossom and tender pods. The plants attained the height of from 12 to 36 inches. Regarding the size, it is worthy of remark, that at Dharwar the plants, according to Mr. Mercer the American planter's statement, only attained a height of 12 to 18 inches, and averaged a crop of 180 to 200 lbs. seed cotton per acre. From the height the plants grow up to here, it is very evident that in a fair season the crop at this place would more than double that of Dharwar. If, after five years' experience, I may venture an opinion upon this subject, I would unhesitatingly say that this and many other parts of Mysore, from the peculiarity of its climate and nature of its soil, is well adapted for the production of a very superior quality of cotton. At this place there are thousands of acres of land fit to grow cotton either by irrigation or by dry cultivation; all that is wanted for producing it equal to American in quality, is European capital and skill. The ryots would cultivate it to any extent if sure of a ready market for the disposal of the kuppas. Although cotton is extensively cultivated all over India, it is gathered and exported so void of care, that, with the exception of what is grown entirely under European management, all other exportations of Indian cotton wool have been condemned in the home market, from the impurities contained in it, and from its usual dirty and soiled appearance. This has been generally attributed to accidents during carriage to the coast, in consequence, as is stated, of there being no, or if any, very bad, roads, and in crossing of rivers: this is, however, an erroneous notion, the actual cause being negligence of the cultivators in the first instance, and dishonesty of grasping dealers afterwards. Ryots are by nature careless, and are the same all over India; and so long as there are purchasers of their dirty produce, it cannot be expected they will improve, but continue indifferent to the quality of their agricultural productions. This indifference is extended to cotton also, which is picked without any care, and thrown in the field during the picking; it is then carelessly gathered up with dry leaves and dirt attached, and in this state is thrown into a corner of the ryot's house, where it is left to accumulate more dirt till taken away by some money-lender or native dealer, who, instead of finding means to free the cotton of this accumulation of dirt, often adds to it, for the purpose of increasing the weight; and for the same reason the cotton, which, with ordinary care, could be carried dry over rivers, is purposely allowed to get wet. This is the true cause for the quantity of dirt and foreign matter found in Indian cotton, and for its usual damaged appearance; if it were the cause, as is generally made to appear, that of bad roads, similar accidents should happen to cotton exported from the interior by Europeans, and indigo, sugar, opium, grain, &c. during transit to the coast, or to salt, Europe piece goods, &c. sent from the coast to the interior. All or most of these articles must be carried on the same roads. That more and better roads are wanted all over India, is a fact I will not take upon myself to deny; but I must deny that the impurity of our cotton is attributable to the want of them. It is beyond a doubt that many parts of India are capable of producing very good cotton; all that is

now wanted is attention to its being picked, and ginned clean, suitable for the home market. This is not in the nature of natives to do; it must therefore be done by Europeans settling in districts where cotton is or can be grown. Encourage the ryots to cultivate it, and purchase the kuppas from them; gin and pack on the spot for exportation. By these means England may expect a supply of good cotton from India. It is not by the superiority of its climate or soil over that of India that America is enabled to rule the cotton market, but by its superior and careful cultivation; and not till the cultivation of cotton in India, like that of indigo, sugar, and coffee, is taken up by Europeans, can any great improvement in the quality or quantity of its produce be expected.

"I remain, dear Sir,

"Yours very faithfully,

"FRED. D. MEPPEN."

"CUDDOOR, *5th June*, 1850."

§ 38. CULTURE IN BELLARY.

We have seen that much of the cotton exported from Madras is brought there from Bellary, forming a great portion of the western cotton of that Presidency. An attempt was made to introduce the American cotton into the district, by detaching Mr. Morris, one of the American planters, from Coimbatore. But on arrival, he was of opinion that neither the neighbourhood of Bellary nor of Adawnie were suited to the culture of American cotton, the native cotton being not more than five or six inches high, and some American plants not higher, though in full flower. He observed, that "about Coimbatore we find the red soil decidedly better adapted for the growth of the American cotton than the black; but we failed in all cases where the plants could not reap the benefit of a sea-breeze." Dr. Wight concluded, that "the stunted appearance of the plants might be owing to late sowing;" Mr. Miller, the Collector, to the failure of rain, which he describes as "having been total, the black lands never once having been thoroughly saturated." The productive powers of the black soil he considered to be very great, and that, in good years, he had seen crops of such exceeding luxuriance, that he could hardly imagine their being excelled, even on the banks of the Mississippi. Mr. Miller, therefore, agreed with Mr. Morris in thinking, that, as the New Orleans cotton plant was not likely to succeed there, it would be preferable to confine their attention to the native plant, and chiefly to the careful cleaning of the cotton; and he believed, that the great cotton contractors of Bellary and also of Adawnie would readily adopt the saw-gin, if it were explained to them in a simple and practical way. By this is probably meant, that the hand saw-gin should be introduced from the neighbouring district of Dharwar, instead of the same efficient but larger instrument moved by cattle or steam power. The experiment was, however, unfortunately put a stop to by the early death of Mr. Morris.

§ 39. CULTURE IN THE NORTHERN CIRCARS.

The Northern Circars were formerly famous for various manufactures of cotton, and the natives still retain a portion of their ancient skill, though the trade has nearly deserted their coasts. But even in those days the cotton was not grown in these districts, but imported from Central India. The Court of Directors early recommended the improvement of the culture of cotton in these regions, but no effect seems to have been produced. Mr. Randall (v. *E. I. C.'s Papers*), at a subsequent period, recommended these districts for the culture of Bourbon cotton, at the same time that he excluded Bellary and Cuddapah, as being too dry. Vizagapatam was subsequently the seat of one of the experimental farms, where the culture seems to have been particularly successful, as the returns per acre are stated, in Dr. Wight's Report on the culture in different districts, to have been large, amounting to 1150 lbs. of seed cotton per acre, probably in consequence of improved culture; for we learn that pruning was employed. In the Cuttack district, as we have seen at p. 259, Bourbon cotton seems to thrive without much difficulty, and it is probable, notwithstanding any former failure, that localities may be found in the Northern Circars suitable for the successful culture of American cotton, if observers will study its requirements in connection with the soil and climate of the several situations, as has been so successfully done in the Tinnivelly district.

Having thus taken a survey of all the cotton districts of India, from Bengal to the North-Western Provinces and the Punjab, and from thence across Central India, including Nagpore and Berar, to the Bombay Presidency and Scinde, we have, in the present account of the Madras experiments, come round in the Northern Circars, nearly to the point from which we started, that is, the moist provinces at the head of the Bay of Bengal. We have seen, that, in most of the districts, the difficulties of the trade consist in the want of local encouragement to the cultivators, while the difficulties of culture with the American cotton, seem to depend on the little attention paid to the nature and wants of the plant, which, in some districts, requires draining and open situations, and, in others, irrigation and shelter. A few subjects only remain for us to mention, before concluding this account of the culture of cotton in India.

§ 40. American Saw-Gins.

Mention has frequently been made of Saw-gins, with which both the native and the American cotton has been cleaned. Several were brought by Capt. Bayles from America; and Mr. Jones, who came over at the same time, constructed at Liverpool, in a few days, a hand saw-gin moved by cog-wheels. Others were subsequently made in this country and sent out to India. Mr. Mercer, as early as October, 1844,* pointed out that the American saw-gin could be altered to clean the cotton of the country; and, in July, he had advocated the setting-up of small saw-gins as preferable to large ones, for introduction into the Southern Mahratta country, "because large and costly gin-houses frighten the cautious natives by their expense."

Mr. Simpson, in Candeish, proposed the construction of saw-gins composed of eight and ten saws. Mr. Mercer, we believe, was the first, and with the aid only of the village artificers, to construct a saw-engine entirely of materials made up in India, with the exception of the saws, which were of English manufacture. Capt. Wingate, Superintendent of the Revenue

* Mr. Simpson has stated, that he was the first to alter the saw-gins to the indigenous cotton, which he did as far back as June, 1842. The manner of working them (by manual labour and fly-wheel) originated with himself, simultaneously with the alterations in the gins.

Survey, reported to Mr. Mansfield, Acting Collector of Dharwar, on the 6th of October, "The superiority of the new gins over the best of the American gins is most decisively established, and is to be accounted for by its parts working more truly, and being better fitted together than those of the American gins. The framing also of the new machine being of teak-wood, and carefully put together, is much stronger and more durable than the pine-wood frame of the American machine;" and in addition to this superiority in point of performance and durability, the new gin has the further recommendation of being cheaper. According to an estimate shown to me by Mr. Mercer, the cost of the new machine will not exceed 150 rupees, which is less than one half of that of the American." (*Return*, p. 533.)

Cottage-gin—In the year 1848, the Manchester Commercial Association, at the instigation of Mr. James Lees, conceived that the culture of American cotton would be greatly accelerated in India if the natives were furnished with a cotton-cleaning machine, which would clean that kind of cotton, and which was cheap enough to come within their means of purchase. The Association having applied at the India House for the loan of a saw-gin, were supplied with a small model of a 25 saw-gin, which had been constructed by Mr. Frost. Mr. Jamieson, of Ashton-under-Lyne, was employed in making one with only four saws. This, when completed, was examined by Mr. Petrie, previously in the service of the East India Company, and for some years in charge of the cotton-cleaning machinery at Coimbatore. He succeeded in making some improvements, to facilitate its working. After this, a further and public trial took place of the machines which had been constructed, when the author was deputed to be present, on the part of the East India Company. The Association had had four of these cottage gins constructed, each containing only four saws, of the kind which Mr. Petrie had found most useful when in India. No. 1 was constructed chiefly of wood, and No. 2 of iron, both having their saws and brushes moved by bands and wheels. No. 3 was moved by cog-wheels; and No. 4 by a pinion and wheel. All were nearly equally efficient; the wooden one less so than the others, probably from the greater amount of friction. But this defect was susceptible of easy amendment. The author considered No. 2 as best adapted for India,—being small and compact, of little weight, moderate in price, and therefore well-suited to fix the attention of the native cultivator, who is easily frightened by the sight of a large instrument and expensive machinery. The author recommended that a considerable number of these instruments should be sent by the Court to India for the following reasons:

"Having shown the efficiency as well as easy working of these cottage gins, it is desirable to inquire whether they are suited to the natives of India. In the first place, these instruments, like the original saw-gin, are especially fitted for the cleaning of American seed cotton, which is not so easily cleaned by the Indian churka. American cotton is not only the most in request at Manchester, but it is also in favorable climates the most profitable for cultivation in India. For, in addition to bringing a higher price both in the Bombay and English markets, it will, with very little extra care in the culture, yield a large quantity of seed cotton per acre, while this seed cotton yields about 9 per cent. more of wool than does the native seed. Its cultivation, however, has not spread so rapidly, except in Dharwar, as might have been expected. This is partly owing to the natives themselves not being able to spin it so easily as their own cotton, while the seed has been stated, I believe incorrectly, to be unfit for feeding their cattle. A part of the delay, however, attending the extension of this culture appears to me to have been owing to the difficulty of cleaning the cotton when grown. As seed cotton is a marketable article only to a particular class, the ryot has no resource but to sell it to the middleman on his own terms, who will allege the difficulty of cleaning and finding a market for a new produce as a reason for giving a lower price for it, if he should agree to buy it. The ryot, moreover, has no inducement to pick his cotton clean, as he does not get a better price for what to the middleman has little value, as he systematically adulterates what he may have bought comparatively clean, with the object of increasing its weight. But if the ryot had the means within his reach of cleaning his cotton as fast as he picked it, he could then avail himself of the advantages of a more extensive market, and be able himself to receive the higher prices which an improved article may be expected shortly to command. The cottage gin is, in my opinion, calculated to effect this object, for its cheapness will allow of its being much more extensively distributed, while a man's own family will be able to work it. This will give the cottage gin a considerable advantage for small farmers, as even the 25 saw-gin requires the labour of ten men to work it efficiently. Its adoption by the natives will, no doubt, be facilitated, in consequence of the superiority of the saw-gin for cleaning cotton being already known in the collectorates of Coimbatore, Dharwar, Belgaum, and Broach, as the engineers and planters sent out by the Court have made up many saw-gins, which have been distributed, and even bought by the native dealers, in some of the above districts."

The Court of Directors ordered 200 of these cottage gins, and Mr. Petrie was employed to superintend their construction. As several modifications were made after the instrument had been seen by the author, the following account refers to the saw-gin in its improved state, and as represented in figs. 1 and 2 in the accompanying plate, where, in No. 1, the cover being removed, the saws and brushes are seen; and in No. 2, a part of the hopper being removed, the saws are seen projecting beyond the grating. The weight of the saw-gin was finally reduced to 75 lbs., and its length to about 2 feet, being about 20 inches in height at the hopper, and 16 inches high over the brushes. The four parallel 10-inch circular saws (*b*) project into the hopper (*a*), where the seeded cotton is placed. The saws, in revolving, draw the fibres of cotton through the grating, when the seeds fall down, as at (*d*). The cotton, when passed through, is brought into contact with the 12-inch brushes, which, coming successively in contact with the saws, brush off the cotton, which is blown out at (*c*) by the current of air formed by the rapid revolution of the eight brushes. The saws and brushes are put in motion by wheels and bands turned by two winches, one on each side, which may be moved by two children. The grating or hopper may be moved up or down, backwards or forwards, so as to do light or heavy work; but Mr. Petrie found, that if the saws projected too far, though the gin would clean a larger quantity of cotton, it cut the staple, and rendered the cotton of less value. Mr. Petrie made the following report of the working of the machine after the improvements he had made:

	Quantity of kupas cleaned per man per hour.	Price of cleaning per candy of 500 lbs.	Cost of wear and tear of machinery in every bale of cotton cleaned.
MACHINE.	pounds.	rupees.	d.
Cottage gin . .	16	2·13	16·16
Hand gin . . .	10·71	3·14	19·16
Indian churka . .	3	5	4·16

When these saw-gins were made, it was stated that they were unsuited to India; because cotton is not cleaned by the ryots. But, in some districts, it is so cleaned; in fact, the customs in different parts of so vast a country may differ so much, that what is unsuitable to one place may be most appropriate to another. No difficulty had been experienced in disposing of these saw-gins in some of the districts, (*v.* Dharwar.)

Dr. Wight mentions, that he had received the cottage gins sent out by the Court, and found that they did their work so well, that he could easily have employed a couple of hundred, and had ginned about 4000 lbs. of cotton with eight of them.

Mr. Frost, who had been sent out as a mechanical engineer to India by the Court of Directors, and had first been stationed at Agra, having applied to return to the country, was again sent out by the Court, and attached to the Experiments at Dharwar, where he arrived in February, 1847. He, as we have seen (p. 365), immediately applied himself to repairing the saw-gins which were out of order: since then in constructing many new ones of all sizes, and in inventing a small hand-gin.

The author received a letter from Mr. Frost, dated 21st November, 1848, in which he gives some account of his new instrument, in the following extracts:

"I doubt not but you will like to have my opinion upon the failure of the American cotton and increase of the native cotton plantation; to give which, I must explain to you, that all the cotton grown in this part of the country is generally sold by ryots (cultivators) to the sowkars (merchants,) the latter being the owners of the American gins, and the former, having no means of cleaning the American cotton which they may have grown, are compelled to sell the American cotton in an uncleaned state to these native merchants, submitting themselves to all their impositions, which, from what I have learnt, I can assure you, are very great; whereas the native cotton they can clean in their own way, and sell to a greater advantage. This I am convinced is the sole cause I can account for the failure of the American cotton. (This refers to the diminished culture of 1848.)

"To remove the above-mentioned cause, and render the cultivation of American cotton more extensive, some kind of small and light gin would suit. For this purpose, I accordingly directed all my attention and endeavours for the invention of a small gin; and I am happy to say that I have succeeded in inventing a small hand-gin, which I presume to say will relieve these poor natives from impositions of the merchants, as most of them will be able to buy the newly invented gins, as each of them will not cost more than 30 rupees.

"Now, to give you an idea of the gin newly invented by me, and the quantity of work it can perform, I must inform you that it was examined by Mr. Bell, Collector of Dharwar, Captain Wingate, of the Engineers, Superintendent of the Revenue Survey, and Mr. Blount, the American cotton planter, and tried by them two successive days, to see what quantity of work it would do, and the following was the result:

1st day it cleaned	1 mound	(26 lbs.)	in	35 minutes.
2d	,,	,,	,,	34 minutes.

"On seeing which, the gentlemen were much satisfied, and highly approved of the gin.

"The gin can be worked by two boys or two women. I got it to work by two boys, and then it cleaned in 10 hours 400 lbs. with the greatest ease.

"Your most obedient servant,

"H. FROST,

"*Engineer of the Government Cotton Experiments, Dharwar.*"

"DHARWAR, 21*st November*, 1848."

Several saw-gins were, at an early period of the experiments, bought by natives on their own account, but they seemed anxious to get rid of them again. Mr. Mansfield was of opinion, that "the wisest course was for government to show the utmost readiness to relieve the natives of their bargains, whether actually or virtually concluded;—what led the natives to wish to get rid of the gins, for the possession of which they at one time appeared desirous, is not perhaps easily ascertained. They are an ignorant people, timid and suspicious; sharp-sighted, certainly, where profit is to be gained, yet without enlarged views even in mercantile transactions, and full of prejudices towards anything new. The time had probably not arrived when the native merchants could appreciate the value of the saw-gin; and the large price of those received from America, afford grounds for doubting whether they would prove a good speculation. The production of a cheaper article in this country, will, I trust, go far to remove this difficulty."

Mr. Mansfield's anticipations have been realized, for a disposition to purchase saw-gins on their own account has been

A. FOOT ROLLER. B. COMMON CHURKA. C. BROACH CHURKA. D 1 2 COTTAGE SAW GIN. 3 4 SAWS & BRUSH.

displayed by the natives. Sixteen had been sold to them at the end of the year 1848, and about fifty more since that time. The demand for saws had so greatly increased, that the Bombay government applied for 1000 saws to be sent them by the overland route. This was done by the September mail of 1850.

Mr. Blount, in answer to queries, states the following as the prices at which the gins, including the driving wheels, bands, and all other materials, are sold at the Dharwar manufactory :

			Rs.
25-saw gins			225
20	"		220
18	"		200
14	"	10-inch saw	160
14	"	12 "	180
10	"	old repaired	100 to 120
7	"	8-inch saws (Mr. Frost's)	40

The gin of seven saws is constructed for forty rupees, may be worked in an open shed or veranda, and can clean from ten to twelve maunds (228 lbs.) of American cotton, and fifteen to eighteen maunds of native, with the labour of two men and a boy; and this Mr. Blount considers the best adapted to the Southern Mahratta country, though he is perfectly aware of the advantages of larger machines, and of cattle or steam power for other situations.

The cotton can now be cleaned by these instruments at the rate of about three to five rupees per candy of 784 lbs., the same quantity cleaned by the foot roller and churka costing eight or ten rupees. Mr. Landon, as we have seen at p. 442, has reduced the expense of cleaning to 2r. 6a. per candy.

Some little injury is no doubt done by the saws (especially when these are quite new); but this is more than compensated for by the celerity and cheapness with which the operation is performed; but the damage is upon the whole so slight, as not to render the cotton objectionable to the manufacturer. A little modification in the instrument renders it equally suitable to the native cotton. The iron grating through which the edges of the saws project when revolving, draw in the cotton, leaving the seeds behind. If the openings of the grating are not sufficiently small, the seeds will be drawn through with the cotton; this is prevented by diminishing the openings, that is, proportioning them to the size of the seeds.

The great difficulty with the natives is to convince them of the advantage of keeping the cotton clean when they have got it so. Mr. Blount says: "The difficulty is to keep the natives from mixing the impurities which have fallen from the cotton during the cleaning process, with the wool. They cannot bear the idea of some loss to get a superior article, and gather the motes from under the gin, which are always more or less mixed with seed, and put them in with the cleaned cotton." When cleaned, it is merely pressed into bags at a cost of about seven annas per candy; no presses being yet in use in the district, though some had been introduced during the experiments of 1829-38, (v. *E. I. C.'s Papers*, p. 88.)

Cotton screw-presses were sent out by the East-India Company, but do not seem to have been generally approved of (v. *House of Commons' Return*, p. 254); but one of them has been set up, and regularly worked at Coimbatore. Mr. Simpson constructed one in the interior of Candeish (p. 389). Mr. Landon, on his arrival in Broach, constructed a cheap and efficient instrument (p. 441). Mr. Blount proposes making a press to make up bales of about 300 lbs.

§ 41. Further Observations on the Quality of Indian Cotton.

In a preceding part of this work (pp. 21 to 27), the author has referred to the difficulty which he had experienced in forming a correct idea of the value of the indigenous cotton of India for the manufactures of this country. Some stating that it was little fitted for such purposes, and some that it might be used for three fourths of our manufactures. The author, as he has stated at p. 27, was unable, by his inquiries, to obtain any confirmation of the latter opinion. He was, therefore, much surprised at seeing in the printed 'Summary of the Cotton Experiments in the Southern Mahratta Country from 1830 to 1848,' the following passage, in a minute of one of the Members of Council at Bombay:—"I observe with regret, from a perusal of Dr. Royle's paper, which accompanied the Honorable Court's despatch, No. 21, of the 10th of November last, that that gentleman has imbibed views hostile to the continuance of our endeavours to introduce the foreign cotton; at least, that he thinks our greatest attention should be given to the cotton of the country."

In the above extract two statements are made, neither of which, as far as the author himself is aware, is to be found in any of the Reports which he wrote, and which were sent out to India. All of these are printed in the '*Report of the House of Commons' Cotton Committee*' (p. 58 to p. 77); and in all the preference is given to the American cotton in all situations where it will grow. Even in that dated Oct. 1847, p. 66-69, the precedence is given to American cotton; and this was written, as is obvious from its concluding paragraphs, with reference to the experiment instituted by the Agra Government, for the culture of the best kinds of indigenous cotton in situations where the American cotton had already failed. With regard to which cotton is of the greatest importance, and to which most attention should be given, the question depends entirely upon whether it is required for consumption in India, or for export to Europe. For their own purposes, the natives of India are satisfied with their own cotton. But if it is wished to supply the manufacturers of Europe, the question depends entirely upon their decision, and they have now sufficiently marked their opinion by the prices which they give for the Indian-grown American, in preference to the indigenous cotton. But discrepant statements were made even upon this subject in the evidence given before the Cotton Committee. The author has on no occasion recommended the culture of the indigenous cotton in situations where the American kinds will succeed. But if he had done so a few years ago, he would have been perfectly justified from the evidence before him; because the Indian was grown with facility, and the American with comparative difficulty, while the purchasers at first gave no better prices for the one than for the other. A consignment from India, which was composed exclusively of New Orleans cotton, and another which consisted of different varieties, including the New Orleans, were stated to have realized the same price, viz. $3\frac{1}{4}$*d.* per pound, at Liverpool. (v. *Summary*, p. 15.) The Bombay Chamber of Commerce, moreover, on more than one occasion, pronounced the native cotton as superior to the New Orleans (*v.* pp. 356 and 382, from *Summary*, pp. 69 and 111); and at a subsequent period some Bombay agents of Manchester firms gave a higher price for the native than for the American cotton, (*v.* p. 358.) Subsequently to the sales alluded to above, the American sold at better prices; but it was not until the Commercial Association of Manchester took up the subject, that the superiority of Indian-grown American cotton over the best Indian cotton was clearly shown, and has been constantly maintained. The indigenous cotton of certain districts has sufficient good qualities to be used for a variety of purposes, and it would be so used here more extensively if it was sent in a cleaner state to market. This we have shown with respect to both the Broach and the Surat cotton, (*v.* p. 96.) The Coompta or Dharwar cotton was pronounced favorably of by Messrs. Ritchie and Stewart's Manchester and Glasgow friends. So in 1847, some saw-ginned Coompta, sent by Mr. Mercer to Mr. Turner, was pronounced at the North Shore Mills "the best specimen of East Indian cotton we ever worked;" but it had the defect, in consequence of having been badly picked, of being full of small broken fragments of leaf.* The carefully cleaned Tinnivelly cotton, mentioned at p. 98, was also approved of, and subsequent consignments have sold well, as also those of the indigenous Coimbatore cotton, though, in all cases in the last few years, at inferior prices to the Indian-grown American cotton.

Notwithstanding the low prices at which Indian cotton usually sells, in some measure owing to its dirty and adulterated state, it is evident that it possesses some good qualities, and commands very fair prices when sent in a clean state to market. As the author was anxious to get further informa-

* This defect may be easily removed by clean picking, but this the natives will not always do. "Of native cotton I have made every exertion to get 500 candies, and offered an enhanced price if they would gather it clean; but I have not succeeded, the ryots in most instances utterly refusing to make the attempt. I have, however, secured 120 or 150 of clean-picked native cotton. The quantity certainly is not large, but the quality is superior, and worth 2*d.* a pound more than such native as that Mr. Mercer sent to Mr. Turner in 1847. No attempt has heretofore been made or inducement held out to the ryots to pick clean. There are many difficulties in the way of picking native cotton clean, but two thirds of the crop can be had almost without leaf; and if our Bombay dealers would only insist on having clean cotton, it would be got. If I remain here another season, I will get 300 candies of clean-picked native cotton at least."—(*Mr. Blount, in a letter to the author.*)

tion and to endeavour to reconcile the discrepant statements referred to at p. 27, he was glad to avail himself of a kind offer made by W. Burch, Esq., of Sewardstone Mills, Essex, to take with him specimens of the improved cotton from India in one of his visits to the manufacturing provinces. This Mr. Burch was good enough to do last summer, and took with him a specimen of the New Orleans cotton grown at Coimbatore, and two specimens of the indigenous cotton of that district, one cleaned by the churka, and the other by the saw-gin. The information which he obtained he was further obliging enough to incorporate into a written report, from which the following are extracts, in which Mr. Burch calls the New Orleans cotton, grown in India, the Am-Surat.

"I find the East India cotton is termed 'Surat' in our markets; that it is the lowest quality of cotton,—short in staple, and delivered in a very foul and adulterated state,—with, however, a variation in quality of staple, and also in cleanliness. It bears the lowest price in the market, and is used for the commonest description of goods, such for instance, as coarse common calicoes, at 2½*d.* or 3*d.* per yard. It is adulterated with dirt, sand, leaf, cotton-seed, &c. The sand is very detrimental to the machinery, as it is liable to get into the bearings, and, like emery powder, will cause them to wear very fast. The seed is liable to be crushed among the fibres by the cleansing machinery, when it cannot afterwards be separated, and forms burrs in the yarn, which experience shows do not bleach. Both Surat and American, but the Surat in much the greater degree, are foul with pieces of dried leaf, which are difficult to get out, and which make specks in the goods. It is, however, generally found that these pieces of leaf will bleach with the cotton itself. There is a large consumption of what is termed 'waste,' which consists in leavings of American cotton after the finer portion has been separated. The trade of the town of Oldham consists almost entirely in working up this 'waste,' and in 'Surats.' They bear about the same price in the market. The Surat cotton is used to a considerable extent, and more particularly when cotton is dear, for mixing with American, in order to reduce the cost. The mixture of the longer stapled American cotton appears to have the effect of binding together the short stapled Surat, and enables the use of Surat for yarns of such fineness, as the Surat alone would not advantageously make. The great prejudice against Surat, independently of its short staple, arises from its being so very foul, that in the process of cleansing, it loses fully twice as much as American, that is,—the 16 oz. of American yields 14 oz. of yarn, the 16 oz. of Surat only 12 oz. of yarn; and this, of course, reacts on prices.

"Secondly, as regards the future consumption of East India cotton, provided it can be sent into the market in an improved state. And here, at the outset, I think it desirable to point your attention to the state of the cotton market in Manchester at this time, and to contrast it with the state of the market at the time you made your inquiries there, as affording some explanation of the difference between the opinions given you and the very decided and general opinions I received, that a very largely increased quantity of cleaned Surats could be advantageously used." Again, "decidedly, that if Surats could be brought to the market like the sample I showed them, a very largely increased quantity would be consumed."

Of the three samples which Mr. Burch took, the second, cleaned by the saw-gin, was not approved so well as the first, (the churka-cleaned.) "It was a general opinion, that the staple had been shortened or cut in the cleaning, which, whether it may have arisen from the inexperience of the manipulators, or that the saw-gin is unsuited to the staple, is a subject worthy attentive consideration."

"The other two samples, the churkaed Surat and the saw-ginned Am-Surat, gave great satisfaction. The Am-Surat was stated to be equal in quality to good American Boweds, and to be then worth in the market from 7¾*d.* to 8*d.* per lb.—suited, in fact, for all purposes for which that quality of American cotton is used. The other sample was stated to be worth from 5¾*d.* to 6*d.*, and several Oldham manufacturers who examined it stated, that they would much rather use that than the waste they consume so largely. Some persons, indeed, would at first scarcely believe it to be Surat, from its appearance being so different to the ordinary Surat of the market.

"In order to be as definite as possible, I endeavoured to learn what quantity of cotton was now worked up for the more common purposes, such as the Surat I showed would be applicable to; and on this point I asked the opinion of a considerable number of manufacturers and others. The general opinion appeared to be, that rather more than one third of the whole quantity consumed in this country was used for such purposes,—say, in numbers, about 600,000 bales. I endeavoured then to obtain opinions as to the quantity that could be disposed of at a fair price in the market, provided it could be supplied equal in quality to the two well-cleaned kinds I showed, and stating at the same time, that 3½*d.* would pay all concerned in the production and importation. The answer I received from several was: 'Any quantity.' I requested, however, something more definite, and received a decided opinion, from parties of standing, which was countenanced by others, that the market could take 10,000 bales per week of each kind. Others, however, appeared to think 20,000 bales per week a very large quantity, but that a great increase might and would undoubtedly take place. It was stated, that the manufacturers of this country could now take 35,000 bales per week, and could rid the quantity of goods produced without overloading the markets; and if they had a full supply of cotton at a moderate price, from the natural consequent development of manufacture, that consumption would speedily increase.

"This kind of information, you will perceive, was precisely what you required; and I accordingly endeavoured to obtain opinions so extensively, that, in giving you my own impressions, I should not be liable to mislead you.

"I think there is no doubt whatever, that if cotton, such as my samples, can be delivered in this country at a moderate price, there would be a very largely increased consumption of the Surat, and that the Am-Surat would enter fairly into competition with the American; and there would be a large consumption of that also.

"Firstly, from improvement in the cotton itself. I feel quite justified in expressing my belief, from the reception which your samples received, and the opinions expressed by manufacturers who were actually at present using the Surat in quantity, that there would be a great increase in consumption; to what extent is of course hypothetical. Although the Oldham manufacturers stated that they would *prefer* using Surat, such as my sample, yet the 'waste' American would not be thrown away. By way, however, of giving a definite opinion, I will say, that the ordinary consumption of Surat cotton would, as a consequence of improvement and cleanliness, be immediately increased to 300,000 bales per year; that is to say, its better standing in the market, consequent on its improvement, would, under the *present* development of manufacture, and, leaving out of consideration the present dearth of cotton, give it legitimately that increased ordinary sale, at satisfactory prices relatively with other kinds of cotton, and at such price relatively with the foul Surat, as would repay the additional care and labour bestowed on it.

"Secondly, from development of manufactures. The continued increase in the cotton manufacture, although not constant from year to year, has, as regards periods of several years, assumed the importance of a recognised and established fact, and is fairly entitled to be taken into consderation and allowed in any estimate of future circumstances. Nothing is more likely to assist manufactures than a free supply of good and cheap cotton; and, although the staple of the cotton from the indigenous plant of India appears only suited for the commonest purposes, yet it is, perhaps, for those purposes,—for the supply of the million,—that the greatest development of manufacture may be expected. Of course, in the lower class of manufactures, cheapness is a most essential consideration, and this recommendation the Indian cotton possesses in an eminent degree; for it appears it can be brought to this market as cheap or cheaper than any other kind. It is, therefore, a fair inference, that in the development of manufactures, the Surat cotton will bear its full share of increase, varying, of course, from year to year, but still a progressive average. It is, I think, quite within the mark, to state the probable average increase on an improved Surat cotton at 40,000 bales per year for several years; but of course it will depend much on the amount of increase from other quarters."

"The third part of my communication has reference to the price which, in the future, may probably be obtained for East Indian cotton in this market.

"Taking the general range of prices for several years past, I endeavoured to learn if there was a fair prospect that such improved Surat as my sample would fetch an average of 3½*d.* or over. My impression, from what I gathered, was, that the average would be over 3½*d.*, in perhaps the following manner:—Suppose a period of six years; it might be expected that the price one year would be 3*d.*; two years, 3½*d.*; two years, 4*d.*; and one year, 5*d.*; which, you will observe, will give an average of nearly 4*d.*, without mentioning the present extreme price, which, as I stated before, was 5¾*d.* to 6*d.*

"If a large supply of clean Surats could be now delivered in the market, there is no doubt that it would restrain the price of American. The effect would be felt in qualities for which the Surats are not applicable. The Surat at 5*d.* would be mixed with Orleans at 8*d.*; the 8*d.* Orleans would be mixed with other cotton at 1*s.*; and the 1*s.* would be mixed with higher qualities. This process of mixing is always carried on to a greater extent when cotton is high; and as by this means the pressure for American would be lessened, the effect would be, to restrain the prices generally.

"But there appears, besides what I have noticed, and beyond the ordinary effect produced on prices by the fluctuations of supply and demand, to be a general and gradual fall in the prices of commodities all over the world, and which has continued for a great many years.

"I see no reason to expect otherwise, and think, therefore, it would be hazardous to give an opinion, that the cotton of India will continue, for any *great* length of time, to bear the prices it has hitherto borne. If the general depreciation continue, its price must necessarily fall with the prices of other commodities.

With respect to the obstacles which interfere with a regular supply of improved cotton from India, Mr. Burch observes:

"Of these, I think the most important consideration is the last-named. Having had the benefit of reading the first portion of your essay, it does appear to me, that the difficulties of the case are such as can only be met, either by small efforts gradually increased in a great length of time, or be successfully combated immediately by a powerful combination here, which should be enabled to trade and contract with the natives of India for their cotton, paying them fair remunerating rates, encouraging the most industrious by assistance, taking them as much as possible out of the hands of the small adulterating factors, establishing depôts, and in all cases examining the cotton, and giving certificates of cleanliness, to accompany it into the market."

§ 42. Alleged Impediments to the Increased Supply of Cotton.

In the concluding paragraph of the above statement, it is evident that Mr. Burch refers to a preceding part of this work (p. 91), where the author has treated of "the difficulties of improving Indian cotton." The great difficulty is the indifference of the cultivators themselves to what others consider of great importance, that is, to keeping the cotton clean when it has been grown, whether carefully or not. Even if they require their cotton for domestic use, they will rather subject themselves to the expenditure of extra time and labour in cleaning it, than take a little trouble in picking it carefully and in keeping it clean. When the cotton which they grow is intended for sale, the ryots have little enough encouragement to bestow more care, either in growing or in picking their cotton, for they usually get no better price for a good and clean, than they do for an indifferent article. The native purchasers not valuing clean cotton as a commodity that will bring a higher price, but as one that will bear a greater degree of adulteration. In the accounts of Tinnivelly and of Broach, we have seen the extent to which the evil has reached, so as, in the latter, to require the interposition of the authorities. But systematic adulteration ought to be punished by fine and confiscation wherever it is practised.

The only effective remedy for this and for most of the other difficulties which prevent the extension and improvement of cotton culture is the settlement in cotton districts of Europeans or their properly instructed agents, who would encourage the natives to grow their cotton with more care and unmixed with other injurious crops, as well as pick it as clean as possible off the bushes, and then separate the seeds, either with the small saw-gins or the most efficient of the churkas, and this without allowing the admixture of dirt from whatever source; or the planter may purchase the seed cotton, and himself clean it with some of the larger instruments. The advanced price which such cotton will always command in the home market will allow of a higher degree of remuneration being given to the cultivator by the European or his agent; the more especially as he will be able to absorb the profits now derived by the series of middlemen. This course has been recommended as the only one likely to be beneficial by almost every one who has written on and is practically acquainted with the subject. The same parties would be able to encourage the ryots to try the culture of American cotton in all suitable situations, and be able, if they would study the principles of culture, to ascertain the causes of any failures, and point out how these might in future be avoided. The same parties might further act as agents for the transmission, from the coast into the interior, of European and other goods. This is already a profitable trade, and might, no doubt, be greatly extended.

One impediment, that of roads, is so frequently mentioned, and no doubt operates as an obstacle in some districts, an agent could not himself remedy, but representations to the local governments would not be without effect, when so much attention is paid to the subject. But though the author would be sorry to write one word which could be construed as being in opposition to one of the first essentials for improving the resources of a country, that is, the making of good or of passable roads, yet the difficulties appear to the author, from extreme cases being taken, to have been greatly exaggerated. For the cotton crops being grown in the rainy season, and the cotton ripened in the dry weather, it is during this season that traffic takes place, and before the accession of the usual rains; less substantial roads therefore are sufficient for traffic in most instances, as has been stated by many, well acquainted with India. In America great difficulties are frequently experienced in consequence of the traffic from the farms to rivers or railways taking place in the beginning of winter, when the roads have been described to the author as being frequently in an almost impassable state, and such as would entail considerable expense if the planter did not employ his farm cattle at a time when they can do no other work, in conveying the cotton. Other things besides roads require to be taken into consideration. This subject has been already referred to (p. 60), and the districts there mentioned have been subsequently treated of in detail. We have seen that many districts near the coast, though this is the most favorable situation, produce no cotton, while others at a distance from it, whence the cost of carriage is considerable, make it their principal culture. Thus in Bengal, where the natives are anxious to cultivate cotton, and the Government have made experiments for a number of years, it has not yet been grown as a profitable crop, though it is cultivated in the far distant North-western and Central provinces, whence it used to be, and still is, brought, though in smaller quantities, for the weavers of Bengal and of Benares. In the Bombay Presidency again, the districts of Broach and of Scinde produce cotton, while the equally maritime districts of Tannah and of Rutnagherry produce none. So in the country above the Ghauts, the districts of Poona and Ahmednuggar, though having the advantage of one of the best made roads, grow but small quantities of cotton, while Candeish and Dharwar, which are the least easily accessible of the Bombay districts, are those which are making the most strenuous efforts to grow American cotton. So also in the Madras Presidency we see Coimbatore and Tinnivelly famed as cotton districts, while others which lie along the coasts produce little or no cotton, though it is brought from the distant province of Bellary, even over what are described as bad roads. The territories of Nagpore and of the Nizam, constituting a great part of Central India, grow larger quantities, though this has to be carried on bullocks, whence this is usually adduced as the ordinary mode of conveying cotton in India, though, as has been seen, it is the exception, and not the rule. The construction of cart roads through the territories of both the above powers and through those of the Company, would no doubt greatly benefit the cotton trade of Central India until a railway can be constructed.

According to other statements, however, the fiscal regulations or the land rent or tax, as it is called, forms the greatest of all the impediments to the culture of cotton in India. From the confidence with which the statements are made, it is difficult to suppose that they can be otherwise than well founded, and yet nothing can be more contradictory than the statements of others who are certainly as well acquainted with the subject. The high rate of this land rent or tax, as it is called, and the varying demand from year to year are stated as the great obstacles to cultivation, and would certainly prove so if they were founded in fact. But other authorities state that the so-called land-tax is kept within the limits of a fair rent, and that the only changes which are made at the annual settlements are remissions on account of failures of crops or on account of land not having been cultivated which had been taken up for cultivation. The only way to reconcile these contradictory statements is to suppose, what no doubt is true of some instances, that exceptions occurring in particular localities are adduced as the general rule of the country, and that descriptions which were applicable to some other localities many years ago are not so at the present time; because, as the author is well aware, changes have been made and are constantly going on, and not the less judiciously because they are effected by degrees and in comparative silence. The author is himself personally acquainted only with the Bengal Presidency, in the lower provinces of which the permanent settlement exists, but as far as he has ever been able to learn, not much to the benefit of the actual cultivators of the soil, who may have their rents increased by the Zemindar under whom they rent, and between whom only and the Government is the settlement permanent. In the north-west provinces the settlements used to be for five years; but since the author was there, the thirty years' settlement has been introduced, much to the satisfaction of the cultivators, and it has conduced so much to the extension of cultivation as to cause the country to appear to be "spoilt" in the eyes of sportsmen. But even previous to the thirty years' settlement, the author received the rent of three villages for the support of the Saharunpore Botanic Garden for a series of years without any increase or decrease. The districts of the Bombay Presidency were under a different system, but there also long leases are being introduced as fast as the means will allow, as is fully explained in the printed "Official Correspondence on the System of Revenue and Assessment in the Bombay Presidency." In the Madras Presidency again, both a permanent and a ryotwar system exists. Respecting the effects of the latter, opinions are as discrepant as on other points. As there is considerable difficulty in understanding so complicated a subject, and which varies so much in different parts of India, the author considers himself fortunate in having been able to induce a gentleman who thoroughly understands the subject to favour the public and himself with the following *general* statement on the Land Revenue of India, in which many of the difficulties of the subject are clearly explained.

NOTE ON THE LAND REVENUE OF INDIA.

As the circumstance that a large proportion of the revenue of British India is derived from an assessment on the land, (commonly, but erroneously, designated a Land-*Tax*,) has been urged as one of the principal impediments to the extension of the growth of Cotton for the supply of the European markets, it may be desirable to devote a few pages to a consideration of the effects which such a mode of obtaining revenue is calculated to produce.

The land assessment of India has its foundation in the immemorial practice of all Oriental States to reserve a portion of the produce of the soil to defray the expenditure of the Government. From the most ancient Hindoo records which have descended to us, it would appear that the right of the sovereign to demand from the cultivator of the soil one-sixth of the produce, in ordinary times, was unquestioned; and that, in the event of war, this proportion might be increased to one fourth.* The Mohammedan conquerors of India, finding the latter rate in force at the time of the country coming under their dominion, are stated to have constituted one fourth of the produce as the standard assessment; but, although the proportions above given are undoubtedly to be found in the works of the most ancient law-givers, it may reasonably be doubted whether they were ever adhered to in practice; and, at all events, it is certain that by various names and under different pretences, abwabs or cesses were, from time to time, added to the original assessment, by which the pressure on the cultivator was materially augmented.

The Government share of the produce was doubtless originally collected in kind, and converted into money through the agency of contractors or farmers of the revenue. The exaction of a fixed share of the produce of all lands, however varying in fertility, must obviously operate with great inequality. Suppose a piece of land to be capable of producing in average years a crop of 400 bushels of grain by the application of an amount of labour which would require the consumption of 200 bushels to maintain it in efficiency, while another piece of land of inferior quality would, by the application of the same quantity of labour, yield a return of only 240 bushels; it is clear that the former would, under the exaction of one fourth of the produce, leave a balance remaining to the cultivator of 100 bushels, while the latter would actually entail on him a loss. Circumstances of this description would be felt in practice long before the principles on which they depended were clearly perceived; and it is not improbable that such considerations, in addition to the obvious convenience to the Government of obtaining its revenue in cash, instead of produce, might have led to the conversion of the shares of grain into assessments in money, by which means the anomalies inseparable from the sharing system might also in some measure be corrected.

It must be remembered that in India, as in other Asiatic

* One fourth of the crops, being the amount of tax leviable during war, is represented by the Greek historians to have been the proportion contributed by the cultivators to the sovereign at the time of Alexander's invasion of India.

countries, the rent of land has never, strictly speaking, been private property. Although the soil itself may have been considered the property of individuals, the rent, or more correctly, a share of the produce, has always been regarded as the fund from which all public expenditure was to be defrayed. The distinctive feature of all the changes which, within the last few years, have been introduced into the revenue administration of India, consists in the important fact that the assessment, instead of being based on the gross produce of the soil, has been laid on the net rental, without reference to the nature or quantity of the actual produce in any given year. The cultivator is consequently at liberty to grow any crop he pleases, without the demand of Government being in any way affected thereby. It would be beside our present purpose to pursue the subject further; but, considering that the principle acknowledged and constantly inculcated by the home Government, and sedulously followed out by the authorities in India, that the assessment should be always kept within the rent; and admitting the now universally recognized position of our political economists, that rent does not enter into the price of agricultural products, it seems incontrovertible that a system of revenue administration which demands only a portion of the rent cannot raise the price of produce, an effect which the exaction of the entire rent, on the part of individual land-holders, would not produce.

Where, as in a great portion of British India, the revenue is paid to the officer of Government directly by the occupier of the soil, the assessment may amount to the whole rent, leaving to the cultivator only the means of subsistence after defraying his farming expenses, without having any tendency to limit cultivation. In other parts, where an intermediate agency exists, and where the revenue is received into the Treasury through the hands of middlemen, designated Zemindars, Talookdars, &c., it is requisite that the amount demanded by the State should leave a sufficient profit to compensate them for the risk and trouble of collection, the actual contributors being at the same time secured by law from undue exactions. In respect to the ryots, the class who live by the cultivation of the land, the objects to be kept constantly in view are: First, that the demand should be moderate, in short, that it should be kept strictly within the limits of the rent which they could afford under average circumstances to pay to a landlord, whether Government or Zemindar. To secure moderation, the rate should be fixed at an amount considerably below that which a general survey or examination of the lands would seem to point out as a proper assessment; and no safer guide in this respect can probably be found than the ascertainment of what the lands had previously paid for a series of years. The inequalities of a moderate assessment will soon become adjusted by an alteration in the marketable value of the lands; but over-assessment, or, in other words, placing on the land a demand in excess of the natural rent, can only end in absorbing the capital of the cultivators, and in their consequent impoverishment and ruin; and in the loss to the State of the revenue which it had previously derived from the produce of those lands which its exactions had thrown out of cultivation.

Secondly, it is essential that the demand should not be liable to increase at the pleasure of the Government; that, at the least, before the commencement of the cultivating season, the ryot should know with certainty what he will be called upon to pay for the occupation of his lands during the ensuing year. On this circumstance must depend his calculations of profit; with this knowledge he is in the position of a tenant farmer in England, holding his lands from year to year. An arrangement of this sort is absolutely necessary, as no man can be expected to exert himself to cultivate his lands to the best advantage, if he feels that any surplus, which he may obtain over and above his immediate wants, is liable to be torn from him at the pleasure of the revenue officer. In such a case, with the rents fixed from year to year, the land would have no tendency to go out of cultivation; but, at the same time, the demand being fixed only for the year, the ryot would have no inducement to expend money in improving his holding, so as to increase its productive powers, the demand of the State being liable to be increased in the event of his farm being permanently improved. It would, therefore, appear to consist with good policy to give to all occupiers of the soil an interest of such duration as to induce them to expend capital in its improvement, by affording them the opportunity of reimbursing themselves the money so applied with reasonable profits.

A permanent money settlement, like that in operation in Bengal, is in fact permanent only as against the State. Assuming that, at its commencement, an Estate produces to the Zemindar an income equivalent to 10,000 rupees, he agreeing to pay 8000 rupees in silver to Government, thus leaving him a profit of 2000 rupees; so long as the relative values of silver and agricultural produce remain unaltered, he may continue to hold his estate, and pay his revenue; if silver should fall in value 100 per cent. relatively to agricultural produce, he would be in the receipt of 20,000 rupees per annum; while the sum covenanted to be paid to the Government would remain the same, and his profit would amount to 12,000 rupees per annum; but if, on the other hand, silver should rise in value 50 per cent., the same money payment of 8000 rupees would still be due from him, while the proceeds of his estate would amount in money only to 5000 rupees. Under this arrangement, the Zemindar has all the advantages of a change of circumstances, while the Government must of necessity submit to all the loss.

The general principle on which the land revenue is based, having been thus stated, it may be desirable to describe, as briefly as possible, the different systems at present in force in the various parts into which our Indian territory is divided, so as to give the reader the means of judging how far those systems accord with the principles suggested in the foregoing remarks.

In the permanently settled Provinces of Bengal, Behar, Orissa, and Benares, the assessment is fixed only as regards the payments to be made by the great landholders* to the State. The actual cultivators of the soil, although their hereditary right to hold their lands at the ancient rates is professedly guaranteed to them by the law, are, in fact, merely tenants at will; the Zemindars have no difficulty in ejecting

* Sudder Malgoozars, or those who pay their revenue directly, and without any intermediate agency, into the collector's treasury. The amounts so paid are in some instances small, but, generally speaking, include the dues of a large number of cultivators. The fixed revenue paid to Government by the Rajah of Burdwan, for his Zemindary, amounts to about £200,000 sterling per annum.

them from their holdings, by raising their rents to an amount which they are unable to pay; and, knowing the extreme reluctance of the cultivators of India to quit the lands which their forefathers tilled, and aware that they would submit to any exaction rather than be forced to such an extremity, there can be little doubt (and *no* doubt seems to be entertained by those whose local knowledge best qualifies them to form a judgment on the matter), that the rents actually paid by the ryots to the Zemindars in the settled provinces are exorbitant, although, from the best information which it has been possible to obtain, there is the greatest reason to believe that the revenue paid by the Zemindars to the government falls short of one half of the gross rental. It is, nevertheless, under this system where the actual cultivators are rack-rented, while the landlords pay to Government a fixed revenue, said to amount to only four annas, or six pence per beegah, that the production of indigo and opium, the great exportable staples of the Bengal Provinces, has increased to an extent which can scarcely find a parallel, except in the instance of the supply of cotton from the United States of America. It would here be out of place to discuss the merits of the measure usually known as the Permanent Settlement of Bengal. The intentions of its framers were doubtless in the highest degree pure and benevolent; but there can be little question that it accomplished a revolution in the state of landed property greater than was probably ever effected by any measure of Government in any other country, and that the immemorial rights of the ryots to the possession of their ancestral lands were effectually destroyed, and handed over by due process of law to the Zemindars, with whom alone the settlement was made. The right of the Khoodkast ryot to occupy his lands on the payment to the state of a moderate assessment, can scarcely admit of a doubt; while it is, to say the least, extremely questionable whether the Zemindar, whom our laws have constituted the possessor of the soil, had, in fact, any proprietary interest whatever in the land included in his Zemindary, and whether he was anything more than the farmer or collector of the revenue, remunerated by a commission on the amount remitted to the treasury, and as such, entitled doubtless to a fair compensation for the loss of the profits of which he was deprived by the introduction of a new system of revenue administration.

In the north-western Provinces of the Presidency of Bengal, extending from the boundary of the permanently-settled districts to the north-western frontier of our Indian empire, the system now in force differs materially from that just described, in so far as the rights of the actual proprietors and cultivators of the soil are concerned. In this portion of territory a regular survey and classification of the lands have been carried out; an assessment has been formed on the data thus obtained, with especial reference to the rates of rent actually prevailing in the districts, and the amount thus ascertained has been declared unalterable for a term of thirty years. Unlike, however, the hasty and little considered arrangements preliminary to the Permanent Settlement of Bengal, the determination of the assessment was preceded by an inquiry into the rights of all the parties claiming a beneficial interest in the land or its produce; these rights have been recorded, and the records thus framed are available for the decision of questions which may hereafter arise before either the revenue or judicial authorities: the settlements have been made either with the superior holders (Talookdars), or with the actual proprietors (Zemindars),* as circumstances might render expedient. In the former case, the amount to be paid to government by the Talookdars has been determined, while, at the same time, the rates which they are at liberty to demand from the Zemindars or under-tenants, have been also fixed and recorded; in the latter case, where it has been thought proper to exclude the Talookdar from the management of the land, an allowance under the name of Huq Talookdaree,

* Much of the confusion which exists with regard to Indian revenue affairs arises from the same term being used in different parts of India to designate classes of persons, possessing a totally different interest in the land. In Bengal proper, the Zemindar is the large proprietor, with whom the permanent settlement was made, and who pays a fixed revenue to Government; in the North-West Provinces, the Zemindar is the resident cultivator, possessing a proprietary interest in the soil, and commonly paying his revenue through the medium of a Talookdar; in the Madras Provinces, the term is not commonly used, except in the Northern Circars, when it generally denotes a person holding much the same relation to the Government as the Zemindar of Bengal: while, under the Bombay Presidency, the word is used exclusively to designate the persons holding hereditary district or village offices, such as those of Patell, Koolkurnee, Tullatie, &c.

has been assigned to him for the period of the settlement, amounting generally, in the first instance, to about 18 per cent. of the net revenue, but liable to be reduced at the expiration of the present term of settlement to 10 per cent.

In these Provinces the amount in money to be paid to the State by landholders of all classes is fixed for thirty years, but at the expiration of that period the assessment will be subject to modification, either in the way of increase or decrease; and in determining this question, one of the main elements to be considered, will be the rise or fall of price of the principal agricultural products. With this view a register of prices has been ordered to be kept in all the districts. In some parts, from different causes, such as the diminution of population by previous wars, the imperfect cultivation of the land owing to the want of industry or agricultural skill of the castes by which they are principally inhabited, or other similar circumstances, the lands are known to be assessed at a rate below their actual capabilities, and in such case they may fairly be subjected to a higher payment on the revision of the settlement without any undue pressure on the population. It is believed, however, to be the opinion of those most conversant with the subject, that on the expiration of the present term of settlement, no very material change is likely to be required.

It must, however, be borne in mind, that, although the present settlements will probably not be much disturbed, a considerable increase of revenue may be looked for from the waste lands, which will, in course of time, as population increases, be brought into cultivation, and more especially from the effects of the vast works of irrigation now in progress, such as the Ganges canal (the estimated cost of which is about a million and a half sterling), and from the canals in the Punjab and elsewhere, by which the water necessary for cultivation will be secured to immense tracts of land, now entirely dependent on the uncertain supply of the monsoon rains, and for the benefits of which the cultivators willingly pay a water-rent, more than sufficient to compensate the Government for the cost of the original construction and the annual maintenance of the works in a state of efficiency. Throughout these Provinces, it is believed that the effect of the settlement has been, to fix on the lands a payment to the State of about two thirds of the gross rental.*

In most of the Provinces subordinate to the Presidency of Madras, the mode of obtaining a revenue from the land differs materially from those which have just been described. The ryotwarry system, as it is commonly called, in contradistinction to the zemindary system, is a term which implies simply that the Government deals directly with the ryots or proprietary cultivators, instead of collecting the revenue due from their lands through the agency of middlemen, such as Zemindars, Talookdars, &c. It is obvious, that the mere circumstance of the revenue being levied directly from the cultivators, instead of through intermediate agency, does not necessarily render the pressure of the assessment more burdensome. But it must be remembered, that when the Zemindar or Talookdar has his own payments to Government fixed, and his receipts from the under-tenants undetermined and liable to increase, he has a strong temptation to raise his rents to the utmost; while the officer of Government, who has the management of a ryotwar district, has no similar interest, except in so far as the realization of an increased revenue may be supposed to raise his character in the estimation of his official superiors. The power which he possesses in this respect is extremely limited, and, whatever may have occasionally, though rarely, occurred in the earlier periods of our rule, when the true principles of revenue administration were but imperfectly understood, no collector could now hope to recommend himself to the Government by such means.

The Madras revenue system (not including the Northern Circars, and some other portions of the Presidency which were settled on permanent rents, but, from failure of payment, are gradually falling into the hands of Government, and, as they lapse, are being assessed on the ryotwar principle,) differs from those previously described in the following respects. The agency of middlemen is dispensed with, and every cultivator who has a proprietary interest in the soil pays his revenue directly to Government. The land is classified, first, as irri-

* A clear and trustworthy account of the mode in which the revised settlement of the North-Western Provinces was formed, and of its results, may be found in an able paper, published in the '*Calcutta Review*,' and since reprinted in a separate form.

gated and unirrigated, and then according to its various degrees of fertility; a fixed rate is applied to every class of land, which is not subject to alteration so long as the land remains in the class assigned to it by the survey records. Lands not cultivated, or not engaged for at the commencement of the cultivating season, are subject to no payment to the State.

In explanation of what is above stated, it is necessary to observe, that lands classed in the collector's books as *wet* or irrigated land, and as such liable to a certain rate of assessment, are entitled to be relieved from that payment if the means of irrigation fail, and at once fall, either permanently or temporarily, into the class of *dry* or unirrigated land. On the other hand, land recorded as *dry*, or not subject to natural or artificial irrigation, may be raised to the class of wet land, if means are found for supplying it with water. If those means are furnished by the State, as, for instance, by tanks or canals, the land is at once liable to be subjected to the higher rate of assessment. If, on the other hand, the means are supplied by the proprietor, the land continues to be held by him at the original rate, until a sufficient time shall have elapsed to compensate him fully for the outlay which he may have incurred in improving his property.

The assessment on lands, which, although engaged for, are not, from the state of the season, brought under cultivation, or have failed to produce a remunerative crop, is, at the discretion of Government, guided by the reports of the local authorities, under the Hookumnamah, or general cultivation rules for the district, entirely or partially remitted.

The circumstances above briefly noticed are those which render necessary what has been called the annual settlement of the districts under the Madras Presidency, an arrangement which seems to have produced a general impression that the government assessment is liable to yearly variation, and that it is in fact raised or lowered at the sole pleasure of the revenue officer. This impression is, however, altogether the reverse of the truth. The rates on all classes of land are fixed for ever; and so long as the land remains in the same condition, the settlement is as permanent as that of Bengal, although made with the ryots or cultivators instead of with zemindars or middlemen. All cultivated land, whether *wet* or *dry*, is subject to a certain assessment, the amount of which is equally well known to the cultivators and the revenue officers; the latter have no power whatever to increase the government demand; but, under certain recognised regulations, they have the power to remit the whole or a portion of it. The so-called annual settlement under the Madras Presidency, to which much undue importance has been attached, has for its object merely the ascertainment of the extent to which the government demand ought, under the particular circumstances of the season as brought to the notice of the government officer, to be reduced or altogether abandoned, and never (except in the occasional case of land being cultivated, and the knowledge of it fraudulently withheld from the revenue authorities,) that of increasing that demand. In short it differs little from the *audit* of a landlord in this country, when the tenantry, unable from loss of crops through adversity of season, from fall of prices, or from other causes, are unable to pay the stipulated rents, and are allowed such a remission as the landlord or his agent may deem equitable and conducive to the interests of both parties.

Under the Presidency of Bombay, a different system again prevails. Until a comparatively recent period, the revenue administration of this portion of country was based on that which we found established under the native governments to which we succeeded. Little more was done than to correct abuses, to remedy inequalities, and to consolidate into one demand the various cesses which, under different names, had been added to the original assessment, and, in particular, to endeavour to make the amount payable by the ryot fixed and determinate, so as to leave him no longer at the mercy of the native revenue officers. To do more than this, a regular survey and assessment of the whole country was required; and the peculiar talents and qualifications requisite for such a task were not easily to be found. For several years, however, this operation has been in active progress; and the entire success which has followed its execution, so far as it has yet been carried, redounds greatly to the credit of the officers concerned in its execution. This most important operation has now been completed in the Collectorates of Belgaum, Dharwar, Poona, Sholapore, and, to some extent, in others; and, as means for its prosecution are found available, is being gradually extended to the districts to the northward of the Presidency.

Under the revised system, the lands of every village are in the first instance accurately measured and classified, field by field; when these operations are completed, the settling officer has the more difficult task of fixing the rates to be applied to all the various classes of land, as determined by the survey. In fixing these rates, he takes into consideration those paid in the adjoining districts, making due allowance for any disturbing circumstances, such as the greater or less regularity in the recurrence of the periodical rains, the nature of the soil, the vicinity of large markets, and having particular regard also to the amount actually collected under the former system from the district in preceding years, so far as authentic records supply the information. The rates proposed by the settlement officer, are reported through the proper channels to Government, with the reasons on which his estimate of the capabilities of the district is based; and if those reasons are considered satisfactory, the settlement receives the sanction of Government, and is confirmed for a period of thirty years, at the expiration of which term it will be again subject to revision. The rates, thus fixed, are applied to every field in the district, according to its previously ascertained measurement and classification. Each field is assessed at a fixed sum, not liable to alteration for a term of thirty years, and demandable only when the field is cultivated. The owner may improve it in any manner by the application of his labour or capital, all the advantages accruing therefrom for the term of thirty years being entirely at his own disposal, without any inquiry or interference on the part of the officers of Government. At the expiration of that time, the State may, if it see fit, claim a share in the benefits arising from those improvements; but even in this case the Bombay ryot, in the revised districts, is on no worse footing than that of a farmer in European countries holding his lands on a thirty years' lease.

In the unrevised districts of Bombay, the information relative to the state of the land revenue is less complete and satisfactory. The assessments are in many cases unequal, if not excessive, and lead to the necessity of large annual remissions, which are not strictly dependent on fixed rules, as in the Madras Provinces, but give great scope to the discretion of the collector, and, it may be feared, to the venality of the inferior revenue officers. There is, however, the strongest ground for assuming that, even in those districts, the land revenue does not operate as an obstacle to the production of cotton, whatever its effect may be on the general well-being of the agricultural classes. In the great cotton-growing Province of Broach, the assessment is confessedly high, and urgently requires revision, which, even if it did not lead to a reduction of the aggregate amount, would certainly tend to correct inequalities which are acknowledged to exist. Yet even here, the high assessment has no effect in reducing the cultivation of cotton. Under the system of rotation of crops prevailing in this province, cotton should be grown in the same soil only once in three years; but the cultivation returns show that more than one-third of the area of the district is every year devoted to that description of cultivation. The statements officially furnished by the local officers are to the effect that, under the present system of agriculture, the supply of cotton from Broach cannot be materially increased. The diminished importation of cotton from this province, which has been much dwelt on, must, therefore, be founded on some other cause than the pressure of the land revenue.

The actual rates of assessment paid in many parts of India have been already stated in this work, and it is needless to recapitulate them. The main point for consideration is whether they fall above or below the natural rent of the land. That they leave a surplus profit, and frequently a large one, to the landowner, is undoubted in the lower and north-western provinces of the Presidency of Bengal, lands brought into the market, whether by public or private sale, being always able to command a considerable price, a fact which would be inconsistent with the supposition that the demand of the State exceeded or even equalled the rental, so as to leave no profit to the purchaser. In the ryotwarry districts of the Madras and Bombay Presidencies, the transfer of lands by public sales is uncommon; but it is known that landed property is highly valued, and the proprietary rights of the Meerassedar, or owner of the land, when under any circumstances exposed to sale, seldom fail to meet with a ready purchaser. In thinly populated districts, where the extent of land is much beyond the wants of the present number of cultivators, and where the waste cultivable land is at the disposal of Government, and any person willing to embark in its cultivation may obtain it on lease (cowle,) on terms which enable him to reimburse himself all the expenses of bringing it under culture before it becomes liable to the ordinary assessment, it is probable that the old cultivated lands may not possess saleable value, although the assessment on them may be much within their capabilities of payment.

Assuming, then, that the land assessment of India is generally within, and never, save in rare and exceptional cases, in excess of the natural rent, it remains to be considered whether its amount can affect the production of cotton rather than that of any other agricultural product. Over-assessment, or in other words, the exaction of an amount beyond the natural rental, or that revenue which under ordinary circumstances the land is capable of yielding, whether to the Government or to an individual landowner, must lead to the rent being in part paid out of capital, to the consequent impoverishment of the cultivators, and to the gradual restriction of cultivation. So long, however, as the land remains in cultivation, the substitution of one kind of produce for another is no evidence of over-assessment, but is merely a proof that the new cultivation is more profitable than that previously pursued. This transfer of land from the cultivation of cotton to that of grain is stated to have taken place in the United States of America to a considerable extent, since the abolition of our restrictive Corn Law: and the same change might occur in the cotton-growing Province of Broach, without leading to any other inference than that the cultivation of grain was more profitable to the farmer than that of cotton, a result which is stated to have occurred in the adjoining district of Surat. In Broach, as has been already remarked, the acreage of land under cotton cultivation is, if not larger, as large as the recognised principles of agriculture, as applied in that district, will allow. There is little, if any, culturable land which is not already under the plough. Supposing that any given number of acres, hitherto employed in the cultivation of cotton, were transfered to the cultivation of some other product of agriculture, would it not obviously arise from the circumstance that that other product yielded a larger remunerating return to the farmer than the cotton which he had previously produced? No reduction of the assessment could affect the relative profits of the two kinds of produce. If, at an assessment of ten shillings the acre, the cultivation of cotton cannot be pursued with advantage, while that of wheat or jowarry yields a beneficial return, how can the reduction of the assessment to five shillings the acre alter the proportion between the two cultures? It is clearly impossible, —the reduction of the assessment may be a boon to the producer, if he is himself the proprietor of the land; if he is not, it will find its way, in the form of an increase of rent, to the superior landlord; but it cannot operate to induce him to cease cultivating the article which yields him the largest profit, in order to supply its place by another which is less remunerative.

These remarks lead us to observe, that rent, of which the land assessment is intended to be (and which, speaking generally, it is), only a part, cannot be created or controlled by administrative arrangements or legislative enactments. It arises naturally from the increase of population in particular localities, and the consequent augmented demand for the products of agriculture, the new comers having to work out their subsistence from lands either naturally less fertile, or less advantageously situated in relation to the means of disposing of the produce, than those previously occupied. The immemorial appropriation of a portion of this rent by the State, cannot effect the economical conditions of the payment of rent, *per se*, whether demanded by the State, or, as in occidental countries, by a class of persons called landlords. In fact, in all countries sufficiently populated to require that lands of different degrees of fertility should be brought into cultivation, in order to furnish the necessary supply of food to the population, rent arises spontaneously, and if relinquished by the State, is simply transferred to individual landowners.

In the preceding observations it has been assumed, that the land-assessment of India falls within, or at least does not exceed, the fair rental of the lands under the present circumstances of the country. If this assumption be admitted as correct, it would be useless to restate the arguments by which it may be shown that the assessment, or that portion of the rent which is paid to the Government, does not enter into the cost at which the articles cultivated on it are produced; and it will be sufficient to refer the reader to the work of most recent date and of highest authority, in which that and other cognate questions are discussed, viz., "Principles of Political Economy," by John Stuart Mill, Esq., First Edition, 1848, Book ii, chap. 16.

The conclusion to which these considerations lead, is, that the Indian land assessment is in fact no tax, and that in so far as it supplies the means of furnishing a fund for the necessary expenditure of the Government, the people are to that extent relieved from taxation. About three fifths of the whole revenue of India is derived from the land assessment, the remainder being supplied by custom-duties, an excise on salt and spirits, the opium monopoly, and some other minor items. If by the extension of cultivation, the land revenue should at some future time increase to such an amount as to enable the Government to dispense with all other sources of income, India would be in the enviable condition of defraying all its public expenditure from its own resources, while its population would be subjected to no sort of taxation whatsoever. Labour might put forth its fullest energy, and capital expand itself to the utmost without being called on for any contribution towards those expenses which in other countries are defrayed out of burdens laid on the industry, past or present, of their inhabitants.

Profits on Imports of the Experimental Cotton.

Having shown that, notwithstanding numerous failures, there has still been sufficient encouragement to warrant success being permanent, if means are adopted to ensure it, it is desirable, in taking only a general view, to show that there are reasonable grounds for expecting that the measure which we advocate, that of dealing directly with the ryots, will be profitable as well as effective. Some of the transactions, as already mentioned, have proved profitable both to the Indian Government and to individuals, even when they purchased the cotton in the Bombay market. But it is necessary to ascertain whether this was an accidental occurrence, or one which could be relied on as an ordinary circumstance, by following the course indicated. The late Chairman of the East India Company, Major-General Sir A. Galloway, shortly before his lamented death, addressed the Court of Proprietors on the subject of cotton culture in India, in the following words:

"The Court had heard a great deal about cotton cultivation in India, and had received complaints on that subject from Manchester. They had been making every exertion to promote the cultivation of cotton, and he was only astonished that they had shown so much perseverance in doing so. He was happy, however, to say that their efforts had been crowned with complete success. They had undertaken to purchase cotton from the people of India, in order to show the Manchester manufacturers that they had only to send out agents in order to do likewise, with profit to themselves. The transactions of the kind in which the Court had been engaged had realised an immense profit. For instance, 300 bales, purchased in India at £1431, had, when sold in Manchester, brought £2126. Every charge had been made, including the agent's commission, and yet there remained a profit of £695. In another instance, £5670 had been paid for a supply of cotton at Bombay, which had sold in England, deducting every expense, at £6963, thus leaving a profit of £1292. There was no subject in which the Government of India took a deeper interest than in improving the internal communication of the country, by establishing roads and railways."

The transactions to which the chairman alluded were, probably, the first to native cotton, per 'Elizabeth Jane,' from Coimbatore, in 1847; and the second to New Orleans cotton, grown in Dharwar, and shipped per 'Quentin Leitch.' These are not isolated instances. Mr. Petrie, the mechanical engineer, who put up and kept in order the cotton cleaning machines at Coimbatore, and who was also employed in purchasing cotton from the natives, and cleaning it for sending to this country, stated, in his evidence before the House of Commons' Committee, that he purchased 6 bales of cotton from the New Orleans seed, from the natives in the Coimbatore district, and that the cost and charges were £28 19*s.* 11*d.*, and the profits on the transaction were £18 0*s.* 11*d.* He stated, that he had also sent home Bourbon cotton, in 1843, and had it sold here by a broker, and that it yielded him some 20 per cent. upon the outlay. He stated, moreover, that he had several other accounts, and they all prove that the gin-cleaned cotton sells better in England than the cotton cleaned by the native method, and that "considerable profit was realized in all the cases, and in every year."

Proceeding from Coimbatore to the Dharwar district, we have seen that its cotton (by the "Quentin Leitch,") yielded profit to all concerned. Mr. Blount, in forwarding about 600 bales of the crop of the year 1848 to this country, wrote to the author, "that its cost, laid down in Liverpool, will not exceed $3\frac{1}{2}$*d.* per lb., and the native cotton $3\frac{1}{4}$*d.* This cotton, imported in the "Brahmin," was sold at Manchester,—the American for 5*d.*, and that from Belgaum for $5\frac{1}{4}$*d.*, while the indigenous Dharwar cotton sold for $4\frac{3}{4}$*d.* per lb.

The crop of 1849, which has since arrived, and which has already been mentioned as costing, the American $3\frac{78}{100}$*d.*, and the native $3\frac{1}{2}$*d.*, has not sold worse than the cotton of previous years, but, like them, has yielded a handsome profit.

With regard to the province of Guzerat, which is so completely established as a cotton country, we have seen that the crop of Broach and Surat of 1847-48 was highly esteemed in this country. The crop of 1848-49 was not less favorably thought of, for it sold in Manchester for $5\frac{1}{4}$*d.* a lb., to the extent of 427 bales, costing, as would appear from a statement by Mr. Landon, the superintendent in Broach, about 2*d.* per lb., landed in Bombay, while the Surat cotton cost not quite $2\frac{1}{4}$d., and sold for $5\frac{1}{2}$*d.* A portion of the cheapness is, no doubt, due to the diminution of expense in cleaning, for Mr. Landon says, "An average out-turn of 1755 lbs. of clean cotton by each gin per diem is without a parallel in the history of cotton cleaning in India; nor have I heard of any having been cleaned before at the low rate of Rs. 2 and 6 annas per candy of 784lbs. Each candy of this cotton cost Rs.70 9 an. "One hundred candies of the cotton from Broach was recently sold in Bombay at Rs.94 per candy, showing a net profit of Rs.23 7 an. per candy, or 33 per cent." The remainder of this cotton having been sent to England, was, as before mentioned, sold for $5\frac{1}{4}d.$ to $5\frac{1}{2}d.$ a lb., requiring, however, the charge for freight and the expenses in England to be added to those incurred for purchasing, cleaning, packing, and conveyance to Bombay. Mr. Landon has engaged to send 2000 bales of similar cotton to this country in the present year.

For the details the reader is referred to the account of the experiments in the several districts.

CONCLUSION.

Having carefully considered every point which seemed to be connected with the culture and commerce of cotton in India, and with an attention to details, which to many may appear unnecessary; we may briefly refer to a few of the conclusions at which we have arrived, in order to see what are the prospects of the cotton trade of India being placed on a more extended and yet comparatively secure basis. In these we cannot lay claim to any great novelty, for they are very similar to what may be found stated in two letters published in 'The Times' more than five years ago, which are here reprinted, in order to show that further experience has only confirmed earlier formed conclusions.*

* "COTTON CULTURE IN INDIA.

" *To the Editor of the 'Times.'*

"SIR,—In the '*Times*' of this day, which, however, I have only seen this evening, I observe an extract from the '*Washington Union*,' headed 'Cotton, the Great Staple,' in which, referring to 'the result of the celebrated experiments made by the East India Company in the cultivation of cotton in the East,' the editor says, 'The English experiment has signally failed. It was made under the most favorable auspices in different parts of India. It has succeeded in none of them.' The editor then proceeds to say, that this failure, and the annexation of Texas, make 'the greatest interest of Great Britain, the most important branch of her manufacturing system, dependent upon us. In the same proportion, of course, it gives us every advantage in competition with her. It gives us wealth in peace and power in war.' The wish, no doubt, is father to the thought; but that the song of triumph is somewhat premature, and that the editor is hallooing before he is out of the wood, I hope to show by the statement of a few facts.

"The experiment was, as the editor observes, commenced under favorable auspices

First the American and Indian cottons have been shown to belong to distinct species of plants; and that the staple of the former seems to be naturally longer and stronger than that of the latter, at least in the situations where, and modes in which they are at present respectively grown.

'by ten experienced American planters from the cotton region of the United States.' They were distributed in three parties, one to each Presidency, and in districts celebrated for the production of native cotton. It was hoped, from the great distance, nearly twenty degrees of latitude, between the extreme points, there would have been sufficient variety of soil and of climate to afford results which would be applicable to the intermediate country.

"The experiment consisted of two very distinct parts:—1st, the cleaning; 2d, the growing of cotton.

"The natives of India are well known to be careless in the picking, the cleaning, and packing of their cotton. The Indian cotton, however, has many good qualities, and would be employed by our manufacturers to a much greater extent, if it were supplied in a clean state in large quantities. The application of the American gin by Americans to the cleaning of Indian cotton has been completely successful at Coimbatore, at Dharwar, and at Broach. The cotton has been freed of leaves, of seeds, of sand and dirt to the extent of nearly one fourth, which had to be carried from the field to the factory, and upon which carriage and freight have usually to be paid, as well as upon the cotton. The operation has been performed with the skill and celerity to be expected from the experience of the Americans employed, with very little injury to the staple, and the cotton has sold in the Liverpool market at nearly the price of New Orleans cotton. I mention this fact prominently, because, without a quick and effective method of cleaning cotton, no very great or rapid extension can take place in cotton cultivation.

"With respect to the culture of American cotton in India, the success of the experiment has not been so uniform; for, though it has failed in some places, it has succeeded and is succeeding in others, and the information obtained has shown us the districts best suited to the culture. India is a country of such great extent and diversified soil and climate, that a culture which is suited to one part, is sure to fail in another, unless corresponding differences in treatment are adopted. Thus, in the north-west Provinces of Bengal, very fair native cotton is grown, and a very good return per acre is obtained; but there the American cotton plant did not succeed well, apparently owing to two very dry seasons, when rain fell for only about six weeks, instead of, as usual, for three months. But even there cotton may, I believe, be as successfully grown as in Egypt, in the same latitude, by adopting the same method, that is, irrigating the plant in proportion to the dryness of the climate; and this the great Dock (Doab) Canal, when completed, will render an easy operation. In the moist and rich parts of Bengal, the American plants run too much into leaf. This might be obviated by variation in culture; but the insects are unfortunately also very destructive to the American cotton. But even there some varieties of cotton, either indigenous or exotic, may be found suitable to the soil and climate.

"In the Madras Presidency, the experiments at Coimbatore, which is far from a favorable situation for American cotton, have been proceeding successfully; for the

One of the American species, that yielding the New Orleans cotton, now yields the great mass of the cotton of commerce, and the deficiency or excess in its crops controls the prices of all other cottons and the demand in a great measure for Indian

cultivation has been going on for some years with the acclimated American seed. The cotton remains of good quality, and the superintendant (not an American) is confident that he can carry on the cultivation with profit; and if he can do so, the natives will be still more able to do so, for they are good cultivators, and much more economical than any European.

"But none of these sites are within what is considered the true cotton district of India—that is, the country above the Ghauts, as the Mahratta country, Deccan, Candeish, Nagpore, and Hydrabad, often all comprehended in the term Central India. There the elevation of the table land, with the modifying influence of the several ranges of mountains, produces a peculiarity of climate which is equally removed from the excessive moisture of Bengal, or the parching drought of Northern India. With a favorable climate there is also abundance of the excellent cotton soil of India; and thence the cotton culture has extended almost of itself, and will go on extending in proportion to the encouragement given by the capital and energy of European merchants. About twenty years since, some excellent cotton was grown at Dharwar, in the Southern Mahratta country. One of the American planters has established himself at this place, and finds it well suited to the cultivation of American cotton. The culture, indeed, has been yearly increasing: it was at first 600 acres; then 3000; last year 7000 acres were under cultivation in the Government farms by the ryots and by some German missionaries, in different parts of the district, with New Orleans cotton. This year seed has been engaged for not less than 15,000 to 20,000 acres, and the intelligent American planter writes, that not less than a million of pounds will be produced this year. The important fact is, that the culture is increasing, and has been taken up by the natives. He further states, that the ryots find it the most profitable unirrigated crop they have, and they can sell it for about a penny a pound. They get more of the American than of their own cotton per acre, and they get a better price for it, without extra expense in cultivation. Much of what has been grown by the ryots has been bought by the Government, is being cleaned, and will be sent to Liverpool. The planter further states, that 'there is no better short-staple cotton than that of Central India, when it is fairly handled, and gets the ghost of a fair chance.'

"In conclusion, I would only remark, that as the season for sowing cotton in the different parts of India varies from June to October, intelligence might at any time be sent of any approaching necessity for extended cultivation, at the same time that the supply of Cotton for China might be diverted to this country, as well as some of that retained for consumption in India. But as all this would afford an inadequate supply, it is of vital importance to the cotton manufacture and trade of this country that it should be placed on a more stable, by having a more extended, foundation. The investment of some British capital in the cotton trade of India would have this effect; that is, if a few Europeans, or their agents, would settle in the cotton districts, make advances to the natives, induce them to pick their cotton more carefully, and to keep it clean. Gins, or cotton-cleaning machines, must at the same time be established cotton in its present condition. This, we have seen, is imported in considerable quantities when American cotton is dear, and in greatly diminished ones when the latter is abundant and cheap.

in sufficient numbers in suitable localities, as well as screws for packing. If all this were done, there is not the smallest doubt that great extension and improvement would take place in the cotton culture of India, especially if one of the numerously-projected railways were to pass into the cotton district, and bring the cotton to the sea-coast in a few days, instead of, as is now the case, some months after the crop has been collected, by which a whole season is yearly lost. A great impression would be produced, and felt, perhaps, even in America, and the English merchant and manufacturer rendered much more independent, not only of war (which the American editor has mentioned), but also, as America is 'cursed with slave labour,' of the civil commotions and slave insurrections, which are among the possible contingencies, and to which he has not alluded. Trusting that you will excuse this lengthened epistle, on account of the importance of the subject,

"I have the honour to be, your obedient servant,

"INDOPHILUS.

"LONDON; *Nov.* 30, 1845.

"CULTURE AND COMMERCE OF COTTON IN INDIA.

"*To the Editor of the Times.*

"SIR,—In the '*Times*' of the 22d of November appeared a letter, headed 'East India Cotton,' and signed 'Amicus,' in which I hardly recognised my cognomen, as it is printed 'Judophilus,' especially as the writer ascribes to me a statement, of which I can see no traces in my letter, that is, that 'the Anti-Slavery Society was about to move in this matter.' I would, however, beg permission to correct a misprint in my letter, that of 'Dock' for Doab Canal, as it gives me an opportunity of alluding to that work, which is to irrigate a belt of country five miles in breadth and several hundred in length, from or near Hurdwar to Allahabad. It was surveyed and reported on by Captain Cautley, superintendent of canals, recommended by Lord Auckland, and sanctioned by the Court of Directors, in the midst of the difficulties of the Affghan war. It is to be hoped that it has not since dragged its slow length along because it has been thought needless. It appears to me the greatest of the works of peace which has ever been entered on in the East, as it will, under Providence, render famines impossible in the north-west provinces, and facilitate the culture of cotton, sugar, corn, &c.; at the same time that it will, I believe, improve the climate,—inasmuch as it would diminish the degree of transition from the furnace-like aridity of the hot weather, to the hothouse moisture of the rainy season.

"With respect to the substance of your correspondent's letter, there is no doubt that India produces abundance of cotton. Its millions of inhabitants are clothed in home-grown cotton—in the hot weather in calico and muslins; in the winter in cotton-padded coats. Instead of blankets they cover themselves with quilts, and in place of doors and glazed windows they hang up curtains padded with cotton; while

In a former part of this work (p. 64), which was finished at the beginning of the year 1850, it was stated, that "we have no doubt that, in the present year, they (that is, the imports of Indian cotton,) will be as high as they have ever been;" and,

tents and tent-ropes, covered carriages, the housings of elephants and of horses, are all made of cotton cloth, besides its being applied to a variety of other purposes,—all indicating a very large production of this Indian necessary of life, in addition to the surplus provided for export to this country and to China.

"If each village, therefore, that now grows cotton, were to increase its cultivation to a small extent, its supply would, even in a single season, be enormously increased. An improvement in the price might effect this. The encouragement of companies or of individuals might, in a short time, produce it, and perhaps to a much greater extent, by confining their attention to particular, that is, to such as are favorable, districts.

"But it will naturally be inquired, is all this cotton fit for the use of the Manchester manufacturer, or can it be made so by the simple process of careful cleaning? Much of it is good enough for all purposes, but some, no doubt, is short in staple and rough in texture, probably from being grown in very dry situations. It has often been disputed whether the 'webs of woven air,' for which the natives of Dacca are still famous, are owing to their fineness of finger or the superior quality of their cotton. Something is probably due to both. But much fine cotton is produced in India. Some of that which formerly formed a part of the Company's investments was highly approved of in this country. A good deal of what is now known as Surat cotton is also of excellent quality; but there is reason to believe that this is produced in Central India, and reaches Surat by a circuitous route. One of the American planters particularly describes the cotton of Oomrawuttee, near Nagpore, as fine in quality and long in staple, and the cotton of Central India in general as excellent cotton, and requiring only to be properly picked and carefully cleaned.

"Your correspondent says, that the finest cottons never reach even Bombay—'in consequence of the enormous expense attending the land carriage;' but, surely, if the inferior cottons can pay this cost, the superior may do so; but, the fact is, that the weavers in the interior give a better price than the exporters at Bombay.

"The American planter describes the culture also as easy, even with the American cotton, where the climate is favorable; and that seems to be the case with the whole of Central India, where there are immense tracts of what is emphatically called 'cotton soil.' He considers the natives of the Southern Mahratta country as good cultivators, and that they would beat any European or American, unless he adopts their methods; and then they will beat him on the score of economy. But, in everything that relates to the cleaning, packing, and sending to market, he adds,—'We can use them up.'

"Your correspondent inquires, why is not an East Indian cotton company established? No good reason can, perhaps, be assigned. It may be too, matter of fact for the delusive propensities of the day,—cotton being produced and producible in much greater quantities in India, while it is required in immense quantities in England; it would seem that the supply might long ere this have equalled the demand. This, however, will not apply to the natives of India, who know little of at p. 83, that the importations "will be to a greater extent, as the unfavorable prospects of the American crop were early known to some, and orders sent to India for cotton." That these anticipations have been fully confirmed, we may see by comparing the imports of the year 1850, with those of the year

what occurs beyond their own immediate neighbourhood, and rejoice in doing only as their forefathers have done for ages before them. They are to be taught rather by example than by precept, and in that are not very unlike English farmers. They may be incited, however, by those who will go among them, or will make them advances. This has been done to some extent by the Parsee merchants, and hence partly the increase of cultivation, but still very far from what is practicable. It may be objected, that the Bombay merchants are not likely to leave to companies at a distance the reaping a profitable harvest from off fields which they may almost consider their own. But it may with truth be replied, that the whole form but a small body, with a vast variety of objects to attend to. Some say they get a larger profit out of bad, than they could get by improving cotton. At all events, the cultivators in the interior complain that they do not get from them the encouragement of better prices for improved articles of culture.

"Like 'Amicus,' I have no doubt that a company might be advantageously established, with great benefit to this country and to India, and with considerable profit to themselves, if they managed their concerns with but ordinary prudence. The cotton now passes through several hands, which intervene between the planter and the manufacturer. The profits of all might be realized by those who would buy from the one and sell to the other. Europeans could in the first instance purchase only the cotton grown by the natives in the districts where it is most abundantly produced; but if they made contracts and paid advances, then they might induce them to grow only from the best seed, either native or American; cultivate with still more skill, and pick the cotton with care at the fittest time, and take care that it was kept clean. Subsequently, if they pleased, they might establish small model farms. The principal outlay would be in establishing groups of gins for cleaning and presses for packing in favorable situations, by which the cotton could be quickly cleaned in large quantities, and sent to market properly packed, as well as freed from the immense quantity of dirt which now increases the expense both of carriage and of freight. If the railway to which 'Amicus' alludes were established towards the centre of the great cotton districts, another great impulse would be given to cotton culture. Of the myriads of bullocks now employed in carriage, some would make shorter trips to the gin-houses, others would plough 'fresh fields' and graze on 'pastures new.'

". . . . . . But the free labour of the mild but apathetic Hindoo requires to be excited by the vivifying influence of English capital, at the same time that his exertions are supported by the indomitable perseverance of Englishmen. As the time has come and the opportunity is favorable, it requires only to be taken advantage of with effect; in which case we may hail the cloud in the west as the harbinger of sunshine for the east.

"I have the honour to be yours obediently,

"INDOPHILUS."

1849, as given in the Circular of Messrs. Tetley, dated London, 31st December, 1850, where the former not only exceed the latter to the extent of 127,059 bales, but are higher than they have ever been:

	1849.		1850.
Import of American	1,477,512	..	1,182,970
" Brazil	163,445	..	171,359
" Egyptian	72,727	..	79,376
" West India, &c.	9,485	..	5,264
" East India	182,079	..	309,168
Total	1,905,248	..	1,748,137
Exported	256,300	..	272,400
Home Consumption	1,586,608	..	1,513,007
Average per week	30,512	..	29,096
Stock 31st December	558,390	..	521,120
Prices of Upland do.	$5\frac{1}{2}d.$ @ $6\frac{3}{4}d.$	..	$7d.$ @ $8\frac{1}{4}d.$

Indian cotton is, no doubt, possessed of sufficient good qualities to be used for the manufacture of calicos, which wear better than those of English manufacture, as well as of muslins, which have been admired in all ages, and almost justify the poetical expression of "webs of woven air," "dew of night," "running water," and similar expressions applied to them by the natives of the East, and which an English manufacturer complimented, when he wished to disparage, by calling them the "shadow of a commodity."

Indian cotton is, however, from the shortness of staple, not well suited for all the purposes of the English manufacturer; but it is much more depreciated than it need be, from the dirty and adulterated state in which it is sent to market. When these defects are avoided, it sells in the English market at fair prices, and if continued to be so sent, would be used in greatly increased quantities. It has been shown that it can be laid down in Liverpool with some profit at $3\frac{1}{2}d.$ a pound, from Bundlecund, Broach, Candeish, Dharwar, Coimbatore, and Tinnivelly; districts which are within the Company's territories, and most of them near the sea or river. It may even be imported at nearly the same price from the far distant territories of Hyderabad and Nagpore. But it is essential that the cotton should be sent in a clean state. If this is not done the expenses will have to be paid on dirt as well as on cotton, while a lower price will be realized in the market.

American cotton is, however, that which is most valued by the manufacturers of this country, and is also the kind which is most profitable to the cultivator in districts where the climate is suitable. Repeated experiments having been made by the East India Company during a series of years, to introduce the culture of American cotton into India, and without any permanent effects being produced, it has been inferred that failures will follow the present or any future attempts. But in former experiments good cotton was produced, and there is no reason to believe at a greater comparative cost than in the present experiments, while in some districts the American plants then introduced have become so naturalized as to be taken for indigenous kinds, and the staple, after so many years of acclimatation, has been considered nearly equal to that of New Orleans cotton. The present experiments might have resulted in failure, if it had not been for the determined perseverance with which they have been carried on in districts where there appeared no sufficient physical obstacles to success, as in Dharwar, Belgaum, Candeish, Coimbatore, and Tinnivelly. In these districts cotton has been grown from American seed, which has been highly valued by manufacturers as well fitted for their purposes, and has been bought by them at prices which have been amply remunerative, both to cultivators and to importers. The cost, as shown in the details given under the heads of Dharwar and Coimbatore, was not more than for native cotton, that is, about 3½*d.* a pound, laid down in Liverpool. The price realized has never been less than this sum, even before the cotton had attracted attention; since then it has frequently sold for 6*d.* and 6½*d.*, and of late for 7*d.* and 7½*d.* The profits realized by Government, even upon the comparatively small quantities, have in the Dharwar district nearly balanced the cost of the experiments. Merchants could no doubt have realized larger profits; but in future the cultivators will expect to share more largely in the better prices arising from the increased value of this cotton in the English market. The extent to which the cultivation has been carried, in consequence of the encouragement held out, first by Government, and lately by the agents and orders of merchants, is so considerable, that it is expected that not less than 9000 bales of American cotton will be sent through Dharwar to this country in the present year. In Belgaum and Candeish the culture is also extending. In the Madras Presidency, however, the natives have taken but slowly to the culture of American cotton. But the presence of European agents would remove their prejudices, and as the cotton is better, and the expenses not greater than in Dharwar, there is sufficient encouragement both for cultivators and for merchants.

In discussing the questions relating to the causes which interfere with the extended culture and commerce of cotton in India, we showed that the cultivator had little encouragement to grow that which was in such irregular demand for the English market, and that the manufacturer here was little inclined to use a cotton, which besides being shorter in staple, was sent to him in a dirty and adulterated state. He therefore abstains from using it, unless when compelled by the high price of American cotton. We have also shown that there was little chance of the natives themselves doing much in picking their cotton carefully, or in keeping it clean, and that therefore the presence of European agents among them was essential to encourage the ryots to do even that which is so much for their own advantage. Such agents would moreover, be able to counteract the influence of the local dealers and money lenders, and the opposition of the Brahminical caste to all kinds of innovation and improvement.

The settlement of Europeans or their agents in the cotton districts, with the express purpose of encouraging the natives to improve the cultivation of their own or to grow the American cotton, is the measure which has been recommended as the one thing essential for the extension and improvement of this great staple. As the trade has been described to be profitable, it appears remarkable that no planters should have established themselves for an object which is considered of such importance by the manufacturers of Lancashire. Within the limits of the Bengal Presidency there are numbers of Europeans settled in various parts, many of whom have made experiments in cotton culture, as recorded in the '*Transactions of the Agricultural*

Society of India.' In North West India we have seen Mr. Hamilton Bell undertaking the culture, on an extensive scale, of what he conceived to be the best kind of indigenous cotton, in a situation where American cotton would not succeed without the aid of irrigation. But the Agra-grown cotton was not approved of at Manchester. Mr. Bruce, again, long resident in the Doab and Bundlecund, and accustomed to the culture and commerce of cotton, has offered to supply (p. 307) manufacturers here with American cotton at 4*d.* or $4\frac{1}{2}$*d.*, and native at 3*d.* or $3\frac{1}{2}$*d.* a pound.

On the Bombay side of India the American planters employed by Government in the Dharwar district, long complained that their efforts were not seconded by the merchants of that Presidency sending agents or orders into the districts, which would encourage the ryots to grow American cotton in preference to their own. The sales of the American cotton, both in Bombay and this country, raised its price by degrees in the district; but still it was chiefly bought by Government agents. Mr. Turner, the President of the Commercial Association of Manchester, took great pains (v. *Summary*) to instruct his agents in Bombay of the great value of the American cotton grown in Dharwar, and gave orders for its purchase. But to be effectual these orders required to be executed in the district itself. This also Mr. Turner arranged to have done; but his orders and those of his friends, could not be executed, because the native dealers had at last become fully aware of the value of American cotton. Some of them stimulated, no doubt, by the orders of their employers in Bombay, were purchasing it at a high price, 100 rupees a candy, where a few years since they would not give half that sum for that quantity. One of the Bombay houses, is mentioned in a private letter, as having sent an agent into the district. A few months since a gentleman called upon the author, previous to departing for India in order to join one of these houses, and who stated, that he was to be stationed in the interior, either in Dharwar or in Candeish, for the express purpose of carrying on the cotton trade in direct communication with the cultivators. In the Broach district, though the American cotton does not succeed there, Mr. Landon has established himself as a purchaser of native cotton, which, by attention to careful picking and cleaning, he conceives may be sent to market in a state to compete with the Uplands variety of American cotton. While in the Government service he greatly improved the working and economy of the saw-gin. Since then, it is understood, he has introduced steam power for the propulsion of his machinery, as indeed it was always his intention to do. Into the district of Candeish, Messrs. Stewart, Ritchie, & Co., of Bombay, have sent an agent, and have agreed to purchase as many saw-gins as can be supplied by the Government factory at Dhurrumgaum. Such an agent, besides purchasing native cotton, will be able to encourage the growth of American cotton, for which, as we have seen, parts of the district are well suited. It is to be hoped that the planters now sent into Sattara, Surat, and Ahmedabad, will be sufficiently successful to induce some Europeans to establish themselves as cotton planters on their own account. It is also to be hoped that means may be adopted for picking and cleaning the good cotton of the far distant provinces of the Nizam territories, and also for introducing the American cotton into the Berar Valley, as Captain M. Taylor is so successfully doing in the principality of Shorapore.

In the Madras Presidency, Mr. Hughes long since established the culture of Bourbon cotton, and his successors have carried it on, though it is not now sent of such good quality as formerly. Mr. Fischer has for many years been established in the district of Salem, as an agent for the purchase of cotton for the European market; but the natives have not been induced to take up the culture of American cotton. Mr. D. Lees has, however, shown that New Orleans cotton may be successfully cultivated in the most barren parts of the Tinnivelly district, and has sent for his nephew to go on with the culture, as we learn from the '*Manchester Guardian.*' His success and his statements have encouraged another Manchester man to determine upon proceeding to India to commence the culture of American cotton in the same district, as he intimated only a few days since at the India House. Besides this, offers have been made in India for the purchase of the machinery for cleaning cotton, which has been set up by the Indian Government at Coimbatore, and this offer the author has learnt, originates in Manchester, as the proposer has lately stated to the home authorities. The establishment of a few energetic Europeans in different districts, interested in the improvement of the cotton of India, the author feels satisfied is all that is required greatly to extend and to improve the Culture and Commerce of Cotton of all kinds in India.

The author begs to conclude the subject by quoting some of his observations on the same subject published in the year 1834, which will show that he has always relied on the principles advocated in the present work.

"I have no doubt that by the importation of foreign, and the selection of native seed, attention to the peculiarities not only of soil, but also of climate, as regards the course of the seasons, and the temperature, dryness, and moisture of the atmosphere, as well as attention to the mode of cultivation, such as preparing the soil, sowing in lines, so as to facilitate the circulation of air, weeding, ascertaining whether the mixture of other crops with the cotton be injurious or otherwise, pruning, picking the cotton as it ripens, and keeping it clean; great improvement must take place in the quality of the cotton. Experiments may at first be more expensive than the ordinary culture, the natives of India, when taught by example, would adopt the improved processes as regularly and as easily as the other; and as labour is no where cheaper, any extra outlay would be repaid fully as profitably as in countries where the best cottons are at present produced."—(*Illustrations of Himalayan Botany*, p. 97.)

APPENDIX.

PAPERS REFERRING TO THE PROPOSED CONTRIBUTIONS FROM INDIA FOR THE INDUSTRIAL EXHIBITION OF 1851.

BY J. FORBES ROYLE, M.D.

(1849.)

EXTRACTS FROM A REPORT BY MESSRS. COLE AND FULLER TO H.R.H. THE PRINCE ALBERT,

President of the Society of Arts, &c. &c.

Of Preliminary Inquiries into the Willingness of Manufacturers and others

TO SUPPORT

PERIODICAL EXHIBITIONS OF THE WORKS OF INDUSTRY OF ALL NATIONS.

"Before concluding this Report, we would inform your Royal Highness, that, as it appeared likely that the East Indies would be able to contribute very largely to the division of the Exhibition proposed to consist of Raw Materials, it was deemed advisable to confer with Sir Archibald Galloway, K.C.B., the Chairman of the East India Company, and some of the principal officers of the India House. The Chairman cordially entered into the proposal, and thought he might undertake to say that the Court, when the subject was brought before them, would give their cordial co-operation in promoting your Royal Highness's proposal in every way.* For his own part, he said he

* "In a subsequent letter the Chairman of the East India Company says: 'I beg to inform you that I communicated to the Court of Directors the conversation which I had with you on the subject of the proposed Exhibition of the Works of Industry, which His Royal Highness the Prince Albert is desirous to institute in the year 1851. I have the satisfaction of acquainting you, for the information of His Royal Highness, that the Court expressed their entire concurrence in the views which I then suggested, and that they will be prepared to give their cordial co-operation in carrying out the wishes of His Royal Highness, by obtaining from India such specimens of the products and manufactures of that country as may tend to illustrate its resources, and add to the interest of the Great National Exhibition of which His Royal Highness is the patron.' (Signed) 'A. GALLOWAY.'"

would be happy at once to make any preliminary inquiries of the Governor-General, even by the next mail, if it were desired. He suggested that a communication should be opened with Dr. Royle, the head of the Botanical department, and in charge of the correspondence relative to the natural productions of India. Dr. Royle has been so obliging as to furnish a communication on this subject, which will be found in the Appendix, No. 3. The Chairman expressed his desire to be informed further on the subject. Mr. Melvill, the Secretary, said that the East India Company had always exhibited the utmost desire to promote the interests of Art and Science, and he instanced the establishment of magnetic observatories in India, made at the suggestion of the British Association. He was sure there would be every disposition throughout India to assist. Mr. Peacock, Examiner of India Correspondence, pointed out that raw products would be perhaps the chief feature, as British manufactures had supplanted the native manufactures so extensively. At the same time, he enumerated various manufactures still produced in India, such as goldsmiths' work, metal-work, ivory-work, pottery, mosaics, shawls, muslin, carpets, &c., and he thought these would furnish a considerable show. Perhaps some of the rich Parsees would be induced to exhibit specimens. It was remarked by others, that there would be mutual advantages of great importance both to India and this country: to India in calling forth new products and directing attention to the subject, and to this country in furnishing suggestions, &c. and new materials for manufactures.

The following is the communication referred to in the above Report:

"*On the Exhibition of Raw Products and Manufactured Articles from India.*

"INDIA, vast in extent and diversified in surface, is remarkable as the cradle of one, at least, of the nations who earliest practised the arts and cultivated the sciences which characterise civilization, and from whence these travelled to the West, and, perhaps, also to the East. Its present inhabitants continue to venerate sciences which they know only by name, and practise arts of which they know not the principles; and this with a skill not only remarkable for the early period at which it attained perfection, but also for the manner in which it has remained stationary for so many ages. This can be explained only by the fact, that the son was unable to add to the manual dexterity of his father, and could not improve an art which he knew only as a routine process. But when Commerce was in its infancy, or dealt only in the most precious commodities, these arts could not have been practised unless India had contained within itself all the raw materials which Art could convert into useful articles or elegant ornaments. Without cotton, the so-called 'webs of woven air' could have had no existence. Without numerous barks, woods, and flowers, dyeing could not have been practised, and calico-printing would probably not have been invented. If an Indigofera had not been indigenous, indigo would never have derived its name from India, nor have afforded us the proof, in the stripe of mummy-cloth, of the early commercial intercourse between its native country and Egypt. Neither would sugar have been arranged by the Greeks with honeys, nor the Indians described as those who 'bibunt tenera dulces ab arundine succos,' unless they had had the cane-like saccharum as a plant of their country. Neither in Persia would the proverb of 'giving an Indian answer,' have been considered equivalent to a cut with an Indian sword, unless the Hindoos had possessed the ore which enabled them to manufacture their far-famed *wootz* steel; and gunpowder is likely to have been invented at an early age only in a country where 'villanous saltpetre' is abundant.

"Besides these, India possesses an immense number, both of animal and of vegetable, as well as of mineral substances, well fitted for arts and manufactures of every kind; and the country has often been described as capable of producing, within its own limits, almost all the useful products of every other quarter of the globe. But it is difficult for a manufacturer to ascertain whether India, or any other foreign country, contains any substance which may be useful even for his own purposes; for it is unknown in the markets of his country, and no mention is made of it in the price currents of its commerce. If it should be included in a foreign catalogue, it is by some name that is unknown to him, and in the explanation of which dictionaries often lend no assistance; for the authors, usually acquainted only with words, attempt to define things of which they have no knowledge. Manufacturers, brokers, and merchants, are moreover, in this country, generally unacquainted with the natural sciences which would, in many cases, lead them to the discovery of new products. Finally, our commercial tariffs and custom-house officers, instead of facilitating, threw, until very recently, unreasonable obstacles in the introduction of new and unknown products.

"There appear only two available methods by which a manufacturer can be made acquainted with the existence of foreign products likely to be useful in his business: one is, by the collection of such information as is obtainable respecting them, and arranging it according to the most prominent properties of such substances. When these are so arranged, it is comparatively easy for any one to ascertain whether India, or any other foreign country, contains any useful or ornamental product which might be employed instead of, and be cheaper than, that already in use.

"Thus, among clothing and cordage plants, an inquirer might search for substitutes for hemp and flax.

"Among timber trees he would find described the different kinds of wood.

"Among the plants which yield oil and fatty substances he would find the means of supplying the wants of those who cannot go to the expense of a high-priced animal oil.

"So among gums, resins, colouring matters, tanning substances, the manufacturer might seek for a new and more efficient agent to answer his purpose, or find a cheap substitute for what he already employs.

"But with the most simple arrangement and clearly conveyed information the manufacturer generally would feel little interest about unknown natural products and their strange names, unless he had an opportunity of seeing and of personally examining them. Then a glance of his practised eye, or the slightest handling of a new substance, informs him whether it is likely to be of use for his purposes. The collection, therefore, of such substances, and arranging them also, as above, according to their properties, is the only method calculated at once to interest the public and to give such confidence to the manufacturer as to induce him to submit them to trial. Their exhibition, therefore, is calculated not only to be of great use to the manufacturer, but of essential benefit to such countries as possess many little known products possessed of valuable properties, and procurable in large quantities at a cheap rate, if a demand could be created for them. India, already the *Koh-i-noor* of the British crown, could contribute to such a collection so large a number of such products as would prove incontestably how valuable an appendage it is of the British Empire during peace, and how much more so it might become, in case of war with more than one nation. Though the writer possesses many of these products in small quantities in his own collection, a little preliminary notice, and the concurrence of the authorities, would be required to procure them for the purposes of general exhibition.

"As India produced the raw material and manufactured it into a costly article, gold and silver have, from the earliest times, been required to purchase this combination of the gifts of nature with the creations of art; but mechanical invention has deprived the Hindoos of many of the advantages of their position, and they have, in a great measure, lost the commerce which they had themselves created, especially as some of their products were subjected to discriminating duties, which amounted to a prohibition on import into this country. Hence their foreign commerce has not advanced, as might have been anticipated, from the enjoyment in many parts of long-continued peace. But fashion, which here is as fickle as the wind, is in the East as steady as their monsoons, and has fortunately preserved some of their manufactures in their pristine excellence, and which, in any general collection of manufactures, would enable those of India still to hold a conspicuous place.

"For instance, though the muslins of Dacca may not now be produced of as fine a quality as formerly, those of Chunderee are still highly esteemed by the natives of rank and wealth.

"So the embroidered muslins of Dacca, the brocades of Benares, and the worked shawls of Delhi, will bear comparison with any other goods. The shawls of Cashmere still remain unrivalled.

"The workers in gold and in silver still produce chains of matchless beauty, and their filagree work would display that delicacy of hand for which the Hindoos have so long been famous.

"The wootz steel, the various arms, the works in copper and brass, and in the different little known metallurgic compounds, the inlaid metals, and the endless variety of images, would display many instances of ingenuity and skill.

"A collection even of Indian toys would not fail to be interesting to many, as would the works in Ivory, ebony, and sandal-wood, which, indeed, still continue to be esteemed in Europe.

"Sugar, as manufactured from the common date, the palmyra, or the sugar-cane, and from different parts of India:

"Indigo in its different states, and opium from the hills and from the plains, from Patna and Malwa, would interest others.

"And to these we could now add tea from the Himalayas, which will rival that from China.

"To these, numerous other manufactured articles, both in their finished and unfinished state, could be added. The whole would form a collection which would be most interesting to the public, if exhibited even by itself, and could not fail to form a most important part of any general collection.

"J. FORBES ROYLE, M.D."

"EAST INDIA HOUSE, *August* 1849."

The author having been desired by the Chairman of the East India Company to submit his views on the desirableness of India contributing to the Great Exhibition of 1851, and on the mode in which the collection should be made, occupied himself, in the autumn of 1849, in taking a general view of the raw products and manufactured articles of different parts of India, and then presented the following Report, with the accompanying Memorandum and Classified Lists of the kind of things which it seemed desirable that India should contribute to the Great Exhibition :—

"The proposed Exposition of Raw Materials, Manufactured Articles, and Inventions of All Nations, novel in idea and grand in conception, will be an occasion when the latent resources of distant provinces and the skill of the least-known artist may compete with the produce of the most favoured regions or the works of the most successful genius. It will enjoy the advantage, moreover, of having almost everyone you could wish for as spectators; for few, either of the commercial, manufacturing, literary, scientific, or fashionable worlds, will omit to visit what can hardly fail to be one of the most interesting displays the world has ever seen. The only fear is, that it may become overwhelming from its magnitude.

"The Exposition is to consist of—

Raw Materials.
Machinery and Mechanical Inventions.
Manufactures.
Sculpture and Plastic Art generally.

"In contributing to such an Exhibition, it is desirable, as far as India is concerned, to ascertain, first, what would prove eventually of the greatest benefit to the country; and secondly, what will be of interest for the Exposition. Though India might contribute something in all the above departments, as, for instance, Sculpture, as practised in the rude representations of the Hindoo Pantheon, and Invention, as exemplified in the several machines which they were probably among the first to apply to various arts and manufactures, it is only under the head of Raw Materials and Manufactured Articles that the products of India will hold a conspicuous place, in the present day, among the accumulated products of the world. A more extensive knowledge among European manufacturers of the Raw Products of the Indian soil could hardly fail to increase its commerce; while an exhibition of its manufacturing skill may still extort admiration, without, perhaps, increasing the demand for Dacca muslins or for Benares brocades, or in making these more fashionable.

"First, with regard to Raw Materials, it is well known that India has often been described as capable of producing within its own limits almost all the useful products of every other quarter of the globe. So Mr. Hume, on a recent occasion, is reported to have stated, that 'He thought the present proposal would be attended with great benefit to India. We were not yet aware of half the raw materials which that country could furnish to our manufactures.' Indeed, if we consider the extent of territory and its diversified surface, together with our knowledge of the fact, that the natives of India have from early ages practised a great variety of useful arts, and this without the import of raw products, it is evident that these must have been produced within the limits of the Indian soil. But if we inquire what these products are, or where they are to be seen, we shall find that the few that are known or can be met with in commerce may almost be counted on the fingers. It is, indeed, remarkable how little the various products of India are known in Europe, or, indeed, to Europeans in India. Lands are surveyed, traversed by roads and intersected by canals, for the purpose both of facilitating transit and of increasing produce; the plants and many of the minerals of the country have been collected and named; and yet the products of plants or of animals, or the educts of minerals, form no object of study or inquiry except to a few. Men of science have usually thought such subjects unworthy their notice, and merchants have neglected them because their properties were unknown. If any planter, more energetic than his neighbours, sent anything new to the European market, it was usually thrown aside by the broker, and reported on as 'of no value,' or as 'unknown in the market,' though, in many cases, the manufacturer would have been glad to receive them, especially if accompanied with any account of their properties or the uses to which they were applied in their native country, with a notice of the quantities and prices at which they could be imported.

"It would not be difficult to show, that there are few of our manufactures which would not be benefited by such imports, and that there are few parts of India which could not send something which would be beneficial to the senders and useful to the importers. But it is requisite that the selection should be made with a knowledge of what is required, and accompanied with such information as manufacturers consider essential.

"The present seems a most fitting occasion in which much may be done, and what is done made extensively known. The opportunity, therefore, should not be lost. But it is difficult to advise how the work should be prosecuted, and by whom. To send general and necessarily vague instructions to the Governments in India would, I fear, not be productive of any great practical benefit. For to whom are these instructions to be subsequently addressed, and by whom are the substances to be collected together, with the required information. The officers of government do not usually pay any particular attention to such subjects, and there are districts in which no European merchants or planters are settled. To prepare specific instructions, applicable to the different parts of India, would involve as much labour as is required for collecting the materials for a book on the Commercial Products of India. For instance, in preparing such specific instructions, it would first be necessary to fix on the substances which are important enough to warrant their being collected and subsequently exhibited. In doing this, we must determine on the name which is to be used. A scientific name will be known only to a few; a native name will, in most cases, be applicable only to particular districts.

"Without this minuteness, I fear, little of what is now generally unknown will be brought to light, and therefore no great benefit can be produced to the country. If general directions are given to send everything, then the same thing will be sent from a variety of districts, and those generally which are already well known, and the collection be so common-place as to be of little use to the country or creditable to the Government.

"In the observations which I wrote when Mr. Cole visited the India House on deputation to announce this great project, I stated my views on the mode in which such a collection was likely to be most useful to manufacturers. I may, therefore, be allowed to adduce them on the present occasion."

The Report then concluded with an extract from the above observations respecting Raw Materials, and with something to the same effect respecting the Manufactures of India.

The following Memorandum and Lists, having been prepared by the author, were lithographed in the India House, and sent to India with the Court's despatch by the mail of the 7th of January, 1850.

List of Raw Products and Manufactured Articles, suggested to be sent from India for the Grand Exposition of 1851.

"Taking it for granted, that it is desirable to exhibit a collection of the Products and Manufactures of India at the Grand Exposition in 1851, it is yet difficult to determine the extent to which this should be carried. To confine it to substances already well known, would disappoint those who expect to see much that is new; while, to exhibit only unknown products, would limit the interest to a comparatively few. Considering, therefore, what may prove of interest to the Exhibition and of ultimate benefit to India, and display at the same time the natural riches of the country and the skilful ingenuity of its inhabitants, I have prepared the following lists, as an index of the extent to which the exhibition may be carried.

"As general instructions might be misapprehended, I have thought it desirable to draw up a specific list of Raw Products and of Manufactured Articles, so as to give an idea of the kind of things which may be exhibited, without intending to mention all that India produces, or wishing to exclude any that it might be thought desirable to send. Of the substances enumerated, many are produced or may be obtained at a great variety of places; but it is necessary to select only one or a few of these, in order to avoid the accumulation of useless duplicates. Some might, no doubt, be most easily obtained as commercial articles in this country; though we might not always be able at the time to get the best specimens of each. A few might be borrowed from individuals or from museums, but a great many of the articles enumerated can only be obtained by being specifically written for, and, in some cases, to particular individuals who are favorably situated or are well acquainted with the subject of research. Some of the products and manufactures, such as the spices of Penang and of Travancore, the indigo and sugar of Bengal, will probably be sent for exhibition by planters and merchants in India, if a notification to that effect is published. The native princes of different parts of India would also be very likely to send the products and manufactures of their respective countries, if the objects of the Exposition are explained to them by the several political agents.

"Some of the manufactured articles (as the finest muslins) will require some time for their preparation; and these, as well as some others, can only be obtained when specially ordered. Most of the others in use by the natives of India may be obtained at any time.

"The directions to be sent for making such collections, depend so much upon the individuals to be employed in making them, that I find it difficult to avoid being diffuse, where I wish only to be precise. The quantities in which the raw products are sent must depend in some measure on the nature of the substance, but also on the instructions which are to be immediately issued by the Executive Committee of the Royal Commission. Of the majority of the substances, a pound or two will be sufficient; but of any which require to be submitted to preliminary processes of manufacture, a larger quantity will be necessary, and the expense in either case will be but small. Of the manufactured articles, only single specimens of the more expensive articles would be required, unless in cases where two or more places are famous for the same kind of manufacture, or individuals wish to contend for prizes, of which some will, I believe, be awarded at the discretion of the Royal Commission.

"In the accompanying Lists, the different products are arranged, some according to their uses (as Dyes and Tanning Substances), and others according to their proximate principles (as Starch, Gums, Resins, Oils, &c.) One arrangement is not incompatible with the other, as the uses to which these may be and are applied depend entirely upon their chemical composition. In sending, therefore, any new substance, it will be necessary to define the class to which it is intended to belong, or to mention the uses to which it is applied by the natives of India. All, as they arrive, will require appropriate sorting and careful labeling, and some will be benefited by passing through some of the preliminary processes, to which they would be subjected if they were to be employed in any of our manufactures.

"Drs. Falconer, M'Clelland, Jameson, and Mouatt might render considerable assistance in collecting the products of the Bengal Presidency; Dr. Wight and Captain Ouchterlony in Madras; and Drs. Gibson, Giraud, and Stocks in the Bombay Presidency."

The author might have added the names of many others, as of Dr. Hunter of Madras, and of Dr. Carter at Bombay; but an accident prevented his making some additions and corrections to his lists before they were ordered to be printed off, in order to be in time for the mail by which they were despatched.

MINERALS, WITH SOME CHEMICALS.

Combustibles—Acids and Acid Salts—Alkalis and Alkaline Salts—Earths and Earthy Salts—Metals Proper, and Metallic Ores.

VEGETABLE KINGDOM.*

Used as food and stimulants chiefly.
- Agricultural Products.
- Dried Fruits and Seeds, used as Food.
- Substances used in the Formation of Drinks.
- Fermented Liquors and Distilled Spirits.
- Intoxicating Drugs.
- Spices and Condiments.
- Starch-like Substances.

Used in the chemical arts chiefly.
- Gum and Mucilages.
- Resins.
- Gum Resins.
- Volatile Oils and Perfumes.
- Fatty Oils and Vegetable Butters.
- Dyes.
- Tanning Substances.

Medicines.

Fibrous—Clothing and Cordage Materials.
Woody—Timber and Fancy Woods.

ANIMAL KINGDOM.

Hoofs, Horns, &c.
Wool, Hair, &c.
Silk.
Skins and Hides.
Fats and Oils.
Isinglass.
Wax.

Honey.
Musk and Castor.
Lac Dye and Resin.
Coral.
Shells.
Pearls.
Birds' Nests.

MANUFACTURED ARTICLES.

Twine, Thread, and Rope.
Fabrics of Cotton and of Pāāt.
" Silk.
" Silk and Cotton.
" Wool, and Shawl Wool.
Manufactured Articles of Feathers, Horn, Ivory, Shell, and Lac.
Worked Muslins, Shawls, and Brocades.
Brass and Copper Utensils, Inlaid Metals.

Gold and Silver Ornaments.
Cutlery and Fire-arms.
Glass Ornaments and Lacquered Toys.
Pottery and Stone Images.
Mats.
Paper.
Dyed Articles.
Soap.
Sealing-Wax.
Leather.

TOOLS AND IMPLEMENTS.

Such as employed by the weavers of muslins, the distillers of atr of Roses; the Drill Plough, &c.

---

* The arrangement here given of the useful products of the Vegetable Kingdom by the author, was subsequently adopted by the Committee appointed by the Royal Commissioners, but they removed "Intoxicating Drugs" to the neighbourhood of "Medicines." In the Lists lately published, however, for the use of the Head Juries, "Intoxicating Drugs" occupy the same place as in the present arrangement. "Distilled Spirits," mentioned here, are excluded from the Exhibition. The author has adopted one group, that of "Cellular Substances," from the arrangement of the Committee on the Vegetable Kingdom.

I. MINERALS, WITH SOME CHEMICALS.

COMBUSTIBLE MINERALS.

Diamonds	Punna, Bundlecund, Mallavilly, Golconda, Masulipátam.
Sulphur	Cutch, Scinde, Nepal.
Petroleum (Asphaltum, Naphtha,)	Assam, Rangoon.
Amber	Cutch, Assam.
Coal	Tenasserim, Burdwan, Silhet, Beerbhoom, Assam, along Nerbudda.

ACIDS AND ACID SALTS.

Citric Acid, from lemons and limes, might be sent either pure or as citrate of lime.
Tartaric Acid, from tartar, &c., the juice of the grape, or from tamarinds.
Oxalic Acid, from the salt in the leaves of gram, *Cicer arietinum.*

ALKALIS AND THEIR SALTS.

Salt, Common (chloride of sodium)	Tumlook, Balasore, Tanjore.
„ or Samur	Samur or Samur Lake.
Rock Salt	Salt range of Punjab.
Borax	Kemaon and Gurhwall, from Tibet.
Khara Noon (sulphate of soda)	Gyah, Tirhoot, &c.
Sal Ammoniac (Nuosadur)	Saharunpore.
Potash and Pearlash, from ashes of any plants, the ashes of wood fires, &c.	
Saltpetre	Sarun, Tirhoot, &c.
Mineral Alkali	Bombay.
Soda, from ashes of species of Salsola and Salicornia	on the Coromandel coast.
Syjee, or Carb. of Soda	in Tirhoot.
Oosur Salt	Mirzapore, &c.
Lanee Kharee	Scinde.
Natron	from Lonar Lake, in lat. 20°, lon. 76° 30′.

EARTHS AND EARTHY SALTS.

Baryta, Sulphate of	Lundour.
Magnesia, Carbonate of	Bellary.
Alum	Cutch, Scinde.
Amethysts	Central India.

Cornelians, Agates, Moss Agates, &c.	Kaen river, Baroda.
Garnets	Himalayas.
Stilbite and Heulandite, &c.	Vindya Range.
Corundum (Koorun)	Mysore, Carnatic.
Potstone (Bullagum)	Mysore.
Talc	Mysore and Central India.
Felspar, White	Bangalore.
Potter's Clay	Cuddapah.
Ochre	Mysore, Jaulnah.
Indian Red, or Red Earth	Bombay.
Tourmaline	Madras.

METALS AND METALLIC MINERALS.

Manganese	Ajmere.
Iron :—	
Magnetic Iron, Ore	Koondra (near Quilon), Malwan, Koompta.
Iron Ores	Salem, Nellore, Burdwan, Sagur, Himalayas.
Iron :—	
Plumbago	Himalayas.
Wootz Steel	Madras, Bombay.
Sulphate of	made at Shahabad, &c.
Copper :—	
Ores	at Colastry in N. Arcot, Nellore, Kemaon.
Sulphate of, and Verdigris	Bazars.
Lead :—	
Sulphuret of, or Galena	Khalsee and Ajmere.
Litharge and Red Lead	in Bazars.
Zinc	from China only.
Tin, Oxide of	Tennasserim.
Antimony, Sulphuret of	Moulmein, Nepal, Borneo.
Mercury :—	
Sulphuret of, or Cinnabar	Nepal.
Calomel and Corrosive Sublimate	in Bazars, of native manufacture.
Arsenic :—	
White	Nepal, from Tibet.
Sulphuret of, or Orpiment, Red and Yellow	Nepal and Kemaon, from Tibet.
Gold	Assam, Warrigaum, &c. Foot of Himalayas.
Platinum	Burmah.

II. VEGETABLE KINGDOM.

AGRICULTURAL PRODUCTS.

Cereals, as Rice, Wheat, Barley, Millets, &c.
Pulses, as Gram, Dholl, Peas, Beans, &c.
Oil Seeds, as Sesamum, Linseed, Mustard, &c.

A complete collection of the Grains and Pulses in use as articles of diet in India, would form a very interesting feature of any general collection of Agricultural Products, and would at all events show the great number of little-known grains and pulses upon which the natives of India subsist; but, as it is desirable that these should be seen only in a fresh state, they should not be sent until after the next harvest, before which lists with synonymes will be prepared in detail.

The Pysee and Julalya Wheats of the Nerbudda Valley; the Wheat, Barley, and Buckwheat of the Himalayas; the two former grains from the Neilgherries, and Oats from the North-west Provinces, together with the finest specimens of Patna and of Pilibeet Rice, would be interesting to Agriculturists and Merchants at any time.

DRIED FRUITS, AND SEEDS USED AS FOOD.

Plantains and Bananas, dried.	
Berberries, dried (*Berberis aristata*)	Himalayas.
Almonds, both *Sweet* and *Bitter*	N. W. India and Bombay.
Apricots (Khoobanee)	" from Kunawur and Caubul.
Plums (aloo Bokhara)	" from Caubul.
Raisins (Monukka, Kishmish, Bedana)	" from Istaulik, &c., Aurungabad.
Figs (Unjeer)	" from Caubul.
Dates (Choohara)	Bombay, from Persian Gulf.
Pistacio Nuts (Pista)	N. W. India, from Caubul, &c.
Pine Nuts (neoza, chilghoza), *Pinus Gerardiana*	" "
Walnuts (Ukhrot)	" and Himalayas and Cashmere.
Cocoa Nuts, dried Kernels (copra)	Bombay, from Malabar Coast.
Litchis, dried	Calcutta.

VEGETABLE SUBSTANCES USED IN THE FORMATION OF DRINKS.

Tea, of different kinds	from the Kemaon and Deyra Plantations, in the Himalayas.
Tea	from Assam.
Coffee	Chota Nagpore, Malabar, Travancore, and Mysore.
Cocoa Seeds (*Theobroma Cacao*)	Calcutta Botanic Garden.
Hops	Deyra Doon and Bangalore.

FERMENTED LIQUORS AND DISTILLED SPIRITS.

Toddy, from Date and Palmyra Trees, Cocoa Nut, Caryota urens (Bhyni).
Urak, from Kujoor or Wild Date.

Dharoo, from Muhwa (*Bassia latifolia*)	Burdwan, Sarun, Cuttack, &c.
Bengal Rum	Calcutta, &c.

INTOXICATING DRUGS.

Opium	Patna, Benares, Malwa, Himalayas.
Ganja	Bengal and Himalayas.
Tobacco	Bhilsa, in Scindiah's Territory, Travancore, Masulipatam, Rajamundry, Coimbatore.

SPICES OR CONDIMENTS.

Areca, or Betle Nut	Jessore, &c., Malabar.
Betle Leaf, or Pan	Bengal, Malabar.
Bay Leaf, Indian (tej-pat) . .	Assam, Nepal.
Cassia	Cochin, Malabar, Cossia Hills.
Cassia Buds	Cochin, Tellicherry.
Cinnamon	Quilon, Tellicherry.
Cloves	Penang.
Mace and Nutmegs	Penang, Mergui.
Cardamoms	Malabar.
„ Wild	Mysore.
„ Large	Nepal, Ghazeepore from Hills.
Pepper	Travancore, Malabar.
„ Long	Bengal.
Capsicum, Chillies, and Cayenne .	Bengal and Nepal.
Ginger	Kemaon, Rungpore, Quilon, Malabar.
Turmeric	Bengal, Travancore.
Star Anise	Calcutta, from China.
Faghureh, or Tejbul (Jabrong in Assam)	Assam, and Himalayas.
Coriander	Bengal.
Cummin	Bengal.

FECULA, OR STARCH-LIKE SUBSTANCES.

Arrow Root (true, from *Maranta arundinacea*) .	Calcutta.
„ „ or Tikoor, from *Curcuma* . .	Patna, Sagur, and South-West Frontier.
„ „ the same, or a different kind .	Mysore, Vizagapatam, and Ganjam.
„ „ do. do. . .	Cochin, Tellicherry.
Sago	Sincapore.
Sago?	Travancore, Mysore, Wynaad Jungle.
Sago-meal, *Phœnix*	Cuttack Mehals.
Salep (Salib Misree)	from Hurdwar Fair.
Nelumbium Seeds	Bengal.
Singhara Seeds, *Trapa bispinosa* . . .	Patna, Cashmere.
Yams, Sweet Potatoes, &c. . . .	Bengal.
Ceylon Moss	Ramnaad.

SUGAR.

Sugar, from Sugar Cane, *Saccharum officinarum*	Jessore to Saharunpore. Excellent Dobarrah Sugar in Burdwan.
Date Sugar, *Phœnix sylvestris*	Dacca and Bombay.
Palmyra Sugar, *Borassus flabelliformis* . .	Madras.
Cocoa-nut Sugar, *Cocos nucifera* . . .	Cochin, Madras, Straits.
Ejoo or Gomuti Sugar, *Saguerus Rumphii* .	Straits.
Neepah Sugar, *Nipa fructicans* . . .	Arracan and Straits.
Manna, kinds of	Bombay.

GUMS.

Babool Gum (Gond babool)	Masulipatam, Scinde, &c.
Keekur (Gond Keekur)	Madras, Saharunpore.
East India Gum, *Ægle Marmelos?* . . .	Bengal.
Seriss Gum (Seriss ke gond)	Saharunpore.
Sem Gum (Sem ke gond)	Do.
Tragacanth (Kuteera)	Madras and Saharunpore.

MUCILAGE, &c.

Linseeed (ulsee), *Linum usitatissimum* . .	Bengal.
Quince (bih-dana), *Cydonia vulgaris* . .	Bombay.
Tookhm balungo, *Dracocephalum Royleanum* .	Saharunpore.
Isufghol, *Plantago Isufghola*	Do.
Soap Berries, *Sapindus*, species of.	

RESINS.

Amber (Kah-roba)	Cutch, Assam, and Kemaon.
Copal (Soondroos), *Vateria indica* . . .	Canara.
Animi	Bombay, from Africa.
Dammer (ral and dhoona), *Shorea robusta* .	Balasore, foot of Himalayas.
Mastic (mustagee)	Bombay.
Resin?	Beerbhoom.
Peynie (pandum), *Vateria indica*	Canara.
Theetsee, *Melanorrhœa usitata*	Assam.
Wood Oil (gurjun, dhoona-tel), *Dipterocarpus turbinatus, &c.*	Chittagong.
Turpentine (gunda biroza), *Pinus longifolia* .	Saharunpore.
Deodar Oil (Kelon ke tel), *Cedrus Deodara* .	Himalayas.
Benzoin (Loban)	Straits, Sumatra.
,, a kind of?	Malabar.
Liquid Balsam of Storax (Rosa mallas), *Rus. Samala?*	Islands of Red Sea.
Caoutchouc, *Ficus elastica*	Assam.
Gutta Percha	Sincapore.

GUM-RESINS, &c.

Myrrh (moor), *Balsamodendron Myrrha* . .	Bombay, from Africa.
Bdellium (googul), *Balsamodendron* . . .	Scinde.

Olibanum (Saleh gond), *Boswellia thurifera* .	Shahabad, &c.
Ammoniacum (ooshk) and	Scinde and Punjaub.
Fetid Gum-Resins, as Assafœtida (hing), Galbanum (barzed), &c.	"

ESSENTIAL OILS AND SUBSTANCES USED AS PERFUMES.

Atr, or Atter of Roses	Ghazeepoor.
Grass, Oil, or Oil of Spikenard (roosa ke-tel) .	Sagur.
Oil of Kayapootee, *Melaleuca Cajaputi* . .	Straits.
" Keora, *Pandanus odoratissimus* . .	Bengal.
" Cinnamon, *Cinnamomum zeylanicum* .	Quilon.
" Cassia, *Cinnamomum*, species of . .	Malabar?
" Sandal Wood, *Santalum album* . .	Do.
" Aloes Wood, *Aquilaria Agallochum* .	Bengal, from Naga hills.
" Lemons	Saharunpore.
" Anise	Calcutta.
Perfumed Oils, as of Jasmine, Hursinghar, &c.	Ghazeepore.
Oil of Turpentine (from Gunda biroza), or *Pinus longifolia*	Saharunpore.
Spikenard true (Jatamansi. Balchur.) . .	Nepal, Himalayas.
Khus-khus, or Vetiver, *Anatherum muricatum* .	India.
Putchapat (Pogostemon Patchouli) . . .	Malay Peninsula.
Putchuk, or Koot, Costus of ancients . .	Cashmere.

FATTY OILS AND VEGETABLE BUTTERS.

Cocoa-nut Oil (Naryul), *Cocos nucifera* . .	Calcutta, Malabar.
Linseed Oil (ulsee ke-tel), *Linum usitatissimum*	Bengal.
Sesamum Oil, Gingelly, (suffed til-ke-tel), *Sesamum orientale*	Madras.
Hutsella, Black til of Deccan, (Kala til-ke-tel), *Verbesina sativa*	Bombay.
Ramtil, *Guizotia oleifera*	Bengal.
Castor Oil, *Ricinus communis*	Patna and Bombay.
Poppy Oil (Post-ke-tel)	Patna.
Apricot Oil (Choohara and zurd aloo ke tel) .	Himalayas.
Ground Nut Oil (Moongphullee-ke-tel), *Arachis hypogœa*	Bengal.
Oil of Ben (Sohunjna), *Hyperanthera Moringa*	Bombay.
Sunflower, *Helianthus annuus*	Bengal.
Bastard Saffron (Kurrur-ke-tel. kundar), *Carthamus tinctorius*	Bengal, Bombay.
Mustard, Oil of, kinds:—	
Kalee Surson, Surson, Tira, Toria v. Kurwa, Raee — Species of Sinapis, &c.	Bengal.
Karunj Oil, *Pongamia glabra*	Bombay.
Bitter Oil (Woondel), *Calophyllum inophyllum*	Do.
Vegetable Tallow, *Vateria indica* . . .	Canara.
Muohwa or Bassia Oil, *Bassia latifolia* . .	Bengal.
Illiepie Oil, *Bassia longifolia*	Madras.
Butter of Ghee tree, *Bassia butyracea* . .	Almora.
Oil of *Prinsepia utilis*	Gurwhal.

Acids and Alkalis yielded by Vegetables—(*see* MINERAL KINGDOM.)

DYES.

Annotto, *Bixa orellana*	Dacca.
Aal (Aal, ach), *Morinda citrifolia, &c.* . .	Bundlecund and Sagur.
Chay root, *Oldenlandria umbellata* . . .	Dyndygal, Nellore, Masulipatam.
Chulchuliera (Lichen, species of) . . .	Himalayas, Scinde.
Madder, Indian, (Munjeeth,) *Rubia Munjistha*	Assam, Nepal, and Bombay. Scindiah's Territory, Quetta, &c.
Myrobolans (Hur and Behara), *Terminalia Sp.*	Bengal.
Safflower (Kusoombha), *Carthamus tinctorius* .	Dacca.
Sappan Wood (Bookum. Putung), *Cæsalpinia Sappan*	Mergui, Malabar.
Red Saunders, *Pterocarpus santalinus* . .	Madras.
Red Wood, *Adenanthera pavonina* . . .	Madras.
Logwood, *Hæmatoxylon campechianum* . .	Calcutta Botanical Garden.
Lodh, *Symplocos racemosa*	Himalayas.
Barberry Wood and Root, *Berberis Lycium, aristata, &c.*	Do.
Turkey Berries, subs. for, *Rhamnus, Sp.* . .	Do.
Turmeric (huldee), *Curcuma longa* . . .	Bengal, Malabar.
Roum v. Room, a blue dye, *Ruellia, Sp.* . .	Assam.
Indigo, *Indigofera tinctorum.*	Bengal, Madras.
Indigo, *Wrightia tinctoria*	Madras.
Black Vegetable Dye	Nepal and Burmah, Shan.

Dyes at Ganjam, Benares, Delhi, &e.

TANNING SUBSTANCES.

Babool Bark, *Acacia arabica*	Bellary, Scinde.
Catechu, Cutch, *Acacia Catechu*	Sarun, &c.
Terra Japonica "	Bombay, and Straits.
Gambeer, *Uncaria Gambeer*	Straits.
Gall Nuts, *Quercus infectoria*	Bombay.
Kino, *Pterocarpus Marsupium*	Tellicherry, Mysore.
Pulas Kino, *Butea frondosa*	Indian Jungles.
Turwur, *Cassia auriculata*	Bellary, Hoonsur.
Mangrove, *Rhizophora, Sp.*	Scinde.
Pomegranate Rind, *Punica Granatum* . .	Kemaon, Scinde.
Tamarisk Galls. *Sumrut-al-asl*	Scinde.
Dividivi, *Cæsalpinia coriaria*	Calcutta.

MEDICINAL SUBSTANCES.

Opium	Patna, Benares, Himalayas, Malwa.
Aconite, *Aconitum ferox*	Himalayas.
Cocculus indicus	Malabar.
Gamboge	Wynaad.
Quassia, Indian	Himalayas.
Senna	Tinnivelly, Coimbatore, Bombay, Agra, Saharunpore.
Colocynth	Bombay.
Nux Vomica	Bengal.
Stramonium	Do.
Henbane	Saharunpore.

Croton	Straits.
Castor Oil	"
Aloes	Arabia, Soccofra, East Coast of Africa, and India.
Chiretta	Himalayas.
Kreyat	Peninsula.
Colchicum	Bazars, N. W. India.
Sarsaparilla, *Smilax*, *Sp.*	Himalayas, Bombay.
" substitute for, Hemidesmus indicus .	Dindigul, Tinnivelly.
Rhubarb	Himalayas and Tibet.
Juniper Berries	Do.
Pomegranate Root	Do.

CELLULAR SUBSTANCES.

Shola, *Æschynomene paludosa*	Bengal.
Birch Bark, (Betula Bhojputra) . . .	Himalayas.

CLOTHING AND CORDAGE MATERIALS.

Cotton, New Orleans, experimental . .	from	Dharwar, Coimbatore, Candeish.
" Bourbon	"	Rutnagherry, Coimbatore, Tinnivelly.
" Native	"	Dacca, Tinnivelly, Surat, Broach, Omerawatty.
" " (bhoga)	"	Garrow and Chittagong Hills, and from hills near Mymensing.
Hemp (the true), *Cannabis sativa*		Gurhwall and Kemaon.
Flax (the true), *Linum usitatissimum* . .		Monghyr, Mymensing.
Hemp, Indian, *Hibiscus cannabinus*		Bengal and Bombay.

" *Sun* in N.W. India; *Maesta-pat*, Bengal; *Ambari*, Bombay.

" " *Crotalaria juncea*	Bengal and N.W. India.

" *Sunnee* in N.W. India; *Sun* in Bengal; *Ghore-Sun*, ex Roxb.

Tag. Conkanee Hemp.

Jute or Pāāt, *Corchorus capsularis* . . .	Bogoorah, and other parts of Bengal.

Ghea nelta pat and *teeta pat* in Bengal.

" " *Corchorus olitorius*	Bogoorah, and other parts of Bengal.

Bunghie-pat in Bengal.

Dhanche, *Æschynomine cannabina*	Bengal.
Maloo, or Maljhun, *Bauhinia racemosa* . .	Kemaon, &c.
Jetee, *Asclepias tenacissima*	Rajmehal.
Rhea, *Urtica tenacissima* . . . . . / " " *nivea*	Assam.
Grass Cloth of China	Assam?
Coir, or Cocoa-nut Fibre, *Cocos nucifera* . .	Malabar and Calcutta.
Ejoo, or Gomuti, *Saguerus Rumphii* . .	Straits.
Manilla Hemp, *Musa textilis*	Calcutta Botanic Garden.
Plantain Fibre, *Musa paradisiaca*	Dacca.
Pine-apple Fibre, *Bromelia Ananas*	Silhet, Assam, Dacca.
Bow-string Hemp (moorva), *Sanseviera zeylanica*	Bengal.
Moonj, *Saccharum moonja*	Bengal.
Bhabhur, *Scirpus cannabinus*	Kemaon.

Spiral Vessels, used as Lamp-wicks, *Nelumbium and Nymphæa*	Madras.
Split Stems for Mats of mooeto patee (*Phrynium dichotomum*)	Bengal.
Matting Materials (vora), *Papyrus Pandorei.*	

TIMBER AND FANCY WOODS.

Teak, *Tectona grandis*	Malabar and Moulmein.
Deodar, *Cedrus Deodara*	Himalayas.
Cypress, *Cupressus torulosa*	Do.
Ebony, *Diaspyros, Sp.*	Mysore, &c.
Sissoo, *Dalbergia Sissoo*	Calcutta.
Blackwood, *Dalbergia latifolia*	Salem, &c.
Saul, *Shorea robusta*	Doon, &c. Forests.
Poon, *Calophyllum*	Malabar.
Soondree, *Heritiera minor*	Delta of Ganges.
Babool, *Acacia arabica*	Scinde.
Tamarisk, *Tamarix*	Do.
Boorans, *Rhododendron arboreum*	Himalayas.
Huldoo, *Nauclea cordifolia*	Foot of do.
Box, *Buxus emarginatus*	Himalayas.
Dhamnoo, *Grewia elastica*	Kheree Pass.
Mohroo, *Quercus dilatata*	Himalayas.
Satin Wood, *Chloroxylon Swietenia*	Peninsula.
Sandal Wood, *Santalum album*	Malabar.
Mahogany, *Hæmatoxylon campechianum* . .	Calcutta Botanical Gardens.
Bamboos	Eastern Frontier of Bengal.
Canes	,,

The timber woods of India are very numerous, and of great importance in the country itself; but few would bear the expense of transport to Europe, from the great distance of most of the forests from the sea. A large collection of Indian woods are already in the India House, having been sent by Drs. Roxburgh and Wallich. Good specimens of a few of the above would be much valued.

III. ANIMAL SUBSTANCES.

Hoofs, Horns, &c. :—

Deer Horns.	
Buffalo Horns.	
Horn Tips	Burdwan.
Bones.	
Ivory	Mymensing, Assam, Madras, Bombay.

Wool, Hair, &c. :—

Sheep's Wool	Mysore, Hurryhur, Chittledroog, Jaulnah, Hansi, Himalayas, Quetta, Punjab.
Shawl, Goat's Wool	Tibet.
Chowries, or Cow-tails	Rungpore, &c., from Tibet.
Furs.	

Silk:—	
Silk, common	Mooshedabad.
Tusseh	Burdwan, &c., Assam.
Skins or Hides:—	
Buffalo Skins	Mymensing, Cuttack.
Hides generally	Balasore, Burdwan, &c.
Fats, Suet, Lard:—	
Tallow	Bengal.
Fish Oil	Tellicherry.
Isinglass, &c.:—	
Fish Maws	Calcutta, Mergui, Malabar, Scinde.
Shark Fins	Mergui, Cannanore, Scinde.
Wax	Bengal, Patna, &c.
Honey	Do.
Musk, &c.:—	
Musk	Kemaon, &c., from Tibet
Castor	in Bazaars.
Civet	„
Ambergris	Calcutta, Bombay.
Lac:—	
Lac Dye	Mirzapore, &c.
Shell Lac	Do.
Coral, Red and White	Bombay.
Tortoise Shell.	
Pearls	Persian Gulph and Ceylon.
Shells (Chanks and Cowries)	Ramnad.
Beche de Mer	Mergui.
Birds' Nests	Tavoy and Mergui.
Cantharides (Blistering Beetle)	Bengal.

IV. MANUFACTURED ARTICLES.

Cordage, Twine, &c.	
Twine and Thread, of Cotton and of Silk	Gyah, &c.
Ropes of Coir, &c.	Calcutta.
„ true Hemp	Kemaon.
Strong Canvas of Kemaon (of true Hemp?)	Do.
Coarse Canvas and Gunny Bags	Dacca, Hooghly.
Coir Bedding and Coir Mats	Chicacole.

COTTON :—

Cotton Cloths of various kinds, including Table-cloths, &c.	Patna, Dacca, Masulipatam, Saharunpore.
Do. by Nunpoorees at	Silhet.
Muslins (jam-dana, mulmul, Khas, &c.)	Dacca, Mymensing.
Mahmoodie Muslins	Chunderi.
Sutrunjees, or Cotton Carpets	Rungpore, &c.
Red Curwah	Allahabad.
Neigilli Cloth, made of *pat*	Rungpore.

SILK :—

Silk Cloths	Bauleah, Moorshedabad.
Corahs, &c.	Rungpore.

MIXED MATERIALS AND EMBROIDERY :—

Silk and Cotton.	
Musroo, muldye, putnee.	Maldah, Dacca, Boorhanpore.
Loongees, cotton, silk, and gold thread	Falta and Scinde.
Fabrics of Shawl Wool, as *puttoo*, &c.	Loodiana, Kemaon.
Shawls	Loodiana, Cashmere.
Brocades (Kinkhobs)	Benares, Boorhanpoor.
Worked Muslins and Embroidery	Dacca.
Muslins worked with Silk and Gold	Peytun.
Worked Cashmere Shawls	Delhi.

WOOL :—

Toose, Woollen Cloth	Ghazeepore.
Blankets	Mysore, Saharunpore, Himalayas.
Carpets	Mirzapore.
Feather Tippets and Muffs, &c.	Commercolly.

METAL :—

Brass and Copper Utensils, and of mixed Metals, as of vidry	Midnapore, Mirzapore, Gyah, &c.
Works in inlaid Metals	Do.
Gold and Silver Ornaments (as Bracelets, Ear-rings, &c.)	Dacca, Midnapore, Vizagapatam, Trichinopoly, Gyah, Delhi.
Cutlery and Native Arms (as Bows, Arrows, Spears)	Gyah, Monghyr, &c.
Fire-arms, in imitation of European	Monghyr.
Saddles and Saddle Cloths	Delhi, Lucknow.

ANIMAL SUBSTANCES, &c. :—

Horn Ornaments and Utensils	Gyah, Vizagapatam.
Shell Ornaments	Dacca, Midnapore.
Lac and Glass Ornaments	Gyah.
Ivory carved Ornaments, &c. Ebony and Sandal-Wood Boxes, &c.	Silhet, Moorshedabad, Vizagapatam.

SMALL MANUFACTURES, &c. :—

Lacquered Toys	Patna, Gyah.
Dyed Articles of Silk and Cotton	Benares, &c.
Mats of the finest quality	Silhet.
Paper	India generally.
„ of Hills made of Burrowah, a species Daphne	Nepal, Kemaon.

Small Manufactures, &c.:

Glass	Gyah.
„ and Glass Ornaments	Dacca.
Soap	Do., Saharunpore.
Sealing Wax	Do., Mirzapore.
Leather	Calcutta and Hoonsoor.
Pottery of peculiar shapes	India generally.
„ from peculiar materials	Sarun.
Stone Cups and Images	Gyah, &c.

Tools and Implements employed in different trades, as the Loom of Dacca, the Drill Plough of the West of India, Distilling Apparatus for Atr of Roses.

On the arrival in India of the Despatches from the Court of Directors, Committees were directed to be established in different parts of the several Presidencies by their respective Governments. The result has been, the transmission from India of extensive collections both of Raw Products and of Manufactured Articles from the different parts of that wide-spread empire, as will be seen at the Exhibition.